— A —
DICTIONARY
— OF —
AUSTRALIAN
COLLOQUIALISMS

A

DICTIONARY

OF

AUSTRALIAN

COLLOQUIALISMS

G.A.WILKES

NEW EDITION

SYDNEY UNIVERSITY PRESS
in association with
OXFORD UNIVERSITY PRESS AUSTRALIA

© M. O. Wilkes 1978
First published 1978

Second edition revised and reset 1985
This edition revised and reset 1990

National Library of Australia
Cataloguing-in-Publication data:

Wilkes, G. A. (Gerald Alfred), 1927–
A dictionary of Australian colloquialisms.

New ed.
ISBN 0 424 00178 0.

1. Australianisms – Dictionaries. 2. English language –
Australia – Terms and phrases. I. Title.

427.99403

Cover design by Jennifer Johnston
Cover illustration by Mini Goss
Typeset by Abb-typesetting Pty Ltd, Collingwood, Victoria
Printed by Impact Printing, Victoria Pty Ltd
Published by Sydney University Press in association
with Oxford University Press,
253 Normanby Road, South Melbourne, Australia

Preface

A Dictionary of Australian Colloquialisms was first published in 1978, and reissued in a revised and much enlarged edition in 1985. In presenting the 1985 edition in a concise format, I have omitted some material of ephemeral or marginal interest, and reduced the number of citations. At the same time I have introduced about one hundred new entries, and updated some two hundred others.

I am grateful to all those who over the years have written with queries or suggestions about Australian colloquialisms, and I hope that this correspondence may continue.

G. A. Wilkes
University of Sydney

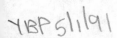

Abbreviations

Acland	L. G. D. Acland 'A Sheep Station Glossary' (1933) in *The Early Canterbury Runs*, Christchurch 1951.
A.F.L.	The Australian Football League.
Baker 1941	Sidney J. Baker, *A Popular Dictionary of Australian Slang*, Melbourne 1941.
Baker 1943	Sidney J. Baker, *A Popular Dictionary of Australian Slang*, 2nd edn, Melbourne 1943.
Baker 1945	Sidney J. Baker, *The Australian Language*, Sydney 1945.
Baker 1953	Sidney J. Baker, *Australia Speaks*, Sydney 1953.
Baker 1959	Sidney J. Baker, *The Drum Australian Character and Slang*, Sydney 1959.
Baker 1966	Sidney J. Baker, *The Australian Language*, Sydney 1966.
Barrère and Leland	A. Barrère and C. G. Leland, *A Dictionary of Slang, Jargon and Cant*, 2 vols, Edinburgh 1889–90.
EDD	*The English Dialect Dictionary*, ed. Joseph Wright, 6 vols, Oxford 1898–1905.
Franklyn	Julian Franklyn, *A Dictionary of Rhyming Slang*, 2nd edn, London 1961.
Grose	Francis Grose, *A Classical Dictionary of the Vulgar Tongue*, London 1785, 1788, 1790, 1811.
Hotten	John Camden Hotten, *A Dictionary of Modern Slang, Cant and Vulgar Words*, London 1859, 1860, 1864.
HRA	*Historical Records of Australia*, Series I, 33 vols, Sydney 1914–25.
HRNSW	*Historical Records of New South Wales*, 7 vols, Sydney 1892–1901.
HRV	*Historical Records of Victoria*, 3 vols to date, Melbourne 1981–.
Lawson *Prose*	Henry Lawson, *Collected Prose*, ed. Colin Roderick, 2 vols, Sydney 1972.
Lawson *Verse*	Henry Lawson, *Collected Verse*, ed. Colin Roderick, 3 vols, Sydney 1967–9.
Mathews	M. M. Mathews, *A Dictionary of Americanisms*, Chicago 1966.
Morris	Edward E. Morris, *Austral English A Dictionary of Australasian Words Phrases and Usages*, London 1898; facsimile reprint Sydney 1972.
O'Brien and Stephens	S. E. O'Brien and A. G. Stephens, 'Materials for a Dictionary of Australian Slang 1900–1910', Sydney, Mitchell Library MS Q427.9/0.
obs.	obsolete
OED	*The Oxford English Dictionary*, 20 vols, Oxford 1989.
Partridge	Eric Partridge, *A Dictionary of Slang and Unconventional English*, 2 vols, London 1970.
Ramson	W. S. Ramson, *Australian English An Historical Study of the Vocabulary 1788–1898*, Canberra 1966.
SND	*The Scottish National Dictionary*, 10 vols, Edinburgh 1932–76.
Turner	G. W. Turner, *The English Language in Australia and New Zealand*, 2nd edn, London 1972.
Vaux	'A Vocabulary of the Flash Language' (1812) in *The Memoirs of James Hardy Vaux*, ed. Noel McLachlan, London 1964.
V.F.L.	The Victorian Football League.
Wentworth and Flexner	Harold Wentworth and Stuart Berg Flexner, *Dictionary of American Slang*, 2nd Supplemented edn, New York 1975.

A

abo *n. & a.* Australian Aboriginal. Not always intended as derogatory, but now increasingly taken to be so [abbr.]

1922 *Bulletin* 5 Jan. 22: I was sheltering from a hailstorm under the verandah of the pub, and among my fellow refugees was an abo. who had been to the mission school.

1934 Jean Devanny *Out of Such Fires* 18: 'Wouldn't take long to get back to the abo state. A few hundred years, perhaps?'

1958 Gavin Casey *Snowball* 118: 'You wait till he gets a bit older. Them abos always go t' the pack,' a cynic told him.

1982 *Sun-Herald* 14 Nov. 70: In Moree, the Aborigines are 'the dark community' or, more crudely, 'the Abos'.

acca An academic

1977 K. S. Inglis *Meanjin* 90: Accas and Ockers: Australia's New Dictionaries [heading]

1982 *Sydney Morning Herald* 3 Sep. 12: N.S.W. University market day . . . Intended for the whole community, not just accas (academic persons).

1984 *Age* (Melbourne) 23 Mar. Weekender 10: Ackers up from the university who read Saturday's 'Sydney Morning Herald' (it used to be the 'Guardian') at half-time.

ace Probably a variant of *arse*: the expression **on one's ace** means 'alone, left to one's own resources', and could be associated with the score of 'one' in dice.

1906 Edward Dyson *Fact'ry 'Ands* 298: 'Would yeh believe it, that tin was tickin' like forty watches, 'n' when Sniff stirred it, you'd think it was full iv live dried peas, 'n' was rattlin' on its ace.'

1908 E. G. Murphy *Jarrahland Jingles* 58: Brim's in London on his 'ace'.

1934 Archer Russell *A Tramp Royal* 213: 'They're capable of good work at times,' said a 'boss cattleman' to whom I had applied for his opinion of the merits and demerits of the aboriginal as stockman, 'but you've got to be with them. Send 'em out "on their ace" and they'll probably "go camp" under the first shady tree they come to.'

acid, to put the ~ on To make the kind of demand (for money, information, or sex) that will either yield results or eliminate that possibility [f. *acid test*]

1906 Edward Dyson *Fact'ry 'Ands* 215: Evidently it was Mr Cato's intention to try the acid on Feathers again.

1925 Arthur Wright *The Boy from Bullarah* 16: 'He owes me anything up to a score of quids . . . I'm going to put the acid on.'

1948 Ruth Park *Poor Man's Orange* 165: 'I'll tell every feller I know she's easy, and she won't be able to go down the street without having the acid put on her.'

1966 Patrick White *The Solid Mandala* 147: 'And a woman like that, married to such a sawney bastard, she wouldn't wait for 'em to put the acid on 'er.'

see **hard word**

acre (acher) Buttocks, backside [? f. appearance]

1938 Heard in conversation.

1966 Baker 169: *acre* The anus. [as World War II slang]

1971 Frank Hardy *The Outcasts of Foolgarah* 18: Wiping between his toes [after a shower] and falling on his acre.

1973 Roland Robinson *The Drift of Things* 164: Because they used to surf in the nude and lie among the flowering tea-trees on the sides of the valley sunbathing, one shack dweller . . . called his shack 'Sunburned Acres'.

Acre, the Dirty Half see **Dirty Half Acre**

Adelaide River Stakes The exodus from Darwin to the Adelaide River following the Japanese bombing raid of 19 February 1942

1966 Douglas Lockwood *Australia's Pearl Harbour* 143: Men unquestionably ran away, but they were not only airmen. The leaders in what later became known as the Adelaide River Stakes included civilians who had not been under direct attack.

adjective, the great Australian see **Australian**

Adrian Quist see **Quist**

Adventure, the Great see **Great**

1

aerial pingpong Australian Rules Football: *jocular* [f. the long kicks and high leaps which are features of the game]
1965 Frank Hardy *The Yarns of Billy Borker* 43: Melbourne Mick would say, 'Australian Rules draws bigger crowds in Melbourne than Rugby in Sydney.' 'What?' Sydney Sam would say, 'that's not football, mate, it's aerial ping-pong.'
1973 *Sun* (Sydney) 4 Apr. 93: Aussie Rules, or aerial pingpong as it is sometimes called, is being telecast live from Melbourne by Nine.
1980 *West Australian* (Perth) 2 Apr. 7: The game cynics call 'aerial ping-pong'.

Akubra Hat [brand name]
1930 *Bulletin* 23 Jul. 16: Hamlet himself stirs pity in the soft-hearted boy, who is overheard to remark that the 'Prince is taking a bit of a risk getting about in the cold without his Akubra'.
1972 Patrick White *The Eye of the Storm* 450: The solicitor was looking at her from under the brim of his Akubra.
1981 *Australian* 11 Mar. 9: These days, even plain-clothes demons don't wear the snap-brim Akubras which villains found such a useful tip-off.

alas! milfissed the balfastards see **balfastards**

Albany Doctor A cool and refreshing breeze [place-name in W.A.]
1922 Edward Meryon *At Holland's Tank* 162: The south breeze, better known in those parts as the Albany Doctor, had arrived.
1937 A. W. Upfield *Mr Jelly's Business* 57: The 'Albany Doctor' people called it, because the strong cool wind from Albany way swept clear the bodily and mental languors brought on by the heat of the long day.
1983 John K. Ewers *Long Enough for a Joke* 105: The nights cool with often a blustering southerly the locals called 'the Albany doctor'.
see **Fremantle doctor**

Alberts, Prince Rags wound about the feet in place of socks [f. the alleged poverty of Prince Albert before he became Victoria's consort: listed by Partridge as nautical]
c. **1888** 'Sam Griffith' *Old Bush Songs* ed. Stewart and Keesing (1957) 203: I knew his feet were blistered/From the Alberts that he wore.
1903 Joseph Furphy *Such is Life* (1944) 39: Unlapping from his feet the inexpensive substitute for socks known as 'prince-alberts', he artistically spread the redolent swaths across his boots to receive the needful benefit of the night air.

alec, aleck A stupid fellow, an ass [f. *smart alec* U.S. 1865 Mathews]
1944 Lawson Glassop *We Were the Rats* 168: 'I reckon if I got stomach ache all you alecks would know almost before I did.'
1946 Margaret Trist *What Else is There?* 90: 'If a man goes on the booze and belts you up, you know where you stand. But when they start in preachin' I kind of feel a big aleck.'
1962 Alan Seymour *The One Day of the Year* 64: 'He looked such a big aleck, marching along as though he'd won both wars single-handed.'

Alf The uncultivated Australian (the opposite to **Roy** q.v.) now being superseded by **ocker** [see quot. 1965]
1960 Murray Sayle 'As Far As You Can Go' *Encounter* May 28: The Australian worker, the 'Alf' as we call him.
1965 E. Morris 'Reliques of Sope' [Neil C. Hope, d. 1964] *Nation* 27 Nov. 21: Middle-class 'Roys' in sports cars and yachting jackets, and red-necked 'Alfs' who want to fight those who swear in front of ladies. (It was Sope who invented the now-ubiquitous term.)
1974 *Australian* 23 Nov. 21: He does not want to show his films in the film workshop-co-op settings and they are too way out for your ordinary Alf.

Alfred, Royal An elaborate swag [? f. Alfred, Duke of Edinburgh who toured Australia 1867–8]
1902 Henry Lawson 'The Romance of the Swag' *Prose* i 501–2: The weight of the swag varies from the light rouseabout's swag, containing one blanket and a clean shirt, to the 'Royal Alfred', with tent and all complete, and weighing part of a ton.

Alfreds, Prince As for **Prince Alberts**
1896 Henry Lawson 'Stragglers' *Prose* i 92–3: Occasionally someone gets some water in an old kerosene tin and washes a shirt or pair of trousers, and a pair or two of

socks – or foot-rags (Prince Alfreds, they call them).

Alice the Alice Springs N.T.; more recently 'Alice'
1901 F. J. Gillen *Diary* (1968) 92: I was sleeping on a canvas covered stretcher which I procured at the Alice.
1933 R. B. Plowman *The Man from Oodnadatta* 140: 'I just dropped on them quite unexpectedly. I didn't know they had left the Alice.'
1944 Frank Clune *The Red Heart* 16: Arrived at 'The Alice' by plane, I decided to investigate the rumour of Lasseter's resurrection.
1961 Jack Danvers *The Living Come First* 16: 'I met them in Alice a while back.'
1982 *NT News* (Darwin) 1 May 28: Alice swings toward home units [heading]

alkie An alcoholic [abbr.] [also U.S.]
1964 Bruce Beaver *The Hot Sands* 16: Ben Tickell, the regular night porter, was an alkie if ever she had seen one.
1971 Rena Briand *White Man in a Hole* 31: Kind-hearted, he'd share ... his last cigarettes with the alkies at the Front Bar.
1975 Elizabeth Riley *All That False Instruction* 126: 'Tried to think what I'd feel like if I was a sixty-odd alkie.'

all about Collective term for workforce on a station, esp. Aborigines [Pidgin]
1908 Mrs Aeneas Gunn *We of the Never-Never* 302: Cheon was announcing dinner in his own peculiar way. 'Din-ner! Mis-sus! Boss! All about!' he chanted.
1935 Mary and Elizabeth Durack *All-About The Story of a Black Community on Argyle Station, Kimberley* [book title]
1956 Tom Ronan *Moleskin Midas* 235: 'What this yarn allabout got where you going to send my boy to whitefeller school?' she demanded.

all alone like a country dunny see **dunny, shouse**

all prick and ribs like a drover's (shearer's, swaggie's) dog i.e. lean but eager
1971 Frank Hardy *The Outcasts of Foolgarah* 35: To see them at work, Little Tich all prick and ribs like a swaggie's dog.
1981 *National Times* 25 Jan. 24: He was like a drover's dog, all —— and ribs.

alley A marble [f. *alley* a choice marble or taw OED 1720–1865]
1 *To pass (toss) in one's alley* To give in, die
1916 C. J. Dennis *The Moods of Ginger Mick* 109: But if I dodge, an' keep out 'uv the rain,/An' don't toss in me alley 'fore we wins.
1933 Norman Lindsay *Saturdee* 23: 'This book says a bloke kicked the bucket, an' Bill says it means a bloke pegged out, so what's it mean?' 'Means a bloke passed his alley in.'
1960 Jack McKinney *The Well* in *Khaki Bush and Bigotry* ed. Eunice Hanger (1968) 228: 'Don't sling in yer alley, missus. There's a good time comin'.'
2 *To make one's alley good* To make the grade, improve one's status or prospects
1924 C. J. Dennis *Rose of Spadgers* 160: That 'e 'ad swore to get me one uv those / Fine days, an' make 'is alley good with Rose.
1952 T. A. G. Hungerford *The Ridge and the River* 109: 'That's all right,' Shearwood said soberly. 'It makes Wilder's alley good, but it doesn't win any popularity stakes for you.'
1975 Xavier Herbert *Poor Fellow My Country* 362: Berated Pat for taking up the cause of a scab in order to make his alley good with a designing female.
see **marble**

alt Follower of an alternative lifestyle
1981 *Age* (Melbourne) 15 Sep. 11: The North Coast is the heart of alternative lifestyles, but there are no visits to communes. We are efficiently informed that there are no votes in hippies and 'alts'.

amateur players, a trap for see **trap**

amber fluid, liquid Beer
1959 *Bulletin* 4 Feb. 35: Dutchy and I were still wary of the amber fluid, but were getting a bit gamer with it.
1965 John Beede *They Hosed Them Out* 185: We grogged on till closing time; it was evident that we all had one thing in common – a liking for the amber liquid.
1980 *NT News* (Darwin) 24 Jan. 6: There'll be 360 meat pies and 30 kilos of snags to demolish, washed down with 40 cartons of amber fluid.

amster, ampster Confederate of the manager of a sideshow, with the task of attracting custom [rhyming slang *Amsterdam* = *ram* q.v.]

1941 Kylie Tennant *The Battlers* 181: As soon as the showman begins to shout: 'All right, the show is commencing Roll up! Roll up!' . . . the amster rushes eagerly up to the ticket window and says: 'Right-o, mister, I'll have a ticket.' He pretends to pass his money over, and is handed a ticket. His brother-amsters form into an impatient queue behind him and file into the tent at the head of the multitude who, like sheep, will follow the leader, but will not be the first to pay their money.

1957 D'Arcy Niland *Call Me When the Cross Turns Over* 101: Barbie, playing ampster, went up and bought a bottle.

1975 Hal Porter *The Extra* 244: A shady Soho club patronised by dips, amsters, off-duty prostitutes.

Anglo An Australian of Anglo-Saxon descent: *usually derogatory* [also U.S.: an Anglo-American as distinct from a Mexican-American]

1986 *Sydney Morning Herald* 30 Aug. 5: Many of her [Italian] friends refuse to confront the problem and end up with a deep feeling of resentment to 'Anglos'.

angora sc. goat, usually in the phrase 'act (play) the angora': *obsolescent*

1899 *Truth* 8 Oct. 5: Refrain from playing the giddy ox, the antic angora, and the cowardly, foul-mouthed dirty devil generally.

1922 Henry Lawson 'The Last Rose of Winter' *Prose* i 906: He had that lovable expression of a Bushman admiring his mate making a giddy angora of himself.

1945 Cecil Mann *The River* 142: 'And you, Clarkey – you, you great angora – standing there, leaning on the rail, scared stiff.'

ankle-biter Child

1981 *Sun-Herald* 2 Aug. 167: The middle-aged Petula Clark does the Julie Andrews bit, skipping and trilling over the edelweiss with the Von Trapp ankle-biters.

1984 *Sydney Morning Herald* 26 Jan. 9: Travelling overseas with an ankle-biter has its advantages. It keeps you out of museums, cathedrals and temples and shows you the raw side of life: playgrounds, supermarkets, laundrettes and public toilets.

Anthony Horderns, Thursday or see **Thursday**

Anzac The code address adopted by General Birdwood in Egypt for the Australian and New Zealand Army Corps in 1915, and used by him in naming the landing-place at Gallipoli 'Anzac Cove'. Used colloquially in various senses:

1 The beachhead, or the campaign more generally

1915 C. E. W. Bean Diary 29 Apr. in *Gallipoli Correspondent* (1983) 83: The jealousy that existed between N.Z. and Australia in Cairo vanished at one blow on the first day at Anzac – vanished utterly as far as the men were concerned.

1936 Miles Franklin *All That Swagger* 447: They remain incapable of instructing the rising generation that the glories of Anzac were as empty as all military glory down the centuries.

1970 Donald Horne *The Next Australia* 153: One even hears rumours of homosexuality at Anzac.

2 A member of the Australian and New Zealand Army Corps

1916 Let. in Bill Gammage *The Broken Years* (1974) 156: So three cheers for the Anzac and the early ending of this sinful game.

1939 Herbert M. Moran *Viewless Winds* 163: The only other drinker was a grey-haired man with a hard cadaverous look who wore the badge of an original Anzac.

1962 Alan Seymour *The One Day of the Year* 73: 'When we went in there we was nobody. When we come out we was famous. [*Smiles*] Anzacs.'

3 An Australian soldier in a later war, esp. on service overseas (sometimes close to 4)

1943 *Khaki and Green* 107: Greetings such as 'You'll do me, you big bronzed Anzac' are not encouraged.

1982 *Sydney Morning Herald* 6 Feb. 3: Smaller role for Anzacs in Sinai [heading] Australia's contribution to the Sinai peace-keeping force will be only about half as big as originally planned.

see **bronze gods**

4 A stereotype of the Australian male

1957 Randolph Stow *The Bystander* 21: 'It's just the way I am. The lean bronzed Anzac type. Don't you agree?'

1965 Eric Lambert *The Long White Night* 8: Most of them had come to the hall straight from the pubs. They were dinkum diggers and bronzed Anzacs all over again. They were perpetuating the Australian Myth.

1982 *Sydney Morning Herald* 21 Jan. 17: Not so long ago, male cosmetics and skin

care products were a definite no-no for the average bronzed Anzac.
5 See quot. 1980
1980 *Sun* (Sydney) 26 Feb. 37: In the food game, an Anzac is a chicken, lamb, porker or calf that has lost a limb, or been badly damaged (wounded in action) on the processing line.

AO The Australian Opera
1984 *Australian* 15 Aug. 8: Not every opera lover stays an AO supporter [heading]

aorta Strine version of 'they ought to'
1971 Frank Hardy *The Outcasts of Foolgarah* 129: *They* ought to (in strine, aorta) give a man a fair go – but they won't. So what do you do? . . . tell them aorta go and get well stuffed.
1982 Ross Gittins *Sydney Morning Herald* 3 Jun. 6: It is not good enough for us PAYE captives to sit around tut-tutting and crying 'aorta do something.

Apple Isle, the Tasmania [f. crops]
1947 C. K. Thompson *Yes, Your Honour!* 231: Sir Richard must have had a terrible set on Tassie, because in 1836 he again tried to push Kinchela on to the Apple Isle as a puisne judge.

apples, everything's In good order, under control [? f. *apple pie order*, or rhyming slang *apples and spice = nice*]
1952 T. A. G. Hungerford *The Ridge and the River* 44: 'How's it going, Wally? Everything apples?'
1961 Frank Hardy *The Hard Way* 132: 'For Pete's sake keep mum about it. 'She's apples,' the worker replied, with another demonstrative wink.
1966 Hal Porter *The Paper Chase* 251: 'Listen, mate, here's the problem. Mascot at five thirty. Passport photographs first – here's the address. While that's happening, can you collect my luggage at Usher's, buy me sixty cigarettes, and pick me up at the photographer's?' Sydney taxi-drivers are the world's best. 'She'll be apples, mate.'
see **sweet, jake**

Argentinian road, the The road to the Banana Republic
1987 Senator Peter Walsh *Sydney Morning Herald* 22 Sep. 8: 'We've been a lucky country for a long time, not so lucky any more and if we don't challenge most of the absurd notions that the majority of Australians have about what they are entitled to and what's essential to them and what isn't then we are going down the Argentinian road.'

aristocracy, bunyip see **bunyip**

arse 1 Effrontery, 'cheek', as in the phrase **more arse than Jessie** q.v. [? f. 'hide']
1963 John Cantwell *No Stranger to the Flame* 76: 'The johns'd never have the arse to frisk every house in a dump like this – people'd feel their word was being doubted.'
1979 John Singleton *Bulletin* 11 Sep. 86: Since the place was set up 25 years ago there have been less than 200 visitors in total and I only got there through sheer arse and lots of it.
2 Equivalent to 'tail' (U.S.): sexual access to women (quot. 1958 also includes sense 3)
1958 Frank Hardy *The Four-legged Lottery* 188: 'See all the snooker balls going the pockets – he had more arse than a married cow playing snooker, I can tell you.'
1979 Colin Johnson *Long Live Sandawara* 53: The only thing he doesn't like is that it is keeping the girls from plying their trade openly, and that means less free arse.
3 Good luck
1963 Frank Hardy *Legends from Benson's Valley* 73: 'They've had the luck of Eric Connolly all night,' Darky said sheepishly. 'Our turn for a bit of arse.'

arse, get the; be arsed out To be dismissed
1966 Baker 366: *Got the arse at Bulli Pass* [as one of a number of sayings based on place-names]
1969 William Dick *Naked Prodigal* 19: 'What's up?' I asked. 'They give me the arse,' he answered loudly.
1983 Laurie Clancy *Perfect Love* 238: 'She's been playing around with half the town. So I went home and gave her the arse.'

arsehole, to To dismiss someone peremptorily
1965 William Dick *A Bunch of Ratbags* 153: 'It's orright when yuh young, but when yuh get a bit old and yuh can't keep up . . . they'll arsehole yuh!'
1974 David Ireland *Burn* 125: They want

to clear us right out. Arsehole us completely.

arseholes, ugly as a hatful of   see **hatful**

arse in gear, get one's   To pull oneself together
1975 Robert Bennett *The Big Ruck* 54: 'I may be able to smooth things over for you if . . . you apologise to Ferguson and also pull your arse into gear.'
1989 Grant Kenny *Sun-Herald* 17 Dec. 65: 'I was on the phone minutes after her [Lisa Curry's] butterfly win to offer my congratulations. The only advice she gave me was to get my arse into gear and win the semifinal.'

arsey   Lucky [f. **arse** 3]
1968 Stuart Gore *Holy Smoke* 30: 'The old man come up on the lottery or something?' 'No . . . He'd have to be pretty arsey, wouldn't he?'
1978 Richard Beilby *Gunner* 87: 'Just lie back an' take it easy. Ya got a homer, mate, you arsey bastard.'

Arthur or Martha, not to know whether one is   A state of confusion
1957 D'Arcy Niland *Call Me When The Cross Turns Over* 52–3: 'Don't try the Barcoo spews. A cow of a thing. Get a feed into you, and then you want to chuck it up again. You chuck it up and you're right as pie till you eat again. And so it goes on. You don't know whether you're Arthur or Martha.'
1965 John Beede *They Hosed Them Out* 104: 'Probably freeze your knackers off,' said Bill sceptically. 'I only tried swimming once over here and didn't know if I was Arthur or Martha when I came out.'
1980 Jessica Anderson *The Impersonators* 192: She flopped into a chair and fanned herself with a hand. 'I still don't know whether I'm Arthur or Martha.'

artist   Expert, specialist, addict, esp. in expressions like 'bull artist', 'booze artist' [f. *artist* an adroit rogue; a skilful gamester U.S. 1890 OED]
[**1895** Cornelius Crowe *The Australian Slang Dictionary* 4: *Artist* a cunning thief or gamester.]
1919 W. H. Downing *Digger Dialects* 9: *Artist* 'One-star artist' – a second lieutenant.
1938 Xavier Herbert *Capricornia* 379:

'We'll take a couple of bottles with us. Joe's a champion booze-artist.'
1951 Dal Stivens *Jimmy Brockett* 49: Bill was fond of telling us he'd be able to retire in a few years, but he'd always been a bull artist.
1976 Helen Hodgman *Blue Skies* 93: 'Proper grog artist, I was. A regular flaming piss artist, that was me all right.'
see **merchant**

arvo   Afternoon [abbr.]
1927 *Sun* (Sydney) 9 Oct. 'Sunbeams' 1: I told young 'Ocker' Stevens to come up and say that so I could go shooting with him with his new pea rifle this arvo.
1958 H. D. Williamson *The Sunlit Plain* 41: 'Going up to see the cricket match this arvo?' Hattie asked, yawning.
1965 Patrick White *Four Plays* 121: 'Later on this arvo I'm gunna take Ernie out and buy him a good time.'

ashtray on a motorbike, useful as an see **useful**

Ash Wednesday   Wednesday 16 February 1983 (Ash Wednesday) day of bushfires in S.A. and Victoria, with the loss of 71 lives
1983 *Sydney Morning Herald* 18 Feb. 2: The Ash Wednesday Disaster [heading]
1984 *Australian* 28 Jan. Mag. 4: The threat of more devastating Ash Wednesdays is always part of the Australian landscape.

ask, a big   A difficult target
1985 Brian Woodward and John Wright *Up the Parramatta Road* 23: He had set an ask of $17,990, which was really stretching things.
1989 *Sunday Telegraph* (Sydney) 7 May 123: A premiership, a State of Origin jumper and belting Canterbury at Penrith Park. Three big asks, but if they all happen, won't the phone be ringing off the hook then.

Aspro   1 Associate-professor, in academic slang [abbr.]
2 A nickname
1983 *Newcastle Herald* 1 Jun. 3: Various lazy people scattered through the Hunter Valley [are] called Aspro, Morphia and Opium: the slow working dopes.

Athens of the North, South   Any Australian city with cultural pretensions, esp. a University city, as ironically viewed by any other

1983 *Australian* 26 Feb. 12: Armidale, 'the Athens of the north', is still seething since last year's street demonstration, when 3000 locals protested over a Fraser Government order to amalgamate the University of New England with the nearby College of Advanced Education.

1983 *Australian* 6 Aug. Mag. 20: It's not as though the leading intellectuals in the Athens of the South are taking hemlock: more your local Claytons, on the basis that the next Adelaide Festival is the one you have when you're not having one, according to some local pessimists.

Auntie The Australian Broadcasting Commission; from 1983 the Australian Broadcasting Corporation [f. nickname of the BBC]

1967 Heather Chapman *Sunday Mirror* (Sydney) 12 Mar. 84: But in the case of Miss Cobb people know she's never stuffy, pretentious, dull or high falutin'. She is, in fact, one answer to the ABC's Old Aunty image.

1984 *Sydney Morning Herald* 5 May 1: Its managing director, Mr Geoffrey Whitehead, spoke of getting dynamism into the ABC, and said: 'If she is going to be Auntie, then she will be Auntie Mame.'

Aussie *n. & a.* 1 An Australian, usually with nationalistic overtones, as in phrases like 'a dinkum Aussie', 'a dinky-di Aussie' [abbr.]

1918 *Aussie The Australian Soldiers' Magazine* 18 Jan. 1: In short, make him a dinkum Aussie.

1934 Steele Rudd *Green Grey Homestead* 191: He's sure she's selected the right man for her husband – 'a good, industrious, God-fearing dinkum young Aussie'.

1940 Arnold Haskell *Waltzing Matilda* 164: Unlike so many who find success, she [Melba] remained a 'dinkum hard-swearing Aussie' to the end.

1971 Hal Porter *The Right Thing* 51: 'Both of them [the housekeepers] fell for dad, first the Pommy one, and then a dinky-di Aussie one.'

2 Australia

1918 *Aussie The Australian Soldier's Magazine* 18 Jan. 1: To the Australian Soldier the name Aussie stands for his splendid, sea-girt, sun-kissed Homeland, and his cobbers are always Aussies.

1945 Diary 16 Sep. Stan Arneil *One Man's War* (1980) 264: We embark tomorrow morning to go to dear old Aussie.

1974 *Australian* 15 Aug. 10: 'Cheers from A Sunburnt Country!' the advertisement trumpets. 'Toast your Pommie mates with a gift from good old Aussie! Great beers, Hardy's fine wines, and Vegemite for the kids!'

Aussie Rules Australian Rules Football (first played in 1858)

1973 Max Harris *The Angry Eye* 63: Aussie Rules remains in its condition of benign stagnation.

1983 Wally Lewis *National Times* 13 May 50: 'A lot of people will bag Aussie Rules, calling it a sheila's game, but the guys that are playing it are top class sportsmen, there's incredible skill involved.'

Australia, the The Hotel Australia, built in 1891, demolished in 1971, long regarded as the leading Sydney hotel

1900 Henry Lawson 'Mr Smellingscheck' *Prose* i 234: We had a well-to-do whisky together, and he talked of things in the abstract. He seemed just as if he'd met me in the Australia.

1968 Stuart Gore *Holy Smoke* 47: 'Here they are still standin' up . . . as cool as if they all had a foot on the brass rail in the Australia.'

1981 Maxwell Grant *Inherit the Sun* 360: He hoped Sir James hadn't found anywhere more satisfactory. 'Not unless you're rebuilding the old Australia,' Red said.

Australia for the Australians A slogan used in a variety of contexts:

1 As a call for national unity or individuality

1868 Archbishop John Bede Polding *Pastoral Letter* [responding to anti-Catholic feeling at the attempted assassination of the Duke of Edinburgh] in *Documents in Australian Catholic History* ed. P. O'Farrell (1969) i 428: The unhappy creature, who attempted the life of our Prince and guest, professes to be a Catholic . . . But will any man of sense believe that his crime was Catholic? . . . Australians we should all be. We owe it to each other, we owe it to duty, we owe it to Christianity. And I say, Australia for the Australians, our sole and sufficient nationality under the rule of our ever good and gracious Queen, whom with her Royal Family may God in his infinite mercy long preserve to us.

1898 A. B. Paterson 'Johnny Riley's Cow' (A Ballad of Federation) in *Singer of the Bush*

(1983) 306: It's Australia for the Australians – one people east and west.
2 As a plea for the interests of the native born
1889 A. B. Paterson *Australia for the Australians.* [pamphlet opposing the concentration of land in the hands of a few, and advocating protective tariffs]
1911 E. M. Clowes *On the Wallaby Through Victoria* 172: Australia ... needs to open its arms, to enlarge its sympathies, and to get rid, once for all, of that 'precious only child in the world' idea by which it seems each year to grow more completely engrossed – I mean the 'Australia for the Australians' ideal.
3 As an expression of anti-imperialist sentiment
1888 *The Republican* 8 Feb. 5: Australia for the Australians. [article on the Australian Republican league, which advocated the abolition of the office of Governor, nationalization of the land, federation of the colonies under republican rule]
1902 A. G. Stephens 'Australia for the Australians' *Bulletin* 25 Jan. Red Page [article questioning the influences of the British in Australia: 'Let young Australia come to the front with the motto of Australia for the Australians. This question of independent national development overshadows all others.']
4 As expressing opposition to coloured immigration: the motto of the *Bulletin* from 21 April 1888 (following the anti-Chinese issue of 14 April) to 30 April 1908
1888 William Lane *White or Yellow?* in *Boomerang* 31 Mar. 9: 'Australia for the Australians!' shouted Colonel Withers ... 'We'll teach the yellow rascals which race has got to go!'

Australia for the White Man Motto of the *Bulletin* from 7 May 1908 until 30 November 1960, indicating support for the White Australia policy
1974 Desmond O'Grady *Deschooling Kevin Carew* 122: Australia for the white man. He should have shown the note to the dumb Chink without letting it out of his hand.

Australian adjective, the great Bloody q.v.
1894 *Bulletin* 18 Aug. 22: The *Bulletin* calls it the 'Australian adjective' simply because it is more used, and used more exclusively by Australians, than by any other allegedly civilised nation.

1899 W. T. Goodge *Hits! Skits! and Jingles!* 115: '——!' / (*The Great Australian Adjective!*) [poem title]
1939 *Daily Telegraph* (Sydney) 23 Jan. 7: Legal opinion upholds the ruling of Mr Atkinson S. M. that the Great Australian Adjective is sometimes offensive but not indecent.
1944 *Daily Telegraph* (Sydney) 7 Jul. 8: The great Australian accent, and the greater Australian adjective, are two of the best advertisements Australia has in other parts of the world.

Australian as a meat pie see **meat pie**

Australian dream, the great The hope of owning one's own home
1981 *Sun-Herald* 22 Nov. 55: The Labor Party of today is firmly committed to the great Australian dream of owning one's home.
1990 *Australian* 17 Feb. Weekend 1: This is the mortgage belt, where mostly first-home buyers have sought the Great Australian Dream – a home of one's own.

Australian novel, the great The novel that is always still to be written, or identified
1941 A. J. A. Waldock *Southerly* Nov. 34: Do people still muse on 'the great Australian novel' for which we wait? Casey, I believe, has it in him to write it.
1948 A. W. Upfield *An Author Bites the Dust* 133: 'Her work is much appreciated by the discerning and we are still expecting her to produce the Great Australian Novel.'
1970 Patrick White *The Vivisector* 112: 'Well, good luck to you, kid! I'm going to write the Great Australian Novel.'
1980 *Australian* 20 Dec. Mag. 13: Helen Garner ... hasn't written the Great Australian Novel, but yet in her own frame of reference is tackling more than most.

Australian salute The movement of the hand in brushing away flies
1972 Ian Moffitt *The U-Jack Society* 65: I flopped a hand at the flies (the Australian salute).
1976 *Australian* 9 Mar. 3: A sexually-mutated blowfly developed by CSIRO scientists in Canberra could lead to the demise of the great Australian salute.
see **Barcoo salute, Queensland salute**

Australian Ugliness, the Great A

phrase developed from the title of Robin Boyd's book of 1960, on the vulgarity of design in the ordinary Australian environment, from architecture to automobiles: since applied mainly to suburbia.

1960 Robin Boyd *The Australian Ugliness* [book title]

1981 Leonie Sandercock and Ian Turner *Up Where, Cazaly?* 130: In the 1950s the spread of car ownership reinforced and multiplied those tendencies and that preference for low density living, otherwise known as suburban sprawl or, by some, as the Great Australian Ugliness.

Australia's national game see **national game**

awake see **wake up**

axe-handle A unit of measurement, in country areas: *obsolescent*

1977 *Australian* 11 Apr. 6: A big woman, but not a big man, would be described as being 'two axe handles across the arse.'

1979 Sally Morrison *Who's taking you to the Dance?* 199: She wouldn't wear that suit. Two axe handles across the beam if you ask me.

1982 *Sun-Herald* 19 Dec. 127: 'There was this giant Yugoslav bodyguard there, about four axe-handles across the chest and he had to wrestle with them to keep them away.'

ay see **eh**

B

babbler, babbling brook Cook, esp. one cooking for a number of men, as in the army or in the outback [rhyming slang]

1919 W. H. Downing *Digger Dialects* 9: *Babbling Brook; Babbler* An Army cook.

1932 Leonard Mann *Flesh in Armour* 96: The new tins hadn't been properly cleaned out by the babbler.

1956 Ruth Park and D'Arcy Niland *The Drums Go Bang!* 71: The shearers . . . drew as their lucky last a wizard cook from Sydney who could throw cream-puffs together with one hand and carve the roast with the other, while he washed up with his feet. Or so it seemed. He was voted one of the best babbling brooks in the business.

1964 *Sydney Morning Herald* 25 Apr. 11: 'If I keep this pretty woman babbler on my books next year I'll have to get an older team.'

bach see **batch**

back block 1 A block of land further from water or grass, and so less favourable to settlement.

1874 Rolf Boldrewood *My Run Home* (1897) 265: 'A regular "back block", if ever there were one – all rock and mountain.'

2 *The backblocks* Regions remote from settled areas

1888 Overlander *Australian Sketches* 65:

Jim Brandon's Christmas on the Back Blocks and what came of it [story title]

1902 Henry Lawson 'The Shearer's Dream' *Prose* i 312: They were part of a theatrical company on tour in the Back-Blocks.

1925 Seymour Hicks *Hullo Australians* 198: 'You haven't seen Australia if you haven't seen the back blocks.'

1944 Gilbert Mant *You'll be Sorry* 31: Bill was a gawky lad from the back-blocks who had this day seen Sydney for the first time.

1970 Barry Oakley *A Salute to the Great McCarthy* 78: 'Where ya from, kid? The backblocks? Flash boy from the paddocks?'

back blocker An inhabitant of the back blocks

1870 *Argus* 22 Mar. 7: 'I am a bushman, a back blocker, to whom it happens about once in two years to visit Melbourne.' [Morris]

1898 David W. Carnegie *Spinifex and Sand* 149: Strong and hard, about thirty-five years of age, though, like most back-blockers, prematurely grey.

1907 Alfred Searcy *In Australian Tropics* 125: If a crowd of overlanders and back-blockers happened to be present, things would be made lively, for . . . they would hardly give up all the liquor without a strong protest.

back country The areas remote from settlement, usually further inland [U.S. 1746 Mathews]

c. **1801** Gov. Hunter *HRNSW* iii. 820n.: A report which some artful villain in the colony had propagated amongst the Irish convicts lately arrived, 'That there was a colony of white people at no very great distance in the back country – 150 or 200 miles – where there was abundance of every sort of provision without the necessity of so much labour.'

1893 Simpson Newland *Paving the Way* 198: I presume you will continue the examination of the back-country with all the hands available, it is useless trying to track her in that thick scrub.

1921 K. S. Prichard *Black Opal* 69: His father, James Henty, had taken up land in the back-country, long before opal was found on Fallen Star Ridge.

1956 A. W. Upfield *The Battling Prophet* 140: 'Us people from the Back Country can always look after ourselves. How long have you been in Australia?'

back, Mediterranean see **Mediterranean**

back of Bourke see **Bourke**

backside, sparrows (geese, peacocks, swallows) flying out of one's see **sparrows**

back to the cactus see **cactus**

back up *v.* To repeat an action, esp. in obtaining a second helping of food
1932 Let. 2 Feb. in *The Wasted Years?* ed. Judy Mackinolty (1981) 120: It appears that owing to men backing up and getting double issues, by means of visiting two towns at short distances apart on dole days, the police were ordered to make dole issuing orders between the hours of 11 o'clock and 12 o'clock.
1966 Elwyn Wallace *Sydney and the Bush* 79: 'They were all backing up for a second lot so I thought I'd go one better and have a third go.'
1981 *Sydney Morning Herald* 14 Sep. 7: On Friday night . . . Ian is a barman at a restaurant at the Rocks from 7 pm to 12.30 am. He backs up on Sunday afternoon.

back up *n.* A second helping

1946 Rohan Rivett *Behind Bamboo* 330: *Backup*, second helping. *Backup king*, man always chasing second helpings.
1953 T. A. G. Hungerford *Riverslake* 199: He raised the blackened tray above his head . . . 'Who'll be in a back-up?'
1971 Frank Hardy *The Outcasts of Foolgarah* 19: 'We fed yer. Right? And we know you appreciate it because you always have a back up of everything.'

bag To disparage, 'knock'
1975 *Australian* 11 Nov. 10: 'He [the TV critic] said his wife loved the show and I said yeah but you're always bagging it and he said, yeah but we've got to sell papers somehow.'
1977 *Sydney Morning Herald* 23 Sep. 7: He is now bagging Mr Fraser at every opportunity, saying he is the worst Prime Minister the Liberals have ever had.
1981 *Australian* 20 Oct. 3: It pains me to report that Choice, journal of the Australian Consumers' Association, bags Vegemite for having too much salt in it.

bag, get a Reproach to a cricketer who has dropped a catch
1925 Seymour Hicks *Hullo Australians* 246: If a man who is fielding misses a catch they tell him to get a bag.
1969 Leslie Haylen *Twenty Years' Hard Labor* 70: When annoyed at some bad play Evatt yelled out 'Get a bag'.
1975 Xavier Herbert *Poor Fellow My Country* 1239: 'Sometimes you'd think you were listening-in to a commentary on a cricket-match or something, and expect someone to yell *Get a Bag!*'

bag, in the See quot. 1982
1941 Baker 7: *Bag, in the* (Of a horse) not intended to win.
1982 Joe Andersen *Winners Can Laugh* 148: Sam rejected many offers from the smart bookmakers to put him in the bag, meaning that, in return for preventing a horse from winning, a rider received a percentage of the money the bookmaker won on the race as a result of the arrangement.

bagman 1 An itinerant carrying his possessions with him. This is the broadest sense of the word, covering both the tramp (cf. **swagman**) and the traveller on horseback (**bagman 2**).
1904 Henry Lawson 'The Last Review'

Verse ii 63: Thought he [Steelman] was an honest bagman.
1910 C. E. W. Bean *On the Wool Track* 220: When a man says he met a 'traveller' or a 'bagman' in the bush he does not mean a commercial traveller. He means a man making his way from station to station, probably a man on horseback with his kit in his bag.
1941 Kylie Tennant *The Battlers* 19: 'Well, this (*adjective*) song was about an (*adjectival*) bagman who was getting himself a bit of meat ... The busker nodded somewhat contemptuously. 'Waltzing Matilda, the Australian National Anthem.'
2 A mounted swagman: esp. in N.T. and W.A.
1911 E. S. Sorenson *Life in the Australian Backblocks* 72: Two terms that are often confused one with the other are swagman and bagman. The first is a footman, the other a mounted man who may have anything from one to half a dozen horses. Though both are looking for work, they move on very different planes; the latter is considered a cut above the former, and looks down with a mildly contemptuous eye on the slowly plodding swagman.
1966 Tom Ronan *Once There Was a Bagman* 31: The bagmen, the horse-borne wanderers, the one purely unique type Australia ever produced.
3 An unemployed itinerant in the depression of the 1930s
1931 Let. of 8 Dec. in *The Wasted Years?* ed. Judy Mackinolty (1981) 116: It is a common occurrence to see bagmen jumping the rattler from this siding.
1965 Frank Hardy *The Yarns of Billy Borker* 49: 'I joined the army when war broke out. Came straight off the track. The sixth Divvy was made up mainly of bagmen, first steady job we ever had was getting shot at.'

Bagman's Gazette A fictitious publication containing news and rumours; graffiti left by itinerants [f. *bagman* 2]
1954 Tom Ronan *Vision Splendid* 266: 'If the Bagman's Gazette,' decided Mr Toppingham, 'was an actual news sheet and not just a figure of speech, I'd advertise for the old beggar in the agony column.'
1957 W. E. Harney *Life Among the Aborigines* 183–4: We passed the windmills and tanks that stretch along the way to water the herds as they travel, and on the big black iron sheets of the squatters' tanks one could read the 'Bagman's Gazette' which is the escape

channel for the grievances of the travellers as they go by ... Each tank we passed had its 'news', and only when a boss passed by and saw his name in a headline would he get the tank re-tarred.

bag of shells   see **shells**

bag, out of the   As for **out of the box**
1954 T. A. G. Hungerford *Sowers of the Wind* 44: 'It was all done with one bloody bomb – that's what makes it one out of the bag. One place that's been skittled is like any other, otherwise.'
1961 Tom Ronan *Only a Short Walk* 135: She was something out of the bag, was Hetty.

bag-swinger   A street prostitute
1953 Baker 124: *Bag swingers* who solicit custom from sailors are said to *cover the waterfront.*
1968 Stuart Gore *Holy Smoke* 79: 'What they call a bag-swinger, down in the city.'

bag system, the   In the depression of the 1930s, the issue of a bag of groceries each dole day to the unemployed.
1963 Frank Hardy *Legends from Benson's Valley* 176: Ernie Lyle read two of the small signs 'Work not Charity', 'Down with the Bag system'. A chord in his heart responded: bags of groceries at Ambler's store, margarine, bulk tea, the cheapest brands thrust into your hand without choice or ceremony.

bag your head, go and   Expression of disagreement, rejection, dismissal
1930 J. S. Litchfield *Far-North Memories* 168: 'Why didn't you tell that lunatic old government to go and bag its silly old head?'
1951 Dymphna Cusack and Florence James *Come In Spinner* 246: 'Aw, go bag your head. It makes me want to puke when I hear you fellows going on with all this purity bunk.'
1976 Dorothy Hewett *This Old Man Comes Rolling Home* 42: 'Ah! Go and bag your 'ead!'
1982 *Sydney Morning Herald* 19 Aug. 7: Fraser the cynical vote-buying survivor told Fraser the nice guy to go bag his head.

bags, rough as   Uncouth, to outward appearance
1919 W. H. Downing *Digger Dialects* 42: *Rough as bags* See 'Rough stuff'. *Rough stuff*

An undisciplined, reckless, indecent, disorderly or disrespectful person or thing.

1929 K. S. Prichard *Coonardoo* 22: 'Ted was as rough as bags,' Geary said; 'a good-looking, good-natured bloke who could neither read nor write.'

1948 Patrick White *The Aunt's Story* 34: Tom Wilcocks was as rough as bags. His neck was red and strong. The pollard had caked hard on his hard hands.

1970 Cynthia Nolan *A Bride for St Thomas* 133: She was a good organiser, but as a nurse she was rough as bags.

1984 Marion Eldridge *Walking the Dog* 89: 'Rough as bags,' people said of Raelene, and in the same breath, 'heart of gold.'

bail up All the senses illustrated seem to have been current simultaneously, although 3 gained more currency as 'bailing up' came to be associated more with highways
1 'To secure the head of a cow in a "bail" while she is milked ... *Austral..* and N.Z.' (OED 1847–1950)
2 In bushranging, to hold the victims under guard, confine them or tie them up
1843 *Sydney Monitor and Commercial Advertiser* 21 Jan. 2: On last Wednesday week, two armed bushrangers went into Grovenor's public house ... they pulled out pistols, 'bailed up' the whole of the family and proceeded to plunder the house ... about 10 o'clock, Mr Grovenor was enabled to free himself.
1862 Horace Earle *Ups and Downs* 82: A plan at that time not unusual amongst bushrangers in their dealings with their victims, namely 'bailing them up', or securing them to trees, and leaving them thus to starve.
3 Equivalent to the highwayman's 'Stand and deliver'
1852 G. C. Mundy *Our Antipodes* i 179: 'Bail up – or you're a dead man,' resounded from behind a thick tree, through a fork of which a double-barrelled gun covered the driver's head.
1853 Mrs C. Clacy *A Lady's Visit to the Gold Diggings of Australia in 1852–53* 127: I cannot quite realise the terrified passengers being driven through the Black Forest, but can picture their horror when ordered to 'bail up' by a party of Australian Turpins.
1895 Rolf Boldrewood *The Crooked Stick* 6: As the coach came abreast of them the man on the grey turned towards it, and, with a raised revolver in his hand, shouted, 'Bail up!'

4 More generally, to hold at bay, arrest the progress of, 'corner'
1859 Henry Kingsley *Recollections of Geoffry Hamlyn* iii 152: And they [the bushrangers] were bailed up in the limestone gully; and all the party were away after them.
1870 Rachel Henning *Letters* ed. D. Adams (1963) 239: [The creek] had risen so that he could not get back, and was 'bailed up' in Stroud for two days.
1919 W. K. Harris *Outback in Australia* 3: Five miles further on ... a road maintenance man bailed me up. 'The mailman said he saw your roan colt tied up near my shanty. Did you have a feed?'
1949 Ruth Park *Poor Man's Orange* 91: Brought up in Surry Hills, she felt there wasn't a drunk in the district she couldn't have handled if he bailed her up.

bake it See quots [services slang]
1968 Geoffrey Dutton *Andy* 14: 'I'm going to need to use one of them latrine buckets pretty soon' ... 'Will you *shut up* and just bake it for a minute or two.'
1970 Richard Beilby *No Medals for Aphrodite* 167: No movement round the lines except to the latrines and then only in dire necessity – 'Bake it, fella if you don't want your head shot off.'

baker, floury   see **floury baker**

balander See quot. 1978 [f. Macassarese]
1946 W. E. Harney *North of 23°* 121: He [the Malay] would land on the beach, and, advancing to the spot where Alf sat resplendently dressed ... would thrice bow his head to the 'ballander'.
1978 *Australian* 6 Oct. 7: Balander ... is an Aboriginal name for a white man – corruption of the word Hollander. The tribes of Arnhem Land knew the tough, phlegmatic Dutchmen of the East Indies before Cook was born. Now a balander means any white man.
1982 Alan Powell *Far Country* 36: The word 'balander', originally referring to the 'Hollanders', was adopted widely in Arnhem Land to designate all white men.

balfastards, alas! milfissed the An exclamation indicating the failure of some action, from an anecdote 'A hulfunting we will golfo' current among Australian soldiers in World War II (communicated by L. Bottomley).

Another version is given in Baker (1945: 274).

c. **1944** A rififleman jumped into a trulfuck with his gulfang to shoot dulfucks swilfimming on the walfater, he raised his rififle and ailfaimed at the dulfucks. Balfang! Balfang! went the rififle. Flalfap! flalfap! went the dulfucks. 'Alas! milfissed the balfastards!' said the rififleman.

Another version is reported by Mr O.C. Uden of Glenunga S.A., from an RAAF source. A man goes to the doctor to be treated for stuttering, and as he can pronounce 'alf' without a stutter, he is encouraged to insert that in each word. He later gives an account of a hunting trip: 'Halfow Dalfoctor. I was walfading along a ralfiver stalfalking dalfucks . . .'

ball-bearing cowboy   See quot.
1980 Rod Ansell *To Fight the Wild* 46: That's one thing about being a 'ballbearing cowboy', for having taken to chasing cattle in a vehicle instead of on a horse.

ball tearer   Someone or something exceptional, for good or bad qualities
1973 Jim McNeil *The Chocolate Frog* 25: 'I mean you bein' pinched for street fightin' . . . yer must be a real little ball-tearer.'
1978 *National Times* 27 May 29: He [Mr Neville Wran] gets to the theatre, and of what he's seen lately Ron Blair's play about the Christian Brothers stood out as a 'ball-tearer'.
1984 *Sydney Morning Herald* 26 Mar. 2: He [Nick Greiner] thought the Opposition might have done better in the country and not quite as well in the city. 'The result in the city shows that corruption is a ball-tearer in the city.'

Balmain boys don't cry   Statement by N. K. Wran at the NSW Conference of the ALP on 11 June 1983
1983 *Sun-Herald* 12 June. 2: Premier Neville Wran yesterday told of the 'anguish and indignity' the Street Royal Commission was causing him . . . 'You know Balmain boys don't cry – we're too vulgar and too common for that and probably vote Labor anyway.'
1984 Nick Greiner *Sydney Morning Herald* 25 Feb. 12: We all know that Balmain boys don't cry, but they certainly bleat a lot.

Balt   An immigrant to Australia from the Baltic countries (and Poland and Holland) after World War II: *derogatory* [f. *Balt* a

native or inhabitant of one of the Baltic states OED 1878: not used pejoratively]
1949 *Sydney Morning Herald* 11 Aug. 1: Yesterday Mr Calwell launched a campaign to get Australians to drop the terms 'D.P.s', 'Displaced Persons' and 'Balts' and to call these migrants 'New Australians'.
1953 T. A. G. Hungerford *Riverslake* 32: A dozen of them, six Poles and the rest a mixture of Lithuanians and Ukranians and Latvians and Estonians, big and small, old and young, dark and fair, but indistinguishable now in their nonentity. Balts.
1959 Dorothy Hewett *Bobbin Up* 150: 'Look at them bloody Balts, all with their heads down and their arses up,' old Betty grumbled . . . 'They'll never be Aussies while they keep that up. They'll work us all outa a job.'
1981 Peter Corris *White Meat* 45: When the migrant rush from Europe got going after the war we called them all 'Balts' wherever they came from, but this one looked like the genuine article.

Bananaland   Queensland: *jocular* [f. crop]
1893 Henry Lawson 'Hungerford' *Prose* i 106: The post office is in New South Wales, and the police barracks in Bananaland.
1946 *Sun* (Sydney) 4 Aug. Suppl. 15: They reckon as he [Captain Cook] sailed away he gave one look back at the coast of Bananaland and said: 'Strewth, I'm glad to give that dump back to the blacks.'
1973 Patrick White *The Eye of the Storm* 185: 'Don't yer remember that, Florrie, from Banana land?'
Bananalander   Queenslander: *jocular*
1887 *Bulletin* 26 Feb. 67: He made all the arrangements for being married on that day, and his friends rallied up to congratulate him, and see him through, after the custom of the simple Bananalanders.
1886 Percy Clarke *The 'New Chum' in Australia* 66: A Queenslander is . . . distinguished by the title of 'banana-man'.

bandicoot *n.*   Used in phrases suggesting misery or destitution [f. the animal]
1845 R. Howitt *Impressions of Australia Felix* 233: 'Poor as a bandicoot', 'Miserable as a shag on a rock', & c.; these and others I very frequently heard them make use of.
1859 Henry Kingsley *Recollections of Geoffry Hamlyn* iii 83–4: 'That Van Diemen's bush would starve a bandicoot.'
1877 Rolf Boldrewood *A Colonial Reformer* (1890) 442: He hadn't had a soul to

talk to for three weeks, since the muster began, and was as miserable as a bandicoot.

1934 Steele Rudd *Green Grey Homestead* 18: 'Spring Gully!' he'll snarl. 'That country is no good for you; 'twouldn't feed a bandicoot!'

1946 K. S. Prichard *The Roaring Nineties* 81–2: 'Was as miserable as a bandicoot, felt like chucking up prospecting and trying to get a job . . . on the mines.'

1980 Densey Clyne *Sydney Morning Herald* 12 Aug. 7: I don't know where the term 'miserable as a bandicoot' came from. They do wear rather long faces, but it's through bone structure rather than disposition.

see **boudoir bandicoot**

bandicoot *v.* To remove potatoes from below the surface, leaving the top of the plant intact [f. the animal's burrowing habit]

1898 George Dunderdale *The Book of the Bush* 102: 'You bandicooted my potatoes last night, and you've left the marks of your dirty feet on the ground.'

1944 M. J. O'Reilly *Bowyangs and Boomerangs* 2: There was a general rule in our district . . . that swagmen might be allowed to go into the paddocks and 'bandicoot' potatoes. The interpretation of 'bandicooting' is that the swaggie could scratch a hole round the potato plant, pick out a few big ones, and hill up the plant again to allow the remainder to mature.

1987 Barney Roberts *Where's Morning Gone?* 42: 'What about taking him a butt of potatoes and a few swedes. It might stop the old reprobate from sneaking down to bandicoot some of ours?'

bandicoot on a burnt ridge, like a A state of loneliness and deprivation

1900 Henry Lawson 'Joe Wilson's Courtship' *Prose* i 546: I mooched around all the evening like an orphan bandicoot on a burnt ridge, and then I went up to the pub and filled myself up with beer, and damned the world.

1935 H. R. Williams *Comrades of the Great Adventure* 36: Abdul, shorn of his finery . . . low in condition, like a bandicoot on an ironstone ridge.

bandy, knock someone To worst completely, leave flabbergasted [listed by Partridge as 'tailors': from ca. 1860]

1899 W. T. Goodge *Hits! Skits! and Jingles!* 165: 'You can talk about yer sheep dorgs,' said the man from Allan's Creek, / 'But I know a dorg that simply knocked 'em bandy!'

1934 F. E. Baume *Burnt Sugar* 59: 'You're seventeen, and could knock me bandy.'

1948 Ruth Park *Poor Man's Orange* 174: 'If I hear you slinging off at her again, I'll knock you bandy, honest to goodness I will!'

1968 Craig McGregor *People, Politics and Pop* 43: What do most of his [the taxi-driver's] passengers feel about the heat? 'Why, it knocks 'em bandy,' he says.

bang like a dunny door see **dunny**

bangtail muster See quots 1888, 1938

1888 W. S. S. Tyrwhitt *The New Chum in the Queensland Bush* 61: Every third or fourth year on a cattle station, they have what is called a 'bang tail muster'; that is to say, all the cattle are brought into the yards, and have the long hairs at the end of the tail cut off square . . . the object of it is, to take a census . . . unless marked in some way, it would be impossible to distinguish those that have been through the stockyard from those that have not.

1938 Francis Ratcliffe *Flying Fox and Drifting Sand* 331 n.: In a bangtail muster every beast rounded up has the tuft of its tail docked to prevent its being counted twice. This is the only way of getting an accurate tally on an unfenced run several hundreds or thousands of square miles in area.

1951 Ernestine Hill *The Territory* 391: 'We're sellin' Merryfield, an' now the buyers have asked for a bang-tail.'

Banjo, the The pen-name of A. B. Paterson (1864–1941), used in his contributions to the *Bulletin* from 12 June 1886; nickname of anyone surnamed Paterson

1896 *Bulletin* 3 Oct. Red Page: An English weekly declares that Becke is popularly known as the Kipling of the Pacific. 'Banjo' and Lawson have also been identified as more-or-less Kiplings.

1903 Joseph Furphy *Such is Life* (1944) 348: Sir Francis Head, one of the five exceptions to this rule – Gordon being the second, 'Banjo' the third, 'Glenrowan' the fourth, and the demurring reader the fifth.

banjo 1 A frying pan [f. shape]

1900–10 O'Brien and Stephens: *Banjo* a bush name for a frying pan.

2 A shovel
1919 W. H. Downing *Digger Dialects* 10: *Banjo* – a shovel. *Swing the banjo* – dig.
1942 Gavin Casey *It's Harder for Girls* 224–5: All his mother's big ideas, and mine, too, wouldn't keep him off the handle of a banjo if that was what he was suited for.
1973 Donald Stuart *Morning Star Evening Star* 110: He was alongside me swinging his banjo.
3 A shoulder of mutton
1919 W. K. Harris *Outback in Australia* 146: Called at his particular station for the proverbial free ... 'banjo' (shoulder) of mutton.
1925 *Sydney Worker* 3 Jun. 13: The mutton was not of super-excellent quality, but Johnny was rarely known to part with a 'banjo' without getting good value in return.
4 Popular name for the fiddler ray [f. shape]
1979 *Age* (Melbourne) 2 Nov. Weekender 21: Their haul included banjo and gummy sharks.

banker A river with the water up to or overflowing its banks, esp. in the expression 'run a banker'
1848 W. H. Haygarth *Recollections of Bush Life in Australia* 129: Now that I take a second glance at the river, its waters look very muddy, which is a sure sign of its being high, not to say a 'banker'.
1877 Rolf Boldrewood *A Colonial Reformer* (1890) 410: The river was high, had come down a 'banker', and any further rainfall might bring down a flood such as the dwellers in those parts had not seen for many a day.
1889 Henry Lawson 'The Ballad of the Drover' *Verse* i 27: Till the river runs a banker / All stained with yellow mud.
1927 Steele Rudd *The Romance of Runnibede* 88: The Station Creek rose to a banker – rose till it spread itself a quarter of a mile on either side, carrying down logs and uprooted trees and the carcases of dead bullocks.
1956 Kylie Tennant *The Honey Flow* 209: Cobberloi Creek was running a banker.

bar, can't stand (won't have) a ~ of Can't tolerate on any terms [? f. *bar* in music]
1945 Margaret Trist *Now that We're Laughing* 25: 'I can't stand a bar of these people that visit you and must have a bath

every day to show you how clean they are.'
1962 Gavin Casey *Amid the Plenty* 149: 'Not that I'd have a bar of a bloke who'd lie to his mates, but it's different with that other mob.'
1973 *Australian* 4 May 2: Dr Arnold said that doctors would be violently against direct billing. 'They won't have a bar of it,' he said.

barbecue, a chop short of a As for **a shingle short** q.v.
1984 *Sunday Independent* (Perth) 6 May 36: The tragedy of that premise is that it automatically assumes that all in charge of prisons are a chop short of a barbecue.

barbed wire Fourex beer, esp. in Darwin [f. xxxx symbol]

barbie A barbecue [abbr.]
1976 *Australian* 14 Aug. 20: He propounded the natural and national virtues of the Aussie beach barbie with beer and prawns, and the big chunder.
1981 *Age* (Melbourne) 19 Jun. Weekender 4: The barbie glows hotly in the cool, river-scented night air as the volunteer short order cook prepares to bung on the snags, hamburgers and giant T-bones.

Barcoo rot A skin ulceration similar to scurvy
1870 E. B. Kennedy *Four Years in Queensland* 46: Land scurvy is better known in Queensland by local names, which do not sound very pleasant, such as 'Barcoo rot', 'Kennedy rot', according to the district it appears in. There is nothing dangerous about it, it is simply the festering of any cut or scratch on one's legs, arms or hands. [Morris]
1903 Joseph Furphy *Such is Life* (1944) 201: The backs of his hands were pretty bad with the external scurvy known as 'Barcoo rot' produced by unsuitable food and extreme hardship.
1968 Walter Gill *Petermann Journey* 57: He has broken out in clusters of sores on hands and wrists. 'Barcoo rot' undoubtedly.

Barcoo salute See quot. 1973
1973 Patsy Adam-Smith *The Barcoo Salute* title page: 'I see you've learnt the Barcoo salute,' said a Buln Buln Shire councillor to the Duke of Edinburgh. 'What's that,' said

His Royal Highness, waving his hand again to brush the flies off his face. 'That's it,' said the man from the bush. [quotation dated 1953]
see **Australian salute, Queensland salute**

Barcoo sickness (spews, vomit) See quots
1898 Morris: *Barcoo Vomit* painless attacks of vomiting, occurring immediately after food is taken, followed by hunger, and recurring as soon as hunger is satisfied.
1927 M. M. Bennett *Christison of Lammermoor* 62: One of the great hardships of those days [the 1860s] was the sickness brought on by the monotonous food and bread made from tainted flour, every settler supposed it peculiar to his district, and named it accordingly Burdekin, or Belyando, or Barcoo sickness.
1966 *Australian* 3 Jan. 6: The unending irritations of the shearer's life ... barcoo spews and purgatorial insects.

bardie 1 An edible wood grub [*Bardistus cibarius*]
1946 K. S. Prichard *The Roaring Nineties* 200: Kalgoorla brought her toasted bardies to eat. Sally recognized the fat white grubs Maritana used to devour with such relish.
1968 Stuart Gore *Holy Smoke* 82: 'They've been stuck out in the mulga for nearly a week ... livin' on lizards and bardies.'
1983 T. A. G. Hungerford *Stories from Suburban Road* 41: He loved to eat the bardies my father cooked every time we went out for wood – the big, white fat grubs you found in every banksia when it split, with hard brown heads the size of a pea ... He would heat the blade of a shovel over the tea fire and drop a handful of bardies onto it and stir them around with a stick until ... they were done.
2 The exclamation 'Starve the bardies!' (a variant of 'Starve the lizards!') more often encountered in lists of Australianisms than in actual conversation
1941 Baker 8: *Bardies! Starve the*: A popular W.A. ejaculation, synonymous with 'Stone the crows!'
1969 *Pocket Oxford Dictionary* 1020: *Starve the bardies!* excl. of surprise or disgust.

bark, short of a sheet of As for **a shingle short** q.v.

1885 Mrs Campbell Praed *Australian Life* 199: He had always understood that Richard Murray was short of a sheet of bark – the Australian equivalent of 'a tile loose'.

Barker, a Bishop A long glass of beer [f. Frederick Barker, Bishop of Sydney 1845–81, 6′ 5″ in height]
1886 Frank Cowan *Australia: A Charcoal Sketch* 32: Long sleever, Bishop Barker, and Deep-sinker, synonyms of the Yankee Schooner.

Barlow, Billy The inexperienced immigrant who meets with misadventures in the colony [f. the ballad 'Billy Barlow': see *Old Bush Songs* ed. Stewart and Keesing (1957) 53–5]
1843 'Billy Barlow' *Maitland Mercury* 2 Sep. 4: When I was at home I was down on my luck. / And I earnt a poor living by drawing a truck; / But old aunt died and left me a thousand – 'Oh, oh / I'll start on my travels,' said Billy Barlow / Oh dear, lackaday, oh; / So off to Australia came Billy Barlow.

Barn, the Old The Sydney Stadium (closed in 1970)
1973 *Sydney Morning Herald* 13 Feb. 15: It would never have happened at the Old Barn.

barney *n.* An argument, disagreement, fight [f. *barney* A disturbance, dispute, altercation EDD 1891]
1858 Charles Thatcher *Colonial Songster* 68: A barney first commences / With a little bit of 'skiting', / But calling names is not enough, / And so it ends in fighting.
1893 Henry Lawson 'Brummy Usen' *Prose* i 77: 'She was just as self-opinionated as the neighbours, and many a barney she had with them about it.'
1938 Xavier Herbert *Capricornia* 379: 'Joe always plays tunes like that when there's been a barney with the men.'
1981 *Business Review* 11 Jan. 2: Andrew Peacock is planning to pull on a barney with the unions. If he wins the face of industrial relations may never be the same again.

barney *v.* To argue, dispute
1876 Rolf Boldrewood *A Colonial Reformer* (1890) 183: 'If you go barneying about calves, or counting on horses that's give in, he'll best ye, as sure as you're born.

1947 Vance Palmer *Hail Tomorrow* 63: 'No more barneying with pannikin bosses about the length of a smoko or whether the sheep's wet or dry.'

barra Barramundi [abbr.]
1979 *Courier-Mail* (Brisbane) 6 Apr. 20: Controls on barra recommended [heading] The giant perch, or barramundi, one of Australia's top sporting and table fish, may be in danger of being fished out.

barrack *v.* 1 To indulge in noisy comment; to subject to banter; to ridicule, jeer at [f. *barrack* to brag, to be boastful of one's fighting powers N. Irel. EDD. Quot. 1878 may be from *baragouin* (*barrikin*) language so altered in sound or sense as to become generally unintelligible; jargon, 'double-Dutch' OED 1613]
1878 T. E. Argles *The Pilgrim* iv 39: Douglass mumbled over a 'petition' intended for presentation to Parliament, for the edification of assembled toughs and larrikins, but it was received with noisy insult and cries of 'cheese your barrickin' and 'shut up'.
1893 Henry Lawson 'For'ard' *Verse* i 259: There's a broken swell amongst us – he is barracked, he is chaffed.
1934 Vance Palmer *Sea and Spinifex* 285: He had never liked being barracked, he was beginning to lose his temper.
2 In sport, to interject in favour of one side or against the other; to support
1891 Henry Lawson 'At the Tug-of-war' *Verse* i 114: It gave the old man joy / To fight a passage through the crowd and barrack for his boy.
1913 John Sadleir *Recollections of a Victorian Police Officer* 278: They yelled and shouted, some 'barracking' for Jack, some for the sergeant.
1934 Tom Clarke *Marriage at 6 a.m.* 200: When Arthur Gilligan's Test Team came out he 'barracked' for Australia.
1969 William Dick *Naked Prodigal* 93: 'He barracks for the Magpies though, same as me.'

barrack *n.* 1 The product of 'barracking'
1899 *The Rambler* 13 Feb. 2: Bits o' Barrack [heading to column]
1947 Vance Palmer *Cyclone* 14: Donolly was jollying the child about the shriek she had let out, but she did not respond to his barrack.
2 Baroque pearl

1962 Jock Marshall and Russell Drysdale *Journey Among Men* 138: Perhaps more interesting than ordinary pearls, though far less valuable today, are those locally known as 'barrack'. This expression is a corruption of 'baroque'. 'Barrack' pearls may be of fantastic shapes. They are sometimes formed by pearly deposits over fishes, crabs, and other small marine animals that have invaded the shell and died there.

barracker One who 'barracks'
1892 G. J. James *Shall I Try Australia?* 129: In Victoria also, the people are 'football mad', and the youths wear the colours of their favourite club, in a profusion which is apt to mystify the new arrival, these are the 'barrackers', the verb 'to barrack' meaning to audibly encourage their own favourites, and comment disparagingly upon the performance of their opponents.
1925 Seymour Hicks *Hullo Australians* 246: A place they call the Hill is occupied by thousands of barrackers, not soldiers, but fellows who are sure they understand cricket better than the umpires.
1969 Alan O'Toole *The Racing Game* 169: 'Like the football days, eh, Bill? You can't beat having a few barrackers.'

barracks Building on a station for the accommodation of the jackeroos, etc., and marking a division in the social hierarchy
1876 Rolf Boldrewood *A Colonial Reformer* (1890) 100: At a short distance from 'the house', Mr Jedwood's cottage, or hut, as the residence of the proprietor was indifferently designated, stood a roomy, roughly finished building known as the 'barracks'. Here lived the overseer ... Three of the numerous bedrooms were tenanted by young men ... neophytes, who were gradually assimilating the lore of Bushland. To the barracks were also relegated those just too exalted for the men's hut, while not eligible for ... 'the cottage'. Such were cattle dealers, sheep-buyers, overseers of neighbouring stations, and generally unaccredited travellers whose manners or appearance rendered classification hazardous.
1903 Joseph Furphy *Such is Life* (1944) 254. Being a little too exalted for the men's hut, and a great deal too vile for the boss's house, I was quartered in the narangies' barracks.
1963 John Naish *That Men Should Fear* 57: 'You want the barracks or the house?'

asked the driver, with a suddenness that caught me unawares.

barrakin see **barrack**

barrow To start or finish off a sheep for a shearer, as a way of learning to shear [? f. Gaelic *bearradh* shearing, clipping]
 1904 E. S. Sorenson *A Shanty Entertainment* 94: It's a good while since we started, you and me, to get a shed; / 'Ow you barrowed that first year for Marty Kell.
 1964 H. P. Tritton *Time Means Tucker* 39–40: On the advice of the boss of the board, I spent most of the afternoon watching and 'barrowing', that is, finishing off. Bill would shear a sheep to the 'whipping side' then pass it to me and as it was straight going, seven or eight blows would complete the job . . . Soon I was holding my own with the other learners.

bart A girl: *obs.* [unexplained]
 c. **1882** *The Sydney Slang Dictionary* 1: *Bart* A girl, generally applied to those of loose character.
 1899 W. T. Goodge *Hits! Skits! and Jingles!* 150: And his lady love's his 'donah', / Or his 'clinah' or his 'tart' / Or his 'little bit o' muslin', / As it used to be his 'bart'.

bash, have a, give it a Make an attempt at (as in 'give it a burl')
 1959 David Forrest *The Last Blue Sea* 183: 'Yair, it's somebody else's turn to have a bash,' said Lincoln.
 1969 William Dick *Naked Prodigal* 179: 'Reckon you'll be able to do it? I mean it's pretty hard.' 'I hope so. I'm gonna give it a bash, anyway.'
 1979 *National Times* 21 Jul. 15: The news director said 'We're a journo short – want to have a bash?'

bash the ear To harangue, talk incessantly [f. **earbasher**]
 1971 Rena Briand *White Man in a Hole* 26: Other days I'd . . . drown my sorrows at the Front Bar and bash Johnny's ear with my tale of woe.
 1975 Xavier Herbert *Poor Fellow My Country* 30: 'They told me that I'd be lucky if you talked to me at all . . . and just as unlucky if you did' . . . 'They mean you'd regret it, because then I'd bash your ear?'

basket weavers from Balmain See **basket-weaving**

1982 *Sydney Morning Herald* 27 Oct. 24: Mr Unsworth is not alone in hurling the cutting insult at the defenceless trendies. Paul Keating disparagingly referred to them as 'basket-weavers from Balmain'.

basket-weaving The activity identifying the Left wing of the Labor party and its new ideology, in the view of their opponents
 1983 Patrick Cook *National Times* 17 Jun. 51: Back in Australia, the various ALP conferences convened, keeping hundreds of disturbed people off the streets, absorbed in ideological basket-weaving.
 1984 Mungo MacCallum *Sun-Herald* 8 Apr. 52: He marched down to the leafy bower where the Left held its meetings. In it were three or four old men practising their basket-weaving.

bastard None of the senses distinguished is exclusively Australian, but all are so much a part of the colloquial language as to be remarked upon by overseas visitors.
 1 Derogatory, but not necessarily suggesting illegitimacy
 1892 Henry Lawson 'The Captain of the Push' *Verse* i 187n: 'Here's the bleedin' push, me covey – here's a bastard from the bush! / Strike me dead, he wants to join us!' said the captain of the push.
 1929 A. B. Piddington *Worshipful Masters* 46: *Digger* [paraded before an English officer trying to discover who called the regimental cook a bastard] 'You keep on asking us who called that cook a bastard; what we want to know is, who called that bastard a cook?'
 1939 Kylie Tennant *Foveaux* 170: 'A man ought to heave the bastard out on his ear.'
 1974 E. G. Whitlam [addressing the Canberra branch of the ALP] *Sunday Telegraph* 9 Jun. 2: 'I do not mind the Liberals, still less do I mind the Country Party, calling me a bastard. In some circumstances I am only doing my job if they do. But I hope you will not publicly call me a bastard, as some bastards in the Caucus have.'
 1980 *Australian* 16 Aug. 13: When told that Premier Bjelke-Petersen was still on the miners' side in their housing tax fight with Canberra, Mr Tanzer replied: 'You can't help but like the old mongrel sometimes. It's a pity that he's such a rotten, radical, reactionary tory bastard.'
 2 Compassionate, indicating a grudging acceptance
 1903 Joseph Furphy *Such is Life* (1944)

31: 'Seen better days, pore (fellow),' observed Cooper sympathetically, as the ripple of water into the pannikin indicated that the whaler was at the tap.
1931 William Hatfield *Sheepmates* 269: 'I've knocked around a bit in my time, and I'll tell them that don't know him he's a decent sort of a poor bastard.'
1934 F. E. Baume *Burnt Sugar* 249: 'And not a bad old bastard either. Been here twenty-two years.'
1962 Stuart Gore *Down the Golden Mile* 159: Conlon . . . replied casually: 'Ah, he's not such a bad poor bastard.'
1981 David Ireland *National Times* 25 Jan. 25: He wasn't a bad poor bastard, it's just that he wasn't anything in particular and people could take him or leave him.
3 Friendly, affectionate
1882 A. J. Boyd *Old Colonials* 62: 'Now then, Harry, you old ——, what the —— is it going to be? Give it some —— name or other!'
1935 H. R. Williams *Comrades of the Great Adventure* 64: One of the things often remarked on by other British troops was the frequent use by the Australians of the word 'bastard'. In the A.I.F. this expression had a very elastic meaning. So much so that between pals it became almost a term of endearment.
1964 H. P. Tritton *Time Means Tucker* [recalling period 1905–6] 109: A short-necked man, with a chest like a barrel, and arms reaching to his knees, forced his way through the crowd, put his hand out and said, 'Frank, you bloody old bastard!' . . . They pumped his hand, smacked him on the back, swore at him and each other, then took possession of most of the bar.
1981 *Business Review* 18 Jan. 5: When being chummy, don't refer to them as 'you old bastard' or some such. Americans aren't used to being abused as a sign of friendship.
4 Impersonal
1915 Ion L. Idriess, diary in Bill Gammage *The Broken Years* (1974) 77: Of all the bastards of places this is the greatest bastard in the world.
1944 Lawson Glassop *We Were the Rats* 169: It's like one of your mates going out on patrol and not coming back. It's a bastard, but you can't do anything about it.'
1962 Alan Marshall *This is the Grass* 128: Sometimes a man began with a question seeking an explanation of my crutches: 'What's wrong with you?' 'Paralysis.' 'Bastard, isn't it . . . ?'

1983 Arthur Cannon *Bullocks, Bullockies and Other Blokes* 98: In bullocky language: 'There is a tide in the affairs of men, which, taken at the ebb, turns into a real bastard.'
see **Pommy bastard**

bastard from the bush, the An uncivilized interloper who imposes himself on the society he enters. [f. Lawson's poem 'The Captain of the Push' and variants of it; the lines most often quoted are not by Lawson: 'Will you have a cigarette, mate?' said the Captain of the Push / 'I'll have the flaming packet!' said the Bastard from the Bush.]
1962 Stuart Gore *Down the Golden Mile* 216: 'Don't think they'd have a bar o' me any other place, I suppose. Not cultured, eh? The bastard from the bush!'
1975 Xavier Herbert *Poor Fellow My Country* 1079: 'It's you're the bastard . . . The Bastard from the Bush. Get back where you belong!'

bastard, happy (lucky) as a ~ on Father's Day Unhappy, unlucky
1958 Frank Hardy *The Four-Legged Lottery* 128: 'I've got about as much luck as a bastard on Father's Day.'
1974 *Sunday Telegraph* (Sydney) 9 Jun. 30: Those words of the Bank of NSW's Russell Prowse – 'bankers are as miserable as a bastard on Father's Day' provided a touch of humour not normally associated with banks.

bastardization Term applied to initiation ceremonies at colleges, schools etc.
1969 *Australian* 20 Sep. 5: Mr Barnard also asked if the terms of reference of the board of inquiry into Duntroon were wide enough to look into whether 'bastardisation' at the college was condoned by some of the permanent military staff.
1979 *Advertiser* (Adelaide) 7 Mar. 3: Senior cadets at the Fort Largs Police Academy have committed 'bastardisation' outrages on several junior cadets, says the Melbourne 'Truth'.

bastardry See quot. 1945 [f. *bastard* 1]
1945 Baker 156: *bastardry* ill-treatment, injustice, anything unpleasant, especially when done at the whim of a superior officer [World War II slang]
1948 Sumner Locke Elliott *Rusty Bugles* in *Khaki, Bush and Bigotry* ed. Eunice Hanger

(1968) 95: 'You see . . . bastardry all the way along the line.'

1962 David Forrest *The Hollow Woodheap* 195–6: 'As one expert to another, Mr Lucas, I have to admire your particular brand of bastardry.'

1982 David Wilson *Weekend Australian* 6 Feb. 17: For more than a decade, taxpayer financed cultural bastardry has flourished in the name of experimental theatre at Melbourne's Pram Factory theatre.

bastards, keep the ~ honest The role perceived for the Australian Democrats (by their leader Senator Don Chipp) in holding the balance of power in the two-party system

1980 *Sydney Morning Herald* 10 Oct. 7: He [Senator Chipp] maintains that he hates politics but that there is a great need for the Democrats. The cynical realism of the catchcry 'keep the bastards honest' also appeals to an electorate noted for its disdain of politicians.

1984 *Age* (Melbourne) 25 Jul. 12: One aspect of the Mick Young affair that is intriguing is the silence of the Democrats. What has happened to Senator Chipp's election promise to 'keep the bastards honest'?

1984 *Sydney Morning Herald* 13 Oct. 38: I'm not sure why Senator Chipp was included [in the TV programme]. Maybe it was to keep the bastards hypothetical.

bastards, run over the Reported instruction of the N.S.W. premier, Mr R. Askin, when demonstrators lay on the road before President L. B. Johnson's motorcade in Sydney in 1966

1968 *Sydney Morning Herald* 24 Jul. 4: Mr Askin was clapped and cheered yesterday when he told a luncheon meeting [of the American Chamber of Commerce] that he had advised a policeman to run over demonstrators trying to block President Johnson's motorcade in Sydney in 1966. He had turned to the policeman and had said 'Run over the bastards'.

1971 *Sydney Morning Herald* 20 Mar. 3: Mr D. Chipp [Minister for Customs and Excise, reported addressing a dinner of the American Chamber of Commerce in Canberra] 'I would like to think that men of goodwill of my generation have more in common with the agonised student movement than with some of the extreme nigger-flogging reactionaries of the establishment

complete with their "run-the-bastards-down" philosophy.'

1981 *Sydney Morning Herald* 18 Jul. 12: I am going to go down (in history) as the bloke who said: 'Ride over the bastards'. – *Sir Robert Askin, in hospital.*

bat the breeze To engage in idle talk [cf. U.S. *fan the breeze*]

1945 Baker 154: *to bat the breeze*, to gossip or talk. [World War II slang]

1953 T. A. G. Hungerford *Riverslake* 75: 'I've got no time to stand here batting the breeze with you.'

1963 Jon Cleary *A Flight of Chariots* 246: 'What have you two been batting the breeze about?'

batch To do one's own cooking and housekeeping (of a man) [f. *bach* abbr. of *bachelor* U.S. 1870 Mathews]

1882 William J. Sowden *The Northern Territory As It Is* 154: Supposing he lives in a hut and 'batches', this is the kind of bill he is confronted with.

1896 Henry Lawson '"Dossing Out" and "Camping"' *Prose* i 164: He had a partner. They batched in the office, and did their cooking over a gas lamp.

1936 William Hatfield *Australia Through the Windscreen* 234: Rooms in which men 'batch' with all the untidiness of men left to look after themselves in single blessedness.

1955 *Sydney Morning Herald* 6 Sep. 1: 'When I'm batching,' he writes, 'I put on the electric kettle, cook the eggs in it, make the tea, shave and wash up with the same water.'

bathers Swimming costume

1936 H. Drake-Brockman *Sheba Lane* 91–2: He appeared, as he had threatened, in his bathers, and was greeted with cries of 'Bright idea' from everybody.

1942 Gavin Casey *It's Harder for Girls* 152: Most of them were wearing trunks, and my old bathers were baggy as well as out-of-date.

1983 Mr Justice Rowland *West Australian* (Perth) 6 Aug. 4: 'It is the magistrate's task to decide whether the mere standing in a pathway to the beach in summer time with bathers down and penis in hand offends against contemporary standards of propriety.'

see **cossie**

battle (battling) 1 To struggle for a livelihood; to work in low-paid employment (usually with an implication of praiseworthiness or self-congratulation)

1907 Henry Lawson 'The Strangers' Friend' *Prose* i 731: 'The fellers as knows can battle around for their bloomin' selves, but I'll look after the stranger.'

1923 Jack Moses *Beyond the City Gates* 128: When you're cockyin' and battlin' and live on what you grow.

1939 Kylie Tennant *Foveaux* 178: All her life Mrs Thompson had been what she called 'battling for a crust'.

1969 Alan O'Toole *The Racing Game* 156: 'That money would make all the difference between battling and being comfortable.'

2 To cadge, subsist by hawking homemade artifacts; used esp. of itinerants. Not derogatory, from respect accorded those down on their luck or able to live by their wits.

1902 Henry Lawson 'On the Tucker Track' *Prose* i 227: They were tramping along the track towards Bourke, they were very hard up and had to 'battle' for tucker and tobacco along the track.

1941 Kylie Tennant *The Battlers* 75: 'I'm going back to battle for some more rum.'

1944 Alan Marshall *These Are My People* 157: 'I'd been on a bad track and I knew this town was a hard town to battle, so I pulled up a bo and asked him if he knew where I could get a hand-out.'

battle, on the Working as a prostitute

1944 Lawson Glassop *We Were The Rats* 93: The girl was still staring. Perhaps she was, as Eddie would say, 'on the battle'. I had been told some of those girls hung about this lounge.

battler 1 A toiler, one who struggles for a livelihood. Anyone so styling himself asserts his apartness from the affluent class.

1896 Henry Lawson 'Stiffner and Jim' *Prose* i 127: I sat on him pretty hard for his pretensions, and paid him out for all the patronage he'd worked off on me . . . and told him never to pretend to me that he was a battler.

1949 Lawson Glassop *Lucky Palmer* 150: 'I'm no big shot,' he had said. 'I'm a battler. Just a battler having a good trot.'

1964 Donald Horne *The Lucky Country* 25: Australians love a 'battler', an underdog who is fighting the top dog, although their veneration for him is likely to pass if he comes out from under.

1975 *Australian* 12 Aug. 9: There are no signs that the forthcoming Federal Budget will give any help to the small Aussie battler.

2 Someone making a living, not just by toil, but by ingenuity [f. *battle* 2]

1935 F. D. Davison and B. Nicholls *Blue Coast Caravan* 157–8: We met two members of the genus 'battler' . . . they were side-show artists, travelling from one country show to another.

1941 Kylie Tennant *The Battlers* [book title]

3 A prostitute

1898 *Bulletin* 17 Dec. Red Page: A *bludger* is about the lowest grade of human thing, and is a brothel bully . . . A *battler* is the feminine.

1956 Ruth Park and D'Arcy Niland *The Drums Go Bang!* 142: The landlord shrugged casually. 'We got a battler in there,' he said. A battler is Sydneyese for prostitute.

4 See quots

1895 Cornelius Crowe *Australian Slang Dictionary* 7: *Battlers* broken-down backers of horses still sticking to the game.

1922 Arthur Wright *A Colt from the Country* 118–19: Professional punters and racetrack battlers, who manage to make a living of sorts out of the game.

Bay, the 1 In N.S.W., Long Bay Gaol

1918 J. Vance Marshall *Jail from Within* 16: 'If yer lucky yer might get a bite at the Bay tonight,' said the officer with brutal unconcern.

1967 B. K. Burton *Teach Them No More* 169: 'You could serve the whole five years, and you could do the lot at Grafton, or the Bay.'

2 In Victoria, Port Phillip Bay

1855 William Howitt *Land, Labour and Gold* i 29: On the left the Yarra winding down towards the Bay.

1915 C. J. Dennis *The Songs of a Sentimental Bloke* 81: We're honeymoonin' down beside the Bay.

1979 *Herald* (Melbourne) 21 May 1: Searches were going on today for a boy missing in rugged alpine country and a father and son missing on the Bay.

3 In Queensland, Cleveland Bay

1979 *Courier-Mail* (Brisbane) 21 Jul. 28: 'Bay' champ to try it again [heading] Trainer Ray Birse expects eight-year-old Windy Lane to cap an outstanding racing career by winning his second Cleveland Bay Handicap at Townsville today.

4   In N.T., Fannie Bay gaol (now a museum),
or racecourse
1946 W. E. Harney *North of 23°* 115: The
cells of the 'Bay' reminded me of old medi-
eval castles, with clanging doors, huge locks
and thick stone walls painted black.
1980 *NT News* 25 Jan. 20: Bay turns it on
for its bettors [heading] It's free beer again
tomorrow at Fannie Bay and then pony and
train rides on Monday.

Bay 13   See quot. 1981
1981 *Sun-Herald* 11 Jan. 9: Bay 13 is to
cricket lovers in Melbourne what the Hill is
to their counterparts in Sydney. Both are
traditional territory of yobbos who love
cricket and alcohol in more-or-less equal
amounts.
1984 *Age* (Melbourne) 30 May 39: The
notorious Bay 13 produces shafts of Shavian
wit like 'Go home ya Pommie mug'.

Bays, the   In S.A., the Glenelg Australian
Rules team
1979 *Advertiser* (Adelaide) 19 Jun. 20:
Norwood rattled by last quarter Bay revival
[heading] Norwood withstood a spectacular
revival by a gallant Glenelg to win a thrilling
match by nine points at Football park.

bean, pork and   see **pork**

bear, teddy   see **teddy bear**

bear up, do a   To pay court to a woman: *obs.*
[OED 'U.S. colloq.' n.d.]
1899 Henry Lawson 'The Hero of Redclay
Prose i 297: 'I'd been getting on all right with
the housemaid at the Royal . . . I thought it
was good enough to do a bit of a bear-up in
that direction.'
1942 Sarah Campion *Bonanza* 208: 'I was
all set to lay another fiver on your chances o'
gettin' hooked – you looked to be bearin' up
proper, an' no mistake.
1974 Donald Stuart *Prince of My Country*
63: 'Can you imagine old John doin' a bear-up
to a young dolly?'

Bears, the   The North Sydney Rugby
League team [f. the Big Bear supermarket,
which sponsored the club in 1965]
1975 *Sydney Morning Herald* 18 Aug. 9:
Gallant Bears skinned

beaten favourite, head like a   see **head**

beaut   1   Applied to something which is

exceptional in its class, and therefore usually
deserving admiration; vague term of commendation [abbr. *beauty* U.S. 1866
Mathews]
1905 Randolph Bedford *The Snare of
Strength* 223: At the sound all the stallion's
senses were . . . bent in his direction. 'He's a
bute,' said Dunphy. 'Quick as a flash; his
nerves are all on ball-bearings.'
1907 Nathan Spielvogel *The Cocky Farmer*
42: 'Them's Piggy Howe's cows. Best milk-
ers on the plains. That big Allerney gives a
heap of milk a day. She's a beaut.'
1930 L. Lower *Here's Luck* 266: 'An all I
get out of it is a black eye. Look at it!' 'What a
beaut!' exclaimed Stanley admiringly.
1973 Alexander Buzo *Rooted* 46: 'It was a
beaut design . . . He did this incredible white
obelisk anchored into a beaut welter of blue
streaks on a sheet of black strips with this
incredible screen of pink flecks on a beaut
steely surface.' 'Sounds beaut.'
2   In the phrase 'You beaut!', as an interjection of approval
1944 Lawson Glassop *We Were the Rats*
212: 'You beaut!' I cried. 'You bloody
beaut!'
1951 Dal Stivens *Jimmy Brockett* 184:
'You beaut!' he said. 'There's a fortune in
it.'
1962 Gavin Casey *Amid the Plenty* 206:
'I've got a job,' he said. 'You bloody little
beaut!' the grocer roared.
3   Indicating reproach or disapproval
1909 Arthur Wright *A Rogue's Luck* 35:
'You're a beaut,' he said, 'leavin' 'er cobber
like that.'
1948 H. Drake-Brockman *Sydney or the
Bush* 201: 'Mum,' his reproach met her,
'you're a beaut. Wher've you been?'
1953 T. A. G. Hungerford *Riverslake* 238:
'You must've thought I was a beaut, not
sticking with you.'

beauty   Expression of full agreement and
approval, often pronounced 'bewdy'
1969 Thomas Jenkins *We Came to Australia* 243: Ask if they want to go swimming
and they [the children] grin from ear to ear,
leap up and down and yell: 'Yair!' (yes),
'Bewdy!' (Beauty, meaning great idea).
1981 *Australian* 15 Dec. 14: Marsh was
everyone's hero when he declared: 'I'm
an Australian, not a bloody Pom.' Bewdy,
Marshy.

Bedourie shower   see **shower**

beer-up See quots

1919 W. H. Downing *Digger Dialects* 10: *Beer-up* A drunken orgy.

1941 Kylie Tennant *The Battlers* 314: 'If he's on a real proper beer-up,' the Stray whispered, 'he may go on for days.'

1971 Frank Hardy *The Outcasts of Foolgarah* 200: 'He moved in today and they're havin' a big beer-up tonight to celebrate.'

beg pardons, no No apologies, no quarter

1906 Edward Dyson *Fact'ry 'Ands* 198: ''Twas quick business down below here, 'n' no beg-pardons with Bunyip. He downed on his victim like er flash.'

1932 Leonard Mann *Flesh in Armour* 96–7: The Fritzes began to put up their hands – too late for most of them. No 'beg pardons'.

1965 Jack Dyer *'Captain Blood'* 27: There was little of the present-day spite . . . simply he-man encounters, straight-out fights and no beg pardons.

behind In Australian Rules Football, a kick that does not pass cleanly through the goal posts, or that goes between the goal post and the behind post: worth one point

1880 'The Opening Ball' *Comic Australian Verse* ed. G. Lehmann (1975) 2: 'Forward Carlton!' is now the cry, / And we rush it like the wind, / A roar from ten thousand throats go up, / For we've kicked another behind.

1980 *Mercury* (Hobart) 8 Apr. 22: North kicked 10 behinds in the first quarter and eight in the last in a shocking display.

behind, further ~ than Walla Walla see **Walla Walla**

bell sheep A sheep taken from the pen just as the bell rings to signal the end of a shift (important to a shearer trying to increase his tally)

1900 Henry Lawson 'A Rough Shed' *Prose* i 464: He [the shearer] is not supposed . . . to take a sheep out of the pen *after* the bell goes (smoke-ho, meals, or knock-off) but . . . he times himself to get so many sheep out of the pen *before* the bell goes, and *one more* – the 'bell sheep' – as it is ringing . . . The shearers are racing each other for tallies.

1911 E. S. Sorenson *Life in the Australian Backblocks* 245: There is also hard cutting among greedy persons for a bell sheep (the one caught just as the bell is about to ring off.)

Benghazi Handicap (Derby) See quots

1944 Lawson Glassop *We Were the Rats* 135: The confusion that was the retreat to Tobruk early in 1941 – we always called it the Benghazi Handicap – has rarely been equalled in the history of a war full of confused retreats.

1952 Eric Lambert *The Twenty Thousand Thieves* 103–4: The Ninth Division and the remnants of a British armoured division reached Tobruk. The Benghazi Derby was over. In Tobruk they turned to stand before Rommel.

berley *v. & n.* To scatter bait on the surface of the water to attract the fish; the bait so thrown [unexplained]

1855 G. C. Mundy *Our Antipodes* i 388: Anchoring the boats in about thirty feet of water, the first operation was the baiting of the spot – locally termed 'burley-ing' with burnt fish, and with the eggs of sharks when any have been caught.

1882 J. E. Tennison-Woods *Fish and Fisheries of New South Wales* 75: It is usual to wrench legs and shell off the back [of the crabs], and cast them out for berley.

1907 Ambrose Pratt *The Remittance Man* 9: 'They don't seem to be biting this morning,' said the boy. 'You should give 'em some burley.'

1937 Vance Palmer *Legend for Sanderson* 124–5: They had burleyed all their favourite fishing-grounds, mixing a sardine paste and scattering it over the sea-floor.

1965 Thomas Keneally *The Fear* 160: The man had worked considerably closer to us, and was hunting blood worms with a sugarbag full of berley.

1981 *Sunday Mail* (Brisbane) 12 Jul. 55: Handfuls of mixed sand and chopped weed used as burley will often help bring the fish on the bite.

Berries, the The Canterbury-Bankstown (N.S.W.) Rugby League team

1974 *Sydney Morning Herald* 9 Sep. 11: Berries just pip Sharks.

bet like the Watsons see **Watsons**

bib, to stick one's ~ in To interfere, intrude

1952 T. A. G. Hungerford *The Ridge and the River* 57: Here was Wilder, almost a schoolboy amongst them, sticking in his bib.

1960 Jack McKinney *The Well* in *Khaki, Bush and Bigotry* ed. Eunice Hanger (1968) 265: 'What's it got to do with you? Who asked you to stick yer bib in?'

1980 *Sun-Herald* 20 Apr. 46: Then a fourth-grade kid put his bib in. 'She's my girlfriend,' he said.

Bible, the Bushman's see **Bushman's**

bible-basher A clergyman, missionary or any devout person: *derogatory* [variant of *bible-banger, -pounder, -puncher*]

1944 Lawson Glassop *We Were the Rats* 124: 'I doan want any bible-bashing bastard who's never seen me before mumblin' any bull – over me.'

1950 Frank Hardy *Power Without Glory* 32: Devlin would have left him alone if it hadn't been for the 'bible bashers' who spoke from the pulpit and wrote to the press demanding action against the gambling mania.

1976 Alan Reid *The Whitlam Venture* 58: The National Country Party Premier of Queensland, Joh Bjelke-Petersen, whom Whitlam in a fit of petulance described publicly as that 'Bible-bashing bastard'.

bickies, big (small) Applied to sums of money

1981 Barry Humphries *A Nice Night's Entertainment* 188: They might look a bit shonky, but they're prepared to invest big bickies in upgrading the Arab image over here.

1983 Bob Simpson *Sun-Herald* 9 Oct. 72: Boycott also was probably one of the first cricketers to sense the possibilities of big bickies in endorsements and commercialisation and go after them.

Big Australian, the Broken Hill Proprietary Ltd

1979 *Australian* 20 Jul. 11: This campaign has reached its height . . . in the sponsorship of the weekly 60 Minutes current affairs program, which features the company as the 'Big Australian'.

1981 *Age* (Melbourne) 25 Jun. 17: BHP set to report another top profit . . . The Big Australian should easily eclipse the $500 million profit mark – the first time for any Australian enterprise.

Big Brother The Barrier Industrial Council at Broken Hill

1981 *Australian* 3 Nov. 7: Since 1916 the BIC – also dubbed Big Brother – has ruled on all wage negotiations and, few doubted, controlled the workings of the town.

Big Fella, the J. T. Lang (1876–1975) Labor Premier of N.S.W. 1925–7, 1930–2 [? f. nickname given to Michael Collins, Irish republican hero, and the height and presence of Mr Lang]

1971 *Sydney Morning Herald* 5 Jul. 3: 'Big Fella' rejoins ALP after 28 years.

1975 *Sunday Telegraph* (Sydney) 28 Sep. 2: John Thomas Lang known to his friends and enemies as the Big Fella, died in St Joseph's Hospital, Auburn, after being admitted ten days ago for a rest.

big man (men) A powerfully built Australian Rules footballer, often playing in a special position (e.g. ruckman); any Australian Rules player

1963 Lou Richards *Boots and All!* 24: Most of the big men are tough, but rarely do you see two big men clashing or knocking each other down . . . Take Jack Dyer, for instance. He was a very tough big man who broke the collarbones of seven players during his long career, but I'm led to believe that most of these blokes were only about 5 ft. 2 in. and could have played with an African pigmy team.

1965 Jack Dyer *'Captain Blood'* 177: He has to play to his ruckmen because the big men are the key to the game.

1984 *Age* (Melbourne) 26 Sep. 40: Michael Byrne vacated a forward pocket and took over the leading bigman role. He has . . . become respected as one of the new breed of quick, highly skilled ruckman [sic] who have replaced lion-hearted workhorses.

Biggles Nickname of Senator Gareth Evans as Attorney-General in the Hawke Government, after he had authorized RAAF spy flights over the projected Franklin dam in 1983 [f. the aviator in the stories by W. E. Johns]

1983 *Australian* 28 Dec. 9: Gareth Evans: Biggles (after the spy flights) or Garrulous Gareth.

1985 *Australian* 5 Jan. 10: Among the 'exceptional circumstances' under which 'Biggles' released drug crim Peter Fulcher was, I suppose – 'It seemed like a good idea at the time'.

big-note man A bookmaker or punter placing or handling large bets

1950 *Australian Police Journal* Apr. 111: *Big-note man* Wealthy.

1956 J. T. Lang *I Remember* 115: When he was not in Macquarie St, he was operating at Randwick. He became a 'big-note' man. At one stage he was a bookmaker's agent, laying-off bets for one of the leviathans of the day. At other times, he acted as a betting commissioner, placing bets for wealthy patrons.

big-note oneself, come the big-note To attempt to inflate one's status or achievements

1948 *As You Were* 164: Champ had the floor and was apparently 'big-noting' himself regarding his prosperous pre-war days.

1959 Dorothy Hewett *Bobbin Up* 137: 'You don't give a bugger about the workers. You're just big-notin' yourself, carving out a slice of your own particular glory.'

1970 Barry Oakley *A Salute to the Great McCarthy* 65: 'Don't come the big note with me, Fortune, your next sarcasm may be your last.'

1981 *Sydney Morning Herald* 19 Feb. 7: David Hill, the 34-year-old chief executive of the State Rail Authority is reluctant to be interviewed. 'The public doesn't want someone trying to big-note himself,' he said. 'It just wants the trains to run on time.'

Big Run, the Victoria River Downs station, N.T.

1951 Ernestine Hill *The Territory* 231: Flanking the river on both sides for about three hundred miles is the biggest cattle run in the world, Victoria River Downs. With 13,150 square miles until this year, it had an area larger than Belgium, and a steady population of about eight white men as compared with Belgium's eight millions ... With a hundred and seventy thousand cattle, a hundred and fifty black stockmen, and six out-camps – some of them sixty miles from the homestead – the Big Run covers the maze of ranges and creeks in mid-river.

1970 Jock Makin *The Big Run* [book title]

1983 *Australian* 25 May 7: 'The Big Run' as it is known to Territorians, is one of the world's biggest properties; before its subdivision in the mid 1930s, it covered 43,000 sq km – about the size of Belgium. But even today, its size is mind-boggling: about 1.3 million hectares, or 12,000 sq km.

big smoke see **smoke**

bike A promiscuous woman, usually in such expressions as 'the town bike', 'the office bike' [f. *ride* for the male role in intercourse]

1945 Baker 123: A willing girl is sometimes described as an *office bike*, *a town bike* etc.

1951 Dal Stivens *Jimmy Brockett* 178: 'I might have known you were the bloody town bike.'

1972 David Williamson *The Removalists* 36: 'Turned out the tart was the biggest bike in the district.'

1980 Barbara Pepworth *Early Marks* 164: Juicy Lucy is the school bike, everyone's ridden her.

bike, to get off one's To appear to be losing control of oneself

1938 Xavier Herbert *Capricornia* 565: 'I tell you I saw no-one.' 'Don't get off your bike, son. I know you're tellin' lies.'

1952 Jon Cleary *The Sundowners* 237: 'I'm sorry, I didn't mean to get off me bike like that.'

1963 Randolph Stow *Tourmaline* 115: 'You make me sick,' she cried again. 'Don't get off your bike,' he said.

1984 Marian Eldridge *Walking the Dog* 163: 'Don't get off your bike, Joe, I'll pick up your pump,' soothes Mr Kneebone.

bike, gone for a ride on the padre's see **padre's**

Bill and Jim Typical outback Australians in the 1890s, and typical soldiers in World War I: *obs.*

1896 *Bulletin* 31 Oct. Red Page: The harrowing tale of the lost Bill or Jim in the Australian desert whose eyes are picked out by the crows almost before his death-struggle ceases.

1899 Henry Lawson 'Jack Cornstalk' *Prose* ii 44: And so out back, to the land of Bill and Jim, where we carried swags together.

1919 W. J. Denny *The Diggers* 171: The freedom with which 'Billjim' spends his pay not unnaturally adds to the warmth of his welcome.

billabong, on the Out of work and camped on a waterhole: esp N.T. and W.A. [f. Ab. *billabong* waterhole]

1954 Tom Ronan *Vision Splendid* 16: 'The north has got better men than you, better men than me. When it gets a man it generally throws him on the Billabong and leaves him there.

billabong whaler   see **whaler**

billet   A post, job, appointment (at first including lodgings): *obsolescent* [f. *billet* order providing quarters for a soldier OED 1644]

1846 L. W. Miller *Notes of an Exile to Van Diemen's Land* 343: 'What in the name of common sense do you want to get into the *wash-house* for?' I asked. 'Oh, it is a *billet*. The work is light, and performed under cover; and the men get tobacco, and enough to eat into the bargain.'

1865 J. F. Mortlock *Experiences of a Convict* (1965) 101: Mr Jones used his influence to get me made clerk (being one of the best 'billets' for which I was eligible).

1902 Henry Lawson 'The Story of "Gentleman-Once"' *Prose* i 535: 'He got a billet in the Civil Service up-country . . . He commenced to drink again, and went on till he lost his billet.'

1938 Xavier Herbert *Capricornia* 325: She had learnt that Steggles would be going to a Government billet in Singapore when his work in Capricornia was done.

bill-poster, busy as a one-armed ~ in a gale   see **one-armed**

billy   A cylindrical vessel with a wire handle, of various capacities, used in the outback for carrying water and boiling it to make tea, also as a cooking utensil; in suburban Australia mainly a container for milk, when it was delivered in bulk; often fitted with a lid [abbr. of *billycan*. Prob. f. *billy-pot* cooking utensil SND c. 1828: the derivation f. Ab. *billa* water is unlikely; although there is some evidence that *bouilli* tins were used as billies (see quot. 1911), the term itself was current earlier. NZ 1839 OED]

1855 William Howitt *Land, Labour and Gold* i 195: Edward came behind . . . carrying in one hand a gun, in the other a tin kettle or billy, as the diggers call it.

1873 A. Trollope *Australia* ed. Edwards and Joyce (1967) 293: He carries also a pannikin and a 'billy'. The latter is an open pot in which he boils his water and makes his tea . . . A bushman of any refinement has the pannikin for drinking; but the rough old chum will dispense with it as a useless luxury, and will drink his tea out of his billy.

1885 *The Australasian Printer's Keepsake*

16: Camp-fires were blazing in the open air, with pots and billies slung across, pannikins of tea were handed round.

1911 E. S. Sorenson *Life in the Australian Backblocks* 276: Billy is famous . . . He seems to have originated on the Victorian goldfields. The early miners consumed great quantities of French tinned soup, called *bouilli*; and the empty bouilli-cans were used for the same purposes as are now the specially made 'billy-cans'.

1934 Thomas Wood *Cobbers* 77: We drank tea straight from the billy.

1971 Colin Simpson *The New Australia* 483: We had boiled the billy hung from a hook on a tripod of steel rods that folded together – an invention of Dr Oxer's.

1981 *National Times* 10 May 49: Children still dawdle along country roads carrying billies of thick creamy milk.

billy boy

1969 Arthur Fadden *They called me Artie* 7: Another family friend made a job for me as 'billy boy' with his cane-cutting gang near the Pleystowe mill. My main job was to make their tea and, preceding the men, to thresh the cane before it was cut.

1981 *Sunday Mail* (Brisbane) 9 Aug. Color Mag. 7: The host for the evening was usually the 'billy-boy'. At just the right time he threw in handfuls of tea leaves, tapped the sides of the tins with a stick and then lifted them off to fill smaller billies and teapots.

billy, boil the   To make a cup of tea, not necessarily with a billycan; to stop for refreshments

1956 A. W. Upfield *The Battling Prophet* 5: 'Glad to meet you. Come on in and we'll boil the billy.' [an electric jug]

1958 H. D. Williamson *The Sunlit Plain* 5: Except for a break at noon to boil the billy, they had been on the move since dawn.

billycart   1   A type of dog-cart which might be drawn by a billygoat

1922 *Sun* (Sydney) 25 Jun. 'Us Fellers' comic strip in 'Sunbeams': illustration of billycart 1.

1923 *Sun* (Sydney) 14 Jan. 'Sunbeams' 3: Some young 'Beamers ride behind a goat in a billycart when they go out driving.

2   A platform on wheels, with the front axle on a swivel for steering, and sometimes a box-like structure at the rear: a home-made vehicle used by juveniles

1922 *Sun* (Sydney) 11 Jun. 'Us Fellers'

comic strip in 'Sunbeams': illustration of billycart 2, there described as a 'racing cart'.

1959 Eleanor Dark *Lantana Lane* 253: It will be queer . . . when no kids trundle their billy-carts at leisure past our gates.

1980 Clive James *Unreliable Memoirs* 38: Other children . . . constructed billycarts of advanced design, with skeletal hard-wood frames and steel-jacketed ball-race wheels that screamed on the concrete footpaths like a diving Stuka. The best I could manage was a sawn-off fruit box mounted on a fence-paling spine frame, with drearily silent rubber wheels taken off an old pram.

billy, swing the   see **swing**

billy tea   Tea made in a billy, i.e. outdoors, and usually milkless

1897 David McKee Wright *Station Ballads* 17: The spuds and meat were nicely done, the billy tea was made, / With plates and bright tin pannikins the whisky-case was laid.

1943 Maurice Clough *We of the A.I.F.* 45: Men who have lived on billy tea / And damper.

1980 *Sydney Morning Herald* 6 Feb. 1: A new delicacy to join the ranks of damper, billy tea and meat pies? A City department store is now selling barbecued rabbits in its take-away food department.

bimbo   Term applied to a young tramp in the depression of the 1930s, usually with an implication of homosexuality [? f. It. *bambino*]

1966 Elwyn Wallace *Sydney and the Bush* 144: 'That "mate" as you call him is a queer,' Paddy explained. 'You know, a queen. I think they're called "Bimbos" on the track.'

1973 Frank Huelin *Keep Moving* 139–40: The older man claimed the younger as his nephew . . . but we concluded there was also a more intimate sexual relationship – that the younger was the older man's 'bimbo'.

bindi-eye   *Calotis cuneifolia*, a weed noted for its prickles or burrs [? Ab.]

1910 C. E. W. Bean *On the Wool Track* 226: Often the only sign that tells you he is a shearer at all is the scar made by binde-i or some other burr in the fleece on the back of his hand.

1963 Bruce Beaver *The Hot Summer* 113: Continue on her way bare-footed, the blue-

metal chips and bindy-eyes presenting less of a trial to her broad toughened feet.

1981 *Sydney Morning Herald* 10 Jul. 14: Bindii is the curse of lawns during summer. The plants creep through the grass, often unnoticed until the seed-heads ripen and begin sticking painfully into bare feet.

binghi *n. & a.*   White term for an Aboriginal: *derogatory* [Ab. word for 'brother']

[**1847** Alexander Harris *Settlers and Convicts* ed. C. M. H. Clark (1954) 173: 'Poor fellow you, binghi (brother).']

1902 A. B. Paterson 'Pearling Industry at Thursday Island' in *Son of the Pen* (1983) 83: Torres Straits Islanders . . . have great contempt for the 'Binghies' or Australian Aboriginals.

1920 *Sunraysia Daily* (Mildura) 16 Oct. 14: Binghi, Our Black Brother: Several Aspects of Aboriginal Life [heading]

1936 H. Drake-Brockman *Sheba Lane* 167: 'And yer need ter be mighty careful not ter fall fer a binghi tart.'

1964 Mary Durack *The Rock and the Sand* 212: Before long every white family in Broome had acquired a mission educated 'binghi' couple.

see **boong, Jacky**

bingle   A car crash, a 'prang' [? *bingle* a hit in baseball U.S. 1902 Mathews]

1953 Baker 169: *bingle* A skirmish. [as World War II slang]

1966 Baker 253: *bingle* A dent or fracture in a surfboard.

1966 Roger Carr *Surfie* 122: There was this clang of metal on metal and both cars lurched over the shoulder and we nearly went for a bingle.

1979 *NT News* (Darwin) 20 Sep. 7: The congestion wasn't helped by a three-car bingle on Bagot Rd near Nemarluck Drive.

bingy   Belly [Ab.]

1832–4 Joseph Larmer 'Native Vocabulary 1832–4' (MS Mitchell Library) 24: 'Binje' in that neighbourhood is a word applied to the stomach.

1859 Henry Kingsley *Recollections of Geoffry Hamlyn* ii 94: 'Don't fret your bingy, boss.'

1908 *The Australian Magazine* 1 Nov. 1251: Two or three aboriginal words . . . are now found in standard dictionaries . . . but others have remained, and are likely to remain in the category of slang, such as bingy (bin jee), stomach.

1931 William Hatfield *Sheepmates* 243: A well earned poke in the bingie.

1946 W. E. Harney *North of 23°* 188: He was lying on his back, or as the natives say in their quaint way 'Binji upwards', and as his belly rose and fell with his steady breathing, the lads stacked fifty-pound bags of flour upon him. He awoke at the eighth bag!

bird, a dead A certainty, esp. in horse-racing [see quot. 1898]

1889 *The Arrow* 20 Jul. 1: A school-teacher recently asked his class 'What is a moral?' and with one accord came the answer 'A dead bird, sir.'

1898 Morris: *Dead-bird* In Australia, a recent slang term, meaning 'a certainty'. The metaphor is from pigeon-shooting, where the bird being let loose in front of a good shot is as good as dead.

1951 Dal Stivens *Jimmy Brockett* 47: It was betting on a dead bird. We had waited nearly a year for a killing like this.

1979 *Sun-Herald* 18 Nov. 63: 'I'm partial to a 'bird' (a betting certainty) on the race-course, but I am even more keen on the real thing', he told me, pointing to a large aviary in his backyard.

birds, box of see **box**

birth stain The convict origins of Australia, so characterized by Lord Beauchamp on his arrival as Governor of New South Wales in 1899

1899 *Sydney Morning Herald* 11 May 5: Mr Corcoran, private secretary, handed the press [at Albany] the following message from Lord Beauchamp to the people of New South Wales. It is in verse, being an adaptation of a verse of Rudyard Kipling's 'The Song of the Cities':

> Greeting, – Your birthstain have you turned to good,
> Forcing strong wills perverse to stead-fastness,
> The first flush of the tropics in your blood,
> And at your feet success. – Beauchamp.

1903 Joseph Furphy *Such is Life* (1944) 65: This record transports you (saving reverence of our 'birth stain') something more than a hundred miles northward from the scene sketched in Chap. I.

1939 Herbert M. Moran *Viewless Winds* 69: An irate lady among the spectators had expressed herself picturesquely about those birth stains.

Bishop Barker see **Barker**

bite, put the ~ on To seek a loan, scrounge money or food [cf. *bite the ear* borrow OED 1879]

[**1859** Hotten 6: *Bite* to cheat, 'to be *bitten'*, to be taken in or imposed upon.]

1919 W. H. Downing *Digger Dialects* 11: *Bite* (*n.* or *v.*) (1) A borrowing, to borrow. (2) an attempt to borrow.

1935 Kylie Tennant *Tiburon* 120: 'An' the perlice is only makin' themselves more work, see, puttin' chaps off the dole, so they 'ave t'bite people, see?'

1957 Ray Lawler *Summer of the Seventeenth Doll* 98: 'Your money's runnin' out, you know you can't put the bite on me any more, and so here's the new champion, all loaded and ready.'

1978 Richard Beilby *Gunner* 237: 'I'm putting the bite on you,' Gunner explained gently. 'Putting the nips in, touching you for a loan.'

bite your bum Expression of refusal or rejection

1979 Kathy Lette and Gabrielle Carey *Puberty Blues* 30: 'Oh, Johnno, lend us ya . . .' 'Bite ya bum.'

1979 *Australian* 24 Nov. 10: 'We were again able to tell the PJT, the Monopolies Commission and Trade Practices to go bite their bums.'

bitser A mongrel dog

1941 Baker 10: *Bitser*: Anything made of bits and pieces; a mongrel animal.

1949 John Morrison *The Creeping City* 36–7: He called the dog Bitser because, as he candidly confessed to anyone who asked its breeding, it was 'just bits of this and bits of that'.

1958 A. W. Upfield *The Bachelors of Broken Hill* 212: 'Had one [dog] once, though. Black an' tan bitser.'

1968 *Australian* 4 Apr. 20: He lives with two bitser dogs that belonged to his mother.

1980 *Sunday Telegraph* (Sydney) 13 Apr. 36: She took her dog, a small and amiable bitser aged about five.

bitumen, the 1 A tarred road

1953 Baker 137: *one for the bitumen*, a

final round of drinks, i.e. 'one for the road'.
1972 W. A. Winter-Irving *Beyond the Bitumen* [book title]
1974 John Morrison *Australian by Choice* 118: It lay three miles off the bitumen, two miles of dirt road and one mile of winding track.
2 *The Bitumen* The highway between Darwin and Alice Springs
1949 H. E. Thonemann *Tell the White Man* 149: There were the workmen who made a beautiful road [during the war] now called the 'Bitumen'.
1959 Frank McCann *Medicine Man* 63: All the events I am about to describe occurred frequently in those dim, distant days of the era now frequently referred to as 'B.B.' ('Before the Bitumen').
1969 Osmar White *Under the Iron Rainbow* 160: 'We used to get a lot of commercials there, travelling up and down the Bitumen.'* *The Bitumen: The sealed highway from Darwin to Alice Springs.

bitumen blonde Aboriginal girl
1943 Baker 10: *Bitumen blonde* An aboriginal girl or woman.

Black and Whites The Swan Districts (W.A.) Australian Rules team [f. colours]
1984 *Sunday Independent* (Perth) 29 Apr. 72: Swans' glory [heading] In the most dramatic finish one could ever hope to see the Black and Whites fell over the line.

black cockatoos fly over A portent of rain
1963 Hal Porter *The Watcher on the Cast-Iron Balcony* 153: I still believe . . . that rain is on the way when swifts fly low, or black cockatoos fly northwards.
1979 Dorothy Hewett *The Man From Mukinupin* 101: 'Rain's comin' up. I heard the black cockatoos fly over.'

black duck See quot.
1989 *Independent Monthly* Oct. 6: He might have ordered a 'black duck' (a Swan) or a 'barbed wire' (a xxxx).

Black Friday 13 January 1939, day of disastrous bushfires in Victoria when 71 lives were lost; applied to any other disastrous Friday
1969 Thomas Jenkins *We Came to Australia* 117: Neither of these fires was Australia's worst. That happened on Black Friday, January 13th, 1939, when 71 people died in bushfires in Victoria. The flames jumped seven miles at a time and tests . . . recorded a temperature of 1,000 degrees.
1978 *Australian* 13 May 1: It was Black Friday in South Australia. Chrysler shut down its giant car plant, locked the workers out to avoid a mass sit-in protest, and started issuing security cards.

black hat A newly arrived immigrant, inexperienced in the ways of the colony i.e. still wearing city clothes: *obs.*
1876 Rolf Boldrewood *A Colonial Reformer* (1890) 21: 'A "black hat" in Australian parlance means a new arrival.'

Black Jack 1 Sir John McEwen (1900–80), leader of Federal Parliamentary Country Party 1958–71
1966 *The Wit of Sir Robert Menzies* ed. Ray Robinson 65: My colleague Jack McEwen has been nicknamed Black Jack. Now and again I address him as 'Black', and occasionally, when in highbrow mood, I call him *'Le Noir'*. That's only when I don't want other Country Party men to know what I'm talking about.
1984 *Australian* 23 Jul. 10: ALP policy goes 'back to Black Jack' [heading]
2 Sir Frederick Gallagher Galleghan (1897–1971), Commander of Changi Prison Camp 1944–5, promoted to Brigadier on return to Australia
1942 Adrian Curlewis *Of Love and War* ed. Philippa Poole (n.d.) 143: Every night 'Blackjack' comes to our room for supper and we yarn until 0100 hours.

black, living see **living**

black prince A variety of cicada [f. colour]
1951 Dymphna Cusack and Florence James *Come In Spinner* 106: 'Mine's a Floury Baker . . . and mine's a Black Prince.' Young Jack and Andrew held up their fists for her to peep at frosted fawn body and tan-and-black.
1980 *Australian* 29 Mar. Mag. 12: If you find a Black Prince, you can trade it for 20 greengrocers, five yellow Mondays or three floury bakers.

Black Saturday 10 December 1938, a day of severe bushfires in N.S.W.

Black Stump 1 An imaginary last post of

civilization. There have been country properties so called, including one near Coolah N.S.W. dating from 1826, and another at Merriwagga N.S.W. (see *Sun-Herald* 22 Feb. 1970) but these names may have derived from the currency of the expression.

1954 Tom Ronan *Vision Splendid* 264: 'You're looking,' he boasted, 'at the best bloody station bookkeeper this side of the black stump.' [spoken in Adelaide]

1962 Criena Rohan *The Delinquents* 151: 'Good old, sweet old, wholesome, pure little Brisbane, best little town this or any side of the Black Stump.'

1984 Judge O'Dea *West Australian* (Perth) 8 Feb. 3: 'It may not be the greatest claim for compensation this side of the Black Stump. It is a simple broken jaw.'

2 The State Offices block in Sydney [f. appearance]

1970 Jon Cleary *Helga's Web* 263: His office was in the State Government block, a beautiful dark grey tower that the citizens, with the local talent for belittling anything that embarrassed them with its pretensions, had dubbed the Black Stump.

1990 *Australian Business* 21 Mar. 20: Sydney's State Office Block – the black stump – is a valuer's nightmare, given the state of the building and the refurbishment or demolition alternatives it presents.

Black Sunday 6 February 1938, the day of a record number of rescues by life-savers at Bondi beach, when five lives were lost

1982 *Sydney Morning Herald* 19 Jan. 23: One of his [Alf Vockler's] famous feats occurred on 'Black Sunday', February 6, 1938, when with 80 other members of Bondi Club he took part in the biggest surf rescue in Australian history. Time and again he went back into the water to help rescue nearly 300 people trapped in treacherous surf at Bondi. Five swimmers died in one of the country's worst beach tragedies.

black taxi A Commonwealth government car, providing free transport for politicians and public servants

1973 *Sun-Herald* 25 Nov. 112: Fred Daly . . . has ordered a crackdown on official use of the 'black taxis'. He has warned MPs that the long black official limousines will not wait outside flats and hotels if those who ordered them aren't ready.

1975 *Sun-Herald* 3 Aug. 48: Commonwealth cars (flippantly known as 'black taxis'

to those new to power) were used to ferry junior aides to lunch.

Black Thursday 6 February 1851, a day of bushfire devastation in Victoria

1855 William Howitt *Land, Labour and Gold* i 68–9: The great bush-fire of what is called Black Thursday, or Thursday the 6th February, 1851 . . . raged fiercely in these parts.

1855 J. Jenkins *Diary of a Welsh Swagman* (1975) 139: This, the 6th of February, is the anniversary of 'Black Thursday' of 1851, when one half of the state of Victoria was on fire.

Black Tuesday 7 February 1967, day of severe bushfires in Tasmania, when 62 lives were lost

1981 *Australian* 4 Feb. 1: The blaze that swept through Zeehan [Tasmania] yesterday has brought nightmare memories of Black Tuesday – February 7 1967, when 62 people lost their lives in devastating bushfires.

black velvet Aboriginal women, as sexual partners [listed by Partridge as English military slang in the nineteenth century]

1899 Henry Lawson 'The Ballad of the Rouseabout' *Verse* i 360: I known the track from Spencer's Gulf and north of Cooper's Creek – / Where falls the half-caste to the strong, 'black velvet' to the weak.

1929 K. S. Prichard *Coonardoo* 79: 'You're one of these god-damned young heroes. No 'black velvet' for you, I suppose?' 'I'm goin' to marry white and stick white,' Hugh said.

1958 Gavin Casey *Snowball* 17: 'Did you see the girls, when you were out there? . . . The sort of black velvet that makes me sometimes wish I wasn't a policeman.'

blacks, they should give it back to the Expression of disgust at any inhospitable feature of Australia [? f. U.S. 'hand it back to the Indians']

1946 *Sunday Sun* (Sydney) 4 Aug. Suppl. 15: They reckon as he [Captain Cook] sailed away he gave one look back at the coast of Bananaland and said, 'Strewth, I'm glad to give that dump back to the blacks'.

1969 Christopher Bray *Blossom Like a Rose* 75: 'They should give it back to the blacks.' 'What's that?' asked Jake. 'The bloody north,' said Tom.

1971 Colin Simpson *The New Australia* 213: Robin Boyd begins by saying that he often feels that Melbourne should be given back to the blacks.

blades, the The hand shears, used before the introduction of machine shearing
1905 *Old Bush Songs* ed. A. B. Paterson 26: I've shore at big Willandra and I've shore at Tilberoo, / And once I drew my blades, my boys, upon the famed Barcoo.
1910 C. E. W. Bean *On the Wool Track* 195: Most shearers told me the machines were a bit faster and easier than the 'blades'.
1973 Donald Stuart *Morning Star Evening Star* 20: I'd seen a double fleece or two shorn with the blades by a brokendown old blade-shearer.

Blake, Joe see **Joe Blake**

Blamey, a Lady See quots [wife of General Sir Thomas Blamey]
1945 Baker 157: *Lady Blamey* A beer bottle, from which the neck has been removed, used as a drinking vessel. [World War II slang]
1972 *Sydney Morning Herald* 28 Oct. 8: During this time she gave her name to the 'bottle' drinking glass used by thousands of Diggers. She taught them to slice an empty bottle cleanly in half with the aid of kerosene-soaked string. The string was wound round the bottle, and set alight. When the bottle was hot it was plunged into water and would break cleanly. The men used the lower part for drinking.

blanket (rug), Wagga see **Wagga**

Bleak City Melbourne, from a Sydney standpoint
1986 Mark Westfield *Sydney Morning Herald* 13 Jun. 23: One of the worst things about Bleak City is that its entire population (apart from followers of the turf) is obliged to flock at weekends to the aerial pingpong matches to brighten their otherwise mediocre existence.
1990 *Sun-Herald* 25 Mar. 94: Hafey ... has embarked on selling league on the tube to the good burghers of the Bleak City.

blight, sandy see **sandy**

Blind Freddie see **Freddie**

Bliss, Johnny A piss [rhyming slang]
1973 Alexander Buzo *Rooted* 77: 'I

couldn't bear to watch it, so I ducked out for a Johnny Bliss.'

blister A debt, bill [f. *blister* a summons OED 1903]
1888 E. Finn *Chronicles of Early Melbourne* ii 546: As far as the bushmen were concerned, they might certainly be styled 'blisters', for they burned their pockets while they had them. [The term 'blister' wrongly applied to **shinplasters** q.v.]
1934 Vance Palmer *Sea and Spinifex* 14: 'Well, they need every quid they can rake together,' McVeagh defended. 'There's a blister on that boat that won't be worked off unless they strike a few good patches.'
1951 Ernestine Hill *The Territory* 431: [In the bush] never carry a 'blister', a bill or an account ... A rider passing by was an honoured guest, and he couldn't be hounding a man down with bills.

block, do the To make a fashionable promenade, in Melbourne along Collins Street between Swanston and Elizabeth Streets, in Sydney in the area bounded by George, King and Pitt Streets: *obs.*
1869 Marcus Clarke *The Peripatetic Philosopher* 12: The 'doing the Block' is doubtless worthy of censure, 'Collins-street Folly' is foolish enough to be visited with the severest blame.
1887 Fergus Hume *The Mystery of a Hansom Cab* (1971) 58–9: It was Saturday morning and of course all fashionable Melbourne was doing the Block. With regards to its 'Block', Collins Street corresponds to New York's Broadway, London's Regent Street and Rotten Row, and to the Boulevards of Paris. It is on the Block that people show off their new dresses, bow to their friends, cut their enemies, and chatter small talk.
1892 Henry Lawson 'The Drover's Wife' *Prose* i 50: She takes as much care to make herself and the children look smart as she would if she were going to do the block in the city.
1945 Herbert M. Moran *Beyond the Hill Lies China* 131: Challis's mind slipped back to the days when, as a student, he 'did the block' on Saturday mornings. Down George Street and around the Post Office, up Pitt Street, past King Street, and through the Arcade, then back to George Street again.

block, do (lose) one's Of the various expressions in which 'block' is used as 'head' (OED 1635), such as 'knock your block off', the most 'Australian' seems to be 'do your block' i.e. lose rational control from rage, excitement, falling in love. The converse is to 'use your block' i.e. apply all shrewdness and judgement.

1907 Charles MacAlister *Old Pioneering Days in the Sunny South* 19: At this Mr Donovan 'lost his block' completely. 'Clear out of my sight, ye skunks,' he screamed.

1915 C. J. Dennis *The Songs of a Sentimental Bloke* 47: I done me block complete on this Doreen, / An' now me 'eart is broke, me life's a wreck!

1959 A. W. Upfield *Bony and the Mouse* 133: 'Not much of a bushman!' 'Good enough, if he uses his block, to get a long way.'

1970 Patrick White *The Vivisector* 586: 'Orright! Don't do yer block! What else?'

1983 Bert Kelly *Bulletin* 26 Jul. 94: I became nervous that he was about to do his block so I said in my fatherly way: 'Don't get cross, Fred.'

blockee, blocker The owner of a block of land on which grapes are grown [listed by Baker as peculiar to S.A., but also encountered in Victoria]

1900 Let. of 4 Feb. in *Audrey Tennyson's Vice-Regal Days* ed. Alexandra Hasluck (1978) 85: The next day H. & I walked down to see some 'blockers' called Nott who we heard had been nearly burnt out.

1920 *Sunraysia Daily* (Mildura) 23 Dec. 1: A Blocker's Home in Karadoc Avenue, Mildura [heading]

1942 John Shaw Neilson *Autobiography* (1978) 131: I reported the matter to the blocker's wife & I think some measures were taken to help.

1979 *Herald* (Melbourne) 8 Mar. 4: Of course there is work for grape-pickers . . . A fortnight ago there were pickers everywhere and blockies were turning them away.

Bloke, the 1 The man in charge, the boss [f. naval slang for a ship's commander OED 1914]

1966 Tom Ronan *Once There Was a Bagman* 2: Kelly the Nip [imagined giving advice to Ronan, about to lunch on the royal yacht *Britannia*] 'See if you can work me in for a yarn with the Bloke. I'll bite him if you won't.'

2   The hero of C. J. Dennis' *The Songs of a Sentimental Bloke* (1915)

1939 R. H. Croll *I Recall* 163: The Bloke has passed: Oh, dip the lid!

1967 R. D. FitzGerald *Southerly* 261: Remember too that when the one and only Bloke was presented with a son . . . Dennis makes the Bloke say: 'Doreen she says 'e's got a poet's eyes; / But I ain't got no use for them soft guys.'

3   *The Old Bloke* God [outback slang]

1958 Russel Ward *The Australian Legend* 98: I was one of a party of four, driving an old truck through the Musgrave Ranges . . . One of my companions gushed considerably over the beauty of the mountain sky-line, silhouetted against the sunset. An elderly stockman answered drily. 'Yes. The Old Bloke makes a good job of them up this way.'

blonde, bitumen   see **bitumen**

blonde, bushfire   see **bushfire**

bloodhouse A public house with a reputation for brawls, gambling

1938 Heard in conversation.

1953 Dymphna Cusack *Southern Steel* 138: 'Ought to have more sense than to go to the Seven Seas – nothing but a bloodhouse. Always blues there.'

1963 Frank Hardy *Legends from Benson's Valley* 104: He stopped to study the defences of the hotel – not such a bloodhouse as the Royal Oak, but nevertheless addicted to after-hours trading.

1981 Peter Corris *White Meat* 16: We crossed the street and had a beer in the bloodhouse opposite.

Bloods, the The South Melbourne V.F.L. club, later the Swans [f. team colours]

1979 *Herald* (Melbourne) 6 Apr. 26: Bloods are running hot [heading] South Melbourne will beat Richmond at South tomorrow.

Blood-stained Angels, the Former nickname of the South Melbourne V.F.L. club

1984 Audrey Blake *A Proletarian Life* 6: We barracked devotedly for the 'Blood-stained Angels', the South Melbourne team. [recalling the 1920s]

bloody The **great Australian adjective** q.v. is by no means distinctively Australian, but has always been conspicuous enough in the colloquial language to be seen as such by overseas visitors

1833 Trial before the Supreme Court, 9 and 10 December, in *True Patriots All* ed. G. C. Ingleton (1952) 149: John Larnack, being duly sworn, said: on the morning of the 5th November last, I went to the river to superintend sheep-washing; between 12 and 1 o'clock I heard a voice exclaiming – *'come out of the water every bloody one of you, or we'll blow your bloody brains out!'*; on looking behind, I saw three men advancing towards me with guns.

1847 A. Marjoribanks *Travels in New South Wales* 57–8: The word bloody is a favourite oath in that country. One man will tell you that he married a bloody young wife, another, a bloody old one, and a bushranger will call out, 'Stop, or I'll blow your bloody brains out'.

1899 W. T. Goodge ' – !' (The Great Australian Adjective!) in *Hits! Skits! and Jingles!* 115: The sunburnt – stockman stood, / And, in a dismal – mood, / Apostrophised his – cuddy; / 'The – nag's no – good, / He couldn't earn his – food — / A regular – brumby.

1942 C. Hartley Grattan *Introducing Australia* 193: When I asked an old 'cove' when he first arrived in Darwin, he replied, 'Young man, in nineteen bloody eight!'

1969 Patsy Adam-Smith *Folklore of the Australian Railwaymen* 218: One of the witnesses, a fettler, came into the inquiry room and tripped on a mat and said, 'What stupid bastard put that bloody mat there?' And he slung it out the door. 'Bull' Mitchell on the inquiry board said to him, 'None of your bloody swearing here, you just remember that you're at a bloody inquiry and bloody well behave yourself'.

1973 Mr C. Jones [Federal Minister for Transport] *Sydney Morning Herald* 18 Aug. 2: There is going to be some bloody mammoth changes – some mammoth changes which the Budget will disclose. Bloody mammoth changes, that is the only way you can describe them. I think Frank [Crean] has done a bloody good job to stand up to the pace. Bloody oath, he has done a marvellous job in standing up to the bloody pace.

1984 *Australian* 24 Sep. 18: As Bulldog captain Steve Mortimer said at the presentation: 'If you can beat a side as good as bloody Parramatta, then you're a bloody good side.' Bloody oath.

blot Anus, buttocks
1945 Baker 156: *blot* The posterior or anus. [World War II slang]
1965 William Dick *A Bunch of Ratbags* 262: He pushed me away and he gave me a kick up the blot.
1974 David Ireland *Burn* 146: Maybe he'll grab this last chance for some action after sitting on his blot all these years.

blow *v.* 1 'To boast, brag (chiefly dial.)' OED c. 1400–1873: *obsolescent*
1857 *Thatcher's Colonial Songster* 35: About your talents blow, / Mind, that's the regular caper.
1879–80 Ned Kelly 'The Jerilderie Letter' in Max Brown *Australian Son* (1956) 279: He is the man that blowed before he left Violet Town if Ned Kelly was to be shot he was the man would shoot him.
1887 *Tibb's Popular Songbook* 24: The squatters blowed they'd cut the price / To seventeen and six.
1945 Gavin Casey *Downhill is Easier* 41: Ordinary rouseabout labourers don't get many chances to blow out their bags about what good men they are, unless they tell lies.
2 To lengthen in odds, the opposite to 'firm' (horse-racing)
1922 Arthur Wright *A Colt from the Country* 129: 'Ain't Lobitout fav'rit?' he gasped . . . 'No!' snapped the stranger. 'Got blown right out.'
1949 Lawson Glassop *Lucky Palmer* 63: 'I've got the commission for it this end of the ring, and I'm trying to blow the price out.'

blow *n.* 1 Bragging, boasting: *obsolescent* [f. *blow v.* 1]
1868 C. Wade Brown *Overlanding in Australia* 18: He seldom carries out his threats, it is more 'blow' (bounce) on his part than anything.
1885 *The Australasian Printers' Keepsake* 162: A European type, working in Sydney, was grievously galled by the 'blow' of the Cornstalks.
1893 Francis Adams *The Australians* 149: The drawling 'blow' (Anglice, boasting) of the competitive bushman borders on an anger which is so high-strung as to threaten insanity.
2 A stroke of the shears in shearing
1870 Rolf Boldrewood 'Shearing in Riverina' *In Bad Company* (1901) 309: Every 'blow' of the shears is agony to him, yet he disdains to give in.
1885–1914 'Click go the Shears' *Old Bush Songs* ed. Stewart and Keesing (1957) 254: The ringer looks around and is beaten by a blow, / And curses the old snagger with the blue-bellied 'joe'.
1911 E. S. Sorenson *Life in the Australian Backblocks* 223: The blades are pulled back

and the knockers filed down, so the shears will take a bigger blow.
1981 *Australian* 19 Dec. 5: The wider the comb, the more wool a shearer can remove with each 'blow'.

blow the froth off a glass of beer, couldn't see **couldn't**

Blow, Joe see **Joe**

blow, strike a To start or resume work
1974 Sir Robert Askin *Australian* 18 Dec. 9: 'I think it's bad that people can live on high interest rates, like 15 per cent, and can get enough money to live on them without striking a blow.'

blow through As for **shoot through**

blowie 1 A blowfly [abbr.]
1945 Gavin Casey *Downhill is Easier* 204: 'There was clouds o' blowies.'
1973 *Australian* 7 Jul. 16: I love this ripper country / Of funnel webs and sharks / With blowies big as eagles / Where your car gets booked by narks.
2 The blowfish, or toado
1983 T. A. G. Hungerford *Stories from Suburban Road* 74: You rubbed the blowies on the wooden planks of the jetty until they swelled up and then you stamped on them: if you did it right they went off with a bang like a penny cracker.

blow-in A casual arrival: *derogatory*
1937 Ernestine Hill *The Great Australian Loneliness* 32: They [the murals] had been painted by a 'blow-in', an Englishman named Malcolmsen, said to have been a crack steeplechase rider in his day.
1953 T. A. G. Hungerford *Riverslake* 195: A couple of blow-ins from the Causeway, with loud-mouthed women.
1983 *Sun-Herald* 9 Jan. 124: It's a bit like the characters who travel great distances to join the throng at Double Bay on Saturday mornings, only to learn that the locals all do their shopping during the week and that the crowd is made up of blow-ins.

blowtorch applied to the belly The test of political fortitude proposed by Mr Neville Wran (see quot. 1983)
1983 *Sydney Morning Herald* 16 Mar. 7: Asked recently what he thought of Greiner,

Neville Wran said he obviously had ability 'but he hasn't had the blowtorch applied to his belly yet'.
1984 *Age* (Melbourne) 17 Mar. 11: The Premier will have four years in which, to borrow his own expression, to apply the blowtorch to the bellies of his detractors.

bludge *n.* A job requiring no exertion [f. *bludger* 2]
1943 Donald Friend *Gunner's Diary* 18: 'I've been three weeks in hospital with measles.' 'Ah – that's not a bad bludge.'
1949 Lawson Glassop *Lucky Palmer* 154: 'A man's got to earn a living and this is a good bludge.'
1962 Stuart Gore *Down the Golden Mile* 53: 'What a smart bludge he's on, eh? At six thousand a year or whatever it is he gets.'
1974 Desmond O'Grady *Deschooling Kevin Carew* 52: 'You don't like the course?' 'Oh it's all right. Plenty of time for fun and a good bludge.'

bludge *v.* 1 To live on the earnings of a prostitute
1947 Vance Palmer *Cyclone* 26: A secret shame was sapping his spirit. You oughtn't to take money from a woman; it was bludging.
2 To avoid effort and live by someone else's exertions; to acquire something without payment
1931 Vance Palmer *Separate Lives* 264: 'I've stood you too long already, loafing around here, and bludging on your mother.'
1957 Ray Lawler *Summer of the Seventeenth Doll* 37: 'I won't bludge. I'll get a job or somethin'.'
1964 Donald Horne *The Lucky Country* 26: Covering up for an incompetent mate is the usual thing as long as he is considered to be trying and not simply 'bludging'.
1975 Richard Cornish *The Woman Lilith* 25: We cleaned the house, painted the walls ... bludged some furniture.

bludge on the flag To fail in one's duty; to exploit a patriotic cause
1919 W. H. Downing *Digger Dialects* 12: *Bludge on the flag* To fail to justify one's existence as a soldier.
1966 Elwyn Wallace *Sydney and the Bush* 72: Kate collected a war pension – 'bludging on the flag' Pete always called it.

bludger 1 Someone living on the earnings of a prostitute: *obs.* [f. *bludgeoner* OED 1842]

1898 *Bulletin* 17 Dec. Red Page: A *bludger* is about the lowest grade of human thing, and is a brothel bully.

1904 Henry Lawson 'The Women of the Town' *Verse* ii 54: And they profit from the brewer and the smirking landlord down / To the bully and the bludger, on the women of the town.

1946 K. S. Prichard *The Roaring Nineties* 388: Bill led an attack on the French bludger who kept three or four Japanese women in miserable shacks at Kanowna.

1981 *Sydney Morning Herald* 7 May 1: Longley said members who lived off waterfront prostitution were known as 'bludgers'.

2 See quot. 1900–10

1900–10 O'Brien and Stephens: *Bludger* The word has come to be applied to any person who takes profit without risk or disability or without effort or work.

1945 Gavin Casey *Downhill is Easier* 15: 'They don't put many on here, but they don't put many off either, unless they're dinkum bludgers.'

1958 H. D. Williamson *The Sunlit Plain* 21: 'You and your rotten, boozy cobbers! Think I don't see enough of 'em in this place to know what they are? Dirty, greasy mob of bludgers!'

1979 *Sydney Morning Herald* 25 Aug. 3: Auckland, Friday. – A man alleged to have called Princess Anne 'a bloody bludger' told a Magistrate yesterday he had spoken the truth. He said he had been making a political speech and the words were not insulting.

1983 James McQueen *Uphill Runner* 161: Never a bludger, he'd never been that. Thinking: I always paid my way, one way or another.

3 Affectionate, when addressed to friends, like **bastard** 3

1953 Dymphna Cusack *Southern Steel* 266: 'You bludger, ya!' Slap's voice was full of relief.

1965 William Dick *A Bunch of Ratbags* 216: 'Don't be scabs, yuh pack of bludgers, all youse ever think of is money,' Argles laughed.

bludger, dole see **dole bludger**

blue 1 A summons, esp. for a traffic offence [f. colour of paper]

[**1895** Cornelius Crowe *Australian Slang Dictionary* 58: *Piece of blue paper* A summons.

1899 Henry Lawson 'Jack Cornstalk' *Prose* ii 50: He gets on the spree and into a row, and so into trouble that merits the serving on his person of what he calls 'a piece of blue paper'.]

1939 Kylie Tennant *Foveaux* 348: 'Take a look at these blues.' With a flourish he produced a wad of grey summonses which he shuffled like a pack of cards.

see **bluey** 3

2 A quarrel, brawl, particularly in expressions like 'bung (stack, turn) on a blue', 'pick a blue'

1943 *Khaki and Green* 105: The 'blue' started, and you knew you'd be going up. Not the whole reinforcement draft, first time.

1957 Judah Waten *Shares in Murder* 58: 'Want to stack on a blue?' he said looking at her strangely.

1963 Jon Cleary *A Flight of Chariots* 178: 'That's one advantage to being a big bastard – people think twice about picking a blue with you.'

1974 David Ireland *Burn* 28: 'You tryin' to bung on a blue? I'll give you a smack in the chops in a minute.'

3 A blunder, mistake [f. *bloomer*]

1941 Baker 11: *Blue* (2) An error or mistake; a loss.

1957 Randolph Stow *The Bystander* 187: 'I reckon you ought to tell your missus she made a bit of a blue.'

1983 *Sun-Herald* 4 Dec. 168: Labor Party chappies were quick to ... score off Nick Greiner's tactical blue in saying the Opposition wasn't ready to govern yet.

4 Nickname for a red-headed person

1932 Leonard Mann *Flesh in Armour* 37: Blue McIntosh, No. 1, red in the head, a League footballer.

1950 Brian James *The Advancement of Spencer Button* 267: Two single ones ... became just Flora and Blue (she had red hair).

1961 Patrick White *Riders in the Chariot* 252–3: Hair – a red stubble, but red ... 'Blue is what he answers to.'

1981 David Ireland *National Times* 25 Jan. 25: His name was Martin Dangerfield, but everyone called him Blue since his hair was red.

Bluebags, the In N.S.W., the Newtown Rugby League team [f. colours]

1976 *Sunday Telegraph* (Sydney) 6 Jun.

56: Hail the Bluebags! Gallant win over Tigers.
1983 *Sun-Herald* 24 Jul. 120: It'll be a big, emotional, memorable, nostalgic, sad night on Thursday when Newtown Leagues Club has its Bluebags' farewell dinner before selling up and moving to Campbelltown.

blue bird The police 'paddy-waggon' [f. colour]
1939 Kylie Tennant *Foveaux* 415: The two-up school on the corner took no notice of Bramley and Kingston. The only thing that really disturbed the streets was 'the blue-bird', the police car on its rounds.

blue duck Anything which does not come up to expectations; a dud, a 'write-off'
1895 Cornelius Crowe *The Australian Slang Dictionary* 10: *Blue Duck* No good; no money in it.
1902 Mrs Campbell Praed *My Australian Girlhood* 21: 'One evening as he sits smoking outside the hut, without a moment's warning he finds a spear in his chest! Dam'd, but he would have been a blue duck if I hadn't ridden up at that very moment and scared the natives off.'
1917 A. B. Paterson *Three Elephant Power* 131: Time and again he had gone out to race when, to use William's own words, it was a blue duck for Bill's chance of keeping afloat, and every time did the gallant race pony pull his owner through.
1949 John K. Ewers *Harvest* 142: Tolly would ask if there was any news, and Len would shake his head and say, 'No. Looks like a blue duck to me.'
1954 Tom Ronan *Vision Splendid* 252: 'If they'll step up my expense account to include a stenographer, the secretary's job is yours. Otherwise I'm afraid it's a blue duck.'
1978 Ronald McKie *Bitter Bread* 142: He had rung round the usual contacts. But this Saturday had, early, an unmistakable feeling of being a blue duck for news.

Blue Hills Applied to anything that is prolonged [f. the radio serial which ran for 5795 episodes]
1981 *Sydney Morning Herald* 3 Jun. 12: This concerned the Blue Hills saga of Mr Murdoch's bid to take over Channel 10 which was originally knocked back and is now being heard on appeal.

Blue Orchid A member of the R.A.A.F. in World War II, considered to have a more glamorous uniform than the other services: *obs.*
1943 George Johnston *New Guinea Diary* 76: In the hearing of a Port Moresby digger never call a R.A.A.F. pilot [giving much needed air support] 'Blue Orchid'!
1946 Rohan Rivett *Behind Bamboo* 395: *Blue Orchids*, Army chaffing for air force.

blue pointer See quot.
1983 *National Times* 11 Nov. 27: The Surfers Paradise lifesavers were standing in a tanned huddle near the water's edge, wearing their Speedos or 'blue pointers' as they are fondly called.

blue swimmer A $10 note [f. colour, resembling the blue swimmer crab]
1986 Roland Fishman *Greg Matthews* 166: 'Here's a blue swimmer,' Greg says as he hands me $10.
1989 *Sun-Herald* 29 Oct. 90: It cost each member of staff a 'blue swimmer' to partake of the nibblies and drinks.

Blues, the 1 In N.S.W., the Newtown Rugby League team (see **Bluebags**) [f. colours]
1977 *Daily Telegraph* (Sydney) 25 Jan. 30: Newtown . . . are ready to shake off their tag of the 'Battling Blues'.
2 The Carlton A.F.L. team
1975 *Sunday Telegraph* (Sydney) 6 Jul. 42: Blues win as Dons brawl.
3 A team representing N.S.W. in state competition
1976 *Sunday Telegraph* (Sydney) 21 Nov. 72: Red faces is order of the day for the Blues.
4 In Queensland, the Fortitude Valley's Rugby League team
1979 *Courier-Mail* (Brisbane) 20 Feb. 18: Dunn free to stay with Blues [heading] Bustling Rugby League centre Brian Dunn will definitely wear the royal blue of Fortitude Valley's again this season.
5 In S.A., the Sturt Australian Rules team
1979 *Advertiser* (Adelaide) 11 Jun. 16: It was the second time this season that Woodville had beaten the Blues . . . and Sturt discard Larry Krieg had played a crucial role for Woodville.

Blues, the Two 1 In N.S.W., the Parramatta Rugby Union team [f. light and dark blue colours]
1979 *Australian* 30 Jul. 13: Melrose stars

for Two Blues [heading] Star Australian rugby union five-eighth Tony Melrose ... steered Parramatta to a 15–12 win over Manly.

2 In Victoria, the Prahran V.F.A. team
1984 *Toorak Sunday* 10 Jun. 24: Prahran go to Frankston today ... The Two Blues have lost every match since the opening win over Dandenong and are not likely to do any better against the Dolphins.

blue-tongue A shed-hand, rouseabout, or other unskilled worker [f. (*blue-tongue*) *lizard*]
1943 Baker 12: *Blue tongue* A station rouseabout.
1968 L. Braden *Bullockies* 119: He did not have an off-sider with him; he always drove by himself – they used to call off-siders Fridays or blue-tongues.
1975 Les Ryan *The Shearers* 124: 'Righto, you blue-tongues!' he bellowed out. 'Get stuck into it!'

bluey 1 A blanket [f. colour]
1891 Henry Lawson 'Harry Stephens' *Verse* i 409: Another bushman found him with his 'bluey' wrapped around him.
1936 Archer Russell *Gone Nomad* 61: I was ever ready to roll my bluey* and travel the roads again. *Blanket.
1958 *Coast to Coast 1957* 208: To the pack his wife held ready he added a piece of ground-sheet, a roll of newspaper, a bluey, and a heavy pullover.
2 The swag rolled in the blanket
1886 John Farrell 'My Sundowner' *How He Died* (1913) 60: His swag, the orthodox horse-collar 'bluey'.
1905 A. B. Paterson *The Old Bush Songs* 25n: To hump bluey is to carry one's swag, and the name bluey comes from the blue blankets.
3 As for **blue** 1
1965 Graham McInnes *The Road to Gundagai* 242: A uniformed John Hop with a tall patent leather helmet rang the bell and handed me the dreaded 'bluey', the summons for riding a bike without lights.
1974 *Sydney Morning Herald* 5 Nov. 1: After half a century the era of the 'bluey' is over. From now on, thanks to Dataprint, the Police Department's new $66,000 computerised traffic system, offending motorists will receive 'whiteys'. The blue summons paper has been replaced by white computer paper.
4 A cattle dog

1941 Baker 11: *Bluey* Colloquial name of a cattle-dog widely used in Australia.
5 Nickname for a red-headed person
1918 Harley Matthews *Saints and Soldiers* 48: Bluey's face went as red as his hair.
1944 Lawson Glassop *We Were the Rats* 277: I did not bother to ask which Bluey. Every fellow in the A.I.F. with ginger hair was called Bluey.
1975 Xavier Herbert *Poor Fellow My Country* 1120: They were calling her *Bluey*, from the copper curls popping out of her maroon cap.
6 See **Tasmanian bluey**

bluey, to hump To carry one's swag, take to the track [f. *bluey* 2]
1890 Henry Lawson 'Possum' *Verse* i 81: He 'umped his bluey ninety mile an' kum to Bungelong.
1911 E. M. Clowes *On the Wallaby through Victoria* 278: An expression used for what in England we call 'tramping' is 'going on the wallaby', otherwise, 'humping the swag', or 'the bluey', or 'sundowning'.
1919 W. K. Harris *Outback in Australia* 146: All the ... celebrities of the day were 'on the wallaby', 'humping bluey', and called at his particular station.
see **drum, swag**

board The floor of the wool-shed on which the sheep are shorn [f. being constructed of smooth timber; other floors would be earthen]
1870 Rolf Boldrewood 'Shearing in Riverina' *Town and Country Journal* 5 Nov. 11: So unreasoning are they, that an act of simple justice is often the signal for a strike, which includes a third or a half of the men 'on the board', as the shearing floor is by them termed.
1893 Henry Lawson 'Stragglers' in *Prose* i 91: The 'board' is very uneven and must be bad for sweeping.
1908 W. H. Ogilvie *My Life in the Open* 36: A raised floor called 'the board', on which the shearers shear the sheep.
1966 D. E. Charlwood *An Afternoon of Time* 68: In the morning the engine started at seven-thirty and the shearers stooped on the board for the last day.

board, boss over the The man supervising the shearing, the contractor
1893 Henry Lawson 'Ladies in the Shed' in *Prose* i 105: The 'boss over the board' comes

along to tell the men not to swear, 'there's ladies coming'.

1885–1914 'Click go the Shears' *Old Bush Songs* ed. Stewart and Keesing (1957) 254: In the middle of the floor in his cane-bottomed chair / Is the boss of the board, with his eyes everywhere.

1964 H. P. Tritton *Time Means Tucker* 51: The boss of the board was a petty tyrant ... One day I mentioned that he had stood over me from bell to bell, but was howled down; each shearer claiming that he had been the exclusive subject of the boss's attention.

Bob, pig-iron see **pig-iron**

Bob, staggering A newly born calf, hence veal ('bobby veal' in N.Z.) [E. dial. *Staggering Bob* ... A calf just dropped, and unable to stand, killed for veal in Scotland Grose 1785]

1873 Charles de Boos *Congewoi Correspondence* 157: Well, there wasn't nothing handy afore I'd cooled down, and so master Staggerin Bob got orf that time, and I was saved from makin a fooler myself.

1908 Mrs Aeneas Gunn *We of the Never-Never* 173: 'The time I've had with them staggering bobs,' he said, when we pitied the poor, weary, footsore little calves.

1959 Mary Durack *Kings in Grass Castles* 246: They had been forced to dispose of no less than thirteen hundred new-born calves during the trip. It was a complete waste, for stockmen were oddly squeamish about eating veal or 'staggering Bob' as it was known in the cattle camps.

bob (two-bob) in, a See quot. 1931

1931 William Hatfield *Sheepmates* (1946) 172: A bob-in [referring to an episode described thus at 72–3: 'There's too big of a mob fer one man to shout the house on his pat at a zack a pop, so you shove in a deaner a nob and flip the rats an' mice, see? An' the winner clouts on the centre an' weighs in fer the shicker, then rams the bunce down south – that is to say, I forgot you were a new chum – in his kick.' Atherton wondered why someone couldn't have said – 'We subscribe a shilling each, dice for the pool, winner paying out of that for drinks.']

1964 Tom Ronan *Packhorse and Pearling Boat* 178: No one shouted the drinks. The poker dice and box were on the counter and it was 'two bob in and the winner shouts for the mob'.

1986 James McQueen *The Floor of Heaven* 272: His introduction to shearers' pool, the old outback game with two bob in and the first one to jerk off gets the pot.

boco, boko A horse with one eye

1901 'Boko' *The Bulletin Reciter* 157: With his single eye to guide him, very few could live beside him.

1906 A. B. Paterson *An Outback Marriage* 243: 'I'm going to ride the boco.'* *One-eyed horse.

bodger, bodgie *a.* Inferior, worthless, false, counterfeit [f. *bodge* to patch or mend clumsily OED 1552]

1945 Baker 156: *Bodger* Worthless, second-rate (this term is apparently related to English dialect in which *bodge* means to botch or work clumsily). [World War II slang]

1951 Frank Hardy *Power Without Glory* 383: This involved the addition of as many more 'bodger' votes as possible.

1965 William Dick *A Bunch of Ratbags* 64: For having accepted the bodgie coin, he would be obliged to come good out of his pay at the end of the day.

1972 John de Hoog *Skid Row Dossier* 106: 'Oh, I gave a bodgy (false) name, and a bodgy last employer – the whole bloody form I filled out was a bodgy.'

bodgie *n.* The Australian equivalent of the Teddy boy: see quots

1950 *Sunday Telegraph* (Sydney) 7 May 47: 'This youth frequents King's Cross milk-bars with other young hoodlums and known prostitutes,' Vice Squad Constable Thompson said ... [The accused] stood in the dock dressed in the bizarre uniform of the 'bodgey' – belted velvet cord jacket, bright blue sports shirt without a tie, brown trousers narrowed at the ankle, shaggy Cornel Wilde haircut.

1966 Bruce Beaver *You Can't Come Back* 5: A would-be bodgie from Redfern, Sam. About five feet five of tight blue jeans, pea-jacket, long black side-levers, and a bit of the Presley look.

1984 Mike Carlton *Sydney Morning Herald* 29 Aug. 12: In his ACTU incarnation, Mr Hawke would slope into the studio like a retired bodgie, a riot of checks and stripes, sideburns and occasional beard a-go-go, hair slicked down to the rims of his horny spectacles.

bodyline Term applied to the type of bowling used against Australia by D. R. Jardine's team, especially Harold Larwood, in the 1932–33 test series: see quot. 1950

1933 18 Jan. cable from Australian Board of Control to MCC in *John Wisden's Cricketers' Almanack for 1934* 328: Body-line bowling has assumed such proportions as to menace the best interests of the game, making protection of the body by the batsmen the main consideration. This is causing intensely bitter feeling between the players as well as injury. In our opinion it is unsportsmanlike. Unless stopped at once it is likely to upset the friendly relations existing between Australia and England. [The Australian newspapers report 'body bowling' in the text of this cable, not 'body-line']
1933 J. C. Davis *The Referee* (Sydney) 1 Feb. 1: Australia has made her second move in the body-line game and sent it to the Marylebone C. C. at Lord's.
1950 Don Bradman *Farewell to Cricket* 66: Now what exactly was body-line bowling? It was really short-pitched fast bowling directed towards the batsman's body with a supporting leg-side field.

bog see **flybog**

bog a duck, wet enough to see **duck**

bogan Anyone stupid or 'square'; a 'nerd' (given currency by the television character Kylie Mole)
1988 *Bulletin* 5 Jul. 9: Bogans live mostly in the western suburbs of Melbourne and in some particularly dead country towns. They carry baseball bats and wear flannelette, red-checked shirts (ripped) and old ugly oddments in red, black and khaki. For entertainment, they get drunk or high or beat up Yuppies.
1989 *Sydney Morning Herald* 17 Feb. 24: Neil Pickard, the NSW Minerals and Energy Minister, managed not to look embarrassed yesterday while launching his Kylie Mole Don't be a Bogan electrical safety campaign.

Bogan shower see **shower**

bogey, bogie *v.* To bathe, swim [Ab.]
1788 Daniel Southwell papers *HRNSW* ii 699: To dive *Bo-gie*. Ibid. 700: I have bathed, or have been bathing *Bogiè d'oway*. These were Colby's words on coming out of the water.

1830 Robert Dawson *The Present State of Australia* 166: I at length told him we must go, when he said 'Top bit, massa, bogy,' (bathe) and he threw himself into the water, where he enjoyed himself as long as I could stay.
1907 Barbara Baynton *Human Toll* 72: 'Fanny,' she gasped, 'naughty, wicked boys goin' to bogey [bathe] on Sunday are stealin' Aunt's peaches!'
1957 R. S. Porteous *Brigalow* 222: I called 'Bogie dogs. Bogie.' The waterhole was only fifty yards away.

bogey, bogie *n.* A swim, bath, esp. in a river or waterhole
1847 Alexander Harris *Settlers and Convicts* ed. C. M. H. Clark (1954) 132: In the cool of the evening has a 'bogie' (bathe) in the river.
1894 G. N. Boothby *On the Wallaby* 246: Then an hour's sharp tennis . . . prepared the body for the evening bathe, or bogie as it is usually called, after which comes dinner.
1933 R. B. Plowman *The Man from Oodnadatta* 107: While the team went on the white men remained behind to have a bogey.
1973 Donald Stuart *Morning Star Evening Star* 60: Drinking tea, after a bogey and a good feed.

bogey hole A swimming-hole: the ocean rock-pool at Newcastle, N.S.W., is so named officially
1953 Dymphna Cusack *Southern Steel* 94: She and Arthur used to come along here in the mornings on their way to swim in the Bogey Hole.
1983 *Newcastle Herald* 10 Jan. 11: More than 200 people attended the Greek Orthodox Church's Blessing of the Waters service at Newcastle's Bogey Hole yesterday morning. The highlight of the service was when 30 men tried to retrieve the holy cross from the bottom of the old convict-built pool.

bogghi, boggi The handpiece of the shears [? f. resemblance to shape of the *bogghi* lizard]
1952 *People* 13 Feb. 12: *Boggi* Handpiece of shears.
1957 D'Arcy Niland *Call Me When the Cross Turns Over* 47: A time in those summers past when a man could take a bogeye and shear two hundred a day.
1963 *Sydney Morning Herald* 17 Aug. 11:

For the last ten years Darky's . . . renunciation of the 'bogghi' (shearing handpiece) has become a stock joke among his shearing mates.
1975 Les Ryan *The Shearers* 45: 'A man needs a bloody axe, not a boggi.'

bog in To start energetically on any task; to start to eat with a will ('Two, four, six, eight; Bog in, don't wait' is a mock 'grace')
1916 *The Anzac Book* 164: Vaulting the parapet and bogging into a dinkum bayonet charge.
1941 Kylie Tennant *The Battlers* 88: 'There's plenty o' stoo', the Stray offered bountifully. 'Bog in for all you're worth.'
1951 Dymphna Cusack and Florence James *Come In Spinner* 360: He . . . motioned them to the tray. 'Bog in, it's all on the house.'
1975 Les Ryan *The Shearers* 45: Clarrie stood nearby, munching a lamington, apparently disapproving of the two, four, six, eight, bog in don't wait, business going on.

boiler see **old boiler**

boilover An unexpected result in racing, esp. from the favourite not winning
1878 Rolf Boldrewood *An Australian Squire* repr. as *Babes in the Bush* (1900) 175: How often is the favourite amiss or 'nobbled', the rider 'off his head', the certainty a 'boil over'!
1904 Nat Gould *In Low Water* 149: The members of Tattersall's has a wholesome dread of 'one of Hickin's hot pots', and were not as a rule inclined to deal speculatively in the hopes of a 'boil-over'.
1924 *Truth* 27 Apr. 4: One of the biggest boil-overs in the rowing world was Queensland's meritorious win in the interstate eights for the King's Cup at Adelaide yesterday.
1975 *Sunday Telegraph* (Sydney) 8 Sep. 48: Roosters plucked in semi boilover.

boko see **boco**

bolter 1 Runaway convict, bushranger
1844 Louisa Meredith *Notes and Sketches of New South Wales* 132: During our stay at Bathurst, a party of the mounted police went in search of a very daring gang of bushrangers, or, as they are sometimes called, 'bolters'.
1865 J. F. Mortlock *Experiences of a Convict* (1965) 221: Three or four 'old hands'

were pointed out to me as Tasmanian 'bolters', who had made their escape to England and been for another crime again transported.
2 An outsider (applied more recently to one who wins or succeeds)
1941 Baker 35: *Hasn't the bolter's* Used of a person or race-horse that has no chance at all in a contest or situation.
1973 *Sydney Morning Herald* 17 Sep. 1: A South Coast publican who continually spurns the big money of Sydney Rugby League was the 'bolter' in the Australian team announced last night to tour France and England.
1984 *Age* (Melbourne) 6 Jun. 35: Pakenham bolter 'will win the Cup' [heading] The horse at the centre of this ambitious plan is Tasman, a 50/1 shot who returned from obscurity to take yesterday's Korean Horse Affairs Association Handicap.

bomb 1 An old or dilapidated motor-car
1950 *Australian Police Journal* Apr. 110: *Bomb, A* A dud – usually refers to second-hand motor vehicles in poor mechanical shape.
1962 Gavin Casey *Amid the Plenty* 58: The car, they called it! Well, he never wanted to be seen in that old bomb, that was for sure.
1970 Patrick White *The Vivisector* 470: Italians from Temora who are here in a bomb they bought, they want to take us for a ride.
1980 *Mercury* (Hobart) 16 Apr. 6: If ever anyone drove a 'bomb', it was the woman at the wheel of an early-model Holden station sedan spotted by a reader in the city yesterday.
2 In Rugby League football, a refinement of the 'up and under': a high kick at the end of the tackle count designed to land near or over the try line, esp. under the goal posts, so that a player catching it and going to ground will score.
1977 *Sun* (Sydney) 23 Sep. 62: We haven't used many 'bombs'. Last year in the finals we put plenty up and scored from a lot of them.
1981 *Canberra Times* 9 Aug. 6: The 'bomb' has been the most significant tactical innovation in league for 20 years. It is significant because it is an adaptation of union's 'up-and-under', and because it is an attempt to use the kick as an effective try-scoring agent.

Bombay bloomers Men's shorts, long and loose-fitting [? f. resemblance to those worn by the British in India]

1954 L. H. Evers *Pattern of Conquest* 80: The first drink he had of it put him in hospital for three weeks where he spent his time swatting green mosquitoes which he claimed wore yellow socks and Bombay bloomers.

1978 *Australian* 22 Nov. 2: Headline Harry [Jensen] they used to call him in his younger days when as Sydney's Lord Mayor he donned Bombay Bloomers in a vain attempt to persuade Australians to wear more suitable summer gear.

1981 Mike Fitzpatrick *Age* (Melbourne) 5 Oct. 11: The VFL issue [of shorts] this year is worse than last year's, which gave all the players a rash. These ones are Bombay bloomers, a reaction because last year the cheeks of one's behind kept peeping out from them.

bomber, brown see **brown bomber**

bomber, grey see **grey**

Bombers, the The Essendon A.F.L. team [f. proximity to aerodrome]

bombo Cheap wine [*bumbo*, a liquor composed of rum, sugar, water, and nutmeg OED 1748]

1942 Baker 12: *Bombo* Cheap wine.

1948 Ruth Park *The Harp in the South* 255: 'Get back to yer bombo, yer old hag.'

1958 H. D. Williamson *The Sunlit Plain* 17: 'Feel crook,' he mumbled. 'Finished up on the bombo last night.'

1968 Stuart Gore *Holy Smoke* 26: 'He done in the whole issue on sheilas and bombo.'

bommy A bombora [abbr.]

1979 *NT News* (Darwin) 7 Dec. 12: The waters there are clear and less turbulent than further south, with some very interesting bommies and reefs.

1983 *Sun* (Sydney) 16 Dec. 58: Outside fishing remains steady in this area with kingfish on the bommies south-west of Broughton Island.

Bondi, to give someone To beat someone up: *obs.* [f. a fracas between larrikins and the police at Bondi on Boxing Day 1884]

1890 *Truth* 19 Oct. 3: Suppose a live policeman is on the ground while the gay and festive members of a 'push' are 'giving him Bondi'.

1951 Dal Stivens *Jimmy Brockett* 67: Then Snowy got Maxie in a corner and began to give him Bondi.

1973 Ruth Park *The Companion Guide to Sydney* 415: 'Bondi' also means the heavy warrior's club, and the word was incorporated in a now-forgotten fragment of larrikins' cant – 'I'll give you Bondi!' meaning a severe bashing.

Bondi tram, to shoot through like a To make a speedy departure [f. trams running from Sydney to Bondi beach, discontinued in 1961]

1951 Seaforth Mackenzie *Dead Men Rising* 53: He called the rolls . . . looked up to check the inevitable comments from the ranks: 'Shot through like a Bondi tram.' 'Not 'ere today, Sar' Major.'

1962 John Morrison *Twenty-Three* 192: 'He shot through like a Bondi tram the minute the telegram arrived.'

1972 Geoff Morley *Jockey Rides Honest Race* 65: I punched him in the mouth and shot through like a Bondi tram.

bone, to (point the bone) 1 In Aboriginal 'magic', to will an enemy to die

2 Among whites, to place a 'jinx' or hoodoo on someone, single someone out with this purpose

1943 Donald Friend *Gunner's Diary* 21: The bone is pointed at myself and a few others. We are to be transferred to a draft battery.

1965 *Daily Telegraph* (Sydney) 27 Apr. 2: Harold Wilson has pointed the bone at the House of Lords. If they don't pull their heads in, he'll chop them off.

1974 Morris West *Harlequin* 15: When you tell a banker that there are anomalies in his accounts, it is as if you point a bone at him or chant a mortal curse over his head.

bonfire night As for **cracker night** q.v.

1976 *Sydney Morning Herald* 12 Jun. 36: Police had warned against the misuse of firecrackers at traditional Queen's Birthday bonfire night celebrations tonight.

bong see **bung**

bontoger, bontosher, bonzarina (almost nonce-words)

1904 *Bulletin* 14 Apr. 29: A bontosher is a real slasher . . . A bonsterina is a female bonster. Ibid. 5 May 29: 'Bonster' is a corruption of 'Bontojer' pronounced Bontodger,

and 'Bontojer' is a corruption of the two French words *bon* and *toujours*.
1934 Thomas Wood *Cobbers* 212: 'She was a little bonzarina.'
see **boshter**

bonzer Excellent, deserving admiration: *obsolescent* [origin uncertain]
1904 *Bulletin* 14 Apr. 29: A bonser or bonster is comparatively superior to a bons.
1915 C. J. Dennis *The Songs of a Sentimental Bloke* 13: The air is like a long, cool swig o' beer, / The bonzer smell o' flow'rs is on the breeze.
1925 Seymour Hicks *Hullo Australia* 88: 'Strange sayings the Australians have, sir, don't they? I asked Davis this evening what the weather would be like when we reached the other side and he said "Bonser".'
1947 John Morrison *Sailors Belong Ships* 72: 'I've got a bonzer little joint not ten minutes from the station.'
1979 *Age* (Melbourne) 21 Sep. 16: I do not have one friend, even acquaintance, who is anywhere near likely to say 'g'day cobber, like a cold tube? geez I like your sheila, no worries, bonzer sport . . .' etc. as most males do in television commercials.

boofhead 1 A stupid person, a fathead [f. *bufflehead* A fool, blockhead, stupid fellow OED 1659]. The term was given further currency in Australia from a comic strip character with an elongated head invented by R. B. Clark in 1939 and introduced in the *Daily Mirror* in May 1941, running until Clark's death in 1970.
1941 Baker 12: *Boofhead* A fool or simpleton.
1954 T. A. G. Hungerford *Sowers of the Wind* 117: 'Try taking your tweeds off, boofhead!'
1966 H. M. Barker *Droving Days* 81: Alf asked what he meant by B.C. 'Before the birth of Christ, you boof-head,' was the answer he got.
1979 John Summons *Lamb of God* 40: 'I find it hard to believe that Jim would throw an apple at the statue on purpose. He wouldn't be that much of a boofhead.'
2 Anyone with a big head (often with the implication 'fathead'); a horse with head out of proportion
1946 Rohan Rivett *Behind Bamboo* 395: *Boof head*, one with a big head.
1965 John Beede *They Hosed Them Out*

171: Tubby . . . asked, 'Who's that boof-headed old bastard, anyway?' It was an apt description and from then on . . . he was known as 'boofhead'. [referring (in 1944) to a colonel with an 'elongated and horselike' face, p. 168]
1981 *Alan Marshall's Australia* 132: 'What a boofhead of a foal,' he had thought – and so it was named. The foal did indeed have a large head, a hairy head, whiskered like a draught horse.

book A bookmaker [abbr.]
1898 A. B. Paterson 'A Disqualified Jockey's Story' *Singer of the Bush* (1983) 299: He said he reckoned he was stiff, / And all the books was layin' six to four.
1907 *Lone Hand* May 86: The 'books' found themselves unable to lay any odds whatever against the majority of the starters.
1934 Thomas Wood *Cobbers* 97: Charles laid down his fork and said it was a skinner for the books.
1984 *Sun-Herald* 25 Nov. 152: A local rails book was abused by a professional punter.

Booligal Town in western N.S.W. given a place in folklore by A. B. Paterson's poem 'Hay and Hell and Booligal'
[**1787** Francis Grose *A Provincial Glossary* R₈v: From Hell, Hull and Halifax – deliver us. This was part of the vagrant's litany. At Hull all vagrants, found begging in the streets, were whipped and set in the stocks; and at Halifax persons taken in the act of stealing cloth, were instantly, and without any process, beheaded, with an engine called a maiden.]
1901 *The Bulletin Reciter* 193: Hot? Great Scott! / It was Hell, with some improvements, worse than Booligal a lot!
1902 A. B. Paterson *Rio Grande's Last Race* 40: 'Oh, send us to our just reward / In Hay or Hell, but, gracious Lord, / Deliver us from Booligal!'
[**1916**] Oliver Hogue *Trooper Bluegum at the Dardanelles* 58: It was generally thought that he had spent some time in hell, or Booligal, so familiarly did he speak of the infernal regions.
1953 *Caddie A Sydney Barmaid* 172: He told me he'd just come from Booligal, and asked me if I knew where it was . . . 'Surely you've heard of Hay, hell and Booligal?' I remembered then. It was a place of heat, dust and flies.

boomah, boomer 1 A very large kangaroo (*Macropus giganteus*) [f. *boomer* anything
very large of its kind EDD]
1830 *Hobart Town Almanack* 110: We
saw a huge kangaroo ... What did we not
feel when Juno [the hound] snapped the
boomah's haunches and he turned round to
offer battle.
1845 R. Howitt *Australia Felix* 273: A
boomer, or large forester Kangaroo.
1981 A. B. Facey *A Fortunate Life* 81:
The boomer had been hit through the chest
and was dead when we ran to him.
2 Anything of exceptional size
1843 Charles Rowcroft *Tales of the Colonies* iii 97: 'There's one! and there's
another! he's a regular boomah!' [describing
a flea]
1896 Edward Dyson *Rhymes from the
Mines* 102: It was said that a nugget – a
boomer – / Had been found by the Chows in
our shaft.
1936 Miles Franklin *All That Swagger*
413: 'Old Robert's overdraft must be a
boomer.'
1944 'Stan Arneil *One Man's War* (1980)
167: I woke up with a boomer cold (almost
my first in the tropics).
1974 *Sydney Morning Herald* 5 Jun. 17:
The English Rugby League centre kicked
several goals from the 25 metre mark on the
sideline, and one boomer from right on the
halfway mark.

boomerang To move like a boomerang; to
recoil
1901 Henry Lawson 'The Mystery of Dave
Regan' *Prose* i 327: He said that to the horse
as it boomeranged off again and broke away
through the scrub.
1945 Kylie Tennant *Ride on Stranger* 63:
Money must boomerang back to his hand or
it never left it in the first place.
1982 *Age* (Melbourne) 1 Apr. 34: 'We
don't want any action to boomerang against
Australia,' one African official said.

**boomerangs, he could sell ~ to the
blacks** A persuasive personality
1974 Peter Kenna *A Hard God* 23: 'He's a
first class con man. He could sell boomerangs to the blacks.'

boondy 1 A club: N.S.W. [Ab.]
1907 Charles MacAlister *Old Pioneering
Days in the Sunny South* 88: The 'Knulla
Knullas', or 'Boondies', were ironbark
sticks, with a heavy nob on the end, used in

killing 'possums, etc., and sometimes in tribal warfare. Ibid. p. 124: They were mercilessly speared and 'boondied' (beaten to
death with nullas) by the blacks.
1978 *National Times* 2 Jan. 6: They had a
boondi (a club the shape of a baseball bat
carved usually from heavy myall or yarran).
2 A stone (of a suitable size for throwing):
W.A. [Ab.]
1952 T. A. G. Hungerford *The Ridge and
the River* 94: 'See that bastard, practising
grenade-throwing with bits of boondies?'
1957 Randolph Stow *The Bystander* 132:
'He's chucking boondies on the roof!'
3 See quot. 1982
1982 Jack Davis *The Dreamers* 88: 'You
got any *boondah*?' Ibid. p. 141: *boondah*,
money; literally, stone.

boong An Australian aboriginal; New
Guinea native; any Asiatic: *derogatory* [Ab.]
1941 Kylie Tennant *The Battlers* 123:
'These boangs are all too matey,' Thirty-Bob
grumbled. 'If a bit of trouble starts, it's a
case of one in, all in.'
1943 George Johnston *New Guinea Diary*
186: The boys from the Middle East called
them [the natives] 'wogs' at first, because it
was their name for the Arabs. Soon they
learnt the New Guinea army term, which is
'boong'. Before they have been there long
they are calling them 'sport', which seems
to be the second A.I.F.'s equivalent for
'digger'.
1946 Rohan Rivett *Behind Bamboo* 395:
Boong Any Asiatic or coloured person.
Boongs with boots on Japs.
1959 Xavier Herbert *Seven Emus* 58: 'He
might have a lot of boong in him, but he's also
got a lot of the white man.'
1980 *Australian* 8 Jul. 2: On the eve of
National Aboriginal Week, the Victorian Aboriginal community is divided in its reaction
to the Premier, Mr Hamer, referring to Aborigines as 'boongs' at a press conference
last Friday.

white boongs
1979 *Bulletin* 3 Jul. 57: Wingeing Poms
are in a class of their own, but 'white
boongs', as Kiwis are pejoratively, but not
really maliciously, called by some Australians [at Bondi], are starting to be regarded as a race apart.

boot, chewy on   see **chewy**

bootlace 1 See quot.

1933 Acland 363: *Boot Laces.* – Narrow strips of skin cut off by rough shearers, generally when opening up the neck.
2   Jerked meat (i.e. strips of meat cured by exposure to the sun)
1951 Ernestine Hill *The Territory* 107: Food in the pack-bags was flour, tea and four hundred pounds of jerked meat – 'bootlace'.

boot, put in the   To kick an opponent when he is down; to be ruthless in pressing an advantage.
1915 C. J. Dennis *The Songs of a Sentimental Bloke* 42: 'It's me or you!' 'e 'owls, an' wiv a yell, / Plunks Tyball through the gizzard wiv 'is sword, / 'Ow I ongcored! / 'Put in the boot!' I sez. 'Put in the boot!'
1923 Steele Rudd *On Emu Creek* 174: They . . . butted into him, played havoc with his clothes, threw him heavily every time he tried to rise, and put the boot into him.
1939 Kylie Tennant *Foveaux* 247: 'Give it to 'em! Put in the boot, boys!' the onlookers encouraged.
1962 Gavin Casey *Amid the Plenty* 79: 'You stand up to my old lady a bit, if you have to. If you let her get you down she'll put in the boot, don't you worry.'
1982 *Sun-Herald* 7 Mar. 15: After a good start this year, Hawke like others, is eager to put in the boot.

boots and all   An all-out effort; 'no holds barred'
1953 Dymphna Cusack *Southern Steel* 260: 'When you do a thing you go into it boots and all.'
1974 John Power *The Last of the Knucklemen* 72: 'You lift your arse off that floor, mate, an' I'm gonna come wadin' into you – boots an' all!'
1981 *National Times* 6 Dec. 1: The Left's drive for more power has been a 'boots and all' campaign.

boots under the bed   Evidence of a de facto relationship affecting a woman's eligibility for Social Security benefits
1983 Philippa Smith *Sun-Herald* 14 Aug. 119: Past practices of field officers inspecting homes and bedrooms – sometimes called the 'boot under the bed' inspections – were also criticised as an extreme intrusion of privacy.

booze bus   A police vehicle equipped for random breath-testing of motorists, introduced in N.S.W. 17 Dec. 1982
1982 *Sydney Morning Herald* 16 Dec. 2: Police 'booze buses' gear up for the start of random breath tests.
1984 *Age* (Melbourne) 4 Oct. 1: About 1000 drivers will be tested each day by booze buses or normal police cars.

bo peep, have a   Take a look at
1944 Lawson Glassop *We Were the Rats* 79: 'Let's take a bo peep at what they got in the canteen.'
1979 *Herald* (Melbourne) 20 Mar. Herald-form 4: He ought to take a bo-peep at the lot I have to deal with at the pickle factory.

borak, borack   Nonsense, gammon, humbug [Ab.]
1845 Thomas McCombie *Arabin, or, The Adventures of a Colonist* 273: *Borack*, Gammon, nonsense.
1885 *The Australian Printers' Keepsake* 124: Oh, we were bad – no borack, mind, boys.
1961 Tom Ronan *Only a Short Walk* 111: The chief steward was full of borack . . . He wasn't a very good liar, this steward.

borack, to poke ~ at   To ridicule, make fun of
1885 *The Australian Printers' Keepsake* 75: On telling him my adventures, how Bob in my misery had 'poked borack' at me, he said – 'You were *had.*'
1893 J. A. Barry *Steve Brown's Bunyip* 21: They're always a-poking borack an' a-chiackin' o' me over in the hut.'
1915 Louis Stone *Betty Wayside* 268: 'If I catch anybody poking borack at my get-up, they'll hear some fancy English!'
1936 William Hatfield *Big Timber* 245: 'Poke borack at me, would you?' he snarled.
1947 Vance Palmer *Hail Tomorrow* 47: 'For God's sake, leave me alone, Jim. You're always poking borak at me!'
1962 Dymphna Cusack *Picnic Races* 22: 'Makes me ropeable that feller does, poking borak every time he gets a chance.'
see **mullock**

bored or punched, he doesn't know if he's   A state of stupidity or confusion [Australian version of English and Canadian 'he doesn't know if his arsehole's bored or punched': Partridge]
1952 T. A. G. Hungerford *The Ridge and*

the River 120: 'They didn't know whether they were punched or bored, after that, until we got out again at the crossing, where you marked on the map.'

1959 Dorothy Hewett *Bobbin Up* 125: 'You're just a mad militant Snow. You wouldn't know if you was punched, bored or . . .'

1962 Stuart Gore *Down the Golden Mile* 301: 'The noise and the bloody flash . . . he won't know whether his stern's bored or countersunk!'

bore it up them Equivalent to 'sock it to them' [Army slang from World War II]

1951 Eric Lambert *The Twenty Thousand Thieves* 178: 'A provost I got into a blue with in Tel Aviv was barkin' the orders. Christ! Did that bastard bore it up me?'

1963 Lawson Glassop *The Rats in New Guinea* 128: 'Stand fast, Aussies, and bore it up 'em.'

1984 Rod Marsh *West Australian* (Perth) 21 Feb. 79: I handed out a lot of rockets as a captain but I also handed out a lot more praise than most captains. If players did badly I would bore it right up them and if they did well I would heap praise on them

born in a tent see **tent**

boshter, bosker Equivalent to **bonzer**, but never attaining the same currency: *obs.*

1906 Edward Dyson *Fact'ry 'Ands* 1: This was the fifth time Benno had declaimed on the 'boshter' qualities of the unknown.

1915 C. J. Dennis *The Songs of a Sentimental Bloke* 14: The little birds is chirpin' in the nest, / The parks an' gardings is a bosker sight. Ibid. 13: Soft in the moon; such *boshter* eyes!

1925 Arthur Wright *A Good Recovery* 52: 'What a bosker pair of earrings they'll make.'

1959 Gerard Hamilton *Summer Glare* 53: 'Gee, it's bosker, ain't it?' [set in 1920s]

boss, the The headmaster of a school

1950 Brian James *The Advancement of Spencer Button* 61: There was variety in this little world, and no marked unity and solidarity, except, perhaps, in the matter of the Boss. It was the proper thing to slander and malign and hate the Boss – and to say so.

1978 *Quadrant* Dec. 65: The boss, as all the chalkies like to call their headmasters, had insisted on inspecting his class.

1984 Ned Manning *Us or Them* 25: 'The boss asked me to remind you about the shortage of duplicating paper.'

boss cocky see **cocky**

boss over the board see **board**

boss, pannikin see **pannikin**

bot *n.* A sponger, persistent borrower [? f. the bot-fly, which 'bites']

1919 W. H. Downing *Digger Dialects* 13: *Bott* (1) A cadger; (2) A useless person; (3) A hanger-on.

1942 Leonard Mann *The Go-Getter* 124: 'Get out, you bot.' Chris ordered him [the beggar] and got up.

1978 Ronald McKie *Bitter Bread* 39: He was delighted to see the last of him. The bot had already cost him a small fortune.

1982 *Sydney Morning Herald* 12 Feb. 1: It might just have been possible to have chosen a happier name than Bot Australia Ltd for the new merchant bank launched this week.

bot *v.* To borrow, sponge on

1934 *Bulletin* 7 Nov. 46: 'How many's that, sir?' he gazed rheumily into space, 'Six it is; that's three beers I owe y'. Settle up when I sell me next picture.' The notebook went back into his pocket and he sighed with relief. 'Well, that's settled. Never did like *botting* on a bloke.'

1944 Alan Marshall *These Are My People* 174: 'If you get plenty later I'll bot a cigarette off the lot of you.'

1962 Criena Rohan *The Delinquents* 105: Lola, she said, was a botting, bludging little bastard.

1978 Richard Beilby *Gunner* 232: Scruffy though he might be he wasn't going to have Eilie thinking he was botting on Whiteside.

on the bot

1965 John Beede *They Hosed Them Out* 156: To prove that she wasn't on the bot she bought me a drink.

Botany Bay Name applied in the eighteenth and earlier nineteenth century to the penal settlement in Australia (actually Port Jackson), and to Australia as a whole [f. the landing place named by Cook in 1770]

c. **1790** 'Botany Bay. A New Song' repr. in Hugh Anderson *Farewell to Old England* (1964) 35: Who live by fraud, cheating, vile tricks, and foul play, / Should all be sent over to Botany Bay.

1819 Barron Field *First Fruits of Australian Poetry* (1941) 3: 'Botany-Bay Flowers' [poem title]
1859 John Lang *Botany Bay, or True Stories of the Early Days of Australia* [book title]

Botany Bay dozen
1792 George Thompson Jnl *HRNSW* ii 796: If guilty, he is taken to a cart-wheel to receive a Botany Bay dozen, which is twenty-five lashes.

bottle   To hit over the head with a bottle
1955 *Bulletin* 10 Aug. 34: The widgies have worked round the back and one tried to bottle me.
1968 David Ireland *The Chantic Bird* 29: Some of the fellows I know, you don't want to get drunk near them. They'd bottle you for two bob if they thought you were half shot.
1978 Kevin Gilbert *Living Black* 304: 'If he was too big to tackle, somebody bottled him.'

bottle, not full   Not fully informed, not 'all there'
1969 Christopher Bray *Blossom Like a Rose* 223: 'Jake and Brody aren't full bottle on this so tell them what goes on, will yer?'
1981 *Sydney Morning Herald* 1 Aug. 16: I have sometimes wondered, during his trip to London [to cover the royal wedding], if Spike Milligan is still the full bottle.

bottle-oh   An itinerant dealer in empty bottles [f. the cry]
1899 A. B. Paterson 'The "Bottle-oh" Man' in *Singer of the Bush* (1983) 332.
1913 Henry Lawson 'Benno and his Old 'Uns' *Prose* i 803: Benno, a Sussex Street bottle-o ... was an angry bottle-o that day.
1935 Kylie Tennant *Tiburon* 7: Battered old motor-trucks, bottle-oh carts ... paused here for the night.
1943 Margaret Trist *In the Sun* 99: A bottle-o followed him, crying cheerily, 'Bottles, bottles, any empty bottles, bottles, bottles, any kind of bottles.'
1970 Patrick White *The Vivisector* 39: Tommy Sullivan said that Hurt Duffield was the son of a no-hope pommy bottle-o down their street.

bottler   Someone outstanding in his class,

for good qualities or bad [cf. the expression 'His blood's worth bottling']
1876 Rolf Boldrewood *A Colonial Reformer* (1890) 95: 'He's a bottler, that's what he [a horse] is, and if you ever go for to sell him, you'll be sorry for it.'
1952 T. A. G. Hungerford *The Ridge and the River* 122: 'The old bastard! The old hooer! What a bloody bottler!'
1972 Alexander Macdonald *The Ukelele Player under the Red Lamp* 33: The theatre rang with cries of 'Good on yer, Mo!' 'You little bottler!' and other endearments.
1984 *Sun-Herald* 5 Feb. 144: There's a bottler of a row between members and the committee at the Australian Golf Club at Kensington.

bottling
1919 W. H. Downing *Digger Dialects* 13: *Bottling* A phrase expressive of admiration.
1957 Ray Lawler *Summer of the Seventeenth Doll* 35: 'They made Dowdie ganger in his place, and what a bottling job he done.'

bottom   In mining, to reach the level at which either gold will be found, or the mine will prove a failure; to succeed or fail in any enterprise
1853 John Sherer *The Gold Finder of Australia* 181: Having bottomed our hole (the bottom is generally pipe-clay), we pick up a good deal of gold – suppose four ounces – and return to our tent satisfied with our day's work.
1880 Rolf Boldrewood *The Miner's Right* (1890) 55: 'Bottomed a duffer, by gum, not the colour itself, no mor'n on the palm o' my hand.'
1903 Joseph Furphy *Such is Life* (1944) 261: Bottoming on gold this time, she buried the old man within eighteen months, and paid probate duty on £25,000
1969 *Southerly* 61: Towards the end of his life he must have had the feeling that he had 'bottomed on mullock'.

bottom of the harbour   Name for tax avoidance schemes given currency by the McCabe-Lafranchi report to the Victorian parliament in 1982
1982 *Sydney Morning Herald* 5 Jun. 13: The 'bottom of the harbour' scheme was so named because a company once stripped of its assets, was dumped and, like a body in a cement suit, sank never to be seen again.

boudoir bandicoot A promiscuous male
1983 *Sydney Morning Herald* 22 Sep. 14:
Speaking in the Budget debate, Mr
Hodgman said: 'The people of Australia are
starting to wake up to this Prime Minister
... I'm not much impressed by his public
breast-beating about being a reformed alcoholic and a retired boudoir bandicoot.'

bounce, the The beginning of an Australian Rules game, equivalent to 'the kick-off'
in other codes [because the umpire starts the
game by bouncing the ball]
[**1906** Joseph Furphy *Rigby's Romance* ed.
R. G. Howarth (1946) 249: Actual interest in
the game was yet abeyant, and the organ-
isms were collected in idle groups, pending
the inaugural bouncing of the ball.]
1958 Barry Humphries *A Nice Night's
Entertainment* (1981) 18: Had the usual
trouble parking the vehicle ... However,
found a possie in the long run just when I was
thinking I'd be late for the bounce.
1978 *Australian* 3 Apr. 15: Within two
minutes of the opening bounce ... Murray
was reported by field umpire Glenn James.

Bourke, back of Beyond the most remote
town in north-west N.S.W.; in the remote and
uncivilized regions generally.
1898 W. H. Ogilvie *Fair Girls and Gray
Horses* 161: 'At the Back o' Bourke' [poem
title]
1919 R. J. Cassidy *The Gypsy Road* 88:
'I could dump you into the desert at the Back
'o Bourke, and you'd be only a speck.'
1959 Gerald Hamilton *Summer Glare* 89:
I took the attitude that if girls didn't like to
dance with me ... they could go to Bourke or
buggery.
1961 G. R. Turner *A Stranger and Afraid*
95: 'To you there is the City, and all else is
back o' Bourke.'
1981 *Canberra Times* 21 Jun. 3: One of the
customers whose accent was decidedly back
o' Bourke complained that she had mixed up
his order.

Bourke, no work at see **Tallarook**
1968 David Ireland *The Chantic Bird* 43: I
remember I was humming to myself, Things
were crook at Tallarook and there was no
work at Bourke.

**Bourke Street, not to know whether it's
Tuesday or** The Victorian equivalent of
now knowing (in N.S.W.) whether it's **Pitt
Street or Christmas** q.v.: a state of confusion or stupidity
1952 T. A. G. Hungerford *The Ridge and
the River* 4: 'You waste too much time on the
dope. He don't know whether it's Tuesday or
Bourke Street.'
1971 Ivan Southall *Josh* 119: 'I told you he
was dumb. He doesn't know whether it's
Tuesday or Bourke Street.'

bower bird A person with the habit of collecting and treasuring odds and ends [f. the
bird's habits]
1941 Kylie Tennant *The Battlers* 233:
George the Bower-bird ... had the habit of
searching camps for discarded trifles or bits
of rubbish ... old boots or clothes that the
travellers threw away he gathered up as
though they were priceless treasures.
1953 *Sydney Morning Herald* 3 Jan. 6:
Those eccentric bower birds, the students of
Australiana, are uttering shrill little chirrups
of joy.
1966 Bruce Beaver *You Can't Come Back*
164: He put it back in his pocket, just like the
old bower-bird he was.
1973 Patrick White *Southerly* 139: All my
novels are an accumulation of detail. I'm a bit
of a bower-bird.
bower birding
1941 Kylie Tennant *The Battlers* 386: 'I
don't want him bower-birding round this
camp,' Mrs Tyrell complained.
1948 William Hatfield *Barrier Reef Days*
66: 'We couldn't put a thing down and turn
our backs without somebody bower-birding
it.'

Bowral, the boy from Sir Donald Bradman [b. Cootamundra, but his cricketing
career began in Bowral N.S.W.]
1930 Jack O'Hagan 'Our Don Bradman' in
*The Barry Humphries Book of Innocent Aus-
tral Verse* 43: The boy from Bowral hits four
after four.
1962 R. J. Hoare *The Boy from Bowral*
[title of biography]
1983 *Sydney Morning Herald* 27 Aug. 60:
The bat, used during the 1925–26 season,
evoked almost as many memories for
O'Reilly as it did for 'the boy from Bowral',
who scored 985 runs with it.

bowyangs 1 A string tied round the
trouser-leg below the knee [f. *bowy-yanks*
leather leggings EDD]
1893 *Warracknabeal Herald* 22 Sep. 4:

The two straps used to hitch the lower part of labourers' trousers are 'boyangs'.

1907 James Green *The Selector* 10: His moleskin trousers were tied below the knee with boyangs of string.

1939 Leonard Mann *Mountain Flat* 7: His pants were stiff moleskins caught in below the knee by bowyangs.

2 Applied derisively to anything rustic, clownish, out-of-date

1945 *Southerly* ii 14: The story is Romeo and Juliet in bowyangs, set in the Australian countryside.

1969 Don Whitington *The House Will Divide* ix: Menzies ... was aided by the stubborn and intransigent attitudes of Labor leaders like Evatt, Ward and Calwell when it became obvious that Labor's bowyang days were past.

box see **glory box**

box *n.* 1 The female genitals [listed by Partridge as 'low English and Australian: C20']

1949 Alan Marshall *How Beautiful Are Thy Feet* 150: 'I believe Leila's running hot in the box,' said Sadie.

1972 Geoff Morley *Jockey Rides Honest Race* 38: 'Say, she's not real bad after all.' 'Nice big boobs.' 'Nice big box, too, I bet.'

1983 Robert Drewe *The Bodysurfers* 86: I've seen some great tits and some of the bushiest boxes you could imagine.

2 The protector worn by sportsmen, the 'rupture box'

1974 Keith Stackpole *Not Just for Openers* 45: Once, I was hit in the box during a one-day match; an agonizing blow that left me crook for four days. A supporter for the opposing team shouted, 'Weak Australian sod, get up.'

3 A mixing of flocks of sheep which should be kept separate; a blunder, esp. in the expression 'make a box of'

1870 Rolf Boldrewood 'Shearing in Riverina' *Town and Country Journal* 29 Oct. 10: This distinguished them from other sheep in the neighbourhood, in case of a 'box' or mixing of flocks, not always to be avoided where so many thousands and tens of thousands are on the march.

1941 Baker 13: *Box* A mistake or confusion, e.g. 'to make a box of something': to muddle.

box *v.* 1 To mix flocks of sheep which

should be kept separate; to make a mess of something

1873 Rolf Boldrewood 'The Fencing of Wanderowna' repr. in *A Romance of Canvas Town* (1898) 69: Great was the bleating and apparent confusion – two flocks incontinently 'boxed', or mixed together.

1903 Joseph Furphy *Such is Life* (1944) 282: 'Tell him a lot o' his sheep was boxed with ours in the Boree Paddick.'

1934 Mary Gilmore *Old Days: Old Ways* (1963) 97: In the unfenced states of the newly settled country sheep boxed and then had to be sorted out.

1960 *Sydney Morning Herald* 19 Jul. 1: Thurber's moral is Those who live in grass houses shouldn't stow thrones. Emily boxed it.

2 To bet in a way which will cover two or more winning prospects or combinations, for a higher outlay; i.e. instead of taking a number of separate bets, the punter 'boxes' them

1983 *Sydney Morning Herald* 25 Jun. 57: Footy TAB punters will be able to rake in a lucrative dividend this weekend if they 'box' two matches when they take their card. If form is any guide, it appears that there are five almost certain results this weekend ... With an average payout of 135–1, it is worth boxing the two matches in doubt. It will cost a little more, but the end result will be worth it.

boxer The ringkeeper in two-up, who takes a percentage of winnings (his 'box'); sometimes an assistant to the ringkeeper who holds the stakes

1911 Louis Stone *Jonah* 216: The spinner threw down the kip, and took his winnings from the boxer – five pounds for himself and ten shillings for the boxer.

1949 Lawson Glassop *Lucky Palmer* 169: The man running a two-up game takes a percentage of the winnings of the spinner when there is a run of heads, but when tails are falling he depends on contributions from the tail backers. In response to the fat man's appeal for a 'Boxer', a few florins and shillings were tossed into the ring.

1975 Les Ryan *The Shearers* 151: *boxer* One who holds the stakes being wagered at a game of two-up.

box of birds Equivalent to 'in good spirits': N.Z. rather than Australian

1951 Dal Stivens *Jimmy Brockett* 120: I was feeling as happy as a box of birds.

1955 D'Arcy Niland *The Shiralee* 122: 'I

had a mate, but he got himself pinched. And just quietly, I been a box o' birds ever since.'

box, out of the   Exceptional, outstanding
1926 *Sun* (Sydney) 29 Jul. 1: Two out of the box. These Siamese cats are just looking at the world from the box in which they travelled on the Comorin. [caption to photograph]
1941 *Coast to Coast* 63: 'You talk about it as if 'aving kids is somethin' out of the box.'
1975 *Sun-Herald* 9 Nov. 111: To be frank, the novel is nothing out of the box, and neither is the movie.
see **out of the bag**

box seat, in the   In the most favoured position (to succeed, control the situation) [f. the driver's seat on a coach]
1949 Lawson Glassop *Lucky Palmer* 116: 'I jumped him away smartly and had him in the box seat all the way. Cantering just behind Lovely Rose and Murragum at the turn, he was.'
1957 Judah Waten *Shares in Murder* 117: 'They'll do Fenton-Lobby favours now and again, and Fenton'll repay them when he's in the box seat.'
1977 *Australian* 4 Jan. 6: With 15 overs and 56 runs required to win, Australia was in the box seat.

boy, the   The jockey, esp. an apprentice
1881 A. C. Grant *Bush-Life in Queensland* ii 67: Now the boy is lifted on, and John leads his horse down the course a little.
1923 Con Drew *Rogues & Ruses* 152: 'I wish the boy would make a move on the grey,' he muttered. 'He's riding him like as if he wanted to lose.'
1984 *Sydney Morning Herald* 18 Apr. 48: The crowd cheers when he mentions Theo Green, the trainer . . . claps again when he mentions 'the boy', Darren Beadman.

boy from Bowral, the   see **Bowral**

boy, the old   see **old**

boy, you can take the ~ out of the bush, but you can't take the bush out of the boy   See quots. [? Australian variations of an international catchphrase]
1981 *Sunday Mail* (Brisbane) 20 Sep. 60: There's that old saying that you can take a boy out of the bush, but not the bush out of the boy.
1983 *Australian Literary Studies* May 75: Disavowing evaluative criticism, Docker's nomination of a new canon of neglected authors reintroduces evaluation in the allegedly more rigorous guise of a conceptually self-conscious criticism. It has been easier to take the boy out of Melbourne than to take Melbourne out of the boy.
1983 Reg Livermore *National Times* 10 Jun. 29: 'After all, I am from the western suburbs, and like they say, you can take the boy out of Parramatta, but you can't take Parramatta out of the boy.'

bracket   Anus
1986 *Australian* 26 Nov. 6: Mr Wilson Tuckey . . . sought on a point of order to know whether words and phrases used by the Prime Minister during Question Time – 'wankers' and 'sticking a boot up the bracket' – were unparliamentary.

brass razoo, not a   see **razoo**

break it down   A plea to desist from or to moderate some action; an expression of disbelief or disagreement; i.e. 'Give over', 'Come off it'
1944 Lawson Glassop *We Were the Rats* 193: 'There's no other bastard in the world can talk to me like that. For Christ's sake break it down or I'll lose me grip on meself. I'm tellin' ya now. Break it down, see.'
1961 Hugh Atkinson *Low Company* 58: The barman was worried about the noise and kept saying uselessly, 'Now, now, blokes, break it down,' and 'Fair go there, fellars.'
1979 *Advertiser* (Adelaide) 22 Apr. 25: Just the other day I heard a young man in North Terrace say to his mate: 'Hey, break it down. What do you think this is, Bush Week?'

break out   Used of the discovery of a goldfield and the 'rush' following
1856 Frederick Sinnett *The Fiction Fields of Australia* ed. C. H. Hadgraft (1966) 36–7: South Australia, at the time when the Victorian gold fields 'broke out', as the common phrase runs, presented a most remarkable social aspect.
1882 A. J. Boyd *Old Colonials* 130: 'I was out prospectin' on the Palmer just after it broke out.
1901 Rolf Boldrewood *In Bad Company*

30: Labour was scarce, owing to the Coolgardie goldfield having broken out.

breeze, bat the   see **bat the breeze**

breezer   A fart (juvenile)
1973 Patrick White *The Eye of the Storm* 380: 'And lets breezers, as if he didn't know there was anybody else in the room.'
1974 Gerald Murname *Tamarisk Row* 91: Barry Launder has ordered every boy to write in his composition *at the picnic I let a breezer in my pants*, or else be bashed to smithereens after school.

brick   £10 Used most often in gambling, and esp. in the expression **London to a brick** q.v.
c. **1914** A. B. Paterson 'Races and Racing in Australia' in *The World of Banjo Paterson* ed. C. Semmler (1967) 324: 'Pop it down, gents, if yer don't put down a brick you can't pick up a castle.'
1949 Lawson Glassop *Lucky Palmer* 103: 'Tiger' . . . slipped a ten pound note into his hand. 'Here's a brick,' he said in his lifeless voice.
1975 Les Ryan *The Shearers* 69: Moody flashed a roll of notes, peeled one off and handed it to Tricum. 'Put this brick on for me.'

brickfielder   A wind carrying dust with it, originally from Brickfield Hill in Sydney. Confused by Morris with the **southerly buster** or **southerly** q.v.
1833 W. H. Breton *Excursions in New South Wales and Van Diemen's Land* 293: It sometimes happens [in Sydney] that a change takes place from a hot wind to a 'brickfielder', on which occasions the thermometer has been known to fall . . . from above 100 degrees to 80 degrees! A brickfielder is a southerly wind, and takes its local name from the circumstances of its blowing over, and bringing into town the flames of a large brickfield. [Morris]
1859 Frank Fowler *Southern Lights and Shadows* 87–8: The 'Southerly Buster', as this change is called, generally comes . . . early in the evening. A cloud of dust – they call it, in Sydney, a 'brickfielder' – thicker than any London fog, heralds its approach . . . In a minute the temperature will sink fifty or sixty degrees.
1861 H. W. Wheelwright *Bush Wanderings of a Naturalist* 231: In Melbourne a hot-wind day is called a 'brickfielder', on account of the dust, which darkens the sky.
1935 H. H. Finlayson *The Red Centre* 21: A desert . . . whose chief function is to provide material for the 'brickfielder' dust-storms which occasionally cloud the towns.
1962 Stuart Gore *Down the Golden Mile* 192: Behind him . . . the sky looked forbidding, no longer pink but red, charged with a threat of dust straight from the desert heart. 'It's going to be a brick-fielder, Dad!'

bride's nightie, off like a   Making a quick departure; acting promptly
1969 Christopher Bray *Blossom like a Rose* 26: 'Come on youse blokes!' he shouted. 'We're off like a bride's nightie!'
1972 Geoff Morley *Jockey Rides Honest Race* 148: At the furlong the jockey said 'Let's go', and Che Sera went off like a bride's nightie. In a flash she hit the front and won by several lengths.

Bridge, the   The Sydney Harbour Bridge
1937 M. Harcourt *It Never Fails* 241: 'The Bridge is very popular for suicides.'
1949 Ruth Park *Poor Man's Orange* 292: Mumma would no sooner have put Hughie or anyone else in the cold cells on Christmas Day than she would have jumped off the Bridge.

brim, the wider the ~, the smaller the property   Formula for estimating the size of rural holdings
1962 Dymphna Cusack *Picnic Races* 189: 'There's a rule for it: "The smaller the property the wider the brim".'
1966 Craig McGregor *Profile of Australia* 162: 'The wider the brim the smaller the property', as the ironic saying goes.

bring back to the field   see **field**

brinny   A stone of the size thrown by children: *rare*
1943 Baker 14: *Brinny* A stone.
1977 Phil Motherwell *Mr Bastard* 43: I slowly crouch to pick up two brinnies from the ground.

Bris, Brizzie   Brisbane [abbr.]
1945 Cecil Mann *The River* 117: Up in Bris he gets himself shaved at the Barber's down the lower end of Queen Street.
1965 Patrick White *Four Plays* 149: 'Reckon I'll catch the evenin' train to Brizzy.'

1979 Thea Astley *Hunt the Wild Pineapple* 162: Mrs Wacker measured plane distances by noggins. 'It's two beers from Brissy to Townsville,' she announced heartily, 'and then one more to the top.'

1981 *Sunday Mail* (Brisbane) 9 Aug. 2: We think that Tony Murphy, the top cop at Cairns, is coming back to Brissie as an assistant commissioner.

Brisbane, battle of 1 The Rugby League match between England and Australia on 19 June 1932

1979 *Sun-Herald* 17 Jun. 59: Memories of the famous 'Battle of Brisbane' Rugby League Test were far from the minds of the crowd of 18,000 as they started to file from the ground midway through the second half at Lang Park last night.

2 The Rugby Union match between England and Australia in 1975

1979 Steve Finnane *The game they play in heaven* 59: The Test was a good game and a great Australian victory but it will always be remembered for an incident that lasted just a few seconds and earned it the tag, 'Battle of Brisbane'. [Macdougall appearing to kick at Nelmes, on the ground]

Brisbane Line Name given to a military plan to concentrate on the defence of vital areas of Australia, put to the Curtin government in February 1942, which led to claims that the abandonment of Australia north of Brisbane was contemplated (Paul Hasluck *The Government and the People 1942-1945* (1970) 711-17). The plan was attributed to the Menzies government by its political opponents.

1951 *The Calamitous Career of Dictator Bob* [Communist pamphlet] 4: Rather than wage a people's war against fascism Menzies devised the Brisbane Line to give Nth Australia to the Japs!

1967 R. G. Menzies *Afternoon Light* 20: This legend did not prevent the notorious 'Eddie' Ward from concocting a story, months later, that we had prepared plans to base Australia's defence against Japan on a so-called 'Brisbane Line' ... and that we were prepared to retreat ... to the extent of surrendering the northern part of Australia!

1984 *Australian* 2 Jun. Mag. 2: 'It's the old Brisbane Line mentality – everything in the north is dispensable.'

British to the boot heels Statement by Sir Robert Menzies in 1963, subsequently interpreted out of its context

1963 Sir Robert Menzies *Commonwealth of Australia Parliamentary Debates*, House of Representatives, Vol. 40, 29 Oct. 2373: The deal made with the United States of America is probably the most favourable deal ever made by Australia with another country for something that is vital to Australia's defence. It is a very great mistake for anyone to think that this involves being pro-British or anti-British. As I have said before, I am British to the boot heels. I will not be told that I am hostile to what is done in Great Britain. But, like my honorable friend opposite, I have always esteemed my prime duty to be to my own country and to the safety of my own country. On that principle we have acted.

1964 Geoffrey Dutton 'Thoughts, Home From Abroad' *Overland 29* 14: But we, of course, are British to our arse-holes.

1981 *Australian Book Review* Nov. 42: No doubt new nationalism is better than being 'British to the bootstraps'.

Britt, Edgar As for **Jimmies, Jimmy Britts** q.v.

1970 Alexander Buzo *The Front Room Boys* in Penguin *Plays* 22: 'Then he raced out to the john for an Edgar Britt.'

1983 Bruce Dawe *Over Here, Harv!* 101: 'Jeez,' said Wooffer, 'You give me the Edgar Britts, sometimes.'

Broken Hill, the battle of The attack by two Turks on 1 January 1915 on a party of picnickers going by train from Broken Hill to Silverton, resulting in six deaths

bronze (bronza) Backside

1953 Baker 105: *bronzo* Anus (a variation of *bronze*, used similarly).

1959 D'Arcy Niland *The Big Smoke* 164: He roared laughing and gave her a slap on the seat. 'The biggest bronza in the world – and just think, you're all mine.'

1968 Geoffrey Dutton *Andy* 262: 'Some bloody boomers, boy, be in it. But some hairy nosed dumpers as well. One of them set me right on my bronze on the bottom.'

1975 Les Ryan *The Shearers* 104: 'Go and sit on your bronze while we give scabs your jobs.'

bronzed gods 1 Applied to soldiers of the A.I.F. 8th Division in World War II (see quot.

1946); transferred to Australian servicemen generally

1946 Rohan Rivett *Behind Bamboo* 395: *Bronze gods* A.I.F. 8th Division. Term was used by a woman journalist visiting Malaya, and subsequently derisively. *Bronzie* Member of the 8th Division.
1952 T. A. G. Hungerford *The Ridge and the River* 31: 'Oh, you big bronzed bastard, you! What you do in the war, daddy?' Ibid. 186: 'You big bronzed Anzac!' A bitter smile flickered at the corner of Malise's mouth.
1960 John Iggulden *The Storms of Summer* 74: 'You won't be able to keep them out . . . you and all the other great bronzed Anzacs!'
2 The 'bronzed' Australian male (no military association)
1969 Thomas Jenkins *We Came to Australia* 174: These bronzed young gods take turns to watch from the top of a scaffolding tower for anyone in trouble in the sea. If they see a hand raised . . . they will swim to help, churning through the sea as if they were fitted with outboard motors.
1980 *Sunday Telegraph* (Sydney) 13 Apr. 160: We wonder what is happening to the big, bronzed Aussie male?
see **Anzac**

brook, babbling see **babbler**

broomie A broom-hand in a shearing shed
1910 C. E. W. Bean *On the Wool Track* 203: There still remain the burry pieces which were skirted from the fleece at the wool-rolling tables and are lying on the floor. A boy, the 'broomy', sweeps them.
1964 H. P. Tritton *Time Means Tucker* 64: Sam was expert, boss of the board, wool classer, tar boy and broomie, musterer and penner-up.
1975 Les Ryan *The Shearers* 142: 'That stupid broomie . . . oh, Gawd! . . . what a scream?'

brothel Any untidy, crowded or disreputable place
[**1919** W. H. Downing *Digger Dialects* 31: *Knocking-shop:* An untidy or squalid place.]
1946 Rohan Rivett 331: *Brothel of a place,* poor place.
1953 T. A. G. Hungerford *Riverslake* 148: 'Always drunk. He does his work, in a way – enough to get by in a brothel like this. But in normal times he wouldn't be tolerated in a boong's kitchen.'

brothel, piano player in a see **piano**

Brotherhood, the The Brotherhood of St Laurence [f. an order in the Anglican community founded in 1930, increasingly dedicated to social welfare]
1985 Helen Garner *Postcards from Surfers* 89: He bought a mattress at the Brotherhood, and borrowed a blanket.

Brothers The Christian Brothers Rugby Union team (Q.)
1979 *Courier-Mail* (Brisbane) 25 Jun. 16: Uni downs Brothers 16–11 [heading]

brown A penny: *obs.* [f. *brown* a copper coin OED 1812; a halfpenny]
1865 *Queenslanders' New Colonial Camp Fire Song Book* 21: Most others are hard up for browns.
1913 Henry Lawson 'The Kids' *Prose* i 806: But for the chartering of the aforesaid craft . . . there must be 'browns', or 'coppers'.
1946 *Sun* (Sydney) 20 Oct. Suppl. 25: Everybody's jumping about like a double-headed brown had been found at a swy game.

brown bomber In N.S.W., a parking policeman [f. colour of uniform]
1954 *Sun* 8 Jun. 1: New name for the Brown Bomber boys is Walkie-Chalkies.
1968 David Ireland *The Chantic Bird* 61: Next day a brown bomber – a parking cop – gave me a fright.
1975 *Sun-Herald* 23 Nov. 5: New uniform to boost new image for the Brown Bombers . . . The long-standing, long-suffering brown is out. A new bluish-grey is 'in' for the city's parking squads.
1982 *NT News* (Darwin) 11 Jan. 7: A dedicated bomber was seen marking tyres at the Stuart Park shopping centre on Saturday afternoon.
see **grey ghost, grey meanie**

brown dog, fit to kill a An adverse judgement on food, esp. as applied by Senator Ron Elstob in 1982 to the food at Parliament House.
1982 *Sydney Morning Herald* 5 May 3: The much-published interjection that some meals in Parliament House would 'kill a brown dog' was finally laid to rest in the Senate yesterday. Senator Ron Elstob (Lab. SA) apologised 'unreservedly' for his remark.
1984 *Toorak Sunday* 10 Jun. 5: It was the

sort of tucker which in the folklore of this great land of ours is reputed to be able to kill a brown dog at anything up to 15 paces.

brownie A bush cake made with currants and brown sugar
1883 J. E. Partington *Random Rot: A Journal of Three Years Wanderings* 312: It was an amusing sight to see the three of us, each with a huge hunch of 'browny' (bread sweetened with brown sugar and currants) in one hand.
1901 Henry Lawson 'Joe Wilson's Courtship' *Prose* i 541: 'Here's some tea and brownie' . . . Jack took a cup of tea and a piece of cake and sat down to enjoy it.
1919 W. K. Harris *Outback in Australia* 49: Damper, beef and tea sweetened with coarse brown sugar, was the usual fare, with an occasional 'brownie' cake to vary the menu.

brown land, the wide see **wide brown land**

brownout A partial blackout in World War II
1942 A. G. Mitchell 'A Glossary of War Words' *Southerly* i 12: *Brownout* A partial blackout.
1953 Dymphna Cusack *Southern Steel* 81: She hated the brown-out. It would have been better had they blacked-out the city, instead of this half-way business of restrictive light and deceptive shadow.
1980 Emery Barcs *Backyard of Mars* 186: I was walking down Pitt Street toward Attila's shop, thankful for the brownout.

Bruce Name applied by the English to the typical Australian [f. the sketch in 'Monty Python Live at Drury Lane' 1975]
1981 *Bulletin* 6 Jan. 30: Aussie journalist Bruce Page – who confirms every pom's pugnacious conviction that all Australians are called Bruce – is currently under siege at the *New Statesman*.
1982 *Australian* 26 Jun. 13: Prince Bruce for Tech . . . the son of Charles and Di could perhaps be given the opportunity to mix more with the masses by attending a good solid State school such as Brunswick East Tech . . . It could also solve the problem of combing through the centuries for suitable names . . . Bruce Windsor. Now there is a name that combines regal style with the grit and honor of the working person.

brumby 1 A wild horse [Ab. *booramby* wild Ramson 120]
1880 *Australasian* 4 Dec. 712: These our guide pronounced to be 'brumbies', the bush name here [Queensland] for wild horses. [Morris]
1892 Gilbert Parker *Round the Compass in Australia* 44: Six wild horses – warrigals or brombies, as they are called – have been driven down, corralled, and caught.
1982 *Courier-Mail* (Brisbane) 26 Mar. 2: Two more brumbies have been found shot dead in scrub on Moreton Island.
2 A person with such attributes
1911 L. St Clare Grondona *Collar and Cuffs* 98: They were a brumbie lot of rotters, all swagmen, and to all appearances at least, considerably down on their uppers.
1936 Miles Franklin *All That Swagger* 444: 'I'm only a brumby compared with you.'
1974 *Sydney Morning Herald* 16 Aug. 7: He [Dr Cairns] gave long allegiance to the Victorian Executive when it was the brumby of the ALP and the despair of ALP voters who wanted to see Labor back in power.

brush A woman; women collectively [Partridge suggests derivation from pubic hair]
1941 Baker 14: *Brush* A girl or young woman.
1965 William Dick *A Bunch of Ratbags* 226: We were all hanging out of windows, whistling up some of the bits of 'brush' (sheilas) that were walking along.
1967 Kylie Tennant *Tell Morning This* 16: 'Always be leary of the brush. There's many a man thought he was going to stand over some little lowie and now he's either looking through bars or else he's mowing the lawn for her.'
1975 Elizabeth Riley *All That False Instruction* 229: 'Beer first. Brush later.'
1983 T. A. G. Hungerford *Stories from Suburban Road* 87: We still called them 'the tarts', but he called them 'brush' and 'swell kakas'.

brusher, give To abscond without paying one's debts, abandon a task: *obs.*
1878 T. E. Argles *The Pilgrim* 2nd Series No. 10, 5: He subsequently victimized Mr Weber, Post Office Hotel . . . indeed anywhere this penniless Hebrew obtained admission he never failed to give 'brusher' to the confiding boniface.
c. **1882** *The Sydney Slang Dictionary* 2: *Brusher (to give anyone)* To obtain or

borrow something and not pay for it or return it.

1904 Henry Fletcher *Dads Wayback: His Work* 20: 'I s'pose I may as well give it brusher for ter-night,' replied Dan, as he wiped his scythe and walked with Dads to the house.

bubs, the   Kindergarten [f. *bub* infant]
1962 Ross Campbell *Daddy, Are You Married?* 83: 'She's still in the bubs. The bubs are too little for me now,' said Little Nell complacently.
1988 Faith Richmond *Remembrance* 64: Some rows of spidery pot hooks from my brother who's in the Bubs at school.

bucket, drop a ~   See quots [f. bucket used as w.c.]
[**1950** *Australian Police Journal* Apr. 112: *Drop the bucket* Drop the responsibility on to someone else.]
1971 Alan Reid *The Gorton Experiment* 242: In Australian political argot to 'turn a bucket' means to attack someone on personal grounds, usually of a slightly scandalous nature.
1977 *Australian* 26 Nov. Mag. 4: Tipping a bucket is now accepted parliamentary usage for releasing embarrassing information usually accompanied by personal insults, innuendo and allegations which, if made outside Parliament, would clearly be defamatory.
1982 Buzz Kennedy *Australian* 28 Aug. Mag. 8: I have had enough of being expected to smile politely and resolve to mend my ways and the ways of my country simply because precious people from somewhere else flip in, flip out and bucket the place.
bucketing
1982 *NT News* (Darwin) 23 Jun. 4: Mr Whitlam copped a bucketing over his inclusion in a National Aboriginal Conference delegation leaving for Africa tomorrow.

buckle   To arrest [f. *buckle* to unite oneself in wedlock OED 1693]
1961 Hugh Atkinson *Low Company* 187: 'What's yer laggin'? What did they buckle yer for?'
1977 Jim Ramsay *Cop it Sweet!* 17: *Buckled*: Arrested.
1990 *Australian* 24 Mar. Mag. 42: Two big coppers are getting a very large serve from an even larger patron . . . 'Aren't they going to buckle him?' I ask.

Buckley's chance (show, hope)   A forlorn hope, no chance at all [Origin obscure. Connections have been suggested with 'the wild white man' William Buckley, the convict who absconded from Port Phillip in 1803 and lived for thirty-two years with the natives. He gave himself up in 1835 and lived until 1856. Another suggested derivation is a pun on the name of the Melbourne firm of Buckley and Nunn.]
1898 W. H. Ogilvie *Fair Girls and Gray Horses* 70: But we hadn't got a racehorse that was worth a dish of feed, / So didn't have a Buckley's show to take the boasters down.
1903 Joseph Furphy *Such is Life* (1944) 339: Brummy . . . doesn't require to stoop at all – and *his* show is little better than Buckley's.
1915 C. J. Dennis *The Songs of a Sentimental Bloke* 20: I knoo / That any other bloke 'ad Buckley's 'oo / Tried fer to pick 'er up.
1944 Lawson Glassop *We Were the Rats* 44: 'I've got two chances,' I said. 'Mine and Buckley's.'
1963 John Cantwell *No Stranger to the Flame* 156: 'He won't stand Buckley's with that mob.'
1983 *Australian* 11 Jan. 1: Miss Jenny May said civilians who worked at test sites had 'Buckley's chance' of getting compensation because their medical records were not held in one place.

bucks' party, night   An all-male party, esp. before a wedding [cf. *stag* functions US 1843]
[**1907** Alfred Searcy *In Australian Tropics* 367: What grand 'buck sprees' we used to have there, to be sure; a lot of men together, pure fun and frolic.]
1942 Gavin Casey *It's Harder for Girls* 82: Bucks' Party [story title]
1957 Nino Culotta *They're a Weird Mob* 88: 'We're 'avin' a bucks' party fer Jimmy Friday night. Cost yer 'alf a quid fer the grog an' the present.'
1980 *Sydney Morning Herald* 27 Dec. 24: My son had just had a bucks' party at which his friends totally encased him in wall plaster. We have tried soaking him in the bath to no avail. He is being married tomorrow. How do we get it off?

Budgie, the Silver   see **Silver**

Buffs, the   The Darwin Australian Rules team [abbr. *buffalo*]

1979 *NT News* 19 Nov. 24: Buffs biffed [heading] Nightcliff gave Darwin a football lesson by creaming them in every aspect of the game.

bugger *n.* Like 'bastard' and 'bloody', bugger (noun, verb and extensions) is not distinctively Australian, but it is remarked upon by visitors as a feature of Australian speech. Intensive uses like 'bugger-all' and 'burnt to buggery' may be more characteristically Australian than the others. The noun is used as an equivalent to 'bastard' in all its senses; as an equivalent to 'damn' ('I don't give a bugger for that'); and in 'bugger all' as meaning 'nothing' [f. *bugger* 2b a coarse term of abuse or insult OED 1719]

1833 Trial before the Supreme Court 9 and 10 Dec. in *True Patriots All* ed. G. C. Ingleton (1952) 149: There was a general cry among the party coming down to me, of '*shoot the bugger*'.

1944 Lawson Glassop *We Were the Rats* 79: 'Wilson or Macduff. Who cares?' 'I don't give a bugger,' said Eddie.

1952 Jon Cleary *The Sundowners* 153: 'Look at those plains, will you? Miles and miles of bugger all.'

1964 Tom Ronan *Packhorse and Pearling Boat* 35: She had started life at Beagle Bay Mission and on the Bishop's arrival proudly informed him: 'Me properly bloody Catholic bugger, all the same you.'

1973 John O'Grady *Survival in the Doghouse* 63: 'An hour and a half to cook pork chops? They'll be burnt to buggery.'

bugger *v.* 1 Used most often as an equivalent to 'damn'; also (with *up*) 'to make a mess of'; and (with *off*) 'to depart'

1942 C. Hartley Grattan *Introducing Australia* (1944) 171–2: The word bugger is used in numerous forms and contexts. 'Oh, bugger it all.' 'I'll be buggered.' 'Buggered if I will.' 'Bugger him.' 'Oh go to buggery.' 'The silly bugger.' 'I'm all buggered up.' And triumphantly combining all the favorite words, 'bugger the bloody bastard'. English people profess to find Australian men foulmouthed.

1957 D'Arcy Niland *The Shiralee* 14: 'But one time I fell off the train and buggered my insides up.'

2 In the pidgin term 'bagarup'

1975 *Australian* 19 Sep. 1: Prince Charles broke into Pidgin at the end of his speech [in Papua New Guinea] saying 'Af de ren I bagarup mi nau arait' which meant 'Unfortunately rain caused me some inconvenience yesterday, but now everything is all right.'

Bugs Bunny The U.S. war memorial in Canberra [f. resemblance to the rabbit in the cartoon]

1979 *Sun-Herald* 16 Dec. 152: A glance at the American War Memorial, or 'Bugs Bunny' as it is known with no particular affection.

bulk A lot of; on a large scale

1983 Tim & Debbie 'Bali Sketch' in *Brainspace Vol. II* [record]: I learnt bulk about Balinese art through their food.

1984 *Sydney Morning Herald* 19 Jun. 10: Now 34, she says she 'came into bulk parenthood quite late when we moved to Brisbane. You know, the talking to other parents at the barbecues about nappies and kindergartens and all of that.'

1987 Kathy Lette *Girls' Night Out* 15: He mustn't be allowed to think that you don't have bulk other things to do. Or bulk other people to do them with.

bull *n.* 1 A Torres Islander: *obs.*

1934 Vance Palmer *Sea and Spinifex* 29–30: The proffered notes were too much for Charlie, a tough little Torres Islander ... 'Those bulls'll take on anything [McVeagh commented] if they're shown a few quid.'

2 A wharf labourer unfairly favoured for employment: see quots 1961, 1973

1957 Tom Nelson *The Hungry Mile* 80: The employers ... indulging in illegal trafficking of 'bulls' to suit their own ends.

1961 *Sydney Morning Herald* 22 May 2: Under the 'bull' system, wharfies had to front the stevedore, and only the 'bulls' (company men or men who would sling to the foreman) could be sure of catching his eye.

3 Nonsense, pretence, deceit. 'Bull' in a sense close to this is recorded in the OED from 1630, and later in U.S. slang. It would be taken in Australia as an abbreviation of **bullshit** q.v. and **bull artist** and **bull dust** q.v. would have the same implication.

[**1871** W. H. Cooper *Colonial Experience* (MS, Mitchell Library) ii 3: *Joe* Oh talk as much Bullock as you can. *Alfred* Bullock? *Joe* Yes, back yourself to ride anything that was ever foaled, tell any amount of crammers about Buckjumpers.]

1905–12 Joseph Furphy *The Buln-Buln and the Brolga* ed. R. G. Howarth (1948)

[Title of a novella previously called 'The Lyre Bird and the Native Companion']

1917 Les Darcy let. 21 Apr. cit. Harry Gordon *An Eyewitness History of Australia* (1976) 212: This [U.S.A.] is a great country ... But they hand out a tremendous lot of bull – everything they have is a champion of the world or the best in the world.

1951 Dal Stivens *Jimmy Brockett* 171: The old man was always talking about England and calling it the Mother Country and Home, but it sounded all bull to me.

1969 William Dick *Naked Prodigal* 204: As I walked along the street I wondered if she really was in Heaven or whether it was just a lot of bull.

1973 Alexander Buzo *Rooted* 78: 'You might be an arty sort of bloke, but ... you don't bung on the bull like a lot of these blokes you see around the place these days.'

see **confetti**

Bullamakanka An imaginary place which is a byword for remoteness and backwardness, like **Woop Woop** q.v.

1953 T. A. G. Hungerford *Riverslake* 230: 'Hitch out to Bullamakanka and live with the blacks.'

1965 Leslie Haylen *Big Red* 88: People rushing through the countryside by car would grin as they raced through Cooee. Here was the authentic bush town ... Here was Bullamakanka.

1984 *Sydney Morning Herald* 7 May Guide 16: He zooms his voice up and down and round about, as the jocks used to do in Bullamakanka about a century ago.

bull artist see **artist**

bull-bar Protective grid on front of motor-car, truck etc.; or mustering device

1967 John Yeomans *The Scarce Australians* 97: Most beasts had been killed by one blow from the bull bars (the heavy horizontal steel tubing mounted as cattle guards) on the front of a road train.

1971 Colin Simpson *The New Australia* 360: Instead of bulldogging the wild steers from horse-back, Land Rovers and Toyota vehicles are now used to knock them over with what is called a 'bull bar' mounted in front.

bull, couldn't hit a ~ on the backside with a handful of wheat Applied to someone with a bad aim

1954 L. H. Evers *The Pattern of Conquest* 81: 'Ah-h, you couldn't hit a bull in the behind with a bag full of wheat,' said Honest John carelessly.

1970 Richard Beilby *No Medals for Aphrodite* 178: 'Her shoot! She couldn't hit a bull in the arse with a handful of rice!'

1981 *Sun-Herald* 3 May 92: 'When it comes to accuracy, he ... couldn't hit a bull's bum with a handful of wheat.'

Bulldogs, the 1 In Victoria, the Footscray A.F.L. team

1974 *Sunday Telegraph* (Sydney) 11 Aug. 100: Bulldogs chase off the Blues.

2 In N.S.W., the Canterbury-Bankstown Rugby League team (formerly 'The Berries')

1978 *Sunday Telegraph* (Sydney) 19 Mar. 66: On paper, you would say the Bulldogs were in for only another average season.

3 In S.A., the Central District Australian Rules team

1979 *Advertiser* (Adelaide) 14 Apr. 12: Bulldogs select big name.

4 In W.A., the South Fremantle Australian Rules team

1983 *Sunday Independent* (Perth) 14 Aug. 35: There was plenty for ... the South Fremantle supporters to get excited about. The Bulldogs ran away to a comfortable victory.

5 In Queensland, the Western Districts Australian Rules team

1979 *Courier-Mail* (Brisbane) 8 May 22: Power-plus play from Bulldogs.

bull dust 1 Fine sand or dust

1935 H. H. Finlayson *The Red Centre* 126: The loam proved unexpectedly heavy, having a rather spongy texture, like the intumescent clays of the Lake Eyre basin, known locally as 'bull dust'.

1967 John Yeomans *The Scarce Australians* 122: Bulldust is the superfine red-grey dust which develops on the northern roads. Sometimes this lies in drifts, perhaps axle deep.

2 As for **bull, bullshit**

1946 W. E. Harney *North of 23°* 78: 'A chap called Darwin says if yer cut off a man's arm, then his sons and so on for generations, would be born without arms.' 'Bull dust', the Scrub replies.

1953 T. A. G. Hungerford *Riverslake* 121: 'I suppose Bellairs told you that bit of bull-dust about there being spies?'

1971 Frank Hardy *The Outcasts of Foolgarah* 23: No man is so gullible when it comes to a bit of bulldust sprinkled on the old national ethos than the Australian, who really believes the sun shines nowhere else except out of his arse and his beer is really the best.

bull jo see **joe**

bullock To toil as strenuously as a bullock
1875 Rolf Boldrewood *The Squatter's Dream* repr. as *Ups and Downs* (1878) 240: 'Let other fellows, if they're fools enough, do all that bullocking. Wise men buy their work afterwards and cheap enough too.'
1894 Henry Lawson 'The Lost Souls' Hotel' *Prose* i 155: Take a selector who has bullocked all his life to raise crops on dusty, stony patches in the scrubs.
1936 Miles Franklin *All That Swagger* 415: He would now have been in a comfortable school instead of having bullocked himself into an early grave.
1948 H. Drake-Brockman *Sydney or the Bush* 201: Now, what chance was there of giving Dick or Phil or Wally even half the things she'd bullocked for?
1983 *West Australian* (Perth) 7 Oct. 46: Set the reel drag so that a big fish can take line and don't try to bullock it to the shore or boat as though it was a herring or chopper tailor.

bullocky 1 A bullock-driver, teamster
1869 Marcus Clarke 'The Language of Bohemia' repr. in *A Colonial City* ed. L. T. Hergenhan (1972) 162: *bullocky* (a teamster).
1876 Henry Kendall 'Bill the Bullock Driver' *Poetical Works* ed. T. T. Reed (1966) 167: Poor bullocky Bill! In the circles select / Of the scholars he hasn't a place.
1905 Randolph Bedford *The Snare of Strength* 210: The bullocky went round the team and recovered the pole-pin.
1929 K. S. Prichard *Working Bullocks* 11: Red Burke was the youngest bullocky in the Karri to own his team, and one of the best drivers.
1941 Sarah Campion *Mo Burdekin* 143: The bullocky . . . stooped to yell at them as they drew level, cursing in the same breath all his plodding oxen.
2 The language of the bullock-driver
1916 *The Anzac Book* 103: Above it all we were certain we heard fragments of language of the category known in Australia as 'bullocky'.* *Bullocky – stands both for the bullock driver and for his chief gift.

bullocky's breakfast see **bushman's breakfast**

bullocky's joy Treacle
1934 Archer Russell *A Tramp-Royal in Wild Australia* 202; Luncheon and supper are much the same, except that damper and 'bullockys' joy' (treacle) take the place of porridge.
1951 Ernestine Hill *The Territory* 176: 1 case treacle, bullocky's joy.

Bulls The Wide Bay (Q.) Rugby League club
1982 *Sunday Mail* (Brisbane) 21 Mar. 68: The Bulls Cop Blast! Wide Bay rugby league coach Gary Pearson has blasted his players on the eve of the Bulls' opening Winfield State League game against Wynnum-Manly in Maryborough today.

bull, scrub see **scrub**

bullsh, bullshit *n.* As for **bull** 3. Not an Australianism in origin, although very common in the colloquial language; the shortening to 'bullsh' is euphemistic.
1919 W. H. Downing *Digger Dialects* 14: *Bullsh* 1) Insincerity; 2) an incorrect or insincere thing; 3) flattery; 4) praise.
1938 Xavier Herbert *Capricornia* 395: 'This talk of invasion by the Japs is all plain bulsh.'
1959 D'Arcy Niland *The Big Smoke* 159: 'We won't be able to get out for the bullsh in a minute,' jibed the lumberman. 'Look at it – it's up to me knees now.'
1965 Eric Lambert *The Long White Night* 23: 'It's an intangible thing, a sort of veneration for an idea for its own sake. It's hard to put into words. You'd probably call it bullshit.'
1974 John Powers *The Last of the Knucklemen* 96: 'I just want to see if all this "knuckleman" stuff's for real – or bullshit.'

bullshit *v.* To talk 'bull', esp. in seeking to delude or impose
1965 John Beede *They Hosed Them Out* 196: 'Don't bullshit to me – I know how I look.'
1977 Helen Garner *Monkey Grip* 51: 'You're not bullshitting me, are you?'

bull's roar, within a A measure of distance

1973 Patsy Adam-Smith *The Barcoo Salute* 53: The sound of axes rang all the way down through Taroona, past places that hadn't been within a bull's roar of the fire.
1984 Mike Carlton *Sydney Morning Herald* 1 Feb. 10: La Humphrey at the opera is consumed by an onslaught of genteelism, a disease which afflicts so many of the Corporation's servants when they come within a bull's roar of Culture For the Masses.

bum to mum See quots: Victorian sporting
1972 Ian Moffitt *The U-Jack Society* 146: Australian Rules, in Victoria, is, of course, a religion which divides man and wife ('Bum to mum' is the standard order for players forbidden intercourse before the big games).
1973 *Australian* 7 Apr. 17: Like the coach [in A.F.L.] who told his team on Fridays, 'well, it's bum to mum tonight boys', because they might wear themselves out in sexual activity.

bumper *n.* A cigarette butt, esp. in the expression 'not worth a bumper'
1900–10 O'Brien and Stephens: *Bumper* A cigarette or cigar stump or butt.
1916 *The Anzac Book* 47: One mornin' early while we was standin' to arms 'e lights up a bumper.
1947 Margaret Trist *Daddy* 164: 'My old man's not going to be worth a bumper that day.'
1983 Ruth Park *National Times* 22 Apr. 27: An elderly neighbour kept all his butts in a jam jar and when out of tobacco would say complacently, 'Gonna peel me bumpers now.'

bundle, drop one's To give up, lose one's nerve, surrender one's responsibilities
1900–10 O'Brien and Stephens: *Bundle* For a competitor to collapse or 'turn it up' is called dropping his bundle.
1906 Edward Dyson *Fact'ry 'Ands* 241: 'He gives er sad cry, 'n' drops his bundle, 'n' goes pluckin' at his 'air.'
1936 H. Drake-Brockman *Sheba Lane* 279: Kent seemed to have come to the end of his tether. He'd dropped his bundle.
1942 Gavin Casey *It's Harder for Girls* 212: 'He dropped his bundle,' said Tom. 'No doubt about it, Sim was right. If they drop their bundles they're gone a million.'
1972 Thomas Keneally *The Chant of Jimmy Blacksmith* 138: 'Panic?' Mort asked. 'Drop your bundle,' McCreadie explained.

1980 Shirley Hazzard *The Transit of Venus* 40: 'We could all give in,' she said, when told that Miss Garside the librarian had completely dropped her bundle.

bundy 1 The 'clock' by which workers 'clock on' and 'clock off', esp. in the expression 'punch the bundy' [f. trade name]
1936 J. L. Ranken *Murder Pie* 73: 'I remember glancing at the bundy clock as I got in.'
1949 G. Farwell *Traveller's Tracks* 16: There are no bitumen roads back there, hardly an up-to-date picture show, no rush hours or bundies to turn life into a milling ant-heap.
1957 D'Arcy Niland *Call Me When the Cross Turns Over* 161: Thousands of men filing down a track ... to the ship-yards ... Through the gates. Punching the bundy.
1961 Mena Calthorpe *The Dyehouse* 140: 'I want you to make sure every man bundies off.'
2 Bundaberg rum, often in the expression 'bundy and coke'
1984 *National Times* 10 Mar. Colour Mag. 6: The 'spirit of the game' was overproof Bundy rum and all players entered freely into it.

bung-eye Sandy blight or similar infection [cf. *bunged up* OED 1622]
1892 G. L. James *Shall I Try Australia?* 242: One pest of the bush and plains is 'Sandy blight' or inflammation of the eyes ... it is also known as 'bung-eye', because ... in the morning, the lids are tightly closed, and require no small amount of fomentation to get them open.
1946 E. L. Grant Watson *But to What Purpose?* 127: He mentioned a kind of ophthalmia, known locally as 'bung-eye', which was very common both amongst natives and whites.

bung (bong), to go Originally to die, then to break down, go bankrupt, cease to function [Ab. *bong* dead]
[**1847** J. D. Lang *Cooksland* 430: A place called *Umpie Bung*, or the dead houses, where there had once been a Government Settlement, now long abandoned.]
1857 F. Cooper *Wild Adventures in Australia* 58: I asked him what had become of 'Solomons'? 'Boung!' said he, making use of the Cameleroi term for dead.
1875 A. J. Boyd *Old Colonials* (1882) 73:

Sometimes you've got a horse as is good an' don't suit you, an' you sells him, but just afore you hands 'im over and gets the money, he goes bung* on you. *Dead.

1901 Henry Lawson 'Telling Mrs Baker' *Prose* i 416: The world might wobble and all the banks go bung, but the cattle have to go through – that's the law of the stock-routes.

1933 R. B. Plowman *The Man from Oodnadatta* 122: 'I heard that their well has gone bung, and their garden is completely ruined.'

1946 Dal Stivens *The Courtship of Uncle Henry* 109: 'The radio's gone bung again and I'm just fixing it.'

1982 *NT News* (Darwin) 15 Jul. 7: Downturn in the bauxite industry seems to be reflected in the choice of name for South Weipa's main street in N.Q. – Gonbung.

bung it on, to To put on 'side'
1963 Alan Seymour *The One Day of the Year* 48: 'Well, she bungs it on a bit don't she? . . . the young lady's too lah-dee-dah for us.'

1969 William Dick *Naked Prodigal* 187: These flash bastards . . . give you the shits bunging on side like they do.

1973 Alexander Buzo *Rooted* 78: 'When I had my one and only exhibition in an art gallery, there was a whole lot of scientists there, bunging it on.'

bunji See quots [Ab. W.A.]
1980 *Daily News* (Perth) 26 Sep. 11: James said that a 'bunji' man was a white man who patronised hotels like Cleo's in Fremantle, looking for sex with Aboriginal women.

1981 Archie Weller *The Day of the Dog* 64: They've been off with some bunji man grinding it into them for a few dollars.

1985 *National Times* 12 Apr. 20: They were Bunji men . . . Today the term, widely used by the Aboriginal people around Perth, refers to the lonely, alcoholic old white men who wander the parks and back streets seeking 'black velvet' – sexual solace from Aboriginal women.

bunny A 'muggins', dupe, person with no mind of his own; in cricket, a player who is no batsman [f. the timidity and helplessness of the rabbit]
1943 Baker 16: *Bunny* A simpleton or fool, an easy victim for exploitation.

1950 Jon Cleary *Just Let Me Be* 14: 'But you wait and see I'm not gunna be like all them bunnies over there for the rest of my life.'

1965 Wally Grout *My Country's Keeper* 41–2: Once again, at Johannesburg, in the fourth match of the tour, I was one of the 'bunnies'.

bunyip Monster of Aboriginal legend, supposed to haunt water-holes; any freak or impostor [Ab.]
1848 W. Westgarth *Australia Felix* 391: Certain large fossil bones . . . have been referred by the natives . . . to a huge animal of extraordinary appearance, called in some districts the Bunyup . . . It is described as of amphibious character, inhabiting deep rivers, and permanent waterholes, having a round head, an elongated neck, with a body and tail resembling an ox.

1852 G. C. Mundy *Our Antipodes* ii 18–19: Did my reader ever hear of the Bunyip? (fearful name to the Aboriginal native!) a sort of half-horse, half-alligator, haunting the wide rushy swamps and lagoons of the interior . . . a new and strong word was adopted into the Australian vocabulary. Bunyip became, and remains, a Sydney synonym for *imposter, pretender, humbug,* and the like.

1903 Joseph Furphy *Such is Life* (1944) 244: 'He heard "Hen-ree! Hen-ree!" boomin' an' bellerin' back an' forrid across the bend in the dark, an' he thought the boody-man, an' the bunyip, an' the bashee, an' (sheol) knows what all, was after him.'

1956 A. D. Hope *Sydney Morning Herald* 16 Jun. 15: 'The Bunyip Stages a Comeback'. The bunyip of Australian literature is the mythical great Australian novel.

bunyip aristocracy D. H. Deniehy's derisory description of W. C. Wentworth's plan for a colonial peerage in 1853; varied to apply to any similar attempt to imitate British institutions.
1853 *Sydney Morning Herald* 16 Aug. in *Select Documents in Australian History* ed. C. M. H. Clark (1955) 342: [Report of speech by D. H. Deniehy on the proposal to establish a colonial peerage] Here they all knew the common water mole was transformed into the duck-billed platypus, and in some distant emulation of this degeneration, he supposed they were to be favoured with a bunyip aristocracy.

1976 *Australian* 14 Jun. 7: The grafting of knighthoods on . . . the Order of Australia is a laughable concession to bunyip snobbery.

1981 Max Harris *Weekend Australian* 21 Nov. Mag. 7: The bunyip aristocracy [The Old Families of Adelaide] were not as sure of themselves as their feeble imitation of their English betters made them seem.

Burdekin duck See quots 1945, 1951 [f. river and district in Queensland]
1945 Tom Ronan *Strangers on the Ophir* 39: A meat fritter known in the Kimberleys as a 'Burdekin Duck', and on the Burdekin as a 'Kimberley Oyster'.
1951 Ernestine Hill *The Territory* 426: 'Burdekin duck', meat fritters.

burglar, gin see **gin burglar**

Burke and Wills, cover more ground than See quot. 1984 [f. the two explorers who crossed the continent from south to north and perished on the return journey]
1984 *Sunday Independent* (Perth) 18 Nov. 43: 'He's covered more ground than Burke and Wills' is the stock condemnation of a racehorse wandering all over the track.
1985 *Sydney Morning Herald* 4 Feb. Guide 1: Bert Bryant became the king of the extravagant image. Horses would . . . 'cover more ground than Burke and Wills'.

burley see **berley**

burl, give it a To make a trial of, risk an attempt [f. *birl* a rapid twist or turn EDD 1892]
1924 *Truth* 27 Apr. 6: *Burl* To try anything.
1935 Kylie Tennant *Tiburon* 72: 'Come on,' Kahn murmured to Johnny as the crowd increased, 'give it a burl!'
1952 T. A. G. Hungerford *The Ridge and the River* 3: He pointed upwards to the threshing palm-fronds. 'Give it a burl?'
1964 George Johnston *My Brother Jack* 34: 'Even if you know you can't bloody win you still got to have a go. You'll always be pissin' into the wind, but that don't mean it isn't worth givin' it a burl.'

burn *v. & n.* To drive fast, esp. in an exhibitionist and competitive fashion [f. 'burning' tyres]
1963 Gunther Bahnemann *Hoodlum* 155: He parked his bike at the kerb and waited. Soon the others burned around the corner as if hunted by the devil in person.
1970 Jack Hibberd *White with Wire Wheels* in Penguin *Plays* 164: 'He . . . wants to know how the Valiant performs. I've promised to take him for a burn when I've driven it in.'

burn, Chinese see **Chinese**

burnt stick, better than a poke in the eye with a see **poke**

burst (bust) A spree, prolonged drinking bout, esp. in the phrase 'on the burst' [cf. *burst* an outburst of drinking EDD 1861; *bust* U.S. 1843 Mathews]
1852 *Select Committee on the Management of the Goldfields* 97: One-third of the miners are incorrigible drunkards . . . they frequently fall into good claims, and make large hauls in the course of the week, they then go 'upon the burst' as they call it, and drink until all their earnings are 'knocked down', and then go to work again.
1911 E. M. Clowes *On the Wallaby through Victoria* 106: Men still go 'on the bust', cheques are planked down, and 'shouting' – the Australian equivalent for 'treating' – indulged in till all the money is finished.
1942 Gavin Casey *It's Harder for Girls* 98: 'He was a real damn nuisance, allus in arguments an' stayin' on th' burst for as much as a fortnight at a time.'
2 A sudden spurt by a football player
1976 David Ireland *The Glass Canoe* 145: Danny's on the burst and swerves just before taking a pass from the half.

Bus, the Old see **Old**

bush *n.* The 'woods' or 'forest'; the unsettled or sparsely settled areas generally; the country as distinct from the towns [f. Dutch *bosch*]
1826 James Atkinson *An Account of the State of Agriculture and Grazing in New South Wales* 64: Very few of the stock owners have sufficient land to support the whole of their stock, and are therefore obliged to have recourse to the unoccupied tracts in the interior . . . they go into the interior, or *bush*, as it is termed, beyond the occupied parts of the country, usually procuring the assistance of some of the black Natives, as their guides.
1833 W. H. Breton *Excursions in New South Wales* 46: The only convenient way of travelling in the 'bush'* is on horseback. *Bush is the term commonly used for the

country *per se*: 'he resides in the Bush', implies that a person does not reside in, or very near, a town. It also signifies a forest.

1853 S. Mossman and T. Banister *Australia, Visited and Revisited* 62: The term 'bush', as it is used in Australia, is indiscriminately applied to all descriptions of uncleared land, or to any spot away from a settlement, as a person in England would speak of the country when they are out of town.

1892 Henry Lawson 'The Bush Undertaker' *Prose* i 57: And the sun sank again on the grand Australian bush – the nurse and tutor of eccentric minds, the home of the weird, and of much that is different from things in other lands.

1950 Brian James *The Advancement of Spencer Button* 134: 'What's the good of your degree if they are going to send you to the bush?'

bush *v.* In the expression 'to bush it', to camp out in the bush; put up with the hardships of bush life

1827 W. J. Dumaresq in *Fourteen Journeys* ed. G. Mackaness (1950–1) 99: Not being provided for *bushing it*, in these early forests, we made up our minds to return. [OED Suppl.]

1838 T. Horton James *Six Months in South Australia* 157: A young man, not afraid of bushing it.

1853 S. Mossman and T. Banister *Australia Visited and Revisited* 132: It was a matter of choice for us to 'bush it' and if we were travelling the same journey again, and well provided, we should often prefer it to putting up at some inns.

bush-bashing Driving through the bush (esp. with four-wheel drive vehicles, trail bikes) where there are no roads

1967 Len Beadell *Blast the Bush* ix: Short cuts through mulga scrub (known as 'bush-bashing') can be an interesting experience but is attended with real dangers.

1978 *Sydney Morning Herald* 8 Sep. 22: The days of laissez-faire bush-bashing are drawing to a close. There's a new perception of what must be done to preserve our natural heritage.

1982 *Age* (Melbourne) 18 May 26: Once you have bashed a bit of bush there is not a lot to do in Alice.

bush carpenter A rough and ready carpenter

1859 C. Calvert *Cowanda* 5: Every room

boasted some three or four doors, beneath which – for bush-carpenters never manage to make things fit – the winter's winds whistled in chorus.

1882 Rolf Boldrewood *Robbery Under Arms* (World's Classics 1949) 10: It was a snug hut enough, for father was a good bush carpenter, and didn't turn his back to anyone for splitting and fencing, hut-building and shingle-splitting, he had had a year or two at sawing, too.

1942 John Shaw Neilson *Autobiography* (1978) 108: Frank had stayed behind ... doing some additions to my father's place. He is a pretty good bush carpenter.

bush dunny See **dunny, country dunny**

1983 Mike Carlton *Sun-Herald* 18 Sep. 143: Changi makes Sydney airport look like a bush dunny.

bushed Lost in the bush; having lost one's bearings generally

1844 *Georgiana's Journal* ed. Hugh McCrae (1966) 124: Even with the aid of his compass, Captain Reid thinks we ran the risk of being bushed for the night.

1870 Marcus Clarke *His Natural Life* ed. S. Murray-Smith (1970) 620: It seemed that the streets were endless, and that once entangled in that maze, he would be 'bushed' indeed.

1887 *All the Year Round* 30 Jul. 68: 'To be bushed', of course, simply meant at first to be lost in the bush, but now it is applied to a person in any mental or physical difficulty or muddle.

1907 Barbara Baynton *Human Toll* 42: Boshy paused, but his hearers were again bushed as to his drift.

1965 Patrick White *Four Plays* 344: 'We reckoned on following the track down Hermit Valley ... but got a bit bushed.'

1980 Murray Bail *Homesickness* 228: 'I got bloody bushed in the subway on the way back.'

bushfire blonde See quot. 1943: World War II slang

1943 Baker 17: *Bushfire blonde* A red-haired girl.

1956 Ruth Park and D'Arcy Niland *The Drums Go Bang!* 121: The bushfire blonde is a mother now, / She has a little bub.

1984 Jack Hibberd *Squibs* 130: 'I love bushfire blondes.'

bushfire, get on like a Applied to a rapidly developing friendship, or to any project that proceeds apace [variant of *like wildfire*]
1942 Sarah Campion *Bonanza* 184: They get on like the proverbial bushfire.

bush, to go Used of an Aboriginal disappearing from his habitat, and so jocularly of anyone 'making himself scarce', with variants like 'head for the scrub', 'take to the mallee', 'take to the tall timber' qq.v.
1908 Mrs Aeneas Gunn *We of the Never-Never* 170: Maudie, discovering that the house was infested with debbil-debbils, had resigned and 'gone bush'.
1926 K. S. Prichard *Working Bullocks* 110: 'Duck Hayes told us you had gone bush. And that's the last we heard about you till a couple of months ago.'
1961 Patrick White *Riders in the Chariot* 383: Alf Dubbo now went bush, figuratively at least, as far as other human beings were concerned.
1984 *Sydney Morning Herald* 24 Mar. 6: A farmer 'went bush' for nine days after shooting a neighbour in a dispute over water supplies and boundary gates, the Central Criminal Court was told yesterday ... After the shooting Elford ran off and lived for nine days in the bush, surviving on birds' eggs and sour lemons.

bush lawyer See quot. 1926
1848 Let. cit. in W. S. Parkes *Village on the Wollombi* (?1968) 17: He has squandered by law-suits and intemperance a considerable property ... and for some years past has solely subsisted ... acting the part of what is termed a Bush Lawyer ... writing of petitions, and whatever he can procure.
1868 C. Wade Brown *Overlanding in Australia* 68: He summoned us because he was put up to it by the old hand, who is a bit of a bush lawyer.
1926 James Vance Marshall *Timely Tips for New Australians: Bushlawyer* A man who gratuitously voices legal opinions although possessing no qualifications for doing so.
1967 Frank Hardy *Billy Borker Yarns Again* 135: In the old days in the bush, there were no registered lawyers, so some half-shrewd mug, usually a barber, would set himself up to advise all and sundry. So now anyone who throws around a lot of free advice is called a bush lawyer.

bush liar A teller of tall stories

1893 Henry Lawson 'Stragglers' *Prose* i 93: Every true Australian bushman must try his best to tell a bigger outback lie than the last bush-liar.
1957 R. S. Porteous *Brigalow* 83: As a yarn spinner and bush liar Wagga had no equal.

bushman, Piccadilly see **Piccadilly**

Bushman's Bible The *Bulletin* (pre-World War I)
1888 *Bulletin* 15 Dec. 5: 'The Bulletin is the Bushman's Bible.'
1903 P. F. Rowland *The New Nation* 204: A back-blocks' shearer once told him that 'if he only had 6d left, he would buy the *Bulletin* with it.' Whatever may be thought of the anti-religious and separatist principles of this 'Bushman's Bible', it must be conceded to have done a very real service to Australia.
1958 Nancy Cato *All the Rivers Run* 67: He took the *Bulletin*, the bushman's Bible, and read all the hints for the man on the land.

bushman's breakfast Variously described as 'a drink of water and a good look around', 'a hitch in the belt and a good look around', 'a shave and a shit and a good look around': echoed in the title of the Phillip Theatre review of the 1960s, 'A cup of tea, a Bex and a good lie down'.
1945 Baker 81: *bullocky's breakfast* A hitch in the belt and an attention to natural requirements.
1981 *Sydney Morning Herald* 18 Nov. 8: We must ... applaud TCN 9's attempt to break new ground with the Sunday morning current affairs, and I was quite prepared to have a drink of water, a good look around, and settle to a two-hour bash.

bushman's cement See quot.
1977 Athol Thomas *Bulls and Boabs* 112: The stones were bonded together with a mortar made from antbed mixed with water – the bushman's cement.

bushman's clock The kookaburra, whose laugh is heard at dawn and sunset
1846 C. P. Hodgson *Reminiscences of Australia* 165: Laughing Jackass ... is well and truly stiled the Bushman's clock.
1853 John Sherer *The Gold Finder of Australia* 102: With the first peep of dawn we were roused by the laugh of the jackass-bird – an extraordinary creature, which passes by

the name of the Bushman's Clock, and which is rarely heard to give utterance to its merry note at any other hour of the day.
see **settler's clock**

bush medicine Reliance on the natural remedies provided by the bush
1982 *Australian* 6 Feb. 17: Interest in bush medicine has been revived by the publication by the Department of Health in Darwin of a dossier of indigenous plants in the Top End which have long been used by Aborigines to cure their ailments.

bush oysters See quot. 1971
1971 *Bulletin* 27 Nov. 48: Eating bull's testicles, or 'bush oysters' as they're known.

bush pickles See quot. 1962
1962 J. Marshall and R. Drysdale *Journey Among Men* 170: Bush pickles . . . are made by stirring a bottle of Worcester sauce into a large tin of plum jam.

bushranger 1 A man with some official task or responsibility in the bush (the English 'ranger')
[**1798** Matthew Flinders *Voyage to Terra Australis* (1814) cxxxv: This little bear-like quadruped is known in New South Wales, and called by the natives, *womat, wombat,* or *wombach,* according to the different dialects, or perhaps to the different rendering of the wood rangers who brought the information.]
1805 G. Caley to Sir Joseph Banks *Banks Papers* vol. 20 cit. Ramson 142: If the Bush rangers will always bring plants from the remote parts of their tours, I can form a good idea of what distance they have been.
2 A law-abiding citizen skilled in bush-craft, a bushman
1805 Gov. King *HRNSW* v 725: The whole of their story [of exploration] is so contradictory that I should not have inserted these particulars but to prove what little confidence can be put in this class of what is locally termed bushrangers.
1825 *Australian* 17 Feb. 1: We regret much that ever Mr Hume allowed such a person as Mr Hovell, who knows so little of the interior of the country, and possessed of such poor abilities as a bushranger, to be of his party.
1827 P. Cunningham *Two Years in New South Wales* ii 157: If pushing into a country at a distance from settlers, a pack-horse with

provisions ought to accompany you. A steady white man who is a good bush-ranger, and a black native, complete your train.
3 A runaway convict trying to survive in the bush, not always by preying on others.
1801 James Elder MS Journal cit. *Australian Literary Studies* Jun. 1966, 214: One of these Bushrangers [concerned in stealing a boat] was Williams.
1819 Let. in *True Patriots All* ed. G. C. Ingleton (1952) 82: Men at this settlement reduced to the last stages of despair, frequently run into the woods and live upon what nature in her uncultivated state affords the wild productions of the forest . . . A man of the name of Creig, actually asserts, that . . . he beheld, leaning against a tree, a skeleton of a man, with a musket by his side, also against the tree, and which he supposes to be a *bushranger,* like himself. Many are compelled from hunger to give themselves up, and very frequently so starved that they can scarce crawl upon their hands and knees.
1838 John Curtis *The Shipwreck of the Stirling Castle* 81: During his journey he fell in with a 'bush ranger' (that is a runaway convict) who had escaped from the penal settlement at Moreton Bay several years before, and had now united himself with a tribe of natives.
4 One who evades the law by keeping to the bush, and maintains himself by robbery (whether an escaped convict or not), usually a member of a gang: the commonest sense
1806 *Sydney Gazette* 16 Nov. 1: BUSH-RANGERS. As the daring spirits of these desperate offenders occupies much serious attention at the present moment, we enter into the following particulars . . . Five sheep have disappeared in the course of one night, notwithstanding every vigilant exertion of the stock keepers and guards . . . Night and day they have been harassed by their daring visitors, their huts plundered as well as their flocks, & their provisions carried off.
1816 *Hobart Town Gazette* 23 Nov. 1: Soon after, the party were alarmed by the appearance of the Bush rangers, headed by *Michael Howe,* & his gang of 8 runaways.
1867 J. R. Houlding *Australian Capers* 380: Bushrangers who stopped them, then rifled the coach and passengers' pockets, and read all the letters in the mail bags that were interesting to them.
1880 J. C. Crawford *Travels in New Zealand and Australia* 6: About this time I had occasion to go to Yass, and on my return was, as they say, 'stuck up' by two bush-rangers.

5 A business enterprise exploiting the public

1951 Dymphna Cusack *Say No to Death* 52: 'Bushrangers, aren't they? Ned Kelly was a gentleman compared with most of the landlords around here.'

1954 *Coast to Coast 1953–54* 160: When she overheard Sam [a junk dealer] described as a bushranger she spun around aggressively ready to do battle for her husband's honour.

bushranging

1822 James Dixon *Narrative of a Voyage to New South Wales* 45: Men rendered desperate retreat to the woods; or as it is termed, go a bushranging, and rob to supply their wants, and often commit worse crimes.

1827 P. Cunningham *Two Years in New South Wales* i 194–5: Some [convicts] disgusted with restraint and steady labour, will occasionally take to the woods, and subsist by plundering the settlers around, with whose convict-servants they are frequently leagued. This method of robbery is denominated 'bush-ranging'; it has been a severe scourge in Van Diemen's Land.

1939 Kylie Tennant *Foveaux* 425: Bud Pellager . . . had taken to a mild and lucrative form of bushranging as owner of a garage on the Main Western Highway.

bush shower A shower, originally improvised e.g. from a kerosene tin hung in a tree, later manufactured on similar principles

[**1937** Ernestine Hill *The Great Australian Loneliness* 97: 'You'll have to get up at piccaninny daylight for your bath,' I had been told further south. 'It's a shower in a tree.' But . . . the shower had been fenced in with roofless tin walls, and only a white cockatoo in the tree above bent an inquiring eye.]

1984 *Sunday Independent* (Perth) 22 Apr. 6: There'll be a billy tea and pork and beans and a bushman's shower slung from a tree.

bush, Sydney or the   see **Sydney**

bush, take the   1   To abscond (of convicts); jocularly 'to decamp'

1827 P. Cunningham *Two Years in New South Wales* ii 190–1: Indeed without the aid of that magic care-killer, the pipe, I believe the greater portion of our 'pressed men' would 'take the bush' in a week after their arrival.

1897 Thomas Archer *Recollections of a Rambling Life* 100: I jumped out of one of

the back windows and 'took the bush', hiding behind a big gum tree.

1907 Charles MacAlister *Old Pioneering Days in the Sunny South* 118: A Strathaird convict – one Joe Green – had 'taken to the bush', as it was called, and it was reported that he was prowling in the vicinity of the 'Irishmen's Station'.

2   To become a bushranger

1844 Louisa Meredith *Notes and Sketches of New South Wales* 59: They do frequently evade the vigilance of their guards, and, 'taking the bush', that is, running away into the forests, they often become formidable in their attacks on travellers in the lonely roads up the country.

1859 John Lang *Botany Bay* 156: The career of these men, who took to the bush . . . was a very remarkable one. There was not a road in the colony . . . upon which they had not stopped and robbed travellers.

1875 Rolf Boldrewood *The Squatter's Dream* repr. as *Ups and Downs* (1878) 165: 'Well, they say taking to the bush is a short life and a merry one,' grumbled out Redcap.

bush telegraph   1   An informant alerting bushrangers to the movements of the police

1878 *Australian* i 507: The police are baffled by the false reports of the confederates and the number and activity of the bush telegraphs. [Morris]

1882 A. J. Boyd *Old Colonials* 175: In Queensland we have no bushrangers. There are no convict shepherds – no bush telegraphs – none of the thousand and one conveniences for securing the safety of these gentry.

1899 G. E. Boxall *The Story of the Australian Bushrangers* 238: The Press . . . continued to urge the necessity for suppressing the 'bush telegraphs' and other sympathisers of the bushrangers.

2   The passing of information (not illicit) by unofficial channels e.g. word of mouth; any message so received

1895 Henry Lawson 'Black Joe' *Prose* i 255: The nearest squatter's wife . . . arranged (by bush telegraph) to drive over next morning with her sister-in-law and two other white women in the vicinity, to see Mary decently buried.

1961 Patrick White *Riders in the Chariot* 381: She had acquired a numerous clientele, through her dealings in bottles, as well as by bush telegraph.

bush tucker Food obtained from the bush environment, as distinct from rations or European food

[**1827** P. Cunningham *Two Years in New South Wales* ii 158: Your muskets will furnish you with birds of various kinds; – and with a brace of good grayhounds you will never lack kangaroos and emus; so that your *bush*-fare is a true sportsman's feast.]

1935 Mary and Elizabeth Durack *All-About* 90: They come up to the homestead for their stock of supplies – beef, tea, sugar and flour. They can kill what 'bush tucker' they come upon, but this is a holiday and they need not go out of their way to hunt.

1962 Jock Marshall and Russell Drysdale *Journey Among Men* 169: The great majority have come to regard the eating of 'roo or other bush tucker as putting oneself on the subsistence level of tribal aborigines.

1978 H. C. Coombs *Kulinma* 228: Some communities found that their only cash income was that derived from old-age pensions and child endowment. Where the environment continued to provide generous supplies of 'bush tucker' this was sometimes enough to provide bare subsistence.

bush week 1 In the expression 'What do you think this is, bush week?' as a protest or complaint: sometimes drawing the juvenile retort, 'Yes, and you're the sap'.

1945 Baker 76: The time honoured chant of derision, *What's this, bush week?*

1949 Lawson Glassop *Lucky Palmer* 37: 'I get smart alecks like you trying to put one over on me every minute of the day. What do you think this is? Bush Week?'

1958 Tom Ronan *The Pearling Master* 309: 'What's the strong of pulling up in the middle of a block? What do you think this is? Bush week?'

1966 H. F. Brinsmead *Beat of the City* 26: 'You can just nail it back on again proper. What do you think this is, bush week?'

2 Name given to organized celebrations, esp. end-of-term student festivities at the Australian National University, Canberra.

1980 *Mercury* (Hobart) 4 Jan. 6: The Deddington Carnival to be held this weekend will turn into Bush Week if the organisers have their way. Part of the Tasmanian Fiesta celebrations, the carnival on Saturday may become a full week of bush activities. A major part of the carnival is the chopping events.

1981 *Canberra Times* 14 Aug. 8: Mr Dobson recalled that in past Bush Weeks a

magistrate had been worth 100 points in the scavenger hunt.

bushwhacker A backwoodsman; someone lacking in social graces or in acumen

1900 Henry Lawson 'Joe Wilson's Courtship' *Prose* i 544: He said I'd spoilt the thing altogether. He said that she'd got an idea that I was shy and poetic, and I'd only shown myself the usually sort of Bush-whacker.

1938 Xavier Herbert *Capricornia* 384: 'You've been readin' newspapers, which from start to finish are only fit for the purpose we bushwhackers use 'em for when we've read 'em.'

1959 Gerard Hamilton *Summer Glare* 68: She was only sixteen, a real bushwhacker, short, buxom and stupid, with little or no education.

1971 Rena Briand *White Man in a Hole* 17: 'It's the smallest dugout in Coober,' he said, 'but good enough for an old bush-whacker like me.'

bushwhacking

1935 H. H. Finlayson *The Red Centre* 24: To Giles the Englishman – after weeks of bush-whacking in the mulga farther north – these views appealed with special force.

bush work See quot. 1882

1882 Rolf Boldrewood *Robbery Under Arms* (World's Classics 1949) 102: Fencing, dam-making, horse-breaking, stock-riding, from making hay to building a shed, all bushwork came easy enough to us.

1936 A. B. Paterson 'The Shearer's Colt' in *Song of the Pen* (1983) 678: 'I'm a bushman, I can do any sort of bush work.'

1940 Ion L. Idriess *Lightning Ridge* 73: 'Used to bush work?' 'Yes. Fencing, breaking-in, ringbarking, mustering, burr-cutting, crutching.'

bush worker

1911 E. S. Sorenson *Life in the Australian Backblocks* 249: There are plenty of good classers among bush workers, who . . . take any other work offering between shearing, including boundary-riding, tank-sinking, and fencing.

1940 Ion L. Idriess *Lightning Ridge* 62: Bush workers often make a country town their base. They 'get known'.

bushy, bushie (bush-head) An uncomplicated bush-dweller, as distinct from a townsman

1887 *Tibb's Popular Song Book* 1: 'Bushy in Town'. Have you noticed in the city, / With the Sydney going push, / How they often stare and giggle, / At us chaps from down the Bush?

1900 Henry Lawson 'A Gentleman Sharper and Steelman Sharper' *Prose* i 226: 'We're two hardworking, innocent bushies, down for an innocent spree.'

1949 John Morrison *The Creeping City* 241: 'I'm only a bush-head. I'm not supposed to have the intelligence to put two and two together.'

1973 Max Harris *The Angry Eye* 70: Warm-hearted, open-minded bushies are thin on the ground.

buster see **southerly buster**
1911 Louis Stone *Jonah* 80: The air was still hot and breathless, but little gusts of wind began to rise, the first signs of a coming 'buster'.

busy as a one-armed bill-poster (milker) see **one-armed**

but Used with the force of 'however' or 'though' at the end of a sentence
1938 Eric Lowe *Salute to Freedom* 157: She had so few words to express her feelings. 'I love you – won't you kiss me, but!'

1957 Gerard Hamilton *Summer Glare* 112: 'Gee, they're lucky but, ain't they?'

1962 Stuart Gore *Down the Golden Mile* 218: 'I always seem to miss th' bastards . . . I've given a couple of 'em a bloody good fright but.'

1977 Mary Gage *The New Life* 25: 'Two nuns took us. I'm not a Catholic or anything like that but.'

butcher A measure of beer [see quot. 1898]
1898 Morris: *Butcher* n. South Australian slang for a long drink of beer, so-called (it is said) because the men of a certain butchery in Adelaide used this refreshment regularly.

1945 Baker 168: *Butcher* is Adelaide slang; in the early days it was used for a glass containing about two-thirds of a pint. In modern times the size has dropped to about half a pint.

1958 A. W. Upfield *The Bachelors of Broken Hill* 130: He ought to be in this pleasant saloon bar reading a paper and enjoying the best cigarettes with long 'butchers' of beer.

1971 Rena Briand *White Man in a Hole* 108: Johnny grinned and ordered three butchers.

1979 *Advertiser* (Adelaide) 6 Apr. 3: The Acting Prices Commissioner, Mr D. G. Selth, said yesterday the price of 170-millilitre (butcher) and 425-millilitre (pint) glasses and 370-millilitre Echo bottles would increase by 1c.

butcher's, butcher's hook Crook, in the senses 'angry' (go crook) or 'ill, out of sorts' [rhyming slang]
1918 *Kia Ora Coo-ee* 15 Aug. 5: A certain New Zealand Regiment, camped on the Jordan flats, recently came under the eagle eye of brother 'Jacko', who immediately went 'butcher's hook' or 'ram's horn'.

1941 Baker 16: *Butcher's, to be* To be angry, annoyed (*about* something). Often 'go butcher's at' (i.e. 'go butcher's hook' or 'crook').

1951 Dal Stivens *Jimmy Brockett* 126: As soon as Sadie came in I went butcher's hook. 'What's this bloody nonsense about a studio, Sadie?' I said.

1980 *Sun-Herald* 2 Nov. 92: Those feeling a bit butcher's are advised to avoid this black comedy.

buttinski An inquisitive or interfering person: *obs.* [U.S. 1903 Mathews]
1924 *Truth* 27 Apr. 6: *Buttinski* An intruding person.

1947 H. Drake-Brockman *The Fatal Days* 120: 'What you wanter speak t' young Ed for? You're a butinski.'

1966 Baker 222: *buttinski* A term used among telephone mechanics for the hand telephone used for cutting in on private phone calls.

buy into, to To involve oneself, esp. in trouble or conflict
1951 Ernestine Hill *The Territory* 438: 'Can't you buy in on the conversation over there, Jack?'

1956 *Australian Signpost* ed. T. A. G. Hungerford 185: 'I don't think it woulda come to much if the mug Pongo hadn't bought in.' 'Private Smith,' I told the major, 'thinks the situation was aggravated by the interference of an English soldier.'

1977 Kenneth Cook *The Man Underground* 122: 'As soon as we open the campaign we have Charlie on the air every day, buying in on everything that's going on.'

buzznacking Moving about, esp. in an officious way [? f. *busk*, to cruise about, tack about OED 1665: nautical and dial.]
1865 Henry Kingsley *The Hillyars and the Burtons* 175: 'And I'll have it done, too, and not be kep' busnacking here in the rain.'
1903 Joseph Furphy *Such is Life* (1944) 353: 'Magomery, he's buzznackin' roun' the run as usual.'
1907 Barbara Baynton *Human Toll* 152: 'You a-bein' sich a sheep-dog a-busnackin', an' a-blatherin', an' a-barkin' roun' urdles day an' night.'

B Y O (G) Bring your own (grog): 1 Legend on informal invitations to a party, notice in restaurants without a liquor licence
1975 *National Times* 23 Jun. 5: B.Y.O. diplomat. The Australian Government last week paid for itself to be a 'guest' at a cocktail party given by the Japan-Australia Society . . . in Tokyo.
1982 *Townsville Daily Bulletin* 26 Mar. 4:

The walk will begin at 10.30 a.m. from the Ranger's house. A midday BYO barbecue will follow.
2   Container for carrying liquor
1980 *Sun-Herald* 24 Feb. 29: The insulated B.Y.O. holds two bottles or four large drink cans. Looks smart and has a removable wine chiller, too. $12.99.
3   Type of restaurant
1981 *Sun-Herald* 24 May 132: Vive le BYO – it's a great way to dine.
4   Applied to things other than liquor
1980 *Australian* 16 Aug. 13: It is the problem of BYO toilet paper, to be brought in by some members to beat a ban imposed on the [S.A.] Parliament by the Australian Government Workers' Association.
1982 *Australian* 8 May 19: The coroner . . . censured the police for arming themselves with home-made or, as one lawyer sardonically described them, BYO weapons . . . It was commonplace for weapons, such as cut-down shovel handles to be available for use by police.

C

cab, first ~ off the rank   The first to take advantage of an opportunity
1977 *Australian* 19 Jul. 10: It is unlikely the Ranger partners will agree to new terms without concessions, such as being first cab off the rank if, as expected, the Government agrees to limited mining.
1982 *Sun-Herald* 15 Aug. 122: First cab off the rank this week was a luncheon fashion parade in Sydney Uni's Great Hall.

Cabbage Garden (Patch)   The colony or state of Victoria: *jocular* [f. size and crops]
1889 J. H. Zillman *Australian Life* 30: 'The cabbage garden', old cynical Sir John Robertson, of New South Wales, once called Victoria. [Morris]
1903 Joseph Furphy *Such is Life* (1944) 43: 'You are a native of the colonies, I presume?' 'Yes, I come from the Cabbage Garden.'
1934 Thomas Wood *Cobbers* 144: People in other States call Victoria, rudely, the Cabbage Patch, and make a show of looking for it

on the map with a magnifying glass. Victorians smile a stiff smile.
1970 *Australian* 31 Oct. 3: 'Cabbage patch history' was the way a leading historian yesterday described the Victorian Government's bicentenary awards – now the centre of a growing literary row.

cabbage-tree mob   Precursors of the **larrikin** q.v. [f. *cabbage-tree hat*]
1852 G. C. Mundy *Our Antipodes* i 53–4: There are to be found round the doors of the Sydney theatre a sort of 'loafers', known as the Cabbage tree mob . . . These are an unruly set of young fellows, native born generally . . . Dressed in a suit of fustian or colonial tweed, and the emblem of their order, the low-crowned cabbage-palm hat, the main object of their enmity seems to be the ordinary black headpiece worn by respectable persons, which is ruthlessly knocked over the eyes of the wearer as he passes or enters the theatre.
1894 James T. Ryan *Reminiscences* 223: Ned Sadler, bootmaker, of Sydney, was a

wonder; he was a great politician, and belonged to the 'Cabbage Tree Mob', as they were then called.

1907 Charles MacAlister *Old Pioneering Days* 178: He earned the enmity of the 'Cabbage-tree Hat' mob on account of the part he took in securing the conviction of the Myall Creek (Aborigines) massacre in 1838.

cacker An undersized mudcrab (W.A.): phonetically the same as *kaka*, a young girl

1983 *Sunday Independent* (Perth) 21 Aug. 47: Cacker-catchers . . . are generally recognisable by the size of their buckets, and their habit of indiscriminately slaughtering as many undersized fish and crustaceans as they can.

cactus, back to the To return to one's familiar haunts, usually away from the city: catch-phrase of the comedian 'Mo' (Roy Rene) in the McCackie Mansions series of the 1940s

1945 *Coast to Coast 1944* 174: He got in the car and started the engine. 'Well, it's back to the cactus,' he said.

1980 *Sydney Morning Herald* 31 Dec. 7: We are today back to the cactus as our Antipodean friends would say.

Cairns, the battle of The forcible ejection of unemployed campers from the Parramatta Park showground, Cairns, on 17 July 1932

calabash A promissory note issued by bush-storekeepers and others: see quots. The name suggests that the calabash had the same brittleness as the **shin plaster** q.v., as though inscribed on the shell of a gourd.

1917 R. D. Barton *Reminiscences of an Australian Pioneer* 159: Everyone was paid by orders, 'calibashes' we used to call them, drawn on himself by the person paying.

1938 *Smith's Weekly* 12 Nov. 6: Mention of 'shin-plasters' recently in 'Smith's Weekly' suggests a mention of 'Calabash'. This was a form of currency in the early days, and was originally an order for a small amount, drawn upon some agent of the drawer and payable at various dates after presentation. Finally a calabash became an IOU for sums under one pound.

call To broadcast a race description

1949 Lawson Glassop *Lucky Palmer* 247: 'There's no better race caller in Australia than "Lucky Palmer". When he was only

fourteen he used to call the races from the verandah of a house.'

1979 *Sun-Herald* 24 Jun. 70: Sport? Cyril [Angles] called it all – the horses, dogs, trotters, boxing, wrestling, foot running, cycle racing. You name it and somewhere along the way Angles 'called' it.

Callan Park A psychiatric hospital in Sydney; used figuratively to represent any such institution

1904 Henry Fletcher *Dads Wayback: His Work* 35: 'No one out o' Callan Park, or who ought ter be there, ever does take it that way.'

1959 Dorothy Hewett *Bobbin Up* 163: 'Life's hard enough for everyone without puttin' up with a mad kid inter the bargain . . . You feel as if you're orf to Callan Park yourself.'

1982 *Sydney Morning Herald* 10 Apr. 23: 'Why I'm not in Callan Park I'll never know.'

camp 1 To rest, lie down

1847 Alexander Harris *Settlers and Convicts* ed. C. M. H. Clark (1954) 130: A flock of sheep 'camping', as the shepherds call it, under the shade of a tree from the noontide heat.

1980 *Australian* 23 Aug. Mag. 1: Close to the road a small herd of prize-winning shorthorns are 'camping' in the early morning sun under a tree.

have a camp

1899 Steel Rudd *On Our Selection* 127: Sometimes Dan used to forget to talk at all – he would be asleep – and Dad would wonder if he was unwell. Once he advised him to go up to the house and have a *good* camp.

1961 Noni Braham *The Interloper* 85: He took out the tarpaulin. 'You have a camp while I boil the billy.' Margaret stretched out gratefully.

1979 Bill Scott *Tough in the Old Days* 39: He stretched luxuriously on the grass as the sun warmed his bones. 'Think I'll have a camp,' he said.

2 To die

1898 Henry Lawson 'Dust Thou Art' *Prose* i 325: 'I can imagine . . . the chaps rubbing their hats off, and standing round looking as if it was their funeral instead of mine, and one of 'em saying, maybe, "Ah well, poor Jack, he's camped down at last!"'

Camp, (the) The original settlement at Sydney Cove, or Hobart: *obs.*

1790 Daniel Southwell let. 20 Aug. *HRNSW* ii 724: He [Governor Phillip] treats us with more affability, and is all at once so polite as to beg of my only companion, Mr Harris, and self, whenever we come to camp, to let him have our co[mpany].

1827 P. Cunningham *Two Years in New South Wales* ii 70: It is the old resident – he who still calls Sydney with its population of twelve thousand bustling inhabitants *the camp* – that can appreciate these things: he who still recollects the few earth-huts and solitary tents scattered through the forest brush surrounding Sydney Cove (known properly then indeed by the name of 'The Camp').

1843 Charles Rowcroft *Tales of the Colonies* i 27: I met nothing between *camp*, as Hobart Town was then called, and New Town.

Campbell, Lady An alternative name for **Paterson's Curse**, q.v.

1983 *Australian* 25 Jun. 10: A certain Lady Campbell, during the construction of the Great Southern Railway through Western Australia in 1889 also helped by introducing it [*Echium plantagineum*] as a garden flower at her home not far from Broomehill. It then followed the construction of the line.

canary 1 A convict; his yellow clothing [f. *canary bird* a jailbird, or person kept in a cage OED 1673]

1827 P. Cunningham *Two Years in New South Wales* 88 117: Convicts of but recent migration are facetiously known by the name of *canaries*, by reason of the yellow plumage in which they are fledged at the period of landing.

1870 Marcus Clarke *His Natural Life* ed. S. Murray-Smith (1970) 548: We can't bring him off . . . in his canaries. He puts on these duds, d'ye see.'

1876 Rolf Boldrewood *A Colonial Reformer* (1891) 49: 'I goes up to the corporal, "I say, mate", says I, "can't you get your canaries off the track here for about a quarter of an hour, and let my mob of cattle pass?"'

2 A gold coin [f. *canary bird* guineas Grose 1785]

1853 Mrs C. Clacy *A Lady's Visit to the Gold Diggings of Australia in 1852–53* 91: For the sake of the uninitiated, I must explain that, in diggers' slang, a 'canary' and a half-sovereign are synonymous.

1895 Cornelius Crowe *The Australian Slang Dictionary* 14: *Canary Bird* a convict; a gold coin.

3 One hundred lashes

1859 John Lang *Botany Bay* 40: There were slang terms applied to these doses of the lash: twenty-five was called a 'tester'; fifty, a 'bob'; seventy-five, a 'bull'; and a hundred, a 'canary'.

canary, couldn't knock the dags off a sick see **couldn't**

Cane Toads, the The Queensland Rugby League team, in State of Origin matches with N.S.W.

1986 *Sun-Herald* 1 Jun. 71: In 1986, as the man says, 'you ain't seen nothin' until you've experienced an evening of sheer emotion and unrelieved mayhem [in a State of Origin match at Lang Park] as the self-styled *Cane Toads* yell themselves hoarse booing and hooting and gleefully abusing the despised *Cockroaches* from the south.

captain See quots

1959 *Bulletin* 21 Jan. 33: 'Whatever you say, dad,' Joey said. 'You're the captain [in charge of the drinking money].'

1972 John de Hoog *Skid Row Dossier* 125: Stiffs have . . . 'captains' (leaders of bottle parties).

1974 John Powers *The Last of the Knucklemen* 63: 'I'll be the captain for a round of beers.'

1978 Kevin Gilbert *Living Black* 302: 'Have you seen 'em bludging up to a captain* who's just come onto the mission with money in his pocket?' *The reserve people's name for a white man who visits them to trade money or grog for sex.

carby The carburettor [abbr.]

1957 Nino Culotta *They're a Weird Mob* 47: 'Carburettor, matey,' said Joe. 'We'll start on the carby.'

1963 Gunther Bahnemann *Hoodlum* 187: 'Wait a minute, that carby's been flooding. It's dripping like a watering-can.'

cardie A cardigan [abbr.]

1974 Patrick White *The Cockatoos* 169: She had torn her winter cardy on a nail.

1984 *Sydney Morning Herald* 26 May 42: The receptionist is a genteel North Shore matron of a certain age in spectacles and lemon hand knit cardie.

Cardinals The West Perth (W.A.) Australian Rules team [f. ecclesiastical red in the team colours]
1980 *Daily News* (Perth) 14 Jul. 26: East Perth coach Grant Dorrington denied the Royals took the field against West Perth with the intention of bashing the Cardinals off their game.

cark (it), to To break down, die [? f. *croak*, or the 'cark' of the crow]
1982 Nancy Keesing *Lily on the Dustbin* 50: A 'stiff dunny' is dead or, in other words 'has carked it'.
1983 Mike Carlton *Sydney Morning Herald* 4 May 8: If there was a bum camera shot or lighting effect that carked, it surely escaped me.
1984 Leo Schofield *Sydney Morning Herald* 17 Mar. 37: Meanwhile over in London they're flogging off the last of the D'Oyly Carte company's costumes. The tradition that we thought would die hard has carked completely.
see **kark**

carn Phonetic representation of 'Come on', esp. of an Australian Rules supporter ('Harry Carna' was the hero of a comic strip on Australian Rules by Peter Russell-Clarke which ran in the Melbourne *Herald and Weekly Times* from 25 March 1972)
1968 Bruce Dawe 'Life Cycle' *An Eye for a Tooth* 42: When children are born in Victoria / they are wrapped in the club-colours, laid in beribboned cots, / having already begun a lifetime's barracking. / Carn, they cry, Carn . . . feebly at first.
1981 Ian Turner and Leonie Sandercock *Up Where, Cazaly?* 5: A deep-throated roar comes from the crowd: 'Carn the Tigers . . . Carn the Blues.' The umpire blows his whistle, bounces the ball, and the game is on. At this moment, Melbourne comes to life.
1984 *Age* (Melbourne) 23 Mar. Weekender 11: Pick your spot and enjoy the passing parade, and the game. Carna Mighties!

carrion A term applied to bullocks, horses, most often collectively: *derogatory* [f. *carrion* poor, wretched or worthless beast OED 1634 *Obs.*]
1835 *Colonist* 22 Jan. 28: Passing the hut of a poor settler . . . he heard the man's wife addressing an old scarecrow of a mare in some such terms as the following:– 'Bad luck to you, you old rottern carrion!'
1901 Henry Lawson 'The Little World

Left Behind' *Prose* i 376: The same sunburned, masculine women went past to market twice a week in the same old carts and driving much the same quality of carrion.
1903 Joseph Furphy *Such is Life* (1944) 7: 'Where did you stop las' night? Your carrion's as full as ticks.'

caser Five shillings: *obs.* [f. Yiddish *kesef* silver: also English and U.S.]
1849 Alexander Harris *The Emigrant Family* (1967) 104: 'A caser (a dollar) if you give him a night of it; and four if he gets what'll make him quiet.'
1901 Henry Lawson 'Send Round the Hat' *Prose* i 471: He rolled the drunkard over, prospected his pockets till he made up five shillings (or a 'caser' in Bush language), and 'chucked' them into the hat.
1950 *Australian Police Journal* Apr. 112: *Caser* 5s.

cashed up Well supplied with money
1930 L. W. Lower *Here's Luck* 163: 'Straight from the Never-Never by the look of him. Is he cashed up?'
1959 D'Arcy Niland *The Big Smoke* 200: 'One of these days when I'm real cashed up like, I'm gonna get myself one of them trombones. They're great.'
1973 John Morrison *Australian by Choice* 127: I . . . came back to Melbourne well cashed up, and for a few leisurely weeks lived well.

Casket, the The Golden Casket, the Queensland State Lottery
1934 Thomas Wood *Cobbers* 135: A was for Australia, B for Bradman, C for the Casket.[1] [1]The Golden Casket. A State lottery started by the Queensland Government; supported now nearly all over the Commonwealth.
1962 David Forrest *The Hollow Woodheap* 8: 'Murder!' screamed the newsboy, 'Casket.'
1981 *Sunday Mail* (Brisbane) 17 May 2: I've spent the last few days thanking my lucky stars. No, nothing like a Casket win. I drove through a radar trap without being pulled up.

Cassa A Casanova [abbr.]
1943 Baker 18: *Casa* A masher (R.A.N. slang)
1957 Ray Lawler *Summer of the Seventeenth Doll* 55: 'To listen to her you'd reckon

I was the biggest Cassa in the North. It ain't as bad as that.'
1982 *National Times* 16 May 22: 'Every guy here is a real Cass'(anova), Camille, 23, a travel consultant warned me. 'They're right up themselves. Especially the first officers and pilots.'

castor A hat: *obs.* [f. *castor* a hat of beaver or rabbit fur OED 1640–1849; *castor* a hat Grose 1785]
1812 Vaux: *Castor* a hat.
1899 W. T. Goodge *Hits! Skits! and Jingles!* 151: When a 'castor' or a 'kady' / Is the name he gives his hat.

castor Similar to 'jake', 'sweet': *rare* [? f. *castor sugar* hence 'sweet']
1945 Baker 156: *castor* Good, excellent. [as World War II slang]
1963 John Cantwell *No Stranger to the Flame* 103: 'How is he today?' 'Castor, now you're arrived,' Max said easily.
1980 Maj. Peter D. Rothwell *Sydney Morning Herald* 3 Jan. 6: In the action where 'Simmo' [Warrant Officer Ray Simpson] won his Victoria Cross [in Vietnam, May 1969], when the situation appeared hopeless, Ray crawled over to me amid the intense enemy fire, and said 'Don't worry, skipper, she will be castor', and it was.

cat 1 A beast without spirit, esp. a race-horse who lets the punters down
1877 Rolf Boldrewood *A Colonial Reformer* (1891) 386: 'They're not a very gay lot to look at now. But I shouldn't wonder to see you knocking ten pounds a head out of some of those cats of steers before this day two years.'
1982 *Sun-Herald* 14 Nov. 86: 'He went into the line sideways, so I told someone after the race that I thought Bernborough was "cat".'
2 In sport, a player who cannot stand up to punishment; any weak person
1978 *Sun-Herald* 1 Jul. 70: 'He's a cat. Bloody big cat. Can't cop it and the other forwards know it. They'll give him plenty'
1984 *Sydney Morning Herald* 15 May 2: 'It is very difficult to prove a rape in prison . . . If you allow it to happen in jail you are identified as a cat – the weak person – and you become the subject of that sort of thing all the time. You're considered fair game.'
3 In prison slang, a homosexual
1958 Frank Hardy *The Four-legged Lottery* 117: Each cat [in prison] has her female

name: Amber, Maude, Rosie . . . Each has her favourite boy friends, who compete for her favours. They colour their hair with peroxide stolen from the hospital . . . They borrow books from the library and use the red colour off the covers for rouge and lipstick.
1974 Robert Adamson and Bruce Hanford *Zimmer's Essay* 31: The big losers in the prison politik are the 'cats', who will not accept feminine status, but who are weak and so are raped, or coerced into cock-sucking. They do not receive the chivalry accorded queens.

Cats, the The Geelong A.F.L. team
1976 *Sunday Telegraph* (Sydney) 11 Apr. 74: Olsson has Cats on rampage.

cat, whip (flog) the To give way to feelings of chagrin, frustration, regret; to reproach oneself [OED records *whip (jerk, shoot) the cat* to vomit 1609–1830. This expression seems closer to 'kicking the dog' as a way of venting spleen.]
1847 Alexander Harris *Settlers and Convicts* ed. C. M. H. Clark (1954) 193: And now it was my turn to 'whip the cat'.
1878 G. H. Gibson *Southerly Busters* 68: Though William by the 'cat' was whipped, / He never 'whipped the cat'.* *To 'whip the cat' signifies, in native parlance, to weep or lament.
1901 Henry Lawson 'A Double Buggy at Lahey's Creek' *Prose* i 595: I 'whipped the cat' a bit, the first twenty miles or so, but then I thought, what did it matter?
1932 K. S. Prichard *Kiss on the Lips* 184: 'I been whippin' the cat, thinkin' I'd missed seein' the mare do her gallop.'
1951 Dal Stivens *Jimmy Brockett* 255: Then I started whipping the cat for not having thought of it before.

catch and kill one's own To rely on one's own resources in dealing with problems, without appealing to outside authority: a motto given prominence by the Federated Ship Painters and Dockers Union (see quot. 1975)
1973 Jim McNeil *The Old Familiar Juice* 69: 'It's all a caser catch 'n kill yer own in their joint . . . or else yer can attach yerself, like, ter someone who'll do all the battlin' and bring home the goodies ter yer.'
1975 T. B. Gordon, Federal Secretary of the Federated Ship Painters and Dockers

Union, in Transcript of the Royal Commission into Alleged Payments to Maritime Unions, 17 Feb. 2642-3, cit. in Royal Commission on the Activities of the Federated Ship Painters and Dockers Union *Discussion Paper: Media Bias and the Victorian Branch* (1982) 105: *Mr St John*: What about the thefts and fires, have there been any charges made in respect of those offences? – No, we catch and kill our own. 'Is that a serious remark, Mr Gordon?' – Well, we look after our own end of the business always. We do not get much assistance from the authorities. They have not been able to track a herd of elephants through a field of snow up to date.

caught in a circular saw see **circular saw**

Cazaly, up there A cry of encouragement or congratulation, commemorating the V.F.L. player Roy Cazaly (1893–1963) noted for his high-marking
1943 Baker 85: *Up there, Cazaly!* Used as a cry of encouragement. (Cazaly was a noted South Melbourne footballer, whose speciality was high marking.)
1965 *Daily Telegraph* (Sydney) 18 Feb. 42: The other states and the Northern Territory play football – 'Up there, Cazaly'.
1979 *Sun* (Sydney) 27 Jul. 57: Melbourne has found a bestseller to match Come On Aussie, Come on. It's called Up There Cazaly, a song to promote VFL football. It sold 30,000 in one week.

cement, bushman's see **bushman's**

Centre, the Central Australia, sometimes the Red Centre
1901 F. J. Gillen *Diary* (1968) 149: She has a somewhat pleasant face of a type not common amongst the natives of the Centre.
1936 W. Hatfield *Australia through the Windscreen* 119: Throughout the whole of the Centre not a spot of rain fell between 1923 and 1930.
1974 *Australian* 18 Oct. 20: How red the Centre this summer?
Centralia
1930 *Bulletin* 8 Jan. 19: Some cattle on a Centralian station.
1982 *NT News* (Darwin) 7 Jun. 12: Centralian beef is better. So goes the theme which will be used for Centralian cattle producers at this year's N.T. expo.

Centre, the Red see **Red**

century, go for the To try to shear 100 sheep in a day
1905 'Another Fall of Rain' *The Old Bush Songs* ed. A. B. Paterson 28: For some had got the century who'd never got it before.
1957 'The Backblock Shearer' *Old Bush Songs* ed. Stewart and Keesing 258: To-morrow I go with a sardine blow / For a century or the sack.
1964 H. P. Tritton *Time Means Tucker* 92: Dutchy went for the 'century' and just failed. [recalling 1905–6]

chain, drag the To lag behind: used first in shearing, but now most commonly of a drinker who does not keep up with his group at the bar
1933 Acland: *Drag the chain, to* To be the slowest shearer in a shed.
1941 Baker 25: *Drag the chain* To be slow, to be inferior, to 'tail' the field in any work or contest.
1954 Tom Ronan *Vision Splendid* 124: 'Pass the bottle, Top, you're draggin' the chain.'
1968 Geoffrey Dutton *Andy* 146: 'Rooster here's way behind; dragging the bloody chain. He's due to set 'em up.'

chair, to be in the To be the one responsible for a round of drinks
1966 Baker 230: *to be in the chair* To be the person who pays for the next round of drinks (the pertinent question is often *Who's in the chair?*)
1972 Geoff Morley *Jockey Rides an Honest Race* 18: 'Just to show you what sort of a fellow I am, I'll go first in the chair.'
1974 John Powers *The Last of the Knucklemen* 78: 'Who's in the chair?' 'Me. My shout.'

chalkie 1 A schoolteacher
1941 Baker 17: *Chalk-and-talker* A schoolteacher
1953 T. A. G. Hungerford *Riverslake* 29: 'I was a chalky before the war – just couldn't settle down to it again, after.'
1972 Richard Magoffin *Chops and Gravy* 46: Kev is a bushie too, although he's a chalkie. He teaches at a boarding school in Charters Towers.
2 Post clerk in a stock exchange
1984 *West Australian* (Perth) 10 Jan. 44: Maureen Lang started at the [Melbourne] exchange 11 years ago as a 'chalky'. She

remembers feeling quite self-conscious up on the catwalk posting buyers' bids and sellers' offers on the trading boards.

champagne, Northern Territory see **Northern**

charge like a wounded bull, the heavy brigade etc. To charge high prices
1944 Randolph Bedford *Naught to Thirty-three* 177: Charles Troedel . . . charged me like the Light Brigade, or a herd of wounded buffalo. But he was the best of all the printers I ever used.
1969 Osmar White *Under the Iron Rainbow* 37: The Americans have access to the duty-free and tax-free stocks of the service canteens, while the Australians must do . . . their drinking in a pub which is said in the local vernacular to 'charge like a wounded buffalo'.
1978 *Australian* 11 Nov. Mag. 12: London restaurants, the better ones, charge like the heavy brigade.
1982 *Sun-Herald* 28 Feb. 144: Now we know why Telecom charges like a stuck boar.

Charities The government lottery set up in W.A. in 1932
1962 Stuart Gore *Down the Golden Mile* 166: 'After a turn-out like *that* I reckon you should have –' 'A ticket in Charities', Joyce completed for her.
1972 G. C. Bolton *A Fine Country to Starve In* 244: Jack Scaddan . . . was entrusted with the legislation setting up a government lottery, with 2s 6d tickets and a first prize of £3000. This was the famous Charities Consultation, which took its place beside Queensland's Golden Casket and Tasmania's 'Tatts' as the average Australian's dream of sudden wealth . . . Before long it passed into common speech, and anyone wanting to give the strongest support to a debatable remark would say, 'I wish I were as sure of winning Charities'.
1983 T. A. G. Hungerford *Stories from Suburban Road* 6: 'You get down on your hunkers and ask him to let us win the Charities. Or we'll soon be in Queer Street.'

charity moll (dame) An amateur prostitute who does not charge a professional rate; any woman who thus deprives the professional of trade
1953 Baker 125: An amateur harlot or one who undercuts regular professional prices,

with little thought for the consequences of this deflationary activity, is called a *charity dame* or a *for-free*.
1962 Criena Rohan *The Delinquents* 104: 'Remember,' she warned, 'no charity moll capers with my men.'

charlie A girl [f. rhyming slang *Charlie Wheeler* = *sheila*. Perhaps related to *charlies*, English slang for breasts.]
1949 Lawson Glassop *Lucky Palmer* 41: 'Charlie?' asked Eric. 'What do you mean by Charlie?' 'Your Charlie,' repeated Max. 'Your canary.' 'Canary?' 'Ay, don't you speak English? Your sheila!'
1951 Dal Stivens *Jimmy Brockett* 102: The stocky little Charlie Wheeler said to me, 'I'm having a party soon and you must come along.'
1972 Geoff Morley *Jockey Rides an Honest Race* 61: There's plenty of charlies over here. The town is built for tourism and this has caused an influx of waitresses, barmaids, chambermaids, housemaids and other assorted frilly trillies.
1983 David Foster *Plumbum* 305: Some cunt'll steal your mags while you're chock-a-block up your charlie.

chase up a cow see **cow**

cheerios Cocktail frankfurts [Queensland and N.T.]
1982 *NT News* (Darwin) 15 Jun. 19: Cheerios $2.49 kg.

cheque The total sum received, esp. for work done by contract, or from the sale of some crop
1857 F. Cooper *Wild Adventures in Australia* 66: Drawing my 'cheque' from Wilder, I felt my exchequer sufficiently strong to allow of my embarking in another career, namely, that of an overlander.
1901 Henry Lawson 'His Brother's Keeper' *Prose* i 517: He was 'ringer' of the shed at Piora Station one season and made a decent cheque.
1922 Herbert Scanlon *Bon Jour Digger* 31: I myself was taking a trip on the results of my huge wool cheque.
1936 Archer Russell *Gone Nomad* 68: So was our mob delivered at last. The drover received the cheque that was due to him and Moleskin, Pilot and I were paid off.
1975 *Sydney Morning Herald* 20 Dec. 19: Australia's wool cheque for the first half of

the 1975–76 wool selling season is estimated at $367.2 million.

chequed up Well supplied with funds in the form of a cheque
1940 Ion L. Idriess *Lightning Ridge* 126: They'd reappear again in six months time, 'chequed up' and smiling.
1966 Tom Ronan *Once There Was a Bagman* 84: 'You fellows should be well chequed up and if you don't speculate you won't accumulate.'
see **cashed up**

cherry Virginity [listed by Partridge as the hymen; also U.S.]
1959 Dorothy Hewett *Bobbin Up* 158: 'And don't bank on your sailor boy comin' home to you ... I lost me cherry on the kitchen table to a sailor once. I was fifteen.'
1974 Robert Adamson *Zimmer's Essay* 46: 'My tip is, do it easy. You have a good time in there. They'll have your cherry before you know it.'
1984 *National Times* 30 Nov. 17: 'Perhaps she has been seduced and because of conscience concludes in her own mind that the only way she can live with the fact that the cherry has been plucked is in the case where it has been taken against her will.'

Chesty Bond Comic strip figure devised in 1938 by Ted Moloney, running in the *Sun* from March 1940, advertising the Bond's athletic singlet (marketed in 1926)
1953 Dymphna Cusack *Southern Steel* 328: Anne rolled over lazily and stared into his face. 'Hop in yourself, Chesty Bond.'
1971 Frank Hardy *The Outcasts of Foolgarah* 195: He swaggered down the hill, ... black hair bristling out of his chesty bond singlet.
1984 *Sydney Morning Herald* 30 Jan. Guide 9: 'What do you get when you match up Dolly Parton with James Bond? ... A chesty Bond, of course.'

chewy on your boot See quots: Victorian sporting
1966 Baker 370: *Hope you have a chewie on your boot!* Used to express a wish that a football player kicking for goal misses because there is chewing gum on his boot.
1975 *Sydney Morning Herald* 8 Nov. 4: Mr Hawke puzzled the crowd when he described their reaction to the Khemlani disclosure as 'You were wrong, chewy on your

boot.' He did not seem to realize that he had used an Australian Rules cat-call.

chiack, chiacking *n.* Good-humoured banter; jeering, esp. collective
[**1859** Hotten: *Chi-ike*, a hurrah, a good word, or hearty praise; [added 1865] a term used by the *Costermongers* who assist the sale of each other's goods by a little friendly though noisy commendation.]
1853 C. R. Read *What I Heard, Saw and Did on the Australian Goldfields* 148: The 'skyhacking'* to which the police were subject when sent round to inspect people's licenses, was brought on principally by their own individual over-bearing conduct. *Blackguarding
1869 Marcus Clarke 'The Language of Bohemia' in *A Colonial City* ed. L. T. Hergenhan (1972) 159: The hissing of gallery, or the gods, is called *chy-ike*.
1885 *The Australasian Printers' Keepsake* 154: One toff, who fancied himself, still kept poking borack, but Steve stopped his chyacking pretty quick, for he hauled off and let him have it.
1959 Gerard Hamilton *Summer Glare* 96: The boys made a few unhelpful suggestions and quite a bit of chyacking went on.
1984 Marian Eldridge *Walking the Dog* 170: When their chiacking got too much I would go out and talk to the turkeys.

chiack *v.* To 'chaff', tease; to ridicule
1893 J. A. Barry *Steve Brown's Bunyip* 21: 'They're always a-poking borack an a-chiackin' o' me over in the hut!'
1896 Henry Lawson 'Across the Straits' *Prose* i 200: There were several pretty girls in the office, laughing and chiacking the counter clerks.
1931 Vance Palmer *Separate Lives* 14: 'They've been chiacking me about my cold feet.'
1967 K. S. Prichard *Subtle Flame* 105: The rowdy bodgie youths kept seats near this group, chiacking the buxom, brassy-haired waitress as she rushed around with a trayload of dishes.

Chinaman, I must have killed a Explanation of any bad luck
1898 George T. Bell *Tales of Australian Adventure* 12: 'By Jove, G.T., old man, you've got such hard luck. You must have killed a Chinaman.'
1923 Con Drew *Rogues & Ruses* 116: 'I've

got a mocker hung on me.' Pinkey laughed. 'Been killin' a Chinaman?' he queried.
1940 Ion L. Idriess *Lightning Ridge* 115: 'We must have killed Chinamen, or looked cross-eyed at a black cat,' growled Tom.
1984 Don'o Kim *The Chinaman* 131: 'How's your fishing?' 'Not so good, mate.' 'Why, you didn't kill a Chinaman, did you?'

Chinese burn The burning sensation given by grasping someone's wrist in a two-handed grip and twisting the skin in opposite directions: *juvenile*
1937 Encountered in conversation.
1980 Clive James *Unreliable Memoirs* 35: Mears's favourite means of persuasion was the Chinese Burn. Grasping your hand in one of his, he would twist your wrist with the other.
1983 *Sydney Morning Herald* 7 May 38: He [L. W. Lower] rabbit chops and Chinese-burns the language, reducing it to dreadful puns, playground non-sequiturs and crazy jokes.

Chink, Chinkie A Chinaman: *derogatory*
1876 A. J. Boyd *Old Colonials* (1882) 233: Our colonialised 'Chinkie', as he is vulgarly termed (with the single variation 'Chow').
1896 Edward Dyson *Rhymes from the Mines* 101: Here, I state that all Chinkies are vicious / And I hate them like fever and snakes.
1939 Kylie Tennant *Foveaux* 85: 'Went to a herbulist . . . He give me something that took it away. Wonderful them Chinks are.'
1951 Dal Stivens *Jimmy Brockett* 90: We've got the best country in the world and the best people, and we don't want any Chinks or other foreigners butting in on us.
1969 William Dick *Naked Prodigal* 5: He didn't seem a bad bloke for a chinky-chink.
see **Chow**

chip, dry as a Extremely dry [1631 Ben Jonson *The New Inn* iv.i.3–4: 'As dry as a chip! Good Jug, a cast o' thy name, / As well as thy office; two jugs!']
1889 Ernest Giles *Australia Twice Traversed* ii 30: Bunches of a thin and wiry kind of grass, though white and dry as a chip.
1957 Morris L. West *Kundu* 68: 'Drink your tea then. You're as dry as a chip.'
1984 John Hooker *The Bush Soldiers* 192: 'This place is as dry as a chip, I wonder what the buggers drink.'

chips, to spit see **spit chips**

Chloe, drunk as Very drunk
[**1823** Jon Bee *Slang A Dictionary of the Turf, the Ring &c* 27: 'Drunk as Chloe'; she must have been an uproarious lass.]
1892 Barcroft Boake 'How Polly Paid for her Keep' *Bulletin* 6 Feb. 10, repr. in *Where the Dead Men Lie* (1897) 69: Drunk! with my loved ones on board, drunk as Chloe!
1945 Cecil Mann *The River* 43: Drunk as Chloe on the potent cognac of that green and pleasant isle.
1956 Kylie Tennant *The Honey Flow* 188: They would get as drunk as Chloe and probably end up in a fight somewhere.
1979 Bobbie Hardy *The World Owes Me Nothing* 115: I'm out in the street then, drunk as Chloe, and abusing this constable.

chockablock See quots
1971 Frank Hardy *The Outcasts of Foolgarah* 80: 'They caught me at it once on the sofa in the living room, caught me right in the bloody act with a woman who came in to do the cleaning; chocker-block up her, I was, going for me life.'
1979 Robert Drewe *A Cry in the Jungle Bar* 146: It was as if he and Gigi had been the couple caught red-handed. On the job. Chocka – as the old schoolboy expression succinctly put it – chockablock.
1983 Clem Gorman *A Night in the Arms of Raeleen* 44: 'She come home early one night . . . caught me scorin' ten from the usherette up the local pictures. Chock-a-block.'

choco 1 See quot. (World War I slang)
1919 W. H. Downing *Digger Dialects* 16: *Chocs* The 8th Brigade ('Tivey's Chocolate Soldiers'). Originally an abusive name; now an honourable appellation.
2 A member of the Militia, which did not serve outside Australia and its territories (World War II slang)
1942 *Salt* 14 Sep. 35: 'You labelled him a 'choco', because he did not fight / You thought he didn't have the guts to stick up for the right.'
1944 Lawson Glassop *We Were the Rats* 261: I told myself that I had misjudged the chocos.
1968 Geoffrey Dutton *Andy* 91: 'You are all volunteers. Your country called you and you came. Not a chocko amongst you.'

Chocolate Soldiers The Penrith R.L.

team, from team colours, and because they are supposed to melt when the heat is on.

1983 *Australian* 11 Mar. 22: 'Even then [in 1976],' Brohman recalled yesterday, 'Penrith players were referred to as "chocolate soldiers". Let's face it – the club's record is not good.'

choko vine over a country dunny, couldn't train a see **couldn't**

choof To move; more often **choof off**, depart: *jocular* [echoic]
1965 Frank Hardy *The Yarns of Billy Borker* 61: So they choof to the travel agency and buy two one-way air tickets to Mexico.
1971 David Ireland *The Unknown Industrial Prisoner* 83: 'We were choofing along Highway One about forty-five or fifty.'
1979 Bobbie Hardie *The World Owes Me Nothing* 156: 'If my presence is going to cause trouble . . . I think I'll choof off.'

chook 1 A domestic fowl [f. *chook* a call to pigs, or occas. to poultry EDD]
1855 William Howitt *Land, Labour and Gold* ii 139–40: They overtook a huge and very fat hen . . . they tied chucky up in a handkerchief, and rode on.
1900 J. C. L. Fitzpatrick *The Good Old Days* 71: A game rooster that could massacre twenty of your neighbours' domestic chooks in as many minutes.
1935 Kylie Tennant *Tiburon* 44: 'Chook! Chook! Chook!' she called to the fowls.
1983 *Weekend Australian* 23 Apr. 13: One of the Premier's aides let slip one of Mr Bjelke-Petersen's stock phrases whenever approached by journalists or when attending a press conference: 'Here are my chooks – I'd better feed them.'
2 A woman (*jocular*)
1915 C. J. Dennis *The Songs of a Sentimental Bloke* 80: 'She's too young – too young to leave 'er muvver's nest!' / 'Orright, ole chook,' I nearly sez.
1959 D'Arcy Niland *The Big Smoke* 45: 'Funny old chook. I can get on all right with her, I think.'
3 Nickname of anyone called Fowler
1911 Louis Stone *Jonah* 126: 'Me name's Fowles – Arthur Fowles,' replied Chook.
1967 Len Beadell *Blast the Bush* 141: 'Chook' Fowler, driving the old D7, heaped up a barrier of dirt.
chookery, chookhouse, chook raffle
1908 Henry Fletcher *Dads and Dan between Smokes* 129: 'I've seen quite a number

o' coves start a chookery; some few battles along, far more comes a cropper.'
1982 *Sydney Morning Herald* 19 Jul. Guide 5: Describing the elation of a young jockey on his return to the scale after a winning ride, Mr Tapp said, 'I tell yer what, mate – he's got a smile on like a carpet snake in a chookhouse.'
1979 *Australian* 30 Jun. 11: Poor Dick Hamer, Premier of all Victoria – he started the week looking as if he couldn't run a chook raffle let alone a State budget.
1984 *Sun-Herald* 22 Apr. 66: After a fundraising chook raffle after yet another St Kilda loss, one disappointed supporter jibed: 'Why don't you raffle the players and play the chooks?'

chooks turn into emus and kick your dunny down see **emus**

choom An Englishman: *jocular* [f. dialectal pronunciation of 'chum' as a mode of address]
[**1916** *The Anzac Book* 31: 'Have you got any badges, choom?']
1919 W. H. Downing *Digger Dialects* 16: *Choom* An English soldier.
1952 Jon Cleary *The Sundowners* 134: 'The Chooms have been telling us what's wrong with us ever since they came out here with the First Fleet.'
1962 Stuart Gore *Down the Golden Mile* 24: 'Me old pal the choom. And how would you be, Squire?'
1974 *Sun-Herald* 9 Jun. 17: Chooms make a few blues over Strine.

chop Share, allocation, esp. in phrase 'get in for one's chop' [f. *chop* slice, cut OED 1640]
1919 W. H. Downing *Digger Dialects* 16: *Chop* Share. 'To hop in for one's chop' – to enter in, in order to secure a privilege or benefit.
1949 Lawson Glassop *Lucky Palmer* 104: 'Ginger's chop was twenty-six quid.'
1966 D. H. Crick *Period of Adjustment* 21: 'Tell him his quid today'll be worth ten bob tomorrow, so he better get in for his chop.'

chop, no No good [f. *first, second chop* OED 1823]
1864 J. F. Mortlock *Experiences of a Convict* (1965) 23: I was in Australasia, dragging a handcart (reckoned 'no chop') when informed of it.

1882 Rolf Boldrewood *Robbery Under Arms* (World's Classics 1949) 13: There's good and bad of every sort, and I've met plenty that were no chop of all churches.
1955 John Morrison *Black Cargo* 174: 'I've heard he's no chop, Rory.' 'No chop? – he's a bastard.'

chop, not much   Unimpressive, inferior
1849 Alexander Harris *The Emigrant Family* (1967) 369: 'Oh, he's not much of a chop, I must say.'
1903 Joseph Furphy *Such is Life* (1944) 9: 'Mac's no great chop.'
1928 Miles Franklin *Up the Country* (1966) 13: 'That old parson is not much chop, I don't reckon,' he confided.
1957 Ray Lawler *Summer of the Seventeenth Doll* 125: 'What I'm offering is not much chop, but – I want to marry you, Ol.'
1973 Alexander Buzo *Norm and Ahmed* 25: 'They've improved a lot, these clubs. Twenty years ago they weren't much chop, just a place to go when you wanted to get out on the grog.'

chop short of a barbecue, a   see **barbecue**

chopper   1   i.e. chopper tailor, fish not yet full size
1980 *Weekend News* (Perth) 8 Nov. 49: Most of the bigger tailor are being taken on mulies and lures, with the smaller choppers in the river falling victim to whitebait.
2   A cow sold for pet food
1984 James McQueen *Uphill Runner* 2: The barren ones [cows] had been sold as choppers at the end of the summer.
1985 *Newsletter* Nursing Mothers' Association of Australia March 22: Even dairy cows vary in the quantity of milk produced – from the champion blue ribbon milk producer to the 'chopper'.

Chow   A Chinaman: *derogatory* [f. *chow-chow* OED 1845]
1864 *Thatcher's Colonial Minstrel* 72: 'The Chinaman's Fate'. Chow Chow his hands with glee did rub.
1908 Henry Fletcher *Dads and Dan between Smokes* 4: 'Give out yer washin' to a Chow.'
1921 K. S. Prichard *Black Opal* 59: 'Michael says he works like a chow.'
1970 Patrick White *The Vivisector* 77:

Like one of the Chinese beans the Chow had given them at Christmas.

Chrissy   Christmas [abbr.]
1972 Geoff Morley *Jockey Rides Honest Race* 229: Forgot to mention the Chrissy party at work.
1981 *Australian* 19 Jan. 9: 'Sorry, matey, but you can't expect us blokes to have a mechanic on duty on a Saturday arvo, just after Chrissie,' the garage attendant said.

christening, like a moll (streetgirl, gin) at a   To be ill at ease, flustered, confused [variant of the English 'As demure as an old whore at a christening' Grose 1811]
1938 Eric Lowe *Salute to Freedom* 370: It was this, the thought of Carl's utter inaptitude, which made him laugh . . . As useless as a whore at a christening!
1954 Bant Singer *Have Patience, Delaney* 114: You got me floundering like a streetgirl at a christening.
1965 Thomas Keneally *The Fear* 192: 'Come on, Cec' the gunner roared to his mate. 'Talk about a gin at a bloody christening!'
1970 Richard Beilby *No Medals for Aphrodite* 31: 'Why don't you get going? You're mucking around like a moll at a christening.'

Christmas hold   See quots
1953 Baker 132: *Christmas hold* A hold applied by grabbing an opponent's testicles (a 'handful of nuts') [prison slang]
1964 Tom Ronan *Packhorse and Pearling Boat* 125–6: Joe came in low, looking for that grip which the west coast black fellow learned from that other clean fighter, the Jap: The Christmas hold (the handful of nuts).
1981 *Australian* 2 May Mag. 7: A woman in a dental surgery, lying on the dentist's couch, put the Christmas grip on the dentist. When the dentist winced with pain, as anyone would wince if a Christmas grip were put upon him, she said, 'We are not going to hurt each other are we, Mr Dentist?'

Christmas, what else did you get for   [also U.S.] Derisory retort to a motorist sounding his horn at another (as though playing with a new toy)
1962 David Forrest *The Hollow Woodheap* 102: The horn honked . . . 'What else did you get for Christmas, Jack?' said Pudden sternly.

1981 *Daily News* (Perth) 19 Jan. 5: What *else* did you get for Christmas? Christmas is over – but for many the memory lingers on, as unsightly and unwanted weight. If you have a weight problem, the Weight Control Centre can help.

chromo   A prostitute: *obs.* [?f. cosmetics]
1938 *Smith's Weekly* 31 Dec. 12: As Tilly remarked, 'Wot can you heckspect from a chromo, whose forefathers was never married.'
1949 Ruth Park *Poor Man's Orange* 200: The chromo next door got her money easy in dark doorways.
1953 Kylie Tennant *The Joyful Condemned* 166: 'He's one of those big he-men that go sneaking around the park waiting to snitch some chromo's handbag. Just a pie-eater.'
1975 *Bulletin* 4 Oct. 4: It is a pity the word 'chromo' is old Australian slang for prostitute (I never knew why). It would be an apt term for a colour television addict.

chuck   Used in the sense of 'stage' or 'throw' (as in 'throw a fit') in a variety of expressions: **chuck a seven, chuck a doubler, chuck a heartie** (have a heart attack), **chuck a mental** (have a mental attack)
1908 see **seven, throw a**
1946 see **doubler, chuck a**
1980 Encountered in conversation ('He was out in the toilet chucking a heartie')
1985 Judy Johnson *Sun-Herald* 17 Feb. 163: Apart from chucking the occasional mental (as she [a teenage daughter] used to call it) I usually grinned and tried to make home a place you wanted to be.

chuck off   As for **throw off** q.v.
1915 C. J. Dennis *The Songs of a Sentimental Bloke* 22: Me! that 'as barracked tarts . . . An' chucked orf at 'em like a phonergraft!
1922 Arthur Wright *A Colt from the Country* 140: 'What y' chuckin' off about?' he growled.
1958 A. E. Manning *The Bodgie* 76: Your friends 'chuck off' at you for being a 'goodie-goodie'.

chunder   To vomit; a term given currency by the Barry McKenzie comic strip [variously explained as an abbreviation of 'watch under' (see quot. 1965) and as rhyming slang *Chunder Loo* = *spew* from Chunder Loo of Akin Foo, a cartoon figure in a long-running series

of advertisements for Cobra bootpolish in the *Bulletin* from 8 Apr. 1909]
1950 Nevil Shute *A Town Like Alice* 76: 'The way these bloody Nips go on. Makes you want to chunda.'
1965 Barry Humphries 'Barry McKenzie' *Times Literary Supplement* 16 Sep. 812: His favourite word to describe the act of involuntary regurgitation is the verb to chunder. This word is not in popular currency in Australia, but the writer recalls that ten years ago it was common in Victoria's more expensive public schools. It is now used by the Surfies, a repellent breed of sunbronzed hedonists who actually hold chundering contests on the famed beaches of the Commonwealth. I understand . . . that the word derives from a nautical expression 'watch under', an ominous courtesy shouted from the upper decks for the protection of those below.
1973 Alexander Buzo *Rooted* 91: She put a plate of rissoles down in front of me the other night and I chundered all over them.
1983 *Sun-Herald* 31 Jul. 48: I'm certainly not in favour of our Foreign Minister turning into a kind of diplomatic ocker, delivering verbal chunderings to sensitive Asian neighbours.

Churches, the City of   see **City**

chutty   Chewing gum
1941 Baker 18: *Chutty* Chewing gum.
1956 Ruth Park and D'Arcy Niland *The Drums Go Bang!* 9: 'Thought maybe you was just friends,' said the woman, taking out her chutty and parking it on the door-frame.

cigarette swag   A very thin swag, indicating destitution
1943 Baker 20: *Cigarette swag* A small swag carried by a tramp when he comes to a city.
1955 Alan Marshall *I Can Jump Puddles* 158: 'He was humping a cigarette swag,' explained The Fiddler. 'We all dodge blokes with a swag like that. They never have anything. They bot on you for the lot.'
1966 Tom Ronan *Once There Was a Bagman* 235: I was in my twenties and at least did have a couple of horses and some gear. Hughie was well in his sixties, with nothing but a cigarette swag.

circular saw, like being caught in a   Metaphor for female promiscuity
1937 Ernestine Hill *The Great Australian*

Loneliness 63: 'I understand you can give evidence regarding the paternity of this child,' rapped out the magistrate. 'Oh, I wouldn't say that,' said Con modestly; 'you see, it's this way. If you were injured by a circular saw, could you pick out the particular tooth that did the damage?'
1956 Tom Ronan *Moleskin Midas* 236: 'And gins never know properly who fathers their kids. It'd be like getting your hand caught in that circular saw ... and saying what tooth it was that cut you.'

City of Churches, the   Adelaide, S.A.
1873 A. Trollope *Australia* ed. P. D. Edwards and R. B. Joyce (1967) 647: Adelaide has been called a city of churches.
1967 Sir Robert Menzies *Afternoon Light* 347: The genial 'barrackers' of Adelaide – the 'City of Churches' – raucously inquired whether he could 'do with a pint'.
1983 *Australian* 27 Jul. 7: Savage undercurrents in the City of Churches ... Is Adelaide the Australian capital of bizarre sexual crime against the young?

Claytons   'The drink I have when I'm not having a drink' (the commercial for Claytons, 'a full bodied non-alcoholic drink made from African kola nuts and citrus essences')
1982 *Sunday Telegraph* (Sydney) 28 Mar. 176: Who's the press secretary working out of the NSW parliament whose press-gallery nickname is Clayton ... because he's the press secretary you're having when you're not having a press secretary?
1983 *West Australian* (Perth) 24 Aug. 17: Senator Don Chipp said it was a Claytons budget – the sort of budget you have when you're not having a budget.
1990 *Australian* 25 Jan. 2: Hawke hits Claytons campaign trail [i.e. before an election has been announced]

cleanskin   1   An unbranded beast
1881 A. C. Grant *Bush-Life in Queensland* i 206: These clean-skins, as they are often called, to distinguish them from the branded cattle, are supposed to belong to the cattle-owner on whose run they emerge from their shelter.
1928 W. Robertson *Coo-ee Talks* 174: The sergeant of police declared that Jarvis's skill as a lifter of 'clean skins' (unbranded cattle) was only excelled by the cunning of his lubra.
2   A person without a police record
1907 Alfred Searcy *In Australian Tropics*

112: The men I met with were good, honest, and hard working, although perhaps it might have been as well for a clean skin to fight shy of some of them.
1950 *Australian Police Journal* Apr. 111: *Cleanskin* A person without convictions – (One who, as it were, has been lucky.).
1984 *Sun-Herald* 24 Jun. 11: Cameron's death was almost certainly ordered because the drug gang had no further use for the former 'clean skin' they had recruited and it was feared he would give evidence against them.

clever country   see **lucky country**

clinah, cliner   Girlfriend, sweetheart: *obs.* [? f. G. *kleine* little]
1895 *Bulletin* 9 Feb. 15: I'm ryebuck and the girl's okay. / Oh, she's a good iron, is my little clinah.
1899 W. T. Goodge *Hits! Skits! and Jingles!* 150: And his lady-love's his 'donah' / Or his 'clinah' or his 'tart'.
1913 Henry Lawson 'The Old Push and the New' *Verse* iii 82: They were faithful to a clinah, they were loyal to a pal.
1916 C. J. Dennis *The Moods of Ginger Mick* 72: Wiv me arm around me cliner, an' me notions far frum wrong.
1928 A. W. Upfield *The House of Cain* 79: 'I 'elped to get 'is clinah out of quod for what she and 'im did for me.'
see **kleiner**

clip, the   'The whole quantity of wool shorn in any place, or in one season' (OED 1825–67)
1840 T. P. MacQueen *Australia as she is and may be* 34: The clip will be from 1469 head at 3 lb each.
1850 B. C. Peck *Recollections of Sydney* 22: The clip this season, in New South Wales, falls very short of the average of many years past.
1925 C. E. W. Bean *On the Wool Track* 229: But every Australian State except Western Australia now has its own sales, and at which nearly the whole of the Australian clip is now disposed of.
1948 K. S. Prichard *Golden Miles* 32: She ... heard about the fine property Bill owned: how many sheep it ran and how well their clip had sold at the last wool sales.
1975 *Sydney Morning Herald* 20 Dec. 19: Australia's wool clip sells for $367.2m.

clock   To strike, hit in the face or head

1941 Baker 18: *Clock, to* To strike with the fist.
1956 F. B. Vickers *First Place to the Stranger* 135: 'Somebody will clock that bastard one day.'
1966 Bruce Beaver *You Can't Come Back* 7: 'You're no mate of mine. I very nearly clocked you back there, but I don't want to fight you or anyone else.'
1973 *Sun-Herald* 25 Mar. 108: Dick Woolcott, 46, the man whom Mr McMahon clocked with a squash racquet in America last year.

clock, bushman's, settler's see **bushman, settler**

clocker Someone who times a racehorse with a stopwatch, esp. at training gallops [U.S. 1909 Mathews]
1895 Nat Gould *On and Off the Turf in Australia* 117: Ruses are resorted to at times to deceive or out-general the 'clocker' on the look-out for a good gallop.
1980 *Daily Mirror* (Sydney) 1 Apr. 111: She's an absolute flying machine and today made clockers look twice when she recorded 35 sec for her boom task.

close up Almost [Pidgin]
1883 Edward M. Curr *Recollections of Squatting in Victoria* 349: All top ropes, of course; but were, as I heard, close up fly-blown [i.e. nearly penniless).
1929 K. S. Prichard *Coonardoo* 316: She was 'close up finish 'm', she knew, as the trooper had said.
1935 Mary and Elizabeth Durack *All-About* 97: 'I bin go mad and kill that Masha. Might 'im close up dead now.'
1946 W. E. Harney *North of 23°* 257: She is panting hard when she arrives, and complains about how she is 'close up been lose 'em wind.'

clucky Thinking of having a baby; indulging in sentimental feelings about parenthood; behaving in a maternally protective way
[**1839** Grose *Glossary of Provincial and Local Words* 32: *Cluckish*, said of a hen when inclined to sit. Kent.]
1941 Baker 18: *Clucky* Pregnant.
1980 David Williamson *Travelling North* 34: 'Moya Simpson's just had another one and it's made me clucky.'
1984 Paula Duncan *New Idea* 10 Mar. 5: 'I've always wanted a child. I've never been anything else but clucky.'

coach, who's robbing this Equivalent to 'Don't interrupt' or 'Don't interfere' [Quot. 1971 refers to the anecdote that Ned Kelly held up a stage coach and announced that he would rob all the men and rape all the women. When a male passenger protested that he should take the money but leave the women alone, a female voice piped up 'Who's robbing this coach, you or Mr Kelly?'. Ned Kelly held up no coaches, and the story is also told of Jesse James, who announced that he would rob all the women and rape all the men. When a passenger suggested that he'd got it wrong, a young man with a fluty voice interpolated 'Who's robbing this coach, you or Mr James?']
1945 Baker 250–1: Disapproval or disagreement is indicated by . . . *who's robbing this coach?* *Reputed to be associated with bushranging days, this expression is equivalent to 'mind your own business!'
1951 Eric Lambert *The Twenty Thousand Thieves* 206: Chip's boom shattered the sudden tensity of feeling among them. 'Who's robbing this coach? Do you want to hear the news or not?'
1971 Frank Hardy *The Outcasts of Foolgarah* 17: He carried on a dialogue with himself, his voice muffly-mimicky deep in the helmet. 'I'm going to rob all the men and fuck all the women': 'You can't do that, you dreadful man': 'Who's robbing this coach, you or Mister Kelly?'
1977 *Australian* 1 Dec. 8: Apart from raising the question as to which of Labor's four Treasurers-elect is robbing the coach, where does this leave Labor policy – except in tatters?

coach, coacher Docile cow or bullock used as decoy to attract wild cattle
1874 W. H. L. Ranken *Dominion of Australia* 110: To get them [the wild cattle] a party of stockmen take a small herd of quiet cattle, 'coaches'.
1947 W. E. Harney *North of 23°* 28: We would find the small wild mobs, in mustering which, coachers – decoy cattle – would be used.
1967 John Yeomans *The Scarce Australians* 37: The docile cattle are called coaches, or coachers, because they coach the wild cattle in the right behaviour.

coat, on the 1 In disfavour, getting 'the cold shoulder'
1941 Baker 18: *Coat, on the* (of a man) To be sent to Coventry.

1949 Alan Marshall *How Beautiful Are Thy Feet* 219: 'Girls that are too easy are on the coat with me,' went on Ron.
1973 Fred Parsons *A Man Called Mo* 47: he stepped back a pace, and fingered his lapel. It was the 'He's on the coat' sign, a gesture of supreme contempt.
2 Used of a bet that is not genuine, made by arrangement to alter the odds
1949 Lawson Glassop *Lucky Palmer* 66: He held the lapel of his coat between his right thumb and forefinger and shook it. 'On the coat, them bets of mine, of course, Norm,' he said, making it clear they were not genuine.

coat, pull (tug) the 1 Not to make a genuine effort [f. *coat* 2]
1977 *Sunday Telegraph* (Sydney) 2 Jan. 45: Although there are many who believe he pulls the coat in Sheffield Shield, that's as far from the truth as you can get.
2 To act as an urger (horse-racing)
1977 Jim Ramsay *Cop It Sweet* 23: *Coat tugger:* Race-track urger.
1984 *Sydney Morning Herald* 19 Oct. 30: In racing parlance a 'coat puller' is someone who gives misleading advice at the track, stopping a punter backing his own selection which usually wins. Losing punters often take out their ire on their 'coat-pulling' mates.
3 To warn (criminal slang)
1975 *Bulletin* 26 Apr. 44: 'One of the old rorters up the Cross tugged me coat a week ago. His mail was that if I didn't weigh in soon I'd be gathered for sure.' Ibid. 46: The expression derives from the system of signals shoppies use in large stores; rather like the bookmakers' tick-tacking. One of these signals is tugging at the lapels of the signaller's coat, signifying danger.

Coathanger, the 1 The Sydney Harbour Bridge: *jocular*
1940 Dorothy Auchterlonie *Kaleidoscope* [7]: Twinkle, twinkle little stars / On a million motorcars, / Along the Harbour Bridge so high, / Like a coat-hanger in the sky.
1957 Sydney Hart *Pommie Migrant* 51: 'Ah,' I countered, jestingly, 'That's what the Melbourne folk call the 'coathanger', isn't it?'
1983 Kate Fitzpatrick *Sydney Morning Herald* 18 Jun. 31: I like it here [in Melbourne] but I'd give anything for a glimpse of the old coat-hanger.
2 A head-high tackle

1982 *NT News* (Darwin) 18 Aug. 36: Brothers Rugby League Club wants a Northern Suburbs player cited for a deliberate head-high tackle ... It claims the player delivered the coathanger tackle to the centre, Brian McSkimming, two minutes before half time.

cobar A penny, a copper: *obs.* [f. name of copper-mining town]
1898 *Bulletin* 1 Oct. 14: A penny is a 'Cobar'.
1911 E. S. Sorenson *Life in the Australian Backblocks* 36: When Jack makes anything for the pet creation, you can bet your bottom Cobar he will put all his ingenuity into it.

cobber Friend, mate: *obsolescent* [f. *cob* to take a liking to anyone EDD]
1895 *Bulletin* 9 Feb. 15: Oh she's a good iron, is my little clinah; / She's my cobber an' I'm 'er bloke.
1910 Henry Lawson 'The Rising of the Court' *Prose* i 660: For the sake of a friend – of a 'pal' or a 'cobber'.
1916 *The Anzac Book* 151n: *Cobber* – Australian for a well tried and tested pal.
1933 F. E. Baume *Tragedy Track* 178: 'Can you imagine your old cobber on the talkies?'
1965 Barry Humphries 'Barry McKenzie' *Times Literary Supplement* 16 Sep. 812: His vocabulary is borrowed from a diversity of national types and words like 'cobber' and 'bonzer' still intrude as a sop to Pommy readers, though such words are seldom, if ever, used in present-day Australia.
cobber up
1923 Jack Moses *Beyond the City Gates* 29: 'Oh, fair,' said Jimmy, cobbering up in true Australian style.
1954 T. A. G. Hungerford *Sowers of the Wind* 51: I thought I might cobber up with them, but ... they don't even know that I'm alive.
1964 Tom Ronan *Packhorse and Pearling Boat* 213: On the trip down I tried to cobber up with the old fellow.

cobbera (cobra) Skull, head: *obs.* [Ab.]
1793 J. Hunter *An Historical Journal* ed. J. Bach (1968) 271: *Caberra,* The head.
1844 Louisa Meredith *Notes and Sketches of New South Wales* 98: 'Good way up cobbra' means 'head high up'.
1881 A. C. Grant *Bush-life in Queensland* i 31: The black fellow who lives in the bush bestows but small attention on his 'cobra', as

the head is usually called in the pigeon-English which they employ.

1899 George Boxall *The Story of Australian Bushrangers* 243: Gilbert dismounted, turned over Parry's body, and remarked coolly, 'He got it in the cobbera. It's all over with him.'

cobbler 1 The sheep left to the last in shearing, as the roughest to shear [f. pun on *cobbler's last*, ? and 'cobbled' appearance of the fleece]

1870 Rolf Boldrewood 'Shearing in Riverina' *In Bad Company* (1901) 315: The 'cobbler' (or last sheep) was seized.

1910 C. E. W. Bean *On the Wool Track* 193: There is gradually left a bunch of animals with wrinkles stiffer than door mats. The stiffest, wrinkliest, is 'the cobbler', because he sticks to the last.

1961 George Farwell *Vanishing Australians* 96: Its name is The Cobbler – a term which, in sheep talk, means the sheep that is hardest to shear.

2 The cobbler-fish, *Gymnapistes marmoratus*, with long rays like a cobbler's strings

1832 G. F. Moore *Diary of ... an Early Settler in Western Australia* (1884) 136: There is another species, somewhat in the nature of an eel, with a sharp spine it can erect at pleasure; this is caught only in the fresh water, and is called a cobbler, a kind resembling it in salt water is named catfish.

1937 K. S. Prichard *Intimate Strangers* 154: When it was a cobbler, he called to the children to keep back until Prospero had hacked off the ugly brown head with its poisonous sting.

1983 *West Australian* (Perth) 19 Sep. 1: Cobblers forced the closure of Sorrento beach, north of Perth, yesterday.

cock it up Used of a woman offering herself sexually

1961 Xavier Herbert *Soldiers' Women* 202: 'He's waitin' out there, and lookin' that nervous that if you cocked it up to him he'd put his hat over it and run.'

1963 Don Crick *Martin Place* 164: 'If they cock it up, what do they expect?'

1975 Richard Beilby *The Brown Land Crying* 210: 'You thought you had something on me, didn't you? You thought I'd cock it up to you.'

cockatoo *n.* 1 A sentinel or lookout, usually acting for those engaged in some illegal activity [f. belief that a flock of cockatoos when feeding posted a sentry to warn of approaching danger]

1828 P. Cunningham *Two Years in New South Wales* (2nd edn) ii 288: It being a common trick [among convict work gangs] to station a sentinel on a commanding eminence to give the alarm, while all the others divert themselves, or go to sleep. Such are known here by the name of 'cockatoo-gangs', from following the example of that wary bird.

1859 Henry Kingsley *Recollections of Geoffry Hamlyn* ii 141: Many a merry laugh went ringing through the woodland solitudes, sending the watchman cockatoo aloft to alarm the flock.

1949 Lawson Glassop *Lucky Palmer* 2: Snedden, the 'cockatoo', a little rat-faced unshaven man with stooped shoulders, whose job was to watch for the police.

1981 *Sun-Herald* 1 Nov. 152: Funny thing about the crackdown on casinos. All the big known gambling houses in the City area are closed, but cockatoos are still operating outside most of them.

2 A small farmer, usually with some overtone of disparagement, because of the cockatoo's inferiority to the squatter or because of his ingrained habits of thrift [see quots 1853, 1867]

1853 William Howitt, *Land, Labour and Gold* (1855) i 320: We were also very near being led into a dilemma by a mischievous cockatoo settler. Most agricultural settlers are thus styled by the squatters, because, I suppose, they look upon them, with their enclosures, as plunderers and encroachers on their wild woods, settling down upon them, as the cockatoos do on the ripening corn.

1883 R. E. N. Twopeny *Town Life in Australia* 244: A 'cockatoo' is a selector who works his piece of land out in two or three years, and having done nothing to improve it, decamps to select in a new district.

1954 Miles Franklin *Cockatoos* 3: Both had fallen to the rating of cockatoos, or farmer-selectors, through inability to keep on the higher ledge of squattocracy.

3 A convict from Cockatoo Island: *obs.*

1870 J. L. Burke *The Adventures of Martin Cash* 123: He's the bravest man that could choose from Sydney men or Cockatoos*. *This name was applied to a body of desperate men, who were imprisoned on Cockatoo Island.

see **cocky**

cockatoo *v.* 1 To act as a sentinel
1954 L. H. Evers *Pattern of Conquest* 216: 'You'd better stay down and cockatoo for us today.'
2 To take to the life of a cockatoo
1875 Rolf Boldrewood *The Squatter's Dream* repr. as *Ups and Downs* (1878) 245: A farm! Fancy three hundred acres in Oxfordshire, with a score or two of bullocks, and twice as many black-faced Down sheep. Regular cockatooing.
3 To perch on a fence
1876 Rolf Boldrewood *A Colonial Reformer* (1890) 224: The correct thing, on first arriving at a drafting yard, is to 'cockatoo', or sit on the rails, high above the tossing horn billows, and discuss the never-ending subject of hoof and horn.
1894 Ethel Turner *Seven Little Australians* 194: But everybody else had gone to 'cockatoo' – to sit on the top rail of the inclosure and look down at the maddened creatures.

cockatoo fence (improvised from crude materials), **cockatoo gate** (see quot. 1934), **cockatoo's weather** (ensuring the longest working hours) [f. **cockatoo** *n.* 2]
1867 Charles de Boos *Fifty Years Ago* 101–2: She ... sheltered herself as well as she could under the rough logs of the cockatoo fence.
1899 Steele Rudd *On Our Selection* 15: A cockatoo-fence was round the barley, and wireposts ... round the grass-paddocks.
1934 Thomas Wood *Cobbers* 140: They [the cockies] work a few hundred acres apiece, and give their name to a gate made from two bits of stick and a length of barbed wire. A maddening structure. It falls down when you open it and will not stand up to be closed.
1933 Acland: *Cocatoos weather* Fine by day and rain at night; or, sometimes, fine all the week and wet on Sunday.

Cockeyed Bob Sudden squall in N.W. Australia
1894 *The Age* 20 Jan. 13: On the approach of an ordinary thunderstorm or 'Cock-eyed Bob' they [the natives of the north-west of W.A.] clear off to the highest ground about.
1921 E. L. Grant Watson *The Mainland* 218: Often the silent heat of midday was disturbed by fierce gusts of wind known locally as 'Cock-eyed-Bobs'. These swifts and currents of air, not more than a yard or two in width, rush roaring across the levels, carrying a cloud of red dust with them and whirling along broken boughs.
1936 W. Hatfield *Australia through the Windscreen* 219: Only a few luggers were in [Broome] for the long 'lay-up' during the season of the treacherous 'willy willies' or 'Cock-eye Bobs' that come roaring out of a calm sea in those north-western waters anytime from December till March.
1980 *Daily News* (Perth) 16 Jul. 2: A cock-eyed-bob hit the small community yesterday afternoon, smashing windows, ripping roofs apart and sending tree branches flying.

cockrag Loincloth worn by Aboriginals
1964 Tom Ronan *Packhorse and Pearling Boat* 46: Joe, clad in Malay style sarong, with a grey flannel shirt hanging down outside it ... at night put on the cockrag and joined the blacks in their corroboree.
1971 Keith Willey *Boss Drover* 144: 'Proper naked buggers – not even cockrag.'

cockroaches, the see **Cane Toads**

cocktail hour See quot.
1964 *Sydney Morning Herald* 25 Apr. 11: Shearers, avid readers of the women's papers, refer ironically to their beer and rum sessions after work as the cocktail hour.

cocky A cockatoo farmer, usually with an overtone of disparagement, from the sometimes wretched existence led by the cocky, from his reputation for exploiting hired help, from the contempt of the grazier or the stockman for those who scratch the earth [**cockatoo** *n.* 2]
1877 Rolf Boldrewood *A Colonial Reformer* (1890) 262: 'If it wasn't for these confounded cockies,' said Mr Windsor, 'that big flat would be a first-rate place to break 'em into.'
1900–10 O'Brien and Stephens: *Cockatoo* or cockie, which form is mostly used – has become fixed as an epithet for small farmers. Among bushmen a 'cockie' is synonymous with everything poor and mean. A cockie's clip, in shearing, is equivalent to shaving a sheep ... Though 'cockie' practically covers every settler under the status of squatter, it more especially applies to the small selectors who hold from forty up to one hundred and fifty acres of land ... On many cockies' farms poultry, milk, butter and eggs are either unknown or positive luxuries.

1936 William Hatfield *Australia through the Windscreen* 241: Up in the saddle a man conceives a lofty disdain for grubbing in the soil . . . What? Get down and drive a plough? Be a miserable cocky? – Not on your life!

1963 Frank Hardy *Legends from Benson's Valley* 15: He looked what he was: a taciturn recluse, the meanest of all the mean cockies in Bungaree.

1982 *Sydney Morning Herald* 3 Aug. 7: The image of the whingeing cocky, driving a Mercedes and worrying about missing his annual ski-trip . . . is likely to be replaced . . . as the drought is prolonged.

cane cocky, cow cocky, fruit cocky, spud cocky, tobacco cocky, wheat cocky (referring to main source of income)

1973 Harold Lewis *Crow on a Barbed Wire Fence* 79: 'Dreaming of bein' a cane cocky still, Bluey?'

1914 Henry Lawson 'A Reconnoitre with Benno' *Prose* i 833: Cobb and Co's coaches . . . ran from Mudgee to Wallerawang nearly as fast . . . as the miserable cow-cocky train . . . The district . . . grows nothing now save cows and rabbits, and breeds nothing save increasingly hateful and well-to-do cow-cockyism.

1941 Kylie Tennant *The Battlers* 351: 'Some of these fruit cockies down on the irrigation might come at it.'

1973 Frank Huelin *Keep Moving* 36: 'When we get among the spud cockies you can make a wagga from spud bags.'

1971 *Bulletin* 15 May 68: Australia's powerful tobacco cockies.

1941 Kylie Tennant *The Battlers* 7: 'My father was one of those half-starved wheat-cockies out from Temora.'

cockying Following the life of a cocky

1923 Jack Moses *Beyond the City Gates* 128: When you're cockyin' and battlin' and live on what you grow.

1942 Eve Langley *The Pea Pickers* 236: 'I'm cow-cockying now, Steve, and I don't get any days off.'

1947 Vance Palmer *Hail Tomorrow* 6: 'Cockying, eh? Kill a pumpkin every Saturday night to keep you and your family in food for next week.'

cocky, boss A person eminent among nonentities; someone enjoying the exercise of petty authority, usually with some element of assertiveness implied

1905 Joseph Furphy *Rigby's Romance*

(1946) 49: A grazing paddock, consisting of frontage land, purchased or stolen by a squatter in the good old times, and now rented by a local boss-cockie.

1918 *Kia Ora Coo-ee* 15 Nov. 18: If ever I'm on my uppers in civvy life, I'll easy be able to hold down a job as boss cocky of a restaurant – one of those three-courses-for-a-tanner shows.

1920 Frank A. Russell *The Ashes of Achievement* 256: 'That's the boss cocky of all musical critics, isn't it? Hasn't he written reams exposing the ignorance of the whole profession?'

1945 Tom Ronan *Strangers on the Ophir* 138: 'The mob was with Nolan tonight. Why? Because I've been Boss Cocky too long.'

1973 Max Harris *The Angry Eye* 131: Bob Hawke, the boss cocky of the ACTU, is a colourful force in the Australian social scene.

cocky on the biscuit tin, like the See quot. 1981

1981 *National Times* 1 Feb. 14: 'Left out like the cocky on the biscuit tin' . . . dates from the precellophane days when Arnott's biscuits were sold from a tin embellished with a parrot emblem. The cocky was on it and not in it; so the phrase describes a loser or someone left out.

1982 *Sydney Morning Herald* 24 Dec. 19: The expression *like the cocky on the biscuit tin*, applied to the non-participant, to someone in a merely decorative or even impotent role, may have been current for as long as the advertisement for Arnott's biscuits.

1983 *Australian* 14 Oct. 9: Russ Hinze recently said of Liberal MP Rosemary Kyburz that she was about as effective as a cockie in a biscuit tin.

Cocky Corner The National Country Party representation in the Federal parliament

1973 Alan Fitzgerald *Old Fitz's Unparliamentary Handbook* [30]: It was a change to listen to the quiet presentation of the honourable member for Berowra (Mr Edwards) which contrasted with the continual cacophony of cackling and caterwauling we have heard from the cockies' corner in recent weeks.

1984 Maximilian Walsh *Sydney Morning Herald* 17 Apr. 9: The approach of Messrs Page, Fadden and McEwen still guides the present occupants of Cocky Corner in the House of Representatives.

cocky's friend Fencing wire
1930 K. S. Prichard *Haxby's Circus* 239–40: Dan and the boys with hammer, nails and fencing wire, 'the cockie's friend', mended seats and fixed up stakes.

cocky's gate See quot. 1935
1935 R. B. Plowman *The Boundary Rider* 196: Some of these were what is known as 'cockies'' gates – the curse of all travellers. Instead of a pair of wooden gates swung on hinges, these gates consist of several wires and a piece of wood. At one end the wires are fixed to a gate-post. At the other they are attached to an upright stick at intervals to correspond with those on the gate-post at the opposite end. In between are usually two sticks or droppers to keep the wires apart. The end stick, when the gate is closed, rests on the ground with its end inside a loop of wire attached to the second gate-post. Another such loop holds the top of the stick.
see **cockatoo gate**

cocky's joy Golden syrup [see quot. 1910]
1910 C. E. W. Bean *On the Wool Track* 64: Cocky's joy is golden syrup in 2 lb tins, costing sevenpence – four times as cheap as jam and six times as portable.
1952 *Sydney Morning Herald* 12 Dec. 1: A customer asked for a tin of golden syrup. 'You know, Cocky's Joy.'
1965 Leslie Haylen *Big Red* 49: Cocky's joy or golden syrup was good on home-made bread smoking hot from the camp oven.

coconut black See quot. 1983
1983 *Sydney Morning Herald* 14 Feb. 7: One word used in the north-west [of N.S.W.] is 'coconut blacks', Aborigines who, according to the radical blacks, are 'dark on the outside and white inside'.

coit see **quoit**

cold as a polar bear's behind see **polar**

cold as mother-in-law's breath see **mother-in-law's**

cold gold A can of beer [f. 'Shake hands with a cold gold', the advertising slogan for Tooth's KB Lager from 1974]
1982 *Sun-Herald* 5 Dec. 87: Typical was one mother's reaction as 'cold gold' in hand,

she fiercely instructed her freckle-faced little monster to 'keep jumping up and down in front, so that nanna will see you on the telly'.
1985 *Bulletin* 14 May 32: They'd empty the joint quick as the first cold gold at the butcher's picnic.

coldie A can or bottle of cold beer
1957 Nino Culotta *They're a Weird Mob* 126: 'Coupla coldies in the fridge', he said.
1981 *Sunday Mail* (Brisbane) 15 Feb. 18: There's nothing he would like more than to join his mate Lenny and share a few coldies in the dressing room later.

collar and cuffs As for **cuffs and collars**
1901 Miles Franklin *My Brilliant Career* 28: The teacher, better known as old Harris, 'stood up' to the inspector. The latter was a precise, collar-and-cuffs sort of little man.

collar, soft An easy job: *obs.*
1903 Joseph Furphy *Such is Life* (1944) 225: 'Soft collar we got here – ain't it?'

collect To be hit by, collide with, 'cop'
1945 Roy Rene *Mo's Memoirs* 51: I can remember someone aiming half a brick at him. It just missed. You were liable to collect anything in those times.
1965 William Dick *A Bunch of Ratbags* 268: 'Yuh rotten mug,' screamed Ritchie at the driver of an oncoming car who hadn't dipped his lights and practically collected us.
1984 *Age* (Melbourne) 25 Apr. 19: Quinlan said he had marked on Fitzroy's half-forward line, dummied around the player on the mark, had a bounce and was kicking the ball with his left foot when he was 'collected' . . . 'I didn't see him. He made contact with the right side of my body and I was knocked to the ground. It was a solid bump,' Quinlan said.

Collins St grazier, farmer The Victorian equivalent of a **Pitt St farmer** q.v.
1971 Barbara Vernon *A Big Day at Bellbird* 114: 'Unfortunate farmers like Atkins forced off their land so that Collins Street graziers can take over!'
1974 *Australian* 16 Jan. 10: Pitt and Collins Streets farmers are costing Australia between $10 and $15 million a year in lost tax, according to the Bureau of Agricultural Economics. What a surprise.

1983 Georgia Savage *Slate & Me and Blanche McBride* 156: The plane belonged to a Collins Street farmer who used a place in the hills as a tax dodge.

Collins, Tom   See quots
1895 Cornelius Crowe *The Australian Slang Dictionary* 86: *Tom Collins*, a fellow about town whom many sought to kill for touching them on 'sore points'; he was said to frequent the hotels, he always managed to vanish before his destroyer, as he was imaginary.
1903 [Joseph Furphy] *Such is Life Being Certain Extracts from the Diary of Tom Collins* [book title]
1951 R. G. Howarth *Southerly* 72: The pseudonym 'Tom Collins', which Furphy adopted as a contributor in the nineties to the Sydney *Bulletin* derives from a mythical bush character who was reputed to start all the idle rumours and tara-diddles heard in the Riverina country.

colonial boy, a wild   The bushranger of the ballad 'The Wild Colonial Boy' (*Old Bush Songs* ed. Stewart and Keesing (1957) 39); anyone sharing the same characteristics.
1958 Russel Ward *The Australian Legend* 153: To the pastoral workers, to the free-selectors, to lower-class people in general, and usually to themselves, they [the bushrangers] appeared as 'wild colonial boys', Australians *par excellence*.
1959 A. W. Upfield *Bony and the Mouse* 108: 'A wild colonial boy, no woman was ever going to tame him. So he said a million times.'

colonial experiencer, colonial experience man   A young Englishman of good connections sent out to gain 'colonial experience', viewed with some cynicism by native Australians because he is an amateur in his work, and not really of their world
1876 Rolf Boldrewood *A Colonial Reformer* (1890) 95: 'You've really hired yourself to drive travelling sheep! Not but it's a sensible enough thing to do, still you're the first 'colonial experience' young fellow that it ever occurred to.'
1886 P. Clarke *The New Chum in Australia* 295: I remember on one occasion a planter put a new 'colonial experience'* man on to 'boss' a gang of black ladies. *Colonial experience is equivalent to apprenticeship of the new chum.
1903 Joseph Furphy *Such is Life* (1944)

347: The well-educated, well-nurtured and, above all, well-born, colonial experiencer, fresh from the English rectory.
1938 Francis Ratcliffe *Flying Fox and Drifting Sand* 122: 'When I was in Bundaberg forty years ago there was a "colonial experience" named Thompson.

colonial goose   See quots
1898 Morris 94: Colonial Goose, *n.* a boned leg of mutton stuffed with sage and onions.
1953 *Sydney Morning Herald* 20 Jun. 7: Colonial Goose is another truly Australian national dish. It is boned leg of mutton stuffed with sage, onions and breadcrumbs, and baked.

colonial oath, my   Emphatic affirmation or agreement [euphemism for 'My bloody oath']
1870 Marcus Clarke *His Natural Life* ed. S. Murray-Smith (1970) 413: 'There ain't a dodge going that he ain't fly to.' 'My colonial oath!' says Tom.
1882 Rolf Boldrewood *Robbery Under Arms* (World's Classics 1949) 381: 'My colonial oath, Dick, you're quite the gentleman.'
1893 Henry Lawson *Prose* i 78: 'His Colonial Oath' [story title]

colour, the   sc. of gold or opal: the indication of success to the miner
1859 W. Kelly *Life in Victoria* i 222: They had not, to use a current phrase, 'raised the colour'.
1882 A. J. Boyd *Old Colonials* 130: He could manage to get 'the colour', *i.e.*, small grains of gold, almost anywhere he tried, but only very rarely did he get anything approaching payable gold.
1944 Brian James *First Furrow* 44: The last shaft he'd sunk . . . A rank duffer – not a colour in it.
1962 Dymphna Cusack *Picnic Races* 76: She considered likely-looking rocks that showed nothing she had learnt to recognize as 'colour'; not even a streak of pyrites that would give her a momentary thrill.

combo   A white man co-habiting with an Aboriginal woman: N.T. and W.A.
1896 W. H. Willshire *The Land of the Dawning* 72: The *Sydney Bulletin* holds the proud sway over all Australian print productions. It not only reaches the combos and stockmen of Central Australia, but it reaches

lepers on isolated islands, lighthouse keepers that are difficult to approach.

1926 K. S. Prichard *Working Bullocks* 47: 'Combo, I call him, gin shepherder . . . combo's what they call a man tracks round with a gin in the nor'-west.'

1958 Gavin Casey *Snowball* 51: 'You know what combo means?' 'Joker that lives with black-gins, ain't it?'

1971 Keith Willey *Boss Drover* 46: The trouble was that the travelling combo was always on the lookout to snaffle somebody else's lubra.

come at 1 To take on, agree to, attempt (against obstacles)

1919 W. H. Downing *Digger Dialects* 17: *Come at* (vb.) Undertake.

1941 Kylie Tennant *The Battlers* (1965) 346: The Apostle, having failed in his tentative efforts to sell the truck, was persuaded to drive it to a bigger town and find a better market. 'Some of those fruit cockies down on the irrigation might come at it,' Thirty-Bob advised. 'You leave it to me.'

1957 D'Arcy Niland *Call Me When the Cross Turns Over* 92: 'No, Barbie, he wouldn't come at it. I know him.'

1965 Colin Johnson *Wild Cat Falling* 108: 'I said I'd never come at that again. Not after last time.'

2 To stomach, bear, tolerate

1962 Jock Marshall and Russell Drysdale *Journey Among Men* 169: 'My blackfellas eat it . . . I just couldn't come at it, thanks all the same.'

1978 Margaret Tucker *If Everyone Cared* 38: Although I have not eaten these wriggling delicacies [witchetty grubs] since I was a child, I can say there is nothing to compare with them for taste. However, I could not come at it now.

1981 Patrick White *Flaws in the Glass* 67: It has always surprised me that Joyce with her nice wit could have come at any of that.

3 To 'try on', presume

1961 Nene Gare *The Fringe Dwellers* 176: 'What's she comin at, sendin a baby off ta some mission?'

1969 D'Arcy Niland *Dead Men Running* 92: 'He wants to give me fourpence each for them . . . What's he coming at?'

1981 A. B. Facey *A Fortunate Life* 286: This made me see red. I said, 'What in the hell are you coming at? Are you trying to get cheap labour?'

come down Flow in flood (of a river) [N.Z. 1863 OED]

1868 C. Wade Brown *Overlanding in Australia* 7: Whole plains are inundated with water almost instantaneously by the 'coming down' of the Darling.

1911 C. E. W. Bean *The 'Dreadnought' of the Darling* 22: The skipper knew the river was coming down on him, and he had been taking in his cargo the day before for all he was worth.

1969 Osmar White *Under the Iron Rainbow* 135: 'A big river, the Drysdale. Six hundred yards wide in the Wet.' 'Must be a ripper when it comes down.'

come down in the last shower, I didn't see **shower**

come good To turn out well (in a reversal of form) [cf. 'come to good', *come v.* 45g OED]

1952 T. A. G. Hungerford *The Ridge and the River* 50: If Wilder came good, it would be off his own bat – nothing that anyone else could say or do would make any difference.

1967 Kylie Tennant *Tell Morning This* 13: 'You're going to be all right, love. Don't you worry. From now on things are going to come good.'

1973 Harold Lewis *Crow on a Barbed Wire Fence* 72: 'He works for himself and one day his farm will come good, as they say out here.'

come in on the grouter see **grouter**

come it See quot. 1812

1812 Vaux 233: *Come it*: to divulge a secret; to tell anything of one party to another; they say of a thief who has turned evidence against his accomplices, that he is *coming* all he knows, or that he *comes it as strong as a horse*.

1882 Rolf Boldrewood *Robbery Under Arms* (World's Classics 1949) 171: 'The knockabouts and those other three chaps won't come it on us for their own sakes.'

1893 James Demarr *Adventures In Australia* 175: After telling him the whole story he replied, that someone had been 'coming it on me' (informing of me).

see **guts, come one's**

come the raw prawn see **prawn**

come to light with To produce, as though from resources [N.Z. 1917 OED]
1956 Tom Ronan *Moleskin Midas* 260: 'He says if you don't come to light with a few quid soon he's goin' to summons you.'

comic cuts, comics Guts [rhyming slang]
1951 Eric Lambert *The Twenty Thousand Thieves* 235: 'I want two quid in the guts! Gentlemen, I require two fiddleys in the old comic cuts!'
1963 Frank Hardy *Legends from Benson's Valley* 26: 'What time would it be?' Arty asked. 'Be nearly midday – according to my comic cuts.'

commando, cut-lunch see **cut-lunch**

compo Worker's compensation: payment for time lost from an injury at work, or for a permanent disability so caused [abbr.]
1941 Kylie Tennant *The Battlers* 373: 'They've got nice rest-rooms for them who faints, and if you do slice your hand, they put you on compo ... Compensation money while it heals.'
1969 William Dick *Naked Prodigal* 130: Brian had worked at the brick works once and had gotten burnt and was off on compo for a six week spell.
1974 *Australian* 26 Sep. 4: Compo plan changes will cost millions.

confetti, cowyard, farmyard, Flemington See quot. 1941
1941 Baker 22: *Cowyard confetti* as for 'bullsh'. Ibid. 31: *Flemington confetti*: Rubbish, piffle, 'bullsh'. [from the Flemington stockyards]
1951 Dal Stivens *Jimmy Brockett* 230: You could pull the wool over his eyes if you talked enough Flemington confetti about the woes of the working class.
1973 *Sun-Herald* 30 Dec. 35: Lots of farmyard confetti has been spoken and written about this young man's selection.
1981 *Age* (Melbourne) 4 Aug. 16: 'Cowyard confetti' my long deceased great-uncle would have called it when in polite company.

connie A tram conductor or conductress, esp. in Melbourne
1943 Baker 21: *Connie* A tram conductor (Melbourne slang).
1978 *Australian* 1 Sep. 1: The entire tramways network in Melbourne could come

to a halt by the weekend because a conductress – or 'connie' – refuses to join the union.

Connolly, the luck of Eric A noted punter (d. 1944) and a byword for luck in betting
[**1949** Lawson Glassop *Lucky Palmer* 149: 'They're hard to pitch all right ... Eric Connolly reckons he's known only one certainty in his life and that got beaten.']
1958 Frank Hardy *The Four-legged Lottery* 134: Jim Roberts announced his amazing win of approaching two hundred pounds ... and Tom Roberts said: 'Well, I'll be damned. We've got an Eric Connolly in the house!'
1963 Frank Hardy *Legends from Benson's Valley* 73: 'They've had the luck of Eric Connolly all night,' Darky said.

contract A difficult assignment
1953 T. A. G. Hungerford *Riverslake* 156: God, what a contract –... Kerry's not going to appreciate being told what to do.
1954 Tom Ronan *Vision Splendid* 157: 'It would be a contract to put bullocks up that hill with the morning freshness on them. They'd never face it to-night.'
1957 Vance Palmer *Seedtime* 174: 'Great woman, your sister,' said Donovan emphatically. 'Not many girls her age would have taken on a contract like that.'

cooee, within In easy reach of; (negatively) nowhere near [f. *cooee* as an Aboriginal call to someone at a distance]
1876 A. J. Boyd *Old Colonials* (1882) 284: 'When you are starved, and are not within cooey of a meat-safe or a bread-bin.'
1887 *All the Year Round* 30 Jul. 67: A common mode of expression is to be 'within cooey' of a place. Originally, no doubt, this meant to be within the distance at which the well known 'cooey', or bush cry, could be heard; now it simply means within easy reach of a place.
1928 Arthur Wright *A Good Recovery* 63: Within cooee of the house, covering a patch of cleared country, stood the shearing shed.
1950 W. M. Hughes *Policies and Potentates* 43: Darling Harbour – the goods depot within cooee of the present Central Station.
1984 *Australian* 6 Jan. 1: Only a romantic 19th century Irish stone farmhouse within cooee of wild surf could qualify as the perfect honeymoon hideaway for the leader of the

Federal opposition, Andrew Peacock, and his wife Margaret.

Coolgardie   A Coolgardie safe: see quot. [f. placename in W.A.]

1945 Elizabeth George *Two at Daly Waters* 32: To keep food cool we had a home-made Coolgardie – a frame covered with hessian, and with long strips of flannel hanging over the sides and resting in water to syphon and keep the hessian wet and cool.

1973 Jack Hibberd *A Stretch of the Imagination* 8: 'Relax, pal, while I repair to the Coolgardie and knock up a snack.'

cop   A noun from the verb *cop*, meaning to be on the receiving end of something, and rarely encountered without a qualifying adjective e.g. 'a good cop' could be a piece of good fortune or a satisfactory job, 'a sure cop' would be a betting certainty

1898 A. B. Paterson 'A Disqualified Jockey's Story' *Singer of the Bush* (1983) 300: I know three certain winners at the Park– / Three certain cops as no one knows but me.

1915 C. J. Dennis *The Songs of a Sentimental Bloke* 67: An' then I tells 'er 'ow I got a job, / A storeman down at Jones' printin' joint, / A decent sorter cop at fifty bob.

1963 Hal Porter *The Watcher on the Cast-Iron Balcony* 99: The political fancy-men . . . the confidence men on a soft cop.

cop it sweet   To accept a penalty without complaint

1965 Jack Dyer *Captain Blood* 115: The committee of the club copped it sweet, a sure sign that the old fire was gone.

1979 *Herald* (Melbourne) 17 May 48: Jockey Malcolm Johnston said he wasn't bitter over the month suspension AJC stewards imposed on him . . . 'It's just one of those things and you have to cop it sweet,' Johnston said.

1988 *Canberra Times* 19 Feb. 20: Caddies at the Masters at Huntingdale yesterday copped it sweet – and wore their issued plus-twos. Twenty-four hours earlier they were close to revolt.

cop, silent   see **silent cop**

Cop this, young 'Arry   A catch-phrase of Roy Rene ('Mo') in the McCackie Mansions sketches, before giving Harry a clip under the ear. The original words were 'Young Harry,

cop this!' The expression could now be used jocularly by someone passing a cup of tea.

1962 John O'Grady *Cop This Lot* 99: 'Cop that, young Harry,' Dennis said.

1976 *Australian* 15 Jan. 2: The script [for the Roy Rene revival] apparently is incomplete. Hence Spears' cheeky inscription on hand-bills advertising the Adelaide production: 'Cop this young Harry'.

1981 *National Times* 4 Jan. 29: It's vital for the future of quality TV to find out what it was about Bridge [*Water Under the Bridge*] that turns viewers off. Well, cop this, young 'Arry: *they never turned on.*

coppertail   The opposite to the **silvertail** q.v.

1890 A. J. Vogan *The Black Police* 116: The genus termed in Australian parlance 'silver-tailed', in distinction to the 'coppertailed' democratic classes.

1905 Randolph Bedford *The Snare of Strength* 317: Charley Byers, being merely a clerk, danced at the Mechanics' Institute with the Coppertails.

1941 Baker 20: *Coppertail* A member of the proletariat, one of the hoi polloi.

cordie   A Duntroon cadet: see quot. 1984

1980 Christopher Lee *Bush Week* 2: Cordies were very regimental, and one day we were told they would make up the cream of Australia's new army. They would always open doors for women.

1984 *Age* (Melbourne) 12 Apr. 11: Cadets are nicknamed 'cordies' around Canberra because they have to rely on corduroy for casual wear, jeans being outlawed as unbecoming to an officer.

corduroy *n. v. a.*   To bed a road with logs to make it passable in wet weather; a road so constructed: *obsolescent* [f. the ribs in the fabric U.S. 1882 OED]

1860 Mrs A. McPherson *My Experiences in Australia* 292: The well-known though somewhat apocryphal tale of a traveller on a Canadian Corderoy road, whose right of treasure trove in a hat which he observed moving about on the surface of a bog by the roadside, was disputed by its submerged wearer.

1889 J. I. Hunt *Hunt's Book of Bonanzas* 71: The course of true love began to partake of the nature of a 'corduroy' road in the wet season.

1911 E. S. Sorenson *Life in the Australian Backblocks* 183: One teamster I remember 'corduroyed' a bog on the Tatham Road with smothered bullocks.

1938 Eric Lowe *Salute to Freedom* 359: Robin slowed the car down to take the corduroy crossing of Beni creek.

1968 L. Braden *Bullockies* 122: In those days we used to corduroy the roads (lay logs across the soggy spots) and sometimes the spars would wear through in places.

corn, on the In prison [f. the hominy diet]

1949 Lawson Glassop *Lucky Palmer* 76: 'We look like doing three months on the corn.' 'The corn?' 'Yeah. The prison porridge.'

Corner, the (the Corner Country) The area at the junction of the borders of N.S.W., Queensland and S. A.

1928 Arthur Upfield *The House of Cain* 84: 'It will be all of a fortnight before we strike "The Corner" of N.S.W.'

1932 William Hatfield *Ginger Murdoch* 1: Birdsville, Bedourie, and Betoota . . . form a rough triangle and The Corner proper, and its border, unlike the arbitrary State divisions, is flexible and undefined, so that folk as far away as Goyder's Lagoon down in South Australia and even at Innamincka on Cooper's Creek may claim without dispute to belong to The Corner.

1981 *Sydney Morning Herald* 5 Sep. 12: Today is Tibooburra's day, and best wishes to it from all of us. The faraway little capital of The Corner country, 425 km west of Bourke and near the junction of the NSW, South Australian and Queensland borders, is celebrating its centenary.

cornflakes packet see **where did you get your licence?**

Cornstalk 1 A native-born Australian youth (as distinct from an emigrant) especially if tall and slender: *obs.*

1827 P. Cunningham *Two Years in New South Wales* ii 116: English and Colonial born, the latter bearing also the name of *corn stalks* (Indian corn), from the way in which they shoot up.

1834 George Bennett *Wanderings in New South Wales* i 341: The Australian ladies may compete for personal beauty and elegance with any European, although satirized as 'corn-stalks' from the slenderness of their forms.

1852 G. C. Mundy *Our Antipodes* (2nd edn) i 45: Cornstalk is the national nickname of the Australian white man.

2 Someone born in N.S.W., as distinct from the other states: *obsolescent*

1885 *The Australasian Printers' Keepsake* 162: A European type, working in Sydney, was grievously galled by the 'blow' of the Cornstalks.

1887 *All the Year Round* 30 Jul. 67: A native of New South Wales is known as a 'cornstalk', because the men generally grow tall and thin.

1957 Sydney Hart *Pommie Migrant* 51: 'Never say that to anyone in New South Wales, or you'll be laid out as flat as a pancake!' he warned me . . . Couldn't the Cornstalks take a joke?

correct weight Announcement after a race that placings are confirmed and bets can be paid (as jockeys and placegetters have weighed in at the correct weight)

1913 Ambrose Pratt *Wolaroi's Cup* 120: I . . . rode jauntily into the enclosure, but I was not really happy until I heard the steward say the magic words, 'Correct weight'.

1983 *Newcastle Herald* 1 Apr. 1: Mr Haigh told Mr Waterhouse that correct weight had been declared and the placing could not be changed.

1990 *Sun-Herald* 1 Apr. 56: It took until Thursday for the actual declaration of correct weight but everybody knew the result [of the Federal election] from the start of the week.

corroboree A gathering or celebration: *jocular* [f. *corroboree* as Aboriginal dance]

1859 W. Kelly *Life in Victoria* ii 62: I derived a wicked enjoyment in the corrobborie [a colonial ball] as far as I was personally concerned.

1867 J. R. Houlding *Australian Capers* 134: A policeman danced a 'corroboree' in the roadway with his arms working.

1885 *The Australasian Printers' Keepsake* 98: There was a corroboree next day of bosses, clickers, and readers.

1926 J. Vance Marshall *Timely Tips for New Australians: Corroboree* An aboriginal dance. Commonly used in the colloquial to describe a noise or uproar.

1980 Thomas Keneally *The Cut-Rate Kingdom* 58: Each of them must have, during one or other of the Sunday afternoon corroborees at the Gaiety Theatre, seen herself as potentially John Mulhall's wife.

cossie A swimming costume [abbr.]

1926 J. Vance Marshall *Timely Tips for New Australians: Cossie* A sea-side term applied to a swimming costume.

1959 Dorothy Hewett *Bobbin Up* 30: He imagined them lying on the dark sand behind the rocks at Bondi, undoing the straps of her cozzie, his hands full of her breasts.

1975 Les Ryan *The Shearers* 76: 'Oh!' she hesitated. 'Haven't got a cossie.'

see **bathers**

cot case Someone incapacitated, esp. by drink: *jocular* [f. hospital term for patient needing to be confined to bed]

1932 Leonard Mann *Flesh in Armour* 219: Sergeant Burke was boozing and often no better than a cot case.

1958 Vince Kelly *The Greedy Ones* 213: 'You're tougher than I thought ... I expected you to be a cot-case for quite a few hours.'

1961 Barry Humphries *A Nice Night's Entertainment* (1981) 54: To tell you the truth, Beryl was beginning to look very peaky and I thought, if this goes on much longer she'll be a cot-case.

couldn't blow the froth off a glass of beer, find a grand piano in a one-roomed house, knock the dags off a sick canary, knock the skin off a rice pudding, pick a seat at the pictures, tell the time if the town hall clock fell on top of him, train a choko vine over a country dunny Various expressions for incompetence

1981 *Australian* 24 Oct. 17: 'They couldn't,' Mr Wran said, referring to both Mr Dowd and Country Party Leader, Mr Leon Punch, 'blow the froth off a glass of beer.'

1981 *National Times* 25 Jan. 23: It sums up the inefficiency of the local copper at the time: 'He couldn't find a grand piano in a one-roomed house.'

1983 *Newcastle Herald* 28 Apr. 2: Mr Tickener told a meeting of graziers and shearers ... that graziers knew nothing about shearing and were not qualified to speak on the subject. 'Ninety per cent of cockies couldn't knock the dags off a sick canary,' he told the meeting.

1984 *Sunday Independent* (Perth) 12 Aug. 48: The pilot, if you don't mind, is the geriatric Burgess Meredith who couldn't knock the skin off a rice puddin'.

1984 *Australian* 20 Aug. 18: Sydney rugby union coach Peter Fenton said yesterday the national selectors 'couldn't pick a seat at the pictures' after the shock omission of backrower Peter Lucas.

1962 Gavin Casey *Amid the Plenty* 17: 'You wouldn't know what the time was if the Town Hall clock fell on you.'

1981 *National Times* 29 Mar. 2: 'He [a football coach] couldn't train a choko vine over a country dunny.'

see also **homing pigeons, kick in a stampede, paper bag, revolving door**

country dunny see **dunny**

country dunny, couldn't train a choko vine over a see **couldn't**

Country, the Lucky see **Lucky**

country, the sunburnt see **sunburnt**

cove This is a term from English thieves' slang (OED 1567); the two senses of it derived in Australia are given by Vaux in 1812: 'the master of a house or shop, is called *the Cove*; on other occasions, when joined to particular words, as *a cross-cove, a flash-cove, a leary cove* &c., it simply implies a man of these several descriptions.'

1 The proprietor, station-manager, man in charge

1845 Thomas McCombie *Arabin* 47: He asked if it was far to the home-station of his master. 'Not very far,' replied the shepherd. 'Will the gentlemen have retired?' inquired Dr Arabin. 'Let me see – will the cove have gone to bed, Jim?'

1882 Rolf Boldrewood *Robbery Under Arms* (World's Classics 1949) 114–15: 'To put up a yard at the back of a man's run, and muster his cattle for him! ... But suppose the cove or his men come across it?'

see **bloke**[1]

2 A chap, fellow; at first as in thieves' slang, but later without any of the associations of this fraternity

1849 Alexander Harris *The Emigrant Family* (1967) 66: 'I thought it was some swell cove.'

1915 C. J. Dennis *The Songs of a Sentimental Bloke* 34: A cove 'as got to think some time in life / An' get some decent tart, ere it's too late.

1938 *Smith's Weekly* 19 Nov. 10: A cove I know in Wagga wants a truck driver.

1965 Patrick White *Four Plays* 105: 'Any

of you know if a cove name of Boyle lives anywhere around? Ernie Boyle.'

cow 1 Anything disagreeable or deserving vilification. The more intensive form is 'a fair cow' [? f. the English *cow* as an insult to a woman]

1864 *Thatcher's Colonial Minstrel* 14: Called each one of them [the bullocks] an old cow, / Whilst blows thick and fast he kept dealing.

1897 Hume Nisbet *The Swampers* 205: 'Police after him too . . . Me know them, the blooming cows.'

1902 Henry Lawson 'Lord Douglas' *Prose* i 497: 'I vote we kick the cow out of the town!' snarled One-eyed Bogan.

1914 *Bulletin* 1 Jul. 47: Then he jerked his head back at the weather outside. "S goin' to be cow of a day.'

1933 R. B. Plowman *The Man From Oodnadatta* 248: 'It's not so bad coming down the river . . . But it's a fair cow going up.'

1942 Gavin Casey *It's Harder for Girls* 13: The girls about the place were pretty uppish, and she must have had a cow of a time.

1964 George Johnston *My Brother Jack* 121: 'How's the job with the baker?' 'It's a fair cow,' he said.

2 An object of compassion, as in the phrase 'the poor cow'

1933 Norman Lindsay *Saturdee* 164: Peter was sure the poor cow had never had a sit with girls in all his life.

1945 *Coast to Coast 1944* 167: 'That poor cow's in a bad way.'

cow, hunt (chase) up a To find a dry patch in the bush, usually with a sense of sexual opportunity

1957 John O'Grady *They're a Weird Mob* 144: 'Gunna be a bastard tryin' to find a dry spot.' 'Hunt up a cow.'

1959 Gerard Hamilton *Summer Glare* 80: We delighted in following couples at night when they went 'chasing up a cow', as courting was commonly called, for couples mostly began their night's love-making by wandering around looking for a sleeping cow that they could disturb to claim the warm patch of earth where it lay.

cow, Malley's see **Malley's**

cowal A lake, or a swampy depression supporting vegetation [Ab.]

1882 Charles Lyne *The Industries of New South Wales* 213: The homestead . . . is not far from . . . the shores of a lake which in this part of the Colony is called, in the language of the aborigines, a 'cowall', or 'cowell'.

1901 Rolf Boldrewood *In Bad Company* 19: Wading girth-deep through the subsidiary watercourses – billabongs, cowalls and such.

1910 C. E. W. Bean *On the Wool Track* 251: If one got bogged in a creek or cowal (which is a small tree-grown, swampy depression often met in the red country).

1934 Jean Devanny *Out of Such Fires* 220: They [the horses] could be trusted not to move far from the little shade afforded by the cowal.

cowboy See quots

1933 Acland 371: *Cowboy* The boy who milks, etc. Not the romantic American horseman.

1961 Noni Braham *The Interloper* 46: Next to the natives, Margaret had discovered the cowboy was considered the lowest form of life on the station, and was nevertheless one of the most essential. He was supposed to milk the cows, separate the milk, empty 'Tumbling Tommy' (the garbage-tin), feed the chooks, fill the stove, and do all the little lowly chores everyone else scorned.

cowyard confetti see **confetti**

crab-hole A hole supposedly burrowed or inhabited by a land-crab: mainly Victorian

1848 Let. in G. Goodman *The Church in Victoria* (1892) 72: Full of crab-holes, which are exceedingly dangerous for the horses. These are holes varying in depth from one to three feet, and the smallest of them wide enough to admit the foot of a horse . . . These holes are formed by a small land-crab and then gradually enlarged by water draining into them. [Morris]

1903 Joseph Furphy *Such is Life* (1944) 16: Price and Cooper, being cooks, had kindled an unobtrusive fire in a crab-hole, where three billies were soon boiling.

1967 Len Beadell *Blast the Bush* 49: Having been there with the black-fellow and driven about the clearing, I knew it was free of crab holes or hidden ruts.

see **gilgie**

crabs, draw the To attract unwelcome attention, esp. enemy fire [? f. *crab* as abbr. of 'crab-louse', or *crab* to interfere (Vaux 1812)]

1932 Leonard Mann *Flesh in Armour* 260:

The Tommy captain lit a cigarette and I lit my pipe [in an air raid]. The young wench reckoned we would draw the crabs.

1959 Dorothy Hewett *Bobbin Up* 41: 'And we don't like 'em under age, draws the crabs.' [police]

1974 *Bulletin* 16 Mar. 17: When Prime Minister Whitlam last week told rural members of the Federal Parliamentary Labor Party that they should have expected the abolition of the superphosphate bounty because it was 'in the Coombs report', he really drew the crabs.

crack a fat see **fat**

crack hardy To put on a brave front in misfortune

1915 C. J. Dennis *The Songs of a Sentimental Bloke* 66: A fool 'oo tried / To just crack 'ardy, an' 'old gloom aside.

1935 R. B. Plowman *The Boundary Rider* 239–40: Old Bill was a great believer in 'cracking hardy'.

1946 K. S. Prichard *The Roaring Nineties* 147: Living from day to day in the heat and glare as if you were withering and drying up inside, but must crack hardy and joke about it to show your grit.

1980 *Sydney Morning Herald* 6 Oct. 7: Mr Fraser had been cracking hardy about the results of the first two polls ... which showed a similar but less dramatic trend.

crack it To succeed in some enterprise, esp. sexual [f. 'cracking a safe', 'cracking a code', etc.]

1941 Baker 23: *Crack it* To record success in an amorous affair.

1948 Sumner Locke Elliott *Rusty Bugles* in *Khaki, Bush and Bigotry* ed. Eunice Hanger (1968) 61: 'Hello, Darky ... so you cracked it again I hear.'

1963 Lawson Glassop *The Rats in New Guinea* 115: 'You wouldn't even crack it with a nymphomaniac.'

1973 Alexander Buzo *Rooted* 78: 'Keep on with your art, mate. You'll crack it one day, I'm sure of it.'

1982 *NT News* (Darwin) 12 Mar. 17: This pair have been round a while and never quite cracked it.

cracker 1 The tip of a stockwhip

1876 Rolf Boldrewood *A Colonial Reformer* (1891) 224: Pipes were lit, stockwhips greased and garnished with resplendent crackers, and all hands strolled in leisurely fashion towards the stockyard.

1905 Randolph Bedford *The Snare of Strength* 256: 'Ere's a cracker, Daven, for your whip; them spiders make the best crackers in the world.'

2 A worn out horse, sheep, bullock

1950 *Sydney Morning Herald* 21 Jul. 1: A puzzled reader asks 'What is a cracker?' He sends a report of a cattle sale which says ... 'stores from £7 to £10; crackers sold for less'. Well, this sort of cracker is a worn-out cow – bottoms in the cattle world.

1965 E. O. Schlunke *Stories of the Riverina* 63: 'Ever seen such a bunch of old crackers?' he said, laughing contemptuously [at the sheep]. 'Fit for nothing but the meat cannery.'

3 A brothel

1963 John Naish *That Men Should Fear* 143: My Aunt Helen worked in a cracker in Munro Street. Worked as a madam or a moll.

cracker, not worth a, haven't got a No evidence has been found for Baker's identification of a 'cracker' with a one pound note (adopted in the OED Suppl.). The word 'cracker' is used for a worn-out cow, and for an attachment to the end of a stockwhip, but neither of these is a likely explanation. The U.S. 'cracker' (a biscuit) would have been unfamiliar to Australia until after World War II. As 'cracker' is found only in negative expressions – cf. 'skerrick' and 'razoo' – it may not refer to anything positive i.e. there is never a report of anyone who *does* have a cracker or *is* worth a cracker. Not to have a cracker is to be completely out of funds, not to be worth a cracker is to be worth nothing at all.

Vaux records 'cracker' in 1812 as 'a small loaf, served to prisoners in jails, for their daily subsistence', but there is no other occurrence of the word in this sense in Australian English.

1934 W. S. Howard *You're Telling Me!* 300: 'What about money?' shade number two asked doubtfully. 'We haven't got a cracker.' [OED]

1942 Gavin Casey *It's Harder for Girls* 162: 'He's got guts, anyway,' said Sayers. 'I didn't think he was worth a cracker.'

1957 Judah Waten *Shares in Murder* 29: 'I've heard her husband didn't give her a cracker when he divorced her.'

1980 *Daily News* (Perth) 22 Dec. 40: 'The

pub safe had been knocked off the night before. That left us stranded in Wiluna without a cracker.'

cracker night The night of Empire Day (24 May) celebrated with a bonfire and fireworks; later transferred to Commonwealth Day and the Queen's Birthday, now the Saturday of the Queen's Birthday weekend
1953 Ruth Park *A Power of Roses* 184: 'Just twenty-seven years ago I met me missus on Cracker Night.'
1980 *Mercury* (Hobart) 3 Jun. 4: We don't usually run 'lost and founds' in this column, but a dog missing since 'cracker night' is an exception.

crash hot Outstanding; in the forefront; up to the minute [f. variant of *shit-hot*]
1956 Encountered in conversation.
1973 Alexander Buzo *Rooted* 86: 'You'll like it here, Gary's a good bloke and his Mum cooks a crash hot rissole.'

crash through or crash A principle advanced by E. G. Whitlam as Labor leader
1972 E. G. Whitlam TV interview with David Frost: 'When you are faced with an impasse you have got to crash through or you've got to crash' cit. Laurie Oakes *Whitlam PM* (1973), p. 122.
1983 Mr Justice Macken *Sydney Morning Herald* 6 Jul. 5: It is no small thing for a company as important as Comeng to decide unilaterally to make major variations en masse to the contract of employment of its workers and to hope by a policy of 'crash through or crash' to render due processes ineffective.

crawl To ingratiate oneself with those in authority: *derogatory*
1881 A. C. Grant *Bush-Life in Queensland* ii 45: He had crawled his way up in 'the foorce' to his present distinguished position from obscurity.
1908 Giles Seagram *Bushmen All* 31: He, being free from 'side' and from any suspicion of toadyism or 'crawling' was generally liked by the men.
1933 Frank Clune *Try Anything Once* 168: I was accused of 'crawling to the Pott's Pointers'.
1969 William Dick *Naked Prodigal* 247: 'I

didn't crawl to him . . . I wouldn't crawl to no bastard for nothing.'

crawler 1 A sheep, cow or other animal that is laggard, weak or docile: *obs.*
1853 *Letters from Victorian Pioneers* ed. T. F. Bride (1898) 218: On this run, out of 1,500 head of cattle, all had been driven off but about 30 'crawlers'. It was many weeks before they were re-mustered.
1868 C. Wade Brown *Overlanding in Australia* 2: Many [sheep] die, particularly such as are old, or weak, technically termed out here the 'crawlers'.
2 A shepherd, from the slowness of his activities, and from the contempt of those who worked on horseback: *obs.*
1853 S. Mossman and T. Banister *Australia Visited and Revisited* 64: As we approached him [the shepherd] at a walking pace, we could not but contemplate his peaceful occupation, so much in accordance with the stillness of the Australian wilderness . . . you find him a long-bearded, bronze-featured 'crawler', as he is termed in the colony.
1857 F. Cooper *Wild Adventures in Australia* 50: Fit only for shepherding – the one employment despised by all classes in a country where the strongest reproach was to be a 'crawler'.
3 A 'slowcoach', loafer, shirker; also unspecific term of contempt: *obs.*
1837–8 *Report from the Select Committee on Transportation* ii 75: The clever knaves among the convicts very seldom fell into such an unfortunate predicament as these refuse of the convicts get into on road-parties. The cant name for these among the prisoners themselves was 'the crawlers'. They were scarcely able to work, people whom no settlers wished to employ.
1849 Alexander Harris *The Emigrant Family* (1967) 32: 'You'll have the pick of a score every day; shepherds, tradesmen, and men that never were men yet; good men and crawlers.'
1924 Rann Daly *The Outpost* 80: 'They're to protect the crawlers who come here to make easy money.'
1931 Miles Franklin *Back to Bool Bool* 265: 'Flaming crawlers!' he commented . . . 'I don't know what to make of the young people to-day. They're born dead.'
4 Someone who toadies to the boss, or any superior
1892 William Lane *The Workingman's Paradise* 104: 'And you'd get more inclined

to humour the boss every time you had to try again [for a job].' 'Naturally. That's how they get at us. No man's a crawler who's sure of a job.'
1902 Henry Lawson 'Lord Douglas' *Prose* i 494: 'As for turning blackleg – well, I suppose I've got a bit of the crawler in my composition (most of us have), and a man never knows what might happen to his principles.'
1934 J. M. Harcourt *Upsurge* 165: The head of her department said that he had no complaint to find with her – though he had recanted after he had seen his master, the bloody crawler.
1953 *Caddie A Sydney Barmaid* 135: 'I'm sick of working amongst that mangy lot of crawlers. I'm satisfied they've got legs on their bellies.'
1973 Roland Robinson *The Drift of Things* 92: 'Don't try to get in good with the boss. He knows what "crawlers" are.'

cray Crayfish, usually regarded as a delicacy
1916 C. J. Dennis *The Moods of Ginger Mick* 46: 'An we'll 'ave a cray fer supper when I comes marchin' 'ome.'
1959 Dorothy Hewett *Bobbin Up* 13: 'Crays and a bottla beer. It's the drunks' special for Saturdee night.'
1972 David Williamson *The Removalists* 27: 'I can walk out of this station tonight, grab myself a cray and half a dozen tubes, get home, sit m'self down in front of the box and watch the wrestling.'

creamie 1 A cream-coloured horse
1887 *Tibb's Popular Songbook* 28: He likes all lively hacks, / He's very partial to the creamies, / And he'll mate up with the blacks.
1902 Henry Fletcher *The Waybacks in Town and at Home* 105: 'Der yer mind Jack Clark comin' ter our place er ridin' er bag o' bones he called a creamy?'
2 A quarter-caste Aboriginal girl; any girl of apparently mixed blood (see quot. 1887 above)
1937 Ernestine Hill *The Great Australian Loneliness* 33: The belles of the village and a few 'creamies', as the half-castes and *multum in parvo* are affectionately called.
1962 Criena Rohan *The Delinquents* 12–13: The other children called her the Creamy. She had come from Singapore with her mother early in '42.
1975 Xavier Herbert *Poor Fellow My*

Country 52: 'I'm using the term Black Velvet not simply to apply to full-blooded women, but any of obvious aboriginal strain, 'yeller girls', or 'creamy pieces', as they're called, half and quarter.'

Creek, the 1 The Albion Park Q. sand circuit, closed to gallopers 30 Dec. 1981
1956 *Sydney Morning Herald* 17 Jul. 52: Last week I visited Albion Park, known to racegoers as 'The Creek'.
1981 *Sunday Mail* (Brisbane) 15 Feb. 5: 'Close the Creek? Fair dinkum?' Old Tom Harper couldn't believe his ears . . . It took a minute or two to convince Tom the Albion Park racing will come to an end and the racecourse will be redeveloped as a trotting complex.
2 In N.T., Tennant Creek
1979 *NT News* (Darwin) 19 Sep. 3: Boring event at Creek [heading]

Creeker A horse able to perform well at Albion Park
1979 *Courier-Mail* (Brisbane) 21 Feb. 21: 'He looks a natural Creeker, but also goes well on the grass.'

cringe, the cultural The phrase invented by A. A. Phillips to describe the denigration by Australians of their own culture, and their attitude to subservience to the culture of overseas countries
1950 Arthur Phillips 'The Cultural Cringe' *Meanjin* 299: Above our writers – and other artists – looms the intimidating mass of Anglo-Saxon culture. Such a situation almost inevitably produces the characteristic Australian Cultural Cringe.
1971 *Australian* 14 Oct. 10: [editorial on the appointment of the Duke of Edinburgh as President of the Australian Conservation Foundation] The cause of Australian conservation deserves better than to be set back into the mould of the great Australian cultural cringe.
1984 *Sydney Morning Herald* 23 Mar. 20: Cultural cringe is alive and well in Melbourne.

cronk Out of order, unsound; dishonest, fraudulent; also 'run cronk' (run a dishonest race), 'go cronk' (go wrong, break down): *obs.* [f. *crank* one that is sick or ill OED 1567; G. *krank* sick, ill]
1889 Rolf Boldrewood *Nevermore* (1892) 271: 'From the look of him . . . I shouldn't be

surprised if there was something "cronk" about him, for all his gold-buying.'

1894 Henry Lawson *Letters* 57: Things went cronk shortly after my arrival in Sydney.

1934 F. E. Baume *Burnt Sugar* 58: 'It all sounds pretty cronk to me.'

1958 Jack Lindsay *Life Rarely Tells* 213: 'Not that I believe in doing anything cronk.'

crook 1 Ill, out of sorts, debilitated

1898 *Bulletin* 17 Dec. Red Page: *Krook* or *kronk* is bad.

1915 C. J. Dennis *The Songs of a Sentimental Bloke* 88: An' then, I sneaks to bed, an' feels dead crook.

1934 Thomas Wood *Cobbers* 19: 'Tell the Gov. I can't come today; I'm crook in the guts.'

1955 Patrick White *The Tree of Man* 185: 'Are the burns bad? We must dress them. Tell me,' she said, 'do they feel crook?'

1969 William Dick *Naked Prodigal* 22: 'He's been drivin' her mad since he's been off with his crook back.'

1984 Marian Eldridge *Walking the Dog* 10: 'Colin dipped out on school today. Reckons he's got a crook throat.'

2 Defective, disagreeable, unattractive

1915 Let. in Bill Gammage *The Broken Years* (1974) 44: Sand in your tucker, in your ears, nose, everywhere, and anywhere, it was real crook.

1983 Leo Schofield *Sydney Morning Herald* 29 Jan. 27: Unlike Dame Joan's dress, which looked better on tele than it did in real life, those horrible banks of ill-assorted and appallingly arranged blooms looked crook on the box but worse in the hall.

see **Tallarook**

crook, go To upbraid, abuse

1911 Louis Stone *Jonah* 190: 'Yer niver 'ad no cause ter go crook on me, but I ain't complainin',' cried Chook hoarsely.

1915 C. J. Dennis *The Songs of a Sentimental Bloke* 113: Goes crook on life, an' calls the world a cheat.

1944 Lawson Glassop *We Were the Rats* 207: 'Then I thinks she'll go crook on me for speakin', seein' that we ain't been introduced.'

1965 Patrick White *Four Plays* 150: 'Dad says Mr Masson is liable. He went real crook.'

crooked maginnis see **maginnis**

Crooked Mick see **Mick**

crooked Hostile, averse to

1870 J. R. Houlding *Rural and City Life* 3: 'Her is getting plaguey crooked herself.' 'Crooked! What are you talking about, Stubble? There isn't a better shaped girl in –' 'Stop, stop, Peggy! it was her temper I was talking about, not her limbs.'

1949 Lawson Glassop *Lucky Palmer* 87: He shuddered when he said 'working'. 'That work,' he said. 'I'm crooked on that.'

1959 Xavier Herbert *Seven Emus* 101: 'It's no good talking religion to Bronco. He's dead crooked on it.'

1980 *NT News* (Darwin) 23 Feb. 7: The thing he was really crooked about was the standard of dress of some of the gamblers – shirts open to the waist and so on.

croppy 1 An Irish convict (from the rebels of 1798, who had their hair cut short in sympathy with the French Revolution)

1800 *HRA* I ii 581: That he hath often been in company with Holt when drinking inflammatory and seditious Toasts – 'Success to the Croppies' and other improper Expressions were made use of by Holt, that he had asked the Witness if there was a rising of the Irish if he would not join them . . . that Holt then said 'You are an Irishman, Kennedy, and we will all go home in one ship together'.

2 A convict; a runaway convict; a bushranger

1809 *HRNSW* vii 216: It is high time that some fresh Governor should have arrived here before this as such doings was never known – pardons to the worst of characters, Croppeys, and thieves.

1848 H. W. Haygarth *Recollections of Bush Life in Australia* 9: Robbed of his horse, valise . . . by the well-known 'croppies' – 'Black Joe' or 'Irish Tom'.

Cross, the 1 The Southern Cross

1931 Miles Franklin *Back to Bool Bool* 43: The Cross was twinkling southwards.

1939 Kenneth Slessor *Five Bells* 15: Night and water / Pour to one rip of darkness, the Harbour floats / In air, the Cross hangs upside-down in water.

1968 Stuart Gore *Holy Smoke* 15: 'Look at the old Cross, shining away up there.'

2 King's Cross, Sydney

1946 Dal Stivens *The Courtship of Uncle Henry* 184: 'What a dump,' Jack said. 'The Cross will look good after this.'

1951 Dymphna Cusack and Florence James *Come In Spinner* 58: 'Us girls have got a flat together up at the Cross.'
1966 Elwyn Wallace *Sydney and the Bush* 138: People in Sydney . . . always say 'Down the 'Loo' or 'Up the Cross'.

Cross, when the ~ turns over When the Southern Cross has tilted from an eastern to a western orientation, indicating the end of a drover's watch (see *Southerly* 1975 33–7)
[**1881** A. C. Grant *Bush-Life in Queensland* i 217: 'Hadn't you better turn in?' suggests Sam. 'We've good three hours yet by the Southern Cross.']
1951 Ernestine Hill *The Territory* 425: 'Call me when the Cross turns over,' you will hear the drovers say, or 'when the Pointers are clear.'
1957 D'Arcy Niland *Call Me When the Cross Turns Over* 124: 'You know what the drovers say, Mrs Anderson – Call me when the Cross turns over, they say. The Cross turns over for everybody. It marks for some the end of a sleep, for some the beginning.'

crow 1 A woman who is old or ugly: *derogatory*
1925 H. H. Richardson *The Way Home* 84: Between ourselves it makes me feel a proper old crow.
1949 Lawson Glassop *Lucky Palmer* 60: She's no crow, he thought. A real good-looking filly, this one.
1965 Hal Porter *The Cats of Venice* 112: Surprised at the old Pommy crow's interruption he spares a glance.
1970 Jon Cleary *Helga's Web* 21: She would have been quite a looker. 'Why do they kill the good-looking ones? There are plenty of crows around.'
2 A prostitute [It. *cornacchia* means 'a loose woman', and there is a Fr. proverb of the seventeenth century comparing a whore to a crow]
1950 *Australian Police Journal* Apr. 111: *Crow* Prostitute.
1965 Eric Lambert *The Long White Night* 80: 'That big café down on the waterfront. The Universal. The crows hang round it there in droves.'
1979 *Herald* (Melbourne) 14 Apr. 9: 'There are some Broady [Broadmeadows, Vic.] girls out crowing (engaging in prostitution) in St Kilda now.'
1980 Bob Herbert *No Names . . . No Pack Drill* 77: 'What are you, anyway. A Kings

Cross crow. Every Yank in town's been rootin' you.'
see **chromo**

crow, draw the To come off worst in any allocation [f. the anecdote about sharing out the day's shooting, the bag containing a number of tablebirds and one crow, so that someone would 'draw the crow' in his share]
1944 Lawson Glassop *We Were the Rats* 113: 'That poor bloke drew the crow.' Ibid. 207: 'I reckon with sheilas I always draw the crow.'
1952 T. A. G. Hungerford *The Ridge and the River* 75: 'Oh, all right.' Sweet's tone was resigned. 'I always cop the bloody crow.'
1970 Richard Beilby *No Medals for Aphrodite* 169: 'I knew we'd drawn the crow as soon as I seen this place!'

Croweater A native of South Australia: *jocular, obsolescent*
1900–10 O'Brien and Stephens: *Croweater* An epithet applied to the natives or citizens of South Australia.
1903 Joseph Furphy *Such is Life* (1944) 123: The wire parted, and Pup and I were deck passengers, on route for the land of the Crow-eater.
1973 Frank Huelin *Keep Moving* 29: 'South Aus. is the worst State in th' country – bloody crow-eaters!'
1982 *NT News* (Darwin) 29 Nov. 7: Crow-eaters, we've long suspected, are a little different from normal folk.

crows, stone the Expression of surprise, regret, or disgust. Sometimes 'stiffen the crows', or 'stone the crows and stiffen the lizards', occurring most frequently in comic-strip Australian [listed by Partridge as Cockney]
1918 Harley Matthews *Saints and Soldiers* 116: 'Starve the crows,' howled Bluey in that agonised screech of his.
1930 L. W. Lower *Here's Luck* 189: 'Stone the crows!' exclaimed Stanley indignantly.
1942 Eve Langley *The Pea Pickers* 321: 'Stone the crows,' he said faintly. 'What is it?'
1981 *Sun-Herald* 19 Jul. 159: The top honours must go to lanky Bryan Brown, the dinkum Aussie digger. How refreshing it was not to see some sort of ocker caricature blast on to the screen, all stone-the-crows and struth and beaudy.

crows, where the ~ fly backwards to

keep the dust out of their eyes One of the attributes of **Woop Woop** q.v. or any similar locality

1899 W. T. Goodge *Hits! Skits! and Jingles!* 6: 'The Oozlum Bird'. It's a curious bird, the Oozlum, / And a bird that's mighty wise, / For it always flies tail-first to / Keep the dust out of its eyes!

1936 Ion L. Idriess *The Cattle King* 153: 'I couldn't see the township,' growled Bill, 'let alone a mob of cattle. No wonder they call this the place where the crows fly backwards to keep the dust out of their eyes.'

1971 Rena Briand *White Man in a Hole* 137: Posters covered the walls, and there was a sign proclaiming that, 'this isn't the Waldorf, therefore no complaints, please – even the crows fly backwards in these parts'.

cruel (the pitch) To spoil someone's chances [f. *queer the pitch* thieves' slang]

1915 C. J. Dennis *The Songs of a Sentimental Bloke* 16: But wot's the use, when 'Eaven's crool'd 'is pitch?

1922 Edward Dyson *The Grey Goose Comedy Company* 69: 'If I said anythink lars night, I'd only have cruelled everythink. We must think out a plan.'

1951 Dal Stivens *Jimmy Brockett* 142: Things were going well with Sadie and myself and I didn't want to cruel anything.

1971 David Ireland *The Unknown Industrial Prisoner* 83: He never made it. His eagerness for overtime and promotion cruelled him.

crumpet, not worth a Utterly worthless

1944 Lawson Glassop *We Were the Rats* 153: 'He won't be worth a crumpet in action, not worth a bloody crumpet.'

1956 *Bulletin* 24 Oct. 22: 'This fellow we've got now – not worth a crumpet.'

1962 Alan Seymour *The One Day of the Year* 73: 'Ballyhoo. Photos in the papers. Famous. Not worth a crumpet.'

crust, a A livelihood

1908 Henry Fletcher *Dads and Dan between Smokes* 116: 'Common labor, battlin' fer a crust, is willin' ter graft fer a crust.'

1910 Henry Lawson 'The Rising of the Court' *Prose* i 660: Police-court solicitors . . . wrangling over some miserable case for a crust.

1939 Kylie Tennant *Foveaux* 312: 'What's

y'r old man do for a crust?' Curly asked . . . 'Driver a taxi.'

1946 K. S. Prichard *The Roaring Nineties* 211: 'He goes around cadging old clothes . . . as if he were a poor boy willing to do anything for a crust.'

1974 Jack Hibberd *Dimboola* 39: 'What do you do for a crust?' 'I'm a reporter.'

cue, put one's ~ in the rack To retire [f. billiards]

1982 Neville Wran *Sydney Morning Herald* 20 Mar. 13: 'I wouldn't mind being in Federal politics before I put my cue in the rack.'

1982 Alex Buzo *Sun-Herald* 27 Jun. 51: The great moments in commentary, such as the question Rex Mossop asked of Mr Hughes, father of 23.7 percent of the Canterbury team: 'Are you gunna have any more or do you reckon it's time to stick the cue back in the rack?'

cue, to See quot. 1935

1935 R. B. Plowman *The Boundary Rider* 146: 'We have got to cue some of the bullocks in our team that have got tender footed.' . . . Picking up a farrier's tool-box, he . . . took from it a hammer and nails and a flat piece of steel – a cue. This was just large enough to cover one half of the horny part of the hoof from the cleft to the heel, and was about an inch and a quarter wide. On the outside it was fairly thick, but was thinned off to a knife-edge on the inside. Taking the hammer and some shoeing nails, Harry fitted the cut [? cue] to one half of the foot, inserted the point of a nail into a hole, such as is found in a horseshoe, and tapped gently.

1951 Ernestine Hill *The Territory* 324: He cued his bullocks at Cueing Pen Spring.

cuffs and collars The insignia of those set apart from the manual workers, esp. in the bush; a jackeroo or 'dude'

1895 Henry Lawson 'The Grand Mistake' *Verse* i 405: You bushmen sneer in the old bush way at the new-chum jackeroo, / But 'cuffs-'n'-collers' was out that day and they stuck to their posts like glue.

1935 Kylie Tennant *Tiburon* 66: 'I sees this young lady walkin' in an' I says, "There's one of the bourgeoisie, if y' like. One of the real middle-class cuff-an'-collar team."'

1983 *Journal* of Ship Painters and Dockers cit. *Sydney Morning Herald* 26 May 1: We who help keep the ships afloat / No matter the dirt, noise and stench / Are maligned by those in white collar and cuffs / From Parliament, media and Bench.

cultural cringe   see **cringe**

cundy   A stone [Ab.]
1941 Baker 21: *Cundy* A small stone.
1962 Stuart Gore *Down the Golden Mile* 113: 'Look, mine friendt, you are scouting roundt for some big coondies, stones, you know?'
see **boondy**

cunning as a shithouse (sewer) rat   see **rat**

Cup of tea, a Bex, and a good lie down
The title of a Phillip Theatre (Sydney) revue in the 1960s, perhaps echoing the **bushman's breakfast** (q.v.); a stereotype of Australian suburbia
1983 *Newcastle Herald* 4 Jun. 8: When the day was finally over, I collapsed with a Bex, a cup of tea and a good lie down.
1985 *National Times* 8 Feb. 39: In a few months time the Valium experience – like the now-quaint notion of the 'cuppa tea, a Bex and a good lie down' – will be old hat.

Cup, the   The Melbourne Cup
1889 J. Jenkins *Diary of a Welsh Swagman* (1975) 177: This year the Cup was won by a horse named 'Bravo', and he started as third favourite.
1895 A. B. Paterson *The Man from Snowy River* 3: There was Harrison, who made his pile when Pardon won the Cup.
1918 C. J. Dennis *Backblock Ballads* 115: 'I'll lay you ten to one in quids he'll say: "Wot's won the Cup?"'
1942 John Shaw Neilson *Autobiography* (1978) 97: I hung on to it till Cup time, when half a dozen of us were put off as the owners were reducing hands.
1975 *Sun-Herald* 2 Nov. 1: Record $25m gamble hangs on the Cup.

currency   1   The local money used in the colonies, as distinct from sterling (OED 1755)
1813 *Sydney Gazette* 27 Nov. 1: Whereas divers Victuallers, Publicans, and others . . . altered the then subsisting Rate of Exchange between the Bills drawn for the Public Service, and the Promissory Notes issued by different Individuals, known by the Name of Currency, by means whereof great Confusion has been introduced into all Private Dealings and Transactions. Ibid. 2: The above [advertised commodities] to be had wholesale and retail, for sterling money, or negotiable currency bills.
1826 James Atkinson *An Account of the State of Agriculture and Grazing in New South Wales* 132: In the early periods of the Settlement . . . every trader constituted himself a Banker, and issued his promissory notes, which were denominated *currency* of various values . . . When it was required therefore to exchange the Colonial currency against sterling bills . . . the former was always exchanged at a discount.
2   The native-born as distinct from the English immigrant, usually as 'currency lads' and 'currency lasses'
1824 *Sydney Gazette* 26 Feb. 2: Owing to this successful issue, the currency lads are in great glee.
1827 P. Cunningham *Two Years in New South Wales* ii 53: Our colonial born brethren are best known here by the name of *Currency*, in contradistinction to *Sterling*, or those born in the mother-country.
1845 Thomas McCombie *Arabin* 134: Nearly all of the species known as 'currency' are matter-of-fact men, with very few elements of originality in their composition, and ignorant of the pleasure to be derived from the fine arts.
1877 Rolf Boldrewood *A Colonial Reformer* (1890) 342: 'You're a regular Currency lass, Tottie,' laughed Mr Banks, 'always thinking about horses.'

curry, to give someone   To make it 'hot' for him, assault verbally or physically
1941 Baker 21: *Curry, to give someone* To abuse, reprove, express anger at a person.
1944 *Coast to Coast 1943* 124: She was trying to think up what she was going to say from the platform. 'I'm going to give those old tarts a bit of curry tonight, Ron.'
1977 Jeff Thomson *Sunday Telegraph* (Sydney) 30 Jan. 48: My old mate Lennie Pascoe gave the Bananalanders some curry yesterday . . . he shattered the first four wickets for only 16 off seven overs.
1980 *Sun-Herald* 28 Sep. 149: Once upon a time, you could ask someone how they're going, and they'd reply, 'Oh, not bad. The old back's been giving me a bit of curry, but can't complain.'

cut   A stroke of the cane

1890 A. B. Paterson 'My Various Schools' in *Singer of the Bush* (1983) 117: All the others . . . took two cuts of the cane on each hand as per usual.
1933 Norman Lindsay *Saturdee* 144: 'Hold out!' Five apiece they got . . . cuts which extinguished them in a purple mist of anguish.
1965 William Dick *A Bunch of Ratbags* 142: He locked the door and got out his strap and gave me four cuts of it.
1974 Gerald Murnane *Tamarisk Row* 91: She gives them each two stinging cuts and sends them back to their class.

cut Angry, resentful (teenage) [f. *cut up*]
1984 *National Times* 19 Oct. 23: 'Boys who have their flasks of spirits confiscated feel really "cut". They say "He took my bloody alcohol!" They feel humiliated.'

cut-lunch commandos See quot. 1953
1944 Keith Attiwill *Cut-Lunch Commandos* [title of a novel on the public service]
1952 T. A. G. Hungerford *The Ridge and the River* 123: 'Come on! Think I got nothin' to do but wait for a bunch of cut-lunch commandos.'
1953 Baker 170: *cut-lunch commandos* Soldiers serving with a home base unit.
1981 Ross Campbell *An Urge to Laugh* 104: The Barracks staff kept office hours, being known as 'cut-lunch commandos'.

cut out *v.* 1 To separate selected cattle from the herd
1844 *Georgiana's Journal* ed. Hugh McCrae (1966) 127: Mr Jamieson was able to identify some of his own bullocks . . . whereupon, he and Captain Reid, with much shouting and cracking of whips, proceeded to 'cut them out' from the mob.

1918 Bernard Cronin *The Coastlanders* 66: 'He's the best hand at cutting out in a muster that I ever saw.'
2 Used of the completion of a contract job, either of the work coming to an end or of the worker finishing his labours
1882 Rolf Boldrewood *Robbery Under Arms* (World's Classics 1949) 28: 'You and George can take a turn at local preaching when you're cut out' [referring to a fencing contract] Ibid. 83: Jim and I stopped at Boree Shed till all the sheep were cut out.
1892 G. L. James *Shall I Try Australia?* 97: The day before we start to 'cut in' – which is the term for commencing to shear (when we have finished we are said to have 'cut out') – is a busy day.
1919 W. K. Harris *Outback in Australia* 141: Last month, they were in full swing, to-day they will be 'cut-out'.
1958 H. D. Williamson *The Sunlit Plain* 24: He had rested a week since the fencing contract had cut out.
1973 Roland Robinson *The Drift of Things* 102: In those days a man who arrived in town after a long spell of bush work would throw his cheque down on the bar, and say to the publican 'Let me know when that's cut out'.

cut out *n.* The completion of shearing, or other rural work
1911 E. J. Brady *River Rovers* 187: North Yanco shearing shed, where 53,000 sheep were destined to leave their wool before the 'cut out'.
1962 *Sydney Morning Herald* 24 Nov. 12: Later, after the cut out . . . the rep. admitted the sheep were as dry as a punctured water bag.

cut snake, mad as a see **mad**

D

D, dee 1 A detective, or policeman in plain clothes. Also an abbr. for **demon** q.v.
1877 T. E. Argles *The Pilgrim* i 4: After my name and occupation had been entered in a ledger by the educated sergeant, I was searched. The pitiless 'D' took all my property away.

1894 *Bulletin* 18 Aug. 14: The inevitable result will be that each private 'D' will keep his own corroborator on the premises.
1924 C. J. Dennis *Rose of Spadgers* 77: ''E's bein' chased,' she sez, 'by Ds, I've 'eard.'
1930 L. W. Lower *Here's Luck* 152: 'These

two gentlemen,' she repeated 'are private detectives.' 'D's!' shouted Woggo.

1973 Ward McNally *Man from Zero* 109: 'Those bloody Dees were each over fourteen stone.'

2   A D-shaped loop or clip on a saddle [f. *dee* metal loop in harness OED 1794]

1888 W. S. S. Tyrwhitt *The New Chum in the Queensland Bush* 59: On the solitary occasion when it was my lot to swim a flooded creek, my horse did it so well that my lunch in a pouch hanging behind me from the D's of the saddle, was kept perfectly dry.

1931 Miles Franklin *Back to Bool Bool* 280: Each saddle had a quart pot or something else on the dees, and tucker and oil-coats on the pommel.

dacca, dakker   Drugs, esp. marihuana [f. S. Afr. *Dagga*, hemp, cannabis]

1977 *Sun-Herald* 16 Oct. 63: Some new words emerge [among the unemployed youth of the western suburbs] like 'dakker' for drugs.

1982 *Sydney Morning Herald* 18 Sep. 1: At a teenage party you may be offered dacca or spot. Called marihuana by some, it's likely to send you off your face.

Dad and Dave   Title of a radio serial of the 1930s and later, derived somewhat remotely from characters in Steele Rudd's *On Our Selection*: now a byword for a humorous version of unsophisticated rural Australia before World War II

1943 Maurice Clough *We of the A.I.F.* 44: Like 'Dad and Dave' of 'hayseed' jokes.

1974 Geoffrey Blainey *Australian* 4 Oct. 8: On the farmlands the trees were ring-barked in their hundreds of thousands, and behind post-and-rail fences they often stood in their pale cemeteries for five or fifteen years before Dad and Dave burned them down.

1984 *Australian* 23 Feb. 11: If Dad and Dave and Mabel were still battling it out on their selection today the chances are the Australian taxpayer would be footing the bill.

see **Dave and Mabel, Snake Gully**

daddy   The supreme instance, esp. in the phrase 'the daddy of them all' [also English and U.S. ? f. expressions like 'the father of a hiding']

1898 W. H. Ogilvie *Fair Girls and Gray Horses* 54: Though shaky in the shoulders, he's the daddy of them all; / He's the gamest

bit of horseflesh from the Snowy to the Bree.

1902 Henry Lawson 'A Droving Yarn' *Prose* i 357: 'Billy was the daddy of the drovers.'

1942 Jean Devanny *The Killing of Jacqueline Love* 154: 'She was the daddy of all liars.'

1954 Bant Singer *Have Patience, Delaney* 77–8: I been in a lot of wild mix-ups in my time . . . but this is sure the daddy of the whole flaming lot.

1961 Ion L. Idriess *Tracks of Destiny* 80: Of the Territory pioneer women perhaps the 'daddy' of the lot is Mrs Phoebe Farrar.

dag   1   'One of the locks of wool clotted with dirt about the hinder parts of a sheep' OED 1731

1878 G. H. Gibson *Southerly Busters* 179: I'm able for to shear 'em clean, / And level as a die; / But I prefer to 'tommy hawk', / And make the 'daggers' fly.

1899 W. T. Goodge *Hits! Skits! and Jingles!* 42: With leathery necks and dags galore, / A bad machine and a slippery floor, / And how could a shearer want for more?

1933 Acland: *Dag, dags* hard or soft dung hanging from the breech of a sheep. Cutting this off the sheep with an old pair of shears is called dagging.

1971 Frank Hardy *The Outcasts of Foolgarah* 2: Sir Percival Dagg, the sheep millionaire.

2   A would-be dashing and stylish fellow (the sense replaced by **lair** q.v.); a humorist, wag, eccentric

1916 *The Anzac Book* 47: Yes; 'Enessy was a dag if ever there was one!

1932 Leonard Mann *Flesh in Armour* 57: Johnny Wright, a solicitor from a country town, now a bit of a dag, with the habit of going on a real bender now and then.

1946 Kylie Tennant *Lost Haven* 351: He had to be the Alec who was 'a bit of a dag', who always had a joke.

1982 *NT News* (Darwin) 29 Oct. 7: The stories of his outrageous acts abound . . . All in all, quite a wag, or perhaps a dag.

3   Someone untidy in dress or appearance [? f. **dag** 1]

1982 *Australian* 18 May 7: Mr Hay, who describes himself as a 'bit of a dag – perhaps the worst-dressed superintendent in Australia', says he is a humanitarian.

1982 *Southerly* 319–20: The young man in question was stood self-consciously by her side, his new suit marginally too big for him, his hair greased and hurriedly combed back for the photograph ... 'He looks a bit of a dag.'

4 Someone conventional, bourgeois, 'square'

1975 *National Times* 13 Jan. 40: The surf has a glamour the ordinary boy lacks. 'They're dags,' says Colleen Field, of Kelly-ville, of ordinary boys. Despite the repulsive tag, dags are the sort of boy every mother would like her daughter to bring home. At least she knows, by the medium-long hair-cut, that he is a boy. His clothes are tidy, he wears shoes and is known to wear a tie.

1979 *NT News* (Darwin) 24 Nov. 14: *Dag*: a person who isn't 'with it', he's un-cool.

1988 *Sydney Morning Herald* 18 Mar. Metro 15: To some kids the police presence and the tight regulations make the Blue Light scene suitable for dags only.

daggy [f. **dag** 1 and 3]

1981 *Australian* 26 Mar. 3: The Oz man has, by and large, the reputation of being a pretty daggy old dresser.

1987 *Times on Sunday* 7 Jun. 24: Those who did well, from both Salisbury and Burn-side, say that it was a bit daggy to be stu-dious.

daily double See quot. [f. the racing term]

1983 *Sun-Herald* 9 Jan. 124: In some circles, having your wedding at St Mark's, Darling Point and the reception at the Royal Sydney Golf Club is known as the daily double. Another commentator ... suggested that 'trifecta' would be a good word to de-scribe belonging to Royal Sydney and the Black and White Committee, as well as hav-ing a bungalow at our most prestigious beach suburb [Palm Beach].

Dame Nellie, doing a see **Melba**

1984 Rod Marsh *Gloves, Sweat and Tears* 112: I didn't want to officially quit and then discover that I really wanted to play on after all ... I wasn't going to do a Dame Nellie.

damper The form of bread best known to the workforce of outback Australia in the nineteenth century and later, hence used colloquially in phrases like 'worth your damper', 'earn your damper'. [f. *damper* A luncheon, or snap before dinner: so called from its damping, or allaying, the appetite Grose 1785]

1827 P. Cunningham *Two Years in New*

South Wales ii 190: The farm-men usually bake their flour into flat cakes, which they call *dampers*, and cook these in the ashes.

1903 Joseph Furphy *Such is Life* (1944) 327: 'You're not worth your damper at this work.'

1934 Brian Penton *Landtakers* 51: 'You wait till I get out. Your damper'll be dough.'

1961 Patrick White *Riders in the Chariot* 382: 'You are not worth your damper,' she said at once, 'layin' around!'

Dapto dog A wog [rhyming slang] [f. dog-racing circuit at Dapto, N.S.W.]

1987 Kathy Lette *Girls' Night Out* 222: She has decided to marry her father's friend's son, Spiro, a real dapto dog from the Old Country.

dark 'un See quot. 1957: wharf slang

1957 Tom Nelson *The Hungry Mile* 81: Some 25 years back a gang of us refused an order of the Union Co. to come back after the breakfast break for four hours, after doing a 'dark-un' (24 hour shift).

1977 *Sunday Telegraph* (Sydney) 6 Mar. 7: 'For 12 years as foreman I worked a weekly 'darkun' – a 24-hour shift. These shifts were inhuman.'

1982 Wendy Lowenstein and Tom Hills *Under the Hook* 17: 'We was on a darkie, a midnight shift.'

Darling Pea *Swainsonia galegifolia*, a plant which when eaten by cattle sends them mad [f. Darling river and districts]

1889 T. Quin *The Well Sinkers* 101: 'The man's mad!' he said ... 'No ... he's got a touch of what we call the Darling Pea.'

1904 Laura M. Palmer-Archer *A Bush Honeymoon* 349: Darling Pea Madness.

1918 N. Campbell and L. Nelson *The Dinky-Di Soldier* 29: When the Darlin' pea is drivin' men an' cattle off their chump.

1957 *Bulletin* 10 Apr. 11: He is ... dopier than a horse with a gutful of Darling Pea. see **pea**

Darling shower see **shower**

dart Some especially favoured object; a cherished plan or scheme: *obs.*

c. **1882** *The Sydney Slang Dictionary* 3: *Dart* Object of attraction, or enticing thing or event, or a set purpose.

1882 Rolf Boldrewood *Robbery Under Arms* (World's Classics 1949) 46: The great dart is to keep the young stock away from their mothers until they forget one another, and then most of the danger is past.

1911 Louis Stone *Jonah* 60: 'Your dart is ter be King of the Push, an' knock about the streets.'

1924 C. J. Dennis *Rose of Spadgers* 84: 'Wot's yer dart?'

Dart, the old   see **Old Dart**

Darwin stubby   The beer bottle introduced in 1958 with the capacity of 80 fl. oz., changed to 2.25 l in 1973, and to 2 l in 1982

1977 *Australian* 4 Nov. 7: A Darwin Stubby, the mammoth 2.5-litre bottle.

date (dot)   Backside, anus

1959 D'Arcy Niland *The Big Smoke* 41: He said, 'Shove it up your black dot,' and went down the stairs.

1961 Mena Calthorpe *The Dyehouse* 214: 'In your bloody date! What do you think we are?'

1973 *Snatches & Lays* 25: The Australian lady emu, when she wants to find a mate, / wanders round the desert with a feather up her date.

date *v.*   To 'goose' someone

1976 Dorothy Hewett *Bon-bons and Roses for Dolly* 52: 'I was up on a chair fixing the new curtains and he comes up behind and dates me. Large as life. Without a word of a lie. He dates me. Cheeky mug.'

Dave and Mabel   Characters in the radio serial 'Dad and Dave' q.v., and hence a byword for unsophisticated rural Australians before World War II

1973 Frank Huelin *Keep Moving* 39: The boss's daughter – a girl in her early teens – who played Mabel to Stan's Dave.

1975 Hal Porter *The Extra* 212: Their table manners pass muster, their accents aren't affectedly Dave and Mabel.

see **Dad and Dave, Snake Gully**

day, that'll be the   An ironical rejoinder meaning 'That would be worth waiting for' or 'That will never happen'. Accepted by Turner 134 as a New Zealand coinage, but often heard in American films.

1918 *Kia Ora Coo-ee* 15 Aug. 4: Just wait for leave to Aussie. Oh! that'll be the day.

1941 Sidney J. Baker *New Zealand Slang* 50: *That'll be the day!* used as a cant phrase

expressing mild doubt following some boast or claim by a person.

1952 T. A. G. Hungerford *The Ridge and the River* 46: White's derisive laughter sounded through the gloom of the fox-hole. 'That'd be the day!'

1977 Sumner Locke Elliott *Water Under the Bridge* 82: Everythink she said was mean or sarcastic. '*That'll* be the day,' she warned if ever you said somethink hopeful. 'I'll believe *that* when I see it.'

de facto   Someone cohabiting without being legally married [f. the legal term *de facto*, as distinct from *de jure*]

1962 Max Harris *Australian Civilization* ed. P. Coleman 61: Australians prefer to pick themselves up a *de facto*, rather than divorce and remarry.

1972 Dorothy Hewett *The Chapel Perilous* 76: 'You're not one of the great whores of history. You're a de facto, living in a pokey bed-sit in the suburbs.'

1984 *Age* (Melbourne) 9 Jun. 1: De factos may get tax relief [heading] The Federal Government is considering giving the dependent spouse tax rebate to people in de facto relationships.

dead bird   see **bird**

dead finish, the   1   The 'last straw', 'the limit', the ultimate test of one's tolerance

1881 A. C. Grant *Bush-Life in Queensland* i 201: 'He's the dead-finish – go right through a man,' rejoins Sam, rather sulkily. 'Blessed if he didn't – near skiver my hoss!'

1902 J. H. M. Abbott *Tommy Cornstalk* 64: There are few colloquialisms more expressive of wearisome disgust, dissatisfaction and discontent than is 'Dead Finish'. It is almost synonymous with 'the Last Straw'.

1980 Rod Ansell *To Fight the Wild* 110: If some do-gooder had come along and shoved the poor old buggers in a nice clean home, that would have been the dead finish of them.

2   A prickly shrub with yellow flowers

1885 Harold Finch-Hatton *Advance Australia!* 272: On the western slopes, rosewood, myall, dead-finish.

1911 L. St Clare Grondona *Collar and Cuffs* 70: 'Wait-a-bit' . . . 'nevertire' . . . and 'dead finish' – Heaven knows why – are all desert shrubs, the last being, in reality, a prickly undergrowth.

1940 Ion L. Idriess *Lightning Ridge* 30: We'd be thirty miles out in the midst of sombre, rocky hills scantily clothed in Dead Finish, wattle and quandong.

Dead Heart The interior of Australia, from J. W. Gregory's book of 1906
1906 J. W. Gregory *The Dead Heart of Australia* [book title]
1936 Archer Russell *Gone Nomad* 47: 'Dead Heart' though this region may be to some, it was never so to me. To know the gibber lands you must go and live amid their silence.
1961 Kenneth Cook *Wake in Fright* 6–7: Further out in the heat was the silent centre of Australia, the Dead Heart.
1974 David Ireland *Burn* 110: 'I'll tell you where the dead heart of Australia is. It's right back there in the cities. Not out in the sand and the mulga and the stones burning hot under the sun.'

dead horse, working (off) a Working for a return that is immediately consumed in the payment of a debt, and thus for no personal benefit [OED 1638; To work for the dead horse; to work for wages already paid Grose 1785]
1798 David Collins *An Account of the English Colony in NSW* (1975) i 409: Settlers gave assignments on their coming crops of wheat for the different sums in which they were indebted ... to use their own expression, they had now 'to work for a dead horse'.
1847 Alexander Harris *Settlers and Convicts* ed. C. M. H. Clark (1954) 181: Endeavour on the part of the labourer, after having largely overdrawn his account, to get rid of the debt; they call working out such a debt, *riding the dead horse.*
1898 *Bulletin* 17 Dec. Red Page: *Working dead horse* is working to pay off a back debt; or, as a teamster would say, 'This trip has got to pay for a horse that I lost last trip; £20 to make up to pay for the new horse.'
1932 William Hatfield *Ginger Murdoch* 38: 'I'm hobbled here workin' orf a huge dead horse.'
1945 Tom Ronan *Strangers on the Ophir* 37: I've got a dead horse at McGarry's that is as big as an elephant.

deadhouse Room attached to a hotel in which the drunks could sleep it off [f. *deadhouse* morgue]

1876 Rolf Boldrewood *A Colonial Reformer* (1890) 133: I remember coming to myself in the dead-house of a bush inn.
1888 E. Finn *Chronicles of Early Melbourne* ii 547: Another usage grew up with the old hotels ... the attaching of a littered room or deadhouse – not the dreary-looking ghostly morgue, where suicides or accidentally made corpses are laid in state, but a secure, unwindowed, comfortably strawed exterior apartment, into which the bodies of those who got dead-drunk by day or night were stowed away, and suffered to rest in peace and sleep off the debauch.
1922 Arthur Wright *A Colt from the Country* 114: 'Another pint, as you say, and it'd be me f'r th' dead-house.'
1962 Alan Marshall *This is the Grass* 46: 'He has no money and when he goes out to it they toss him into the dead house beside the stable.'

dead marine An empty bottle (of beer or spirits) [? f. *dead men* empty bottles OED 1700; Grose 1785]
1885 J. Brunton Stephens *Convict Once and Other Poems* 308: We had filled a dead marine, sir, at the fam'ly waterhole.
1892 Henry Lawson 'Jones's Alley' *Prose* i 41: A small bony horse, which, in its turn, dragged a rickety cart of the tray variety, such as is used in the dead marine trade.
1948 K. S. Prichard *Golden Miles* 375: 'Woodcartin's not the game it used to be, neither is collectin' dead marines.'
1983 Laurie Clancy *Perfect Love* 100: They were all indistinguishable dead marines to her, horrible brown objects that she hurled violently out into the backyard.

dead men's graves See quot.
1901 Rolf Boldrewood *In Bad Company* 482: I was walking the horses over a curious formation of small mounds, provincially known as dead men's graves.

dead set *adj.* Absolute, utter
1965 Frank Hardy *The Yarns of Billy Borker* 119: 'I'm a real crusader against acid stomach, got a dead-set cure for it.'
1974 David Williamson *The Coming of Stork* 11: 'I bet there's some dead set nymphos around here, boy.'
1981 *National Times* 21 Jun. 3: 'The man was a dead set unionist who tried to help his members and all he got out of it was character assassination.

dead set *adv.* Equivalent to 'fair dinkum'
1979 Kathy Lette and Gabrielle Carey *Puberty Blues* 36: 'Deadset, Kim, Dave's stoked in you.'
1982 John Singleton *Sydney Morning Herald* 6 Feb. 40: 'I've worked bloody hard. Deadset, I was into work at three, four, five in the morning when I started, and I'd be the last to leave at night.'

dead-un A horse not ridden to its full capacity, to ensure better odds when it next races [cf. U.S. and English *stiff 'un*]
1896 Nat Gould *Town and Bush* 225: He has a remarkable way of scenting a 'dead un', or of finding out a non-starter.
1933 Samuel Griffiths *A Rolling Stone on the Turf* 49: 'Well I'm damned!' he exclaimed . . . 'Another bloody dead 'un has come home on me!'
1982 *National Times* 1 Aug. 14: 'You hear a lot about dead 'uns *after* the race,' said Beirne, 'but 99 per cent of it is sour grapes.'

Dean Maitland   see **Maitland**

death adders in one's pocket, to have
see **pocket**

death, packing   see **packing**

death seat 1   In trotting, the position outside the leader, from which it is difficult to win. The horse or reinsman is said to 'sit' in this position
1982 *Australian* 7 Aug. 44: Prince Jade sat behind a different leader (Rhonda's Al), with Local Honored in the 'death seat' – from where he faded while Prince Jade got a miracle rails run in the final stages to win.
1984 *Sunday Independent* (Perth) 17 Jun. 89: 'He was the first pacer to break 2 min on a country track in Australia . . . I sat in the death seat with him and we cruised home.'
2   The seat next to the driver of a car (as most liable to injury in an accident) [also U.S.]
1971 Craig McGregor *Don't Talk to Me About Love* 149: Paula, feet braced against the Mazda floor in case of a head-on smash, in which case she, being in the death-seat, would have the chance for neither mistakes nor regrets.

debbil debbil   see **devil-devil**

deckie A deckhand [abbr.]

1984 *Sunday Independent* (Perth) 18 Nov. 2: This season Judy is a deckie on Brian Bollard's 12.8m crayboat Aqua Lass, working equal halves of the deck with a male deckie.

dee   see **D**

deener Shilling [before the introduction of decimal currency in 1966] [OED 1839]
c. **1882** *The Sydney Slang Dictionary* 3: *Deaner* A shilling.
1901 Henry Lawson 'At Dead Dingo' *Prose* i 452: 'Stumped?' inquired Jim. 'Not a blanky, lurid deener!' drawled Bill.
1923 Con Drew *Rogues and Ruses* 22: 'We couldn't afford a deaner to see an earthquake.'
1942 Gavin Casey *It's Harder for Girls* 55: 'My dad's got plenty of money . . . I can get a few deeners from him easy enough.'
1965 William Dick *A Bunch of Ratbags* 19: One thing about him, though, he knew how to make a deener on the side.

Deep North   see **North**

deep sinker A long glass of beer: *obs.*
1877 T. E. Argles *The Pilgrim* vi 64: These misguided mortals spend in 'deep sinkers' . . . that money which their landladies are daily sighing for – and sighing for in vain.
1886 Frank Cowan *Australia: A Charcoal Sketch* 32: Long-sleever, Bishop Barker, and Deep-sinker, synonyms of the Yankee Schooner.

defence, streaker's   see **streaker's**

deli A delicatessen [abbr.]
1973 Max Harris *The Angry Eye* 164: The deli owner would have to employ a bloke with a pencil and paper classifying every sale.
1975 *Australian* 11 Oct. 25: It was the same with Dean's, a pacesetter in the delicatessen world, operating a 'deli' before anyone really had heard the term.
1982 Doreen Clarke *Roses in Due Season* 73: Listen love, could you nip down to the deli for some fags for me?

delo Delegate, in trade union parlance [abbr.]
1961 *Sydney Morning Herald* 20 May 2: The boys had been battling for gloves, so I went up to the foreman, I'd cut me fingers and that. The pano said 'See your delegate!'

So the delo fronted him and said 'If we don't get gloves we'll walk off!'

demon A policeman, esp. in plain-clothes; a detective [? f. *dee*. The OED Suppl. derivation from Van Diemen's Land is unlikely]
1889 Barrère and Leland: *Demons* (Australian) prison slang for police.
1900–10 O'Brien and Stephens: *Demons* detectives, i.e. plainclothes generally (from D's).
1941 Kylie Tennant *The Battlers* 118: Adelaide had been triumphantly certain that the shearers were 'demons', or plain-clothes detectives.
1961 Tom Ronan *Only a Short Walk* 19: Some smart demon . . . would start getting ideas. And those plain-clothes men knew how to stick to a track once they got on to it.

Demons, the 1 The Melbourne A.F.L. team (previously the Red Demons, and the Redlegs) [f. team colours]
1973 Rev. Alan Walker, in Keith Dunstan *Sports* 230: 'Ladies and Gentlemen gathered here on this great occasion, whichever team we may support – the Saints or the Demons – we can surely agree that we are joined together as brothers in Jesus Christ.'
2 The Perth (W.A.) Australian Rules club
1980 *West Australian* (Perth) 25 Mar. 83: Be a Demon [heading] Join the Perth Football Club now.
3 The North Hobart (Tas.) Football Club
1980 *Mercury* (Hobart) 22 Mar. 54: Lift for Demons [heading] The Schweppes soft drink company will sponsor North Hobart Football Club for $7,000 this season.

dermo Dermatitis, in World War II army slang [abbr.]
1948 Sumner Locke Elliott *Rusty Bugles* in *Khaki, Bush and Bigotry* ed. Eunice Hanger (1968) 52: 'They send you south if you get dermo more than three times bad enough to put you in hospital.'
1972 'Darwin Interlude' *Comic Australian Verse* ed. Geoffrey Lehmann 165: My men are down with dermo and with every tropic curse.

dero A derelict, i.e. someone unemployed and destitute [abbr.]
1973 *Sun-Herald* 8 Apr. 9: 'And you bump into a lot of very strange people – druggies and deros.'
1984 *Sunday Independent* (Perth) 5 Feb.

23: Perth's deros stagger through life and the courts [heading]

derry An alarm, police search; in the expression 'to have a derry on', an attitude of hostility, a 'down', a grudge against [? f. the refrain 'derry, derry down']
1882 Rolf Boldrewood *Robbery Under Arms* (World's Classics 1949) 68: 'Said he knew a squatter in Queensland he could pass him [the stolen stallion] on to; that they'd keep him there for a year and get a crop of foals by him, and when the 'derry' was off, he'd take him over himself.'
1892 Henry Lawson 'A Derry on a Cove' *Verse* i 173: 'It's cruel when the p'leece has got a derry on a bloke.'
1915 C. J. Dennis *The Songs of a Sentimental Bloke* 49: I took a derry on this stror-'at coot / First time I seen 'im dodgin' round Doreen.
1937 Vance Palmer *Legend for Sanderson* 226: 'More interested in his job and in giving his men a fair spin than in raking off big profits. That was why the other contractors had such a derry on him.'
1958 Vince Kelly *The Greedy Ones* 214: 'She's got a derry on Porkreth, too, because he shot up her boy friend.'

Derwenter An ex-convict [f. the convict settlement on the Derwent river in Tasmania]
1853 John Rochfort *Adventures of a Surveyor* 51: The proprietor of our tent (an old Derwenter) stationed himself at the door to receive payment as we departed.
1865 J. F. Mortlock *Experiences of a Convict* (1965) 220: Among the officials were no less than three old 'Derwenters'.

deuce, deucer 1 To shear 200 sheep in a day: someone capable of this feat [f. *deuce* two]
1950 Jack Sorenson *Collected Poems* 32: I thought perhaps he may have chanced to hear / Of how I almost deuced them* at Murgoo. *'Deuce them' – To shear 200 sheep.
1953 Baker 69: *deucer*, a shearer who can shear 200 sheep or more a day.
2 A double shift
1953 Dymphna Cusack *Southern Steel* 138: 'He's doing a deucer,' Landy explained. 'The snipe on the 12 to 4's sick.'
1979 George Stewart *The Leveller* 56: If any of the firemen were sick or injured you were called upon to work a 'Deucer' (two hours of his watch each).

devil-devil An evil spirit, in Aboriginal belief [Pidgin]

1844 Louisa Meredith *Notes and Sketches of New South Wales* 95: I never could make out anything of their religious ideas, or even if they had a comprehension of a beneficent Supreme Being but they have an evil spirit, which causes them great terror, whom they call 'Yahoo' or 'Devil-devil' ... The name Devil-devil is of course borrowed from our vocabulary, and the doubling of the phrase denotes how terrible or intense a devil he is.

1905 Jeannie Gunn *The Little Black Princess* 6: She said that if you had on a red dress when there was a thunderstorm the Debbil-debbil who made the thunder would 'come on' and kill you 'deadfellow'.

1938 Xavier Herbert *Capricornia* 72: A deserted house was a delightful playground, but an occupied house a place to be avoided like a reputed lair of debil-debils.

1983 G. E. P. Wellard *Bushlore* 120: The fire in the entrance [to a mia mia] is a must. Apart from being useful to cook on, it also prevents any debble debble coming in during the night.

devil-devil country Any hazardous terrain

1870 Edward B. Kennedy *Four Years in Queensland* 20: 'Devil devil' country ... is simply one formation of holes and hillocks, in some districts of great depth and size.

1907 Alfred Searcy *In Australian Tropics* 156: I had to work my way through a belt of mangroves, and then on my stomach crawling for some distance over 'devil-devil', or Bay of Biscay country.

1946 Ion L. Idriess *In Crocodile Land* 46: We returned with Fred, an awful ride, jolting over devil-devil country all ploughed up from last wet by countless buffalo hoofs.

1963 Xavier Herbert *Larger than Life* 93: Before the fastest car could get anywhere near him travelling over the devil-devil country of the downs.

devil's number The score of 87 for an Australian cricketer (13 from 100), or any other score including those numbers

1984 *Australian* 17 Nov. Mag. 19: The dreaded Devil's Number for Australian batsmen, 87 runs.

Devine, Tilly see **Tilly**

devo A deviate [abbr.]

1982 *Sydney Morning Herald* 10 Jul. 32: 'They're the spiritual devos (deviates),' says one of the staff.

dice To reject, abandon [f. *dice* To lose or throw away by dicing OED 1618]

1944 Lawson Glassop *We Were the Rats* 50: 'I says, Mrs 'Aliburton, I haven't seen Snow since the day before yesterday. He hasn't diced me, has he?' 'Gee, Shirley,' she says, 'he musta got another girl friend.'

1953 T. A. G. Hungerford *Riverslake* 190: 'You want to make up your mind and dice whatever you don't want.'

1963 Frank Hardy *Legends from Benson's Valley* 213: 'No bastard puts my daughter in the family way then dices her ... and gets away with it.'

dickhead A fool, idiot [f. *dick* penis]

1974 Barry Humphries *A Nice Night's Entertainment* (1981) 147: They'll stitch you up, stick it up you and take you for a dead-set dickhead.

1980 *Bulletin* 28 Oct. 141: The senator also showed a thorough grasp of student parlance, referring variously to his opponents on the library lawn as 'dickheads, thick heads and wankers'.

Dickless Tracy A policewoman [f. Dick Tracy, the cartoon figure]

1967 *King's Cross Whisper* (Sydney) xxxiv 4: *Dickless Tracy*: A woman policeman.

1984 *Sydney Morning Herald* 4 Feb. 37: Mangan is one of 18 policewomen at Darlinghurst (out of 136 police) whom one sergeant calls Dickless Tracys.

dickon 1 An exclamation of disbelief or rejection: *obs.* [? f. *Dickens*]

1894 *Bulletin* 5 Apr. 13: *Witness:* Then he biffed me. *Chief Justice:* And did you stouch him back? *Witness:* No. *Chief Justice:* Dicken. *Witness:* Swelp me.

1911 Louis Stone *Jonah* 68: 'Dickon ter you,' said Mrs Yabsley, 'Yer needn't think they're got up ter kill ter please yous.'

1929 Hal Eyre *Hilarities* 46: 'Those were the days when ... we said "No flies on you", "Dickon to that", and similar things. So you see it was some time ago.'

2 In S.A., an expression of agreement, like 'you bet', 'too right'

1981 *Sydney Morning Herald* 24 Jan. 35: Mr Dutton remembers being laughed at as a boy at school in Melbourne when he used the term 'dicken!' as an expletive rather in the way in which 'my oath!' is usually employed. 'A common term in South Australia,' he said, 'but no one in Victoria ever heard of it.'

Diehards The Fortitude Valleys (Q.) R.L. team
1979 *Courier-Mail* (Brisbane) 24 Feb. 36: Valleys staged a typical Diehard finish to down Souths 12–10.

diff The differential in a motor vehicle
1942 Gavin Casey *It's Harder for Girls* 163: 'The diff's gone.'
1973 Henry Williams *My Love Had a Black Speed Stripe* 13: These sheila drivers . . . who wouldn't know a slipping clutch from a busted diff.
1988 Marian Eldridge *Canberra Tales* 97: 'Better get the diff fixed if you want to get further than Sale, Dad,' Billy says.

dig Abbreviation of **digger** 2, 4 and 5, qq.v.
1929 *Reveille* 31 Aug. 14: The first time I heard 'Digger' was in London, early in 1917, when an American soldier addressed me as 'Dig'.
1932 Leonard Mann *Flesh in Armour* 83: One of the Mth, seated on the ground, cried to Charl, 'Give us a smoke, for Gawd's sake, dig.'
1953 T. A. G. Hungerford *Riverslake* 50: 'What about you, dig?' the big man demanded, pushing his face so close.
1966 D. H. Crick *Period of Adjustment* 170: 'How are yer, dig?'
1972 Dorothy Hewett *The Chapel Perilous* 83: 'Haven't got the price of a drink on you, have you dig?'

dig, pull out ~, the dogs are pissing on your swag see **pull**

digger 1 An Australian gold-miner of the 1850s and later [? f. U.S.]
1852 Lord Robert Cecil *Goldfields Diary* (1935) 36: When the diggers address a policeman in uniform they always call him 'Sir', but they always address a fellow in a blue shirt with a carbine as 'Mate'.
1867 J. S. Borlase *The Night Fossickers* 2: I did not come, however, as a seeker of the yellow metal – I had no ambition to become a digger.
1914 Henry Lawson 'I'll Bide' *Prose* i 826: On the ferry I sat beside a man I took to be an old digger . . . He'd been in Westralia, after

Coolgardie, where I had been – also Papua, South Africa, Klondyke and South America.
2 An Australian soldier in World War I, esp. an infantryman; an Australian soldier in any later war [Unexplained: returned soldiers writing in to *Reveille* for 31 July, 31 August, 30 September and 31 October 1929, including C. E. W. Bean, offer some twenty different accounts of the origin of the term.]
1917 Diary cit. Bill Gammage *The Broken Years* (1974) 241: Some Diggers were walking along the street [in England] when two Tommy officers approached and on coming close to the diggers prepared for a salute . . . The diggers just walked past grinning from ear to ear.
1918 *Aussie* 18 Jan. 11: 'Digger' has taken the place of the time-honoured 'Cobber' in the parlance of the Australian soldier. Anyone know the origin of the new word?
1945 Herbert M. Moran *Beyond the Hill Lies China* 142: A man in shabby uniform accosted Challis: 'Kin yer spare a deaner, Mister, for a digger down on his luck?'
1965 Patrick White *Four Plays* 105: A bit seedy, battered. Good features of the hatchet variety. The Digger type.
1984 *Weekend Australian* 28 Jan. 7: The mines buried in the [Sinai] desert during five wars are a dangerous legacy for today's Diggers and desert dwellers.
3 A private soldier, as distinct from one with any rank
1984 *National Times* 5 Oct. 22: 'You can go into the army as a digger and if you're lucky, 14 years later you might make it to a sergeant.'
4 An Australian who is not a soldier: used as a mode of address like 'mate'
1926 J. Vance Marshall *Timely Tips for New Australians: Digger* A familiar term of address such as 'friend' or comrade. Originally it was only applied to soldiers but now its use is universal.
1934 Thomas Wood *Cobbers* 173: 'What's up, digger?' asked the policeman.
1983 Margaret Jones *Sydney Morning Herald* 5 Aug. 8: No wonder jokey Britons, introduced to an Australian, invariably say in what they believe to be Oz dialect: "Ow are yer, mate, 'ow yer going, digger?'
5 Anyone thought of as showing typically Australian characteristics
1978 *Nation Review* 9 Mar. 20: Don Chipp has chosen to sink the slipper into the image of the sunbronzed digger.
1985 *Sydney Morning Herald* 6 May 42: Allan Border's boys were 'diggers to the

bone, slouching, gum-chewing Aussies who will bow the knee to no one, least of all an Englishman', he [Scyld Berry] wrote . . . There had always been two types of Australians, Berry said. 'The Diggers, anti-English, anti-establishment, anti-everything except amber fluid; and the "Old Australians", Brits abroad, clean-shaven types like Kim Hughes and Terry Alderman.'

digger hat   The slouch hat first worn by Australian soldiers in the Boer War, known as the 'digger hat' after World War I
   1955 John Morrison *Black Cargo* 114: A digger's hat hanging on a nail driven into the mantelpiece.
   1960 Nancy Cato *Green Grows the Vine* 37: He had been wearing, as usual, a battered old Digger's hat, its wide brim pulled down fore and aft.
   1976 *Sydney Morning Herald* 18 Feb. 24: Monique Connolly, the French wife of the Liberal MP for Bradfield, was outstanding in a Dior outfit – an off-white, light wool dress, featuring big silver buttons, a multi-coloured scarf, and matching felt Digger hat with feather band.

Digger, the Little   William Morris Hughes (1864–1952) Australian Prime Minister in World War I, and diminutive in size
   1919 *Daily Telegraph* (Sydney) 15 Sep. 6: The Little Digger [heading] . . . There were wavings of hats and hands and handkerchiefs, and a wild burst of cheers for 'the Little Digger'.
   1952 *Sydney Morning Herald* 20 Oct. 2: No title that he earned was so dear to Mr Hughes as that of 'The Little Digger', and today none will mourn his passing more deeply than the veterans of the first world war.
   1975 *Australian* 25 Jan. 16: The redoubtable Billy Hughes once observed that he trusted only two people – Jesus Christ and the Commonwealth Statistician (The 'Little Digger' incidentally added that he still wasn't too sure about the former).

dike (dyke)   Urinal, lavatory, *esp.* for communal use, as in a school or army camp [f. *dike* ditch or trench OED 847]
   [**1839** Grose *Glossary of Provincial and Local Words* 47: *Dike*, in Scotland, a bank; or even a wall, especially when it surmounts a ditch.]
   1923 Manchon *Le Slang* 104: *Dike*, les cabinets. [OED]

1948 Sumner Locke Elliott *Rusty Bugles* in *Khaki, Bush and Bigotry* ed. Eunice Hanger (1968) 42: 'Make sure you do everything on the double . . . run to mess . . . run back . . . run to the dike.'
   1971 George Johnston *A Cartload of Clay* 138: 'I mean, be orright for a dike, I suppose [the name *Merde Alors*] but funny for a house.'
   1983 Georgia Savage *Slate & Me and Blanche McBride* 2: 'Can I go to the dyke?'

dill   A simpleton, an incompetent [f. *dilly*]
   1941 Baker 23: *Dil* A simpleton or fool (2) A trickster's victim.
   1945 Gavin Casey *Downhill is Easier* 197: 'Them dills'll never find out who done him in.'
   1957 Judah Waten *Shares in Murder* 50: 'You must think I'm a dill if you expect me to take any notice of it.'
   1966 Patrick White *The Solid Mandala* 46: Waldo decided not to listen to any further dill's drivel.
   1982 David McNicoll *Bulletin* 30 Nov. 60: Would I be going too far in saying that there must be some dills in Australia's diplomatic and military outposts?

dilly   Foolish, silly, 'dopey-looking'; having lost one's presence of mind: *obs.* [*dilly* cranky, queer E. dial. OED 1873]
   1906 Edward Dyson *Fact'ry 'Ands* 213–14: 'Who should come sprintin' upstairs but me nibs, pale's er blessed egg, hair on end – fair dilly.'
   1915 C. J. Dennis *The Songs of a Sentimental Bloke* 16: 'If this 'ere dilly feelin' doesn't stop / I'll lose me block an' stoush some flamin' cop!'
   1935 Kylie Tennant *Tiburon* 21: 'Bless you, lady, bless you,' he says, all dilly with joy, see, thinkin' he's on a good thing.
   1949 John K. Ewers *Harvest* 204: 'Cripes, it'd drive a bloke dilly!'

dillybag   Aboriginal word for a small bag or basket, applied to similar small bags made and used by whites
   1876 A. J. Boyd *Old Colonials* (1882) 283: 'What is there in the dillybag?' 'About enough beef and flour for a day's feed, and a pound of tea.'
   1881 Mrs Campbell Praed *Policy and Passion* 179: Lord Dolph . . . armed with a dilly-bag and a trowel, clambered up the precipice to search for roots.

1953 *Sydney Morning Herald* 16 May 5: Mrs Eunice Woolcott Forbes said . . . that her bank account was a 'joint dilly bag' for the transactions of her bankrupt husband . . . and their children.

1980 Emery Barcs *Backyard of Mars* 185: After issuing each of us with three woollen blankets, mess-gear in a calico dilly bag, and a cheap safety razor in a metal box, he said amiably, 'Now you are ready for action'.

ding *n.* 1 An Italian or Greek; a foreigner generally: *derogatory*

1941 Baker 23: *Ding* An Italian.

1948 K. S. Prichard *Golden Miles* 100: Serbs, Bulgarians, Italians and Greeks, who worked on the mines, were gathering in excited groups . . . over the latest news. The Dings, as the northern people were called, and the Dagoes, which included the southern European races, had never fraternised very much.

1957 Randolph Stow *The Bystander* 21: 'She's not a Ding.' 'She says you're not a Greek,' Frank explained . . . 'Or is it an Italian. I never remember which is a Ding and which is a Dago.'

1962 Stuart Gore *Down the Golden Mile* 30: 'He's a Ding for mine. He was born in Italy, wasn't he.'

1971 Rena Briand *White Man in a Hole* 11: 'And them Greeks . . . if yer wanner leave them dirty dings they're gonna run yer outa town.'

1979 George Stewart *The Leveller* 24: This was the beginning of a savage fight involving miners and all foreigners. No matter what race, Slav, Greek, Italian, Maltese, they were all Dings.

2 (also *dinger*) Backside, anus

1948 Sumner Locke Elliott *Rusty Bugles* in *Khaki, Bush and Bigotry* ed. Eunice Hanger (1968) 96: 'In your great dinger, you rotten crawling choco.'

1953 T. A. G. Hungerford *Riverslake* 161: 'why *my* mate, particularly?' 'Hell he thinks the sun shines out of your dinger!'

1972 Geoff Morley *Jockey Rides Honest Race* 209: 'You can get fined or sent to gaol for kicking a cat in the ding, but it's okay if it's a three-month-old baby.'

1980 Bob Herbert *No Names . . . No Pack Drill* 49: 'It's not only 'is MPs that's lookin' for 'im. Our wallopers are too . . . An' they're right up 'is dinger.'

3 A party, celebration [f. *wingding*]

1956 *Sydney Morning Herald* 18 Oct. 1: In New Guinea a party is called a 'ding' and a

house is a 'donga'. So if they have a party at home it's a ding in their donga.

1972 Alexander MacDonald *The Ukelele Player under the Red Lamp* 205: Only there was no beer. Just trayfuls of battery-fluid and cochineal . . . that was the kind of ding it was, all very outer-space and quaint and inconceivably twee.

1984 Max Harris *Australian* 16 Jun. Mag. 10: I'm in favour of stylishness . . . But we mustn't let the newspapers fool us. It has nothing to do with the latest social ding at the Sydney Opera House.

4 A dent, esp. in a surfboard

1963 *Pix* 28 Sep. 62: *Ding*: A hole in the fibreglass sheath of the board.

1979 Kathy Lette and Gabrielle Carey *Puberty Blues* 32: They checked their boards for dings and stood over us as we waxed them.

1984 *Sydney Morning Herald* 23 Apr. 12: Pity about that speck of rust on the door. And that little ding in the front.

ding *v.* To throw away, abandon, give up, esp. in the expression 'to ding it': *obsolescent* [f. thieves' slang: see quot. 1812]

1812 Vaux: *Ding* To throw, or throw away . . . To ding a person, is to drop his acquaintance totally, also to quit his company, or leave him for the time present.

1875 A. J. Boyd *Old Colonials* (1882) 68–9: 'If any man was to try and get along carryin' on the Northern road with only twelve horses, he'd very quickly find he'd have to ding it.

1896 Edward Dyson *Rhymes from the Mines* 74: Ding it? No. Where gold was getting I was on the job, and early.

1903 Joseph Furphy *Such is Life* (1944) 178: 'I'm as weak as a sanguinary cat. I must ding it.'

dingbat 1 An Army batman: World War I slang: *obs.*

1919 W. H. Downing *Digger Dialects* 19: *Dingbat* See Batman. *Batman* An officer's servant.

1932 Leonard Mann *Flesh in Armour* 161: The lieutenant and his dingbat slid down into the trench.

2 Someone eccentric or deranged

1918 *Kia Ora Coo-ee* 15 May 5: There are men who will tell you that they like camels, and I reckon that they ought to be put in the Dingbat Home at Abbassia. There's something wrong with their brains.

1957 Nino Culotta *They're a Weird Mob*

29: 'Some ding bat after that job ... He sounds a bit crackers to me.'
1977 Sumner Locke Elliott *Water Under the Bridge* 71: 'They ought to have him put away in Callan Park with the other ding-bats.'

dingbats, to be, have the To have delirium tremens; to be in an irrational state [N.Z. 1918 OED]
1924 *Truth* 27 Apr. 6: *Dingbats* To be annoyed, D.T.'s.
1925 Arthur Wright *The Boy from Bullarah* 66: 'It's enough to give a fellow the dingbats. I suppose you've been soaking up this damned stuff till it's sent you ratty, eh?'
1943 Margaret Trist *In the Sun* 29: 'May as well take another job soon,' he said, 'a man would only get dingbats hanging around here too long.'
1972 Richard Magoffin *Chops and Gravy* 106: *dings* ding-bats, dee-tees, delirium tremens, the horrors.

dinger see **ding** 2

dingo *n.* Aboriginal word for the native dog, a term of extreme contempt when applied to a man, because of the animal's reputation for cowardice and treachery
[**1855** William Howitt *Land, Labour and Gold* ii 168: The coward dingo of the bush.]
1908 Henry Fletcher *Dads and Dan between Smokes* 116: 'Them townies must be a fair lot o' dingoes.'
1923 Con Drew *Rogues and Ruses* 133: 'You're not goin' to fight! ... I always thought you were a flamin' dingo!'
1944 Randolph Bedford *Naught to Thirty-three* 79: Jock Robertson has a great and affectionate following, although some bushmen called him 'Dingo Jack'.
1962 Tom Ronan *Deep of the Sky* 180: 'Jim Campbell was a different proposition. He was a bloody dingo.'
1973 *Australian* 21 Nov. 11: 'He has shown cowardly instincts by trying to restrain this action,' Mr Anthony said of Mr Whitlam. 'All I can say of him in the Australian language is that he is a dingo.'

dingo *v.* To behave like a dingo (also 'dingo out', 'turn dingo', 'act the dingo')
1935 *Bulletin* 29 May ii: In the second round he 'dingoed', letting us through repeatedly, much to his team-mates' disgust [OED Suppl.]
1945 Margaret Trist *Now That We're Laughing* 133: 'That's the kind she is. Turn dingo on her own sister if it suited her.'
1952 Eric Lambert *The Twenty Thousand Thieves* 335: 'Where is Allison?' 'He dingoed at the last minute.'
1963 T. A. G. Hungerford *Shake the Golden Bough* 217: 'Now you've dingoed, and I wonder just what the hell mates are for.'

dingoes, did they forget to feed the Jocular greeting to an unexpected arrival
1968 Walter Gill *Petermann Journey* 13: He looked up, saw it was me, and barked, 'You again! Christ, ain't they fed the bloody dingoes lately?'

dingo's breakfast A variant of the **bushman's breakfast** q.v.
1983 Tim Vaughan *Sydney Morning Herald* 5 Apr. Good Living 1: My compatriot Pierre and I amused the fellow-travellers by starting the day with a dingo's breakfast, before we strolled to the bar for a more leisurely Spanish breakfast.
1984 *Age* (Melbourne) 16 Jun. Extra 11: A dingo's breakfast, a pee and a look around, is free, which I'm told is popular with tourists on buses.

dink *v.* To carry a passenger on the crossbar of a bicycle, or on a pillion seat (originally from doubling-up on a horse: see **double-bank, double-dink**)
1941 Baker 23: *Dink, to* See 'double dink'.
1959 Gerard Hamilton *Summer Glare* 111: When I was getting my bike out from under the veranda, she came up to me and said, 'How about dinking me home from school?' ... 'All right,' I said. 'Hop on.'
1984 *Age* (Melbourne) 15 Dec. 11: Bowen often used to dink Murphy home from school on his pushbike.

dink *n.* A ride taken by 'double-dinking'
1934 *Bulletin* 5 Sep. 20: The fortunate Melbourne school-kid with a bike ... is asked by his cobbers for a 'dink'.
1965 D. E. Charlwood *All the Green Year* 46: 'I'll give y' a dink.' He drew up with me on his new bike and I jumped on the bar.
1980 *Sydney Morning Herald* 13 Feb. 7: I rode a bicycle, which cramped my style a

little. Girls only start to get interesting after they cease to accept 'dinks' on bikes.

dinkum *n.* 1 Work, toil: *obs.* [E. dial. OED 1891]
1882 Rolf Boldrewood *Robbery Under Arms* (World's Classics 1949) 47: It took us an hour's hard dinkum to get near the peak. Sometimes it was awful rocky, as well as scrubby . . . but there was no help for it.
2 An Australian soldier in World War I: *obs.*
1918 *Aussie* 18 Jan. 3: 'And how often do you get leave to Australia?' asked the inquisitive old lady. 'Once every war,' replied one of the dinkums, 'at the end of it.'
1919 W. H. Downing *Digger Dialects* 19: *Dinkums (The)* The 2nd Division. Also applied to the New Zealanders.

dinkum *a. & adv.* Authentic, genuine, esp. in the expression 'fair dinkum' ('on the level')
1894 *Bulletin* 5 May 13: *Chief Justice:* And did yer stouch him back? *Witness:* No. *Chief Justice:* Fair dinkum? *Witness:* Yes.
1911 Louis Stone *Jonah* 63: 'Garn, ye're only kiddin'!' she cried with an uneasy grin. 'Fair dinkum!' said Jonah.
1922 Arthur Wright *A Colt from the Country* 78: 'It's like a story out of a book,' went on Bucks. 'But it's dinkum.'
1951 Ernestine Hill *The Territory* 433: If from the other side I can do anything for you, Paddy Murray or Bill Sheahan, I will, fair dinkum. Good luck, everybody. [from the will of a N.T. drover]
1984 *Sydney Morning Herald* 3 Mar. 38: Fair dinkum. Last week I saw Don Dunstan wearing a tie.

dinkum oil see **oil**

dinky-di 1 An intensive form of 'dinkum', usually with nationalistic overtones
1918 N. Campbell and L. Nelson *The Dinky-Di Soldier and other Jingles* [book title]
1939 Miles Franklin and Dymphna Cusack *Pioneers on Parade* 41: 'You raise my hopes that there are some real Australians.' 'Yes, we have some,' smiled Prim . . . 'My cousin is a dinki-di specimen.'
1973 *Australian* 19 Sep. 14: If one has the ability to drink oneself into an alcoholic stupor without falling flat on one's face in front of one's mates, one apparently has then

achieved the true blue hallmark of excellence of today's dinky-di Aussie.
2 Abbr. for 'dinky-di Australian'
1981 *Australian* 11 Mar. 2: Bob Ansett's a born-again dinky di now [heading] Bob Ansett, along with his American accent and trans-Pacific worldliness, is in Australia to stay, and to prove he means it got himself naturalised at the Opera House in Sydney yesterday.

dinner, to be done like a To be completely worsted
1847 Alexander Harris *Settlers and Convicts* ed. C. M. H. Clark (1959) 88: 'If we don't give the rain time to wash out the horse-tracks we shall be done like a dinner.'
1853 *Letters from Victorian Pioneers* ed. T. F. Bride (1898) 170: The driver . . . up to his neck in water, calling out to me 'he was done like a dinner'.
1901 *Grip* 5 Dec. [1]: The Southern Rivers 'Done like a Dinner' [headline]
1965 William Dick *A Bunch of Ratbags* 236: 'Chassa came out from behind the counter and done him like a dinner and threw him out the door.'
1980 Blanche d'Alpuget *Monkeys in the Dark* 90: 'They went off half-cocked and got done like dinners.'

dinnyhayser A knockout blow; anything of exceptional size or force [f. the boxer Dinny Hayes]
1907 Nathan Spielvogel *The Cocky Farmer* 14: 'Then I gets a dennyaiser in the eye, and sits down suddenly.'
1946 K. S. Prichard *The Roaring Nineties* 17: He . . . got him dancing mad and blowing like a grampus before he let him have a dinnyazer that knocked him.
1949 Ion L. Idriess *One Wet Season* 141: Here, too, the teamsters have their 'last drink'. A dinnyhayser, at times.
1966 D. E. Charlwood *An Afternoon of Time* 80: 'Gunna be a dinnyheazer of a storm,' said Percy.

dip A punch, thump, delivered to an opposing player in Australian Rules [f. cricketing slang *dip*, hit, slog]
1963 Lou Richards *Boots and All!* 88: Like most Brownlow Medallists, he was still no angel – I saw him have a bit of a dip on more than a few occasions.

dip one's lid, to   To raise one's hat to: (fig.) to salute
1915 C. J. Dennis *The Songs of a Sentimental Bloke* 21: 'This 'ere's Doreen,' 'e sez. 'This 'ere's the Kid.' / I dips me lid.
1930 Jack O'Hagan 'Our Don Bradman' in *The Barry Humphries Book of Innocent Austral Verse* (1968) 43: Don Bradman every Aussie dips his lid to you!
1975 Rodney Hall *A Place Among People* 238: 'I'm here to say I was wrong, I dip me lid to a fellow like you. You're a man.'
1984 *Sydney Morning Herald* 9 Jul. Guide 16: So now three journalists, White, Day and Thomson, own a radio station. Us ordinary journos dips our lids.

dip out (on)   1   To withdraw, renege; fall behind
1952 T. A. G. Hungerford *The Ridge and the River* 56: There wasn't a man in the section who would dip out on a patrol so long as he could drag one leg after the other.
1968 David Ireland *The Chantic Bird* 111: I reckon if I'd ever said things like that when I was a kid, my parents would have stayed alive instead of dipping out, just to hear more.
1983 *Sydney Morning Herald* 29 Oct. 1: The ABC's new managing director will be named probably on Monday – but it won't be Bruce Gyngell, who dipped out of the race yesterday.
2   To be displaced, fail to qualify
1989 *Australian* 18 Mar. 44: Whitney dips out; Campbell wins tour spot [heading] For Whitney, 30, it is the first time since at least World War II that the season's leading wicket-taker has not been chosen for an Ashes tour.

dip your eye (in fat)   A retort expressing derision
1953 T. A. G. Hungerford *Riverslake* 163: 'Dip your eye!' Randolph said with gutter coarseness, putting into the words as much as he could of his dislike of Condamine.
1959 Edward Lindall *No Place to Hide* 189: 'Dip your eye,' I said.

dirt-tin, like a lily on a   see **lily**

Dirty Digger, the   see quots
1973 Mungo MacCallum *Nation Review* 8 Jun. 1041: Keith Rupert Murdoch, better known to his admirers as the Dirty Digger.
1981 *National Times* 3 May 4: For more than a decade, the Dirty Digger, as he is

known on Fleet Street, has been by far the most successful of Britain's press proprietors.

Dirty Half Mile   See quot. 1970
1934 F. E. Baume *Burnt Sugar* 338: Mario could ... mention Bondi and Coogee with detachment and grin knowingly when anyone spoke of the Dirty Half Mile.
1951 Dymphna Cusack and Florence James *Come In Spinner* 189: 'Got above herself, she has. Stuck up in one of them flash joints round the Dirty Half Mile and for all I care, she can stay there and rot.'
1970 Kenneth Slessor *Bread and Wine* 18–19: Woolcott Street has become respectable and changed its name to King's Cross Road ... William Street itself ... has been transformed completely since the days when I walked its length coming back from the Stadium. Then it was less than half its present width, a narrow and somewhat sinister street lined on one side with frowsy terraces and dimly-lit shops. It was the original 'Dirty Half Mile', a title afterwards transferred to Woolcott Street and now without a claimant.
1984 *Sydney Morning Herald* 2 Jul. Guide 16: The *Nightwatch* mike found a trio of buskers near the Dirty Half Mile.

dirty on, to be   To hold in disfavour
1965 Jack Dyer *Captain Blood* 153: I was a bit dirty on being beaten.
1972 Geoff Morley *Jockey Rides Honest Race* 230: There's Deena talking to her boyfriend. I know he's got a bird out in the car waiting for him. She's gonna get dirty if she finds out.
1984 *Age* (Melbourne) 29 Mar. 28: Even without losing money I get very dirty on a team for not winning when everything points to its certain success.

Dirty Reds   see **Reds**

dish, go for the big   To plan a large bet, gamble for a large amount
1949 Lawson Glassop *Lucky Palmer* 74: 'A quid?' he asked scornfully. 'A quid? Only a quid! Cripes, you're playing with their dough now. Go for the big dish.'

dish up   To defeat in a contest, worst completely [f. *dish* To 'do for', defeat completely OED 1798]
1916 *The Anzac Book* 101: He said to me:

'Corporal Wilson, / You've dished up the beggars in style.'
1919 J. Vance Marshall *The World of the Living Dead* 84: Me remish I lorst fer dishin' up a screw.

disperse Euphemism for destroying the natives: *obs.*
1887 E. M. Curr *The Australian Race* iii 20: To an observer of languages, it is interesting to note the new signification of the verb *to disperse*: that when a Black girl of fifteen is shot down she is said to be *dispersed*.
1890 J. A. Barry *Steve Brown's Bunyip* 182: Earliest dawn heralded the pitiless swoop of the native troopers on the quiet camp. His tribe 'dispersed', baby Billy, the sole survivor, was brought to B——.
1918 C. Fetherstonhaugh *After Many Days* 232: One of the native police officers . . . told me that on one occasion when they were 'dispersing' (that was what it was called) some blacks, he saw Jerry, one of his boys, with a little picaninny boy in his hand. He was swinging the little chap round preparatory to knocking out his brains against a tree.

distance, tyranny of see **tyranny**

Dix(er), Dorothy A parliamentary question asked by a member of the Government party so that the Minister may make a prepared answer, to his own advantage [f. 'Dear Dorothy Dix' the newspaper feature consisting of answers to correspondents' problems]
1963 *Australian Financial Review* 31 Oct. 16: Queensland Senator Dame Annabelle Rankin may have been posing a 'Dorothy Dix' (political jargon for a planted question) to Senator Sir William Spooner.
1971 *Australian* 24 Apr. 5: Mr Barnard said Dr Forbes was reading from a prepared statement and obviously answering 'a question that is more commonly known in the House as a Dorothy Dixer'.
1981 *Sydney Morning Herald* 4 Jun. 14: He got his chance with a nice little Dorothy Dixer from the Government backbenches.

do To expend or consume completely; lose or forfeit
1859 Frank Fowler *Southern Lights and Shadows* 48: A wealthy tavern-keeper who came to England with us, used to boast of 'doing' his forty nobblers of brandy a day.

1921 *Aussie* 15 Mar. 54: 'Just done me last dollar up at the swi school.'
1948 Sumner Locke Elliott *Rusty Bugles* in *Khaki, Bush and Bigotry* ed. Eunice Hanger (1968) 34: 'Done the lot . . . Done the flamin' lot. Yeah, done me thirty quid. How's a bloke's luck.'
1959 Dorothy Hewett *Bobbin Up* 117: 'What do you want me to do, do me job cold?'
1974 David Ireland *Burn* 52: 'Don't bet on it, son. You might do your dough.'

do over 1 To bash up, equivalent to U.S. 'work over'; attack and destroy (military)
1944 Lawson Glassop *We Were the Rats* 76: 'Do this galah over,' he whispered in my ear. 'He's a king-hit merchant.'
1965 William Dick *A Bunch of Ratbags* 177: Sometimes they'd eject some of the more rowdy ones of our mob and take them to the station and do them over.
1975 Les Ryan *The Shearers* 103: 'Get goin' before the mob does you over too.'
2 Applied to the male role in intercourse [f. *do with* have intercourse with OED 1175]
1952 T. A. G. Hungerford *The Ridge and the River* 172–3: 'Wait till you see a few of the girls in the villages in the hills, where they haven't been done over.'
1961 Mena Calthorpe *The Dyehouse* 101: 'You're not the first dame that's been done over, not by a long shot.'
1975 Richard Beilby *The Brown Land Crying* 110: 'Anyrate, 'e never done 'er over, if that's what ya worryin' about.'

dob in 1 To inform against, implicate, betray
1957 Judah Waten *Shares in Murder* 173: 'You said you'd go to the police and dob him in unless he coughed up . . . That's the story isn't' it?'
1966 H. F. Brinsmead *Beat of the City* 144: 'But you feel such a rat to tell on her. To dob her in.'
1982 *Australian* 11 Dec. 3: Victoria's 'dob in a druggie' campaign has been hailed as an outstanding success by the Police Commissioner, Mr Doug Miller.
dobber
1958 *Coast to Coast 1957–1958* 201: 'How's his flipping form? Dobber-in Number One?'
1974 John Powers *The Last of the Knucklemen* 95: 'Don't look at me, you bastards! I'm no bloody dobber!'

2 To contribute (probably confused with 'dub in' as in 'dub up')

1954 Tom Ronan *Vision Splendid* 179: 'Very pleased to subscribe. Pity more of the staff aren't home. I'm sure they all dub in.'

1968 Geoffrey Dutton *Andy* 197: 'The ground crew are dobbing in too,' said Rogerson, 'and there should be some other donations.'

1971 David Ireland *The Unknown Industrial Prisoner* 86: 'For the price of few cents a week, we can all have a ticket . . . Dob in, men!'

doco A documentary

1981 *Sun-Herald* 9 Aug. 151: Mr Dunstan has made a series of dockoes on Australia Past, Present and Future.

1982 *Sydney Morning Herald* 2 Oct. 16: Too often a docco is a strung-together report full of sound and flickers but signifying little.

doctor 1 A bush cook, esp. for a number of men [a ship's cook U.S. 1821 OED]

1868 C. Wade Brown *Overlanding in Australia* 71: Grumbling is contagious in its nature, so for this reason alone a good cook, or 'doctor', as he is called, is a necessary individual in a camp.

1908 Giles Seagram *Bushmen All* 192: 'By the way, we've no Doctor. All hands take it in turns to cook.'

1945 Robert S. Close *Love Me Sailor* 144: 'Hey doctor! What about something to eat?'

2 A refreshing sea-breeze, usu. named from a specific place (e.g. **Albany, Fremantle** q.v.)

1914 *World's Standard Dictionary* (Aust. Suppl.): *doctor* (in W.A.) a cool, healthy sea-breeze which blows *bet.* November and April (the summer months).

1976 Max Brown *The Black Eureka* 97: Perhaps on an evening when a Port Hedland Doctor blew in from the ocean they even knew what they sought.

doctor, go for the To make an all out effort, esp. in horse-racing; bet all one's money

1949 Lawson Glassop *Lucky Palmer* 250: 'Passing the seven, Gelignite is only half a length in front of Laughing Water – Jim Minburry seems to be going for the doctor – closely followed by Harristine, Pirate Gold.'

1966 Tom Ronan *Strangers on the Ophir* 80–1: But a jackeroo . . . whose horsemanship was of no standard at all suddenly sat down and started to go for the doctor. With his whip going like a flail and his spurs like pistons he drove his cuddy to the lead.

1976 *Sydney Morning Herald* 20 Apr. 13: 'I decided to go for the doctor rather than let Taras Bulba fight for his head.'

dodge 1 To move cattle or sheep, esp. along a droving track

1881 A. C. Grant *Bush-Life in Queensland* ii 134: Dodging Cows [chapter heading]

1911 E. S. Sorenson *Life in the Australian Backblocks* 167: Dodging the crawlers along is the most disheartening of all stock work.

1936 Archer Russell *Gone Nomad* 27: My cattlecamp and sheep-dodging* days. *Sheep mustering and droving.

2 To acquire dishonestly, as in **poddy-dodging** q.v. [? f. *dodge* a dishonest stratagem]

1965 Tom Ronan *Moleskin Midas* 149: 'For every poddy that's up in the Coronet breakaways there's a dozen blokes trying to dodge it off.'

see **monkey dodger**

dodger Bread, esp. in army, boarding school, etc.: *obsolescent* [cf. *dodge* a large irregular piece, a lump OED 1562]

1919 W. H. Downing *Digger Dialects* 19: *Dodger* Bread.

1950 *Australian Police Journal* Apr. 112: *Dodger* Gaolbread.

1957 Nino Culotta *They're a Weird Mob* 51: Joe said to Jimmy, 'Smack us in the eye with another hunk o' dodger, matey.' Jimmy gave him some bread, but I was unable to see the connection between the request and the reply.

1964 Thomas Keneally *The Place at Whitton* 91: 'A couple of rounds of mouldy dodger and you'll be right.'

doer A 'character', an incorrigible, an eccentric. Often a **hard doer** q.v.

1919 W. H. Downing *Digger Dialects* 19: *Doer* A person unusually humorous, reckless, undisciplined, immoral or eccentric.

1930 L. W. Lower *Here's Luck* 161: 'My crikeys!' he added. 'That young Stanley must be a bit of a doer!'

1958 Hal Porter *A Handful of Pennies* 95: 'A real doer . . . oh, a dag when you got to know him.'

dog 1 An informer; one who betrays his associates, often in the expression 'turn dog' [U.S. 1846 OED]

1864 J. F. Mortlock *Experiences of a Convict* (1965) 78–9: Men betraying their companions or accepting authority over them are often called 'dogs', and sometimes have their nose bitten off – the morsel being termed 'a mouthful of dog's nose'.

1895 Cornelius Crowe *The Australian Slang Dictionary 24: dog* 'to turn dog', to turn Queen's evidence.

1903 Joseph Furphy *Such is Life* (1944) 252: 'I'd be turnin' dog on the station if I took advantage o' your message, to go round warnin' the chaps that was workin' on the paddick.'

1941 Kylie Tennant *The Battlers* 350: 'Old Sharkey turned dog on us, didn't he, Bet? Said he'd get me for abduction.'

1962 Tom Ronan *Deep of the Sky* 30: Always someone would turn up who knew him as the man who had sent his mates to the gallows. No one, free immigrant, currency lad, or old lag, would eat, work or travel with Tully the Dog.

1990 *Sun-Herald* 4 Mar. 17: 'He became known as a "dog". A dog is a very evil person who would even give his mother up for two meat pies.'

2 A dingo (the native dog)

1899 A. B. Paterson 'Father Riley's Horse' in *Singer of the Bush* (1983) 337: It was Hogan, the dog poisoner – an aged man and very wise.

1910 C. E. W. Bean *On the Wool Track* 52: Some forgotten shepherd penned his sheep night after night from the dogs and the natives.

1938 Francis Ratcliffe *Flying Fox and Drifting Sand* 235: I also learned a thing or two about dingoes. In the North-east, at least on those stations I had visited, dogs are no longer a serious pest; but there the story was different.

1979 *Advertiser* (Adelaide) 31 Jul. 14B: Dog fence review [heading] Protection and restoration of the 60-year-old dog fence was being treated as a matter of urgency, the Minister of Land and Environment, Dr Cornwall, said yesterday.

3 A horse or sheep difficult to manage

1945 Baker 175: A *dog* is a horse difficult to handle.

1965 Leslie Haylen *Big Red* 117: The Ape tried giving him 'dogs' to shear. That is, old, rough, wrinkled wethers, knobbly, burry, dusty, hard to shear.

1987 *Sun-Herald* 29 Nov. 81: Schofield, when asked by chief steward Ray Murrihy for his explanation, didn't pull any punches. 'The horse is a dog. Sometimes he gets right back in the field and races badly and other times he can be up with them.'

4 Canned meat i.e. **tinned dog** q.v.

1977 F. B. Vickers *A Stranger No Longer* 25: 'I always keep a few tins of dog on hand, son. The bloody blowflies are so bad you can't keep anything fresh. So just in case the old corn goes green or bad, I've got the dog.'

5 A measure of cold: see quots

1955 *Bulletin* 26 Oct. 13: The frost was just beginning to vanish when one of the abo. 'boys' came up to the homestead from his camp. 'Very cold last night, Billy,' remarked the new governess. 'My oath, missus,' he replied, 'had to put on a couple more dogs.'

1956 Stuart Gore *Overlanding with Annabel* 120: They [dogs] are particularly useful in place of blankets on cold nights. So if a native tells you that it was 'Plurry cold last night – three-dog night', you know what he means.

1987 Gordon Francis *God's Best Country* 70: 'But winter – brrrr – six dog nights all the time.'

Dog Act, the See quot. 1898

1898 A. B. Paterson *Bulletin* 31 Dec. 31: There is an Act compelling a publican to refuse drink to an habitual inebriate. This is locally known as the 'Dog Act' and to be brought under the Dog Act is a glorious distinction, a sort of V.C. of Northern Territory life.

1965 Xavier Herbert *Larger than Life* 217: 'Let me hear of you drunk again, and I'll have you put under the Dog Act.'

1974 Robert Adamson and Bruce Hanford *Zimmer's Essay* 16: Helm was the sort of prisoner that it probably wouldn't hurt to classify insane, to treat for alcoholism under the Dog Act, or certify.

dog, all prick and ribs like a drover's (shearer's, swaggie's) see **all**

dog and goanna rules No rules at all (as in a fight between a dog and a goanna)

1971 *Sydney Morning Herald* 12 May 1: Says a Merimbula reader: A propos of the recent reference to Queensland politics now working under a 'dog and goanna franchise', as an octogenarian I can remember the good

old days when Queensland cemeteries voted almost to a man.
1979 *Australian* 1 Dec. 13: When it comes to takeovers in the business world, Mr Bjelke Petersen wants a Marquis of Queensberry style conduct observed, not the dog and goanna rules and tactics so often displayed in his parliament.

dogbox 1 A compartment on a long-distance train, in a carriage with no corridor
1905 Nathan Spielvogel *A Gumsucker on the Tramp* 43–4: I found at last railway cars worse than the worst Australia possesses. The one I came down here in was a dog box. Under the seat was a collection of old wine bottles and broken lunch baskets, etc.
1958 E. O. Schlunke *The Village Hampden* 115: 'We had to get out of our sleepers into dog-boxes and found we still had over a hundred miles to go.'
1963 Bruce Beaver *The Hot Summer* 128: They found a dog-box all to themselves which meant an uninterrupted half hour between Mundulla and the first stop.
2 A security area in prison for police informers [f. **dog** 1]
1990 *Sydney Morning Herald* 16 Mar. 1: The only safe place for dogs is in a so-called dog box – a special unit reserved for protected prisoners.

Dog Collar Act The Transport Workers' Act (1928) and the Transport Workers' (Seamen) Regulations (providing for the licensing of seamen before they could work), so styled by the Seamen's Union in challenges of 1935–6 and later
1939 *The Seamen's Journal* 1 Sep.: Vicious Acts that we are now shackled with such as the *Crimes Act*, the *Transport Workers' Act* (Dog Collar).
1953 Dymphna Cusack *Southern Steel* 255: 'The Government put the Dog-Collar Act on the wharfies when they refused to load shipments of pig-iron.'
1982 Wendy Lowenstein and Tom Hills *Under the Hook* 62: The Dog Collar Act destroyed the WWF as an industrial power for more than twenty years, until it was repealed by the Curtin Labor Government in 1942.

dogger 1 A hunter of dingoes (native dogs)
1910 C. E. W. Bean *On the Wool Track* 55: He asked to be taken on as a dogger.
1934 Archer Russell *A Tramp-Royal in*

Wild Australia 113: It is along the fences, most often, that the 'wild dogger' sets his traps, into which, more often than the wily dingo, steps the unsuspecting bustard.
1971 Colin Simpson *The New Australia* 489: As a dogger (dingo destroyer) Charlie had shot or trapped as many as 275 dingoes in one year, earning $60 a week plus $4 a 'scalp' (ears and tail).
1984 *West Australian* (Perth) 19 Jan. 45: The Minister for transport, Mr Julian Grill, is pressing for the reinstatement of a dogger for the Salmon Gums area after complaints of attacks by dingoes on sheep flocks.
2 A slaughterer of horses for pet food
1978 *Sun-Herald* 21 May 80: The despised horses being bought by the 'doggers' for the people who manufacture canned pet-food.

dogging Dingo-hunting
1910 C. E. W. Bean *On the Wool Track* 55: A man is generally kept dogging, and the boundary rider gets a few pounds out of occasional scalps.
1928 Arthur Upfield *The House of Cain* 89: 'I bin dogging round Lake Frome.'
1932 William Hatfield *Ginger Murdoch* 167: 'Yes, dogging – dingo-stiffening, you know.'
1965 *Australian* 15 Feb. 8: Peter . . . has been dogging for forty years. In ten years around the Alice they killed nearly 40,000 dogs.

dog, head like a robber's see **head**

dogleg fence See quots
1863 Rachel Henning *Letters* ed. David Adams (1963) 136: It is what is called a 'dog's-leg' fence, made of unbarked saplings, but crossways, and it looks quite pretty as it goes up and down the gullies.
1901 Henry Lawson 'Water Them Geraniums' *Prose* i 577: The clearing was fenced in by a light 'dog-legged' fence (a fence of sapling poles resting on forks and x-shaped uprights).
1934 Steel Rudd *Green Grey Homestead* 75: Crossing your legs to steady yourself, and looking like a section in a dog-leg fence, your eyes will meet Josie's by accident.
1955 Alan Marshall *I Can Jump Puddles* 171: A decayed dog-leg fence, erected from trees felled along its line, encircled the paddock, in which saplings and scrub marked the return of the bush.

dog licence Certificate exempting an Aborigine from the provisions of the Aborigines Protection Act 1909–43, esp. as allowing the holder to drink in a hotel (discontinued in 1967): *derogatory*

1955 F. B. Vickers *The Mirage* 257: 'Monty wants us to get the dog licence – that's the paper they give you . . . If we had this paper, me and you could have walked into that pub and stood at the bar all day and none of 'em could have said a word to us.'

1962 Cynthia Nolan *Outback* 80: If Moonlight had been asked why he had not applied for a Certificate his answer might possibly have been the same as that of the half-caste drover who replied furiously: 'If I've got to have a licence to be equal to a white man I'd rather stay as I am – it would be like taking out a dog licence.'

1978 Kevin Gilbert *Living Black* 297: Before the 1967 referendum, before citizenship, Aborigines could receive these exemption cards – dog certificates – which enabled them to enter a hotel.

dogman A man who rides on the hook of a crane, and directs operations by signals [f. *dog* sb. 7a OED]

1962 Robert Clark *The Dogman and other Poems* 2: The dogman dangles from the clouds, / Astride a beam of swinging air, / Unrealized hero of the crowds, / Whose upturned faces dimly stare.

1965 *The Tracks We Travel* ed. L. Haylen 42: The shrill whistle of the dogman 150 feet above warns us that he is signalling the winding driver to lower away.

1981 *Australian* 14 Oct. 7: Dogmen, who 'rode the hook' (stood on loads being lifted by cranes to direct the driver) in high winds and on ever-higher buildings, were dying at the rate of a dozen a year in the 60's. Riding the hook was unnecessary if two dogmen were employed per crane.

dog, shoot your own see **shoot**

dog's disease Influenza

1919 W. H. Downing *Digger Dialects* 19: *Dog Fever* A mild form of influenza.

1932 Leonard Mann *Flesh in Armour* 218: Half the platoon had had dog's disease.

1953 Baker 166: *dog's disease* Malaria. [as World War II slang]

Dogs, the 1 The Footscray A.F.L. club [abbr. of Bulldogs]

1979 *Herald* (Melbourne) 7 Apr. 34: Dogs

die! Melbourne survived fierce, relentless pressure from Footscray to snare a 12-point victory at the MCG this afternoon.

2 The Canterbury Bankstown Rugby League club

1979 *Australian* 1 Jun. 16: Top 'Dogs' return for Manly game [heading]

dogs are pissing on your swag see **pull**

dog tied up See quots

1906 A. B. Paterson *An Outback Marriage* 178: 'Paddy's 'ad a dorg tied hup 'ere (ie. an account outstanding) this two years.'

1944 Lawson Glassop *We Were the Rats* 83: 'He's left so many dogs tied up all over Australia it's a wonder there're enough of 'em left to hold tin-hare meetings.'

1962 John O'Grady *Gone Fishin'* 124: 'I says what about me three pound six, I haven't got a dog tied up here, have I?'

dog, tinned see **tinned dog**

dole-bludger Someone drawing unemployment benefits even though work is available

1977 *Bulletin* 22 Jan. 14: The last three Labor Ministers have all talked a lot about cracking down on 'dole bludgers' but there is little anyone at the top can do.

1982 *Australian* 18 Nov. 22: Federal parliamentary references to the unemployed have turned about. Some time ago the unemployed were dubbed 'dole bludgers', now they are the 'disemployed' and 'those with no opportunity for commencing employment'.

doley Someone on the dole, in the Depression of the 1930s

1953 *Caddie A Sydney Barmaid* 209: 'You needn't worry about 'im Caddie. 'E's a friend to all us doleys.'

1966 Elwyn Wallace *Sydney and the Bush* 108: 'You track dolies are more trouble than you're worth. Better bloody fed than I am.'

1982 *Sydney Morning Herald* 5 Apr. 6: How do the rest of you poor, frustrated, out-of-work 'dolies' feel?

Doll, the Ray Lawler's play *Summer of the Seventeenth Doll*, first performed in 1955, and taken as marking a renaissance in Australian drama

1963 *Sydney Morning Herald* 16 Mar. 12: 'The Doll' Hits Iceland!
1974 *Southerly* 215: Since *The Doll* naturalism has retained its force in Australian drama.

doll, knock over a To incur the consequences entailed in any activity [? f. the contest of throwing at dolls at a sideshow]
1954 T. A. G. Hungerford *Sowers of the Wind* 142: 'Surely to God he knows that if he throws the ball he's got a chance of knocking over the dolly!' [i.e. contracting venereal disease]
1959 Gerard Hamilton *Summer Glare* 95: 'Knocking a doll' was an old belief among us youths. We had never believed the story of the stork or of the cabbage patch either. Years ago the big boys had told us a much better story. It was that inside all women there was a number of small babies sitting in a row, and when a man, or a boy big enough, knocked one over, it was born after nine months. Thus our saying 'to knock a doll'.

dollar The sum of five shillings (until the introduction of decimal currency in 1966) [f. equivalence of value with the U.S. dollar]
1911 Louis Stone *Jonah* 65: As she was rather suspicious of a wedding that cost nothing, she decided to give the parson a dollar to seal the bargain.
1942 Gavin Casey *It's Harder for Girls* 55: 'I can get half a dollar from dad.'
1964 Tom Ronan *Packhorse and Pearling Boat* 119: With tobacco at twelve shillings per pound he found it hard to send more than a dollar a week up in smoke.

dollar, holey The 'ring' dollar authorized in 1813 by the striking of a circular piece (a **dump** q.v.) from the centre of a Spanish dollar
1849 J. P. Townshend *Rambles and Observations in New South Wales* 10–11: This place [Ulladulla] ... is commonly called 'Holy Dollar'. The origin of the corruption of this native name is this: it used to be the practice to cut the centre out of a dollar, and the middle piece was called 'a dump' and the remainder of the original coin 'a holey dollar'.
1859 See **dump** 1
1984 *Sydney Morning Herald* 28 Jan. 7: A 170-year-old 'holey dollar' fetched $18,275 at a public auction in Melbourne yesterday. The coin was one of 40,000 Spanish coins punched with holes by order of Lachlan

Macquarie in 1814. About 150 'holey dollars' are known to be left. They were used in lieu of a local currency and the centres were punched out to render them worthless outside Australia.

dollar, not the full As for **not the full quid** q.v.
1976 Robert Drewe *The Savage Crows* 8: Was he the full dollar these days?
1983 Peter Corris *The Empty Beach* 86: 'I hear that Freddy might not be the full dollar. He was in Changi, which wouldn't have done him any good.'

dolly's wax, full up to See quot. 1982
1945 See **pussy's bow**
1965 Barry Humphries *A Nice Night's Entertainment* (1981) 85: Everyone was full up to dolly's wax and I was absolutely stonkered, so unfortunately it was hardly touched.
1982 Nancy Keesing *Lily on the Dustbin* 17: When my children were small a man, then in his eighties, sat back from our table after lunch and announced, 'I'm full up to dolly's wax!' It had to be explained that dolls once had delicate, modelled wax heads with a neck shaped so that it could be sewn to a stuffed rag body.

Dolphins, the The Redcliffe (Q.) Rugby League club
1981 *Sunday Mail* (Brisbane) 20 Sep. 1: After joining Redcliffe from Roma in 1964, Beetson helped the Dolphins to their first and only premiership the following year.

don 1 Doyen [f. *don* a leader, first class man, an adept OED 1634–1853]
1898 W. H. Ogilvie *Fair Girls and Gray Horses* 55: He's the don at every muster and the king of every camp.
1901 Henry Lawson *Verse* ii 2: He's a don at peeling spuds.
2 *The Don* Sir Donald Bradman, the cricketer
1949 J. Fingleton *Brightly Fades the Don* [book title]
1965 Wally Grout *My Country's Keeper* 12: 'The Don' looked ageless behind the sticks, and his cover drive was still the most exciting thing in cricket.

dona, donah Sweetheart, esp. in larrikin argot: *obs.* except for the saying 'Don't introduce your donah to a pal' [f. Sp. *dona*, It. *donna* woman]

[**1859** Hotten: *Donna and Feeles* A woman and children.]

1874 *Melbourne Punch* 9 Jul. 276: [legend to a cartoon] *Cad* (yells to friend) 'Yar-icks – Nobby 'ere's Nixon with a new dona!' (Which being interpreted, meaneth that Nixon is paying his addresses to a fresh sweetheart).

1896 Nat Gould *Town and Bush* 103: When they dare not smash windows, they perform upon the faces and bodies of their female acquaintants, familiarly called 'donahs'.

1923 Jack Moses *Beyond the City Gates* 136: But at this moment Bill's donah became hysterical and fainted.

1954 *Bulletin* 14 Jul. 8: Sydney 'Telegraph' has come to light with the diary of the lady who introduced Mrs Simpson to the Prince, while herself in favor (don't introduce your donah to a pal?).

Donald Duck Fuck [rhyming slang]
1967 *King's Cross Whisper* (Sydney) xxxiv 4: *Donald Duck*: Truck. Also that four-letter word.

1987 Kathy Lette *Girls' Night Out* 170: We washed down the meal with Germaine Greers and Donald Ducked on the Rory O'Moore.

done like a dinner see **dinner**

dong *v.* To strike, punch
1916 Let. in Bill Gammage *The Broken Years* (1974) 233: I feel that the Corporal would have failed his manhood had he not 'donged' him.

1939 A. W. Upfield *The Mystery of Swordfish Reef* 228: 'Stop that, Bob, or I'll dong you one.'

1970 Patrick White *The Vivisector* 10: She came up and donged him one with her skinny hand.

1981 *Australian* 28 Apr. 3: England captain Ian Botham threatened to dong him [Henry Blofeld] at Bermuda airport.

dong *n.* A blow
1932 L. W. Lower *Here's Another* 14: How would they like a dong in the gills with a golf ball?

1938 Francis Ratcliffe *Flying Fox and Drifting Sand* 167: I . . . was just about to have a dong at him when the brute changed its mind and shot ahead.

donga 1 A natural depression or gully

[f. S. African *donga* A channel or gully formed by the action of water OED 1879]

1937 Ernestine Hill *The Great Australian Loneliness* 330: *Donga* Depression in sandy country.

1945 Stan Arneil *One Man's War* (1980) 230: Working in the open, in hot, steamy dongas, with fields of tapioca around us, I revel in the simplicity and crudeness of the soil.

1978 *Sydney Morning Herald* 28 Oct. 11: He knows it well . . . Where the bores are, and the dongas (hollow depressions), where salt bush changes to blue bush.

2 A makeshift shelter: see quot. 1972
1956 *Sydney Morning Herald* 18 Oct. 1: In New Guinea a party is called a 'ding' and a house a 'donga'. So if they have a party at home it's a ding in their donga.

1972 Turner 22: *Donga* 'a gully' was current among soldiers in the Second World War, expanding its meaning to include any kind of shelter, until now among the Europeans in New Guinea it is a local word for 'house'. Only *donga* among all these words seems likely to be traceable to the battlefields of the Boer War.

1975 *Overland 62* 7: Like many of the older houses [in Darwin] Bill's little donga has survived in some form, though the roof's gone, and a wall.

3 A portable
1983 *Australian* 7 Oct. 7: The single men call their steel prefab homes dongas – easily demountable for cartage to the next job site.

1986 James McQueen *The Floor of Heaven* 186: I can see row after row of dongas – portable camps that look like old railway carriages, each divided into half a dozen cubicles.

donkey-lick To defeat easily, esp. in horse-racing
1890 A. B. Paterson 'Our New Horse' in *Singer of the Bush* (1983) 109: He sold for a hundred and thirty, / Because of a gallop he had / One morning with Bluefish and Bertie, / And donkey-licked both of 'em bad.

1907 Arthur Wright *Keane of Kalgoorlie* 50: 'What's more, he can donkey-lick a stable full of crocks like Yalgoo.'

1958 Frank Hardy *The Four-Legged Lottery* 42: 'Who won the footie?' 'Ah, Richmond got donkey-licked.'

1984 *Sun-Herald* 30 Sep. 65: Hawthorn donkey-walloped Essendon in last year's one-sided grand final by 83 points.

donkey vote A vote recorded by simply numbering preferences down the ballot paper in the order in which the names appear

1963 *Sydney Morning Herald* 23 Mar. 2: The 'Donkey Vote' in Australia.

1979 *Advertiser* (Adelaide) 12 Mar. 1: Mr Corcoran said the by-election showed the Australian Democrats were a spent force. 'If you take the donkey vote away from them they would be down to about 4 p.c.' he said.

1984 *Sun-Herald* 11 Mar. 168: Remember Rev Fearless Fred Nile getting the number one spot on the Upper House ballot papers for his Call to Australia group at the last election? God's work, said Fred, to help him get the donkey vote.

Dons, the The Essendon A.F.L. team (also the Bombers) [abbr.]

1975 *Sunday Telegraph* (Sydney) 29 Jun. 38: Don's Rally Pays Off.

don't argue The straight-arm warding off movement in Rugby football [f. illustration in the trademark of J. C. Hutton Pty Ltd: see quot. 1977]

1942 Leonard Mann *The Go-Getter* 232: He should have . . . just put a hand in his face and given him a push – a 'Don't Argue' sort of push, like that in the advertisement.

1977 *Australian* 14 Apr. 18: Rugby football fans around the world know the straight-arm fend-off as a 'Don't argue', and its origins go back to the turn of the century. The creator of the symbol was Mel B. Spurr, a pianist, singer, dancer, vaudevillian, monologist, cartoonist and story-teller. Mel Spurr starred in Melbourne's Tivoli, the Athenaeum Hall and the Town Hall in the golden days of vaudeville. Spurr invented the two man symbol and took it to Hutton's Melbourne manager. The 'Don't argue' slogan was quickly evolved, and in a short time became one of Australia's best-known trademarks.

1982 *Sydney Morning Herald* 28 Aug. 30: 'The kid's got everything . . . He has the size and strength to burst through tackles, a 'don't-argue' fend, and he loves scoring tries.'

Dooley, give someone Larry To administer punishment, give a hiding [unexplained, although a connection has been claimed with the pugilist Larry Foley]

1946 Alan Marshall *Tell Us About the Turkey, Jo* 104: I had driven him [the bull]

back a week before and that morning I gave him Larry Dooley.

1969 Patsy Adam-Smith *The Folklore of the Australian Railwaymen* 118: I nodded towards the Governor's train. 'They'll [the mosquitoes] give his nibs larry-dooley tonight.'

doorknock A fundraising campaign for charity which is conducted by seeking donations from door to door [f. the Anti-Cancer Appeal Doorknock of 1958, organized by Don Chipp: see quot. 1978]

1973 *Bulletin* 16 Jun. 22: Winter: season of doorknocks, of middle-aged women smiling winningly on the porch and writing out receipts with cold fingers and blotty ballpoints in the front hall.

1978 Don Chipp in Tim Hewat and David Wilson *Don Chipp* 10: I gathered together a committee of bright young people and I invented the name Doorknock. On the day we had 55,000 volunteers; and that first Doorknock raised £350,000 ($700,000) in two hours.

1984 *Alice Springs Star* 8 Aug. 1: The appeal, launched by Chief Minister, Mr Paul Everingham last week culminates in a Territory-wide door-knock on Sunday.

Dorothy Dixer see **Dix(er)**

dose of salts, go through like a see **salts**

dot As for **date** q.v.

1978 Ronald McKie *Bitter Bread* 104: She did not look or act like a real pro, although with so many amateurs around trailing their dots you could not always tell.

1984 John Hepworth *Toorak Sunday* 10 Jun. 5: Only one bird [in King's Cross] hawking the dot – and she had *pants* on.

dot, wine see **wine**

double-bank 1 To yoke on a second team of bullocks to pull a load out of a bog, or to overcome some similar difficulty

1863 Rachel Henning *Letters* ed. David Adams (1963) 128: I should rather like to see them at the river or some of the bad creeks, where they 'double-bank the bullocks' as it is called: that is, put the whole team, thirty yokes perhaps, on to each dray to drag it over.

1913 John Sadleir *Recollections of a Victorian Police Officer* 168: The teamsters did not travel alone, for there were many places where double-banking was a necessity, and six or more horses in single file might often be seen hauling one load over some bad pinch.

2 (also *double-dink*) To double a load; carry an extra person on a horse or bicycle

1876 A. J. Boyd *Old Colonials* (1882) 77: 'By-and-by, down goes the mare, dead beat . . . so we unpacked her, and double-banked my other mailhorse, and the inspector got along on the first one.'

1882 Rolf Boldrewood *Robbery Under Arms* (World's Classics 1949) 221: 'We must double-bank my horse,' whispers Jim . . . He jumped up, and I mounted behind him.

1933 R. B. Plowman *The Man from Oodnadatta* 223: 'I have only one spare riding camel . . . They could double-bank on him if they liked.'

double dink   as for **double-bank** 2

1941 Baker 25: *Double-dink* To carry a second person on the top bar of a bicycle.

1943 Charles Shaw *Outback Occupations* 120: It was back in the days when the boys were little fellows, still going to school, double-dink on the old brown mare.

1959 Gerard Hamilton *Summer Glare* 105: Once or twice I had double-dinked her home from school on my bike.

see **double bank**

double dipping, double dip   See quots

1983 *Sydney Morning Herald* 22 Apr. 3: This review will take into account 'double dipping' by pensioners who take their superannuation in a lump sum form and then draw the age pension.

1983 Paul Keating *Australian* 27 May 10: 'A trend had emerged in Australia where people took their benefits in a lump sum, arranged their affairs to minimise income and then double-dipped the public purse by taking the age pension.'

double drummer   A variety of cicada [f. sound]

c. **1905** A. B. Paterson 'Done for the Double' in *Song of the Pen* (1983) 248: Certainly the locust was a 'double-drummer', and could deafen the German Band when shaken up judiciously; still, it was dear at the price of a sovereign.

1951 Dymphna Cusack and Florence

James *Come In Spinner* 105: There came the piercing crackle of a cicada. 'He's a double drummer.'

Double Pay   The Sydney suburb of Double Bay [f. shop prices]

1981 *Sydney Morning Herald* 20 Feb. 1: It's yet another irritating example of Opera House tenants' unswerving devotion to Le Rippe Off, on the assumption that everybody who goes to the place is from Double Pay.

1984 *Sunday Telegraph* (Sydney) 25 Mar. 158: This one's not Double Pay [heading] Unbelievable food at realistic prices is what Tony's International restaurant at Double Bay has to offer.

doubler, chuck a   To 'have a fit'

1946 *Sun* (Sydney) 1 Sep. Suppl. 23: When he lamps Sydney he chucks a doubler.

1959 H. D. Williamson *Sammy Anderson Commercial Traveller* 133: 'He chucks a doubler, and finishes up flat on his face in the gutter.'

doughboy   Name given to the colonial versions of the doughboy ('A boiled flour dumpling' OED 1865), most often cooked in fat

1834 Let. in Edward Shann *Cattle Chosen* (1926) 58: Dawson fried some pork, and Phoebe cooked some doughboys for dinner.

1855 William Howitt *Land, Labour and Gold* i 117–18: A suet pudding, called a dough-boy . . . put into the fat, and when ready, beef steaks or mutton chops are fried.

1983 *West Australian* (Perth) 31 Dec. 15: 'We hadn't eaten all day and when we asked for a meal, the farmer boiled us up some doughboys in a kerosene tin.'

doughnut (golden)   1 The vulva

1972 David Williamson *The Removalist* 53: 'We'll be in like Flynn there tomorrow night. We'll thread the eye of the old golden doughnut – no worries.'

1974 Barry Humphries *Barry McKenzie Holds His Own* 33: [Barry is watching an attractive girl] Ohh, I could hit that on the golden doughnut like a plate of porridge.

2 See quot.

1981 *Sydney Morning Herald* 20 Apr. 1: They started their usual entertainment of 'doughnuts'. This involves a motor cyclist spinning his machine in tight circles.

Douglas   An axe [f. brand name]

1901 Phil Moubray *The Swag* 3: From

Bacchus Marsh onwards they 'introduce Douglas' to you. That is, they put an axe in your hand and make you earn your feed.
1966 James Hackston *Father Clears Out* 160: Sometimes on a Sunday morning exhibitions of axemanship (theoretical) were given; right and wrong way to swing Douglas.

dover A bush knife, esp. in the expression 'flash your dover' as an invitation to eat; also food [f. brand name]
1870 Marcus Clarke *His Natural Life* ed. S. Murray Smith (1970) 616: 'Hang up your moke, my young Ducrow, sit down, and flash your Dover.'¹ 1 *Flash your Dover* is essentially *Colonial* slang. The majority of clasp knives imported in to the Australian colonies twenty years ago were made by one 'Dover'. Hence 'flashing your Dover' is equivalent to 'drawing your Toledo'.
1885 *The Australasian Printers' Keepsake* 75: He . . . returned with half a loaf of bread, part of a shoulder of mutton, and some cold potatoes. He roared exultingly – 'Here's the sanguinary dover for yer – now let us have a blooming pint!'
1908 Giles Seagram *Bushmen All* 164: 'He was a loud, red-faced man who used his blooming dover like a shovel.'

down, have a ~ on To have a grudge or prejudice against, to be hostile to [f. thieves' slang: see quot. 1812]
[**1812** Vaux: A *down* is a suspicion, alarm or discovery, which taking place, obliges yourself and *palls* to give up or desist from the business or depredation you were engaged in; to *put a down upon a man*, is to give information of any robbery or fraud he is about to perpetrate, so as to cause his failure or detection.]
1835 *Colonist* 10 Sep. 289: To use the colonial slang, Up comes Mr Cory himself . . . to Sydney, to have a *down* upon us, poor *misfortunate* Editor, for a libel!
1855 Raffaello Carboni *The Eureka Stockade* ed. G. Serle (1969) 14: I, a living witness, do assert that, from that day, there was a 'down' on the name of [Commissioner] Rede.
1863 R. Therry *Reminiscences of Thirty Years' Residence in New South Wales* 122: 'I am very sorry to tell your Grace that there's a great down upon the Romans in this country.'
1896 Henry Lawson 'Stiffner and Jim'

Prose i 127: 'I had a down on Stiffner, and meant to pay him out.'
1907 Ambrose Pratt *The Remittance Man* 185: 'I can't see why you should have such 'a down' on him. How has he offended you?'

Down Under Australia: rarely used by Australians themselves
1886 J. A. Froude *Oceana* 92: We were to bid adieu to the 'Australasian' . . . She had carried us safely *down under*.
1916 *The Anzac Book* 145: He sat down to think, little dreaming that he was fulfilling Macaulay's prophecy concerning the man from 'down under' sitting on the ruins of London Bridge.
1951 Simon Hickey *Travelled Roads* 121: Because I came from 'Down Under', they gave me imposing statistics on petroleum, helium, sulphur, mercury, beef cattle.

drac(k) Unattractive, esp. as applied to women, in phrases like 'a drack sort' [? f. *Dracula's Daughter*]
1945 Baker 127: *Sope* is an old larrikin word . . . the direct antithesis of *bonzer* . . . *Drack* and *bodger* are modern equivalents.
1949 Ruth Park *Poor Man's Orange* 180: He was always stuck with drack types like Dolour Darcy.
1968 Geoffrey Dutton *Andy* 265: 'You blokes get on to some bloody drack subjects.'
1972 *Sydney Morning Herald* 26 Sep. 9: Mr Hardy said he would put aside his memories . . . of meeting Raquel Welch ('A drac sort – not nearly as good looking in the flesh as you would expect').

drag A prison term of three months [thieves' slang: see quot. 1812]
1812 Vaux *Drag* A cart. The *drag*, is the game of robbing carts, waggons, or carriages . . . *Done* for a *drag*, signifies convicted for a robbery of the before-mentioned nature.
1877 T. E. Argles *The Pilgrim* i 6: He expected to receive at the hands of the magistrates a term of imprisonment which he designated as a 'drag' (three months).
1939 Kylie Tennant *Foveaux* 311: 'I got a drag,' he said not too regretfully. Three months was a good deal less than he had expected.

drag the chain see **chain**

dragged, to be To be replaced (by the coach) in an Australian Rules match

1975 Robert Bennett *The Big Ruck* 22: 'You could always drag me off if I don't come up to expectations.'

1986 *Sunday Telegraph* (Sydney) 28 Sep. 123: The Hawks' best move was the use of veteran Rodney Eade to tag damaging Carlton utility Craig Bradley. Eade was so effective that the Carlton player was dragged from the field in the third quarter.

dragged scraming from the tart shop see **tart shop**

Dragons, the The St George (N.S.W.) Rugby League team (also the 'Saints') [f. club emblem]

1974 *Australian* 8 Aug. 20: Dragons will draw extra fire to beat Easts.

draw the crabs see **crabs**

draw the crow see **crow**

dreamtime, the The mythological past of the Aborigines, used colloquially to refer to anything remote, out of touch with the present

1953 T. A. G. Hungerford *Riverslake* 235: Slim and the kitchen and Riverslake seemed to have receded into a dream-time that had no tangible link with the present and the immensity of the revelation that had come over him.

1983 *Australian* 1 Jun. 16: The suggestion that all post-graduate awards should be taxed showed the 'dreamtime mentality' of many senior academics and administrators, according to the Council of Australian Postgraduate associations ... The report had failed to understand the realities of the needs of postgraduates.

drink a horse see **horse**

drink with the flies see **flies**

drongo Someone who is stupid, clumsy, worthless [f. the racehorse described in quots 1946, 1958, 1977. The horse would presumably have been named (before it acquired this reputation) after the swift and alert *drongo* (family *Discruridae*), a bird resembling the starling]

1941 *Salt* 22 Dec. 36: An airforce recruit

is a drongo, and this word, it is suggested, is taken from the name of a large clumsy flying bird found in the Cape York Peninsula.

1946 *Salt* 8 Apr. 22: Drongo a horse foaled in 1921 and retired in 1925 who failed to win a race, and after that anybody or anything slow or clumsy became a Drongo.

1949 Ruth Park *Poor Man's Orange* 181: It wasn't his fault he was a drongo ... He didn't want to have pimples, or a thin neck, or that hair all snowflaked with dandruff.

1958 Tom Ronan *The Pearling Master* 181–2: His continued run of second placings, both in and out of the classroom, brought from a senior of some standing the comment that ... 'Weyland was another Drongo' ... They all knew about Drongo: the colt had been a popular fancy for the previous Derby at Flemington. After a careful preparation ... he had run second. Throughout Oliver's first year at school the horse continued running seconds. He dropped out of the quality races and competed in moderate class handicaps, but he never managed to have his number hoisted first by the judge ... Drongo, first synonymous with a capacity for always being narrowly beaten, gradually changed to be an epithet flung at anything or anybody too cow-hearted to try to win.

1963 Randolph Stow *Tourmaline* 63: 'Put your head back, drongo,' Kestrel said to Byrne.

1977 *Sunday Telegraph* (Sydney) 13 Feb. 120: The 1600 m Drongo Handicap – for apprentice jockeys and horses without a win for more than a year – is raced in memory of a horse who gave his name to the language ... running second in a VRC Derby and St Leger, third in an AJC St Leger and fifth in the 1924 Melbourne [*in error for* Sydney] Cup. The trouble was he couldn't win in 37 starts.

1982 *Sydney Morning Herald* 20 Nov. 29: 'In fact,' Tite told Senator Gareth Evans, who was at Magdalen in the 1960s, 'of all the colonial drongoes – that's the word, is it not? – that ever passed through my hands, Fraser was the greatest.'

droob A 'sad sack', hopeless-looking person [? f. *droopy*]

1945 Baker 156: *drube* A term of contempt for a person. [Army slang]

1948 Ruth Park *Poor Man's Orange* 181: A sick feeling entered Dolour's heart when she saw Harry standing there, his hands thrust into his pockets like packages and a little, saliva-stained fag stuck on his lower

lip. Of all the nice boys going to Luna Park
. . . she had to draw this droob.

drooby

1972 James Searle *The Lucky Streak* 50:
'You'll 'ave to wear something a bit decent
. . . you look pretty drooby in them.'

1981 *Sunday Mail* (Brisbane) 25 Oct. 18:
The party was rotten – drooby creeps,
spooks, twits, bores etc.

drop a bucket see **bucket**

drop one's bundle see **bundle**

drover's breakfast A variation of the
bushman's breakfast

1990 *Sunday Telegraph* (Sydney) 21 Jan.
184: Just as many Aussies will settle for a
Pommy's breakfast – a cup of tea and a
smoke – or a Drover's Breakfast – a look
around and a cough.

drover's dog 1 From Mr Hayden's statement on being replaced as Labor leader by
Bob Hawke shortly before the Federal election in 1983: see quot.

1983 Bill Hayden *Australian* 4 Feb. 1: 'I
believe a drover's dog could lead the Labor
Party to victory the way the country is.'

1983 *Sydney Morning Herald* 14 May 1:
Sir Kenneth's retirement, aged 70, came
fortuitously for the Labor Party: it enabled
the party, having decided at last that Dr Bert
Evatt was no drover's dog, to find a soft landing for him as Chief Justice.

2 Mr Hayden himself

1983 *Australian* 28 Dec. 9: Bill Hayden:
both nicknames, Bellyache Bill and Whingeing Willie, have been dropped. Now it is the
Drover's Dog.

drum *v.* To impart necessary and reliable
information; to set someone straight [see
drum n. 1]

1919 J. Vance Marshall *The World of the
Living Dead* 30: Hurriedly he impressed
upon me the exact location . . . and proceeded to 'drum me up' with the message.

1948 Sumner Locke Elliott *Rusty Bugles* in
Khaki, Bush and Bigotry ed. Eunice Hanger
(1968) 32: 'You never get out of here, mate
– I'm drumming you.'

1969 D'Arcy Niland *Dead Men Running*
105: 'Don't bite me, son. I was only gonna
drum you.'

drum *n.* 1 Information requisite to some

particular situation; reliable information generally, esp. in the expression to 'give someone
the drum'

[**1812** Vaux: *Drummond* Any scheme or
project considered to be infallible, or any
event which is deemed inevitably certain, is
declared to be a *Drummond*; meaning, it is
as sure as the credit of that respectable
banking-house, Drummond and Co.]

1923 Con Drew *Rogues & Ruses* 88: 'But
how do you know that Ding Dong won't be
tryin'?' says the clerk . . . 'Because I got the
drum on the way out to the races,' says
Cracker.

1969 Thomas Keneally *The Survivor* 167:
'I was hoping for the drum on Antarctica, I
was thinking you might cough up some Ant-
arctic quintessence, something that can't be
learnt from the journals.'

1980 *Bulletin* 18 Nov. 132: 'I've just had
the drum,' he whispered, 'that Susan Sang-
ster has bought herself a stunning new outfit
on the grounds that she's going to lead the
Cup winner in and wants to look her best.'

2 A swag, esp. in the expression 'hump
one's drum' [? f. cylindrical shape]

1868 T. Wade Brown *Overlanding in Australia* 64: He is 'humping his drum' (i.e.
travelling) looking up a job.

1887 *All the Year Round* 30 Jul. 66: In
Australia, the 'swag', also sometimes called
a 'drum', is the bundle, generally consisting
of a large blanket rolled up which contains
the personal luggage of the man who carries,
or 'humps' it.

1891 Henry Lawson 'On the Wallaby'
Verse i 134: I am out on the wallaby humping
my drum.

3 A brothel [f. thieves' slang: *Drum*, a
house, a lodging . . . *Flash drum*, a house of
ill-fame Hotten 1860]

c. **1882** *The Sydney Slang Dictionary* 3:
Drum, or Crib House of ill repute.

1894 *Bulletin* 18 Aug. 14: Grog scarce,
'drums' shut.

1944 Lawson Glassop *We Were the Rats*
103: 'There's another drum down here,' said
Eddie.

1951 Dymphna Cusack and Florence
James *Come In Spinner* 254: 'This place has
the rep. for being one of the safest drums in
the town.'

1975 Hal Porter *The Extra* 50: 'What's a
nice boy like you doing in a drum like
this?'

drum, not to run a Fail to perform as
tipped (turf slang)

1942 *Truth* 31 May 2: Ridden by Mc-Menamin, Vanity Fair was always at an unprofitable quotation, more especially when she subsequently failed to 'run a drum'.
1957 Nino Culotta *They're a Weird Mob* 72: 'Makes no difference. 'E never run a drum, anyway.'
1962 Stuart Gore *Down the Golden Mile* 261: 'Backed Sweet Friday for a spin . . . But it never run a drum.'
1978 John Hepworth *His Book* 113: Warrego Willie went like a hairy goat – never even looked like running a drum.

drummer 1 A commercial traveller [U.S. 1827 OED]
1886 P. Clarke *The New Chum in Australia* 124: A 'drummer' – that is, a commercial traveller.
2 The slowest shearer, the one with the lowest tally in the shed.
1898 *Bulletin* 1 Oct. 14: 'To carry the drum' is to be last man in the shed.
1911 E. S. Sorenson *Life in the Australian Backblocks* 240: The drummer, or slowest shearer, is about the only man who doesn't seem to care when supper-time comes.
1964 H. P. Tritton *Time Means Tucker* 92: In his previous sheds he had been drummer all the time.
3 See **double drummer**

drunk as Chloe see **Chloe**

Dry, the The dry season of the year, the months without rain
1882 William J. Sowden *The Northern Territory As It Is* 146: The year has two seasons – the dry and the wet – from May to September, and from October to April, respectively.
1908 Mrs Aeneas Gunn *We of the Never-Never* 219: It was August, well on in the dry.
1938 Xavier Herbert *Capricornia* 115: People scoffed at O'Cannon's cotton, saying at first that it would never see the Wet through, then that it would never live through the Dry.
1965 *The Tracks We Travel* ed. L. Haylen 78: On many such holdings, water has to be drawn from very great depths in the 'dry' in order to keep the cattle alive.

dry as a chip see **chip**

dry as a Pommy's towel (bath-mat) see **Pommy's**

dry-blow, dry-blower, dry-blowing 1 Goldmining terms for the process of separating out the gold when water is unavailable for 'washing': hence any monotonous and unproductive activity
1894 *The Argus* 28 Mar. 5: When water is not available, as unfortunately is the case at Coolgardie, 'dry blowing' is resorted to. This is done by placing the pounded stuff in one dish, and pouring it slowly at a certain height into the other. If there is any wind blowing it will carry away the pounded stuff. [Morris]
1915 J. P. Bourke *Off the Bluebush* 103: 'Do you have any luck at the diggings,' I said / To a dryblower grizzled and grey.
1950 K. S. Prichard *Winged Seeds* 18: Dinny started dry-blowing his reminiscences as if Young Bill . . . had never heard them before.
1967 Kylie Tennant *Tell Morning This* 50: Miss Montrose, who realised that she had struck paydirt at last after so much dry blowing at Grandma's conversation, clicked her tongue to express sympathy and interest.
2 See quot. 1979
1979 David Ireland *A Woman of the Future* 257: I didn't find out till later that some of them can mimic the spasms of ejaculation, and produce nothing. 'Dry-blowing', it's called.

dub A lavatory
1956 Ruth Park and D'Arcy Niland *The Drums Go Bang!* 170: 'A hot-water heater! and a hand basin. And look at that dub!'
1961 Nene Gare *The Fringe Dwellers* 25: 'If ya wanta use the dub it's round the side.'

dubbo Stupid; a stupid person (in N.S.W.)
1973 David Forster *North South West* 17: You've only got to look at all the bushwhacking, nest feathering dubbos we get for Education ministers in this state to know something's wrong with the system.
1980 *Sun-Herald* 27 Jan. 66: In New South Wales, of course, a person wouldn't be yarra, he'd be dubbo.
1982 *Sydney Morning Herald* 10 Jul. 36: Dubbo is an Aboriginal word for 'red earth', which does not explain why, on the east coast, this word is used to describe those who are slightly thick.

duchess To treat anyone 'as a duchess', esp. applied to the courtesies extended by overseas governments to visiting Australian politicians, as though imposing on their naivety

1969 Leslie Haylen *Twenty Years' Hard Labor* 134: Cables from London, telling us about the Labor delegation flashing through London in Rolls Royces, of being 'duchessed' in the Commons or on the lawns at the Palace, didn't exactly send the Labor benches into transports of delight.

1976 *Sun-Herald* 27 Jun. 38: It cannot be said that Malcolm Fraser was 'duchessed' during his memorable stay in Peking. But the flattering, seductive treatment he received did resemble the softening up process thus named to which Australian political leaders visiting London used to be exposed.

1983 *Sun-Herald* 12 Jun. 21: All this – and the fact that Bob bounced Prince William on his knee – ... prompts the thought that Hawke has been duchessed by royalty.

duck, black   see **black duck**

duck, blue   see **blue duck**

duck, Burdekin, Hawkesbury   see **Burdekin, Hawkesbury**

duck, couldn't head a   see **head**

duckhouse, one up against your   A point scored in some way against an adversary: *obs.*

1933 Norman Lindsay *Saturdee* 7: 'You think you hid me cap, so that's one up agen your duckhouse.'

1968 Stuart Goe *Holy Smoke* 52: He says, 'That's one up against your duckhouse, Jonah!'

1981 Ross Campbell *Sydney Morning Herald* 21 Nov. 45: National Trust needed to preserve historic Australian idioms, e.g. 'Shove that up against your duckhouse.'

duck-shoving   Jockeying for position; manipulative action generally

1870 *Notes & Queries* 6 Aug. 111: Duck-shoving is the term used by our Melbourne cabmen to express the unprofessional trick of breaking the rank, in order to push past the cabman on the stand for the purpose of picking up a stray passenger or so. [Morris]

1944 Keith Attiwill *Cut-Lunch Commandos* 115: The moral ... is that he who would trip abroad must learn to conjugate the verb 'to wangle' – I wangle; thou wanglest; he duckshoves; and so on.

1977 *Sun-Herald* 3 Apr. 15: The sensitive

report has been shuffled off to a variety of Public Service committees for more study and evaluation, but all the Public Service duck-shoving will not change the basic arguments.

duck, wet enough to bog a   Extremely wet

1879–80 Ned Kelly 'The Jerilderie Letter' in Max Brown *Australian Son* (1956) 272: The ground was that rotten it would bog a duck in places.

1920 *Bulletin Book of Humorous Verses* 9: And the ground was soft enough to bog a duck.

1934 Thomas Wood *Cobbers* 89: What about them tracks? ... Six inches of rain in three days would bog a duck.

1981 Garry Disher *Approaches* 12: 'This mud's soft enough to bog a duck.'

duff, duffing   Stealing cattle, esp. by branding unbranded calves (**poddy-dodging** q.v.) or by altering brands; poaching grass [f. *duffer*]

1869 E. C. Booth *Another England* 138–9: There was a 'duffing paddock' somewhere on the Broken River, into which nobody but the owner had ever found an entrance, and out of which no cattle had ever found their way ... The man who owned the 'duffing paddock' was said to have a knack of altering cattle brands. [Morris]

1875 Rolf Boldrewood *The Squatter's Dream* repr. as *Ups and Downs* (1878) 162: 'I knew Redcap when he'd think more of duffing a red heifer than all the money in the country.'

1903 Joseph Furphy *Such is Life* (1944) 47: Such a sound at such a time is ominous to duffing bullock drivers.

1938 *Salute to Freedom* 28: 'It's silly to surround cattle duffing with a cloak of romance as many people do. It's straight out theft.'

1964 H. P. Tritton *Time Means Tucker* 102: Never were we refused a bit of grass for our horses (I suppose they knew we would duff it if it was refused).

duffer   1 Someone who steals cattle, esp. by counterfeiting the brands, or branding cleanskins [f. *duffer* One who sells trashy goods as valuables, upon false pretences 1756 OED]

1877 Rolf Boldrewood *A Colonial Reformer* (1891) 352: 'Your husband takes to idle ways and worse, and your children grow

up duffers and planters, and perhaps end in sticking up people.'
1907 Charles MacAlister *Old Pioneering Days in the Sunny South* 252: The latter promptly pulled a burning stick from our camp fire and thrust it into the 'duffer's' face, singeing his red beard and making him howl with pain.
1937 Ernestine Hill *The Great Australian Loneliness* 83: O paralyse the duffer's hand, / When he lifts up his flaming brand.
1984 *Age* (Melbourne) 30 Jun. 17: Some time during the night of 7–8 May a group of duffers drove their truck on to Mr Wheelhouse's 50-hectare farm at Mooroopna, near Shepparton, and stole 28 Hereford steers worth about $13,000.
2   A mine that proves unproductive, esp. in expressions like 'sink a duffer', 'bottom a duffer'
1861 T. McCombie *Australian Sketches* 193: 'It was a terrible duffer anyhow, every ounce of gold got from it cost £20 I swear.' [Morris]
1880 Rolf Boldrewood *The Miner's Right* (1890) 55: 'Bottomed a duffer, by gum, not the colour itself, no mor'n on the palm o' my hand.'
1944 Brian James *First Furrow* 44: The last shaft he'd sunk . . . A rank duffer.
1960 Donald McLean *The Roaring Days* 58: In the drought of '92 he'd sunk a shaft that turned out a duffer as far as silver was concerned.

dummy *n.*   One who acts under his own name on behalf of someone else, to gain an illegal advantage: orig. applied to those employed by the squatters, when their runs were opened to 'free selection', to take up the best areas and so forestall genuine selectors
1865 *Australasian* 23 Jun. 5: There were twenty-two *bona fide* applicants, no dummies, and no certificate holders.
1901 Henry Lawson 'Water Them Geraniums' *Prose* i 578: I had an idea that he wasn't a selector at all, only a 'dummy' for the squatter of the Cobborah run. You see, selectors were allowed to take up land on runs, or pastoral leases. The squatters kept them off as much as possible, by all manner of dodges and paltry persecution. The squatter would get as much freehold as he could afford, 'select' as much land as the law would allow him to take up, and then employ 'dummies' (dummy selectors) to take up bits of land that he fancied about his run, and hold them for him.

1953 *Caddie A Sydney Barmaid* 178: 'This pub's a goldmine and they own three others in the country as well.' . . . 'But how do they get round the licences?' 'Aw, they get over that hurdle by putting in a dummy.'

dummy *v.* **dummying**   To act as a 'dummy'; the system so developed
1873 Anthony Trollope *Australia* ed. Edwards and Joyce (1967) 134: The . . . system is generally called 'dummying' – putting up a non-existent free-selector – and is illegal.
1903 Joseph Furphy *Such is Life* (1944) 35: 'Bob and Bat were dummying on the station at the time, and looking after the Skeleton paddock.'
1936 H. Drake-Brockman *Sheba Lane* 251: Begging the Government to take steps to suppress the dummying of luggers – the practice whereby a white man lent his name (at a price) to a coloured man, who was not allowed by law, to hold a pearling licence.

dummy, to spit the   To give way to a fit of temper, indulge in a tantrum
1987 Peter Ryan *Times on Sunday* 16 Aug. 12: Victorian teacher unions spat out their dummies last week for what may well be their final effort. Tantrums over the years have exposed them as the most greedy, manipulative and shameless of all the industrial rort merchants.
1987 *Sunday Telegraph* (Sydney) 29 Nov. 52: Laurie Brereton's decision to spit his ministerial dummy this week has raised profound doubts about whether he will ever regain his spot.

dump *n.*   1   Coin struck from the centre of a Spanish dollar in 1813, valued at 1s. 3d. [f. *dump* A term familiarly applied to various objects of 'dumpy' shape OED 1770; *Dumps* are also small pieces of lead, cast by schoolboys in the shape of money Grose 1811. (The term seems most often to be applied to the residue of some industrial process)]
1821 *Sydney Gazette* 5 May 2: A Number of BAD DOLLARS and DUMPS having been lately offered in Payment at the Bank of New South Wales, the Public, for their Information and Protection, are hereby apprised that the following Description of illegal Coin is much in circulation: – Dollars and Dumps that are not silver . . .
1826 James Atkinson *An Account of the State of Agriculture and Grazing in New*

South Wales 132: A piece was struck out of the centre of each [dollar]; this centre piece was called a dump, and was put into circulation at fifteen-pence sterling value.
1859 Daniel Bunce *Travels with Dr Leichhardt in Australia* 59: Our first change for a pound consisted of two dumps, two holy dollars, one Spanish dollar, one French coin, one half-crown, one shilling, and one sixpence.
2   Small coins, contemptuously referred to; any trivial amount
1826 *Sydney Gazette* 22 Apr. 2: The offender, who had money in both pockets, very cheerfully paid the fine, observing, 'that was the way to spend dumps'.
1905 Randolph Bedford *The Snare of Strength* 294: 'I'm that thirsty I'd drink with Nosey Bob the hangman. It doesn't matter a dump who pays.'
1981 Bill O'Reilly *Sun-Herald* 13 Dec. 97: From now on you can have your three pronged Australian pace attack ... I wouldn't give you a tuppeny dump for it.
3   A marble
1959 Gerard Hamilton *Summer Glare* 76–7: 'If you an' me were playing dumps' ... 'I see,' he said. 'Dumps are marbles.'

dump *v.*   1   To press bales of wool
1872 C. H. Eden *My Wife and I in Queensland* 98: The great object of packing so close is to save carriage through the country, for however well you may do it, it is always repressed, or 'dumped' ... by hydraulic pressure on its arrival in port, the force being so great as to crush two bales into one. [Morris]
1910 C. E. W. Bean *On the Wool Track* 265: To squash each bale into about two-thirds of its original size by 'dumping' (which means binding it round so tightly that what was formerly its length is squeezed into about the same dimension as its breadth).
2   (of a wave) To break and hurl a surfer down
1938 Jack Moses *Nine Miles from Gundagai* 88: W'en de breakers dumped / Me at Curl Curl.

dumper   A large wave that breaks suddenly and hurls the surfer down, instead of carrying him in to shore
1920 A. H. Adams *The Australians* 185: A dumper is a badly behaved breaker, easily recognisable by the expert, that instead of carrying you on its crest gloriously right up to the beach till you ground on the sand, ignominiously breaks as it strikes the shallow

water and deposits you, smack! in a flurry of sand and water, any side up. Dangerous, too; you might break your arm.
1942 Gavin Casey *It's Harder for Girls* 153: Most of our mob didn't know what to do when they got in front of a 'dumper', but I could still manage them.
1954 Peter Gladwin *The Long Beat Home* 193: 'Not that one,' he yelled. 'It's a 'dumper' ... He saw the wave's crest, instead of sliding, arch enormously and hang, and hurl her down and crash on her.

Duncan   The rolled swag: *rare* [unexplained]
1905 Arthur Bayldon *The Western Track* 56: With tucker-bags and billy-cans and Duncan on their back / They trust to luck to pull them through, and face the Western Track.
1906 H. J. Tompkins *With Swag and Billy* 8: Choice may be said to lie between the knapsack, rucksack, and swag – good old Duncan or Matilda.

dungaree settler   See quot. 1826
1826 James Atkinson *An Account of the State of Agriculture and Grazing in New South Wales* 29: I beg here to be understood as only alluding to the early Settlers, and the lower order of the present – what are technically termed in the Colony *Dungaree Settlers*, from a coarse cotton manufacture of India which forms their usual clothing; a more improvident, worthless race of people, cannot well be imagined.
1847 Alexander Harris *Settlers and Convicts* ed. C. M. H. Clark (1954) 4: It is a common assertion, that the poor Australian settler (or, according to colonial phraseology, the Dungaree settler; so called from their frequently clothing themselves, their wives and children in that blue Indian manufacture of cotton known as Dungaree) sells his wheat crop from pure love of rum.

dunny   A privy, esp. outside [f. *dunnakin* a necessary OED 1790; *dunegan* A privy A water closet Grose 1811]
1947 *Coast to Coast 1946* 216: 'We gotta get some wood from somewhere, or we'll freeze' ... 'We're buggered too – been burnin' the floor boards orf the dunny.'
1952 T. A. G. Hungerford *The Ridge and the River* 18: Right now there might be a Shinto under every bush, and me stuck out like a dunny in a desert.
1974 *Sunday Telegraph* (Sydney) 8 Sep. 9:

Someone once said he [Paul Hogan] was as Australian as a slab off a dunny door.
1982 *Australian* 25 Oct. 9: On Friday night and Saturday, November 12 and 13, Tongala will hold a Burn the Dunny Festival – to celebrate the town's connection to the sewerage.

dunny, bush see **bush**

dunny cart
1980 Clive James *Unreliable Memoirs* 50: I often watched the dunny cart from the front window. As it slowly made its noisome way down the street, the dunny men ran to and from it with awesome expertise.

dunny, country Used in figurative expressions of isolation or conspicuousness
1953 Baker 268: *Loneliness* All by himself like a country dunny.
1976 *Australian* 22 Mar. 26: The influence is there, but it doesn't stick out like the proverbial Australian country dunny.
1982 *NT News* (Darwin) 12 Mar. 17: Two players stood out like the proverbial country dunny for Nightcliff last week.

dunny door, to bang like a
1981 Garry Disher *Approaches* 53: 'There used to be this bird from Mawson at St. Margaret's. Bang like a dunny door.'

dunny man
1962 Hal Porter *A Bachelor's Children* 280: Early in December, one found a card on the lavatory seat:
Enjoy Christmas as best you can,
And don't forget the dunny man.

dunny, kick your ~ down   see **emus**

dunny, useful as a glass door on a   see **useful**

durry   A cigarette [? f. Hindi *dhurri*, a cotton carpet of Indian manufacture]
1941 Baker 26: *Durry* A cigarette butt.
1976 Sam Weller *Bastards I have met* 80: Crot slumped in the saddle, shirt out, feet out of the irons, reins on the horse's neck and a durry stuck to his lip.
1979 *NT News* (Darwin) 24 Nov. 14: *Darryls*: Another name for cigarettes (also Durries).
1984 Ned Manning *Us or Them* 6: STEVE (*stubbing out his cigarette*) Waste of a good durry!

dust   Flour, in bush parlance
1878 G. H. Gibson *Southerly Busters* 25: 'A pint o'dust' – that was his low / Expression meaning flour.
1903 Joseph Furphy *Such is Life* (1944) 256: The storekeeper measured me out a pannikin of dust into a newspaper.
1919 W. R. Harris *Outback in Australia* 146: The proverbial free pannikin of 'dust' (flour).

dust, bull-, heifer-   see **bull, heifer**

dyke   see **dike**

E

each way, two bob   see **two**

Eagles, the 1 The Manly-Warringah Rugby League team (N.S.W.): also the Sea Eagles [f. club emblem, and Manly as a seaside suburb]
1983 *Sun* (Sydney) 15 Aug. 27: Gutsy Eagles floor Bears [heading] Manly stunned North Sydney on Saturday with a 54–16 win.
2 In S.A., the West Torrens Australian Rules team
1979 *Advertiser* (Adelaide) 24 Mar. 20: Eagles sign full back [heading] West Torrens

has gained the services of Richmond defender Barry Grinter.
3 In Queensland, the Windsor-Zillmere Australian Rules team
1979 *Courier-Mail* (Brisbane) 17 Apr. 23: The Eagles won the knocks five to two.

earbash   To talk unremittingly, harangue [World War II slang]
1944 Lawson Glassop *We Were the Rats* 205: 'Are you going to sit there ear bashing all night?'
1953 Kylie Tennant *The Joyful Condemned* 22: 'She was ear-bashing me all over

tea how you came lairizing round at our place like you owned it.'
1981 *Sydney Morning Herald* 31 Jan. 16: Conferring awards on writers is usually a mistake. It encourages them to earbash instead of getting on with their writing.

earbasher A persistent talker, a bore
1946 Rohan Rivett *Behind Bamboo* 396: *Ear basher*, one who talks too much.
1954 *Coast to Coast 1953–1954* 85: He was an ear-basher and a known liar.
1975 *Sydney Morning Herald* 6 Sep. 12: Xavier Herbert is a cantankerous, outrageous old earbasher.
1953 Dymphna Cusack *Southern Steel* 260: 'I think we might as well shut up now and give Pop and Mum a chance. They must be just about sick to death of this earbashing.'
1964 Gavin Casey and Ted Mayman *The Mile that Midas Touched* 23: He didn't need a lot of earbashing from Bill.

earlies, the The early years of settlement in any region: N.T. and W.A.
1933 Charles Fenner *Bunyips and Billabongs* 65: However, the interesting story of the wild adventurers who lived on this remote island in the 'earlies' is not our subject.
1941 Charles Barrett *Coast of Adventure* 140: 'He loved to talk about his wonderful life up here in the Earlies.'
1951 Ernestine Hill *The Territory* 428: 'In those trails of yours, especially in the earlies, I suppose you've often travelled where no white man has ever been before you?'

early opener See quot. 1980
1972 John de Hoog *Skid Row Dossier* 10: We'd finished breakfast and gone for a drink, a quick one, to the Chamberlain Hotel, an early opener.
1980 *Bulletin* 28 Oct. 36: I refer to the early opener: one of those hotels licensed to open their doors at dawn, up to four hours before the rest of the country's pubs serve their first heart-starters of the day. There are 53 early openers in Sydney alone. The early-opening idea caught on in 1955 when 6 pm closing ended in New South Wales. Some licensees whose pubs depended for their custom on the wharves or food markets or other specific industries with early shifts applied for and were granted different trading hours from the general 10 am to 10 pm.
1990 *Australian* 24 Mar. Mag. 40: The

Grand is the last early opener in Sydney's central business district . . . It's the watering hole for the dawn briefcase brigade.

early shower, to take an see **shower**

Eastern States, the The states east of Western Australia (usu. excluding N.T.)
1904 Let. 30 Oct. *Letters from Irish Australia 1825–1929* ed. Patrick O'Farrell (1984) 117: Potatoes here fetch from £4 to £14, the market depending on supplies from Eastern States.
1984 Buzz Kennedy *Australian* 26 May Mag. 24: I was raised in the West Australian belief that everything evil, rapacious and sinful in Australia was in 'the Eastern States'.

easy Having no preference for one course of action over another, usually in the expression 'I'm easy' [listed by Partridge as 'R.A.F. coll.: since ca. 1938']
1942 Gavin Casey *It's Harder for Girls* 229: 'We might as well all stop here now,' said Clara. 'We'd just have to go down and come almost straight back.' 'I'm easy,' said Tom.
1955 John Morrison *Black Cargo* 90: Clarrie looks at me and Bob Grainger. 'What about it?' 'I'm easy,' I tell him, 'but a seven o'clock finish would do me.'
1966 Tom Ronan *Once There Was a Bagman* 191: Ned now wanted me to go to the Depot instead of to Hall's Creek. I was easy.

easy, life wasn't meant to be see **life**

Echuca, no lucre at see **Tallarook**

Edgar Britt see **Britt**

Eels, the The Parramatta Rugby League team (N.S.W.) [one of the Ab. meanings of 'Parramatta' is 'place where the eels lie down']
1974 *Australian* 22 Jul. 18: South's drought against Eels ends.

eh Supposedly used at the end of sentences in the speech of Queenslanders, not necessarily as an interrogative
1976 David Ireland *The Glass Canoe* 164: He was a Queenslander and though this is an interesting fact about any man, some get over it. Eh never did. Eh is pronounced 'ay' as in day. It was a question at the end of

every sentence. That was the way up north Queensland . . . When the boys got tired of calling him Eh they called him Guy, to stir him.

1983 *Australian* 30 Sep. 7: The men wear broad hats, the toilet doors swing outwards and almost everyone ends each sentence with an 'ay' . . . 'G'day Vince. Doing a bit of tripping round this week, ay', says the garage attendant as she fills our car with petrol at 53.9c a litre. Despite the inquisitive 'ay' and the upward inflection, it isn't a question. She had heard on the radio that Vince Lester would be in his electorate.

eighteen 1 An eighteen-gallon keg of beer

1918 George Dale *The Industrial History of Broken Hill* 117: The procession proceeded to the goods station, loaded some foodstuffs and five 'eighteens' of beer, and started back to the mine.

1942 Gavin Casey *It's Harder for Girls* 218: 'We got an eighteen, and plenty o' bottles coming over.'

1971 Frank Hardy *The Outcasts of Foolgarah* 194: 'Two eighteens, twenty dozen hot dogs,' Molly counted to herself, a hostess to the finger tips.

2 An Australian Rules team

1950 Gavin Casey *City of Men* 43: Jack Laycock will be dropped from the Collingwood eighteen next year.

1981 Leonie Sandercock and Ian Turner *Up Where, Cazaly?* 3: At 11.30, the two top Reserve Eighteens play out their Grand Final.

3 An eighteen-footer (i.e. 18-foot skiff)

1982 *Bulletin* 12 Jan. 79: Today, the eighteens are still part and parcel of a Sydney summer weekend out on the harbour.

eighteen-footer An eighteen-foot skiff

1946 Eleanor Dark *Waterway* 99: On Saturdays and Sundays all the eighteenfooters were out; they came racing down the harbour, their white sails fat and straining with wind, their crews leaning out horizontally over the water while they turned round the buoy and went skimming back again.

Ekka, the Brisbane Exhibition Grounds; the annual Exhibition there

1979 *Courier-Mail* (Brisbane) 31 Jul. 22: How to see the Ekka – and survive [heading] An expected 810,000 people will forge optimistically through the Brisbane Exhibition turnstiles this year.

1980 *Sunday-Mail* (Brisbane) 17 Aug. 3: Maternity hospitals in Brisbane report an upsurge in premature births during the annual Ekka. It appears that the Super Loops, Pirate Ship and other similar thrill-seeking sideshows induced quite a few births.

elephant, the The Commonwealth Bank [f. logo used since 1965, in association with the slogan Get With the Strength, on money boxes etc.]

1973 Alexander Buzo *The Roy Murphy Show* in *Three Plays* 112: 'Now it's time for the Commonwealth Bank Passing Competition and you know the rules. Three passes at the target . . . You get ten points for an Elephant's Eye and the Elephant's the symbol of the Commonwealth Bank and it's a pretty good idea to get with the strength.'

1984 *Sydney Morning Herald* 4 Apr. 1: As to whether the 'elephant' will eventually lose its monopoly right in NSW to the banking business of those budding business tycoons – the school-children – Mr Christie conceded that the bank could indeed soon be having to face competition.

embassy, tent embassy An encampment set up by Aborigines on the lawns of Parliament House on 26 January 1972, as a protest against government policies esp. on land rights; any similar demonstration

1972 *Sydney Morning Herald* 29 Jan. 2: Mr Howson . . . attacked a protest on Aboriginal land rights being staged outside Parliament House by members of the Black Power movement. He said . . . there was a disturbing undertone in the use by the protesters of a sign reading 'Aboriginal Embassy'.

1972 Ian Moffitt *The U-Jack Society* 157: Most of us averted our eyes from the Aboriginal 'Embassy' outside Parliament House when we first saw it . . . while the odd racist drove by yelling 'Niggers!'

1983 *Australian* 30 Aug. 3: Members of Sydney's gay community will set up a 'gay embassy' outside the Woollahra home of the NSW Premier, Mr Wran, after the arrest of 11 men at a homosexual club last weekend.

Emma Chisit The Strine equivalent of 'How much is it?'

1964 *Sydney Morning Herald* 30 Nov. 1: Monica Dickens, busily autographing her books in a city store, signed one handed her by a woman shopper. Miss Dickens THOUGHT that the lady then said 'Emma Chisit'. 'Oh,' said Miss Dickens brightly. 'You'd like me to write your name in it?' And she scrawled, 'To Emma Chisit'. 'I asked,' the lady said crossly, 'HOW MUCH IS IT?'

Emmaville express, the   Debbie Wells, the sprinter, born in Emmaville (N.S.W.)
1978 *Australian* 5 Jun. 18: Debbie Wells, the Emmaville Express, rated Australia's most promising woman sprinter in years, is in danger of missing out on the Australian Commonwealth Games squad for Edmonton in August.

emu   See quot. 1966 [f. **emu bobber**]
1966 Baker 237: *emu* A race-course lounger who picks up discarded betting and tote tickets in the hope of finding one which has not been cashed.
1983 *Sun-Herald* 23 Jan. 50: There was an epidemic of emus at Rosehill yesterday . . . 'Perhaps it is a sign of the recession times but I have never seen so many emus picking up discarded tote tickets at a race track' . . . Candrick said.
1984 *Age* (Melbourne) 20 Mar. 50: 'He picks up all the old betting tickets. They call them emus.'

emu-bobber   Someone employed to pick up after clearing or burning-off in the bush (emu-bobbing) [see quot. 1964]
1920 *Bulletin Book of Humorous Verses* 187: A score of 'emu-bobbers' came a-tramping from the Bland.
1959 C. V. Lawlor *All This Humbug* 16: 'Emu bobbing' consisted of gathering up small timber and twigs.
1964 H. P. Tritton *Time Means Tucker* 87: We . . . went to Wingadee to work for a contractor at burning-off. This work is also known as 'stick-picking' or 'emu-bobbing'. A group of men bending to pick up the fallen timber, with heads down and tails up, look very much like a flock of emus.
1973 Roland Robinson *The Drift of Things* 79: I was on 'emu-bobbin'' with him. Tom would axe, cut and stack the big logs . . . I picked up the smaller timber and sticks and threw them on the stacks.

Emu Hilton, the   Term applied to blacks' camp adjoining a white settlement (e.g. in Kununurra valley W.A.)
see **Jesus Hilton**

emu parade   In the army, a parade to clean up an area by 'emu-bobbing'
1941 T. Inglis Moore *Emu Parade* [book title]
1951 Eric Lambert *The Twenty Thousand Thieves* 315: 'Round up some men for an emu parade and parties to tidy up slit trenches and fix guy ropes.'
1982 *Australian* 8 Mar. 48: Gordon rugby union breakaway Greg Owen, after losing part of an ear in a match: 'Can we organise an emu parade to find the rest of my ear.'

emus, may your chooks turn into ~ and kick your dunny down   An expression of ill will
1974 Barry Humphries *Barry McKenzie Holds His Own* 48: Oh, I hope all yer chooks turn to Emus / Kick yer dunny down flat to the grass / I hope yer balls turn to bicycle wheels / And back-pedal up yer arse.
1975 Nev Hauritz *M7 Records MS055*: 'I Hope Your Chooks Turn into Emus and Peck Your Dunny Down' [song title]
1983 *Australian* 15 Jan. Mag. 16: Then there was *I Hope Your Chooks Turn Into Emus and Peck Your Outhouse Down*, another Hauritz composition inspired, like a thousand others, by a chance remark in a pub.

end, to get one's ~ in   To succeed in having intercourse with a woman
1969 William Dick *Naked Prodigal* 243: 'Look, you go and get your end in. I'll be O.K. You take your bird home, orright?'
1972 David Williamson *The Removalists* 117: 'I knew a Marilyn once. Biggest knock in Footscray. Got your end in yet?'
1981 Garry Disher *Approaches* 53: 'Where's your moll, Rymers? Not getting your end in tonight?'

enforcer   In sport, an aggressive player [f. U.S. gangster idiom, esp. as popularized in the television series *The Untouchables*]
1979 Steve Finnane *The game they play in heaven* 4: People began to talk about me as an enforcer – a term borrowed from rugby league and usually used to describe a player who was in a team for his fistic rather than his football ability.
1985 Rex Mossop *Sun-Herald* 8 Sep. 83: 'They . . . have no idea, at this stage, what the front row is all about. It's an enforcer's job, and you need to be a type of standover man, exhibiting sheer physical bloody dominance.'

1990 Max Presnell *Sydney Morning Herald* 13 Apr. 34: Dittman, 'The Enforcer', produced a Moore-like tactic to take the filly Research to the lead.

Enzed, Enzedder A New Zealander [f. N.Z.]
1915 Ion L. Idriess *The Desert Column* (1965) 11: The Australians and En Zeds waited until the Turkish charge was within fifty yards and then every man blazed away.
1949 Lawson Glassop *Lucky Palmer* 83: Approaching the home turn, Reed let the Enzedder go and he shot away with a winning break before you could say 'Phar Lap'.
1952 *Bulletin* 31 Dec. 10: Two Enzedders, E. P. Hillary and G. Lowe, will be included in Colonel Hunt's British Everest expedition, which will have its shot at the hill in the new year.
1983 David Foster *Plumbum* 202: You can buy any Australian girl with that, and a fair percentage of En Zedders.
see **Kiwi**

E.S. Eastern States, from standpoint of W.A.
1981 *Australian* 15 Sep. 16: Places like Victoria, NSW, and Queensland do not really exist in the Sandgroper's mind: instead they are lumped together and described collectively as the ES – or Eastern States.

esky Trade name of portable cooler for drinks, etc. [f. *eskimo* as previously used in trade name of an ice chest]
1971 Craig McGregor *Don't Talk to Me About Love* 152: George and Sonia with a transistor and an Esky beside them in the wilderness.
1976 *Sunday Telegraph* (Sydney) 25 Jan. 26: 'Look, Mate, I don't mind a tidal wave as long as it doesn't knock over my Esky.'
1984 *Sydney Morning Herald* 21 Jan. 1: 'We should have brought the esky to stand on,' one teenage girl remarked to a friend as they strained to catch a glimpse of the ceremony.

ethnic 'designating a racial or other group within a larger system' OED: in Australia, any recognizable member of a non Anglo-Saxon community
1981 *Sydney Morning Herald* 20 Jun. 37: Spokesmen for the Melbourne communities claim that Sir Nicholas . . . is a kind of 'token

ethnic', or an ethnic person in name only (he was born in Coogee of Lebanese parents).
1981 *Age* (Melbourne) 11 Aug. 11: That ethnics suffer persecution in school is no more than what happens in society at large.

euchred Exhausted, destitute, at the end of one's resources [f. *euchre* outwit U.S. 1855 Mathews]
1946 K. S. Prichard *The Roaring Nineties* 34: 'I've got to get water for me horses at the next tank, or we're euchred.'
1952 T. A. G. Hungerford *The Ridge and the River* 143: 'We can't do much more of that.' He pointed down the slope. 'We'd be euchred.'
1973 John Morrison *Australian by Choice* 83: This man has worked hard in Australia for forty years, but he's euchred now.
euchre To ruin, wreck
1974 *Australian* 12 Oct. 19: He sits in the mayoral car ('So many dials and buttons! I hope I don't euchre this thing').

Eulo Queen, the Isabel Robinson, later Gray (d. 1929), mistress of the Royal Mail Hotel at Eulo in south-western Queensland in the 1890s
1892 Barcroft Boake 'Skeeta' *Bulletin* 17 Dec. repr. in *Where the Dead Men Lie* (1897) 90: 'On the Paroo I saw him; he's been / In Eulo a fortnight then, drinking, and driving about with 'The Queen'.
1964 H. P. Tritton *Time Means Tucker* 113: Of all the pub-keepers concerned in the many stories told of 'lambing-down', two women were running equal for pride of place, Mrs Brown of Grawin, and Isabel Gray, 'The Eulo Queen'.

expert, the In a shearing-shed, the man in charge of the machinery; anyone qualified to deal with farm machinery
1910 C. E. W. Bean *On the Wool Track* 195: The expert (the man in the engine-room).
1923 Steele Rudd *On Emu Creek* (1972) 168: Much time and 'language' would be wasted trying to locate the trouble and fix it [the reaper and binder] up, or waiting for an 'expert' to arrive to do it.
1938 Eric Lowe *Salute to Freedom* 113: 'It's the new shearing machines . . . Campbell's expert will be here in a couple of days.'
1964 H. P. Tritton *Time Means Tucker* 40: 'The expert' is another important man in

the shed. He is responsible for the smooth running of the machinery and has to have a thorough knowledge of everything mechanical in the shed.

eyes, pick the ~ out   To occupy the choice portions of a run, in order to make the rest of the territory unusable by another (a technique used in the conflict between squatter and selectors)
1865 *Australian* 23 Jun. 11: As the day advanced [at the land office], and sections were taken up, and the 'eye picked from the area'.

1881 *Adelaide Observer* 22 Oct. 44: His expression about the selectors being free to pick out Mr Gray's eyes was not really so savage as it sounded – only referring to what are called the 'eyes of the run', the watering places and choice blocks.
1934 Brian Penton *Landtakers* 138: 'Ay, like the rest of them – pick the eyes out of the country and leave it.'
1981 Leonie Sandercock and Ian Turner *Up Where, Cazaly?* 213: There is much interstate resentment against Victoria's ability to 'pick the eyes' out of Australian football.
see **peacock**

F

faceless men   Term applied (esp. in the 1963 election campaign) to the non-parliamentary members of the Labor Federal Executive, who held power over the parliamentary representatives
1963 *Sydney Morning Herald* 3 Sep. 2: They will lay themselves open to the same charges they laid against the Opposition Leader, Mr Calwell, in accepting policy directions on North-West Cape from the 36 'faceless men' constituting the special A.L.P. Federal Conference.
1972 Don Whitington *Twelfth Man* 175: He [Mr Whitlam] destroyed the 'faceless men' myth that had dogged Labor like an albatross for years, and was used against every Labor leader whenever other ammunition was lacking.

factory (female)   1   Place of detention for women convicts
1819 W. C. Wentworth *Statistical . . . Description of the Colony of New South Wales* 18: The public institutions [at Parramatta include] . . . a factory, in which such of the female convicts as misconduct themselves, and those also who upon their arrival in the colony are not immediately assigned as servants to families, are employed in manufacturing coarse cloth.
1826 *Sydney Gazette* 18 Mar. 1: Wanted for the Use of the Female Factory at Parramatta, One Ton of Colonial Flax, scutched.
1855 William Howitt *Land, Labour and*

Gold ii 360: We paid a visit to what is called the Female Factory at Ross [in Tasmania], a neat village on the banks of the Macquarie river. This female factory is a depot of the female convicts who are not consigned to particular persons, or who are sent hither by an order from the magistrate for one cause or other. It is at once a house of asylum and correction.
1931 Miles Franklin *Back to Bool Bool* 200: 'Blanche would have been well placed in the Parramatta "Factory" stirring up the inmates.'
2   The Australian National Gallery, Canberra
1982 *National Times* 24 Jan. 23: Among Canberra's glitterati the aggressively shaped bulks of white concrete – relieved only be steel-framed skylights – of Colin Madigan's building have been pejoratively nicknamed The Factory.

fair crack of the whip   see **whip**

fair dinkum   see **dinkum**

fair go   1   The call in a two-up game indicating that all the rules have been satisfied and that the coins may be spun, and at the same time enjoining that there be no hindrance to the spinning
1911 Louis Stone *Jonah* 216–17: The seventh man threw down the kip, and Chook, as if obeying a signal, rose from his seat and

walked into the centre of the ring. He handed five shillings to the boxer, and placed the pennies tail up on the kip. His stake was covered with another dollar, the betting being even money. 'Fair go!' cried the boxer. Chook jerked the coins upward with the skill of an old gaffer; they flew into the dome, and then dropping spinning. As they touched the canvas floor, a hundred voices cried 'Two heads!'

1925 Arthur Wright *The Boy from Bullarah* 17–18: For a few moments the spinner stood waiting, while the players noisily made their wagers, and then again the voice of the ring-keeper rang out. 'Fair go! Set a quid.' All eyes followed the spinning pennies as they rose in the air.

1949 Lawson Glassop *Lucky Palmer* 167: He handed the kip to the spinner . . . placed two pennies, tail up, on it with infinite care and said 'Fair go'. He heard a rustling in a corner, strode over, picked up two ten shilling notes off the canvas, crushed them in his hand, threw them out of the ring over his head, and growled, 'Yous knows the rules. No bets after I say "Fair go". I'm runnin' this game and I'm runnin' it proper'.

2 Any situation or arrangement which meets the basic requirements of fairness, with neither favour nor prejudice being shown; the elementary fair treatment to which anyone must be entitled

1907 James Green *The Selector* 37: 'I'll buy her first, then ride her,' replied Woolham. 'It's a fair go,' Patrickson exclaimed.

1919 W. H. Downing *Digger Dialects* 22: *Fair Go* Equitable treatment, a fair field and no favour.

1945 Gavin Casey *Downhill is Easier* 146: 'He's given me a fair go, so far,' I stated.

1951 J. B. Chifley *The Light on the Hill* 56: I do not think the miners gave the Labor Government a fair go while it was in office.

3 'Fair go!' as an exclamation may be a protest, a plea, a humorous disclaimer: always as though appealing to basic principles

1938 *Smith's Weekly* 31 Dec. 4: When the laugh had gone on long enough, he would silence it by his opening words, 'Fair go, mob'.

1957 Randolph Stow *The Bystander* 187: 'You didn't happen to give her a bit of cheek, I suppose!' 'Fair go, boss,' Fred begged. 'I wouldn't cheek *your* missus. You know me better than that.'

1962 Alan Seymour *The One Day of the Year* 32: *Alf.* Wack and me are old mates. At

the war together. *Jan.* Which one? *Alf.* Fair go. Second.

1970 Jessica Anderson *The Last Man's Head* 133: 'I still think that was him, all right. No – fair go – I think it *could* have been him.'

Falcons The West Perth (W.A.) Australian Rules team, formerly the Cardinals

1983 *Sunday Independent* (Perth) 14 Aug. 37: Sharks Savage the Falcons [heading] East Fremantle . . . took West Perth on and never gave them a chance after half time.

fall in To 'come a cropper', suffer a reverse (through miscalculation)

1894 A. B. Paterson 'How the Favourite Beat Us' *Singer of the Bush* (1983) 221: If I can't get a cropper, by Jingo, I'll stop her, / Let the public fall in, it will serve the brutes right.

1903 Joseph Furphy *Such is Life* (1944) 363: I wouldn't advise you to count upon the institution . . . You might fall-in.

1920 Louis Esson 'The Woman Tamer' in *Dead Timber* 21: 'I fell in. Nine months I done. I was dead innocent.'

fang *v.* To drive a car at high speed

1973 Alexander Buzo *Rooted* 36: 'Let's hop in the B and fang up to the beach.'

1981 *Bulletin* 10 Nov. 43: 'We pick up sheilas, get drunk, steal cars, fang 'em (drive them fast) . . . anyfink!'

1984 *National Times* 14 Sep. 14: 'They've had half a dozen drinks and, you know, they want to impress the girls and their mates at how fast they can fang their car around the corner.'

fangs, put the ~ in To bite q.v.

1919 W. H. Downing *Digger Dialects* 22: Fangs 'To put in the fangs' – to demand money, etc.

1932 Leonard Mann *Flesh in Armour* 250: They were all short of cash . . . 'I'll stick the fangs in him all right,' Tich averred.

1952 T. A. G. Hungerford *The Ridge and the River* 218: 'Give me a smoke,' Wallace suggested. 'If there's one thing I like, it's to sink the fangs into an officer.'

fang *v.*

1975 *Daily Telegraph* (Sydney) 10 Jul. 2: 'What if they'd fanged us for $8000 million?'

1979 *Herald* (Melbourne) 3 Mar. 41: He fanged me for a brick and next thing I know he's shot through all the way to Darwin.

f.a.q. Fair average quality
1929 Sir Hal Colebatch *A Story of a Hundred Years* 249: There is considerable competition for the bagged wheat amongst the agents of the wheat merchants. It is purchased at bushel rates on what is known as the f.a.q. (fair average quality) basis.
1930 Edward Shann *An Economic History of Australia* 311: It is impossible to 'bear' a land boom by selling f.a.q. land for future delivery.
1982 *Sydney Morning Herald* 23 Jun. 8: The questions were faq – when did you first want to enter politics, how do you handle the pressure, how long can you last, what do other people think of you?

Farm, the 1 Australia, usually in the expression 'buying back the farm' (from overseas investors)
1973 *Australian* 10 Apr. 9: According to Mr Baume, 'buying back the farm' is partly government public relations.
1975 *Sun-Herald* 3 Aug. 7: The Minister for Minerals and Energy, Mr Connor, revealed this week his plans to 'buy back the farm' in less than three years.
1981 Maxwell Grant *Inherit the Sun* 350: 'The Government was getting touchy about selling off the farm as it was called, selling off the country to foreign interests.'
2 Monash University, Victoria, as distinct from 'the shop' (University of Melbourne)
1964 *Sydney Morning Herald* 28 Aug. 2: Third University for Melbourne. La Trobe joins 'the Shop' and 'the Farm'.
3 Warwick farm racecourse, N.S.W.
1939 Patrick White *Happy Valley* 240: Interview . . . a bald-faced gelding, won a race at the Farm.
1975 *Sydney Morning Herald* 7 Nov. 14: Two likely 'stars' on trial at Farm.
4 Eagle Farm racecourse, Queensland
1981 *Sun-Herald* 8 Feb. 62: Farm washout [heading] Stewards cancelled the last two races of the Eagle Farm race meeting in Brisbane yesterday.

farmer, Collins St, Pitt St see **Collins St, Pitt St**

farrago of facts, falsity and filth The description of a document before the Petrov Royal Commission, later known as Document J, by Mr W. J. V. Windeyer, chief counsel assisting
1954 *Sydney Morning Herald* 19 May 4: Mr Windeyer said that the document

appeared to be just a 'farrago of facts, falsity and filth'.
1984 Neville Wran *Sydney Morning Herald* 7 Apr. 2: On the basis of this farrago of facts, filth and falsity [the *Age* tapes] . . . the whole integrity of two Labor Governments, one of the greatest judges in the history of the High Court of Australia and other reputations are to be impugned and dragged down.

fat, crack a Achieve an erection
1941 Encountered in conversation
1968 Barry Humphries *The Wonderful World of Barry McKenzie* [56]' 'Pommy Sheilas? Aw, they're apples I s'pose – but the way I feel now I don't reckon [I] could crack a fat!'
1970 Jack Hibberd *White With Wire Wheels* in Penguin *Plays* 224: 'By Christ, if he races her off, it'll be the last fat he ever cracks.'
1976 Robert Drewe *The Savage Crows* 88: When he'd cracked a fat against her . . . 'Hey Stiffy,' she'd whispered in his ear, and giggled.

Father's Day, happy as a bastard on see **bastard**

fats Fat cattle or sheep, intended for market
1896 Thomas Heney *The Girl at Birrell's* 93: The wild station-manager from the North, down in Adelaide with 'fats'.
1903 Joseph Furphy *Such is Life* (1944) 228: 'I come with some fats as far as Wilcannia; an' a drover took charge o' them there.'
1932 Myrtle Rose White *No Roads Go By* 106: A succession of mobs of 'fats' were mustered and started down to market.
1979 *Courier-Mail* (Brisbane) 16 Mar. 4: Twelve months ago good fattening-age store cattle sold for $80 each. Today, as fats, they are meeting increasing demand at $300 and $350 each.

favourite, head like a beaten see **head**

feather duster, a rooster one day and a ~ the next Catchphrase for the uncertainty of (political) success [? f. U.S. See quot. 1972]
1955 *Bulletin* 15 Jun. 7: Calwell has a long memory. Forty years or so ago American 'Life' published a cartoon showing a fed-up

rooster leaning against a barn-door and ruminating, 'What's the use? An egg today – a feather-duster tomorrow'. Speaking on the bill to increase Federal members' pensions he said the public was fickle and members were 'roosters today, and feather-dusters tomorrow'.
1972 A. A. Calwell *Be Just and Fear Not* 266: Years ago I told the House of Representatives a basic truth that I had read in a United States publication. The writer said that a politician is 'a rooster one day and a feather duster the next'.
1984 *Age* (Melbourne) 27 Apr. 13: From rooster to feather duster is a common enough story in politics, but reversing the process as Mr Young has done is very rare indeed.

feature with To achieve sexual intercourse with [given currency by Barry McKenzie comic strip]
1965 Barry Humphries *Times Literary Supplement* 16 Sep. 812: Barry's amorous aspirations are expressed in a desire to 'feature with a lass'.

Feds Members of Federal parliament, as distinct from states; members of the Federal body of a political party, as distinct from state branches; Federal police [parallel to U.S. usage]
1978 *Bulletin* 11 Apr. 14: At the moment they're leaving it all to Joh, whom they can trust to see that the Feds don't pull any swifties.
1980 *Sydney Morning Herald* 11 Dec. 6: Mr Hills has resorted to rule No. 2 in the State politicians' handbook to justify the situation. Rule No. 2 says: If you can't blame The Feds blame your predecessor.
1990 Brian Toohey *Sun-Herald* 7 Jan. 40: The 'Feds' balked at strong indications that their Assistant Commissioner was corrupt.

feeding time at the zoo see **zoo**

fellow, the old see **old**

female factory see **factory**

fence, over the Unconscionable, unreasonable [also U.S.]
1918 *Kia Ora Coo-ee* 15 May 4: 'It's over the blinking fence,' cried one chap, and he voiced the general opinion.
1930 K. S. Prichard *Haxby's Circus* 79: 'Bruiser's over the fence. He *makes* trouble.'

1964 *Sydney Morning Herald* 18 Sep. 11: Some publications which unduly emphasize sex were 'entirely over the fence', the Chief Secretary, Mr C. A. Kelly, said yesterday.

fencing wire, tough as Very tough
1893 Henry Lawson 'Lake Eliza' *Verse* i 252: The grass is tough as fencing-wire, / And just as good for fodder.
1930 Vance Palmer *The Passage* 103: 'He'll last the lot of us out. Tough as fencing wire the old boy's always been.'
1968 Stuart Gore *Holy Smoke* 9: Only a little bloke, picked before he was ripe, but game as Ned Kelly and tough as fencing wire.

fibro 1 Fibro-cement [abbr.]
1946 Margaret Trist *What Else is There?* 167: The house was a dishevelled structure of brick, weatherboard and fibro.
1957 Nino Culotta *They're a Weird Mob* 177: 'No matey. Not fibro. No matter 'ow you do ut, fibro looks like a shack.'
2 See quots
1981 *Sydney Morning Herald* 20 Jun. 1: When Wests play Manly at Brookvale tomorrow, will it be a class struggle as well as a Rugby League match? One could be excused for thinking so after hearing 2GB's advertisements yesterday . . . 'The Western Suburbs fibro set takes on the Manly silvertails,' the station said.
1986 *Sun-Herald* 8 Jun. 5: Both [Paul Hogan and his wife Noelene] were typical westies, the types his present Belrose neighbours might refer to as 'fibros'.

fiddley A one pound note [f. rhyming slang *fiddley did = quid*]
1941 Baker 28: *Fiddley* A £1 note.
1949 Lawson Glassop *Lucky Palmer* 175: 'Here's yer dough. Ninety fiddlies.'
1975 Xavier Herbert *Poor Fellow My Country* 102: 'If I could only lay me hands on two hundred and fifty fiddleys.'

field, to bring (come) back to the To disturb someone's pretensions or delusions, to restore a sense of reality to a situation [f. the distinction between the front runner and the main body in horseracing]
1944 Lawson Glassop *We Were the Rats* 82: 'Don't worry,' said Bert . . . 'The poor bastard's hopeless. He'll come back to the field.'
1954 T. A. G. Hungerford *Sowers of the*

Wind 4: 'Young Mark Flannery should come back to the field.'
1984 *Sun-Herald* 11 Mar. 96: Whenever a comparative newcomer enjoys quick success at some facets of racing, his seniors tag him as 'a lucky, young upstart who will quickly come back to the field'.

fields, the   i.e. the goldfields, esp. W.A.
1942 Gavin Casey *It's Harder for Girls* 198: Up here on the fields he had plenty of sunshine and plenty of good food.
1950 K. S. Prichard *Winged Seeds* 124: Barb Reidy was one of the best bushmen on the fields.
1983 *West Australian* (Perth) 21 Nov. 64: Power line a key in Fields growth [heading] The new power line between Muja and Kalgoorlie is expected to be instrumental in bringing many gold prospects in the Goldfields into production.

fifty   1   A 50 lb. bag of flour (or other commodity)
1904 Henry Fletcher *Dads Wayback: His Work* 20: Dads had gone to Dan Robins' place for fifty of flour.
1914 Henry Lawson 'The Flour Bin' *Verse* iii 103: Though bakers' carts run out – / Still keeps a 'fifty' in it / Against a time of drought.
1959 Donald Stuart *Yandy* 98: 'D'you bring any flour? We're right out this last three days.' 'Yeah, we got two fifties for you.'
2   A glass of half 'old' and half 'new' beer (N.S.W.)
1971 Frank Hardy *The Outcasts of Foolgarah* 76: 'Five schooners of fifty, thanks love.'
1974 *Festival* ed. B. Buckley and J. Hamilton 55: He said he would have his usual middy of fifty.

Fiji uncle   An imaginary rich uncle overseas, backing some venture in which the unwary may be persuaded to invest: *obs.*
1902 Henry Fletcher *The Waybacks* 6: 'Ain't yer got an uncle in Fiji?' demanded Dads, with scorn. 'Ain't yer got two hundred quid to give to the honest man who will trust you to the same amount?'
1914 Henry Lawson 'Mitchell on the Situation' *Prose* i 716: They were both spielers ... Their game was anything weaker or stupider than themselves that had cash or property, and when they were in Sydney their uncles lived in Fiji.

1928 Arthur Wright *A Good Recovery* 9: 'I'm beginning to think that rich uncle is like the one from Fiji, eh, Lance?'

filthy on   As for **dirty on**
1987 *Daily Telegraph* (Sydney) 27 Jul. 55: Martin Bella claimed he was gouged repeatedly by a Balmain player during yesterday's match at Leichhardt Oval ... 'I'm filthy on the bloke – he gets away with it all the time.'

financial   1   In possession of funds
1926 J. Vance Marshall *Timely Tips for New Australians* 11: In Australia, to describe a man as being 'financial' is to describe him as being possessed of means.
1963 Lou Richards *Boots and All!* 197: A majority of them are now putting in licensed bars, which will mean that they are going to be pretty financial clubs [in S.A.] in the near future. Once they do become financial I would say that Victoria could be in trouble as far as their top-line players are concerned.
2   Paid-up, as a member of an organization
1939 *Seamen's Journal* Sep. 1: All members in arrears of their contributions are called upon to make themselves financial and keep financial, so as to ensure that their rights as *Seamen* will always be protected.
1959 Dorothy Hewett *Bobbin Up* 180: 'I'm collectin' for the union. When are you goin' to join Dick?' 'Haven't been financial for two years Nell ... I work too hard for me wages to hand it over to those bludgers.'

fine day for travelling   see **travelling**

fire   In sport, to play to one's full capacity [f. an engine firing]
1977 *Australian* 19 Jan. 22: With three fine quick bowlers you can rest assured one will be firing at any given stage of a Test.
1987 *Rugby League Week* 29 Jul. 7: Bob Fulton is a smart coach and he'll have his team firing until the end of the year.

fire low, and lay them out   The instruction relayed by Lieut.-Col. Tom Price to the Mounted Rifles on 31 Aug. 1890, the day of a mass meeting of unionists in Melbourne during the maritime strike
1890 *Truth* 19 Oct. 1: This is what Col. Price said to the Melbourne Mounted Rifles: '... fire low and lay them out, lay the disturbers of law and order out so that the duty will have to be again performed.'

1892 Henry Lawson *Verse* i 184: 'The Lay-'em-out Brigade' [poem title]
1971 Frank Hardy *The Outcasts of Foolgarah* 229: Lt. Colonel Gravel, receiving the order to fire low and lay them out, took a rifle . . . and fired the bullet shattering Moss's good leg.

firm To shorten in odds, the opposite of **blow** (horse-racing)
1977 *Sun-Herald* 9 Jan. 43: Cool Look opened second favourite at 5–4 yesterday, but under consistent support firmed to start a solid even-money favourite.

Firm, the J. C. Williamson Ltd, theatrical entrepreneurs
1938 *Life Digest* Oct. 97: In the early 'eighties the famous firm known as 'The Triumvirate' came into being. Its components were J. C. Williamson, Arthur Garner and George Musgrove. Later they were invariably termed 'The Firm' and finally after Musgrove separated from Williamson and Garner dropped out, the firm was J. C. Williamson, as it is today.
1945 *Salt* 16 Jul. 25: As acknowledged rulers of the Australian professional stage, J. C. Williamson Ltd. – known as 'The Firm' and consisting of the four brothers Tait – has frequently been attacked on these grounds.
1965 Hal Porter *Stars of Australian Stage and Screen* 279: The Firm's luke-warm, carbon-copy commercial successes which catch the social sheep, and the night-out-at-the-theatre-on-mum's-birthday celebrants.

first cab off the rank see **cab**

First Fleeter One who arrived in Australia with the First Fleet in 1788, usually a convict; a modern descendant of the arrivals on the First Fleet
1830 *HRA* xv 371: Of these, 5 came in the first Fleet. One of these first Fleeters died a few Years ago at the advanced Age of 104 years without having lost a Tooth.
1848 H. W. Haygarth *Recollections of Bush Life in Australia* 93: A man who by his own account, is of so long standing in the neighbourhood as to have been what is called in the colony a 'first fleeter'.
1870 Marcus Clarke *His Natural Life* ed. S. Murray-Smith (1970) 623: Mooney was one of the 'First Fleeters'.
1934 Mary Gilmore *Old Days – Old Ways* 267: In the days of the first fleeters . . . the

hills and shores of Sydney Cove were sheets of flowers.
1977 *Australian* 24 Jan. 2: The Fellowship of First Fleeters will hold its annual dinner to celebrate Australia Day in Sydney on Saturday night.

first Tuesday in November Melbourne Cup day
1895 Mary Gaunt *The Moving Finger* 263: The eventful day came at last, the first Tuesday in November, the day that would be 'cup day' now-a-days.
1983 Donald Horne *National Times* 30 Sep. 4: It is no accident that Australia's two greatest national days are April 25 and the first Tuesday in November.

fit as a mallee bull see **mallee**

fiz-gig A police informer
1895 Cornelius Crowe *The Australian Slang Dictionary* 29: Fizgig a spy for a detective.
1957 Judah Waten *Shares in Murder* 14: He was known as the king of the fiz-gigs: no detective had more informers serving him.
1984 *Sun-Herald* 29 Jan. 47: We described him as a big crim and also a 'fiz gig' – an interesting Australian word that means a grass, an informer.

fizzer Anything which disappoints expectations; a firework which fizzes but fails to explode [? f. *fizzle*]
[**1941** Baker 29: *Fizz out on* To let down, fail in a promise.]
1977 Fred Daly *From Curtin to Kerr* 153: The Petrov episode proved to be a fizzer, but it ruined Evatt.
1983 *Newcastle Herald* 5 Feb. 4: Mr Hawke would either be a great Prime Minister or a great fizzer.

flaming fury An outdoor latrine, periodically 'sanitised' by firing with oil or kerosene
1961 Jack Danvers *The Living Come First* 130: The lavatory was a 'flaming fury' behind the hut.
1982 *NT News* (Darwin) 13 Dec. 7: We have heard of a famous Territory dunny that was known far and wide in the post-war years as 'The Blue Room' . . . For a 'flaming fury' it was something out of the ordinary.

flash as a rat with a gold tooth Very flash

1978 Bill Peach *Sun-Herald* 27 Aug. 59: Eddie [Coogan] is the ultimate lurk-man ... as flash as a rat with a gold tooth. He patronises Ginger, heckles him, attempts at every turn to trip him up or do him down.

1981 *Bulletin* 25 Aug. 53: Most Press descriptions of Grassby over the years had seemed to focus rather unnecessarily on his clothing, implying snidely that he was as flash as a rat with a gold tooth.

1984 *Sunday Independent* (Perth) 3 Jun. 35: Reilly – Ace of Spies has suddenly become as flash as a rat with a gold tooth.

flash one's dover see **dover**

flash jack Someone swaggering in behaviour and possibly ostentatious in dress [f. *flash* dashing, ostentatious, swaggering, 'swell' OED 1785]

1901 Henry Lawson 'The Golden Graveyard' *Prose* i 343: Dave Regan – lanky, easygoing Bush native; Jim Bentley – a bit of a 'Flash Jack'.

1905 *The Old Bush Songs* ed. A. B. Paterson 26: 'Flash Jack from Gundagai'. [poem title]

1934 Archer Russell *A Tramp-Royal in Wild Australia* 41: 'Leave that kind of talk to flash Jacks.'

flat as a tack Very flat, esp. in mood

1965 Jack Dyer *'Captain Blood'* 39: We were as flat as a tack when we met South in the Grand Final and they romped away with the flag.

1976 David Ireland *The Glass Canoe* 60: His beer was still there, flat as a tack.

1983 *Sydney Morning Herald* 13 Jun. 25: 'I rode her in the Brisbane Cup and she went disgracefully,' Quinton said. 'She was as flat as a tack after the hard run.'

flat out like a lizard drinking see **lizard**

flea, so bare you could flog a ~ across it Applied to land bare of vegetation

1866 Rolf Boldrewood 'A Kangaroo Drive' *Cornhill Magazine* xiv 740–1: The vast natural meadow was, as one of the stockmen feelingly observed, 'as bare of grass as the palm of your hand', while another gravely professed his belief 'that you could hunt a flea across it with a stock-whip'.

1903 Joseph Furphy *Such is Life* (1944) 207: The famine was sore in the land. To use the expression of men deeply interested in

the matter, you could flog a flea from the Murrumbidgee to the Darling.

1954 Tom Ronan *Vision Splendid* 61: He told of roads so bare 'you could flog a flea along them with a greenhide whip'.

1972 *Sydney Morning Herald* 10 Apr. 6: I first heard the expression 50 years ago. It was used to describe land so denuded of grass and herbage by drought as to be quite bare and devoid of possible cover, even for a flea ... 'So bare that you could flog a flea across it.'

flick, give (get) the To reject, repudiate, dismiss [rhyming slang: flick pass = arse]

1986 David McNicoll *Bulletin* 7 Oct. 68: Judith Dagworthy, for many years the efficient and popular Press Officer at the Savoy, was unceremoniously given the flick a couple of weeks ago.

1987 *Times on Sunday* 22 Mar. 27: Officially they [prostitutes] could refuse to perform certain sex acts, but unofficially, 'if you refuse too often and lose clients, you get the flick'.

flicker, let her Usu. preceded by 'Okay', and giving the word to start some operation that has been prepared for [? f. starting a reel of film]

1945 Encountered in conversation

1953 T. A. G. Hungerford *Riverslake* 129: 'Right-oh, gents, let 'er flicker.'

flies, no ~ on Applied to someone who is alert and astute [? f. habit of flies to settle on a sluggish beast: also U.S.]

1845 C. Griffith *The Present State of Port Phillip* 78: The person who excites their [the old hands'] greatest respect is the man who is alive to their attempts (or, as they express it themselves, *who drops down to their moves*) and the highest encomium they can pass on such a one is, *that there are no flies about him.*

1932 Leonard Mann *Flesh in Armour* 305: They admitted, though, there were few flies on him.

1961 Hugh Atkinson *Low Company* 121: He was far from being a gawking hayseed ... there were no flies on Byron.

flies, drink with the To drink by oneself in a pub, indicating an unsociable attitude, or the aversion of others

1925 Arthur Wright *The Boy from Bullarah* 114: 'A few days ago a common swaggie, drinking with the flies.'

1944 A. W. Upfield *No Footprints in the Bush* 90: He says he doesn't like drinking with the flies.

1957 R. S. Porteous *Brigalow* 212: 'I've got a bottle of O.P. rum with only two nips taken out of it. Didn't enjoy drinking with the flies.'

flip oneself off To masturbate (of a man)

floater 1 A meat pie in a plate of peas or gravy: esp. S.A. [listed by Partridge as dumpling in gravy or sausages in mash]
1959 *Australian Letters* Dec. 13: She bought me a floater, meat pie in a plate of peas.
1969 Thomas Jenkins *We Came to Australia* 51: The Floater is, believe it or not, a meat pie floating in a plate of pea soup. It is mainly served from pie-stalls in the streets. The true floater aficionado, of course, douses his pie with . . . tomato sauce.
1974 *Australian Women's Weekly* 11 Sep. 67: A floater consists of a meat pie submerged in a sea of pea soup, with a flavouring of tomato sauce or vinegar, depending on taste . . . Floaters were first sold in Adelaide by James Gibbs, a pastrycook who migrated from the English county of Devonshire before the turn of the century. He set up a handcart at the corner of the two busiest streets, Rundle and King William.
2 Loose opal-bearing or gold-bearing rock of low value [f. *float* loose rock brought down by the action of water U.S. 1814 OED]
1903 Joseph Furphy *Such is Life* (1944) 198: The surrounding country had been prospected for a few floaters . . . and there was the jeweller's shop.
1937 Ernestine Hill *The Great Australian Loneliness* 232: It was a 'floater', quite worthless, but an indication of the jewel in the country.
1971 Colin Simpson *The New Australia* 153: Opal fields are usually indicated by stones found on the surface, 'floaters'.
3 On the wharves, men not attached to any gang
1955 John Morrison *Black Cargo* 35: Plenty of men available this morning. Over fifty gangs in, as well as hundreds of floaters. Floaters are the men not attached to gangs.
1982 Wendy Lowenstein and Tom Hills *Under the Hook* 107: 'Blokes that wouldn't join gangs – they just floated around . . . If

anyone was away, they'd send you a floater.'
4 See quot. 1979
1979 *Age* (Melbourne) 24 Dec. 3: Among barristers they're known as 'floaters'. They're the defence briefs that pass from one barrister to another as cases are scheduled for hearing, postponed, rescheduled, postponed again and so on.

flock of homing pigeons, he couldn't lead a see **homing**

flog the cat see **cat**

flogger A stick with streamers attached, for waving by supporters at Australian Rules matches
1982 *Age* (Melbourne) 25 May 34: The VFL may have to take further action against cheer squad members who wield floggers at League matches. Police have written to VFL chiefs making it clear that they believe the floggers to be dangerous and that they fear for the safety of players and umpires. In the early 1970s the League banned the use of floggers. However, in discussions with cheer squad officers, they made a concession and said smaller sticks decorated with streamers and the like could be used, provided they were only waved inside the fence. The mini floggers quaintly known as 'Patty Dukes' (they are short sticks adorned with colored pom-poms) have suddenly blossomed, and, in effect, are identical to the banned floggers.
1985 *Advertiser* (Adelaide) 5 Oct. Review 1: The Peckerettes' small paper floggers have given way to elaborate pom poms, batons, canes and hoops.

flogging parson see **parson**

floury baker A variety of cicada [f. colouring]
1951 Dymphna Cusack and Florence James *Come In Spinner* 106: 'Mine's a Floury Baker . . . and mine's a Black Prince!' Young Jack and Andrew hold up their fists for her to peep at frosted fawn body and tan-and-black.

flow on *n. & v.* The process by which a wage increase granted to workers in one union by the Arbitration Commission results in a similar increase for workers in a related union; a wage increase so gained
1974 *Australian* 12 Oct. 4: $9 metal

award flow-on for building workers ... A Deputy President of the Commission ... decided that last month's $9 increase in the Metal Trades Award should flow on to the Carpenters and Joiners Award.
1984 *West Australian* (Perth) 14 Jan. 30: Farmers are worried that wage flow-ons for farm workers will push up shearing costs.

flute, have the To talk incessantly: *obs.*
1896 T. W. Henry *The Girl at Birrell's* 23: 'You've got the flute properly tonight, Graham,' returned the other. 'You can gas for all hands.'
1908 E. S. Sorenson *Quinton's Rouseabout* 84: 'He never had much to say, though he'd chip in at times when Joe had the flute.'
fluter An incessant talker
1898 *Bulletin* 17 Dec. Red Page: An incessant talker is a *skiter* or a *fluter*, and a request to him to *pass the flute* or the *kip* is to allow someone else to 'do a pitch'.
1959 D'Arcy Niland *The Big Smoke* 178: 'Where's Phil the Fluter now?'

fly, the big men Phrase applied to Australian Rules football, referring to the high leap needed to take a mark
1963 Lou Richards *Boots and All!* 68: Dick stood about 5 ft. 11 in. in his socks, and on top of this he had very long arms, which gave him a decided advantage as a rover, because he could fly for marks against bigger men.
1969 Alan Hopgood *And the Big Men Fly* [play title]
1981 *Australian* 22 Dec. 1: The big men cry as club splits [heading] State representative footballer Stephen Wright broke down and cried when the South Melbourne Football Club crisis worsened last night.
1982 *NT News* (Darwin) 27 Sep. 13: The big words fly ... Melbourne Age writer, Geoff Slattery, looks back on a typical week in Australia's football-mad capital.
see **aerial ping pong**

fly, give it a To chance it, make a trial of, have a go
1919 W. H. Downing *Digger Dialects* 24: *Fly (to give it a)* To make an attempt
1928 Arthur Wright *A Good Recovery* 119: 'I'm willing to give it a fly, but –.'
1934 Thomas Wood *Cobbers* 19: 'We're proud of the Trots in Perth ... They come in for miles, some of 'em, to give it a fly.'
1949 Lawson Glassop *Lucky Palmer* 75: 'We're playing with their dough ... Might as well give it a fly.'

1976 *Sydney Morning Herald* 14 Sep. 2: 2SM's general manager, Mr G. Rutherford, said yesterday that the station was 'just having a fly at something'.
see **burl, go, lash**

flyblown Penniless, destitute: *obsolescent* [? f. the condition of flyblown meat]
1853 C. R. Read *What I Heard, Saw and Did at the Australian Gold Fields* 51: His friend rushes into the billiard room to relate poor Newchum's misery to his fraternity, who deeply regret that it did not fall to their lot 'flyblowing him'.* *Being 'flyblown' is a Colonial term for being 'done up'.
c. **1882** *The Sydney Slang Dictionary* 4: *Fly-blown* To be thoroughly hard up.
1931 William Hatfield *Sheepmates* 161: 'Sit in, some o' yous that aint flyblown – some o' yous that's got a month or two in, an' their IOU's is good, if there's no real Oscar about the joint.'
1966 Tom Ronan *Once There Was a Bagman* 25: 'They'd been on that Katherine railway job, living from pay to pay, and when it shut down they were flyblown.'

flybog Jam: World War I slang, in World War II often shortened to 'bog'
1920 *Aussie* Apr. Glossary: *Flybog* Jam.
1944 Jean Devanny *By Tropic, Sea and Jungle* 214: Sometimes you take a tin of flybog (treacle) with you as a luxury.
1968 Stuart Gore *Holy Smoke* 27: 'I know them cockies! Not even a tin of fly-bog of a Sunday's tea.'

flyer A swiftly moving kangaroo, usually female; a half-grown kangaroo
1826 James Atkinson *An Account of the State of Agriculture and Grazing in New South Wales* 24: The animals of this kind that are not quite full grown are termed flyers; they are exceedingly swift.
1834 George Bennett *Wanderings in New South Wales* i 287: The males of this species [kangaroo] are called by the colonists 'foresters', the females 'flyers'.
1927 Steele Rudd *The Romance of Runnibede* 199: While the halfgrowns, or 'flyers', were swifter than greyhounds, many of the 'old men' were in difficulties.

Flying Fornicator, the See quot. 1979
1979 *Sun-Herald* 1 Jul. 43: The last train back from Sydney [to Wollongong] on Sundays is packed with young people and known to some as the Flying Fornicator.

flying fox An overhead cableway from which buckets etc. are suspended, often as part of an elaborate system; an improvised cableway for conveying things across a gorge or river [f. the bat (Pteropus) so called]

1901 May Vivienne *Travels in Western Australia* 210: To convey the stone along the open cut to the mill there is a wonderful aerial tramway composed of wire cables, on which the trucks run high up in the air; it is a marvellous way of conveyance, but more peculiar still is what is here called the 'Flying Fox', which has an iron bucket on a single rope of twisted wire. Machinery on the top of the shaft and above the crushing mill conveys it to its destination; then the bucket empties as if by magic, and flies back to the bottom of the open cut, a quarter of a mile journey, to be again replenished.

1916 Henry Lawson 'The Passing Stranger at Burrinjuck' *Verse* iii 360: The 'flying foxes', / From the cable tower on the rocky height, / Seem to swerve with their swinging boxes, / Like damaged 'gents' who've been out all night.

1945 Elisabeth George *Two at Daly Waters* 82: A flying-fox was erected, and when the creek was running a banker, I packed sandwiches and cookies in boxes and Jerry and Stumpy took them across on the flying-fox.

1961 Noni Braham *The Interloper* 106: Margaret suddenly noticed wires strung overhead. 'What on earth are they for?' 'A "flying-fox",' Colin explained. 'During the wet, it's the only way they can get supplies.'

flying kangaroo, the The logo of Qantas

1981 *Sydney Morning Herald* 23 Feb. 1: The flying kangaroo has been seen in some odd places lately because of Qantas's union troubles. Passengers on QF1 to London last week found themselves high above the Greenland icecap.

1984 *Australian* 5 Jun. 1: Our flying kangaroo stays aloft [heading] Qantas will unveil a new look for its aircraft today, but despite rumours, the flying kangaroo symbol will not ... be replaced by a koala to appeal to the highly competitive US market where some tourists have mistaken the kangaroo for 'a big white rat'.

flying peanut Nickname of Joh Bjelke-Petersen, formerly Premier of Queensland

[because he is a peanut-farmer and flies in his own plane, piloted by Beryl Young]

1975 *Australian* 3 Dec. 6: Ignoring the 'go home Joh' and 'flying peanut' calls the Queensland Premier appealed to 'that great silent majority'.

Flying Pieman William Francis King (d. 1874), noted for such feats as walking from Sydney to Parramatta and back (thirty-two miles) in six hours, for a wager

1847 *Heads of the People* 31 Jul. 124: Francis King, better known as the flying pieman, undertook last week, without any consideration, except as he states the pleasure of gratifying the ladies, to walk 50 miles in twelve hours, for six successive days.

1907 Charles MacAlister *Old Pioneering Days in the Sunny South* 54: That long-winded wonder, the 'Flying Pieman', whose running feats against the coaches I can vouch for from personal experience.

flying, sparrows (geese, peacocks, swallows) out of one's backside see **sparrows**

Flynn, in like Seizing an opportunity offered, esp. sexual [see quot. 1973]

1963 T. A. G. Hungerford *Shake the Golden Bough* 219: 'You're in like Flynn, and there's no turning back.'

1973 Alexander Buzo *Rooted* 137: *Flynn, in like* (also *in like Errol*), refers to the athletic and sexual prowess of the late Australian-born Hollywood actor.

1975 David Niven *Bring on the Empty Horses* 119: Errol was acquitted [of charges of statutory rape on the *Sirocco* in 1942], but the stigma of rape was attached to him, he never shook it off, and for years he gritted his teeth when hailed with cries of 'In like Flynn!'

forby, four by two A Jew [rhyming slang]

1977 Jim Ramsay *Cop It Sweet* 37: *Forby* ... See Four by Two. *Four by Two*: rhym. Jew.

1984 Sandy Gutman *National Times* 20 Jan. 4: 'Here I am, the full-on forby ('Four-by-two' = Jew) from Vaucluse working out at f – g Parramatta.'

forest devil A stump-pulling device

1915 F. C. Spurr *Five Years under the Southern Cross* 184: Certain portable 'forest devils' have been invented by means of which one man can, with the aid of a lever and a wheel-gear, draw from the ground the most stubborn stump of a tree. Agricultural dentistry – that is what it is!

1951 Ernestine Hill *The Territory* 275: A traction engine and two forest devils trundled down to clear it, the first consequential machinery the north had ever seen.

forester Name given rather indiscriminately to the larger types of kangaroo, but sometimes restricted to *Macropus giganteus*

1804 R. Knopwood *Journal in Historical Records of Port Phillip* ed. J. J. Shillinglaw (1972) 184: Killed a very large kangaroo – a forester.

1826 James Atkinson *An Account of the State of Agriculture and Grazing in New South Wales* 24: The forester is the largest of the common kinds [of kangaroo], frequently weighing 150 lbs. It is seldom found in an open country, delighting in forests that have occasional thickets of brush.

1864 J. F. Mortlock *Experiences of a Convict* (1965) 85: Three or four species of kangaroo – of sizes from the 'Forrester', as heavy as a man, down to the Wallaby, not bigger than a large hare, are found in the 'bush' [of Tasmania].

forklift See quot. 1970 [f. *fork* crutch]

1970 Partridge 1144: *fork lifts.* Two striped cushions placed in the rear window of a car . . . to facilitate rear-seat copulation.

1990 *Sun-Herald* 11 Feb. 123: Carlton was flabbergasted last week to hear of automotive fame for another of his FNN characters, Dimity Fork-Lift. Toyota Forklifts have presented Carlton with a working model of a forklift called 'Dimity'.

form Expected mode of behaviour. To 'know someone's form' is to have summed him up, unfavourably: 'How's your rotten form?' is a jeering reproach, given currency in World War II slang [f. racing form]

1955 D'Arcy Niland *The Shiralee* 129: 'I know your form. I just wanted you to know that I know it.'

1961 Russell Braddon *Naked Island* 13: 'How's his rotten form! Steals anything.'

1981 Barry Humphries *A Nice Night's Entertainment* 189: That van at the bottom of the drive could be a bunch of ASIO pricks. Just their form to come snooping around here.

forties Thieves, swindlers: *obsolescent* [f. 'Ali Baba and the Forty Thieves']

1879 T. E. Argles *The Pilgrim* i 12: A collection of shock-haired ruffians – the dregs of the 'forties' – i.e. forty thieves – of the city.

1893 J. A. Barry *Steve Brown's Bunyip* 21: 'You want to get away amongst the spielers and forties of the big smoke?'

1927 M. M. Bennett *Christison of Lammermoor* 194: Rowdies and 'forties' – gambling sharpers who travelled from shed to shed making five pounds by cheating for every five shillings they earned.

1966 Tom Ronan *Strangers on the Ophir* 76: The usual percentage of spielers and forties, rogues and vagabonds.

forty-foot pole see **pole**

fossick To search out small quantities of gold, esp. in abandoned diggings; to search, rummage for something [f. *fossick* to 'ferret out' EDD]

1852 James Bonwick *Notes of a Gold-Digger* 8: Though most of these may be wrought out, a good living may be got . . . by the newcomer, in a little tin-dish fossicking in deserted holes.

1896 Henry Lawson 'The Man Who Forgot' *Prose* i 158: The swag had been prospected and fossicked for a clue, but yielded none.

1901 May Vivienne *Travels in Western Australia* 187: There are always a lot of men fossicking (looking for gold at the surface) about Bayley's.

1923 Jack Moses *Beyond the City Gates* 119: He started early . . . in order to give himself full time to fossick among likely-looking country.

fossicker One who fossicks

1867 J. S. Borlase *The Night Fossickers* 94: The 'night fossickers' – miscreants who watched for the richest holes during the day, marked them, and plundered them at night.

1911 E. S. Sorenson *Life in the Australian Backblocks* 256: Fossickers, who settle on what they term 'played-out fields', build more lasting homes.

1955 F. B. Vickers *The Mirage* 133: There were still fossickers on the Flat – old miners, on the pension now, but still panning off a few grains of alluvial gold, still hoping to strike it rich, as they had hoped all their lives.

1979 *Australian* 15 Sep. Mag. 3: There is

a certain technique in using metal detectors and in knowing likely spots. The gold rush has created a boom in their sale and most of the new fossickers discuss them and their relative merits in the same way that back in suburbia they would compare the relative performances of different makes of cars.

Four bob Robbo   see **Robbo**

fourpenny dark   A cheap wine [f. price and colour]
1948 *As You Were* 18: He merely treated me to the wintry smile of the dowager duchess being pressed to a fourpenny dark at a pensioners' party.
1967 Frank Hardy *Billy Borker Yarns Again* 5: A week on a fourpenny dark did nothing to make his hand any steadier.
1976 Dorothy Hewett *This Old Man Comes Rolling Home* 11: 'You better watch your step with that fourpenny dark. It'll get you before you know it.'
1981 *National Times* 7 Jun. 39: You could have a fourpenny dark, a small glass of sweet wine, usually muscat.

fourths   See quot. 1838
1834 Let. of 4 May in *The Tanner Letters* ed. Pamela Statham (1981) 80: He has put his sheep out on fourths.
1838 G. F. Moore *Diary of . . . an Early Settler in Western Australia* (1884) 366: I give him also 100 sheep to keep for three years on a fourth share of the increase; to the other man I let 4000 acres for five years, and I give him 200 sheep on fourths.
see **thirds**

fox   1   To pursue stealthily, to 'shadow'
1892 Henry Lawson 'Billy's "Square Affair"' *Verse* i 226: The 'gory' push had foxed the Streak, they foxed her to the park.
1918 Bernard Cronin *The Coastlanders* 174: 'You've been foxing me and Red all the morning . . . I think it's about time you came out into the open.'
2   To chase and retrieve a cricket ball, etc. [juvenile]
1942 Leonard Mann *The Go-Getter* 3: The batsman said, 'You bowled it, you fox it!'
1943 Margaret Trist *In the Sun* 87: Then a ball came down near her and rolled away beyond her. 'Fox it, Eleanor,' called someone, and Eleanor ran swiftly after it.

fox, flying   see **flying fox**

foxie   A fox-terrier [abbr.]

frame   An emaciated animal, esp. horse or bullock [U.S. 1880 OED]
1903 Joseph Furphy *Such is Life* (1944) 249: 'By-the-way, there's four of your frames left – out near those coolibahs.'
1946 A. J. Holt *Wheat Farms of Victoria* 327: 'You raise and kill a decent beast yourself and divide it with your neighbour. When it comes for his turn he picks out some rangy old frame with only hair on it.'
see **carrion**

franger   A condom
1979 Rae Desmond Jones *Walking the Line* 20: The little franger & KY peddler.
1987 *Sydney Morning Herald* 3 Aug. 13: 'If Australians use the word "rubber" for an eraser, what do they call a condom?' Cheshire paused, and then said: 'Well, you could say a franger'.

freckle   The anus
1971 Barry Humphries *Bazza Pulls It Off!* [25]: 'Flop your freckle on the grass there.'
1979 *Australian* 30 Apr. 2: 'I'll punch your flaming teeth so far down your throat that you'll have to shove a toothbrush up your freckle to clean them.'
1987 *Sydney Morning Herald* 2 Jan. Metro 3: She discovered . . . kids who used such terms as freckle-puncher (homosexual) and slopehead (Oriental person) in their daily vocab.

Fred   The ordinary, unimaginative Australian; the average consumer [? a coinage of Max Harris]
1973 Max Harris *The Angry Eye* 21: Even down where the Freds are browsing in their nocturnal pastures, the herd heroes are largely wasted. The John Laws and Brian Hendersons of Fredsville could well be their own men, real individuals down in the jungle of the sub-culture.
1975 *Sunday Telegraph* (Sydney) 20 Apr. 90: The Centura is aimed at what is loosely known as the average Fred market – the ordinary family motorist who wants basic transport for a price and who is not an imported car buff.
see **Alf, Ocker**

Freddie, blind   An imaginary figure representing the highest degree of disability or incompetence, and so used as a standard of comparison [derived by Baker (1953: 53n) from a blind hawker in Sydney in the 1920s]

1944 Dal Stivens *The Courtship of Uncle Henry* 188: 'He doesn't want to go on with tonight. Blind Freddy could see that.'

1966 Betty Collins *The Copper Crucible* 56: 'I know there's a principle involved – blind Freddie could see that.'

1975 Hal Porter *The Extra* 218: All the characters who've been around since Julius Caesar was a pup, and wouldn't fool blind Freddy.

1983 *Sydney Morning Herald* 2 Jul. 3: 'Over the last year even blind Freddie could see the council has been split like the Grand Canyon. Why don't you get together for the good of Mudgee?'

free   In Australian Rules, a free kick

1955 *Bulletin* 14 Sep. 26: What about when a player is too badly injured by an illegal tackle to take the 'free' awarded to him?

1984 Garrie Hutchinson *From the Outer* 186: Fitzy fell over, going for a free, for being pushed in the back . . . And he got it.

Fremantle doctor   See quots

1941 Baker 30: *Fremantle doctor* A refreshing sea-breeze that blows into Fremantle and Perth after hot weather, esp. in the evening.

1972 G. C. Bolton *A Fine Country to Starve In* 2: The 'Fremantle doctor', the afternoon sea-breeze which so often tempered the more than Mediterranean heat of the city in January and February.

1982 *Australian* 2 Jun. 2: The Freo Doc is on the honker . . . It and other westerly zephyrs stink to high heaven – because they are laden with the effluvium of live sheep loaded on ships for export to the Middle East.

see **Albany doctor**

frenchy   A condom [f. *French letter*]

1970 Patrick White *The Vivisector* 188: 'And never found nothun – but a used Frenchie!'

1979 *National Times* 3 Nov. 26: They have a friend who works at a chemist and provides 'frenchies' on discount.

1990 David Malouf *The Great World* 43: Trading had started up again: a packet of cigarette papers and two frenchies for a fountain-pen.

frog   A condom [f. *French letter*]

1952 T. A. G. Hungerford *The Ridge and the River* 23: Having a bath and a shave, getting into clean clothes, whacking a froggie into the kick, to lare up at the dance.

1970 Alexander Buzo *The Front Room Boys* in Penguin *Plays* 40: ' "Jees I forgot the frog", he said . . . I was disgusted. I put my pants back on and told him to take me home immediately.'

1983 Clem Gorman *A Night in the Arms of Raeleen* 45: 'Nine is gettin' yer length in, with a frog on, and both fully stripped, and ten is gettin' yer end in, with no frog, and both fully stripped.'

frog's eyes, eggs   Sago (or sometimes tapioca) pudding

1953 Baker 104: *frog's eyes* Boiled sago.

1983 *Sydney Morning Herald* 21 May 35: Sweets were mostly tapioca, watery junket and stodgy slabs of steamed pudding, labelled frog's eyes, white wobble and tombstone.

front   To appear before, 'front up'

1945 Kylie Tennant *Ride on Stranger* 67: Mr Litchin was . . . making frantic signs to Beryl who fronted him much in the manner of a ruffled kitten.

1950 *Australian Police Journal* Apr. 112: *Front, To* To appear before. 'Front' the court.

1961 *Sydney Morning Herald* 20 May 2: So the delo fronted him and said 'If we don't get gloves we'll walk off!'

1974 John Powers *The Last of the Knucklemen* 29: 'They reckon it's strange you don't front down there any more – not since that night.'

front, more ~ than Myers, Foy and Gibson's   An excessive 'hide', 'cheek', effrontery [f. facade of large departmental stores in Melbourne and Adelaide]

1958 Frank Hardy *The Four-Legged Lottery* 87: 'Must get back to the game. Some of these bastards have more front than Myers; might get their hand caught in the tin.'

1966 Baker 347: *more front than Foy and Gibson's*, said of a person who is extremely daring in his or her demands, or of a girl with large breasts.

1978 Barry Humphries *A Nice Night's Entertainment* (1981) 165: He's a cheeky beggar – always has been – more front on him than Myers.

1983 Clem Gorman *A Night in the Arms of*

Raeleen 30: 'That guy's got more front than the National Bank.'

front page, to put sport back on the   see **sport**

froth off a glass of beer, couldn't blow the   see **couldn't**

fruit for the sideboard   An access of good fortune, esp. extra income for minor luxuries; a racing or other gambling win, which is unexpected or a bonus
1953 T. A. G. Hungerford *Riverslake* 128: He was not afraid that they would ever wake up to it . . . not the poor dopes who came back week after week to buy the fruit for his sideboard.
1973 Alexander Buzo *Rooted* 8 'Some of our blokes were easy picking for those bastards. Fruit on the sideboard. That's what they were.'
1980 *Sun-Herald* 2 Nov. 81: Grey Receiver . . . was going to be the fruit on the sideboard the other day, but Voigt came along on Fantastic Planet to beat him in the closest of camera finishes.

frying pan   1   Applied to one brand superimposed dishonestly on another [f. appearance]
1857 F. Cooper *Wild Adventures in Australia* 104: 'This person was an "old hand" and had got into some trouble . . . by using a "frying pan brand". He was stock-keeping in that quarter, and was rather given to "gulley raking". One fine day it appears he ran in three bullocks belonging to a neighbouring squatter, and clapt his brand on the top of the other so as to efface it.'
1941 Baker 30: *Frying pan brand* A large brand used by cattle thieves to cover the rightful owner's brand.
2   Equivalent to 'small time' (cf. 'tea and sugar' burglar)
1864 J. F. Mortlock *Experiences of a Convict* (1965) 93: Some, unarmed, prowl about, watch the inmates of a dwelling away, and then pilfer. These are called 'frying-pan' bushrangers, being looked upon with much contempt.
1966 Tom Ronan *Strangers on the Ophir* 46: 'Oh, just a frying-pan fighting man who blew in from Coronet with a silver cheque.'

Fuchsias, the   Former nickname of the Melbourne A.F.L. club [f. resemblance of red flowers of the fuchsia to team colours]
1955 *Bulletin* 18 May 26: Melbourne – they used to be called Fuschias [sic], but it's Demons now – remain undefeated in the V.F.L.
1981 Leonie Sandercock and Ian Turner *Up Where, Cazaly?* 148: By the end of the decade Melbourne (who were called the Fuschias [sic] until Checker Hughes changed their name in the 1930s to the Demons) had won another two premierships.

fucktruck   A panel van, esp. with fitted mattress
1979 Rae Desmond Jones *Walking the Line* 19: The boys wearing blue singlets in their striped fuck trucks yelled and pressed down on their horns but Fifi kept going.
1982 John Tranter *Meanjin* 395: How did you adapt / your fuck-truck style of driving to a foreign car?

fuckwit   An idiot
1970 Suzy Jarratt *Permissive Australia* 142: 'Of course they do, you fuckwit.'
1980 Jessica Anderson *The Impersonators* 46: That morning a girl, a heroin addict of seventeen, had said to him, idly, 'Yes, but you're just a middle-class fuckwit, aren't you?'
1983 Rob George *Sandy Lee Live at Nui Dat* 64: 'Listen to me Anderson. You're a fuckwit.'

full   Used in various comparisons to indicate drunkenness
1911 Louis Stone *Jonah* 226: "Ard luck, to grudge a man a pint, with 'is own missis inside there gittin' as full as a tick.'
1951 Dymphna Cusack and Florence James *Come In Spinner* 367: 'She's been as full as a goog, ever since 'er boy friend went back.'
1955 D'Arcy Niland *The Shiralee* 86: 'The same old Lucky. Full as a boot and happy as Larry.'
1959 Hal Porter *A Bachelor's Children* 285: 'I'm going to get full as a State School . . . blind sleeping drunk!'
1961 Patrick White *Riders in the Chariot* 448: 'I bet that nephew of yours will be as full as a piss-ant by eleven!'
1964 Lawson Glassop *The Rats in New Guinea* 151: 'We'll get as full as the family po.'
1983 *Daily Telegraph* (Sydney) 2 Apr. 3: The saying 'as full as a Bourke Street tram'

is soon to take on a new meaning in Victoria, where alcohol may soon be served to passengers as the rails sing by.

full bottle, not the   see **bottle**

full dollar, not the   see **dollar**

full quid, not the   see **quid**

furphy   1   A water-cart made by Furphy of Shepparton, Victoria

1916 *The Anzac Book* 56n: Furphy was the name of the contractor which was written large upon the rubbish carts that he supplied to the Melbourne camps. The name was transferred to a certain class of news item, very common since the war, which flourished greatly upon all the beaches.

1955 E. O. Schlunke *The Man in the Silo* 208: The wood-and-water-Joey came trudging along with a load of water slopping out of the Furphy.

1969 Patsy Adam-Smith *The Folklore of the Australian Railwaymen* 25: Lying there in my bed [in the 1920s] I'd hear the rattle of kerosine tins, buckets, tin dishes, even the rumble of a horsedrawn furphy, the little iron tank on wheels.

2   A rumour thought to have arisen in gossip around the water-cart in World War I (a latrine rumour); any false report

1915 C. E. W. Bean Diary 7 Jun. in *Gallipoli Correspondent* (1983) 126: The place has been full of spy rumours these last few days . . . Blamey has asked me if I can get out a 'Furfies Gazette', with these furfies so exaggerated as to laugh them out of court.

1919 W. J. Denny *The Diggers* 67: We were not quite certain of our destination and 'Furphies'* became rife. *This word is used by Australian soldiers to signify rumours without foundation. It originated in a Victorian camp from the name of the proprietor of the sanitary carts – Furphy.

1946 Rohan Rivett *Behind Bamboo* 371: We sat around all the morning yarning, drawing rations, and hearing optimistic furphies which I was in no mood to believe.

1953 T. A. G. Hungerford *Riverslake* 147: 'Had you heard this furphy about Radinski?'

1982 Dick Klugman *Bulletin* 10 Aug. 5: Please stop repeating the same furphy; it upsets my constituents and causes eager political correspondents for the afternoon papers to ring me at 6 am.

fuzzy-wuzzy   Term applied in World War II to natives of Papua New Guinea working as stretcher-bearers, etc. [Applied to Soudanese in 1892, from appearance of hair OED]

1949 *As You Were* 93: Fuzzy wuzzies have been lauded, and A.N.G.A.U. men who organised and directed them have had some of the praise they earned.

1952 T. A. G. Hungerford *The Ridge and the River* 205: They had already had their reward – a slushy poem written from the gratitude of a soldier's heart and dedicated to them, the fuzzy-wuzzy angels, the Christs with black faces.

1972 John Bailey *The Wire Classroom* 31: These are the Fuzzy-Wuzzy Angels, now known as coons, and of course refused membership or even entry to the club, except as servants.

G

Gabba, the   The Queensland Cricket Association ground at Woollongabba, a suburb of Brisbane [abbr.]

1976 *Sydney Morning Herald* 26 Nov. 13: Test hopes on line at the Gabba.

1981 *Australian* 29 Jun. 1: VFL cracks Gabba record [heading] The Brisbane Cricket Ground attracted a record crowd yesterday when the Victorian Football League came to town.

galah   An ass, nincompoop, sometimes in the expression 'mad as a gumtree full of galahs' [? f. the cockatoo so named]

1944 Lawson Glassop *We Were the Rats* 142: 'When will these galahs wake up? It's a wonder there aren't no gum-trees around fer 'em ter nest in.'

1957 D'Arcy Niland *Call Me When the Cross Turns Over* 39–40: Poor old Dummy, lying in a hospital bed in Port Augusta, pinching the nurses' bottoms and telling the doctors what a lot of galahs they were.

1969 Leslie Haylen *Twenty Years' Hard Labor* 201: One has only to listen to the speeches on Grievance Day to realize that the private member has been reduced to the status of a political galah.

1981 'Stork' Hendry *Sydney Morning Herald* 3 Nov. 31: 'These bloody galahs going around now are bowling feet wide of the stumps and being hailed as good bowlers.'

galah session An interval on the Flying Doctor radio network when anyone may come on to the air, to exchange gossip [see quot. 1961]

1959 Jon Cleary *Back of Sunset* 111: 'You're just in time for the galah session. I never take that meself. Can't stand a bar of a lotta women magging their heads off.'

1971 Robin Miller *Flying Nurse* 103: During the gossip or 'galah' sessions, people can hear the cheerful voices of their 'next door neighbours' – who may be more than 100 miles away.

Galloping Greens see **Greens**

gallows A frame from which the carcass of a slaughtered beast could be suspended

1847 Alexander Harris *Settlers and Convicts* ed. C. M. H. Clark (1954) 159: Another convenience it [the stockyard] must contain is what is called 'the gallows' for hauling up a beast that has been slaughtered, to take the hide off.

1900 Henry Lawson 'The Selector's Daughter' *Prose* i 62: Her father finished skinning, and drew the carcass up to a make-shift 'gallows'.

1955 Mary Durack *Keep Him My Country* 95: The butcher's gallows stood out eerily against the rising yellow moon.

galvo Galvanized iron [abbr.]

1973 Donald Stuart *Morning Star Evening Star* 97: A canoe that you'd made with your own hands from a sheet of galvo.

1977 *Sydney Morning Herald* 5 Mar. 11: Risk drowning yourselves in canoes made from sheets of galvo.

game as Ned Kelly, a pebble, a pissant see **Ned Kelly, pebble, pissant**

game, the ~ they play in heaven Rugby Union football

1979 Steve Finnane *The game they play in*

heaven 168: It would be nice to think of a schoolboy in the year 2007 giving a rugby tourist a similar answer to the one John Lambie got from a Welsh lad in 1976. Lambie asked why rugby played such a special part in the lives of the Welsh. The singsong reply came back as quick as a Gareth Evans pass: 'Why it's the game they play in Heaven, Mr Lambie.'

1983 M. F. Unuk *Australian* 3 Aug. 6: An advertisement which recently appeared in your pages said 'Rugby – the game they play in heaven'. To whom was this information revealed, or has someone returned from heaven? Are there any other games played in heaven? What games do they play in hell?

game, the greatest ~ of all Rugby League football

1973 Alexander Buzo *The Roy Murphy Show* in *Three Plays* 113: 'I must say, Sharon, you've added a touch of glamour to the greatest game of all.'

1982 *Sun-Herald* 28 Feb. 74: 'The greatest game of all', as its followers insist on calling it . . . seems for the moment to be secure from any serious takeover.

gangie See quot.

1983 Wayne Pearce *Daily Mirror* 13 Sep. 55: Premiers Parramatta would be well advised to eliminate what they term the 'gang tackle' from their repertoire. For those not in the know, a 'gangie' is when three or four defenders converge on the ball-carrier and crash him to the ground, presumably to make him think twice the next time he handles.

Gap, the Cliff near South Head (Sydney) which has been the scene of suicide attempts: the offer of 'a one-way ticket to the Gap' is a sign of disfavour

1867 J. R. Houlding *Australian Capers* 223: They stood for a short time, and gazed into the Gap – that fatal chasm.

1925 Seymour Hicks *Hullo Australians* 251: The Gap is a jumping off place for all those who don't believe in the allotted span.

1934 Thomas Wood *Cobbers* 174: 'So they [the intending suicide and the policeman] had a talk about it first. Then they both went over the Gap.'

1975 *Quadrant* Jul. 34: Do you want to be an editor? Yeah, like I want a one-way ticket to the Gap.

garbo A garbage-collector, dustman [abbr.]

1953 Baker 105: *garbo* A garbage man.
1973 *Sun-Herald* 8 Apr. 9: Being a 'garbo' has compensations, according to Joe.
1983 *Sunday Independent* (Perth) 14 Aug. 3: Garbos complain of victimisation [heading]

Garden, Cabbage   see **Cabbage**

Garden State, the Victoria, in the language of tourist advertising, and in the legend on car registration plates

1911 *The Standard of Empire* 3 Feb. 20: Victoria, the Garden State of Australia [advt]
1978 *Sydney Morning Herald* 26 Jun. 1: Victoria, the self-styled Garden State, is definitely taking litter seriously.
1982 *Bulletin* 21 Sep. 12: Victoria may be the Garden State . . . but we all know what you put on gardens.

Gazette, Bagman's, Hominy   see **Bagman's Hominy**

geebung Derisive term for an uncultivated native-born Australian (cf. *stringy bark*); place-name for any remote and primitive locality [f. *geebung* the native plum (*Persoonia*) a small and tasteless fruit]

1874 Charles de Boos *The Congewoi Correspondence* 109: You know morer these things than I do, seein' as I'm only a poor old geebung, as ain't up to the ins and outser politics.
1895 A. B. Paterson 'The Geebung Polo Club' *The Man From Snowy River* 43: It was somewhere up the country, in a land of rock and scrub, / That they formed an institution called the Geebung Polo Club.
1900 Henry Lawson *Prose* i 21: 'Bogg of Geebung' [story title] Ibid. 295: 'He drank again, and no wonder – you don't know what it is to run a *Geebung Advocate* or *Mudgee Budgee Chronicle*, and live there.'

geek *v. & n.* Look [? f. *geck* to toss the head OED 1724]

1919 W. H. Downing *Digger Dialects* 25: *Geek* (vb. or n.) Look.
1954 T. A. G. Hungerford *Sowers of the Wind* 190: 'There's a circus down by the dance-hall, a Jap show,' Waller volunteered. 'What about having a geek at that?'
1970 Jack Hibberd *White With Wire Wheels* in Penguin *Plays* 204: 'It's just a good

solid reliable car. Just have a geek at the figures. It doesn't compare with the Valiant.' see **gink**

geese flying out of one's backside   see **sparrows**

George Female codeword for menstruation [listed by Partridge as meaning defecation]

1979 Sally Morrison *Who's taking you to the Dance?* 43: 'I'm having a baby . . . I haven't had George for two whole months.'
1982 Nancy Keesing *Lily on the Dustbin* 31: Kathy says to Mary 'You lot go on. Don't miss the bus, but I've just remembered I'm out of white bread, and George is calling tonight.' Mary understands that Kathy wants to dash into a chemist shop to buy sanitary napkins.

George Moore's whistle The imaginary whistle the jockey George Moore was supposed to blow to clear the way for a winning run

1982 *Sun-Herald* 10 Oct. 77: 'You'll know that it is Ray Selkrig looking for an inside run, just as George Moore did when he blew his whistle.'
1990 Max Presnell *Sydney Morning Herald* 13 Apr. 34: As the master horseman weaved his way to record-breaking wins, the whistle, it was said, enabled him to get the runs at the right time, in the most unexpected places.

geri A geriatric [abbr.]

1977 *Sydney Morning Herald* 5 Apr. 7: Geris (short for geriatrics) is applied by the young to anyone over 40, and has replaced 'oldies' in the Ocker vocabulary.
1984 *Sydney Morning Herald* 3 May 14: Enrol now in training schemes for the care of our growing legion of gerries.

get down on To steal

1941 Baker 31: *Get down on* To steal.
1948 *As You Were* 136: 'Would you hang on to my pack, Doc? 'Fraid some hungry b—— might git down on it.'
1959 *Bulletin* 27 May 59: 'Some ——'s got down on me rum I planted in the grass under me hut.'

get up To win (of a horse; sometimes a sporting team)

1904 Henry Fletcher *Dads Wayback: His*

Work 100: 'When ther public fancies yer nag's chance, an' puts ther beans on, ther books gives yer ther office, an' that prad don't quite get up that time; though he runs close.'

1949 Lawson Glassop *Lucky Palmer* 48: 'The way you bet you're up for a bundle if the favourite gets up.'

1983 Phillip Adams *Sun-Herald* 9 Oct. 9: 'I can't think of one confronting feature film that has criticised our society and got up.'

getting any? sc. sex: Current in Services slang in World War II, with stock replies

1945 Baker 124: The jocular greeting between man and man, *gettin' any?*

1951 Dal Stivens *Jimmy Brockett* 125: 'Getting any, Jimmy?' he'd asked a couple of nights ago. 'You bet,' I told him. 'I have to put an extra man on.' Ibid. 174: 'Getting any, smacker?' I'd ask him. More often than not he'd come back at me, 'I've got to climb trees to get away from it.'

1973 Alexander Buzo *The Roy Murphy Show* in *Three Plays* 103: 'Morning, Col. Getting any? That's the stuff.'

1984 *National Times* 6 Jul. 5: The Prime Minister's informal contact [on overseas trips] runs to occasional en-route card games lasting for hours with several press favorites . . . and social banter of the 'are yer gettin' any' kind.

getting off at Redfern see **Redfern**

Ghan, the The train which from 1929 to 1980 ran on the narrow gauge track from Marree to Alice Springs (it had previously terminated at Oodnadatta). It connected with a broad gauge track from Adelaide to Port Pirie, and a standard gauge track from Port Pirie to Marree. It was replaced in 1980 by the new Ghan connecting Adelaide with Alice Springs via Tarcoola, on a standard gauge line. [See quot. 1969]

1933 F. E. Baume *Tragedy Track* 21: This train, once known as the Ghan, because it was largely patronised by Afghans going to the then railhead of Oodnadatta, to-day is making history.

1969 Patsy Adam Smith *Folklore of the Australian Railwaymen* 250: The Ghan, that now runs from Port Augusta to Alice Springs but was named back when the line ran only as far as Oodnadatta. Railway literature gives two explanations for the name, one that it was named Ghan because of the many Afghan camel men using it, the other

that it was because of the number of Afghans and their families living at Oodnadatta, the railhead.

1982 *Sydney Morning Herald* 24 Dec. 17: After about an hour the Ghan was shunted down along the platform. It is a gleaming silver train of 16 cars, hauled by two Australian National diesels.

ghost, grey see **grey ghost**

gibber 1 A boulder: *obs.* [Ab. word for 'stone': Morris 1834]

1847 Alexander Harris *Settlers and Convicts* ed. C. M. H. Clark (1954) 87: He did not object to stow himself . . . under the 'gibbers' (overhanging rocks) of the river.

1882 Rolf Boldrewood *Robbery Under Arms* (World's Classics 1949) 62: A kind of gully . . . something like the one we came in by, but rougher, and full of gibbers (boulders).

2 A stone of the size thrown by children

1893 Dan Healey *The Cornstalk* 66: 'Now boys, get your gibbers, here's a man beating seventeen of us.'

1908 E. S. Sorenson *Quinton's Rouseabout* 146: They could all bowl, having practised in spare time with gibbers, using the hut for wicket.

1949 *Coast to Coast 1948* 34–5: He could also hurl goolies, gibbers, and plain bluemetal with devastating accuracy.

1963 John Cantwell *No Stranger to the Flame* 19: 'Some murdering bastard of a kid must have donged it with this gibber and then shot through.'

3 A wind-polished stone, esp. in the phrase 'gibber plain' [almost a technical term in geology, rather than a colloquialism]

1906 J. W. Gregory *The Dead Heart of Australia* 51: Our journey lay mainly over sand plains and 'gibber' plains; these last have a hard brown soil, littered with rough fragments of schist and quartzite.

1938 Francis Ratcliffe *Flying Fox and Drifting Sand* 231: 'Gibbers' are the iron-stained, wind-polished stones that are strewn on the surface of so much of the arid Australian inland.

1959 David Forrest *The Last Blue Sea* 23: His eyes were not cheerful, but hard, hard as a gibber plain under a summer sun.

gidgee A spear made from the wood of the gidgee (gidyea); any long spear

1878 *Catalogue of Objects of Ethno-typical Art in National Gallery, Melbourne* 46:

Gid-jee. Hardwood spear, with fragments of quartz set in gum on two sides and grass-tree stem. Total length, 7 feet 8 inches.
1937 K. R. Prichard *Intimate Strangers* 154: He screwed the fish on the end of the gidgee and raked him, whirling and flapping, into the boat. Prospero seized and pulled the fish off the gidgee.
1983 *West Australian* (Perth) 17 Dec. 3: A boy was rushed to hospital yesterday afternoon with the head of a three-pronged spear embedded in his stomach . . . he accidentally fell on a 'gidgee'.

gig *v.* 1 To look at [see **gig** *n.* 2]
1953 Ruth Park *A Power of Roses* 164: 'A girl don't want people giggin' her when she's just starting to branch out.'
1965 Kylie Tennant *Tell Morning This* 393: 'Let's have some light on it,' his host muttered. 'Can't waste our whole bloody life gigging out of windows.'
2 '? To befool, hoax' (OED 1795); to make fun of
1953 Baker 103: *gig* To tease.
1969 Wilda Moxham *The Apprentice* 149: He scowled. He didn't ever like being gigged.
1977 *Sydney Morning Herald* 17 Sep. 11: Should I win the Alfa Romeo the last thing that will worry me will be being gigged by my neighbours.

gig *n.* 1 'A queer-looking figure, an oddity; *dial.* a fool' (OED 1777–1856)
1945 *Salt* 13 Aug. 11: 'I'm not going to look like a gig for the sake of a few principles.'
1953 T. A. G. Hungerford *Riverslake* 19: He knew that, behind their bland glances, they were saying to themselves, 'Who's this gig?'
1971 Johnny Famechon *Fammo* 72: They were terrible, those early interviews, and my friends used to rubbish me when I made such a gig of myself.
1982 *NT News* (Darwin) 4 Aug. 7: Ever feel a real gig when you misplace your car key?
2 A look, glance [? variant of *geek, gink*]
1924 C. J. Dennis *Rose of Spadgers* 65: 'Is this 'ere coot,' I arsts, 'well knowed to you?' / The parson takes another gig. 'Why, yes.'
1949 John Morrison *The Creeping City* 8: 'You pay sixpence to go in and have a gig at his fern-gully and fishponds.'
1973 Frank Huelin *Keep Moving* 145: 'I

scarpered like a scalded cat – didn't even get a good gig at her.'
3 A **fiz-gig** (q.v.), a police informer
1984 *Bulletin* 19 Jun. 69: Fifty per cent of the Drug Squad's arrests are based on information received and woe betide a user, supplier or anyone else who becomes a dog, a gig.

giggle-house A mental asylum
1919 W. H. Downing *Digger Dialects* 26: *Giggle-house* Lunatic asylum.
1935 H. R. Williams *Comrades of the Great Adventure* 53: 'As silly as the "giggle-house" on a moonlight night.'
1957 D'Arcy Niland *Call Me When the Cross Turns Over* 116: 'Your own brother is half in the rats with worry and anxiety. Unless something's done he'll end up in the giggle-house.'
1973 Frank Huelin *Keep Moving* 169: The 'Giggle-house', a large, barrack-like building once used as a mental home.

gilgai, gilgie 1 'A saucer-shaped depression in the ground which forms a natural reservoir for rain-water. *Ghilgais* vary from 20 to 100 yards in diameter, and are from five to ten feet deep.' (Morris) [Ab.]
1903 Joseph Furphy *Such is Life* (1944) 68: Verifying the tracks of the thirsty bullocks so near the gilgie that it seemed a wonder they hadn't walked into it.
1931 Vance Palmer *Separate Lives* 231: Their horses feeding on Denison's grass and drinking from his gilgais.
1964 Tom Ronan *Packhorse and Pearling Boat* 157: It was just dark when the old packhorse floundered into a gilgai (small billabong).
2 A freshwater crayfish
1944 *Coast to Coast 1943* 174: Watching a gilgie hole he saw after a time the waving antennae and the cautious claws, then the black head and part of the body come out. He threw a bit of bark at the water and the gilgie jerked back into the hole.
1965 Colin Johnson *Wild Cat Falling* 12: 'What say we catch gilgies?'
1982 Jack Davis *The Dreamers* 142: *gilgy*, known as yabbies in the Eastern states; a small, freshwater crustacean. A corruption of *tjilki*.

gin at a christening, like a see **christening**

153

gin burglar A white man who has casual sexual relations with Aboriginal women

1947 W. E. Harney *North of 23°* 77: We had the eternal clash of 'gin burglar' versus 'gin shepherd'.

1971 Keith Willey *Boss Drover* 46: The manager would refer to 'combos' and 'gin burglars' as though they were social outcasts. But let his wife go away for a while ... and he would be down to the blacks' camp in no time.

gin jockey As for **gin burglar**

1955 D'Arcy Niland *The Shiralee* 121: He hated the ignominy of capitulating to a harlot, and a black one at that. Macauley, the gin-jockey, they could say. The black velvet for Macauley.

1975 Xavier Herbert *Poor Fellow My Country* 54: 'They only have to see you treating an Aboriginal woman like a human being to raise the cry *Gin Jockey*.'

1982 Brian Syron *Australian* 30 Aug. 9: 'I'm the product of a gin jockey. They [the whites] see the sins of their forefathers in my face.'

gin shepherd Someone seeking to protect Aboriginal women from white men: *derogatory*

1947 W. E. Harney *North of 23°* 75: The age old instinct to protect his herd was strong in Joe. 'A gin shepherd' the bagmen called him, but Joe only smiled when they called him that, as he knew that here was one who had been unsuccessful in the hunt.

1954 Tom Ronan *Vision Splendid* 58: She had a self-imposed, utterly sincere mission to save the lubras from the lust of the white men. She failed in her endeavour, earned herself the name of the 'greatest gin shepherd in the country', and was eventually responsible for her husband losing his job because he couldn't keep men.

1971 Keith Willey *Boss Drover* 46: The practice of separating the women from the combos was known as 'gin shepherding'.

gin's piss, weak as Very weak

1951 Seaforth Mackenzie *Dead Men Rising* 243: 'Whisky is nothing – what you call gin's water, is it?' 'Gin's – '. Poole stopped himself.

1983 *Australian* 5 Feb. Mag. 1: A new brand of white wine ... can be purchased in Tennant Creek and Alice Springs by tourists who want a really different souvenir. It costs $8 a flagon and bears the label 'Gin's Piss and Yakka Gum'. Maker and bottler unstated.

ging A catapult (juvenile)

1933 Norman Lindsay *Saturdee* 152: Peter took out his ging to make a show of catapulting a stone at a non-existent bird.

1965 Colin Johnson *Wild Cat Falling* 13: I put a stone in the ging and let fly.

1983 T. A. G. Hungerford *Stories from Suburban Road* 20: 'Help me cut the rubbers for my ging, Tommy.'

ginger See quot. 1945

1945 Baker 139: A prostitute who robs a man by taking money from his clothes is known as a *gingerer*. She usually works with an accomplice. *To ginger* and *gingering* are associated terms.

1953 Kylie Tennant *The Joyful Condemned* 5: 'I've just gingered the copper. Give him his pants back when he gets too noisy' ... 'Gingering', or robbing prospective clients, was considered low taste, but after all the man was a copper.

1961 Xavier Herbert *Soldier's Women* 306: 'Call the cops and prove it for yourself. They'd like to do business with the gal who gingered Plug for his roll.'

Gingerbeer An army engineer

1941 Baker 31: *Gingerbeers* The Aust. Engineer Corps.

1951 Eric Lambert *The Twenty Thousand Thieves* 149: 'And minefields! The Ginger Beers have laid so many mines they've lost trace of some of 'em.'

1970 Richard Beilby *No Medals for Aphrodite* 83: 'Who are these people, sergeant?' 'Couple of Gingerbeers, sir. Picked 'em up along the track.'

gink 1 A fellow, 'guy', interchangeable with **gig**: *derogatory* [U.S. 1910 OED? f. *geck, geke* a fool, simpleton 1515]

1924 *Truth* 27 Apr. 6: *Gink* A peculiar fellow.

1939 Miles Franklin and Dymphna Cusack *Pioneers on Parade* 35: 'Quick! Look at that gink over there. Isn't he a cut!'

1954 Bant Singer *Have Patience Delaney* 16: Up front the gink in the blue suit ... stands up and peers after the ambulance.

1971 Barbara Vernon *A Big Day at Bellbird* 185: He understood that long gink with her was her fiancé.

2 A look (? variant of *geck*)

1945 Robert S. Close *Love Me Sailor* 227:

I kept staring so that he could get a gink at me wide awake.

1962 Stuart Gore *Down the Golden Mile* 205: 'Come up to my camp on the way home in the morning and have a gink at it then.'

give away Abandon, give up, cease operations [? f. *give it best*]

1948 Sumner Locke Elliott *Rusty Bugles* in *Khaki, Bush and Bigotry* ed. Eunice Hanger (1968) 98: *Andy:* How's the garden going, Ot? *Ot:* Give it away.'

1955 John Morrison *Black Cargo* 14: 'If it was me I'd give it away,' I say to Tiny. 'He's got Buckley's chance.'

1961 Patrick White *Riders in the Chariot* 408: 'What's wrong with your job, Alf? You haven't given it away?'

1971 Colin Simpson *The New Australia* 157: 'Well, I gave the city away. Best thing I ever did, and my wife agrees.'

glad, gladdie A gladiolus

1968 Barry Humphries *A Nice Night's Entertainment* (1981) 110: Most other invalids get glads or carnies so Beryl said Valda must have really put her thinking cap on.

1972 Ian Moffitt *The U-Jack Society* 154: The breakfast gong has not summoned the tourists yet to the hotel dining-room (vases of gladdies in a funeral pink glow).

Glad, Our Miss Gladys Moncrieff (1892–1976), singer who took leading roles in *Maid of the Mountains* (1921, 1942), *Rio Rita* (1926) and in Gilbert and Sullivan productions

1939 *Life Digest* Mar. 99: A very vital and kindhearted woman is Gladys; everyone's friend, she is known to countless Australians simply as 'Our Gladys'.

1974 *Australian* 20 Nov. 3: Our Glad ill. Gladys Moncrieff has been admitted to a Gold Coast private hospital suffering from a virus complaint.

1984 *Sydney Morning Herald* 15 Oct. Guide 14: It's Livvy – Australia's 'Our Glad' of the eighties – in another cornucopia of song and dance that can only be described as lavishly dazzling.

glass door on a dunny, useful as a see **useful**

glassy, just the Superlative; the one who excels, is most admired: *obsolescent* [f. the 'glassy' as the most prized marble]

1906 Edward Dyson *Fact'ry 'Ands* 166:

'They're all right, ain't they?' asked the man, and he dusted them [the trousers] carefully. 'Oh, they're jist ther glassy.'

1911 Steele Rudd *The Dashwoods* 25: 'I said it would be just the glassy marble – the sort of thing I'd like to be at.'

1951 Dymphna Cusack and Florence James *Come In Spinner* 300: 'Low profits and quick turnover, and this is the glassy marble.'

Gloria Soame The 'Strine' formulation of 'a glorious home'

1965 *Sydney Morning Herald* 6 Jan. 1: The first advertisement in pure Strine reached our 'classified' department yesterday. It advertised a 'gloria soame' of 14 squares, with amenities.

glory box A box kept by young women for storing clothes etc. in preparation for marriage: *obsolescent* (U.S. *hope chest*)

1915 Louis Stone *Betty Wayside* 244: It was her glory box, containing all her treasures that she had gathered together against such a day as this.

1934 F. S. Hibble *Karangi* 110: They came to gossip and rave over the glory-box, being frank in their envy.

1966 Bruce Beaver *You Can't Come Back* 118: 'That's my glory-box . . . I'm saving up things so I can get married and get away from here.'

1975 Rodney Hall *A Place Among People* 149–50: 'She has been buying quite good quality things for her glory box.'

gluepot A depression in which a cart or wagon becomes bogged

1885 *The Australasian Printers' Keepsake* 84: Bullocks to make one more effort to extricate the dray from a 'glue-pot'.

1903 Joseph Furphy *Such is Life* (1944) 55: 'Hello! where's Damper?' 'Stuck in a gluepot, just in front o' the (adj.) hut,' replied Mosey.

1949 George Farwell *Traveller's Tracks* 74: It was only just under water, but underneath was red mud – a real gluepot.

2 A muddy race track

1984 *Sun-Herald* 13 May 63: 'Gluepot' going a hazard [heading]

gnamma see **namma**

go, give it a As for **give it a burl** q.v.

1924 *Truth* 27 Apr. 6: *Give it a go* To make an attempt.

1934 Thomas Wood *Cobbers* 10: 'Besides, we want people from the other side to see our State. Give it a go!'

1950 Gavin Casey *City of Men* 288: With Joe he would be giving himself a chance – the only chance he would ever be likely to get. 'I'll give it a go,' he announced suddenly.

1971 Robin Miller *Flying Nurse* 172: Damascus airport was closed by fog, but . . . I was prepared to give it a go.

go off 1   To be raided by the police, when engaged in something illegal

1941 Baker 31: *Go off* When an hotel or club is raided by the police for permitting gambling or after-hours drinking, it is said to 'go off'.

1949 Lawson Glassop *Lucky Palmer* 5: 'Clarrie, he ain't gone off in six months. Must sling to the cops. Wonder how much he pays 'em.'

1967 Kylie Tennant *Tell Morning This* 10: 'The nice thing about this place . . . is that it's never raided. Number Eighteen went off last week, and the Vice Squad are always in and out of the place two doors down – but us – we never seem to have them.'

1984 *Bulletin* 10 Jul. 49: Mona last went off in December 1983 when she was charged under her real name, Lucy Domingo, and fined $200 for having been the keeper of a brothel.

2   See quot. 1941

1941 Baker 31: *Go off* When a horse is expected or 'fixed' to win a race it is said to 'go off'.

1949 Lawson Glassop *Lucky Palmer* 176: 'A bloke who's got a mare like Laughin' Water is extra welcome. Let's know when she goin' off.'

1976 Sam Weller *Bastards I have met* 104: They had a real hot-pot ready to go off and they played it very cagey.

3   To be stolen

1953 T. A. G. Hungerford *Riverslake* 151: 'I wondered if you'd mind my wireless while I'm in Sydney? If I leave it in my room it'll go off.'

1963 Frank Hardy *Legends from Benson's Valley* 44: 'There's been a lot of wood goin' off from yards round the town lately.'

go the knuckle   see **knuckle**

go through   To abscond, make a swift departure, esp. to avoid some obligation (interchangeable with 'shoot through')

1943 Baker 34 *Go through* To desert from a northern base to the south. War slang.

1949 Lawson Glassop *Lucky Palmer* 79: 'When will you fellows wake to it? Here it is twenty to twelve and you blokes are still believing he'll be here. Can't you see he's gone through?'

1951 Eric Lambert *The Twenty Thousand Thieves* 222: He shrugged. 'I'll probably have to go through meself again.' He said it as though going A.W.L. was as casual a thing as shaving.

1973 Frank Huelin *Keep Moving* 179: *Gone through* Left town.

go under someone's neck   see **neck**

goat, a hairy   A racehorse which performs badly

1941 Baker 34: *Hairy goat, run like a* (used esp. of horses) To perform badly in a race.

1951 Dymphna Cusack and Florence James *Come In Spinner* 40: 'The last one you gave me [as a racing tip] ran like a hairy goat.'

1978 John Hepworth *His Book* 113: When the barrier flew up Warrego Willie went like a hairy goat – never even looked like running a drum.

goburra   The kookaburra: *obs.* [Ab.]

1834 George Bennett *Wanderings in New South Wales* i 222: The natives at Yas call the bird 'Gogera' or 'Gogobera', probably from its peculiar note, which has some resemblance to the sound of the word.

1905 *Old Bush Songs* ed. A. B. Paterson 114: Until they chime in the rude rough rhyme of the wild goburra's song.

Godzone   Australia [f. the use of this heading (for 'God's own country') in a series of articles in *Meanjin Quarterly*]

1966 *Meanjin Quarterly* 133: Godzone (1) The Retreat from Reason [Note:] This is the first of a new series of commentaries on the reality of present-day life and living in God's Own Country.

1976 *Australian* 15 May 21: Godzone's richest acres. A fine-focus on the best addresses in Australia.

1981 Buzz Kennedy *Australian* 14 Dec. 2: The ennui of the jet-setter. I don't know how the beautiful people stand up to it. But cripes – it was bonzer to get back to Godzone.

goer A project, proposal likely to be put into effect or to succeed
1977 *Bulletin* 29 Jan. 29: The film is now finally a goer. Hellwig's money is in and the rest will come from private investment . . . and film commissions.
1980 *Mercury* (Hobart) 31 Mar. 30: 'I've said it before and I'll say it again – without the public's support, this competition can never be a goer.'
1982 *NT News* (Darwin) 15 Jun. 2: Barge service a goer [heading] A monthly barge service from Darwin to Singapore . . . will go ahead despite union opposition.

gogobera see **goburra**

golden doughnut see **doughnut**

golden girl An Australian woman athlete who has won an Olympic gold medal; any outstanding Australian sportswoman [f. the 1956 Olympics, when Australia won the women's relay, and Betty Cuthbert three gold medals]
1956 *Sunday Telegraph* (Sydney) 2 Dec. 3: Golden Girls Triumph in Relay. Ibid. 9 Dec. 1: Australia's four 'golden girls' led the parade of athletes in a moving closing ceremony at the main Olympic stadium today.
1974 *Australian* 7 Aug. 21: Whatever happened to Evonne Goolagong – our golden girl who won this year's Australian tennis title.
1982 *NT News* (Darwin) 9 Sep. 37: Reviving memories of the 'Golden Girls' [heading] With the Commonwealth Games starting in three weeks, Australia's female athletes . . . are reviving memories of the 'Golden Girls', Marjorie Jackson, Betty Cuthbert and Shirley Strickland.

golden hole A very rich mining claim
1855 Raffaello Carboni *The Eureka Stockade* ed. Geoffrey Serle (1969) 176: Below at a depth of 140 feet in a . . . hundred pounds weight Golden Hole.
1861 Horace Earle *Ups and Downs* 290: 'Here's luck, Tom!' . . . 'A golden hole to you, Tom!' sounded from every quarter.
1896 Henry Lawson 'An Old Mate of Your Father's' *Prose* i 67: Poor Martin Ratcliffe – who was killed in his golden hole.
1950 K. S. Prichard *Winged Seeds* 22: 'Everywhere they tapped the reef, she was lousy with gold. They thought they'd struck a golden hole.'

Golden Mile, the 1 See quot. 1971

1901 May Vivienne *Travels in Western Australia* 210: From this place one has a glorious view of the other great mines on the Golden Mile, so-called on account of the marvellous quantity of gold that has been and still is being extracted from its depths – Lake View, Great Boulder, Ivanhoe, Boulder Perseverance, and Golden Horseshoe.
1908 E. G. Murphy *Jarrahland Jingles* 120: He has toiled along the Golden Mile among the cyanide.
1971 Colin Simpson *The New Australia* 557: The Golden Mile lies between Kalgoorlie and Boulder and is an extra-ordinarily rich auriferous reef area that is actually about two miles long and a third of a mile wide and has been mined to thousands of feet.
2 See quot. 1983.
1982 *Sydney Morning Herald* 10 Jul. 35: Behind all this activity run constant rumours about a mass move of the gay establishments from this golden mile of Oxford Street.
1983 *Daily Telegraph* (Sydney) 5 Feb. 21: A trip along that section of Oxford Street that runs from Darlinghurst to Paddington which the gays call 'The Golden Mile'. It starts at the western, city, end at Patchs disco and is generally considered to run out at the Apollo restaurant, Paddington.

goldfish Tinned herrings, as issued to the Services in World War II
1942 *Salt* 25 May 8: *Goldfish* Herrings.
1952 T. A. G. Hungerford *The Ridge and the River* 189: 'Flaming pigeon-pie every day instead of bullamacow and goldfish!'
1962 Jock Marshall and Russell Drysdale *Journey Among Men* 104: 'Tell us about your part in that rather disagreeable goldfish business during the war' . . . 'It was not goldfish,' said Dom quietly. 'The fish is *Nematalosa erebi*, a so-called bony bream. It is, in fact, a true herring – one of the soft-rayed clupeoid fishes.'

golfer A woman's cardigan
1975 Hal Porter *The Extra* 178: Some delightful young Queensland maiden . . . who wears golfers, eats cracknels, and says, 'Oh scissors!'

golly *v. & n.* To spit (juvenile)
1938 Encountered in conversation.
1941 Baker 32: *Gollion* A gob of phlegm.
1975 Les Ryan *The Shearers* 153: *Gobber* Ejaculation of saliva; a golly.
1978 Donald Hutley *The Swan* 48: He drew back from the nose and brought up

from the chest and gollied out into the rain.

gonce Money: *obsolescent* [? Yiddish]
1899 W. T. Goodge *Hits! Skits! and Jingles!* 159: 'The nearest guess will get the gonce as sure as you are there!'
1918 Bernard Cronin *The Coastlanders* 114: 'They know how to treat a gent in them places, provided he has the gonze.'
1930 J. S. Litchfield *Far-North Memories* 8: 'Old dad can't spare any time for frills; but he's got the gonce all right. He's worth more than most of the first-class travellers on this boat.'

gone a million see **million**

gone for a ride on the padre's bike see **padre's**

gone to Gowings see **Gowings**

gone to Moscow see **Moscow**

Gong, the 1 Wollongong N.S.W.
1979 *Sun-Herald* 1 Jul. 42: The 'Gong: . . . a city brave or sad.
1982 *Bulletin* 14 Dec. 52: Down in the 'Gong we're all on the dole / Looking for a job's like climbing a greasy pole.
2 Nickname of Evonne Cawley, née Goolagong
1982 *Sydney Morning Herald* 29 Nov. 22: 'It's good to have you back, Gong,' Martina Navratilova told Evonne Cawley as they shook hands over the White City centre court net.

good-oh Expression of agreement of approval; a state of well-being
1918 *Kia Ora Coo-ee* 15 Aug. 5: 'Fish for dinner to-day, Jack?' 'Good O! What sort?'
1923 Jack Moses *Beyond the City Gates* 166: 'You are to come and help . . . in the eating of the big fat turkey, the sucking pig and the plum pudding. Isn't that good oh!'
1940 Arnold Haskell *Waltzing Matilda* 36: If your companion says 'good oh' you know that he understands and approves.
1958 Frank Hardy *The Four-Legged Lottery* 36: 'Gee it must be good-oh at the races, Dad.' 'It's good-oh, all right.'

good oil see **oil**

good on you Expression of approval, congratulation, goodwill

1908 Giles Seagram *Bushmen All* 84: One man said, 'Good on yer, Mac.'
1922 Arthur Wright *The Colt from the Country* 171: 'Good on you, mate,' he said. 'We'll have a go.'
1935 Kylie Tennant *Tiburon* 273: 'Good on her,' Polly said cheerfully. 'May be the best thing she's ever done.'
1954 *Sydney Morning Herald* 10 Feb. 4: More than 10,000 people at Newcastle Sportsground today clapped and shouted, 'Good on you, Philip,' when the Duke of Edinburgh quickly opened up an umbrella to shield the Queen from the rain. Ibid. 19 Feb. 6: Shouts of 'Good on you, Liz' and 'Good on you, Phil'.
1981 *Australian* 22 Aug. Mag. 8: Of course Lady Diana was a virgin bride – and good on her.

good, to come see **come**

goofy, goofy-footer See quots
1963 *Pix* 28 Sep. 62: *Goofy Foot*: Surfing with the right foot forward.
1964 Bruce Beaver *The Hot Sands* 10: The most remarkable feature of Lou's skill and finesse was his unconventional stance on the board. He was a 'Goofy Footer' – a right foot forward boy.

gooley A stone of a suitable size for throwing (juvenile) [? f. Hindustani *goli* a bullet, ball]
1924 *Truth* 27 Apr. 6: *Gooley* A stone.
1949 Ruth Park *The Harp in the South* 47: 'Someone's been bunging goolies through her window.'
1963 John Cantwell *No Stranger to the Flame* 20: 'I lobbed it with a gooley and knocked it cold.'
1974 David Ireland *Burn* 18: 'Garn, get out of it,' Gunner says, 'before I let fly with a goolie.'

goom Methylated spirits, in Aboriginal parlance
1977 Jim Ramsay *Cop it Sweet* 41: *Goom* Methylated spirits.
1982 *Meanjin* 453: Goom! What a name for methylated spirits.
goomee A metho drinker
1977 Kevin Gilbert *Living Black* 93: 'My uncle was a goomee and when he died it really broke me up.'
1982 *Sydney Morning Herald* 3 Jul. 29: Musgrave Park [in Brisbane] is also the home of the drones, or the goomies, a word

158

used by the Aborigines themselves for a homeless black, and by the whites in a derogatory sense for a metho-drinker.

goon A flagon of wine [urban Ab.]
1982 *Sydney Morning Herald* 13 Nov. 30: Tim Stanford started off drinking with 'the goon'. It's a flagon of moselle or riesling.
1983 *Sydney Morning Herald* 23 Nov. 1: Three flagons of port (known as goons) have been consumed noisily [in Brewarrina] by about 8.30.

Gordon, in more trouble than Speed Beset with extraordinary difficulties [f. the character in the comic strip]
1971 Alan Reid *The Gorton Experiment* 381: Scott, a pathetic figure in some ways, who had been in more trouble than Speed Gordon while Customs Minister, went quietly.
1974 John Powers *The Last of the Knucklemen* 14: We might just find ourselves in more trouble than Flash Gordon.
1980 *Daily Telegraph* (Sydney) 12 Mar. 48: Les Boyd has found himself in more trouble than Speed Gordon since his switch to Manly.

Gorillas, the 1 In Queensland, the Wilston-Grange Australian Rules team
1979 *Courier-Mail* (Brisbane) 28 May 18: Centre half forward Gary Maddison turned in another brilliant performance for the Gorillas.
2 Former nickname of the Fitzroy A.F.L. club
1984 Lou Richards *Sun* (Melbourne) 9 Mar. 31: To give the team a psychological lift and a bit of bite they changed their name to the Gorillas . . . The idea was great – some of the players were built like Tarzan, but unfortunately for Fitzroy they played like Jane.

Government house The residence of the owner or the manager on a sheep or cattle station, as distinct from the **barracks** and the **hut** qq.v., more often just 'the house'
1887 Simpson Newland *The Far North Country* 12: The 'Government House', as the operator's residence is called [at Charlotte Waters Telegraph Station], is the principal building, chiefly remarkable for ugliness and heat.
1896 Henry Lawson 'Stragglers' *Prose* i 91: 'Government House' is a mile away [from the wool shed], and is nothing better than a

bush hut: this station belongs to a company.
1919 W. K. Harris *Outback in Australia* 2: 'Government House' (the owner's or manager's residence) on a big sheep station.
1936 A. W. Upfield *Wings Above the Diamantina* 77: Heading this class trilogy on the average station is the owner or manager, and his family. They reside in what is termed 'government house', the main residence on the property and centre from which it is directed.

Government man A convict
1802 David Collins *An Account of the English Colony in New South Wales* ed. B. Fletcher (1975) ii 19: The following prices of labour were now established . . . A government man allowed to officers or settlers in their own time 10d.
1820 *The Evidence of the Bigge Reports* ed. J. Ritchie (1971) i 85: Mr. Cox has allowed me to have a Government man in consequence of my marriage.
1854 W. Shaw *The Land of Promise* 49: The asperity of the word *convict* shocks their ears, so the more mollifying term of 'government man' has been substituted.
1874 Charles de Boos *The Congewoi Correspondence* 148: As to bandicoots, they're like Government men, they never turn out in wet weather, but keep theirselves snug at home.

Government stroke The indolent working style of a government employee, originally on road work
1855 C. R. Thatcher 'The Bond Street Swell' cit. R. Ward *The Australian Legend* (1958) 117: And then he went upon the roads, / As many a young swell must . . . / You may see him do the Gov'ment stroke / At eight bob every day.
1873 A. Trollope *Australia* ed. Edwards and Joyce (1967) 190: In colonial parlance the government stroke is that light and easy mode of labour – perhaps that semblance of labour – which no other master will endure, though government is forced to put up with it.
1903 Ada Cambridge *Thirty Years in Australia* 216: The labourer naturally prefers the Government stroke, and can be tempted away from that easy and pleasant way of passing his time only by an increased rate of wages.
1949 George Farwell *Traveller's Tracks*

93: Why should the white fellow have a monopoly of the government stroke?
1969 Osmar White *Under the Iron Rainbow* 108: 'Once them New Australians get the idea of the Government stroke and union rules they leave the Aussies for dead when it comes to bludging.'

Gowings, gone to Advertising slogan used in series of cartoons from the 1940s showing scenes vacated in a hurry by those seeking bargains [f. Sydney retail store]
1945 *Sun* (Sydney) 4 Jan. 2: Gone to Gowings [advertisement showing note left by bridegroom, with bride and congregation waiting in the church]
1979 *Sun-Herald* 4 Nov. 29: 111 years and they're still going to Gowing's [heading]

graft *n.* Work, esp. manual labour [? f. *grave* to dig c. 1000 OED; *graft* work of any description EDD 1891]
1853 John Rochfort *Adventures of a Surveyor* 47: Afterwards I could have obtained an engagement in my own profession at 300 l. a year, but, finding that I could make more money by 'hard graft', as they call labour in the colonies, I would not take it.
1935 Kylie Tennant *Tiburon* 199: He was tired of being an agrarian organiser in this west that regarded hard graft and bad food and hard times as just as inevitable as a dust storm.
1957 Sydney Hart *Pommie Migrant* 81: 'What a mug ya are to come 12,000 miles to do this kind of graft for a living.'

graft *v.* To work; to work hard
[**1859** Hotten: *Graft* to go to work]
1892 Harry Morant 'Paddy Magee' *Bulletin* 20 Feb. 14: What are you doing now, Paddy Magee? / Grafting, or spelling now, Paddy Magee?
1900 Henry Lawson 'Drought-stricken' *Prose* ii 96: They were very poor – often lived and grafted on damper, tea, and sugar.
1941 Kylie Tennant *The Battlers* 7: 'He grafted like a team of bullocks, and . . . had me out ploughing and clearing and fencing.'

grafter A hard worker
1901 F. J. Gillen *Diary* (1968) 277: Stephen like his brother John is an old friend of mine and a great grafter.
1918 C. J. Dennis *Backblock Ballads* 29: And though still a steady grafter, he grew restless ever after.

1953 *Caddie A Sydney Barmaid* 12: He was a grafter* and worked out in the bush six days a week. *In Australia a grafter is a very hard worker.

grand piano in a one-roomed house, couldn't find a see **couldn't**

Grannies Variant of **apples** q.v. [f. the Granny Smith apple]
1963 Bruce Beaver *The Hot Summer* 115: 'She'll be Grannies,' cackled the ragged informant.

Granny *The Sydney Morning Herald* (founded 1831 as *The Sydney Herald*) [see quot. 1931]
1851 *The Press* 23 Apr. 189: In the same number of 'My Grannie O', (which we beg to submit as a very good cognomen for the *Herald* and its antiquated and obsolete notions on the subject of government), there is a letter from the honorable member for Northumberland.
1901 Henry Lawson *Prose* ii 125: Even some London Conservative dailies come wonderfully refreshing to me after the *Sydney Morning Herald* ('Grannie').
1931 *A Century of Journalism* 239: The *Herald* has long been affectionately – and sometimes contemptuously – known as 'Granny'. The nickname being supposed to refer to its age, its allegedly conservative methods and the untiring energy with which it has always dealt out advice, comment, and criticism.
1950 Jon Cleary *Just Let Me Be* 241: 'You're beginning to talk like some old spinster,' Harry said. 'You'll be writing letters to Granny Herald next.'

grape on the business, a Someone whose presence spoils things for others; an odd man out [? variant of *gooseberry*]
1941 Baker 32: *Grape on the Business, A* (of a person) One who is a blue stocking, a wallflower or a drag on cheery company.
1944 Lawson Glassop *We Were the Rats* 9: 'I've got nobody to go with. All the girls'll be going with their boy friends and I don't want to be a grape on the business.'
1946 Alan Marshall *Tell us about the Turkey, Jo* 62: She hasn't got a bloke. She is a grape on the business.

grass castles (kings in) 1 See quot. 1878

1878 Patrick Durack in Mary Durack *Kings in Grass Castles* (1959) title page: 'Cattle Kings' ye call us, then we are Kings in grass castles that may be blown away upon a puff of wind.

1984 *Age* (Melbourne) 21 Mar. 11: When the kings in grass castles divided the land among themselves, Aborigines were needed to work the cattle and their dependants were tolerated.

2 The mansions built in Griffith N.S.W. from supposed profits from growing marijuana

1980 Alfred W. McCoy *Drug Traffic* 291: The Grass Castles of Griffith [subheading]

1984 *Sydney Morning Herald* 17 Oct. 15: The murder . . . of Donald Mackay, who had been campaigning against the 'kings in grass castles' of the Griffith marijuana trade, was probably the biggest mistake ever made by organised crime in Australia.

3 See quot. [f. *grass* = inform on]

1987 *Sydney Morning Herald* 25 Apr. 28: It might have been hoped that the Rogers incident would have spurred the Government to press on with the proposal for a gaol solely for prisoners who are informants, the so-called 'grass castle'.

grasshoppers 1 Visitors to Canberra, esp. in tourist groups, as distinct from the permanent residents

1965 *Sydney Morning Herald* 3 Jul. 5: A full bus-load of 'grass-hoppers' (the Canberra term for tourists – 'they eat everything in sight and never have a drink').

2 Interlopers in any community

1989 *Sydney Morning Herald* 26 Jan. Style 1: We quickly discovered that, as 'grass-hoppers' (blow-ins from the city), we would never be considered anything but part of . . . the sudden rural push.

greasy 1 An outback cook; any cook for a collection of men [f. grease on clothes]

1873 J. C. F. Johnson *Christmas on Carringa* 1: Bill, who himself was our *chef d'cuisine* . . . in the vernacular, cook or 'greasy', had on this occasion quite excelled his usual excellence.

1938 *Smith's Weekly* 19 Nov. 22: 'Greasy' was the officers' mess cook, but sad to relate, he was not an expert.

1953 T. A. G. Hungerford *Riverslake* 148: 'God, cooks aren't people!' Carmichael retorted . . . 'I'm going to write a book about greasies one day!'

2 A shearer

1956 F. B. Vickers *First Place to the Stranger* 134: 'When those five greasies get moving they'll shear a lot of sheep.'

1963 *Sydney Morning Herald* 17 Aug. 11: A lot of greasies (shearers) get hen trouble. Some shearers' wives reckon we shearer blokes are either too tired, too drunk or too far away.

1975 Les Ryan *The Shearers* 123: 'The greasier have hung up. Why can't we?'

greasy pig, a In two-up, a throw of tails after a succession of heads

1949 Lawson Glassop *Lucky Palmer* 174: 'Come on, gents, he's done 'em four times. Here's a chance for a greasy pig!'

Great Adventure, the Australian participation in World War I, esp. the Gallipoli expedition

1918 *Kia Ora Coo-ee* 15 Mar. 1: The Great Adventure [heading] April 25th., 1915. What a host of memories the date conjures up.

1935 H. R. Williams *Comrades of the Great Adventure* [book title]

1977 Richard Beilby *Gunner* 117: Too young for the earlier war, too old for this one, they lied and blustered, signed false declarations . . . Perhaps it had been the Great Adventure.

great Australian adjective, novel see **Australian**

Great Divide, the The Great Dividing Range

1907 Charles MacAlister *Old Pioneering Days in the Sunny South* 1: John Hamilton Hume . . . first bore the white man's burden across the Great Divide.

1983 *Sydney Morning Herald* 30 Apr. 29: City folk . . . may forget that there is life beyond the Great Divide. The CWA does not.

Great White Shark The fair-haired golfer Greg Norman

1984 *Australian* 23 Jun. Mag. 3: In the 1981 US Masters he finished fourth, but gained considerable attention with his 'shark hunting' stories, and thus became known as The Great White Shark . . . 'Actually, I never went out hunting sharks at all. I only shot at some when I became irritated that they were eating the fish I was catching. And I only did that a few times.'

Greek's, the The local milk bar, café, etc. (often run by Greeks)

1946 Margaret Trist *What Else is There?* 144: She caught up with Mamie and Teddy outside the Greek's. 'How about an ice-cream?' asked Teddy.

1953 T. A. G. Hungerford *Riverslake* 234: 'Sometimes they eat at the Greek's, down at the Kingston shops.'

1968 Geoffrey Dutton *Andy* 176: Steak and eggs and a cup of ghastly coffee at the Greek's.

1977 Ted Roberts *Lindsay's Boy* in *Five Plays* ed. Alrene Sykes 234: 'Should be out celebrating. What about a feed at the Greeks?'

green and gold Australia's sporting colours in international competition (unofficial until 1984)

1981 *Sydney Morning Herald* 18 May 28: Their lack of heart and fight must have been nauseating to the great players who have worn the green and gold in the past.

1984 *Bulletin* 15 May 124: Prime Minister Hawke's announcement that Australia's official colours were to be green and gold has caused some consternation at the Australian Bicentennial Authority, which has formally colored itself blue and gold.

green cart The van supposed to take people to the mental asylum

1959 Dorothy Hewett *Bobbin Up* 109–10: 'You're mad, that what's up with you. They'll come for you in the green cart one of these days me lady and not before time.'

1975 *Overland 62* 27: The green cart will come for me, and I'll disappear into Callan Park, and that will be some kind of solution.

Green Rats, the Warringah (N.S.W.) Rugby Union club [f. Rats of Tobruk, battling against odds]

1982 *Sun-Herald* 1 Aug. 77: Year of the green rats is coming [heading] For the first time, Warringah look like they could win the Rugby premiership.

Green Season See quot. 1979

1979 *NT News* (Darwin) 3 Nov. 12: It's official! There's no more wet season as far as the tourist people in the Top End are concerned ... As from last month and until March Top Enders will be going through the Green Season. And that's how the tourist people are promoting the old wet season.

1983 *Sydney Morning Herald* 15 Jan. 26: 'The Green' is the Territory's new name for the wet and it's supposed to keep the tourists coming.

greengrocer A variety of cicada [f. colouring]

1951 Dymphna Cusack and Florence James *Come In Spinner* 106: 'Mine's a Greengrocer – look!' Durras opened his hand carefully, showing a cicada with iridescent wings folded back on a body of delicate green.

greenie A supporter of the 'green bans' imposed by the Builders Labourers Federation in 1973 on demolition and development projects considered contrary to principles of 'conservation'; a trendy conservationist

1973 *Nation Review* 28 Sep. 1572: The local greenies have despaired of stopping the dreaded post office tower by indirect means, and have started on a little direct action.

1981 *Age* (Melbourne) 5 Oct. 10: Her father, a retired professor, is leading a battle by greenies to save from 'development' the inner-suburban street in which he lives.

1983 *Sun-Herald* 13 Feb. 24: Organisation for Tasmanian Development posters are chilling: 'Fertilise the SW – bulldoze a greenie'.

Greens, the Galloping The Randwick (N.S.W.) Rugby Union team (also the Wicks) [f. team colours]

1974 *Australian* 26 Sep. 20: Eels to knock gloss off the Greens.

Gregory's *Gregory's Sydney Street Directory*, first published by Cecil Albert Gregory in 1934

1983 Peter Corris *The Empty Beach* 93: My *Gregorys* showed Mark Lane to be a little trickle of a thoroughfare in Clovelly near the boundary with Randwick.

grey In two-up, a double-headed penny, or a penny with two tails [f. English thieves' slang OED 1812–68]

[**1812** Vaux: *Gray*: a half-penny, or other coin, having two heads or two tails, and fabricated for the use of gamblers, who, by such a deception, frequently win large sums.]

1898 *Bulletin* 3 Sep. 32: He'd simply smashed the two-up school / (Assisted by a 'grey'!)

1946 K. S. Prichard *The Roaring Nineties*

387: A spieler had been caught ringing in the grey, a two-headed penny, and the boys were giving him a rough time. Ibid. 125: 'The grey', a penny with two tails.

grey bomber As for **grey ghost**, q.v.
1983 *Newcastle Herald* 8 Feb. 3: Six parking officers, or grey bombers as they are better known, are being trained in Newcastle.

grey ghost A N.S.W. parking policeman, successor to the **brown bomber** q.v. [f. colour of uniform]
1976 *Sydney Morning Herald* 10 Jul. 1: Don't think you can park just anywhere in the City during the national strike – the police will get the Grey Ghosts on the job.
1979 *West Australian* (Perth) 5 Dec. 8: Sometimes derisively and sometimes jocularly referred to as 'grey ghosts', Perth's parking inspectors must rank as one of the most maligned groups in the city.

grey meanie A parking policeman in Victoria [f. colour of uniform]
1971 *Sunday Australian* 1 Aug. 3: Mr McMahon walked into the hotel's lounge and took tea. Meanwhile one of Melbourne's famous 'grey meanies' slapped the ticket on the Prime Minister's car.
1984 *Age* (Melbourne) 3 Apr. 17: Grey meanies, and how to beat them [heading]

greys, Hexham see **Hexham**

grid (iron) A bicycle: *obsolescent*
1941 Baker 32: *Grid (iron)* A bicycle.
1942 Gavin Casey *It's Harder for Girls* 125: 'Here, you go on, on my grid, an' I'll do the walking.'
1955 F. B. Vickers *The Mirage* 114: 'You'll see him wheelin' the grid along the Ninety Mile Beach.'
1977 Helen Garner *Monkey Grip* 9: We . . . disentangled our bikes from the heap outside the kitchen door; my thirty dollar grid, and Clive's blue and silver Coppi racers.

grog General term for alcoholic drink, usually beer [f. *grog* as rum (and water) OED 1770]
1833 George Fletcher Moore *Diary of Ten Years* (1884) 185: With you 'grog' means a mixture of spirits and water, in the ratio of one to three, or one to four – no such thing here – it means unmixed ardent spirits.
1938 Xavier Herbert *Capricornia* 256:

'Sorry – I've knocked your grog over. Let's buy another . . . What are you drinking?' 'Double whiskey.'
1949 Lawson Glassop *Lucky Palmer* 8: 'Likes his beer, does Darky.' Clarrie groaned. 'The grog,' he said. 'He can't beat the grog.'
1953 *The Sunburnt Country* ed. Ian Bevan 126: Grog is beer: and beer, to the A.I.F. is sacred. The first sound heard from any Australian convoy arriving in any foreign port will always be the cry 'How's the beer?'
1973 Alexander Buzo *Rooted* 44: 'Hammo had been on the grog and he didn't give way to his right and this bloke smashed into him.'

grog on To continue steady drinking
1965 John Beede *They Hosed Them Out* 185: We grogged on till closing time; it was evident we all had one thing in common – a liking for the amber liquid.
1979 Bobbie Hardy *The World Owes Me Nothing* 146: The pubs were full of shearers grogging on and waiting for a break in the weather.

grog-up As for 'beer up'
1962 Alan Seymour *The One Day of the Year* 77: 'We're sick of all the muck that's talked about this day . . . It's just one long grog-up.'
see **sly-grog**

Groper As for **Sandgroper** q.v.
1908 E. G. Murphy *Jarrahland Jingles* 29: 'Give me the goblet of good ruddy wine!' / Cried a Groperland Poet who gropes.
1926 J. Vance Marshall *Timely Tips for New Australians: Groper* A West Australian.

Grouper A member of one of the 'Industrial Groups' set up in the Labor Party in 1945–6 to counter Communist influence in the trade unions
1955 *Sydney Morning Herald* 27 Apr. 1: Last year the groupers altered the rules to give two delegates for every 250 members from a State electoral council.
1985 *Sydney Morning Herald* 24 Apr. 5: He [Fred Daly] said that the activities of the 'groupers' meant that he and his mates spent the best years of their political lives in the wilderness.

groupie A participant in the Group Settlement scheme in Western Australia in the 1920s, under which hundred-acre allotments were made to English emigrants in the backward south-west

1972 M. L. Skinner *The Fifth Sparrow* 119: Few of the 'groupies' knew anything about farming at all and the raw land daunted and frustrated them.

1979 Justine Williams *White River* 11: I had to milk three of the cows . . . My mother milked three, my father four, so caring for the total that the authorities provided for each groupie, as they were called.

1983 John K. Ewers *Long Enough for a Joke* 111: The Collie miners were earning good money; the groupies were earning only sustenance.

grouse Excellent, outstanding [origin unknown]

1924 *Truth* 27 Apr. 6: *Grouse* something good.

1944 Lawson Glassop *We Were the Rats* 5: 'You know them two grouse sheilas we've got the meet on with tomorrer night?'

1953 T. A. G. Hungerford *Riverslake* 74: 'Seven o'clock, O.K.?' 'Yeah, that'll be grouse.'

1974 Jim McNeil *How Does Your Garden Grow* 111: 'And then there's the advertising in the papers . . . usually with a grouse sheila in the picture all ready to get her gear off if yer use whatever stuff they're trying to sell yer.'

1982 Ford Ray *Bulletin* 12 Jan. 10: My recollection is that 'grouse' was used in three forms. 1. Grouse, as in 'What a grouse lookin' sheila.' 2. Extra grouse, as in 'That was extra grouse tucker, Mrs Dutton', and finally, the superlative degree 3. THE grouse, as in 'I reckon a cold beer on a scorcher like this would be the grouse!'

grouter, come in on the To seek benefit from a situation not of one's own making, esp. in two-up by withholding any bet until a run of heads or tails indicates that a change must soon occur (hence a 'grouter bet')

1919 W. H. Downing *Digger Dialects* 27: *Grouter* An unfair advantage. 'Come on the grouter' – gain an unfair advantage.

1944 Lawson Glassop *We Were the Rats* 113: 'I reckon you Seventh Div. jokers have come in on the grouter.' I felt ashamed. 'Our turn'll come,' I said. 'We've got to do some more training yet.'

1954 Tom Ronan *Vision Splendid* 230: 'Bloke here headed 'em eight times. Good chance for a grouter.'

1965 Wally Grout *My Country's Keeper* 90:

I saw a cove who had been watching me play the machine step up to it, whip in a few coins, and crack the jackpot. A nice easy way to earn a living. We call that 'coming in on the grouter'.

grunter A promiscuous woman [f. *pig* prostitute]

1973 Alexander Buzo *Rooted* 70: 'I'll line up a bird for you, too. I know a couple of grunters.'

gub, gubbah Aboriginal term for a white

1972 *Sydney Morning Herald* 2 Nov. 12: Mr Gub is . . . the white man. The word is the diminutive of garbage.

1982 *Sydney Morning Herald* 14 Feb. 7: A young Aboriginal woman described last month how she walked into a hotel [in Moree] to find a black man drinking alone with whites. She told him sneeringly that he was a 'gubber lover'.

guernsey, get a To gain recognition or approval; succeed [f. selection in a sporting team]

1918 Let. in Bill Gammage *The Broken Years* (1974) 218: In 1918 troops chosen for an attack 'got their guernseys.'

1964 George Johnston *My Brother Jack* 298: 'As long as you're going to get a guernsey, that's the main thing.'

1981 *Sunday Mail* (Brisbane) 27 Sep. 2: Two well known Brisbane racing scribes were delighted recently to score a guernsey for last Wednesday's plush Horse of the Year bash in Melbourne.

guiver, gyver Flattering pretence; loquacity; general 'carry-on': *obsolescent* [? Yiddish]

1864 *Thatcher's Colonial Minstrel* 13: 'I'll give you the sack pretty quick, / If my wife you offend with your guiver.'

1902 Henry Fletcher *The Waybacks in Town and at Home* 22: 'But yous er bloke as knows ther inside runnin' o' things; tell me, straight, what's this Federation guiver all amount ter?'

1915 C. J. Dennis *The Songs of a Sentimental Bloke* 79: I s'pose the wimmin git some sorter fun / Wiv all this guyver.

1947 Vance Palmer *Cyclone* 68: 'Chuck that cheap guyver, Con. It doesn't suit you. Leave it to the girls in Finnegan's bar.'

1962 Dymphna Cusack *Picnic Races* 19:

'Lotta jumped-up blow-ins putting on more guyver than the Governor's wife.'

gully-raker 1 One of those engaged in **gully-raking** q.v.
[**1865** Hotten 148: *Gully-rakers* cattle thieves in Australia, the cattle being stolen out of almost inaccessible valleys, there termed *gullies*.]
1869 E. C. Booth *Another England* 138: The old fellow had lost his team, and had been seeking them ever since. Hearing that the 'gully-rakers' about were not very particular, he had travelled down the river as far as Shepparton.
2 A long whip
1881 A. C. Grant *Bush-Life in Queensland* i 40: Following up his admonition by a sweeping cut of his 'gulley-raker', and a report like a musket-shot.
1919 W. K. Harris *Outback in Australia* 85: Long whips with short handles, and short whips with long handles, eight strands and upwards, from the redoubtable old 'gulley-rakers' to the exaggerated thong affixed to a hunting crop.

gully-raking The rounding up of un-branded cattle by searching the gullies and other places where they may have been over-looked; illegally appropriating cattle by this practice
1847 Alexander Harris *Settlers and Con-victs* ed. C. M. H. Clark (1954) 140: If he could find an unbranded beast in the bush, had no qualms about making it his own by clapping his brand on it. In this way, by a process technically called 'gully-raking', he had quadrupled the little herd his father gave him.
1857 F. Cooper *Wild Adventures in Aus-tralia* 104: 'He was stock-keeping in that quarter, and was rather given to "gulley-raking". One fine day it appears he ran in three bullocks belonging to a neighbouring squatter, and clapt his brand on top of the other so as to efface it.'

gumleaves, the smell of Symbol of what is authentically Australian, perhaps from the influence of Lawson's short story 'His Country – After All'
1894 Henry Lawson 'His Country – After All' *Prose* i 203: 'The smell of them gum leaves set me thinking.' And he thought some more ... 'What do you Britishers know about Australia? She's as good as England, anyway.'

1947 Margaret Trist *Daddy* 126: She went abroad. Now she's come back a sort of success woman ... Once you get rid of the smell of gum-leaves you can cash in on any-thing.
1982 Bill O'Reilly *Sydney Morning Herald* 23 Oct. 56: As soon as he [Brett Henschell] took his stance and played his first shot past point I detected an almost overpowering smell of gumleaves ... The vigorous manner in which he belts his side-on shots through the off, the purposeful way in which he chances his arm by smacking straight into the pitch of on-side deliveries, all acknowl-edge that he comes from the wide open spaces.

gumsucker A native of Victoria; a native-born Australian [? f. *gumtree*]
1855 William Howitt *Land, Labour and Gold* i 24: Bitten twice by the over 'cute 'gum-suckers' as the native Victorians are called.
1859 Frank Fowler *Southern Lights and Shadows* 24: Your thorough-bred gum-sucker never speaks, without apostrophising his 'oath', and interlarding his diction with the crimsonest of adjectives.
1903 Joseph Furphy *Such is Life* (1944) 44: 'When anybody calls him a Port Philliper, or a Vic., or a 'Sucker, he comes out straight ... 'I'm a Cornstalk, born in New South Wales.'
1914 Nathan Spielvogel *The Gumsucker at Home* 9: I hoped to wander all around Vic-toria, spending a few weeks in each place, and so in the course of four or five years to know all about the land of the Gumsucker.

gumtree, up a In great difficulties, in a state of confusion (like an animal which has been treed) [? U.S. song 'possum up a gum-tree' Mathews 1831]
[**1888** W. S. S. Tyrwhitt *The New Chum in the Queensland Bush* 150: The opossum, more generally known as the possum, as a rule occupies his proverbial position in a gum tree.]
1941 Baker 33: *Gumtree, up a* In trouble, in a quandary.
1945 Gavin Casey *Downhill is Easier* 87: They wanted to know whether or not we'd been kidded up a gum-tree, and they shouted and roared a lot about it.
1973 *Sun-Herald* 25 Mar. 108: Up a gum-tree [heading] During the Yugoslav Prem-ier's visit, energetic policemen went along the shores of Lake Burley Griffin shaking

young gum trees. Security cars in the motorcade were marked with special markings on the roofs, so they could be spotted by police sharp-shooters overhead.

gun *n. & a.* A shearer with a high tally; anyone pre-eminent in some activity [f. *big gun, great gun* OED 1815]
1898 'Whaler's Rhyme' *Bulletin* 9 Jul. Red Page repr. in *Old Bush Songs* ed. Stewart and Keesing (1957) 250: There's brand-new-chums and cockies' sons, / They fancy that they are great guns.
1940 Ion L. Idriess *Lightning Ridge* 152: The 'gun shearer' there was a two hundred-a-day man, the tally of the lowest was over a hundred a day.
1957 D'Arcy Niland *Call Me When the Cross Turns Over* 131: He was a champion at other things too. He was a gun potato-digger and pea-picker.
1986 *Courier-Mail* (Brisbane) 7 Jul. Sports Extra 9: 'Southport are the gun side in the competition and we really worked hard to beat them,' he said.

gundy An Aboriginal hut
1876 Rolf Boldrewood *A Colonial Reformer* (1891) 204: There were a dozen 'goondies' to be visited, and their inmates started to their work.
1908 Mrs Aeneas Gunn *We of the Never-Never* 186: The camp-fires were all around us: dozens of them, grouped in and out among the gundies.
1956 Tom Ronan *Moleskin Midas* 158: 'Men I've known ... Not miserable rats waiting outside a blackfellow's gundy for the buck to send out the gin when he's done with her himself.'

Gundy, no good to Applied to something adverse: *obsolescent* [origin unknown]
1919 W. H. Downing *Digger Dialects* 35: *No good to gundy* Of no advantage.
1922 E. O'Ferrall *Bodger and the Boarders* 46: One of them scrawled 'I don't want none of youre dam sympathy. Out 'ere it's 107 in shade and all that there talk about comin and settin be fires made me sweat like an orse. No good to Gundy.'
1923 Jack Moses *Beyond the City Gates* 128: 'Taint no good to Gundy to see the fluid go, / When you're cockyin' and battlin' and live on what you grow.
1968 Stuart Gore *Holy Smoke* 35: 'This is no good to gundy, they say.'

gungible See quot. [urban Ab.]
1983 *Sydney Morning Herald* 7 Dec. 11: A white person could be mistaken as a gungible (police officer).
1988 Ruby Langford *Don't Take Your Love to Town* 262: I could see Nobby looking very dignified in his navy suit, sitting between two gungabul. [Note: gungabul – policemen.]

gunyah An Aboriginal hut (Morris, 1798), but applied colloquially to shelters improvised by whites
1841 *A Mother's Offering to Her Children* 150: They only went two miles that afternoon; and then encamped: making a snug hut, or gunyah, with boughs.
1853 S. Mossman and T. Banister *Australia Visited and Revisited* 53: He [the gold-digger] would be as much at home lying down in his dirty clothes for weeks together, in a tent or bark gunya, as he was at home in his straw pallet in his mud cabin.
1903 William Craig *My Adventures on the Australian Goldfields* 113: Other shelter and accommodation had, however, to be obtained, and the following day we procured from Spring Creek the necessary calico for a 'gunyah'.
1919 E. S. Sorenson *Chips and Splinters* 12: The sawyers, whose home was a bark gunyah nearby, were tradesmen whose work was important to them.

guts, come (give) one's To inform to the police, or other authority
[c. **1882** *The Sydney Slang Dictionary* 2: *Come it* To inform.]
1945 Tom Ronan *Strangers on the Ophir* 172: 'He'll give away all his guts to try and save his worthless hide.'
1953 Kylie Tennant *The Joyful Condemned* 295: The sullen, big oaf, baited and jeered at by everyone, a man who had 'come his guts to the coppers', was almost driven desperate.
1966 Elwyn Wallace *Sydney and the Bush* 141: 'Me? Come me guts? A top-off?'

guts, in the In two-up, referring to bets placed 'in the ring' as distinct from 'on the side'
1948 Sumner Locke Elliott *Rusty Bugles* in *Khaki, Bush and Bigotry* ed. Eunice Hanger (1968) 30: 'I'll spin 'em for a quid . . . Get set in the guts ... Another two bob for the guts.'
1965 Leslie Haylen *Big Red* 101: Outside

he could hear the gamblers: 'Come on, I want a dollar in the guts.'
1975 Les Ryan *The Shearers* 96: 'Money up or shut up!' Lofty called out. 'Four quid wanted in the guts.'

guts, rough as Extremely rough or uncouth
1966 Bruce Beaver *You Can't Come Back* 118: 'I'm shy all right, but I'm not smooth . . . I'm rough as guts.'
1968 Frank Hardy *Unlucky Australians* 11: 'The old Territorian is a good bloke, rough as guts but his heart's in the right place.'
1978 Helen Hodgman *Jack and Jill* 89: She was getting rough as guts . . . just like her Dad.

guts, the good Reliable information (mainly Services slang)
1919 W. H. Downing *Digger Dialects* 27: *Guts* The substance or essential part of a matter, information.
1948 Sumner Locke Elliott *Rusty Bugles* in *Khaki, Bush and Bigotry* ed. Eunice Hanger (1968) 33: 'Got any good guts on replacements?' Ibid. 57: 'Heard the late good guts on the leave?'
1965 William Dick *A Bunch of Ratbags* 196: 'What about Sharon?' asked Joey. 'How much does she charge, Elaine? Give us the good guts on her.'

gutser, come a To 'come a cropper' (used both literally and figuratively)
1919 W. H. Downing *Digger Dialects* 27: *Gutzer* A disappointment; a misfortune. 'To come a gutzer' – suffer a reverse of fortune.
1936 Miles Franklin *All That Swagger* 381: 'The banks will fetch old Robert a gutser one of these days.'
1963 Jon Cleary *A Flight of Chariots* 179: 'They thought we'd knuckle under, but they came a gutser.' 'A gutser?' 'Came a thud. Made a mistake.'
1973 Patrick White *The Eye of the Storm* 493: He stumbled into a pothole: could have come a gutser.

gutter-gripper A motorist who drives with one arm out of the car window gripping the 'gutter' on the roof
1959 *Bulletin* 14 Oct. 9: The driver who draws some mysterious moral support from gutter-gripping.
1986 *Sydney Morning Herald* 6 Mar. 16:

Even gutter grippers . . . respond to the backbeat with relish. We've all got rhythm.

guzinter A schoolteacher: *obsolescent* [see quot. 1945]
1945 Baker 133: A schoolteacher is called variously a *chalk-and-talker*, *guzinter* (i.e. one 'guzinter' two, two 'guzinter' four, etc.)
1951 Dal Stivens *Jimmy Brockett* 52: I wanted to ask the old guzinter where all his bright boys were today, but I let it pass.

gym Small quantities of gold, esp. if pilfered from the mines [see quot.]
1941 K. S. Prichard *The Roaring Nineties* 209: The miners used to get rid of a bit of gym, which was what they called the gold they got out of a mine with the Gympie hammer. It was easy to get away with in their crib bags or billies.

gympie 1 A nettle-tree [Ab.]
1895 Archibald Meston *Geographic History of Queensland* 55: GYMPIE [place name]. The Mary River blacks' name for the stinging tree.
1938 Francis Ratcliffe *Flying Fox and Drifting Sand* 68: The 'Gympie nettle' of South Queensland, *Laportea gigas*, is replaced in the northern scrubs by a closely allied species, *Laportea moroides*. The chief difference between them seemed to be that the latter possessed an even more terrible touch than its southern cousin.
1959 Eleanor Dark *Lantana Lane* 249: There was a big rock beside a Gympie tree.
2 A hammer [f. place name]
1945 Baker 94n: The single-hand or *Gympie hammer* was also called a *Massey hammer*.
1979 Donald R. Stuart *Crank Back on Roller* 182: He would be . . . good on a windlass or swinging a gympie.
3 A steel drill
1964 H. P. Tritton *Time Means Tucker* 75: hammer and drills (tap and gympie).
1979 Bill Scott *Tough in the Old Days* 129: The four of us were given two fourteen pound sledge hammers and a handful of steel drills, 'gads' or 'gympies' were the colloquial names for these drills.

gyver see **guiver**

167

H

ha ha pigeon A kookaburra (the laughing jackass): *rare*
1941 Baker 34: *Ha-ha Pigeon* A kookaburra.
1962 Jock Marshall and Russell Drysdale *Journey Among Men* 169: Italian migrants have begun to put themselves on the wrong side of the law by eating willy wigtails, jacky winters, kookaburras ('ha ha pigeons') and, in fact, almost everything in feathers.

hairy goat see **goat**

hammer, to be on someone's To pursue, to maintain pressure upon [explained by Baker (1945:286n) as rhyming slang: *hammer and tack = track*]
1942 *Truth* 31 May 12: Someone 'drums' me there's two 'Jacks' on me 'hammer'.
1944 Lawson Glassop *We Were the Rats* 140: 'We can't stop. The Jerries might be right on our hammers for all we know.'
1956 Kylie Tennant *The Honey Flow* 157: 'The only way to get the best out of a dope like Mongo is to keep on his hammer all the time.'
1975 Les Ryan *The Shearers* 5: 'The shearing committee will be on your hammer later on.'

hand, old see **old**

handbag 1 A male not taking a proper manly role, esp. an Australian Rules player
1985 *Sunday Independent* (Perth) 1 Sep. 83: An ocker accent . . . certainly helps when it comes to screaming for your team . . . 'Kill the umpire' and 'What are ya – y'bloody handbag', and 'Carn Swans'.
1987 *Parliamentary Debates House of Representatives* 1 Apr. 1865: *Mr Keating* – The Honourable member [Mr Carlton] will rip up another sheet of paper if we are not careful or stamp his foot and throw his handbag at us.
2 See quots
1986 *Sydney Morning Herald* 13 Jun. 16: In Paris, where Gough Whitlam is finishing up soon as Ambassador to UNESCO, she [Margaret Whitlam] had been, she said, '. . . once again a handbag, something that is taken out as required to match the occasion'.

1987 Kristin Williamson *Times on Sunday* 28 Jun. 25: 'When people ask me what I do for a living, I say that I sleep with the minister,' she [Jan Murray] declared. Was she trying to ruin his career? No, she was probably just fed up with being a handbag.

handbrake on a Holden, useful as a see **useful**

handle A glass of beer, esp. in N.T. (and New Zealand) [f. tankard style glass]
1943 *Bulletin* 14 Apr. 27: The chap who leaves his work or office at 5 p.m. and wants his two or three handles before going home often has to fight his way into a saloon or front bar and stand and wait in a queue, because all lounges and such places are full of females.
1958 *Bulletin* 22 Oct. 8: A young Victorian who asked in a South Australian country hotel for a 'pot' should, he learned later, have asked for a 'handle'.
1982 *NT News* (Darwin) 2 Mar. 1: Beer prices will rise by up to 10 cents a handle following major wage increases to Territory hotel workers . . . The price of a 285 ml handle will jump to an average of 80 cents.

hang up 1 To tether (a horse) [U.S. 1835 OED]
1859 Henry Kingsley *Recollections of Geoffry Hamlyn* i 124: 'Come down off the bridge, my love, and let us talk together while I hang up the horse.'
1900 Henry Lawson 'Bill, the Ventriloquial Rooster' *Prose* i 143: The fellows from round about began to ride in and hang up their horses round the place.
1930 Vance Palmer *The Passage* 281: He hung up his mare at the fence and stumbled over the uncropped grass.
1962 Alan Marshall *This is the Grass* 60: 'Why didn't you hang up your horse outside?'
2 To hang up the shears i.e. stop work
1962 *Sydney Morning Herald* 24 Nov. 12: A shearer putting in a wet ticket, after a majority dry vote, can 'hang up', and go to the huts without dismissal.
1974 Les Ryan *The Shearers* 123: 'The greasies have hung up. Why can't we?'

hanging state, the Victoria, before the abolition of capital punishment in 1975

Hanrahan The persona of John O'Brien's [the Rev. Father P. J. Hartigan's] poem 'Said Hanrahan', whose prophecy was 'We'll all be rooned', whatever the circumstances
1921 P. J. Hartigan 'Said Hanrahan' *Around the Boree Log* 77: 'We'll all be rooned,' said Hanrahan, / In accents most forlorn . . . 'We'll all be rooned,' said Hanrahan, / 'Before the year is out.'
1980 *National Times* 20 Apr. 16: Nixon immediately took what is known in the Prime Minister's Department as 'the Hanrahan option', after the bush ballad which includes the recurring line: 'We'll all be ruined said Hanrahan'. He would not want anyone to think that farmers were well off.
1982 Les Murray *Meanjin* I 122: The tunes or contours of whingeing, the rhetoric of the dying fall or the depressive ul-ul-ulation, the Hanrahan note.

happy as a bastard on Father's Day see **bastard**

happy as Larry see **Larry**

Harbour, our Sydney Harbour, as referred to by the local residents
1883 R. E. N. Twopeny *Town Life in Australia* 19: I suppose that nearly everyone has heard of the beauties of Sydney Harbour – 'our harbour', as the Sydneyites fondly call it.
1892 Francis Adams *Australian Life* 194: When he got to Sydney . . . he set to taking stock of 'their harbour', their town and their people.
1925 Seymour Hicks *Hullo Australians* 242: 'Our 'arbour' as its owners humorously and lovingly call it is indeed a veritable marvel.
1965 Graham McInnes *The Road to Gundagai* 71: 'Our 'Arbour, Our Bridge and Our Bradman' was the Melbourne jibe at Sydney.

hard doer A stronger version of a **doer** q.v.
1926 K. S. Prichard *Working Bullocks* 168: Terrible Tommy's patter and jokes . . . had been on the road as long as he had, but never failed to make the country people laugh – if it was only good humouredly – to see such old hard-doers again.
1947 Gavin Casey *The Wits are Out* 55:

Everybody looked at him with amusement and admiration, and laughed. 'He's a hard doer,' someone said, chuckling.

hard-hitter A bowler hat
1895 J. Roberts *Diary* 7/2: I had long ere this put on my own clothes . . . of the 'masher' type – white shirt, hard-hitter, tight trousers, etc. [OED]
1901 Henry Lawson 'Buckolts' Gate' *Prose* i 440: Jim sat in his shirt-sleeves, with his flat-brimmed, wire-bound, 'hard-hitter' hat on, slanting over his weaker eye.
1951 Dal Stivens *Jimmy Brockett* 51: He had his Sunday clobber on, wore a hard-hitter and carried a stick.
1982 Joe Andersen *Winners Can Laugh* 19: In his frock coat and black 'hard hitter' his was an overwhelming presence.

hard word, put the ~ on Used most often of a man seeking sex (outside marriage) and as the expression for bringing matters to a point, but applied also to other requests that approach an ultimatum [cf. *put the acid on*]
1919 W. H. Downing *Digger Dialects* 28: *Hard word* An outrageous demand. (Put the hard word on)
1936 H. Drake-Brockman *Sheba Lane* 192: 'I loved him, and I found out I wasn't any better than the others when he started to put the hard word on me.'
1939 Kylie Tennant *Foveaux* 359: The landlord tried to make love to her, or, as she termed it, 'put the hard word on her'.
1951 Dal Stivens *Jimmy Brockett* 117: If I'd slung a diamond bracelet her way before I'd put the hard word on her, it'd have been a very different story.
1972 *Sydney Morning Herald* 9 Mar. 'Look' 2: She [Lady Hasluck] deplored the absence of a museum devoted exclusively to historic Australian costumes, and added 'Is it one we should put the hard word on the Government for?'

hatful of arseholes, ugly as a Very ugly
1957 D'Arcy Niland *Call Me When the Cross Turns Over* 139: 'I know the one with the ugly face like a hatful of bronzas. Who's the other?'
1972 Geoff Morley *Jockey Rides Honest Race* 62: The floor as filthy as a hatful of arseholes and sheilas sitting down against the wall.
1985 Robert G. Barrett *You Wouldn't Be Dead for Quids* 188: She was . . . as naive as

they come and uglier than a hat full of arse-holes, but ... after all she was a Queens-lander so she couldn't be all that bad.

hat, to throw one's ~ in first To test the likely reception beforehand
1953 *Caddie A Sydney Barmaid* 248: As he walked in through the back door I said: 'Hadn't you better throw your hat in first?'
1975 Xavier Herbert *Poor Fellow My Country* 343: It was Fay McFee again, de-claring in her brassy contralto that she sup-posed she ought to throw her hat in first, but didn't have one.
1981 *Australian* 25 Apr. Mag. 18: The builder returned with a big smile: 'Should I throw my hat in first?' he asked, as his only concession.

hatter A bushworker who lives and works alone; a bush eccentric [? f. *mad as a hatter* OED 1849]
1853 John Rochfort *Adventures of a Sur-veyor* 66: The Bendigo diggings are suitable for persons working singly ... Such persons are humorously called 'hatters'. They live alone, in a tent often not more than six feet long, three feet high, and three feet wide.
1873 Rolf Boldrewood 'The Fencing of Wanderowna' *A Romance of Canvas Town* (1898) 36: I always hated the 'hatter' or soli-tary shepherd system.
1900 Henry Lawson 'No Place for a Woman' *Prose* i 398: I was surprised to hear of a wife, for I thought he was a hatter.
1935 R. B. Plowman *The Boundary Rider* 82: Among the many station-hands were one or two old hatters. In the kitchen they felt at ease, but for no consideration would they have entered the station sitting-room.
1946 K. S. Prichard *The Roaring Nineties* 27: Ford was a regular hatter ... surly and uncommunicative.

have on, to See quot. 1941
1935 Kylie Tennant *Tiburon* 97: 'I'm a wrestler, I am. 'Ave y' any wrestlers that'd 'ave a bloke on?'
1941 Baker 34: *Have (someone) on* To be prepared to fight a person: to accept a chal-lenge to a contest or fight.
1962 Stuart Gore *Down the Golden Mile* 137: 'I'm as good as some o' you young jokers. I'll have any one of yer on – old and all as I am.'
1980 *Sun-Herald* 6 Apr. 24: 'I never

picked fights, but if someone picked one with me, I'd have them on.'

Hawkesbury rivers The shivers [rhyming slang]
1941 Baker 35: *Hawkesbury rivers* The shivers (rhyming slang).
1951 Dal Stivens *Jimmy Brockett* 72: I had the Hawkesbury Rivers every time I thought of what could happen if the press boys got on to it.

Hawkespeak Term applied in various ways to the utterances of R. J. Hawke, Prime Minister 1983– [f. analogy with Newspeak, etc.]
1 With an implication of 'doublespeak', esp. by political opponents, but often reflecting a careful choice of words which may mislead the unwary
1983 Andrew Peacock *Parliamentary Debates House of Representatives* 26 May 1015: It [the imposition of taxes on lump sum superannuation payments] is the re-emergence of our old bogey, Hawkespeak: the Prime Minister says one thing but really means the opposite ... Not one but several newspapers reported on 16 April that the Prime Minister had stated that there would be no increase in tax on lump sum super-annuation. Yesterday the Prime Minister told the House that these reports were without substance. Later in the day, he de-scribed these reports as 'speculation'. [See comment by Mike Steketee *Sydney Morning Herald* 26 May 1:
On April 15, Mr Hawke was asked at a news conference about the speculation over taxing lump sum superannuation. He replied: 'Because there has been speculation, a num-ber of my ministers have spoken with me and I can say on the basis of conversations I have had, without pre-empting the decision that will have to be made in the Cabinet pro-cedures, that I think you will find that there has been no basis for the speculation.'
The Sydney Morning Herald and other newspapers interpreted the Prime Minis-ter's remarks as ruling out a tax increase for superannuation. The previous day, the Herald and other newspapers reported that Mr Hawke had made the same promise to the ACTU executive.
There was no attempt by the Government to deny the reports, although a close reading of Mr Hawke's comments show that he left himself a way out.]

2 To denote the excessive use of 'in respect of', 'consideration', 'position' etc.

1983 Mike Steketee *Sydney Morning Herald* 25 Jun. 30: On the 11-hour flight back to Canberra, journalists amuse themselves with Hawke-speak renditions, delivered in suitably nasal accents, such as: 'In respect of, foundationally-speaking, our position down the track, the viability of the kangaroo is in place'.

1983 *Sydney Morning Herald* 22 Jul. 1: In respect of Mr Hawke's press conference in Canberra yesterday, the vocabulary of Hawkespeak was fully respected by the P.M. The word 'respect' occurred 26 times.

3 To refer to the use of involved and discursive sentences

1984 *National Times* 14 Dec. 2: If you don't know by now what Hawkespeak is then here is a verbatim excerpt – from the official transcript – of what our Great Communicator drops off-the-cuff as communication:

Journalist: Prime Minister, yesterday in a statement, the Left of the Party said the poor result of the election was caused to some extent by traditional Labor voters being disenchanted, specifically young people.

Hawke: Let me say that I am not commenting upon, if I can be this juxtaposition 'the right of the left', on the basis of results, to talk about the electoral perception of positions. That is for others to do. It is an interesting exercise. But I really want to say this – that I can understand that in that interregnum that a group wanted to express its view. Let me say this, that I expect into the future that the discussion about these matters will be conducted within the Party, within the framework of the Party, and I believe the attitude that was exhibited in the Caucus today was one of acceptance of that position that we have, from myself speaking on behalf of the Ministry, indicated in good faith, that we will be consulting fully with the Caucus, with all sections of the Party ...

Hawks, the 1 The Hawthorn A.F.L. team

1950 *Melbourne Sun* 8 Apr. 3: It was Cazaly who changed Hawthorn's nickname from the 'May-blooms' to the 'Hawks'.

2 In Queensland, the Sandgate Australian Rules team

1979 *Courier-Mail* (Brisbane) 8 May 22: The Hawks stretched their lead to nine points at half-time.

hay Money (modifying the U.S. sense of a trivial amount of money as in 'that ain't hay')

1955 *Bulletin* 10 Aug. 20: We cash the cheque for the poddies and we get a hundred-and-fifty quid each, which in them high and far-off times is a lotter hay.

1962 Gavin Casey *Amid the Plenty* 130: 'We're on the way to get the hay.'

1983 *Sun-Herald* 4 Dec. 168: When all the work ends soon to rejuvenate Randwick racetrack and complete the all-weather training track, $1 million will have been spent in the past six months. Seems a lot of hay.

head a duck, couldn't A disparaging comment on a racehorse

1902 A. B. Paterson 'Sitting in Judgment' in *Song of the Pen* (1983) 81: 'Homeward Bound!' says the fat man. 'Why, the pace he went wouldn't head a duck.'

1925 Arthur Wright *The Boy from Bullarah* 81: 'They raced his legs off after that at all sorts of meetings, but he didn't seem able to head a duck.'

heading them Playing two-up [f. throwing 'heads']

1890 A. G. Hales *Wanderings of a Simple Child* 10: I saw a large crowd of the genus digger, engaged in the refined pastime known to the elite of the back blocks as 'heading 'em'.

1897 Henry Lawson 'The Boss's Boots' *Verse* i 320: Just keep away from 'headin' 'em' and keep away from pubs.

1930 Frank Hives *The Journal of a Jackaroo* 8: On Sunday mornings there would be a 'school' in the backyard of the hotel, when the game of 'heading them' would be indulged in for high stakes.

1959 Anne von Bertouch *February Dark* 69: 'We might just as well take up heading 'em for a living,' said Peter. 'Heading 'em?' said Helen. 'Two-up,' said Max.

1964 *Sydney Morning Herald* 25 Apr. 11: A mob of ringers (station hands) in for a sublimating grog-up and full of beer and nostalgia start 'heading 'em' in the bar.

head like a beaten favourite, a robber's dog, a twisted sandshoe Ill-favoured

1961 Frank Hardy *The Hard Way* 249: 'Have a look at him!' I advised the audience. 'Have a good look at the head on him like a robber's dog.'

1981 *National Times* 25 Jan. 23: A face like a twisted sandshoe.

1982 *Sydney Morning Herald* 27 Nov. 28: When he captures the real Australia in expressions like 'She's got a head like a beaten favourite', McKellar is at his timeless best.

head over turkey   see **turkey**

head, pull your ~ in   Equivalent to 'shut up' or 'come off it' (in schoolboy parlance in the 1940s, 'Pull your head in, they'll think it's a cattle truck', addressed to a passing train, etc.)
1944 Lawson Glassop *We Were the Rats* 111: 'It's no use sayin', "Put ya head in, they'll think it's a cattle truck". It bloody well is a cattle truck!'
1963 John Cantwell *No Stranger to the Flame* 20: 'I know you, Max Sinclair. So pull your silly skull in.'
1974 *Australian* 4 Jan. 1: When reporters continued questions, the Minister for Minerals, Mr Connor became angry and said: 'Give us a bloody chance to work it out. Come off this, pull your bloody head in.'
1981 *Age* (Melbourne) 11 Jul. 3: He said Mr Grassby should 'pull his head in'.

heads, the   1   In N.S.W., the North and South Heads of Sydney Harbour
1802 Matthew Flinders *Voyage to Terra Australis* (1814) 9 May i 226: At one o'clock we gained the heads, a pilot came on board, and soon after three the Investigator was anchored in Sydney Cove.
1867 J. R. Houlding *Australian Capers* 216: 'Catch me in a fishing-boat outside the Heads again, if you can.'
1939 Kylie Tennant *Foveaux* 497: The Saturday afternoon procession of ships passed at slow intervals from the Heads.
1951 Dymphna Cusack and Florence James *Come In Spinner* 86: 'She was born in Manly, and never been outside the heads except on a Saturday afternoon cruise.'
2   Those in authority [listed by Partridge as 'more gen. Colonial than English; very common in the A.I.F.']
1916 C. J. Dennis *The Moods of Ginger Mick* x: If I was up among the 'eads, wiv right to judge the game, / I'd look around fer chance to praise, an' sling the flamin' blame. Ibid. 145: *'Eads (Heads)* The authorities; inner council.
1935 H. R. Williams *Comrades of the Great Adventure* 184: General Birdwood interrupted our game. Two-up was not encouraged by the 'heads'.

1978 Kevin Gilbert *Living Black* 62: 'My brother's a big head at Canberra but I just turned out a drunk.'

health hazard   A phrase, with variants, given currency by the requirement of the Broadcasting and Television Act in 1972 that each advertisement for cigarettes (or cigarette tobacco) broadcast or televised should be followed by the statement 'Medical authorities warn that smoking is a health hazard'.
1972 *Parliamentary Debates House of Representatives* 18 May 2828: [Mr D. J. Hamer moved an amendment] In the proposed section 100A.–(1) omit 'The National Health and Medical Research Council warns that cigarette smoking is dangerous to health'; insert 'Medical authorities warn that smoking is a health hazard'.
1979 *Advertiser* (Adelaide) 28 Feb. 3: Kissing may be a tooth hazard [heading] Kissing may transmit tooth decay, a SA doctor says.
1984 *Sun-Herald* 7 Oct. 107: I have heard that jeans can be a health hazard.

heaps, to give them   To contest strenuously, deal severely with an opponent
1978 *Sydney Morning Herald* 26 Sep. 2: Good Luck Kangaroos (and give 'em heaps) Tooths KB is proud to sponsor the 1978/79 Kangaroo tour of Great Britain and France. And wish players and officials good luck in their quest to keep the Ashes.
1982 *Sunday Mail* (Brisbane) 5 Sep. 80: Punters give Malcolm heaps [heading] Malcolm Johnston was booed after champion galloper Kingston Town was beaten into fourth place . . . at Randwick yesterday.

Heart, Dead   see **Dead**

Heart, the Red   see **Red**

heaven, the game they play in   see **game**

heifer dust   A variant of **bulldust** 2 [OED 1927]
1941 Baker 35: *Heifer dust* Nonsense, 'bullsh'.
1951 Dal Stivens *Jimmy Brockett* 52: If Jimmy Brockett had any say, kids would not have to clutter up their brains with a lot of the heifer dust that is pushed up to them.
1955 D'Arcy Niland *The Shiralee* 96: 'All they could do was take his money and string

him a line of heifer dust as long as your arm.'

heifer paddock A girls' boarding school: *obs.*

1885 Mrs Campbell Praed *Australian Life* 50: 'Next year I shall look over a heifer-paddock in Sydney and take my pick.' N.B. Heifer-paddock in Australian slang means a ladies' school.
1897 Mark Twain *Following the Equator* 221. 'heifer-paddock' – young ladies' seminary.

hen's teeth, scarce as Very scarce [listed by Partridge as 'mostly Australian']

1965 John Beede *They Hosed Them Out* 203: 'You'll find they're as scarce as hen's teeth on this squadron.'
1976 *Bulletin* 16 Oct. 53: 'I'd really like to be in PR or travel, but those jobs are scarce as hen's teeth.'
1980 *Australian* 27 Sep. 40: VFL grand final tickets are as scarce as hen's teeth and fans will try anything to obtain one.

herbs, give it the To give extra power (esp. applied to accelerating a car) [? f. extra taste given by the addition of herbs]

1957 Randolph Stow *The Bystander* 116: 'Go on, give him the herbs. Bet he doesn't even notice you're there.'
1961 *Age* (Melbourne) 20 May Lit. Suppl. 17: One teaser I want explained . . . is 'herbs' for a car's horse power.
1975 Don Townshend *Gland Time* 140: 'Them glands have given him more herbs than a tractor.'

Hexham greys Mosquitoes of exceptional size [f. place-name in N.S.W.]

1895 A. B. Paterson *The Man from Snowy River* 170: They breed 'em at Hexham, it's risky to vex 'em, / They suck a man as dry at a sitting, no doubt.
1964 H. P. Tritton *Time Means Tucker* 12: The Hexham swamps are the home of the famous 'Hexham Greys', the biggest and hungriest mosquitoes in Australia, or maybe in the world. And it is no exaggeration to say there were millions of them.
1983 *Newcastle Herald* 21 Mar. 3: Our friend the Hexham Grey mosquito doesn't deserve his bad reputation. It isn't the grey that puts the bite on unsuspecting gardeners; it's the salt-marsh mosquito. Hexham Greys do bite but the black salt-marsh

mosquito is much more common and more vicious.

Highlanders, the The Gordon (N.S.W.) Rugby Union team [f. the regiment so named]

1979 *Sunday Telegraph* (Sydney) 20 May 107: Highlanders' fling not good enough [heading] Gordon scored two tries to one, had a feast of possession, but still lost 15–11 to Randwick.

Hill, the The uncovered area in front of the scoreboard at the Sydney Cricket Ground

1925 Seymour Hicks *Hullo Australians* 246: A place they call the Hill is occupied by thousands of barrackers . . . who are sure they understand cricket better than the umpires.
1979 *Australian* 2 Jun. Mag. 1: It's enough to . . . cause a cricket connoisseur on The Hill to exclaim 'Oh, well blocked, Boycott!'
1981 *Daily News* (Perth) 19 Jan. 28: The most astonishing discovery of the season was that the mob on Sydney's notorious Hill, in spite of their beery belligerence, are a thin-skinned, sensitive lot who were deeply offended when Richard Hadlee described them as the worst-mannered cricket crowd in the world.

hill, go over the Abscond, clear out (Army slang)

1966 Don Crick *Period of Adjustment* 35: 'If you don't want to be in it, get out,' Jim said. 'Go over the hill.'

hill, the light on the see **light**

Hills, the Surry Hills, a suburb of Sydney, N.S.W.

1966 Elwyn Wallace *Sydney and the Bush* 2: Molly was one of the few who always had plenty of money and to the Hillites she was a good sport with a heart as big as The Hills itself.

Hilton, Emu see **Emu**

Hilton, Jesus see **Jesus**

Hilton, Malabur see **Malabar**

hip pocket in a singlet, useful as a see **useful**

hold a bull (elephant) out to pee, strong enough to

1955 D'Arcy Niland *The Shiralee* 122: 'He'd eat me, you know. Big enough to hold an elephant out, he was.'
1981 *National Times* 25 Jan. 23: The occasional bushman is still to be found who is 'strong enough to hold a bull out to pee'.

Holden, useful as a handbrake on a   see **useful**

holding   In funds
1924 *Truth* 27 Apr. 6: *Holdin'* Possessing money.
1932 William Hatfield *Ginger Murdoch* 29: 'If you want a few bob, I'm holdin' sweet.'
1963 Alan Marshall *In Mine Own Heart* 166: 'How're ya holding?' Darkie asked me, looking intently at me with hard, suspicious eyes. 'I've got thirty bob,' I said.
1980 Jessica Anderson *The Impersonators* 93: His message was: HOW ARE YOU HOLDING? ... 'Oh,' she said ... 'how am I holding for money? I'm quite all right.'

holey dollar   see **dollar**

Holiday Isle, the Tasmania, in the language of tourism
1980 *Sydney Morning Herald* 14 Nov. 1: Column 8 takes exception to the trite slogans appearing on new number plates ... Who needs to be told that Tasmania is the Holiday Isle?

hollow log 1 See quot. 1983
1982 *National Times* 31 Oct. 15: Was he planning to do a Wran, keeping all charges steady while he emptied the hollow logs?
1983 *Bulletin* 12 Jul. 27: They all had good reason for remembering this 'heated' meeting [in August 1977]: it was the first confrontation between the Treasury officials and Wran's advisers over the idea of drawing funds from the State's 'hollow logs' – a process which saw some $230 million scooped from the cash reserves of statutory authorities to support the State's capital works program.
2   A dog, esp. racing [rhyming slang]
1979 *Sun-Herald* 29 Apr. 74: Greyhounds are dills. I reckon they must be the least intelligent of all breeds of hollow logs.

holts, in At grips with; in dispute, quarrelling or fighting [f. *holt* U.S. 1823 OED]
1935 R. B. Plowman *The Boundary Rider* 123: 'Hefty looking brute. Wouldn't like to get into holts with him.'

1952 T. A. G. Hungerford *The Ridge and the River* 83: 'I noticed you and him in holts a couple of times today!'
1966 D. H. Crick *Period of Adjustment* 162: Had I come to holts with him over it, I might have said that I couldn't think of Jim Campion as being part of Furnley's machinery.

home Great Britain, from a colonial standpoint: *obsolescent*
1791 George Barrington Let. of 1 Jul. *HRNSW* ii 784: There are in the bay with us two ships ... which afford us an excellent opportunity of writing home. But, why should I say *home*? What is England, or Ireland, or Scotland to me now?
1834 Charles O'Hara Booth *Journal* 25 Dec. ed. Dora Heard (1981): Enjoyed ourselves – but still the thoughts of Home would come to mind and cause a gloom.
1898 Beatrice Webb *The Webb's Australian Diary* ed. A. G. Austin (1965) 33: He was extremely bitter at the whole tone of Society: its aspiration to go 'Home' and belong to the Prince of Wales' racing set.
1981 *Sun-Herald* 19 Jul. 54: Like it or not, Australia is still linked intimately to Great Britain, the United Kingdom. Many Australians have family links with what used to be called 'home'. Many have professional or philosophical links.

home and dried, home and hosed, home with a rug on Used of successfully completing some enterprise with a margin to spare [f. horseracing]
1918 *Kia Ora Coo-ee* 15 Oct. 14: All being home and dried, 'Shorty' went over to the 'Q. Emma's' to borrow a bit of 'buckshee' sugar.
1934 Thomas Wood *Cobbers* 96: Charles would make a book ... and he would lay two to one port-wine jelly, five to two apple pie. Nine times out of ten he was, in his own phrase, home in the stall with a rug on.
1959 Eric Lambert *Glory Thrown In* 219: 'Look!' he yelled to Christy. 'A and C Companies home and hosed!'
1972 *Bulletin* 26 Aug. 11: The government is home and hosed and can thank the budget.
1981 *Sunday Mail* (Brisbane) 9 Aug. 57: Ideal Planet, having the second start of his career, was 'home and hosed' until Black Shoes came with her unbeatable challenge.

home, kick   see **kick**

homer See quot. 1945 (World War II slang)

1945 Baker 156: *homer* A wound sufficiently serious to cause a man to be sent home.

1952 T. A. G. Hungerford *The Ridge and the River* 173: 'He'll get a homer out of it – perhaps Australia.'

1978 Richard Beilby *Gunner* 87: 'Ya got a homer, mate, you arsey bastard.'

homestead Used in a special sense like **house** q.v. for the residence of the owner or manager on a station, significantly set apart from the barracks and the men's hut [N.Z. 1849 OED]

1903 Joseph Furphy *Such is Life* (1944) 66: I had drawn up to Goolumbulla homestead with six tons of wire. The manager, Mr Spanker . . .

1935 R. B. Plowman *The Boundary Rider* 70: 'Government House' – as the owner's residence is called in the back country. Solidly built of stone and with a broad sweep of veranda across its front, it looked the part of homestead to the largest station in that part of South Australia.

1952 Jon Cleary *The Sundowners* 221: Halstead was a good bloke, better than most bosses; but the homestead was an enemy camp and no worker worth his salt ever stepped across the boundary.

1979 *Sydney Morning Herald* 3 Mar. 12: The homestead is seldom a tin-roofed building sitting in a fenced-off garden wilting in the sun. It is more likely to be a large, modern ranch-style building set in flourishing lawns with a swimming pool and entertainment area.

homing pigeons, he couldn't lead a flock of Comment on R. G. Menzies attributed to W. M. Hughes

1977 Fred Daly *From Curtin to Kerr* 116: Menzies tolerated him [W. M. Hughes]. Probably never forgot the time Billy said Menzies could not lead a flock of homing pigeons.

1980 Alan Reid *Bulletin* 29 Jan. 365: Hughes stabbed a finger in the direction of Menzies' office. 'Him,' he said, derisively. 'Him. Couldn't lead a flock of homing pigeons.' Then he stamped off.

hominy Prison food, used in expressions like 'hominy bus', 'hominy gazette' (gaol rumours)

1895 Cornelius Crowe *Australian Slang Dictionary* 36: *Hominey* prison fare.

1953 Baker 129: The jail tram that runs between Darlinghurst Police Station and Long Bay Gaol is called the *hominy bus*.

1919 J. Vance Marshall *The World of the Living Dead* 85: O, no more I'll quiz The Hominy Gazette for shearin' news / Or'll use the Holy Bible fer me fags.

hooer Possibly a variant of 'whore', but applied to men in a generally derogatory way, like 'bastard'.

1952 T. A. G. Hungerford *The Ridge and the River* 31: Cranky old hooer! White thought, with a wry smile. Always on the bloody job.

1962 Stuart Gore *Down the Golden Mile* 152: 'What the hell's those two silly hooers tryin' to *do* – kill their bloody selves!'

1975 Les Ryan *The Shearers* 63: 'Ar, go to blazes, you drunken hooer.'

hook up To 'pull' a racehorse, deliberately prevent it from winning

1949 Lawson Glassop *Lucky Palmer* 245: 'Owners always want favourites hooked up. I know it all.'

hooks, put the hooks into As for **put the nips into**

hoon 1 A procurer of prostitutes; general term of insult

1938 Xavier Herbert *Capricornia* 338: 'You flash hoon,' he went on.

1953 Baker 124: *hoon* or (by rhyme) *silver spoon* A procurer of prostitutes.

1976 *Cleo* Aug. 33: Hoon is a nebulous sort of word. It means someone living off the girls. He is not a pimp for them, he can be a standover man. It is an insult to be called a hoon . . . something worse than a bludger.

1982 *Sunday Mail* (Brisbane) 20 Jun. 45: They fear bashings and wrecking of their homes by prostitutes and their hoons if they speak out.

2 Anyone given to loutish behaviour

1979 *Herald* (Melbourne) 18 Jun. 4: The hoons have taken over, and somehow we let it happen. In every walk of life the hoons have succeeded, some may be better educated than others, come from better addresses, but they are hoons nevertheless. In some cases they are called the underprivileged; in some cases, the over indulged.

1981 *Sunday Mail* (Brisbane) 8 Feb. 2: A father, taking his son to his new high school after the holidays, couldn't figure out what the untidy and badly dressed group was doing in the grounds. The shock came when he discovered they were members of the staff – teachers and teachers' aides. 'I thought they were hoons,' he said.

1982 *NT News* (Darwin) 15 Sep. 7: The prize hoon who has been shooting at dogs with an airgun at Stuart Park had better lay off in future.

3 Someone driving fast and aggressively
1986 *Sunday Examiner* (Launceston) 13 Jul. 12: As long as the wheels screech on his Torana, the motor screams, the green hand waves in the window and his brain is in neutral, the hoon is happy.

1987 *Australian* 4 Nov. 2: Psychologists have argued that the [Adelaide] Grand Prix may cause what they termed a 'hoon effect' – an increase in the number of accidents by young people encouraged to drive faster and more recklessly.

hoop A jockey [f. hooped colours]
1941 Baker 36: *Hoop* A jockey.
1949 Lawson Glassop *Lucky Palmer* 245: 'It'll be a soda for a hoop like you. It won't be hard to get her beaten.'
1969 Alan O'Toole *The Racing Game* 79: 'We'll see if this hoop of yours has turned up.'
1975 *Bulletin* 28 Jun. 66: He was very fast at writing large-type headlines for the page one – like . . . Star Weds Top Hoop.

Hooray, hooroo Equivalent to 'Cheerio' as a farewell
1870 J. R. Houlding *Rural and City Life* 257: 'We won't come anigh yer house agin to-day; never fear, sir. Hooray!' With that parting salute, away scampered Jerry.
1917 F. J. Mills *Dinkum Oil* 73: There was a vast deal of . . . 'Goodbye Auntie, tool-raloo Bill . . . hooray Dick', and so forth.
1931 William Hatfield *Sheepmates* 238: 'Well, hooroo!' And he was gone in the direction where the fire glowed like a dropped cigarette butt.
1942 Leonard Mann *The Go-Getter* 221: 'So long, Chris.' 'Hooray, boy.'
1959 Anne von Bertouch *February Dark* 193: 'We'll see you later. Hooray.'

hoot Money [N.Z. 1879: see quot. 1896]
1881 G. C. Evans *Stories Told Round the Campfire* 265: Why the very stuff you are now drinking has been bought with 'hoot' obtained from stolen goods.

1896 *Truth* 12 Jan. 4: There are several specimens of bush language transplanted from the Maori language. 'Hoot' is a very frequent synonym for money or wage . . . The Maori equivalent for money is *utu* pronounced . . . with the last syllable clipped.
1938 Xavier Herbert *Capricornia* 301: 'On the construction you could make a pot of hoot in no time.'
1962 Hal Porter *A Bachelor's Children* 185: 'He's got plenty of hoot; has shares in everything from here to Perth.'
1977 *Sun-Herald* 24 Jul. 111: 'It's about a Q.C. and his wife, who live in Point Piper and obviously have lots of hoot.'

hop into As for **slip into**, q.v.
1945 Robert S. Close *Love Me Sailor* 160: 'Did you see young Ernie hopping into Christenson?'
1958 Gavin Casey *Snowball* 207: 'All right, kid, hop into your tucker,' Plugger ordered briskly.

horror budget The 1951 budget of the Menzies government, introduced by Arthur Fadden as Treasurer: so styled by its political opponents
1951 Arthur Calwell *Commonwealth of Australia Parliamentary Debates, House of Representatives*, Vol. 214, 3 Oct. 286: The Prime Minister sees virtue in his budget, but only a month ago he said it would be a 'horror budget'. [Mr Menzies had predicted severe budgetary action after the 12s. basic wage increase on 18 July, and at the end of the Economic Crisis Conference on 31 July.]
1969 Arthur Fadden *They called me Artie* 121: As soon as the referendum was over I introduced my 1951–52 Budget, dubbed 'The Horror Budget' by my political opponents.
1978 *Sydney Morning Herald* 21 Jun. 21: The Government looks to be locked in on an increased deficit for next year . . . That is unless it wishes to bring down a horror budget in August.

horror stretch An ordeal (given currency by the Redex Reliability trials of the 1950s)
1954 *Bulletin* 15 Dec. 9: It [the Canungra jungle-training camp] is the worst horror-stretch in Australia, but . . . when you have traversed it you really feel a ball of muscle.
1986 *Bulletin* 21 Jan. 70: The horror stretches of the past have gone from Queensland roads.
1987 *Sun-Herald* 29 Nov. 103: The horror

stretch finally ended for bookmakers at Rosehill yesterday with most bagmen enjoying winning days.

horse, jump a ~ over the bar, eat or drink a ~   To sell a horse for liquor or supplies
1900–10 O'Brien and Stephens: *Jumping your horse over the bar* to sell his horse or mortgage it to the publican so as to prolong his spree.
1919 E. S. Sorenson *Chips and Splinters* 34: It had been . . . given to a rabbit-poisoner known as 'Billy-the-Rooster' for a skewbald packhorse which Billy had 'jumped over the bar'.
1962 Tom Ronan *Deep of the Sky* 101: When his rations were exhausted he 'ate a horse' – that is, sold one for what he could get and converted the proceeds into supplies.

horse, to sell a   See quots
1939 R. H. Croll *I Recall* 54: You 'sell a horse' by putting in a shilling apiece, one member writes a number down privately, then all count as in a kiddies' game. The person who calls the hidden number scoops the pool and buys the drinks.
1964 Tom Ronan *Packhorse and Pearling Boat* 234: 'Selling a horse' . . . a very simple substitute for the cards and dice and, when there are fourteen in the party, much quicker. The barman collects the two bobs and, on a scrap of paper, writes down a number between fifty and a hundred. Then the party forms up in a group, someone starts counting at any number between one and ten, and whoever calls the figure the barman has written down scoops the pool.

horse, working off a dead   see **dead horse**

hosed, home and   see **home**

hospital pass   A pass exposing the receiver to a heavy tackle, esp. in Rugby League
1985 *Australian* 16 Feb. 18: In rugby, this is known as the hospital pass, the one that arrives just as your opponents hit you.
1987 Evan Whitton *Sydney Morning Herald* 13 Jul. 54: What should be a hospital pass occasionally ends in a try.

hostie   An air hostess [abbr.]
1955 *Bulletin* 10 Aug. 21: We get on the

aircraft and we're on our way. The little hostie is short and dark and beautiful.
1975 *Australian* 26 Mar. 10: For poor old Western Australia, already isolated by flooded railway lines and impassable roads, the final separation caused by the hosties' strike is the last straw.
1982 *Sun-Herald* 25 Apr. 151: Hosties these days are called flight attendants . . . but there is still a cause to be made out for a good-looking bird to flog the coffee and biscuits.

hostile   An 'educated' word used colloquially, like **strife**
1941 Baker 36: *Hostile* Angry, annoyed. Also, 'go hostile at', express annoyance (towards someone).
1951 Seaforth Mackenzie *Dead Men Rising* 85: 'Dammit, that'll mean sleeping in for me. The wife will be hostile about it.'
1958 H. D. Williamson *The Sunlit Plain* 175: 'All right,' Duveen protested in high, aggrieved tones. 'All right, mate. There's no need to get hostile.'
1973 Frank Huelin *Keep Moving* 83: 'We don't want to get hostile about it. Yous got your ideas and I've got mine. Let it go at that.'

hottie   A hotwater bottle [abbr.]
1942 Let. *Australian* 30 Jul. 1988: Mag. 7: Pat's 21st birthday present to me came last night, a lovely red rubber hotty bottle.
1953 *Bulletin* 15 Jul. 9: A sheepish patient confessed that he had drunk the tepid and rubber-flavored contents of the 'hottie', as he had an insatiable thirst, and didn't want to wake sister.
1958 Barry Humphries *A Nice Night's Entertainment* (1981) 17: We'd had a run of late nights and we were pretty fagged so round about ten I filled the hottie and Beryl and I went to bed.

house, the   On a station, the residence of the owner or manager, and so distinct from the accommodation for the station hands (the men's hut), for the jackeroos (the barracks) and others
1869 Marcus Clarke *The Peripatetic Philosopher* 41: At the station where I worked for some time . . . three cooks were kept during the 'wallaby' season – one for the house, one for the men, and one for the travellers.
1876 A. J. Boyd *Old Colonials* (1882) 81: 'The squatters know well enough when a man is fit for the house or the kitchen, and

they consider a gentleman's a gentleman, no matter what he's employed at.'
1893 J. A. Barry *Steve Brown's Bunyip* 202: The dealer, having pretty well cleaned out 'the hut', determined to try his luck at 'the House'.
1921 M. E. Fullerton *Bark House Days* 117: I was a favourite with the men, being even then a reader of the newspapers, I constituted myself the medium by which the huts were supplied with the weeklies as soon as the house was finished with them.
1936 William Hatfield *Australia Through the Windscreen* 64: It is pitiful to see the perturbation on the face of a manager when a presentably dressed traveller pulls up at a station where he must be given accommodation, trying to guess correctly whether the stranger is a 'house' or a 'hut' man.
1954 Tom Ronan *Vision Splendid* 76: He would leave the Big House as soon as it was politely permissible and stroll down for a yarn with the men.

Howe, Jacky Sleeveless flannel shirt [f. shearer (1855–1922) so named]
1930 *Bulletin* 9 Apr. 19: Long Jim was telling us how ... it took nine bars of soap to wash his 'Jacky Howe' flannel.
1949 Ruth Park *Poor Man's Orange* 122: He had finished his tea and was sitting in his Jackie Howe, which is a singlet with the sleeves out of it, and called after a famous shearer, of the blade days.
1985 *Woman's Day* (Sydney) 14 Oct. 53: Not only does 21-year-old Wendy Eveleigh cut a striking figure in her Jacky Howe singlet, but she has well and truly earned the right to wear it as Australia's top female shearer.

hoy Bingo or housie: Queensland [? f. shout]
1975 Bruce Dawe *Just a Dugong at Twilight* 30: The State Crown Law Office, Queensland, was called upon to decide whether the game known as 'Hoy' was illegal or not.
1979 Thea Astley *Hunting the Wild Pineapple* 99: Mrs Waterman ... attended more and more church hoy drives, opened fêtes, launched yachts.

Hoyt's, the man outside The commissionaire outside Hoyt's Theatre in Melbourne in the 1930s, so elaborately dressed as to seem a person of consequence, and jocularly

referred to as the authority for various reports
1950 *As You Were* 90: 'Who's that swearing?' The muffled reply is one of those meaningless army answers – 'The Man outside Hoyts'.
1961 Frank Hardy *The Hard Way* 85: 'Struth, it's funny enough for a fat bludger dressed up like the man outside Hoyt's[1] to come into a prison cell in the middle of the night.' [1]Uniformed announcer outside Hoyt's Theatre in Melbourne who wears a most elaborate uniform.
1975 *Sydney Morning Herald* 5 Jul. 9: We might be better off to abandon pre-selections and elections, and choose our politicians by having the Governor (or the man outside Hoyts) stick pins into the telephone book.

Hughie Name given to God in the outback, esp. in the expression 'Send 'er down, Hughie' used when it is raining hard; also to the deity of the surf [Partridge lists 'Send her down, David']
1918 L. J. Villiers *The Changing Year* 12: Down Hughie* pours *Hughie = the rain.
1922 *Bulletin* 26 Jan. 22: The missionary tackled him [the aboriginal boy] with 'Who made this country, Peter?' 'Dunno' – says Peter – 'was here when I came.' 'Well,' says Parson, 'who is it makes the rain?' Peter knew that all right. 'Ole Hughie,' he answered promptly.
1946 K. S. Prichard *The Roaring Nineties* 30: Miners and prospectors would turn out and yell to a dull, dirty sky clouded with red dust: 'Send her down! Send her down, Hughie!'
1951 Seaforth Mackenzie *Dead Men Rising* 210: 'All you want to do is get married and have kids,' he said. 'Don't worry about the money. Hughie looks after that, my boy.' The Corporal was diverted. 'Who's this Hughie?' he said ... 'Ah,' Gell said, affecting a gravity which was not altogether false. 'You don't say "God", you see, because nobody believes in God but everybody believes in Hughie. I dunno – it's just a thing you hear the boys say.' Ibid. 207: 'Hughie's throwing it down all right.'
1964 H. P. Tritton *Time Means Tucker* 92: With only a couple of thousand to go 'Hughie' answered the prayers of the loppies with a fairly heavy shower. Ibid. 42: To the best of my belief, it was at Charlton [in 1905] that 'Hughie' as the chief deity in the job of controlling the weather came into being.
1984 *Sydney Morning Herald* 31 Jan. 31:

During the award ceremony [for a malibu board-riding contest], an organiser said: 'I want to thank Hughie upstairs (Hughie's the surfie's name for God) for the waves (between 6 ft and 8 ft) and the good weather.'

hum *n.* A cadger, sponger: *derogatory*
1915 J. P. Bourke *Off the Bluebush* 190: If you cannot be a spendthrift, be a hum.
1919 J. Vance Marshall *The World of the Living Dead* 70: Almost beneath the bottom rung of the social ladder there is ... the 'hum', the unskilled derelict or derelict-to-be who stands upon the 'pub' corner kerb, 'bites' all and sundry, and, at regular intervals succeeds in getting lumbered for 'vag'.
1937 *Best Australian One-Act Plays* 163: Generally winds up with ... one of 'em nipping you for a couple of bob ... Perfect hums some of 'em.'
1957 D'Arcy Niland *Call Me When the Cross Turns Over* 136: 'Rigby's a twister. He's a hum and a liar.'

hum *v.* To borrow, scrounge (not used in such a pejorative sense as the noun)
1915 J. P. Bourke *Off the Bluebush* 77: Got no coin to treat a pal! Got no face to hum!
1919 W. H. Downing *Digger Dialects* 29: *Humm* To cadge.
1937 Xavier Herbert *Capricornia* 257: 'You're only humming for a drink. Nick off home.'

hump bluey, the drum, the swag To follow the life of the swagman, carrying one's belongings on one's back
1855 William Howitt *Land, Labour and Gold* i 226: He 'humped his swag', in diggers' phrase that is, shouldered his pack, and disappeared in the woods.
1883 R. E. N. Twopeny *Town Life in Australia* 244–5: He 'humps his drum', or 'swag', and 'starts on the wallaby track', i.e. shoulders the bundle containing his worldly belongings, and goes out pleasuring.
1892 Henry Lawson 'Jack Dunn of Nevertire' *Verse* i 222: He humped his bluey by the name of 'Dunn of Nevertire'.
1911 E. M. Clowes *On the Wallaby Through Victoria* 278: An expression used for what in England we call 'tramping' is 'humping the swag' or 'the bluey'.
1943 Maurice Clough *We of the A.I.F.* 45: Men who have lived on billy tea / And damper, humping their 'bluey'.

1961 George Farwell *Vanishing Australians* 44: 'When I first set eyes on him, he was humping his drum, hoofing it down the road from Tilpa.'

humpy An Aboriginal bark hut (Morris, 1846), but also applied to any rude shelter or hut constructed by a white
1881 A. C. Grant *Bush Life in Queensland* i 133: To dwell in the familiar old bark 'humpy', so full of happy memories. The roof was covered with sheets of bark held down by large wooden riders pegged in the form of a square to one another. [Morris]
1896 Henry Lawson 'In a Dry Season' *Prose* i 79–80: The only town I saw that differed much from the above consisted of a box-bark humpy with a clay chimney, and a woman standing at the door throwing out the wash-up water.
1931 Vance Palmer *Separate Lives* 12: His humpy was on the edge of the settlement, a ragged lean-to made of slabs and old iron that he had built in his spare time out of such scraps as his neighbours discarded.
1961 Nene Gare *The Fringe Dwellers* 27: The humpy was ... a ramshackle arrangement of tarpaulins and scrap-iron nailed to bush timber.
1981 *Australian* 18 Apr. 3: 'In some cases school buildings are non-existent – they are just humpies,' said Mr Lloyd.

hungry 1 Grasping, stingy, often as part of a nickname: *derogatory*
1855 William Howitt *Land, Labour and Gold* ii 294: At one station I asked two men who were resting with their cart by the roadside whose station that was? 'Hungry Scott's' was the reply.
1902 Henry Lawson 'Two Sundowners' *Prose* i 99: They came to a notoriously 'hungry' station, where there was a Scottish manager and storekeeper.
1948 K. S. Prichard *Golden Miles* 74: 'There's some hungry bastards,' the men said, 'making big money on their ore, and never give the poor bugger boggin' for 'em a sling back.'
1981 *Sydney Morning Herald* 27 May 24: One glance at the price of Dom Perignon – $75 – confirms just how hungry Mischa is.
2 Applied to a taxi-driver's shift, esp. at slack periods, which is extended beyond the usual limits to increase the revenue
1986 *Age* (Melbourne) 12 Mar. 17: Fleet operators can allow cars to operate 'hungry' (to be driven by one driver for longer than

one shift). A 'hungry' shift can earn 25 to 50 per cent more than a day shift.

Hungry Mile, the The part of Sussex Street, Sydney, fringing the waterfront, with the office of the Waterside Workers Federation
1930 Ernest Antony *The Hungry Mile* 5: To see Sydney wharfies tramping down the hungry mile.
1957 Tom Nelson *The Hungry Mile* 75: The stretch along Sussex Street was called the 'Hungry Mile' by the wharfies . . . a very apt title indeed.
1973 *Sydney Morning Herald* 2 Aug. 7: When I was much younger the 'Hungry Mile' of Sydney waterfront was an area of glamour.

hunt To drive away, dismiss
1870 Rolf Boldrewood 'Shearing in Riverina' *In Bad Company* (1901): He . . . makes a calculation as to who are unreasonably bad, and who, therefore, will have to be 'hunted'.
1983 T. A. G. Hungerford *Stories from Suburban Road* 118: I'd heard them saying she'd been got into some sort of trouble by Mr Floyd, and that her parents had hunted her.

hunt up a cow see **cow**

hut, the (men's) On a station, the accommodation provided for the station-hands, usually a large structure, but distinct from **the house** and **the barracks** qq.v.
1843 Charles Rowcroft *Tales of the Colonies* ii 258: 'Mr Clover came into the hut,

the men's hut . . . John Buttress did not go on being ordered out: Mr Clover then took him by the collar, and shoved him out of the hut.'
1869 Marcus Clarke *The Peripatetic Philosopher* 41: I have seen as many as twenty able bodied hungry men come up to a home-station with the stereotyped inquiry, 'Want any hands, sir?' and receiving a reply in the negative . . . go merrily down to the 'men's hut' and, having smoked, eat some two pounds of 'fat wether' per man.
1873 A. Trollope *Australia* ed. Edwards and Joyce (1967) 138: The labouring man . . . is sent to the 'hut'. There is a hut at every station, fitted up with bunks, in which the workmen sleep. Here the wanderer is allowed to stretch his blanket for the night – and on all such occasions two meals are allowed him.
1911 E. M. Clowes *On the Wallaby Through Victoria* 103: The shearers live – that is, sleep and eat – in what is known as 'the hut', a long narrow structure with bunks at either side, in two tiers, each bunk just long enough to hold a man.
1931 William Hatfield *Sheepmates* 76: 'Rough diamond, you know, used to be in the Hut – stockman, horse-breaker and all that you know, though I say you can't hold it against a man because he came from the Hut.'

hydraulic (jack) Nickname for anyone with the habit of 'lifting' things, i.e. a thief, esp. on the waterfront
1977 *Sunday Telegraph* (Sydney) 24 Apr. 136: 'They call him Hydraulic – he'll lift anything that isn't nailed down.'

I

iceberg Someone who regularly takes an early morning swim throughout the winter, esp. as a member of a club; anyone who braves the water on a cold morning [f. the Icebergs Club at Bondi, founded in 1929]
1932 L. W. Lower *Here's Another* 12: 'One of the toughest surfs I've experienced this winter. All the Icebergs agreed.'
1964 Tom Ronan *Packhorse and Pearling Boat* 79–80: I admit that I did not join the

icebergs who favoured cold showers even on the bitterest winter mornings.
1974 Geoffrey Lehmann *A Spring Day in Autumn* 174: 'I'm a regular swimmer myself, right in the middle of winter. They reckon I'm the oldest iceberg in Sydney.'
1986 *Sydney Morning Herald* 4 Nov. 1: The Bondi Icebergs Club has started a junior branch – the Bondi Ice-cubes.

identity (old) A resident of long standing in a particular place [N.Z.: see quot. 1874]

1862 *Thatcher's Dunedin Songster* 2: 'The Old Identity' [song title]

1874 Alexander Bathgate *Colonial Experiences* 26: The term 'old identities' took its origin from an expression in a speech made by one of the members of the Provincial Council, Mr E. B. Cargill, who in speaking of the new arrivals, said that the early settlers should endeavour to preserve their old identity. The strangers, who were inclined to laugh at the aboriginals as a set of old stagers, caught up the phrase, and dubbed them 'old identities'. A comic singer helped to perpetuate the name by writing a song.

1880 Rolf Boldrewood *The Miner's Right* (1890) 213: Some of the old identities still survived.

1901 F. J. Gillen *Diary* (1968) 11: Met Harry Pannell an old identity of the interior who has been a teamster on three inhospitable roads since the days of the construction of the line.

1929 Jules Raeside *Golden Days* 42: Volumes could be written about many of the identities of those days.

1973 Alexander Buzo *Rooted* 77: 'I was in the pub having a quiet beer with a few Werris Creek identities, when this bloke came up and started picking a blue with Simmo.'

identity, racing A person of some notoriety with racing connections: *jocular*

1959 *Bulletin* 21 Jan. 33: 'Always pleased to have a drink with a couple of racing identities,' he said, and laughed at his joke.

1989 *Sun-Herald* 17 Sep. 92: In his heyday, 'Hollywood' George Edser hogged the headlines as one of Australia's most colourful racing identities.

1990 *Australian* 21 Mar. 6: Freeman . . . was most often referred to in recent years as a 'colourful racing identity'. It was a standing joke, a euphemism.

igloo, the The Academy of Science building, Canberra [f. shape]

1984 *Sydney Morning Herald* 11 Oct. 9: The igloo – also known as the Academy of Science, perhaps Canberra's most architecturally successful building, blending simplicity and compatibility with the low hills of the capital and rounded contours of the Brindabellas in the distance.

ignore, to treat with To deliberately ignore someone's presence or request

1938 *Bulletin* 6 Jul. 26: The habit of 'treating with ignore' our own industrial experience is quite wrong.

1946 Alan Marshall *Tell us about the Turkey, Jo* 202: At first he treats me with ignore, then he answers me back, then he just looks at me.

1963 John O'Grady *The Things They Do to You* 110: I saw her a couple of times, and attempted to discuss the work and the weather . . . But, as we used to say in those days [in the war], she 'treated me with ignore'.

1983 *Sydney Morning Herald* 27 May Metro 3: When you ask politely for room to pass, you can be treated with cold ignore.

illywhacker A professional trickster, esp. operating at country shows [derived by Baker (1945:138) from *spieler*]

1941 Kylie Tennant *The Battlers* 183–4: An illywacker is someone who is putting a confidence trick over, selling imitation diamond tie-pins, new-style patent razors or infallible 'tonics' . . . 'living on the cockies' by such devices, and following the shows because money always flows freest at show time. A man who 'wacks the illy' can be almost anything, but two of these particular illy-wackers were equipped with a dart game.

1975 Hal Porter *The Extra* 15: Social climber, moron, peter-tickler, eeler-spee, illy-wacker.

imbuggerance An intensified form of indifference

1966 Baker 380: *imbuggerance* Indifference strengthened by allusion to the phrase *don't care a bugger.*

1990 Buzz Kennedy *Australian* 3 Mar. Weekend 16: The likes and dislikes of a Grub street penny-a-liner [Jean Rook] are a matter of profound imbuggerance to me and, I imagine, to most Australians.

improve, on the Improving

1959 Baker 119: *improve, on the* Improving in health or proficiency.

1965 Hal Porter *The Cats of Venice* 144: Had a bout of Bronchitis but on the improve.

1978 John Pringle *Sydney Morning Herald* 18 Sep. 7: I am moved to protest against the increasing tendency to use the appalling phrase 'on the improve' instead of 'improving'. This is particularly popular with one of

the ABC's weather announcers, who regularly tells us, sometimes mistakenly, that 'Sydney's weather is on the improve'.
1984 *West Australian* (Perth) 4 Jan. 92: Regal Martin on the improve [heading] Three-year-old Regal Martin showed improvement with a smart trial over 800m on the wood fibre track at Ascot yesterday morning.

in bad, good   In disfavour, in favour
1958 Peter Cowan *The Unploughed Land* 118: 'I can be in bad over that car.'
1966 Peter Cowan *Seed* 53: 'I've got to be back in time tonight,' she said. 'I'm in bad enough now.'
1989 Sally Morgan *Wanamurraganya* 68: I wanted to stay in good with them and I didn't want to lose my job, so I agreed.

in it, to be   To participate, join in a planned action (in the imperative, usually an appeal to group loyalty)
[**1823** Jon Bee *Slang. A Dictionary of the Turf, the Ring &c.* 105: *In it* – concerned or making part of a gang, or lot.]
1928 Arthur Wright *A Good Recovery* 37: 'It's a queer business,' ventured Trilet, 'and if I'm to be in it, I want to know the strength of it.'
1945 Gavin Casey *Downhill is Easier* 149: 'We're goin' for a couple o' days shootin' in the mornin',' South said to me. 'You'd better be in it.'
1965 William Dick *A Bunch of Ratbags* 198: Elaine continued to try to coax me to come into her place to sleep with her, but I wouldn't be in it.

in like Flynn   see **Flynn**

Indons   Indonesians
1973 Jack Hibberd *A Stretch of the Imagination* (1981) 37: 'The Indon and Kanaka we will civilize.'
1982 *Age* (Melbourne) 30 Jun. 10: End Indon arms aid, inquiry told [heading]
1983 *National Times* 13 May 2: Intriguing is the request recently made by the Indonesian Government to the Department of Foreign Affairs in Canberra. The Indons want to know the sleeve measurement of the Prime Minister, Bob Hawke.

inked   Drunk, incapacitated
1898 *Bulletin* 1 Oct. 14: To get drunk is to get 'inked'.

1919 W. H. Downing *Digger Dialects* 29: *Inked* Drunk.
1951 A. W. Upfield *The New Shoe* 94: 'What is he like when properly inked?' 'Quiet as Mary's lamb,' was the surprising answer. 'Ten beers and he goes to sleep.'
1969 Patsy Adam-Smith *Folklore of the Australian Railwaymen* 85: Driver found well and truly inked and lying down to it.

inland, the   The sparsely settled interior of Australia (often with a capital letter, esp. after the formation of the Australian Inland Mission in 1912)
1890 A. B. Paterson 'Those Names' in *Singer of the Bush* (1983) 126: There were men from the inland stations where the skies like a furnace glow.
1911 E. S. Sorenson *Life in the Australian Backblocks* 282: The majority of inland youngsters have to go through that mill.
1935 R. B. Plowman *The Boundary Rider* 60: The station folk of the Inland know how to dispense hospitality.
1954 Vance Palmer *The Legend of the Nineties* 146: Most of them had been born in the inland and their work of shearing, droving, kangaroo-shooting had given them a certain independence of outlook.

inlander   An inhabitant of the inland
1911 E. S. Sorenson *Life in the Australian Backblocks* 282: There is one thing about the inlander that favourably impresses itself upon those who have to look after a city's water supply, and that is his careful use of the liquid.
1913 John Flynn (ed.) *The Inlander* [journal title]
1944 Archer Russell *Bush Ways* 132: He was a typical inlander, quiet, reliable, an experienced and hardened desert-rider.
1962 Cynthia Nolan *Outback* 33: Interference from outsiders is resented by these inlanders.

Innisfail, in jail at   see **Tallarook**

inside   Within the more settled areas of Australia (in the nineteenth century), the opposite of **outside** q.v.
1864 Rachel Henning *Letters* ed. David Adams (1963) 171: When Biddulph first took up Exmoor it was a very outside run northwards, and when he dissolved partnership with the Tuckers a year after it was valued at £4,000. Now it is quite an inside station, every bit of country is taken up for several

hundred miles round it, and just before he went to Sydney Biddulph refused £25,000 for it.
1910 C. E. W. Bean *On the Wool Track* 27: Whilst the 'inside' stations may grow [sheep] for meat if they care, the 'outside' stations grow for wool.
1949 George Farwell *Traveller's Tracks* 17: Such conditions have eased considerably on the Inside. But on the Outside track they are still the norm, and the bushman remains the sardonic and resourceful character of Australian legend.
1984 *Sydney Morning Herald* 20 Oct. Colour Mag. 24: The Charnleys think they have been out west long enough and next year they will take their two children 'down inside', somewhere east of Bourke.

I.P.   1   Intending purchaser
1876 Rolf Boldrewood *A Colonial Reformer* (1890) 187: I hope the I.P. (intending purchaser) is a good plucked one.
2   Irate parent (visiting a school)

iron *v.*   To 'flatten'
1953 Baker 104: *To iron* To attack or fight (a person) i.e. *to flatten* him.
1965 William Dick *A Bunch of Ratbags* 228: Argles was ready behind the big bloke to king-hit him and iron him out.
1974 Jim McNeil *How Does Your Garden Grow* 126: 'How many [pills] yer take?' 'Told yer. Half a dozen.' 'Oh well, that'll iron yer right out.'
1984 *Sunday Independent* (Perth) 9 Sep. 86: He was absolutely ironed out . . . with a shirt-front bump you could feel in the press box.

iron   Corrugated iron
1877 Let. in *Letters from Grenfell*, ed. G. J. Butland (1971) 74: Many of the towns in the interior of this colony were born of the enterprise of the gold miner and in their infancy are built of calico or bark or iron.
1946 W. E. Harney *North of 23°* 35: Women lived in these places and reared their children in humpies with bag sides and iron roof.
1958 Patrick White *Australian Letters* I iii 39: Even the ugliness, the bags and iron of Australian life, acquired a meaning.
1983 *Sydney Morning Herald* 30 Apr. 32: His modest fibro and iron home in the township was bought on an eight-year term with the repayments of $245 a month.

iron, good   Expression of approval or agreement: *obsolescent* [see quot. 1908: Partridge lists *bad iron* a failure, a mishap, bad luck]
1894 Ethel Turner *Seven Little Australians* 46: 'Good iron!' Pip whistled softly, while he revolved the thing in his mind.
1908 *Australian Magazine* 1 Nov. 1250: 'Good iron', a very Australian approbatory ejaculation, comes from quoits, the players in the old days being wont to call the phrase after the manner of 'good ball' of the cricketers.
1936 Miles Franklin *All That Swagger* 100: 'Good iron! I don't rob little boys.'

iron lung, he wouldn't work in an   The ultimate standard of laziness [f. the artificial respirator which did the patient's breathing for him]
1948 Encountered in conversation.
1971 Frank Hardy *The Outcasts of Foolgarah* 79: Silver Tails who wouldn't work in an iron lung.
1974 Barry Humphries *Barry McKenzie Holds His Own* 27: 'Work! Brits couldn't even spell it. Bloody Poms couldn't work in an iron lung.'
1984 Russ Hinze *Bulletin* 17 Apr. 125: I never recall anybody being able to convince me that he has ever worked in his life, this bloke. I don't think he would work in an iron lung.

Isa, the   Mount Isa, Queensland
1958 *Bulletin* 3 Dec. 45: The coming and going of blokes from the Isa, the Hill, Kalgoorlie and all points in between.
1979 Bill Scott *Tough in the Old Days* 76: 'The Isa' was a town of goats and dogs and red dust, divided down the centre by the railway line and the mine smelters.

Isle, the Apple   see **Apple**

Isle, the Holiday   see **Holiday**

issue, get one's   To be killed
1919 W. H. Downing *Digger Dialects* 29: *Issue* (1) A portion; (2) 'to get one's issue' – to be killed.
1932 Leonard Mann *Flesh in Armour* 77: 'Jack Martin's got his issue.'

issue, that's the   Equivalent to 'That's the lot' [Services slang]
1919 W. H. Downing *Digger Dialects* 29:

Issue (1) A portion; (2) 'to get one's issue' – to be killed.

1930 Frederic Manning *Her Privates We* 351: 'What are you talkin' about?' . . . 'The whole bloody issue,' said Bourne, comprehensively. 'Officers, and other ranks.'

1968 Stuart Gore *Holy Smoke* 26: 'He done in the whole issue on sheilas and bombo.'

it's moments like these you need Minties see **Minties**

J

jack 1 The anus, backside
[**1896** J. S. Farmer and W. E. Henley *Slang and its Analogues* iv 33: *Jacksy-pardy*, the posteriors]
1951 Seaforth Mackenzie *Dead Men Rising* 196: 'He thinks the feller had it [the concealed cord] up his jack . . . It's so thin it'd easily go into the rectum.'
2 *The jack* Venereal disease
1954 T. A. G. Hungerford *Sowers of the Wind* 3: 'Pencillin'll take care of that. They reckon they just pump you full of it, and bingo! No more jack!'
1975 Alex Buzo *Tom* 39: 'I should hop down to the Clinic if I were you. You want to watch out for the jack. Wait on, don't move, I might have some Condy's crystals and a plunger. Didn't they teach you hygiene at Abbotsleigh?'
1989 *Australian* 25 Jan. 34: Asked if he was on antibiotics, he [Pat Cash] said: 'Antibiotics? What for? Got the jack?'
jacked up Infected
1962 Alan Marshall *This is the Grass* 164: 'I got a dose from a sheila I went out with . . . she was jacked up and I was the mug.'

jack of, to be To be fed up with something, to the point of rejecting or abandoning it
1896 Edward Dyson *Rhymes from the Mines* 98: No, you can't count me in, boys; I'm off it – / I'm jack of them practical jokes.
1944 Jean Devanny *By Tropic, Sea and Jungle* 155: I used to like to get on my pat for a week – prospecting you know – but not for more than a week. Too much of it makes you jack of it quick.
1965 William Dick *A Bunch of Ratbags* 69: 'There ain't nothin' much to do, is there? I'm getting jack of these holidays.'
1970 Jessica Anderson *The Last Man's Head* 201: 'You know my feelings about it, I made them clear the other day. I'm jack of it.'

jack up *v.* 1 To give in, collapse [*To jack up* To give up suddenly or promptly OED 1873]
1903 Joseph Furphy *Such is Life* (1944) 178: 'I ain't a man to jack-up while I got a sanguinary leg to stan' on; but I'm gone on the inside, some road.'
2 To reject, abandon [*To jack up* to throw up, give up, abandon OED 1873]
1880 Henry Kendall 'Jim the Splitter' *Poetical Works* ed. T. T. Reed (1966) 159: The nymph in green valleys of Thessaly dim / Would never 'jack up' her old lover for him.
1880 Rolf Boldrewood *The Miner's Right* (1890) 35: Having that morning decided to 'jack up' or thoroughly abandon work at our present claim.
3 To refuse orders, esp. as a collective action (Services slang); to refuse or abandon a task assigned, as though going on a protest strike
1898 Rolf Boldrewood *A Romance of Canvas Town* 253: The half-used plates and dishes were to me as things loathsome. They operated prejudicially upon my dinners in prospect even, as well as upon those which had 'gone before'. So, as a man, a gentleman, and a squatter, I 'jacked up' at the cookery.
1936 Miles Franklin *All That Swagger* 470: 'Grandfather always took Grandma with him everywhere until she jacked up.'
1959 David Forrest *The Last Blue Sea* 38: 'They'll jack-up like they did on the Townsville wharf.'

jack up *n.* The action of refusing orders, esp. if collective
1948 Sumner Locke Elliott *Rusty Bugles* in

Khaki, Bush and Bigotry ed. Eunice Hanger (1968) 94: 'By gee, if I'm not on the next draft I'm telling you there's going to be the biggest jack-up you ever saw.'
1953 *The Sunburnt Country* ed. Ian Bevan 125: This jacking up is a procedure which no army but the Australian could tolerate. It is not mutiny . . . It consists simply of selecting some minor regimental parade or order and boycotting it, to a man, as a public expression of a legitimate grievance.

jackaroo (jackeroo) A young man of good connections working on a station as a cadet to gain experience of station management
1873 Rolf Boldrewood 'The Fencing of Wanderowna' *A Romance of Canvas Town* (1898) 70: 'It's very hard on the poor man . . . You won't want no hand from shearing to shearing except two or three Jackaroos.'
1878 G. H. Gibson *Southerly Busters* 19n: Young gentlemen getting their 'colonial experience' in the bush are called 'jackeroos' by the stationhands.
1917 A. B. Paterson *Three Elephant Power* 49: For assistants, he [the manager] had half a dozen of us – jackeroos and colonial experiencers – who got nothing a year, and earned it. We had, in most instances, paid premiums to learn the noble art of squatting.
1973 Patrick White *Southerly* 136: While I was a jackaroo I used to shut myself up at night with a kerosine lamp and write.
1981 *Sunday Mail* (Brisbane) 22 Nov. 76: At 17 he shipped out to Australia on an assisted passage to become a jackaroo on a station near Dubbo.

jackaroo *v.* To work as a jackaroo
1875 Rolf Boldrewood *The Squatter's Dream* repr. as *Ups and Downs* (1878) 239: 'A year or two more of Jackerooing would only mean the consumption of so many more figs of negrohead, in my case.'
1890 Tasma *In Her Earliest Youth* 152: 'They knock down all their money at first go-off, and then there's nothing for them to do but to go and jackaroo up in Queensland.'
1938 Eric Lowe *Salute to Freedom* 71: Boyd Freeman had gone to the University, and six months earlier John Morgan had left and was now jackerooing on a station in Queensland.
1980 *Australian* 23 Feb. Mag.: A year after he ran away from home to go jackerooing in the Queensland bush the then 14-year-old Jim Killen fell off a horse.

jackass, the laughing The kookaburra, *Dacelo gigas* (Morris 1798)
1827 P. Cunningham *Two Years in New South Wales* i 232: The loud and discordant noise of the *laughing jackass*.
1834 George Bennett *Wanderings in New South Wales* i 138: The peculiar noise of the laughing or feathered jackass (*Dacelo gigantea*), which increases from a low to a loud thrilling gurgling laugh, was often heard.
1902 Henry Lawson 'Lord Douglas' *Prose* i 494: Barcoo-Rot, who took Mitchell seriously (and would have taken a laughing jackass seriously).

Jack the Painter A coarse green tea used in the bush, apt to colour the utensil or the mouth: *obs.*
1852 G. C. Mundy *Our Antipodes* i 329: Another notorious ration tea of the bush is called 'Jack the painter'. This is a *very* green tea indeed, its viridity evidently produced by a discreet use of copper drying pans in its manufacture.
1877 Rolf Boldrewood *A Colonial Reformer* (1890) 413: He drank his 'Jack the Painter' tea milkless, most probably, and flavoured with blackest sugar.
1918 C. Fetherstonhaugh *After Many Days* 30: The Colonial tea had two names, 'Jack the Painter', that was the green tea, and it had a whiff of paint.

Jackey, Jackie Generic name for the Australian Aboriginal
1855 *The Australasian Printers' Keepsake* 26: All the valleys where . . . Jacky Jacky hurled his boomerang.
1898 D. W. Carnegie *Spinifex and Sand* 154: Handed him a plate of scraps for his dinner, calling out, 'Hi, Jacky-Jacky, this one your tucker', to which Jim replied with stern dignity, 'Who the h– are you calling Jacky-Jacky? Do you think I'm a – blackfellow?'
1954 Tom Ronan *Vision Splendid* 216: 'Now a jacky with new clothes every two months and five sticks of tobacco a week can look down on us and he's going to keep doing so.'
1965 Frank Hardy *The Yarns of Billy Borker* 113: 'Just like calling an American negro Sambo, or an Australian aboriginal Jacky. The white man who says it means well, but it's patronising, if you get what I mean.'
1978 *Sydney Morning Herald* 8 Apr. 13: 'I have been treated like a jacky,' he [Senator Neville Bonner] said.

Jacky, to sit up like   To sit up straight, 'as large as life', almost cheekily
1941 Baker 38: *Jacky, sit up like* To behave, sit up straight.
1948 H. Drake-Brockman *Sydney or the Bush* 176: Cripes, the way they sat there, stiff as Jacky, not saying a word.
1958 Peter Cowan *The Unploughed Land* 182: 'Arriving in state today,' he said. 'Sitting up here in the front like Jacky.'
1975 Hal Porter *The Extra* 139: He's telling Edinburgh, and those writers sitting up like jacky in tiers behind him, about the construction of his next book.

Jacko   Generic name for the Turkish soldier in the Gallipoli and Palestine campaigns in World War I
1918 Let. in Bill Gammage *The Broken Years* (1974) 136: Our position is serious as Jacko is giving us chaps a bad time further back & we are pretty well cut off & cant get rations.
1935 H. R. Williams *Comrades of the Great Adventure* 23–4: Impetuosity of the Anzacs was too much for·'Jacko', who steadily gave ground before the vehemence of the onslaught.

jackshay, jackshea   A quart-pot
1881 A. C. Grant *Bush-Life in Queensland* i 209: The party, therefore, carry with them a light blanket apiece, stowed away in the folds of which is each man's supper and breakfast. Hobbles and Jack Shays[1] hang from the saddle-dees. [1] A tin quart-pot, used for boiling water for tea, and contrived so as to hold within it a tin pint-pot.
1911 E. S. Sorenson *Life in the Australian Backblocks* 276: Empty boulli-cans were used for the same purposes as are now the specially made 'billy cans'. Quart pots, jackshays, pannikins, and other relatives followed as a matter of course.
1932 Ion L. Idriess *The Desert Column* 119: Before daylight, we warily returned to the oasis and boiled our jackshays.

Jacky Howe   see **Howe**

jake   All right, in good order, 'apples' [U.S. 1921 Mathews]
1919 W. H. Downing *Digger Dialects* 29: *Jake* Correct.
1932 Leonard Mann *Flesh in Armour* 266: 'I think she was jake.'
1965 William Dick *A Bunch of Ratbags* 242: 'We're all right mate; she's jake.'

1980 Dudley McCarthy *The Fate of O'Loughlin* 236: Jimmy had finished what he had to do on the engine and said 'She's jake now, mate, as good as new!'
jakerloo
1919 W. H. Downing *Digger Dialects* 29: *Jake-aloo:* See *jake.*
1938 Xavier Herbert *Capricornia* 189: 'Not wounded, are you?' . . . 'I'm jakerloo.'

jam, to put on   To adopt an affected speech or manner
c. **1882** *The Sydney Slang Dictionary* 5: *Jam (Putting on)* Assuming false airs of importance.
1888 E. Finn *Chronicles of Early Melbourne* ii 780: 'Putting on jam', a phrase of modern slang, and increasing in popularity.
1901 Miles Franklin *My Brilliant Career* 219: People who knew how to conduct themselves properly, and who paid one every attention without a bit of fear of being twitted with 'laying the jam on'.
1951 Dal Stivens *Jimmy Brockett* 30: Sadie put on a bit of jam when she talked, but not too much.

Jap on Anzac Day, you wouldn't give it to a   The ultimate degree of the unacceptable
1973 Jim McNeil *The Chocolate Frog* 36: *Shirker* Our mate 'ere seems ter *like* people . . . *Tosser Like* 'em! I *reckon* he does! He'd kiss a Jap on Anzac Day . . . red 'ot poof, fer mine.
1981 *National Times* 1 Mar. 2: The booze here is so crook you wouldn't give it to a Jap on Anzac Day.

jerry to, to   To become 'wise' to [U.S. 1908 Mathews]
1911 Arthur Wright *Gamblers' Gold* 111: 'I always thought I'd seen yer somewhere, but I on'y jerried ter yer when yer was dealin' it out.'
1945 Cecil Mann *The River* 26: 'I've just taken a jerry to y'. Never struck me before. You got your woman here.'
1975 *Bulletin* 26 Apr. 44: I should've jerried when the guy gave me a tug.

jersey, get a   As for **get a guernsey**

Jessie, more hide (arse, cheek) than   An excess of effrontery [f. the elephant at Taronga Park Zoo, d. 1939 *aet.* 67]
1951 Dal Stivens *Jimmy Brockett* 130:

'You've got more cheek than Jessie the elephant!' I said.

1965 Eric Lambert *The Long White Night* 81: 'You've got more arse than Jessie,' I told him.

1975 Les Ryan *The Shearers* 143: 'The bastard's got more hide than Jessie,' he said.

1982 *Sun-Herald* 24 Jan. 150: So Bill McMahon gets the old age pension ... It tells you all you need to know about Australia, about the kind of man we put ourselves up to run it, about noblesse oblige Australian style, about the hide of Jessie.

Jesus Hilton, the St Vincent's Private Hospital, Sydney

1984 *Bulletin* 10 Apr. 55: William McMahon: on top again after a stay in the Jesus Hilton [caption to photograph]

Jets, the Former Newtown (N.S.W.) Rugby League team (also the 'Blues')

1974 *Sydney Morning Herald* 15 Jul. 13: Manly ground Jets.

jeweller's shop In mining, a pocket or patch glistening with gold; a rich claim

1855 Raffaello Carboni *The Eureka Stockade* ed. G. Serle (1969) 10: The jewellers shops, which threatened to exhaust themselves in Canadian Gully were again the talk of the day.

1861 Horace Earle *Ups and Downs* 328: The produce was so vast that the holes there ... were known throughout the entire field as jewellers' shops.

1903 William Craig *My Adventures on the Australian Goldfields* 218: They sank over a 'pocket' at the foot of the reef ... and dropped upon a veritable 'jeweller's shop'.

1950 Gavin Casey *City of Men* 57: 'We're on leaders now that are going to take us right into the jeweller's shop.'

1960 Donald McLean *The Roaring Days* 62: 'A jeweller's shop might be under your feet, or it might be a duffer.'

jig To play truant

1967 *King's Cross Whisper* (Sydney) xxxv 6: *Jig* Play truant.

1979 *National Times* 3 Nov. 25: A group from Leichhardt High 'jig' school at the shops, taking care to avoid the police ... 'I you can't nick off sometimes you can find a place to hide, and jig it in the toilets or the change rooms.

1983 *Sydney Morning Herald* 26 Jul. 1: 'I

used to jig school almost every day because I just hated the place, and did not like the teachers very much either.'

jigger 1 A radio set improvised in gaol

1953 Kylie Tennant *The Joyful Condemned* 212: Jake Fletcher ... was not making large sums selling 'jiggers', tiny wireless sets, at five pounds each.

1967 Brian K. Burton *Teach Them No More* 190: 'I'm aware that other fellows in here have jiggers, but that's not good enough for us.'

2 Any device for illegally stimulating a race-horse

1958 Frank Hardy *The Four-Legged Lottery* 172: A jigger is a battery. It is not used in the actual race. A horse is 'hit with it' on the training tracks.

1982 Joe Anderson *Winners Can Laugh* 99: Hand held devices were designed just to make a sound similar to that made by the painful jigger used only in track gallops. When the horse heard the sound during a race it anticipated a coming shock and accelerated in order to avoid it.

3 Anyone 'jigging it', or playing truant

1983 *Sydney Morning Herald* 26 Jul. 1: Sarah was sent to Ormond where she and the 39 other school children there have one thing in common: they are chronic 'jiggers', or truants.

jillaroo Female counterpart of the **jackaroo** q.v.

1943 Baker 42: *Jillaroo* A Land Girl (War slang.)

1969 Osmar White *Under the Iron Rainbow* 100: 'Everybody knows Patsy. She's our little jilleroo.' 'Jilleroo?' 'We call her that. Our little black stock girl.'

1978 R. A. Nicholls *Almost Like Talking* 44: 'She'd been a station cook and a jillaroo, and she was the best horsewoman I've ever seen.'

1984 *Bulletin* 3 Apr. 48: She [Greta Scacchi] worked as a jillaroo before returning to England for three years of drama school.

jim The sum of £1: *obs.* [see quot. 1945]

1906 Edward Dyson *Fact'ry 'Ands* 214: He was tearin' ratty t'raise another jim ... 'Twas only fer a day, he said, cause he was goin' under er operation yes'day ter recover ther lost goblin.

1911 Arthur Wright *Gambler's Gold* 76: It was the loud-voiced winner speaking with a mouthful of saveloy and peas. 'Here's 'arf a jim for y'.'

1945 Baker 109: £1 – *jim* (from the old English slang *jimmy o' goblin*, a sovereign).

Jimmies, Jimmy Brits A fit of nerves; a state of anger [rhyming slang for 'shits', f. the boxer Jimmy Britt, who toured Australia in World War I]

1941 Baker 13: *Brits up, have the* To be afraid, alarmed.

1952 T. A. G. Hungerford *The Ridge and the River* 116: 'I'm sorry, Clem,' he said . . . 'Must be a touch of the Jim-brits.'

1961 Patrick White *Riders in the Chariot* 415: She was not accustomed to see the grey light sprawling on an empty bed; it gave her the jimmies.

1975 Les Ryan *The Shearers* 120: 'Gees!' Sandy exclaimed in awe. 'Has he got the jimmy brits!' 'We're for it,' Lofty said.

See **Britt, Edgar**

Jimmies, Jimmy Grants Immigrants: *obs.* [rhyming slang]

1845 E. J. Wakefield *Adventures in New Zealand* ii 180: Knots of whalers, who had come on a cruise to the new settlement, were loitering about . . . curiously divided between contempt for the inexperience of the 'jimmy-grants,' as they call the emigrants, and surprise at the general industry and bustle prevailing.

1850 J. D. Mereweather *Diary* in *Settlers* ed. John Hale (1950) 184: A young person at table, speaking contemptuously of some newly-arrived immigrants ('Jimmy Grants', I think, was the slang term she applied to them) I asked her how long she had been out herself?

1859 Henry Kingsley *Recollections of Geoffry Hamlyn* ii 154: 'What are these men that we are going to see?' 'Why, one,' said Lee, 'is a young Jimmy (I beg your pardon, sir, an emigrant), the other two are old prisoners.'

1895 James Kirby *Old Times in the Bush of Australia* 144: As soon as he got to camp, he unyokes, and we found out from him that he was a 'Jimmy-grant' (emigrant), and was loaded with stuff for a station.

1963 Xavier Herbert *Disturbing Element* 91: When we kids saw people on the street dressed like that we would yell at them: 'Jimmygrants, Pommygranates, Pommies!'

Jimmy Woodser see **Woodser**

job To punch, clout [f. *job* to peck, dab, stab, prod, punch; in pugilistic language, to strike with a sharp or cutting stroke OED 1537]

1890 A. B. Paterson 'More Reminiscences' in *Singer of the Bush* (1983) 119: Some other choice youths . . . advised our man to 'hold him up and job him', which he did and so won the fight.

1900 Henry Lawson 'Andy Page's Rival' *Prose* i 362: 'I'll find out for you, Andy. And, what's more, I'll job him for you if I catch him!'

1950 Brian James *The Advancement of Spencer Button* 123: 'I'll job you, Sawkins, if you say I boned two bags of lollies.'

1961 Mena Calthorpe *The Dyehouse* 77: 'He jobbed him,' Larcombe said . . . 'Laid him out cold.'

1982 Nicholas Enright *On the Wallaby* 27: A man comes up to me, cap in hand, and says, 'Help me sir, I haven't had a job in weeks.' So I jobbed him.

jockey Someone travelling with the driver of a taxi who can claim to have already hired it if the destination of an intending passenger would mean an unprofitable trip; anyone riding with the driver by arrangement

[**1900–10** O'Brien and Stephens: *Brewer's jocky* Melbourne – a man who rides about with the driver of a brewer's waggon helping him load and unload on the chance of a share of the drinks which fall to the lot of a brewer's man.]

1945 Baker 140: A *jockey* is a taxi-driver's accomplice who pretends to be a passenger in order to encourage legitimate travellers to pay extortionate fares to secure the taxi.

1974 John Powers *The Last of the Knucklemen* 58: 'One of the cattle stations used a helicopter for spottin' stray cattle. I jockeyed for the pilot.'

jockey, gin see **gin jockey**

joe An ant, usu. in combinations like *bulljoe*, *redjoe*

1944 Brian James *First Furrow* 16: A great worker, but with a weakness for ants. Davie always had a pickle bottle for staging heroic contests between red-joes and black-joes – or either of these against twice their number of road ants.

1965 Leslie Haylen *Big Red* 164: 'You'd have written your poetry on an ant bed with your arse bitten off by the bull joes.'

1988 *Sun-Herald* 19 Jun. 104: *Bulljoe*

bites: Rub in the juice from a fresh bracken fern frond, says Mark Day from 2UE.

Joe On the Victorian goldfields, a trooper enforcing the regulations of Governor C. Joseph La Trobe; a warning cry of the approach of a trooper
1854 Raffaello Carboni *The Eureka Stockade* ed. G. Serle (1969) 48: From my tent, I soon heard the distant cries of 'Joe!' increasing in vehemence at each second. The poor soldiers were pelted with mud, stones, old stumps, and broken bottles.
1855 William Howitt *Land, Labour and Gold* i 400: Hermsprong rode away followed by his men, and by the execrations of the whole diggings in that quarter, expressed in the well-known cry of 'Joe! Joe!' – a cry which means one of the myrmidons of Charley Joe, as they familiarly style Mr La Trobe, – a cry which on all the diggings resounds on all sides on the appearance of any of the hated officials.
1919 W. H. Downing *Digger Dialects* 30: *Joey* A military policeman.
1953 *Caddie A Sydney Barmaid* 140: A whistled Joey from a barmaid was the danger signal [of the proprietor's approach].
joeing, being joed
1854 Raffaello Carboni *The Eureka Stockade* ed. G. Serle (1969) 21: A mob soon collected round the hole: we were respectful, and there was no 'joeing'.
1882 A. J. Boyd *Old Colonials* 160: No one wears a coat – if a bank manager even wore a coat he would be 'joed'.* *'Joed', i.e. hooted.

Joe Blake 1 A snake [rhyming slang]
1941 Baker 39: *Joe Blake* A snake.
1951 Ernestine Hill *The Territory* 446: There is little rhyming slang in the Territory. A snake is always 'Joe Blake'.
1964 H. P. Tritton *Time Means Tucker* 88: A snake can look remarkably like a slender branch and several times a day you would see men jump back with a string of curses after almost picking up a 'Joe Blake'.
2 *the Joe Blakes*: see quot. 1969
1944 Alan Marshall *These Are My People* 155: 'You feel nothin' when you're on a bender . . . You get the Joe Blakes bad after a few weeks.'
1969 Osmar White *Under the Iron Rainbow* 153: It's the electricity in the air that gives a man the joe-blakes* just before the Wet. *Rhyming slang: Delirium – Seeing Snakes – Joe Blakes.

Joe Blow A nondescript; the average man; the man in the street [also U.S.]
1955 *Bulletin* 27 Jul. 6: Had Mr Casey been plain Joe Blow and gone and shot an eagle there wouldn't have been the slightest fuss.
1966 Peter Mathers *Trap* 73: You couldn't tell him from Joe Blow.
1978 Hal Porter *Overland 71* 25: It's more than probable that such symbolic and vocal *bêtises*, outrageous to me, aren't even dimly apparent to Mr and Mrs Joe Blow.

joes, the A fit of depression
1915 C. J. Dennis *The Songs of a Sentimental Bloke* 41: It gimme Joes to sit an' watch them two!
1942 Leonard Mann *The Go-Getter* 97: The weather's bad enough to give a man the joes.
1955 Mary Durack *Keep Him My Country* 182: 'Soothing!' Millington exclaimed. 'It fair give me the joes.'

joey 1 A baby kangaroo, carried in the mother's pouch [Morris 1839]
2 A baby, an infant
1887 *All the Year Round* 30 Jul. 67: 'Joey' is a familiar name for anything young or small, and is applied indifferently to a puppy, or a kitten, or a child.
1948 K. S. Prichard *Golden Miles* 75: 'A girl never knows when she'll be bringin' home a joey if she goes with you.'
1955 D'Arcy Niland *The Shiralee* 27: 'Got a joey with yer, have yer? And what's your name, young 'un?'
1968 Stuart Gore *Holy Smoke* 42: 'Along comes young Daniel, not much more'n a joey at the time, but pretty shrewd for his age.'

joey, wood and water see **wood and water**

John, John Hop A cop [? f. *gendarme* and rhyming slang]
1909 Edward Dyson *Fact'ry 'Ands* 99: 'He had er John in tow . . . ther policeman was fer me.'
1923 D. H. Lawrence *Kangaroo* 356: 'Police!' snarled Jack. 'Bloody John Hops!'
1958 H. D. Williamson *The Sunlit Plain* 25: 'I hope she hasn't got that dirty, greasy john hop with her.'
1975 Xavier Herbert *Poor Fellow My Country* 1151: Brumby Toohey . . . had the

Provosts after him now, instead of the Johns as of old.

Johnny Bliss see **Bliss**

Johnny-cake Similar to damper, but closer in size to a scone: made basically of flour and water, and cooked in the ashes or in a pan [f. the name of a flat cake of corn bread U.S. 1739 Mathews]

1846 G. F. Angas *Savage Life and Scenes in Australia and New Zealand* i 161: Our cook had not been idle: there were 'damp-ers', 'dough-boys', 'leather-jackets', 'johnny-cakes', and 'beggars-in-the-pan'.

1862 Rachel Henning *Letters* ed. D. Adams (1963) 102: Tom lit a great fire and made some beautiful 'johnny-cakes' – thin soda cakes which are baked in about ten minutes and are the best bread you ever ate.

1893 Henry Lawson *Letters* 53: No work and very little to eat: we lived mostly on Johnny cakes and cadged a bit of meat here and there.

1954 Tom Ronan *Vision Splendid* 76: 'When he got back I was living on Johnny cakes and lizards.'

1964 H. P. Tritton *Time Means Tucker* 121: 'Yair,' he said, 'I'd be flatter than a Johnny cake.'

Johnny Raw A new chum, novice, new recruit [colonial application of *Johnny Raw* nickname for an inexperienced youngster OED 1813]

1845 Thomas McCombie *Arabin* 248: 'I think,' said Arabin, 'you have managed to get very cleverly out of a scrape.' 'Yes, I am no Johnny Raw,' replied the other.

1888 E. Finn *Chronicles of Early Melbourne* ii 905: The 'Expirees' regarded the others with a feeling of pitying contempt, a species of simpletons who should have stayed at home. They called them 'Johnny Raws' and 'New Chums'.

1908 *Australian Magazine* 1 Nov. 1251: A 'jackeroo' (a new chum on a station out for colonial experience) is supposed to be 'Jacky Raw' with a kangaroo's tail as it were.

joke A dishonest scheme

1870 J. R. Houlding *Rural and City Life* 292: 'I'm sorry we have gone so far with the joke, for I don't believe I can ever actually like her, let alone love her.'

1913 Ambrose Pratt *Wolaroi's Cup* 120: 'Straight to you, Tommy. You were in on the joke.'

1956 Tom Ronan *Moleskin Midas* 180: 'Seein' that you was in the joke of stealing them in the first place, I don't suppose you're worrying much about getting them back.'

1988 *Sydney Morning Herald* 1 Sep. 7: To Mr Fitzgerald's evident disgust, Herbert de-fined a 'joke' as a corrupt system in which criminals, SP bookmakers in this case, paid police for protection.

joker A fellow, chap [N.Z. 1868 OED]

1900 Henry Lawson 'Meeting Old Mates' *Prose* i 165: 'I haven't seen him for more than three years. Where's the old joker hanging out at all?'

1929 Herbert Scanlon *Old Memories* 13: 'If it wasn't for me, you two jokers would never have got a spot.'

1942 Gavin Casey *It's Harder for Girls* 218: 'What're you jokers doing tonight?' asked Winch. 'Like to come to a party?'

1965 Eric Lambert *The Long White Night* 88: 'Don't you recognize this joker?' 'Why should I? Who is he?'

jonic, jonnik Genuine, fair, reliable: *obsol-escent* [E. dial. *jannock* fair, straight-forward OED 1828]

1870 J. R. Houlding *Rural and City Life* 237: 'Bravo! Bob,' said Ben. 'That was joanac.'

1923 Jack Moses *Beyond the City Gates* 112: I'm camping down in Logan's, at the old pub in the Glen, / Where the fluid's always jonick.

1935 H. R. Williams *Comrades of the Great Adventure* 163: 'You don't say so!' said Elliott feigning surprise. 'Yes, it's jonick,' continued Peter.

1953 T. A. G. Hungerford *Riverslake* 166: 'Got the knife right into him.' 'Jonic?' 'Jonic!'

1968 Stuart Gore *Holy Smoke* 65: 'That's jonnick, ain't it?' 'Yes. Ridgey-the-didge, mate.'

journo A journalist [abbr.]

1971 *Southerly* 271: Many who met Sles-sor in his more formal and conservative moments would have regarded him as the most journo of journos.

1981 *Sunday Mail* (Brisbane) 27 Sep. 2: Junkets for Journos are not all they are cracked up to be.

judge, salute the see **salute**

jug handle see **monkey 2**

Julia Creek, things are weak at see **Tallarook**

jumbuck A sheep [Ab. or Pidgin]
1824 Let. 26 Jan. cit. W. S. Ramson *Australian English* (1966) 107: They smacked their lips and stroked their breasts, 'boodjerry patta! murry boodjerry! – fat as jimbuck!!' i.e. good food, very good, fat as mutton.
1843–63 Charles Harpur 'The Kangaroo Hunt' in *Poetical Works* ed. Elizabeth Perkins (1984) 510: Jimbuc is an aboriginal name of a little shag-haired species of kangaroo which is peculiar to mountain copses. It may be called the mountain wallaby . . . The Blacks of the Hunter call the sheep jimbuc, no doubt from a resemblance, however remote, arising out of the hairy shagginess of the one and the woolliness of the other.
1895 A. B. Paterson 'Waltzing Matilda' in *Singer of the Bush* (1983) 250: Up came the jumbuck to drink at the waterhole, / Up jumped the swagman and grabbed him in glee.
1934 Brian Penton *Landtakers* 26: 'What's a thousand of them poor jumbucks to me?'
1983 *Sydney Morning Herald* 13 Sep. 15: The idea is to promote lamb by controlling production and processing from the time of lambing until the chops, roasts, lamburgers and spare ribs hit the plate in the Big Jumbuck restaurant chain.

jump a horse over the bar see **horse**

jump, take a running ~ at yourself Equivalent to 'get lost', 'go to blazes'
1941 Baker 75: *Take a run at yourself* Run away! Go to the devil!
1977 *Sunday Telegraph* (Sydney) 22 May 59: We can only hope that when this unlikely Pommie lot get here they manage to take a series of running jumps at themselves.

jump up A sudden steep rise in a road: mainly N.T. and W.A.
[**1844** Louisa Meredith *Notes and Sketches of New South Wales* 70: The main portion of the road is *bad* beyond an English comprehension; sometimes it consists of natural step-like rocks protruding from the dust or sand one, two, or three feet above each other, in huge slabs the width of the track, and over these 'jumpers', as they are pleasantly termed, we had to jolt and bump along.]

1894 G. N. Boothby *On the Wallaby* 189: A little later the line crossed the Burdekin River, by means of what seemed to us a most dangerous bridge, technically termed a 'jump up' . . . The descent on one side and the ascent on the other are very steep.
1948 H. Drake-Brockman *Sydney or the Bush* 230: Buncker turned the wheel sharply to avoid a jump-up in the track.
1964 Tom Ronan *Packhorse and Pearling Boat* 151: On the first stage out from Hodgson we climbed a jump-up: not a cliff, nor an escarpment, nor a bluff, but in the magnificently adequate basic English of the cattle country, a jump-up.

jump up whitefellow An expression reflecting an Aboriginal belief that those with white skins are reincarnations of dead blacks
1830 Robert Dawson *The Present State of Australia* 158: 'When he makes blackfellow die,' I said, 'what becomes of him afterward?' 'Go away Englat (England),' he answered, 'den come back white pellow.' This idea is so strongly impressed upon their minds, that when they discover any likeness between a white man and any one of their deceased friends, they exclaim immediately, 'Dat black pellow good while ago jump up white pellow, den came back again.'
1882 A. J. Boyd *Old Colonials* 198: The trooper had a suspicion that if shot, his deceased relative would not 'jump up whitefellow'.
1927 M. M. Bennett *Christison of Lammermoor* 109: One old gin wanted to claim Munggra [Christison] as a defunct brother who had 'jumped up white fellow'.

jungle juice See quot. 1945
1945 Baker 157: *jungle juice* Any alcoholic beverage concocted by servicemen in the tropics.
1948 Sumner Locke Elliott *Rusty Bugles* in *Khaki, Bush and Bigotry* ed. Eunice Hanger (1968) 75: 'He hasn't half been on the jungle juice.'
1968 Geoffrey Dutton *Andy* 268: The Americans had two bottles of bourbon and one of jungle juice made from fermented coconut milk and surgical alcohol.
see **snake juice**

just quietly see **quietly**

K

kadoova, off one's Deranged, off one's head: *rare* [? f. *cady, kadi* hat]
1941 Baker 50: *Off one's kadoova* To be silly, cranky, stupid.
1946 Dal Stivens *The Courtship of Uncle Henry* 72: I reckoned then Thompson was a bit off his kadoova.

kaka A girl (in juvenile slang, W.A.)
1978 T. A. G. Hungerford in *Memories of Childhood* ed. Lee White 44: We were hanging thirstily on his startling disclosures about the parts and purposes of what we still called 'the tarts' but which he referred to as 'the brush' or the 'swell kakas'.

kanga 1 Money [? f. rhyming slang *kangaroo = screw*]
1969 Alan O'Toole *The Racing Game* 6: 'On account of you being a mighty bloke, and sending Ape that kanga without asking any questions, we're all agreed on one thing. You're getting the biggest share.'
1978 Eunice Hanger *2D and Other Plays* 44: 'Your daughter's got a bit of kanga, but, hasn't she?' 'Kanga?' 'Cash. That's what they say in the bush.'
2 A jackhammer [? f. 'hopping' motion, also brand name]
1975 *Sun-Herald* 20 Jul. 13: A bone-shaking ride on a 'kanga' – a jackhammer, to the uninitiated.
3 see **skip, skippy**
kangas see **Kangaroos**

kangaroo 1 To move jerkily (used of a car when the engine is warming up)
1964 *Sydney Morning Herald* 14 Sep. 1: Be on the lookout for a grey car kangarooing through the Manly area. Mrs – has just received her driver's licence.
1971 Craig McGregor *Don't Talk to Me about Love* 187: The car ... jerked and kangarooed off into the night.
2 To defecate in a kangaroo-like posture
1955 D'Arcy Niland *The Shiralee* 115: It ended up with the injunction in snaggled capitals: Kangarooing it Not Allowed. And in smaller letters: Remember others have to sit where you shat.
1987 Kathy Lette *Girls' Night Out* 59: My mother had only imparted a few pieces of wisdom ... *never* sit on a public toilet seat.

Not wanting to contract any trendy venereal fauna, I kangaroo-ed it. Poised there in a crippled leapfrog, I craned to decipher the graffiti on the top of the door.

Kangaroos, the 1 The Rugby League team representing Australia internationally
1933 *Sydney Morning Herald* 14 Sep. 12: The Australian Rugby team, the 'Kangaroos' beat Yorkshire today by 13 points to nil.
2 The North Melbourne A.F.L. team
1975 *Sunday Telegraph* (Sydney) 10 Aug. 55: Roos catch the Tigers in hectic scramble.
Also **the kangas**
1979 *Herald* (Melbourne) 21 Apr. 36: Kangas bounce back.
3 The touring Australian Rules team
1984 *Australian* 28 Jul. 56: The National Football League executive gets no points for its move earlier this week of declaring the national Australian football team to tour Ireland in October the 'Kangaroos'. The Kangaroo tag has been worn by our national rugby league team overseas with distinction since 1908.

kangaroos in one's top paddock, to have
See quots
1908 *Australian Magazine* 1 Nov. 1250: If you show signs of mental weakness you are either balmy, dotty, ratty or cracked, or you may even have white ants in your attic or kangaroos in your top paddock.
1946 Dal Stivens *The Courtship of Uncle Henry* 70: Talked like a toff himself, he did, but he had kangaroos in the top paddock, as you'll see.
1981 *Sydney Morning Herald* 7 Nov. 44: None of the patients appears to have any more kangaroos in the top paddock than the people one meets at work or in the pub.

kark (it), to As for **cark it**
1977 Richard Beilby *Gunner* 302: 'That Wog ya roughed up – well, he karked.'
1984 *Sydney Morning Herald* 7 Mar. 47: 'She's finally karked it!' [a truck breaking down]. 'C'mon ... We'll have to hoof the rest!'
1984 *Sunday Independent* (Perth) 17 Jun. 48: His friend and co-explorer stopped a

shovel-nosed spear in the midriff and karked it.

Kath, Kathleen Mavourneen An indefinite period (from the refrain of the song, 'It may be for years, it may be forever'): applied to a gaol sentence, and by transfer to an habitual criminal [listed by Partridge as 'An indefinitely long term of imprisonment' (N.Z. 1914), and 'The hire purchase system' (Anglo-Irish 1932)]
1903 Joseph Furphy *Such is Life* (1944) 201: Heaven grant that that parting may be a Kathleen Mavourneen one.
1941 Baker 40: *Kath* An indeterminate gaol sentence, *Kathleen Mavourneen* . . . An habitual criminal.
1951 Simon Hickey *Travelled Roads* 38: One hawker owed £75 to his supplier . . . and called to tell him that he was on a Kathleen Mavourneen (it may be for years, it may be forever) trip to Beirut.
1983 *Sydney Morning Herald* 20 May 16: Only two on a lengthening list of the Bowen Basin's 'Kathleen Mavourneen' mines whose development could be for years or could be forever.

Kelly 1 An axe [brand name]
1941 Baker 40: *Kelly* An axe.
1968 Stuart Gore *Holy Smoke* 94: 'A man'd better be reckoning on a bit of shut-eye, if he's going to be any good on the kelly in the morning.'
1982 *NT News* (Darwin) 15 Jun. 7: Our anthropologists, many with a large 'Kelly' to grind, would have us believe the Aborigine to be Superman, Tarzan and JC in one package.
2 Nickname for a crow
1935 Henry G. Lamond *An Aviary on the Plains* 51: As we leave the camp Kelly the Crow, being the sanitary contractor of the bird world . . . floats down to inspect the small litter we've left.
1980 *Mercury* (Hobart) 28 Jun. 6: Replies to a questionnaire sent to all pasture protection boards in the State [of N.S.W.] indicated firm support for the economic value of the crow and advocated its protection as an important force for control of grass grubs . . . 'Kelly' the crow was a good bird to have about.
3 See quot. 1953
1953 Baker 142: *kelly* A tram or omnibus inspector.
1980 Clive James *Unreliable Memoirs* 155: The inspectors [on the buses] were

called Kellies, after Ned Kelly, and were likely to swoop at any time.

Kelly, Ned see **Ned Kelly**

Kenso 1 Kensington, a suburb of Sydney, N.S.W.
1949 Lawson Glassop *Lucky Palmer* 24: 'Might be Kenso or Victoria Park or even Moorefield or Warwick Farm.'
2 The University of New South Wales (at Kensington)
1972 Geoff Morley *Jockey Rides Honest Race* 10: You enrol at Kenso High School (in-joke) and pay your fees. You go to Uni five nights a week and work here five days a week.

kero Kerosene (paraffin) [abbr.]
1938 Xavier Herbert *Capricornia* 148: 'Take it and buy some tucker and kero.'
1969 Osmar White *Under the Iron Rainbow* 76: These times with kero refrigerators and bottled gas it was different.
1973 Frank Huelin *Keep Moving* 171: A shallow wash dish made from another cut-down kero-tin.

kick To accelerate (of a racehorse); usu. in the expressions 'kick away', 'kick clear'
1980 *Sun-Herald* 8 Jun. 57: Winter's Dance made the home turn awkwardly and appeared to get on the wrong leg. Her supporters had given up hope as the leaders kicked away.
1983 Phillip Smith *Sun-Herald* 17 Apr. 65: 'I was confident that we had Veloso covered but it was the opposite – he just kicked clear and won easily.'

kick, he couldn't get a ~ in a stampede (stable) Reproach to an inadequate Australian Rules player
1981 *National Times* 25 Jan. 23: The Australian Rules footballer who 'couldn't get a kick in a stampede'.
1984 *Sunday Independent* (Perth) 1 Apr. 72: They couldn't win a kick in a stable.

kick on To carry on, with just enough funds for the purpose
1949 Lawson Glassop *Lucky Palmer* 153: 'I knew him when I used to slip ten bob out of the till . . . so he could kick on with it.' 'You can often kick on with ten bob,' said Lucky judicially.
1957 Ray Lawler *Summer of the Seventeenth Doll* 50: 'What about all those times

when you've carried me – every year when I've run dry down here you've kicked me on?'

kick the tin To make a contribution [? f. rattling of collection box]
1966 Baker 230: Such suggestions as *kick the tin* . . . to the person who is due to buy drinks.
1969 Leslie Haylen *Twenty Years' Hard Labor* 36–7: He [Mr Chifley] gave me £50 for my campaign funds out of his own pocket and said, rather unnecessarily I thought, 'I'm kicking the tin for a few others as well so you needn't mention this.'
1976 *Sunday Telegraph* (Sydney) 30 May 34: When A.L.P. president Bob Hawke was appealing for money to help pay the Federal election campaign debt of $300,000, the NSW Labor Party was claiming it could not afford to 'kick the tin'.
1987 *Sydney Morning Herald* 12 Jun. 1: To a greater extent than ever before, business is perceived to be kicking in the tin for Labor – Bob Hawke's very own white shoe brigade.

kidstakes Pretence, nonsense; as an exclamation, equivalent to 'Fiddlesticks': *obs.* [f. *kid* to hoax, humbug OED 1811]
1916 C. J. Dennis *The Moods of Ginger Mick* 88: Mick reads the boys them ringin' words o' praise; / But they jist grins a bit an' sez 'Kid stakes!'
1919 W. H. Downing *Digger Dialects* 30: *Kidstakes* Insincere flattery; inveiglement; a wheedling or deceitful speech or action.
1938 Xavier Herbert *Capricornia* 567: 'I didn't see him, I tell you.' 'You told his Ma you did.' 'That was only kidstakes.'
1990 David Malouf *The Great World* 31: He came at times like a small child, hugging her waist and hanging on. 'None of that,' she would tell him. 'You're all kidstakes. That's all that is.'

killer A bullock or sheep to be killed for meat
1897 I. Scott *How I Stole over 10,000 Sheep in Australia and N.Z.* 9: 'You know the killers, don't you?' . . . i.e. the sheep the boss used for his own mutton at the house. [O.E.D.]
1929 K. S. Prichard *Coonardoo* 112: Warieda had gone out after a killer, cut up the beast and given everybody in the uloo his or her share.
1949 *Coast to Coast 1948* 149: 'The killers

are in the paddock behind the pen. You can leave the meat hanging.'
1966 Tom Ronan *Once There Was a Bagman* 36: Most of my time seemed to be spent chasing killers . . . In between meat-chasing trips I was supposed just to find myself something to do.

kill our own, we catch and see **catch**

Kimberley cool Applied to beer drunk at the temperature of the atmosphere [f. the early days of the Ord scheme, when beer was drunk by construction workers from the drums in which they kept it]

Kimberley Formal A dress style for men requiring shirt and shorts, shoes and socks

Kimberley mutton, oyster, walkabout See quots [place-name in N.W. Australia]
1945 Tom Ronan *Strangers on the Ophir* 39: A meat fritter known in the Kimberleys as a 'Burdekin Duck', and on the Burdekin as a 'Kimberley Oyster'.
1959 Jon Cleary *Back of Sunset* 167: The roast goat, Kimberley mutton, as it was called.
1971 Keith Willey *Boss Drover* 72: Horses . . . would die in hundreds from what we called the Kimberley walkabout. This was a disease which set a horse walking, round and round and up and down, knocking into trees and rocks and never stopping to eat, until in a few hours or days he would literally have walked himself to death.
1976 Roland Robinson *The Shift of Sands* 348: 'They [the donkeys and mules] don't get the Kimberley walkabout disease that kills off the horses. The C.S.I.R.O. reckon it's caused by a plant called 'Croatalaria'. We call it rattle-pod.'

Kinchela, putting ~ on them See quots: *obs.*
1897 *Bulletin* 25 Sep. Red Page: 'Putting Kinchela on 'em' is evidently inspired by the fact that one Kinchela, some years ago, wrote and published a pamphlet on the art of sharpening and 'keeping' shears.
1911 S. E. Sorenson *Life in the Australian Backblocks* 233: The blades are pulled back and the knockers filed down, so the shears will take a bigger blow. This is called 'putting kinchler on them', from the fact that it was first adopted by John Kinsella, who died in Armidale about August 1902.

kinder Kindergarten, esp. pre-school (Victoria)

1978 *Herald* (Melbourne) 5 Sep. 9: A Kinder Group Wants to Expand [heading] The International Montessori Association wants to expand its educational program in Australia. The association . . . has six kindergartens and two primary schools in Melbourne suburbs.

1983 Morris Lurie *Seven Books for Grossman* 100: Little Norbert and little Hermione and little all the rest of them, are all tucked nicely away in their kinders and creches and day-care centres.

kindy Kindergarten, esp. pre-school [abbr.]

1969 Lyndall Hadow *Full Cycle* 189: The house was vapid when he was at work, the children at school, Philip at morning kindie.

1980 *Daily News* (Perth) 17 Oct. 44: Lorrelle Holman (5), of Mt Pleasant, is learning pots about the animal kingdom, thanks to her local kindy. Her proud dad Ken says the kids were issued with tadpoles last week.

1984 *Sun-Herald* 17 Jun. 154: 'Same thing with my kids,' I said. 'I told them almost from kindie that they had to be *dying* before they didn't go to school cos I was working.'

king In combinations like 'cattle king', 'shepherd king', 'squatter king', 'wool king'

1908 W. H. Ogilvie *My Life in the Open* 25: Tyson, the Queensland cattle king, who died a few years ago.

1936 Ion L. Idriess *The Cattle King: The Story of Sir Sidney Kidman* [book title]

1875 Rolf Boldrewood *The Squatter's Dream* repr. as *Ups and Downs* (1878) 277: Entering the parlour in a suit of rough tweed, he felt much more like a shepherd king of the future than the death-doomed pioneer . . . of the preceding few days.

1921 William Baylebridge *An Anzac Muster* 26: 'I am settling portions of my holding with embryonic sheep-kings – those ambitious trouble-hunters I spoke of.'

1891 Francis Adams *Fortnightly Review* Oct. 542: All the old profuse hospitality, the hunts and dances and four-in-hands of the squatter kings, live now but as a dim tradition.

1869 *Australian Journal* Jul. 685: *Wool King* A squatter.

1900 Henry Lawson 'Middleton's Peter' *Prose* i 257: The Australian squatter is not always the mighty wool king that English and American authors and other uninformed people imagine him to be!

king *v.* Abbr. of **king-hit** q.v.

1959 Gerard Hamilton *Summer Glare* 97: 'Ken kinged him.'

1962 Alan Marshall *This is the Grass* 144: 'If a bloke comes at you buttoning up his coat you always king him when he's on the last button. It's just common sense.'

1975 *Bulletin* 26 Apr. 45: 'He kinged a floor-walker.'

King Billy The imaginary patriarch of the Aboriginal race; nickname for any Aboriginal singled out from the rest

1898 D. W. Carnegie *Spinifex and Sand* 190: Finding the water that King Billy (for so had we named the Buck) eventually took us to.

1902 Henry Lawson 'A Bush Publican's Lament' *Prose* i 467: An' supposin' Old King Billy an' his ole black gin comes round at holiday time and squats on the verander.

1920 E. S. Sorenson *Sunraysia Daily* (Mildura) 16 Oct. 14: It is a libel on the race to take the degenerate King Billy, who loafs about the towns, as a criterion, embodying as he does the results of rum, opium, tobacco and other vices of the white man.

1975 Richard Beilby *The Brown Land Crying* 35: 'You'll see Captain Cook coming ashore from the South Perth ferry . . . And I suppose there'll be a few Aborigines, King Billy and his nulla-nullas and spears.'

king-hit *n.* A knockout punch; a surprise punch, probably unfair

1924 *Truth* 27 Apr. 6: *King-hit* The winning blow in a fight.

1935 H. R. Williams *Comrades of the Great Adventure* 192: Swung with terrific force, the unusual weapon scored a 'king-hit' which spreadeagled the second 'Jack'.

1960 Ron Tullipan *Follow the Sun* 128: 'He's a king-hit merchant, always has been, and when he misses the surprise shot, he doesn't get a second free one with a bloke like me.'

1984 *Sun* (Melbourne) 16 Jul. 3: The reported player had been bashed in the face by a 'king hit' which started the brawl.

king-hit *v.* To deliver a knockout punch, or a surprise punch, probably unfair

1962 Stuart Gore *Down the Golden Mile* 277: 'King-hit me, the bastard,' he muttered. 'With me own gun!'

1972 John Bailey *The Wire Classroom* 140: The previous cop at Wendi who had been known to king-hit a native who had spat on the pavement near his wife.

1980 *Daily News* (Perth) 25 Sep. 39: Ruck-rover Wayne Cormack was 'king hit' behind the play early in the third term.

king-pin   The leading figure, most import-ant person [U.S. 1867 OED ? f. *king-bolt* a main or large bolt in a mechanical structure OED 1825]

1907 Charles MacAlister *Old Pioneering Days in the Sunny South* 262: The notorious Frank Gardiner – the King-pin of Australian bushrangers – so began his stirring ca-reer.

1915 C. J. Dennis *The Songs of a Sentimen-tal Bloke* 102: But 'struth! 'E is king-pin! The 'ead serang!

1938 H. Drake-Brockman *Men Without Wives* 78: 'Andy, where is old man Lovatt?' 'Out on the run. For the moment I'm king-pin.'

1957 Judah Waten *Shares in Murder* 99: 'Then he must be the biggest fence of the lot. The kingpin. The daddy of all fences.'

kings in grass castles   see **grass cas-tles**

kip   The small flat piece of board from which the coins are tossed in two-up [cf. *kep* to catch EDD 1781; *keper* a flat piece of wood secured in the mouth of a horse to prevent his eating the corn EDD 1897]

1898 *Bulletin* 17 Dec. Red Page: The kip is the piece of wood used in 'two-up'.

1911 Louis Stone *Jonah* 215: The spinner placed the two pennies face down on the kip, and then, with a turn of the wrist, the coins flew twenty feet into the air.

1949 Lawson Glassop *Lucky Palmer* 167: He handed the kip to the spinner ... placed two pennies, tails up, on it with infinite care and said 'Fair go'.

kipper   An Englishman (Services slang in World War II) [f. the prominence of kippers in English diet. See also quots 1946, 1962]

1946 *Daily Telegraph* (Sydney) 22 Jan. 11: Hansen told Mr Goldie, S. M. that the girls called them 'Pommies' and 'kippers'. 'I understand that in Australian "kipper" means two-faced and gutless,' Hansen ad-ded.

1954 T. A. G. Hungerford *Sowers of the Wind* 204: 'The kippers have got orders not to go about alone now.'

1962 J. Marshall and R. Drysdale *Journey Among Men* 190: This unlovable trait has led to the application of the expression *Kipper* to a certain type of Englishman. A kipper, by virtue of its processing, has become two-faced with no guts.

1975 *Bulletin* 30 Aug. 63: The Australian naval slang term for a Pommy matelot is – or was – 'bloody kipper'. Retrospective lower-deck etymology gives the derivation as 'A two-faced bastard with no guts'.

kiss and ride   See quot. 1975

1975 *Sydney Morning Herald* 16 Jan. 6: The kiss-and-ride system – the wife drops her husband off at the station or terminal, keeps the car for her own use during the day, and picks him up at night.

kitchen tea   A pre-wedding party to which the guests bring some items of kitchen equip-ment as a gift

1934 Tom Clarke *Marriage at 6 a.m.* 17: Tom Rawlings led me off to see the bride at a 'kitchen tea' ... it was so called because each guest brought a kitchen utensil as a wedding-gift.

1943 Kylie Tennant *Time Enough Later* 200: 'I beg of you, restrain them from any idea of visitings and junketings and grue-someness in the form of kitchen teas.'

1980 *NT News* (Darwin) 9 Jan. 19: A Traditional Kitchen Tea was held for last Saturday's bride Sue Jennings ... Guests took along gifts for the bride's future home which will be in Darwin.

Kiwi *n. & a.*   A New Zealander [f. the bird unique to New Zealand OED 1918]

1935 H. R. Williams *Comrades of the Great Adventure* 210: 'We're darned lucky we are not all beaten up like your Kiwi friend.'

1965 *Daily Telegraph* (Sydney) 13 Apr. 64: We never had less than 150 Aussie and Kiwi girls on our own temporary staff.

1982 *Sydney Morning Herald* 18 Mar. 6: There is a view that New Zealand has made a significant contribution to the number of drag queens at the Cross. 'Kiwi fruits' is the term used, I'm told.

kleiner   As for **clinah** q.v.

1899 W. T. Goodge *Hits! Skits! and Jingles!* 17: Well, spare me days, kleiner, I love yer!

knobtwister Bookmaker [f. the knobs for controlling the betting board]
1984 *Sun-Herald* 25 Nov. 152: At Canterbury on Wednesday two rails knobtwisters were reprimanded for not betting each-way when they should have.

knock *n.* An act of intercourse; a promiscuous woman [f. **knock** *v.* 1]
1965 William Dick *A Bunch of Ratbags* 199: I had caused him to miss out on a knock many weeks ago with Elaine, and he had never forgiven me. Ibid. 158: To tell your best mate that one of his family was a knock was unethical and uncalled for.
1972 David Williamson *The Removalists* 117: 'Never turn down a knock, Russy boy. Tomorrow you might get run over by a tram.'

knock *v.* 1 To copulate with [OED 1598], in Australia more common in expressions like 'knock off', or 'do a knock with' (to strike up an acquaintance, seeking favours)
1933 Norman Lindsay *Saturdee* 138: 'Supposin' I was to do a knock with girls, what 'ud I say to them?'
1969 William Dick *Naked Prodigal* 112: 'She all right? Does she look like she knocks?'
1971 Frank Hardy *The Outcasts of Foolgarah* 15: 'Well, he's not knocking orf my sister-in-law and that's for sure.'
2 To disparage, criticize, find fault with [U.S. 1896 Mathews]
1892 William Lane *The Workingman's Paradise* 85: 'Admit it's a business concern and that everybody growls at it, it's the only paper that dares knock things.'
1903 Joseph Furphy *Such is Life* (1944) 32: 'Hold on, hold on,' interrupted Mosey. 'Don't go no furder, for Gossake. Yer knockin' yerself bad, an' you don't know it.'
1920 *Sunraysia Daily* (Mildura) 6 Nov. 7: Don't knock too hard, Mick ... for the love of Australia don't deny the existence of story-writers at least as capable ... as those of other English-speaking countries.
1958 E. O. Schlunke *The Village Hampden* 233: 'She seemed to be so nice and friendly. I wasn't going to knock my good luck.'
1981 *Australian* 17 Oct. Mag. 2: Knocking – like sunshine, fresh air and punting – is as Australian as lamingtons.

knocked, knocked out Killed or wounded in action (Services slang)
1917 Diary cit. Patsy Adam-Smith *The Anzacs* (1978) 215: We just go into the line again and again until we get knocked.
1932 Leonard Mann *Flesh in Armour* 312: 'Corporal Jeffreys knocked, sir,' he said.
1944 Lawson Glassop *We Were the Rats* 128: 'If a section leader got knocked, somebody ... would just take over and the rest would follow without question.'

knock back *v.* 1 To reject
1918 *Kia Ora Coo-ee* 15 Jul. 12: Have you ever got arrangements completed for your holidays to commence on a Monday at home, and then about six of your fellow workers got sick on the Saturday, and you have been knocked back?
1938 Eric Lowe *Salute to Freedom* 267: 'It's just that I don't want you to feel disappointed if you get knocked back.'
1966 Tom Ronan *Strangers on the Ophir* 46: 'I knocked him back for credit and put him to sleep with a special drink.'
2 To drink, consume [OED 1931]
1962 J. Marshall and R. Drysdale *Journey Among Men* 164: He took the top off one [bottle] and poured himself a glassful. He knocked this back in one hit.
1975 Don Townshend *Gland Time* 231: He was knocking back the grogs at an alarming rate.

knock bandy see **bandy**

knock down *v.* To spend (esp. a cheque) until funds are exhausted, generally on liquor
1853 C. R. Read *What I Heard, Saw and Did on the Australian Goldfields* 98: A volume might almost be written on the ridiculous manner in which this class of people squander away their money; many, I have heard boasting at the diggings, as to the shortness of time in which they could 'knock down' a thousand or two pounds, and return to the diggings, without sufficient to buy a pickaxe.
1883 E. M. Curr *Recollections of Squatting in Victoria* 348: 'All I've heard of was a Devil's River lot, six or eight of them, knocking down their cheques at Young's.'
1891 Henry Lawson *Verse* i 135: For the bushman gets bushed in the streets of a town, / Where he loses his friends when his cheque is knocked down.
1946 Ion L. Idriess *In Crocodile Land* 209:

'A bushie had blown in that day and started to knock down his cheque.'

knock out To earn [N.Z. 1871 OED]
1881 A. C. Grant *Bush-Life in Queensland* i 31: These were part of the Ipswich tribe, and knocked out a precarious living by hunting in the bush and begging in the town.
1896 Edward Dyson *Rhymes from the Mines* 93: Yet Jo contrived to knock out bread and butter, / And something for a dead-broke mate.
1975 *Bulletin* 30 Aug. 16: What about the school-teacher, the young computer programmer or plumber knocking out about $200 a week.

knock over a doll see **doll**

knockabout man A station-hand doing odd jobs; a rouseabout
1868 Marcus Clarke 'Swagmen' repr. in *The Peripatetic Philosopher* (1869) 41: At the station where I worked for some time (as 'knock-about man').
1880 Rolf Boldrewood *The Miner's Right* (1890) 60: 'If we don't make a rise before that time, we shall have become wages men, bush-rangers, or knock-about-men on a station – farm-labourers.'

knockback *n.* A refusal; rejection of an overture, often sexual [E. dial 1902 OED]
1919 W. H. Downing *Digger Dialects* 31: *Knockback* A refusal.
1933 Frank Clune *Try Anything Once* 25: There was no need for any further hands about the place. This was rather a blow, but already I was getting used to knock-backs and I felt that something or other would turn up.
1957 Ray Lawler *Summer of the Seventeenth Doll* 101: 'Yeh – you, the great lover that's never had a knock back.'
1975 Les Ryan *The Shearers* 76: 'Please yourself,' he said, looking like Humphrey Bogart after a knock-back. 'I'll be around.'

knockdown, the An introduction [U.S. 1865 OED]
1916 C. J. Dennis *The Moods of Ginger Mick* 149: *Knock-down* A ceremony insisted upon by ladies who decline to be 'picked up'; a formal introduction.
1938 *Bulletin* 6 Jul. 48: 'Another bloke gave me a knockdown to 'im.'
1950 Jon Cleary *Just Let Me Be* 9: 'She'll never give you a knock-down while you're

just a milkman. You'll have to go up in the world.'
1981 *Sun-Herald* 1 Mar. 97: 'Crikey, that's a grouse-looking little sheila over there, Sal. Any chance of a knockdown to her later on?'

knocker 1 Common sense: *obs.*
1900 Henry Lawson 'Two Larrikins' *Prose* i 231: 'The old woman might have had the knocker to keep away from the lush while I was in quod.'
2 Someone addicted to fault-finding, disparagement of what others praise [f. **knock** *v.* 2]
1923 Jack Moses *Beyond the City Gates* 154: The 'knocker' of his home town is, on this line of deduction, a 'knocker' of his Empire; a destroyer of thought, labour, and enterprise.
1961 *Meanjin* 399: 'For one terrible moment I thought you were going to be a knocker. In Merulga there's no place for knockers.'
1982 *Age* (Melbourne) 1 Jul. 12: Fellow Melburnians, how much longer are we going to honor our reputation for being the world's greatest 'knockers'?

knocker, on the Promptly, on demand, esp. in the expression 'cash on the knocker' [listed by Partridge as English slang for 'on credit']
1962 Jon Cleary *The Country of Marriage* 297: Sid was a man who wanted cash on the knocker.
1975 *Australian* 12 Aug. 9: 'He has to pay cash on the knocker for everything he buys, but he has to wait two or three months for payment from the big firms.'

know more than one's prayers see **prayers**

knuckle, go the To punch, fight
1944 John Devanny *By Tropic, Sea and Jungle* 160: I always got on well with the blacks, because I never went the knuckle on them, and never interfered with their women.
1959 D'Arcy Niland *The Big Smoke* 15: 'He reckoned you could go the knuckle a bit.'
1975 Richard Beilby *The Brown Land Crying* 156: 'Old Sam goin' the knuckle. Well, whaddya know.'

knuckle sandwich A punch in the mouth

1973 Alexander Buzo *Norm and Ahmed* 2: 'He tried to hang one on me at Leichhardt Oval once, so I administered a knuckle sandwich to him.'

koala bear 1 A member of the militia in World War II, who originally could not serve outside Australia: *derogatory*
1943 Baker 45: *Koala bear* A Militiaman. (War slang.)
1945 Baker 152: An attempt was made in October 1942 to pin the name *koala bears* on the militia, 'because you can't shoot at 'em and you can't export 'em,' but the term has small currency.
1984 *Sydney Morning Herald* 30 Jun. 13: Conscripts or 'chocos' or 'koalas' as they were called (chocos because they were supposed to be chocolate soldiers and koalas because they were not expected to be exported or shot at) were part of the militia force which met, stopped and drove back the Japanese landing at Milne Bay.
2 Nickname for an unappreciative male [cf. **root** *v.* 1]
1976 David Ireland *The Glass Canoe* 31: She christened the Koala Bear, who eats roots and leaves.
see **wombat** 2

kooka 1 Kookaburra [abbr.]
1923 Jack Moses *Beyond the City Gates* 18: The carolling of the magpie and the laughter of the kookas heralded dawn.
1968 David Ireland *The Chantic Bird* 123: A kooka was on the verandah sill, his cocked head very still.
1980 *West Australian* (Perth) 3 Mar. 6: The dear old 'kooka' should be removed from the protected list and then removed from Western Australia to give the small fry a chance in their own habitat.

2 The Kookaburra brand of cricket ball used in Australia, esp. in test cricket
1986 *Sun-Herald* 30 Nov. 85: A Kooka differs in four respects from the traditional ball: its core, its finish, its shape and, most important, its stitching.

koori An Aborigine (a term applied by Aborigines to themselves)
1834 L. E. Threlkeld *Australian Grammar* 87: Ko-re, Man, mankind.
1894 Ethel Turner *Seven Little Australians* 207: 'A tall young Koree who was coming that way saw the wipparoo, and with one blow from his strong nulla-nulla, which, being interpreted, meaneth a club, cut its head from its body.'
1978 Robert J. Merritt *The Cake Man* 12: 'See'n I'm a Kuri. The Australian Aborigine, that's who I am and what I am.'
1983 *Sydney Morning Herald* 7 Dec. 1: 'If a Koorie (Aboriginal) gets off a train at Central, he can come to Eveleigh Street and see someone he knows,' explained one prominent Aboriginal.

Kremlin, the See quot. 1981
1981 *Australian* 3 Nov. 7: Broken Hill takes its orders from the Kremlin ... Otherwise known as the Trades Hall, it is headquarters for the Barrier Industrial Council.

k's Kilometres
1984 Robert Caswell *Scales of Justice* 31: 'The cars could have driven twenty or thirty k's.'
1987 Howard Jacobson *In the Land of Oz* 326: 'Turn left at the lights,' she said, 'and go straight. If you're not in Cairns after 370 ks you're on the wrong road.'

L

LA Low alcohol [abbr.]
1979 *Sydney Morning Herald* 17 Dec. 1: It will be Sydney's first LA (low alcohol) Christmas. How will it go?

La Stupenda see **Stupenda**

lady, white see **white**

lady's waist A 5 or 7 oz glass of beer [f. shape]
1941 Baker 42: *Lady's waist* A gracefully shaped glass in which beer is served (2) Whence, the drink served.
1954 *Sydney Morning Herald* 8 Nov. 2: Calling for an appropriately named Sydney 'lady's waist' in Adelaide would

probably result in being hauled off to gaol.

1978 Ronald McKie *Bitter Bread* 85: He could not even afford a lady's waist, and that was the smallest glass you could buy.

lag *n.* 1 A convict or ex-convict, esp. if transported

1812 Vaux 249: *Lag* A convict under sentence of transportation. Ibid. 255: *Old lag A man or woman who has been transported, is so called on returning home, by those who are acquainted with the secret.*

1845 Charles Griffith *The Present State and Prospects of the Port Phillip District* 76: The old hands are men, who, having been formerly convicts, (or lags as they are generally termed) have become free by the expiration of their sentences.

2 **lagger** A police informer

1974 Robert Adamson and Bruce Hanford *Zimmer's Essay* 31: Maitland also houses the cretins, and the laggers who would be killed if they were left in cells among crims they had lagged upon.

1975 *Sydney Morning Herald* 3 Jul. 11: A lagger is someone who puts people in to the police.

lag, be lagged *v.* 1 To be transported as a convict; to be arrested and convicted

1812 Vaux 249: *Lag* To transport for seven years or upwards.

1847 Alexander Harris *Settlers and Convicts* ed. C. M. H. Clark (1953) 127: He was a great low-lived looking ruffian, not long 'lagged' (transported).

1879–80 Ned Kelly 'The Jerilderie Letter' in Max Brown *Australian Son* (1956) 283: It only aids the police to procure false witnesses and go whacks with men to steal horses and lag innocent men.

2 To inform on someone

1847 Alexander Harris *Settlers and Convicts* ed. C. M. H. Clark (1953) 187: 'I thought it was – (the overseer), and if it had been, I would have knocked him on the head and put him into a hollow log before he should be *lagged* (transported) me.' [The speaker had already been transported: the interpolated explanation is probably a misunderstanding.]

1973 Jim McNeil *The Chocolate Frog* 34: 'You won't never alter the fact that yer lagged yer mate! Be as sorry as yer like . . . but yer lagged 'im.'

lair A showoff; a flashily dressed person; a

term of general contempt (esp. 'mug lair') [see **lairy**]

1935 Kylie Tennant *Tiburon* 106: He was also considered something of a lare among the girls.

1944 *Coast to Coast 1943* 51: He saw a mug-lare with a yellow tie ogle the girl.

1958 Gavin Casey *Snowball* 208: He didn't want to dress like a lair, and he rejected the brilliant blazer and the too-pale grey slacks he'd bought.

1974 John Powers *The Last of the Knucklemen* 30: 'I don't get hustled into punch-ups with two-bob lairs.'

1979 *Sunday Telegraph* (Sydney) 25 Mar. 9: Prince Charles flew out of Perth for Canberra yesterday leaving behind a shaken co-driver. 'I'd reckon he'd be a lair on the road,' grinned Danny Tenardi, who rode with the prince in a huge iron ore truck.

lair around, lair up To behave like a lair, dress like a lair

1952 T. A. G. Hungerford *The Ridge and the River* 23: Having a bath and a shave, getting into clean clothes . . . to lare up at the dance.

1955 H. Drake-Brockman *Men Without Wives and Other Plays* 83: 'He's a trimmer. Always laring around. No good to girls.'

1975 Xavier Herbert *Poor Fellow My Country* 397: 'Better go and wash yo'self.' 'Sure,' said Nobby. 'Think I'm goin' leave the lairin' up all to you?'

lairize To behave like a lair

1953 Kylie Tennant *The Joyful Condemned* 22: 'She was ear-bashing me all over tea how you came lairizing round at our place like you owned it.'

1965 Wally Grout *My Country's 'Keeper* 139: Most people thought I did it 'lairising' – being a show-off, as we say at home. It seemed to them I had caught the ball and spilled it only when throwing it in the air, a favourite flourish of 'keepers.

1981 *Bulletin* 19 May 65: The crew raced for stretchers, first aid kits, splints. The mountain men looked on impassively. 'He was lairising,' they said.

lairy Flashily dressed; (of colours) bright and showy: *obsolescent* [? f. *leery* wideawake, knowing, 'fly' OED 1796]

[**1859** Hotten 58: *Leary* flash, or knowing. *Leary bloak* a person who dresses showily.]

1906 Edward Dyson *Fact'ry 'Ands* 160: Minnie piped something to the effect that she would disdain to be 'found drownded with a bloke what don-up 'is 'air dead leary', next morning the elaborate festoons had disappeared from Chiller's brow, and his hair was parted with the oily precision characteristic of Sunday-school superintendents and reputable young barbers.
1932 Leonard Mann *Flesh in Armour* 291: 'Who've we got?' 'Lairey Ridley.' They laughed . . . Captain Ridley had been a recognized hard-doer. His helmet was tilted rakishly over his left ear and his tunic and light coat were of the ultra fashionable style.
1949 Lawson Glassop *Lucky Palmer* 142: 'You ought to see the rug I got for Bunny. All done in my colours, red, green, and gold. Classy, eh? Some of the boys reckon it's too lairy, but I reckon it's a beaut.'
1975 Rodney Hall *A Place Among People* 13: Chick nodded in the direction of a newcomer heading for the bar, 'That's a lairy rig-out isn't it?'

lamb down To defraud a 'chequed up' bushman by keeping him drunk until his funds are supposedly exhausted [f. helping a ewe to give birth]
1869 Marcus Clarke *A Colonial City* ed. L. T. Hergenhan (1972) 162: *To lambdown* – that is, to make drunk and incapable – of course originated with some shepherd.
1888 E. Finn *Chronicles of Early Melbourne* ii 546: The publican's harvest consisted chiefly in fleecing (or 'lambing down', as it was technically termed) the stockmen, bullock-drivers, shepherds and shearers who made periodical trips to Melbourne for a 'spree' or to 'knock down their money'.
1902 Henry Lawson 'A Bush Publican's Lament' *Prose* i 469: 'Someone's sure to say he was lambed down an' cleaned out an' poisoned with bad Bush liquor at my place.'
1945 Tom Ronan *Strangers on the Ophir* 27: 'How the hell is the publican going to make a crust if the travellers won't let themselves be lambed down?'

land, man on the   see **man**

landing, the   The landing at Gallipoli on 25 April 1915
1916 *The Anzac Book* 1: 'The landing' By a Man of the Tenth [heading]
1945 Herbert M. Moran *Beyond the Hill*

Lies China 125: A mere boy from Heggity's Lane won a high decoration for his conduct at 'The Landing'.
1958 *Bulletin* 25 Jun. 10: He was 16 a few days before the Landing.
1983 T. A. G. Hungerford *Stories from Suburban Road* 99: He'd been Wounded at the Landing, and we all called him Soldier Tom.

larrikin   1   A young street rowdy [*larrikin* a mischievous or frolicsome youth EDD Suppl.]
1877 T. E. Argles *The Pilgrim* I viii 5: Here, packed like sardines, are a motley crew of that hideous excrescence of blind-alleys and right-of-ways – the Sydney Larrikin – and the female companion he so much affects.
1888 J. A. Froude *Oceana* 138: There is an idle set at the lower end of the scale: noisy, riotous scamps, who are impertinent to peaceful passengers, and make rows at theatres, a coarse-type version of the old Mohawks – they call them *Larrikins*.
1896 Henry Lawson 'A Visit of Condolence' *Prose* i 32: 'How dare you talk to me like that, you young larrikin? Be off! or I'll send for a policeman.'
1911 Louis Stone *Jonah* 67–8: They were dressed in the height of larrikin fashion – tight-fitting suits of dark cloth, soft black felt hats, and soft white shirts with new black mufflers round their neck in place of collars – for the larrikin taste in dress runs to a surprising neatness. But their boots were remarkable, fitting like a glove, with high heels and a wonderful ornament of perforated toe-caps and brass eyelet holes in the uppers.
1980 *West Australian* (Perth) 14 Jan. 3: After recent reports of larrikins and drunkenness at Rottnest, it was relatively quiet on the island this weekend, with no problems at the hotel.
2   In a more favourable sense, as though referring to authentically 'Australian' characteristics of non-conformism, irreverence, impudence (projected on to the larrikin as romanticized by Lawson and C. J. Dennis)
1974 *Sydney Morning Herald* 29 Jun. 11: The heroine with a larrikin streak [article on Joan Sutherland]
1983 *Bulletin* 30 Aug. 28: Certainly, Hinze's larrikin public image leaves a lot to be desired.

Larry Dooley   see **Dooley**

Larry, happy as Completely happy [origin obscure]

1905 Joseph Furphy *Rigby's Romance* ed. R. G. Howarth (1946) 62: 'But now that the adventure was drawing to an end, I found a peace of mind that all the old fogies on the river couldn't disturb. I was as happy as Larry.'

1910 Henry Lawson *Prose* ii 216: And Frank Myers – 'As happy as Larry in Castlebarry.'

1946 K. S. Prichard *The Roaring Nineties* 369: 'I'm as happy as Larry to be on the job again,' Alf exclaimed eagerly.

1983 Georgia Savage *Slate & Me and Blanche McBride* 128: He dumped me in the main street and went off as happy as Larry.

lash, have a To take part in something, make an attempt at

1941 Baker 42: *Lash at, have a* To make an attempt at (something).

1948 Ruth Park *Poor Man's Orange* 222: The blithe pipings of old men who safe [from the fight] up on their balconies, leaned over rails and exhorted everyone to 'ave a lash.

1970 Jack Hibberd *Who?* in Penguin *Plays* 146: 'We might even have a lash at some juicies ourselves.'

last shower, didn't come down in the see **shower**

later, see you An expression of farewell (not a proposal for a later meeting)

1942 Gavin Casey *It's Harder for Girls* 75: 'Well,' I said, 'I'd better get along.' 'Yes,' said Phil. 'I gotter pick up some packages. See you later.'

1948 William Beard *'Neath Austral Skies* 177: ''Ooray,' returned the drover, shaking Ralph's hand. 'See you later!'

1987 Howard Jacobson *In the Land of Oz* 317: The great distinctive Australian expression, 'See you later', which causes so much confusion when it's used to non-Australians who aren't expecting to see you again for another six months, if ever at all.

laughing jackass see **jackass**

lay-by *n. & v.* To secure an item for sale by making a deposit and paying instalments until the full price is paid, without interest charges, the goods being taken only when payment is complete

1930 *Sydney Morning Herald* 16 Oct. 4: Avail yourself of our Lay-by service. [Hordern's advertisement]

1932 *Sydney Morning Herald* 5 Dec. 1: A New Service! / 'Lay-By' at Farmer's / Lay-Away-a-Gift Plan! / Farmer's now assist with a practical, worryless 'Lay-By'.

Begin tomorrow and lay a gift away each day until your list is completed. Farmer's grant you ample time in which to pay the balance without any hardship on your purse. When your thoughts, in future, turn to 'Lay-By', think of Farmer's quality stocks now easily within your reach.

1978 *Sydney Morning Herald* 9 Jan. 1: The widespread acceptance of credit cards is marking the demise of laybys, which have dropped from 6 per cent of total sales to about 1 per cent.

lead a flock of homing pigeons see **homing**

leaping Lena Nickname of the train running from Birdum to Darwin

1940 Ernestine Hill *The Great Australian Loneliness* 124: There is a train a week in the Territory . . . They call it Leaping Lena. One terminus is Birdum, three shacks in the bush, and the other the first breaker of the Indian Ocean ... The Sentinel – Leaping Lena's official name – is a string of scarcely glorified cattle trucks.

1945 G. H. Johnston *Pacific Partner* 149: When Australia declared war, Leaping Lena had to be entrusted overnight with vital military movements. In fact, she became the only troop train in the Northern Territory.

1962 J. Marshall and R. Drysdale *Journey Among Men* 44: Jouncing from side to side in this machine, which he informed us was known as Leaping Lena or the Abortion Express.

leatherjacket A kind of pancake, made from dough and fried in fat

1846 G. H. Haydon *Five Years in Australia Felix* 151: A plentiful supply of 'leatherjackets' (dough fried in a pan).

1853 S. Mossman and T. Banister *Australia Visited and Revisited* 126: 'Leatherjackets' – An Australian bush term for a thin cake made of dough, and put into a pan to bake with some fat. The term is a very appropriate one, for tougher things cannot well be eaten.

1894 Henry Lawson *Prose* i 52: 'I wish I had just enough fat to make the pan siss; I'd treat myself to a leather-jacket; but it took three weeks' skimmin' to get enough for them theer dough-boys.'

leatherneck   A rouseabout in a shearing shed, etc.: *obsolescent*
   1898 *Bulletin* 1 Oct. 14: The rouseabouts [are] 'leathernecks'.
   1941 Baker 43: *Leather-neck* A station 'rouseabout'.

leghorn, white   see **white leghorn**

leg-opener   Alcohol, esp. wine or spirits, thought of as making women more vulnerable sexually
   1959 Dorothy Hewett *Bobbin Up* 93: 'Gotta bit of leg opener in the back seat of the heap.'
   1965 Leslie Haylen *Big Red* 133: There was a bottle of wine or two there for a birthday party or for the women at Christmas time. Shearers had been known to buy a bottle of Charlie's 'leg opener' to knock off a sheila.
   1979 Helen Garner *Age* (Melbourne) 23 Nov. 20: My mother had told me that Pimms No. 1 cup was 'what they called a leg-opener'. I only dimly visualised what this could mean.

lemony   Annoyed, peeved [? f. sourness]
   1941 Baker 31: *Go lemony at* To become angry, express anger towards someone.
   1944 Dal Stivens *The Courtship of Uncle Henry* 75: He's as lemony as hell when he opens the door and doesn't say a word to me.
   1968 Stuart Gore *Holy Smoke* 35: 'They went real lemony on 'im!'

lesbo   Variant of **leso**, q.v.
   1961 Xavier Herbert *Soldiers' Women* 235: 'She's a lesbo, I think. She took a shine to me right away.'

leso   A lesbian [abbr.]
   1976 Dorothy Hewett *The Tatty Hollow Story* 118: 'What's up with you? Are you a leso or something?'
   1978 *Australian* 24–5 Jun. Mag. 12: It all ends in the great united cry of 'Up the Lesos', shouted with beer cans held aloft in militant Les-Power salute.
   1983 *National Times* 22 Jul. i 37: 'And *Gay*! What an insult to the poofs and lezzos who made this country what it is today!'

level playing field   See quot.

1989 Alan Peterson *Sydney Morning Herald* 27 May 83: *a level playing field* is common now for a fair go.

licence, where did you get your   see **where**

lid, to dip one's lid   see **dip**

Life. Be In It   Slogan of a fitness campaign launched in November 1975 by Brian Dixon, Victorian Minister for Youth, Sport and Recreation, with a series of television commercials conceived by Phillip Adams and featuring the cartoon character **Norm** (q.v.), becoming a national campaign on 1 November 1977.
   1975 *Age* (Melbourne) 24 Nov. 2: The Minister for Youth, Sport and Recreation, Mr Dixon, yesterday launched a five year plan to make healthier Victorians ... The Life – Be In It campaign with a budget of $200,000 for the first stage up to June next year, is the first attempt in Australia to use modern marketing and advertising techniques to sell fitness ... Advertisements, pamphlets, posters, stickers and iron-on transfers all bearing the Life – Be In It logo will go throughout the State from today.
   1980 *Daily News* (Perth) 16 Dec. 44: A festive card has turned up for the Life. Be In It organisers ... Norm and his pals are shown with haloes, under the message, 'Hark the herald angels sing, Life. Be In It and do your thing'.

life, go for your   An expression of encouragement, as though guaranteeing no interference
   1928 Arthur Wright *A Good Recovery* 128: 'I'll get plenty of witnesses from the west as soon as ever they're wanted. Go for your life, cobber; I'll be ready.'
   1947 Gavin Casey *The Wits are Out* 27: 'I'd just as soon have sherry,' Myra said. 'Then get a bottle and go for your life,' Bill said.
   1988 James McClelland *Stirring the Possum* 240: Before he launched his takeover bid ... Murdoch called on Hawke and was apparently encouraged to go for his life.

lifesaver   Officially a member of a Life Saving Club; more colloquially one of the stereotypes of the Australian male
   1969 Thomas Jenkins *We Came to Australia* 174: You can see the Lifesavers sitting up in their tower. All volunteers, these bronzed young gods take turns to watch

from the top of a scaffolding tower for any-one in trouble in the sea. If they see a hand raised . . . they will swim to help, churning through the sea as if they were fitted with outboard motors.

1972 Geoff Morley *Jockey Rides Honest Race* 170: I could feel the soft fleshiness of you when my strong Australian life-saver arms held you, and it was strangely erotic.
1984 *West Australian* (Perth) 13 Jan. 23: Not all surf lifesavers are 6-foot, macho men with broad shoulders, bulging biceps and sun bleached hair. The WA beaches are also ser-viced by slim, lithe, athletic women.

life wasn't meant to be easy A saying associated with Malcolm Fraser, Australian Prime Minister (1975–83) [cf. the proverb 'Life is not all beer and skittles'; Longfellow, 'Life is real! Life is earnest' ('A Psalm of Life'); G. B. Shaw *Back to Methuselah* (World's Classics 1945) 263: 'Life is not meant to be easy, my child; but take courage: it can be delightful']
1970 *Australian* 1 Apr. 11: As a farmer in Victoria's Western District he [Mr Fraser] felt life was too easy. 'I don't believe life is meant to be easy.'
1981 *Times* (London) 16 Mar. 6: Perhaps he [Mr Fraser] has gained his most notorious reputation for either his obsession with the horror of Russian expansionism or for having once allegedly said 'life wasn't meant to be easy', which had been requoted hundreds of times. Did he actually say it? The Prime Min-ister smiled reflectively and said: 'I said something very like it. It's from *Back to Methuselah* by Bernard Shaw.'

light, come to ~ with To produce, as though from reserves [NZ 1917 OED]
1920 Thomas A. White *Diggers Abroad* 52: A look at their clothes brought three to light.
1956 Tom Ronan *Moleskin Midas* 260: 'He says if you don't come to light with a few quid soon he's goin' to summons you.'
1967 Alan O'Toole *The Racing Game* 31: 'Been waiting about over two years now for old Whisper to come to light with some of it.'

light on Sparsely supplied, of short weight [? abbr. of *light on the ground*]
1944 Lawson Glassop *We Were the Rats* 122: 'You're a bit light on too, aren't you?' 'Purely a temporary state of poverty, Rey-nolds old boy.'

1954 Tom Ronan *Vision Splendid* 76: 'A month later our rations were starting to get a bit light on.'
1973 Frank Huelin *Keep Moving* 133: 'Yous blokes waitin' f'r a feed?' the cook asked, thrusting his head out of the galley. 'Might be a bit light on.'
1980 *Daily News* (Perth) 16 Jul. 590: 'We have an abundance of depth in half-forwards, rucks, and wingers but we are light-on for back-up rovers.'

light on the hill, the The symbol of the socialist objective of the Australian Labor Party
1949 J. B. Chifley policy speech *Sydney Morning Herald* 15 Nov. 4: We do say that it is the duty and responsibility of the commu-nity, and particularly those more fortunately placed, to see that our less fortunate fellow citizens are protected from those shafts of fate which leave them helpless and without hope. This is the objective for which we are striving. It is, as I have said before, the bea-con, the light on the hill, to which our eyes are always turned, and to which our efforts are always directed.
1967 R. G. Menzies *Afternoon Light* 129: The Socialist objective, his 'light on the hill', must not be blotted out or obscured in this way.
1984 *Australian* 13 Apr. 6: Coalition fails to put a light on the hill [heading]

like Used to suggest approximation, tenta-tiveness in any statement
1945 Robert S. Close *Love Me Sailor* 129: 'That cask looks as if it might have gone bad like, sir,' said the cook.
1949 Lawson Glassop *Lucky Palmer* 153: 'That's the latest new-fangled subject they teach 'em at school – Sarcasm, a branch of English like.'
1979 Patrick White *The Twyborn Affair* 201: 'She could talk about their homes, their clothes – their divorces, by the hour. It was her religion like.'

lily on a dirt-tin, like a See quot. 1970
1970 Partridge 1391: *shag on a rock, standing out* – occ. *sitting – like a;* or . . . *like a lily on a dirt-tin;* or, rarely, . . . *like a beer bottle on the Coliseum.* These pic-turesque Australian similes, dating from, resp., ca. 1930, 1935, 1945, bear three dis-tinct senses: Lonely, as in 'He shot through and left me sitting like a shag on a rock'; conspicuous, as in 'It stood out like a lily on a

dirt-tin'; incongruous, as in 'He was as out of place as a beer bottle on the Coliseum.'
1982 Nancy Keesing *Lily on the Dustbin Slang of Australian Women and Families* [book title]

line 1 A line of patter, a 'technique', esp. in such expressions as 'doing a line', 'selling a line' for a male approach to women [also U.S.]
1933 Norman Lindsay *Saturdee* 242: 'I suppose you're going with Elsie Coote, aren't you?' 'Oh, yes, I'm doin' a line with her,' said Peter.
1951 Dymphna Cusack and Florence James *Come In Spinner* 364: 'My dear, he's a wow. And what a line! He calls me his little dream-dust and kisses me as though I was made of glass.'
1961 Nene Gare *The Fringe Dwellers* 286: 'I'm gunna do a line with the little gel that wants to go to Perth with me.'
2 A girl or woman, as an amorous prospect
1944 Lawson Glassop *We Were the Rats* 5: 'You seen that new blonde barmaid at the Royal? A real good line.'

Line, Brisbane see **Brisbane**

Lions, the 1 The Fitzroy A.F.L. team (from 1957)
1976 *Sunday Telegraph* (Sydney) 18 Apr. 55: The Lions led by eight points by half-time.
2 The Subiaco (W.A.) Australian Rules team
1980 *West Australian* (Perth) 19 May 59: Lions find their roar . . . Subiaco played with courage, confidence, and a fierce desire to win.
3 The Brisbane soccer team
1978 *Sunday Telegraph* (Sydney) 30 Apr. 94: Penalty miss lets Lions in.

lippie Lipstick [abbr.]
1940 Encountered in conversation.
1965 Hal Porter *The Cats of Venice* 139: 'Is there any lippy on the snowy tats?' And she bares her brilliant teeth at Mum like a poster Polynesian.
1983 *Sydney Morning Herald* 19 Dec. Guide 1: On radio, Miss Buttrose sounds as though she is wearing a sunfrock, bit of lippie and a pair of orthopaedic sandals.

Lithgow flash, the Miss Marjorie Jackson (b. 1932), of Lithgow N.S.W., winner of Gold

Medals for the 100 and 200 metres sprint at the Olympic Games in 1952.
1952 *Sydney Morning Herald* 10 Aug. 1: A pennant with the words 'Lithgow Flash' flew from the bonnet. At the rear was a banner with the words 'Hail, Marjorie Jackson'.
1979 *NT News* (Darwin) 22 Sep. 3: 'She was trying to get away,' he said. 'But with her weight and size, no one could compare her to the Lithgow Flash.'

little Aussie battler, the Anyone (preferably not tall) seen in the role of underdog, while exhibiting genuine Australian characteristics
1979 *Sun-Herald* 12 Aug. 54: I do not think one could seriously quarrel with Mr Murdoch's 'Australianism', even though I do find his 'little Aussie battler' act a bit rich.
1982 Blanche d'Alpuget *Robert J. Hawke* 285: His [Hawke's] very ordinariness – his flashy suits, flat voice, friendly manner and vulgar humour – had been among his greatest advantages with crowds, because he appeared so like everyone else, only more so: the quintessential Australian, the little Aussie battler.
1984 *Sunday Times* (Perth) 5 Aug. 96: Jon Sieben, 'the little Aussie battler' from Brisbane who was on the dole before the Olympics, beat the world yesterday in one of the greatest rags to riches upsets in Olympic swimming history.

Little Digger, the see **Digger**

little mate, my see **my**

liver, shit on the see **shit**

living black Following the Aboriginal way of life
1937 Ernestine Hill *The Great Australian Loneliness* 244: I stumbled upon . . . Mrs. Jackie Forbes, otherwise Witchetty, the only authentic case to date of a white woman 'living black' with the tribes.
1949 John K. Ewers *Harvest* 194: 'It's all right for a white boss in peace-time,' he said. 'But our boys [in New Guinea] are living black. They're not used to it.'
1977 Kevin Gilbert *Living Black* [book title]

lizard 1 A shepherd; a man maintaining boundary fences (and so crawling along or stretching out in the sun)
1908 Giles Seagram *Bushmen All* 127:

The term 'lizard' was one rather contemptuously applied to the shepherds by the horsemen.

1931 W. Hatfield *Sheepmates* 120–1: 'You're goin' in the camp, aren't you? – Not goin' lizardin'?' . . . 'Yes,' said Hallett, 'you'd be better out in the camp with me than crawlin' around a fence like a fly-catcher lizard.'

1937 Arthur Upfield *Winds of Evil* 174–5: 'What bloke wouldn't be depressed at coming down to a fence lizard! . . . Come down to fencin' and you want to know why a bloke's depressed.'

2 The handpiece of the shears [f. resemblance to a lizard]

1979 Keith Garvey *Tales of My Uncle Harry* 37: 'The sheep was dead in no time, and the young fellow panicked. He pulled the lizard out of gear, and rushes down the board.'

see **bogghi**

3 A flathead [f. resemblance]

1980 *Weekend News* (Perth) 27 Dec. 44: Some great flathead have been landed during the week. Touching the scales at well over a kilo the old lizard is one of the best table fish around.

4 The penis

1979 Steve Finnane *The game they play in heaven* 86: Most conversations are about women. A country voice cuts across the others: 'Did you give the lizard a run, mate?'

1987 Kathy Lette *Girls' Night Out* 167: 'You've really got him gallopin' the lizard. Been wankin' himself to death, poor bastard.'

lizard, flat out as a ~ drinking Working 'flat out', without a moment to spare

1944 Jean Devanny *By Tropic, Sea and Jungle* 227: The mother [kangaroo-rat] went one way and the young one another . . . It ran straight, as flat out as a lizard drinking.

1951 Dal Stivens *Jimmy Brockett* 70: The Wednesday of that week I was flat out like a lizard drinking when the phone rang.

1970 Max Harris *Australian* 10 Jan. 14: Have you ever copped the way those girls serve the community at the Sydney Telephone Exchange? Flat out like lizards drinking, all day long.

1984 *Age* (Melbourne) 25 Apr. 3: Myers, Coles and McDonald's stores all reported very brisk trading. One McDonald's franchise-holder said he had been 'as flat out as a lizard drinking water'.

lizards, stiffen (starve) the An exclamation of astonishment, protest, disbelief: sometimes 'Stone the crows and stiffen the lizards' (comic strip Australian)

1944 Lawson Glassop *We Were the Rats* 204: 'God starve the lizards,' said Eddie, 'another dud. Reckon half their bloody shells are duds.'

1965 Eric Lambert *The Long White Night* 89: 'Starve the bloody lizards!' breathed Clancy. 'Now I've seen the lot!'

load of, get a Take notice of, get an 'eyeful' of [U.S. 1929 OED]

1941 Baker 44: *Load of, get a* To take notice of, understand.

1959 Dorothy Hewett *Bobbin Up* 178: 'Get a load of that, when she bends over!'

1975 Les Ryan *The Shearers* 14: 'Hey Lofty! Get a load of that!' he said, as a blonde salesgirl in white uniform entered.

lob (in) To arrive, turn up

1915 C. J. Dennis *The Songs of a Sentimental Bloke* 56: 'Twas at a beano where I lobs along / To drown them memories o' fancied wrong.

1931 Vance Palmer *Separate Lives* 220–1: 'When I lob home,' said Chook, 'd'you know the first thing I'll do?'

1950 K. S. Prichard *Winged Seeds* 24: 'You never knew who'd lob into the camp.'

1983 *Australian* 9 Jul. Mag. 20: Ken Myer is nuts about all things Asian and will be interested in finding a place for Clive when he lobs back in the next month or so.

lock on with, to To fight (juvenile)

1959 Gerard Hamilton *Summer Glare* 107: When I looked around they were fighting – 'locked on' as we called it. Ibid. 108: 'Why did you lock on with Nancy this arvo?' I said.

logs, the Gaol: *obs*. [f. timber used in construction]

[**1802** David Collins *An Account of the English Colony in NSW* ed. Brian Fletcher (1975) ii 1: The governor . . . resolved on constructing a strong and capacious Log Prison at each of the towns of Sydney and Parramatta . . . he called upon every officer, settler and housekeeper within the above-mentioned districts, to furnish a certain number of logs for this purpose.]

1870 Marcus Clarke *His Natural Life* ed. S. Murray-Smith (1970) 784: 'Tommorow

morning – Mac, we'll have all these fellows comfortably in the logs.'
1903 Joseph Furphy *Such is Life* (1944) 369: 'It seems sort a' hard lines when a man's shoved in the logs for the best three months in the year for a thing he never done.'

lolly A sweet, esp. coloured [abbr. of *lollipop*]
1854 Catherine Spence *Clara Morison* (1971) 278: Fanny ran away to the nearest lolly shop, and all her brothers and sisters followed her.
1883 R. E. N. Twopeny *Town Life in Australia* 54: You will see babies without number left in the blazing sun, some hanging half-way out of their perambulators, others sucking large painted 'lollies' or green apples.
1900 Henry Lawson 'The Songs They Used to Sing' *Prose* i 37: We got lollies (those hard old red-and-white 'fish lollies' that grocers sent home with parcels of groceries).
1931 Vance Palmer *Separate Lives* 64: Coloured lollies in bottles that made the mouth water.

lollyboy The vendor of a tray of sweets and ice cream at the cinema
1951 Frank Hardy *Power Without Glory* 460: Above the mumble of five thousand voices could be heard the calls of the drink and lolly boys with their trays.
1971 G. Johnston *A Cartload of Clay* 45: The lights came on for interval and the lolly boys were shuffling raucous with their trays.
1981 *Sydney Morning Herald* 28 Nov. 40: The advertising man Bani McSpedden wore white. A white jacket with vanilla coloured revers, the kind lolly boys used to wear at Saturday matinees, white pants and white Gucci sneakers.

lolly, do the To lose one's temper, presence of mind
[**1859** Hotten 60: *Lolly* the head.]
1941 *Active Service* 111: We only hoped that Ernie would have enough common lolly to make some tea without burning it.
1959 Dorothy Hewett *Bobbin Up* 178: 'Keep an eye on me machine will you Jeanie. S'pose we'll haveta keep it goin' now Dick's doin' his lolly.'
1962 Criena Rohan *The Delinquents* 132: 'Don't start talking to me as though you

were a plain-clothes cop,' said Lola, 'or I'm liable to do the lolly.'
1983 *Australian* 26 Mar. Mag. 16: 'In Britain they had seen Richard Carleton's *Nationwide* interview with Hawke in which Hawke did his lolly.'

lollywater Soft drink, esp. if coloured
1945 Baker 231: *lolly-water* Soft drink. [as an example of derivation from pidgin]
1948 Sumner Locke Elliott *Rusty Bugles* in *Khaki, Bush and Bigotry* ed. Eunice Hanger (1968) 56: 'Only one bottle of lolly water per man.'
1953 *The Sunburnt Country* ed. Ian Bevan 127: The greatest indignity that ever befell the hapless defenders of Darwin was not the Japanese air-raids ... [but] that its garrison was issued not with beer, but with bottled cordial. This they christened, contemptuously, 'lolly water': and weed killer could not have been more detested.
1984 *Age* (Melbourne) 9 Jun. 11: The nearby sandwich shop sold only lolly water and Big M, neither of which I would be caught dead with.

London to a brick on A statement of betting odds (a brick = £10) popularized by the racing commentator Ken Howard (1914–76)
1965 Frank Hardy *The Yarns of Billy Borker* 108: 'Close: but Magger by a head,' the course announcer Ken Howard says, 'London to a brick on Magger.'
1974 *Sydney Morning Herald* 1 Jan. 2: A Howard trademark was his confident prediction of the winner in a tight finish – 'It's London to a brick on.' ... Where did the expression 'London to a brick on' come from? 'I don't know, but I probably picked it up in the billiards halls when I was younger,' he said. 'I used to meet a lot of Damon Runyon characters, listen to their talk and pick up some of their expressions.'
1983 *Australian* 11 May 15: A senior Customs official told the spirit industry recently that higher taxes were 'London to a brick on' unless a miracle happened.

long oats see **oats**

long paddock, the The stock route, as opposed to the stockowner's holding
1933 Acland 386: *Long paddock, the.* – Slang for the road. People turn stock out on it, or travel them on it, to get cheap grazing.
1979 *Age* (Melbourne) 8 Nov. 3: 'From

here [Queensland] to Victoria is the "long paddock". You put your cattle on the road for 180 days from Queensland to Echuca, and by the time they get there, they're nice and fat.'
1982 *Australian* 21 Sep. 9: They've put their stock in the long paddock – the old stock routes and the open road.

Loo, the Woolloomooloo, a Sydney suburb
1893 Daniel Healey *The Cornstalk* 39: Tim Bunyip was of Austral birth, / Born at the classic 'Loo.
1930 *Bulletin* 24 Dec. 42: 'I'm off back home to me job and the 'Loo.'
1959 Dorothy Hewett *Bobbin Up* 15: The shabby, genteel poverty of bed sits and bed and breakfast, running downhill into the slummy rabbit warrens of Paddo and the Loo.

look, take a ~ at A wry injunction intended to draw attention to the realities of a situation
1943 Dymphna Cusack *Morning Sacrifice* 27: 'Take a look at me, cherub, and remember that nothing comes to the woman who waits.'
1957 Ray Lawler *Summer of the Seventeenth Doll* 78: 'Glamorous nights! I mean – look at us.'
1959 Eleanor Dark *Lantana Lane* 21: 'By golly!' they will snort bitterly. 'Just take a look at us, and then take a look at the graziers! They have it all taped.'

loop, the The City Circle Loop Service of the Melbourne underground, linking Flinders St, Spencer St, Flagstaff, Museum and Parliament
1981 *Australian* 30 Apr. 9: Tedium-racked tourists have been known to ride the Paris Metro in the hope of exhilarating encounters with muggers or rapists. But what is that to the daily adventures offered by the Melbourne loop? Boarding it is an odyssey into the unknown, a grand roulette in which destination and arrival time is decided by a quirk of fate. The colourful cries of commuters making their third successive and non-stop circuit of the city have to be heard to be fully appreciated.

loppy A rouseabout
1898 *Bulletin* 1 Oct. 14: The rouseabouts [are] 'leathernecks', 'spoonbills', 'loppies', or 'Jacks'.

1964 H. P. Tritton *Time Means Tucker* 92: With only a couple of thousand to go 'Hughie' answered the prayers of the loppies with a fairly heavy shower.

Louie A fly, from 'Louie the Fly' in the Mortein commercials of the 1960s and later
1967 *Billy Borker Yarns Again* 2: 'Who's Louis the Fly?' 'The ringkeeper at Tommo's Two-up School; had buck teeth like the fly in the T.V. commercials. His mates used to say to him: 'I hate Mortein. Louis hates Mortein.'
1980 Peter Luck *This Fabulous Century* 347: The 'Louies' we see in television commercials are actually raised in science laboratories.

lousy Tight-fisted, parsimonious, stingy
1946 *Under the Atebrin Moon* 80: 'Mine's a brandy ... an' you hav'n' gotter by lousy with it, neither.'
1959 H. D. Williamson *Sammy Anderson Commercial Traveller* 135: 'Bottle of Swiller's, please,' he says. Right. 'Large or small?' you say. 'Small,' he says. He's a bit lousy, see.

lower than a snake's belly see **snake**

low heel A prostitute; a woman of easy morals
1939 Kylie Tennant *Foveaux* 311: In this crowd of low heels, quandongs and ripperty men, she looked at her ease and yet not of them.
1951 Dal Stivens *Jimmy Brockett* 56: Sheilas generally get round in pairs. If you do see a sort on her own it's an even chance she's a pro or a lowheel.
1965 John Beede *They Hosed Them Out* 193: My well-bred low-heel declared it was the first time she'd been done on the floor and voted it an exceedingly diverting experience.

lowie
1967 Kylie Tennant *Tell Morning This* 16: 'There's many a man thought he was going to stand over some little lowie and now he's either looking through bars or else he's mowing the lawn for her.'
1979 *Sydney Morning Herald* 3 Mar. 13: A group of bikies ... stagger in and out, beer cans in hand, chatting up the 'loweys' who hang about beside the entrance waiting to be picked up.

luck of Eric Connolly see **Connolly**

Lucky Country, the The Australia of the 1960s, from a book of that title (1964) by Donald Horne
1969 *Australian* 13 Sep. 11 C: Illegitimacy in the Lucky Country.
1970 Donald Horne *The Next Australia* 19: When I invented the phrase 'The Lucky Country' it was quickly misunderstood as it quickly caught on ... So a phrase that was intended as an ironic rebuke became a phrase of self-congratulation.
1990 R. J. Hawke *Business Review Weekly* 16 Mar. 45: No longer content to be the lucky country, Australia must become the clever country. [Labor policy speech]

Lucky Shop, the The TAB, in Victoria
1979 *Age* (Melbourne) 19 Dec. 24: He was intrigued by the number of people at the so-called 'Lucky Shop' frittering away all kinds of money on undisciplined quadrella betting.
1982 *Sun-Herald* 7 Mar. 144: Victoria's TAB (quaintly called lucky shops).

lucky, strike me A catch-phrase of the comedian Roy Rene ('Mo') and the title of a film in which he starred in 1935
[**1859** Hotten *Strike me lucky!* a simple form of an oath common amongst the lower orders when making a bargain, and appealing to their honour.]

lumber To arrest, imprison
1812 *Vaux* 251: A man apprehended, and sent to gaol, is said to be *lumbered*, or be *in lumber*, or to be in *Lombard street*.

1896 Edward Dyson *Rhymes from the Mines* 77: This job, I think, just saved me from being lumbered on the vag.
1951 Dal Stivens *Jimmy Brockett* 94: Every time I see a bloke being lumbered, I want to pitch in and help him. I've never had much time for cops.
1968 Stuart Gore *Holy Smoke* 58: 'That's about the strong of 'em ... cunnin' as sewer rats when they're trying to lumber someone under the Act.'

lurk 1 A dodge, a scheme, stratagem
[**1859** Hotten 61: *Lurk* A sham, swindle, or representation of feigned distress.]
1945 Tom Ronan *Strangers on the Ophir* 37: 'There was a good lurk picking up horses inside and working them through here and up to Camooweal.'
1951 Dal Stivens *Jimmy Brockett* 113: It might be a good lurk to float it into a company and get out while the going was good.
1980 *Mercury* (Hobart) 11 Apr. 5: Greedy medicos discover a new lurk.
lurk-man
1980 Clive James *Unreliable Memoires* 97: He was something of a lurk-man, but he had the additional quality of humour.
2 A job, occupation (close in implication to 1)
1915 C. J. Dennis *The Songs of a Sentimental Bloke* 20: I found 'er lurk / Was pastin' labels in a pickle joint.
1953 T. A. G. Hungerford *Riverslake* 189: 'I dunno why you don't take up teaching again. That's your lurk.'
1962 Alan Marshall *This is the Grass* 159: 'What's your lurk, anyway?' 'I just knock around,' I said ... I added, 'I'm a clerk.'

M

mad as a cut snake Out of one's mind; extremely annoyed
1920 Louis Esson 'The Drovers' in *Dead Timber* 34: 'The boss is as mad as a snake – he was flourishing his greenhide and cursing like thunder and lightning till we got 'em together again.'
1932 William Hatfield *Ginger Murdoch* 30: 'But you're mad!' said Mick, 'mad as a cut snake!'

1975 Don Townshend *Gland Time* 148: 'Never seen anythin' like it. Mad as a cut snake she was.'
see **silly as a two-bob watch**

mad as a meat-axe As for **mad as a cut snake**
1934 'Leslie Parker' *Trooper to the Southern Cross* (1966) 78: I was as wild as a meat-axe.

1946 *Coast to Coast 1945* 252: 'The cow's mad – mad as a meat-axe!' Jack said with conviction.
1984 Max Harris *Weekend Australian* 28 Jul. Mag. 4: John McArthur is ruled out. He was monomaniac, if not as mad as the proverbial meat-axe.

mad, he went ~ and they shot him Jocular reply to a request for anyone's whereabouts (World War II slang)
1944 Lawson Glassop *We Were the Rats* 47: 'I just came in for a yarn with Happy. Where is he?' 'If ya referrin' ter Mr Simpson he went mad and they shot him.'
1953 *The Sunburnt Country* ed. Ian Bevan 129: '*He went mad and they shot him*' is the routine answer to any superior seeking the whereabouts of a subordinate.
1975 *Woman's World* 8 Oct. 71: Father was unusually late home, having been held up in a traffic jam. Five-year-old-son, tired of waiting for Dad, announced, 'Perhaps he went mad and they shot him.'
see **went through like Speed Gordon, gone for a ride on the padre's bike, went for a crap and the sniper got him**

mad mick see **mick**

madwoman's custard (knitting, lunchbox), all over the place like a In complete disarray
1953 T. A. G. Hungerford *Riverslake* 18: 'What a joint! All over the place like a mad woman's knitting.'
1957 D'Arcy Niland *Call Me When the Cross Turns Over* 199: 'In the end he was blood from head to hocks and all over the place like a mad woman's custard.'
1973 Alexander Buzo *Norm and Ahmed in Three Plays* 10: 'I floored this bloody Kraut. Really laid him out. He was all over the place like a mad woman's lunch box.'

mag *v.* To talk: *derogatory* [1778–1885 OED]
1899 W. T. Goodge *Hits! Skits! and Jingles!* 168: In every town, you'll notice, there is someone with a rat, / Who forever keeps on magging of some place like Mulga Flat!
1941 Sarah Campion *Mo Burdekin* 35: 'Sure, they all mag – men 'n wimmen alike.'
1957 Nino Culotta *They're a Weird Mob* 19: 'I can't stand 'ere maggin' ter you all day.'

1973 Alexander Buzo *Norm and Ahmed* in *Three Plays* 23: 'Just to talk to someone, that's all I want. And when I do find someone to talk to, I just mag away like an old woman and ruin everything.'

mag *n.*
1913 C. J. Dennis *Backblock Ballads* 198: *Mag*, vulgar raillery.
1919 W. H. Downing *Digger Dialects* 33: *Mag* (vb. or n.) Chatter.
1934 Brian Penton *Landtakers* 382: 'I thought it was your mag I was hearin',' she said.
1961 Barbara Jefferis *Solo for Single Players* 30: There's this time every morning when they can get on their radios and have a good mag to each other.'

maginnis, a crooked A hold (as in wrestling) that puts an opponent at a complete disadvantage: *obs.* [derived by Baker (1966: 126) from a wrestler called McGinnis]
1900–10 O'Brien and Stephens: *putting the McGinnis on* To put an opponent or combatant hors-de-combat. A grip or hold that cannot be unlocked or resisted.
1903 Joseph Furphy *Such is Life* (1944) 15: 'You see, Tom,' he remarked to me, 'this fixter'll put the crooked maginnis on any fence from 'ere to 'ell.'

maggot, dead as a Inert, incapacitated, quite dead
1949 *As You Were* 156: 'Dead as a maggot,' Jerry assured him. 'An eighteen-pounder shell hit her fair in the guts.'
1954 Tom Ronan *Vision Splendid* 93: 'As dead as a maggot,' he commented.
1965 William Dick *A Bunch of Ratbags* 73: 'He's dead orright, dead as a maggot.'
1976 David Ireland *The Glass Canoe* 15: Someone hit one of Danny's mates with an iron bar. Dropped him cold as a maggot.

maggoty Angry, bad-tempered [*maggoty* freakish, whimsical OED 1678–1864]
1919 W. H. Downing *Digger Dialects* 33: *Maggotty* Angry.
1951 Dal Stivens *Jimmy Brockett* 31: I didn't need to, but I shaved every day and my old man made me maggotty by asking me one day, 'Do you shave up or down?'
1959 David Forrest *The Last Blue Sea* 74: 'He's down there in the R.A.P. going maggotty about doctors and Japs and boongs.'

magnoon Crazy, mad: Services slang in World War I and II [f. Arabic]

1918 *Kia Ora Coo-ee* 15 Mar. 9: A 'magnoon' Waler is next to ride with every chance of a fall.

1919 W. H. Downing *Digger Dialects* 32: *Macnoon* (Arab.) Mad.

1944 Lawson Glassop *We Were the Rats* 191: 'They're *magnoon* blokes who think it's an honour to die for their Fuehrer.'

magpie A halfcaste [urban Ab.]

1982 Brian Syron *Australian* 30 Aug. 9: 'It's difficult if you're a "magpie". You cop it from both sides.'

1988 Ruby Langford *Don't Take Your Love to Town* 231: It was about an Aboriginal man, his white wife and their 'magpie' son.

Magpies, the 1 in N.S.W., the Western Suburbs Rugby League team [f. black and white colours]

1976 *Sunday Telegraph* (Sydney) 11 Apr. 58: Magpies breakfast on the Berries.

2 In Victoria, the Collingwood A.F.L. team

1963 Lou Richards *Boots and All!* 12: I was born into a Magpie family and reared in the Magpie nest, kicking tin cans and paper footballs around the streets of Collingwood and Abbotsford.

1974 *Sunday Telegraph* (Sydney) 8 Sep. 84: Magpies get home easily.

3 In S.A., the Port Adelaide Australian Rules club

1978 *Sunday Telegraph* (Sydney) 17 Sep. 103: Port Get Up in Late Burst [heading] The Magpies were 28 points down going into the last quarter, but stormed home.

4 In Queensland, the Southern Suburbs Rugby League club

1979 *Courier-Mail* (Brisbane) 16 Apr. 17: Young Magpie centre Mal Meninga calmly booted a goal to give Souths a 9–7 win.

5 In N.T., the North Darwin Australian Rules club

1979 *NT News* (Darwin) 19 Nov. 23: Magpies flutter to earth . . . North's slogan for the season 'Fly high with the Magpies' looks to be degenerating into a sick joke.

6 In Tasmania, the Glenorchy Australian Rules club

1980 *Mercury* (Hobart) 25 Jan. 23: New secretary for Magpies [heading] Mr Stan Waler is the new secretary of the Glenorchy Football Club.

mail Rumour, report, esp. a racing tip

1966 Baker 77: Along with the variations *mulga mail* (or *wire*), it can mean a source of rumour.

1975 *Bulletin* 26 Apr. 44: 'His mail was that if I didn't weigh in soon I'd be gathered for sure.'

1984 *Age* (Melbourne) 19 Sep. 38: 'I had never heard of the horse [Fine Cotton] before. I didn't receive any special "mail" on it, but I've gone to races all my life – money speaks all languages.'

Mainland, the Australia, from a Tasmanian standpoint

1934 Thomas Wood *Cobbers* 164: They are tied to Australia – 'the mainland', they call it . . . 'the mainland' is an object of suspicion, envy, and dislike.

1958 Christopher Koch *The Boys in the Island* 15: He lived in an island. At six years old he knew about that. He heard it at school, and knew about it from Uncle Charlie's talk about the Mainland, Australia.

1975 Don Townshend *Gland Time* 33: The mainland was foreign to him and always would be foreign. On Monday morning he flew back to Tasmania.

maintain the rage see **rage**

Maitland, Dean A silent person [f. the film *The Silence of Dean Maitland*, 1914 and 1934, based on the novel by Maxwell Grey]

1948 Sumner Locke Elliott *Rusty Bugles* in *Khaki, Bush and Bigotry* ed. Eunice Hanger (1968) 88: *Ot:* Poor old Dean Maitland . . . *Vic:* There must have been a lot on his mind. I never saw him speak the whole time he was here.

1969 R. S. Whitington *The Quiet Australian* 98: The twenty-two players were far too tense to talk during the twenty-minute break. Twenty-two 'Dean Maitlands' sipped their tea in silence.

makings, the Tobacco and cigarette papers [N. Amer. 1905 OED]

1938 Eric Lowe *Salute to Freedom* 420: He pulled the inevitable 'makings' from his tunic pocket and started to roll a cigarette.

1958 H. D. Williamson *The Sunlit Plain* 17: 'Got the makings on you?' Eddie . . . handed over a tin of tobacco and papers.

1981 Maxwell Grant *Inherit the Sun* 327: He put his firearm down and took the makings from his shorts pocket.

Malabar Hilton Long Bay gaol, N.S.W.
1988 Clive Galea *Slipper* 86: 'If ever two young tearaways were destined for a return visit to the Malabar Hilton it was us.'

mallee, the Equivalent to 'the scrub' in expressions like 'take to the mallee' [f. the mallee scrub in Victoria]
1958 E. O. Schlunke *The Village Hampden* 127: 'They're going to lynch you, Rogerson,' Harry told him, grinning. 'You'd better take to the mallee before they come for you.'

Mallee bull, fit as a Extremely fit; Victorian [see quot. 1974]
1962 John Morrison *Twenty-three* 163: 'How's Bubby?' 'Fit as a Mallee bull! Got another tooth . . .'
1974 Jim McNeil *How Does Your Garden Grow* 45: *Mick*: Ha! (*Posing*) Fit as a mallee bull! Ibid. 141: *A mallee bull* is thus a beast toughened by spartan living conditions.
1981 *Sun-Herald* 14 Jun. 151: He looked as fit as a Mallee bull.

mallee root A prostitute [rhyming slang]
1941 Baker 45: *Mallee root* A prostitute.

Malley's cow See quot.: N.T.
1951 Ernestine Hill *The Territory* 441: 'By the look o' the sun I better get a move on, missus. I'm Malley's Cow. I'm a goner!' Ibid. 445: *Malley's Cow** A person gone away. *Back in Monaro folklore one Malley in a mustering-camp was told to hold a particular cow. When the boss came back and asked for it, Malley grinned. 'She's a goner,' he said.

Maluka, the The chief, the boss [Ab.]
1905 Jeannie Gunn *The Little Black Princess* 3: I was 'the Missus' from the homestead, and with the Boss, or 'Maluka' (as the blacks always called him), was 'out bush', camping near the river.
1928 Martin Boyd *The Montforts* 238: 'You'd better come and see the Maluka.' 'What's that?' ventured Raoul. 'It's aboriginal for headmaster.'
1971 Keith Willey *Boss Drover* 140: An aboriginal with me said: 'Pickum grass, Maluka.'
1983 *NT News* (Darwin) 1 Jan. 6: Anthony Thomas is a quiet, self-effacing man. And that is probably the reason the Chief Minister overlooked him in the realignment of responsibilities. A source close to the

Maluka told me he was unaware of the fact that Anthony is a vet.

man in white see **white**

man, the old see **old**

man on the land, the A rural producer (other than an employee on wages). The phrase is emotionally toned, allowing both the implication that he is the possessor of staunch qualities, and that he may be acquisitive of subsidies and given to whingeing. The Man on the Land was the heading to a column in the *Bulletin* for many years.
1917 Robert D. Barton *Reminiscences of an Australian Pioneer* viii: The greatest trouble that the man on the land has had . . . is the shifting policy of governments with regard to our various holdings.
1923 Jack Moses *Beyond the City Gates* 23: The 'man on the land', in pursuit of his daily vocation, has much to contend with, hardships to encounter that would break the spirit of the average man.
1940 Ion L. Idriess *Lightning Ridge* 128: Every drover knows that the most suspicious man in the world is the Man on the Land – when travelling stock are about.
1984 *Bulletin* 13 Mar. 102: We heard a lot of eloquence from farmers about the many fine qualities of the 'man on the land', how he was morally superior to city slickers and how dedicated he was to the production of export income – not for his but for the country's good.

manatj As for **monarch, monaych** q.v.
1982 Jack Davis *The Dreamers* 143: *Manatj*, police, literally 'black cockatoo'. The dark peakcap uniforms of the early police caused them to be compared to this bird.

manchester Used as *n.* and *adj.* to apply to Manchester goods (i.e. cotton materials) from at least the 1920s
1955 *Bulletin* 2 Feb. 56: Special bargain offers from our Manchester section (advt)
1969 Thomas Jenkins *We Came to Australia* 124: Light bulbs were called globes and the linen department the manchester department.
1983 Max Harris *Bulletin* 29 Nov. 90: My wife experienced an episode of some confusion, if not embarrassment, in the John Lewis department store in London recently. She had just concluded a transaction and was

asked if she would take her purchase with her. 'No,' she said, 'just hold it. I have to go to manchester but I'll be back in a while.' A baffled sales assistant informed madam that it was quite a long way to Manchester. My wife insisted that it was merely on the second floor. The assistant looked as if she should be calling in some nice men with white coats to take her away.

mangle A bicycle (juvenile) *obs.* [? f. humorous resemblance]
1941 Baker 45: *Mangle* A bicycle
1965 Graham McInnes *The Road to Gundagai* 122: 'Where's the grid?' 'My bike!' 'Yeah, the old mangle; isn't this where we left it?' [recalling the 1920s]

Mankad, to To run out a batsman at the non-striker's end, for moving up the wicket before the ball has been bowled (Vinoo Mankad dismissed W. A. Brown in this way in the 1947/8 test series)
1982 *Australian* 17 Nov. 22: In the 1978–79 Perth Test against Pakistan, Sikander Bakht backed up too far and was 'Mankaded' by Alan Hurst.
1983 *Australian* 1 Oct. 44: When Devlin again left his crease, Pascoe twisted and threatened to 'Mankad' the batsman.

mantle of safety The Rev. John Flynn's phrase for the protection given to outback Australia by the Flying Doctor service.
1927 *The Inlander* (ed. John Flynn) Oct. 70: To all who have battled for this 'Mantle of Safety' to spread over isolated pioneers we tender our sincerest gratitude.
1947 Ernestine Hill *Flying Doctor Calling* 146: This should add a very sympathetic touch to the 'Mantle of Safety' already provided by the presence of the doctor and the transceiver sets.
1961 Noni Braham *The Interloper* 2: 'The Flying Doctor spreads a mantle of safety over the whole area.'

Maoriland New Zealand [f. Maoris as the original inhabitants]
1868 J. R. Houlding *Australian Tales* 207: Perhaps, seeing so many others going to Maori-land, stimulated me to hasten away too.
1896 Henry Lawson 'Steelman's Pupil' *Prose* i 209: They battled round together in the North Island of Maoriland for a couple of years.
1930 *Bulletin* 2 Jul. 11: Everyone had

contributed at least one good lie except the man from Maoriland.

map, throw a See quot. 1945
1945 Baker 135: *throw a map, to* To be sick.
1978 *Australian* 25 Mar. Mag. 5: I failed to find 'throw a map', a term much in use in the 'fifties. Persistent map-throwers were known as cartographers.

marble, to make one's ~ good To make the grade, confirm or improve one's status or prospects (cf. *alley*) [N.Z. 1926 OED]
1950 Brian James *The Advancement of Spencer Button* 162: 'He's trying to make his marble good, all right.'
1963 Don Crick *Martin Place* 223: 'Take my tip, if you wanter make your marble good: say nothing.'

marble, to pass in one's To give up, die
1908 *Australian Magazine* 1 Nov. 1250: Instead of dying you can 'chuck a seven', 'pass in your marble', or 'peg out'.
1916 Diary 31 Oct. cit. Bill Gammage *The Broken Years* (1974) 173: I absolutely threw my marble in and if it wasn't for the thought that I was on active service I think I would have wasted a cartridge on myself.
1961 George Farwell *Vanishing Australians* 77: He . . . went into a coma, and it was some time before the coves he was shouting woke up that he'd really passed in his marble.
see **alley** 2

Marble Bar, till it rains in Indefinitely [f. W.A. town of low rainfall]
1943 Douglas Stewart *Ned Kelly* in *Four Plays* (1956) 172: 'And we'd have held this country against the troopers / Till it rains in Marble Bar!'

March, the The march of ex-servicemen on Anzac Day
1945 Cecil Mann *The River* 136: Clarkey is not in the March this year.
1962 Alan Seymour *The One Day of the Year* 79: 'We started at a pub in King Street straight after the march.'

Mardi Gras A carnival held at any time of the year [f. *Mardi Gras* (Shrove Tuesday) as a festival]
1958 *Bulletin* 22 Jan. 10: The popular translation is just *Mardi Gras* = 'beano'.

1977 *Sunday Telegraph* (Sydney) 16 Jan. 76: A closing highlight of the Festival of Sydney will be a huge Mardi Gras at the Haymarket on the night of Saturday, January 29.
1984 *Australian* 3 Feb. 7: The Rev. Troy D. Perry author of *The Lord is my Shepherd and He Knows I'm Gay*, will be special guest at Sydney's Mardi Gras ... All the Mardi Gras needs now is a gay ayatollah.

marines, dead see **dead marines**

mark, marking Abbr. of 'earmark', generalized to cover the whole process of earmarking, docking and castrating lambs; also a euphemism for 'castrate'
1826 Let. in *Mortmain* ed. E. Fitz-Symonds (1977) 125–6: Some of the stolen sheep newly ear marked returned to the flock and claimed their mothers ... For the sheep delivered to Lindsey and Jenkins your Memorialist received cattle from the Herd of their Master Mr. Lord, and was to have had some more after the cutting and marking had finished.
1883 Edward M. Curr *Recollections of Squatting in Victoria* 153: Shortly after taking charge I marked two thousand lambs.
1911 E. S. Sorenson *Life in the Australian Backblocks* 143: When the pens are full there is a blessed respite while the lambs are marked ... The markers are ranged on the outside of the pen, and operate on the lambs as they are dumped on the rail by the catchers, who hold a foreleg and a hindleg in each hand. Knives and teeth are used alternately by the operators.
1982 *Sydney Morning Herald* 8 May 13: As he signed the last departmental file yesterday ... Killen remembered the blessed relief he felt long ago at the end of a long, hot morning marking (castrating) a couple of thousand lambs the old way (dragging them out with your teeth).

market, go to To behave in a violent or angry way (superseded by **go to town**)
1870 Rolf Boldrewood 'Shearing in Riverina' *Town and Country Journal* 12 Nov. 13: He slackens the rein, and saying, 'Go to market now old fellow,' sits the wild plunge of the colt like a Mexican vaquero.
1898 *Bulletin* 17 Dec. Red Page: To *get narked* is to lose your temper; also expressed by *getting dead wet* or *going to market*.
1948 K. S. Prichard *Golden Miles* 29: 'She

goes to market when I get shickered,' Bill admitted.
1951 Frank Hardy *Power Without Glory* 35: 'I have me instructions, so it's no use going to market on me.'

Maroons, the 1 A sporting team representing the state of Queensland, esp. in Rugby League football [f. team colours]
1973 *Sydney Morning Herald* 12 Jul. 13: A Blue Day for the Maroons.
2 Former nickname of the Fitzroy A.F.L. club
1984 Lou Richards *Sun* (Melbourne) 9 Mar. 31: When I first played against them they were known as the Maroons.

Marvellous Melbourne Melbourne as described by G. A. Sala (see quot. 1885)
1885 George Augustus Sala 'The Land Of The Golden Fleece' VII *The Argus* 8 Aug. 5: Life is a perpetual perhaps. Yet I am enabled to be tolerably well assured that it was on the 17th March in the present year of grace, 1885, that I made my first entrance, shortly before high noon, into Marvellous Melbourne.
1891 Edward Kinglake *The Australian at Home* 145: Marvellous Melbourne, but fifty years old, grown to be bigger than its sister Sydney which is twice its age, is justly entitled to make a place among the cities of the world of first rank and importance.
1910 *Marvellous Melbourne – Queen City of the South* [title of film screened at Spencer's Modern Picture Theatre, Melbourne, 22 Nov.]
1984 *Age* (Melbourne) 10 Apr. 23: Somewhat tensely clutching his SR45 emergency life-support system, our columnist Garrie Hutchinson begins his historic hike along Marvellous Melbourne's southeastern trunk sewer.

mary A girl or woman [Pidgin]
1876 A. J. Boyd *Old Colonials* (1882) 234: They [the natives] fail to comprehend how it is that a Chinaman who is 'baal white fellow' can get a white woman for a wife. They say, 'Chinaman got'im white Mary; blackfellow get'im white Mary.'
1919 W. H. Downing *Digger Dialects* 56: *Mary* Woman [under heading Papua (Pidgin English)]
1931 Vance Palmer *Separate Lives* 68: 'White mary no walk about all day. She belonga one boss, sit down longa one house.'
1956 Tom Ronan *Moleskin Midas* 326:

'Harness up the buggy and take this Mary back to town.'

mate 1 A working partner; an habitual companion; a fellow-participant in some corporate activity (always a man)
[**1859** Hotten 62: *Mates* The term a coster or low person applies to a friend, partner or companion. 'Me and my mate' did so and so, is a common phrase with a low Londoner.]
1845 C. Griffith *The Present State . . . of Port Phillip* 79: Two [bushworkers] generally travel together, who are called mates; they are partners, and divide all their earnings.
1864 James Armour *The Diggings, the Bush and Melbourne* 23: After much talk about the perfidy of former mates, he said that . . . he would take me for a partner.
1899 Henry Lawson 'Crime in the Bush' *Prose* ii 35: Then there is the unprovoked, unpremeditated, passionless, and almost inexplicable bush murder, when two mates have lived together in the bush for years, until they can pass days and weeks without exchanging a word.
1953 *The Sunburnt Country* ed. Ian Bevan 126: No cry rings louder in the A.I.F. than this . . . 'Don't bludge on your mates'.
1960 Donald McLean *The Roaring Days* 1: 'My mate' is always a man. A female may be my sheila, my bird, my charley, my good sort, my hot-drop, my judy or my wife, but she is never 'my mate'.
1983 *Sydney Morning Herald* 13 Jun. 12: Mr Hayden observed that the word 'mate' is 'an expression of deep loyal male friendship', but in NSW 'it's like the mafia presenting you with a bunch of flowers'.
2 As a mode of address, indicating equality and friendliness
1852 Lord Robert Cecil *Goldfields Diary* (1935) 36: When the diggers address a policeman in uniform they always call him 'Sir', but they always address a fellow in a blue shirt with a carbine as 'Mate'. 'Mate' is the ordinary popular form of allocution in these colonies.
1862 Arthur Polehampton *Kangaroo Land* 99: A man, who greeted me after the fashion of the Bush, with a 'Good day, mate'.
1981 *Age* (Melbourne) 20 Jul. 9: Lear, disgusted with the nature of man, cries out: 'Let copulation thrive'. From the back stalls came a shout of 'Too bloody right mate' and the audience went wild.
3 As a neutral or hostile mode of address, to someone not an acquaintance

1855 Rafaello Carboni *The Eureka Stockade* ed. Geoffrey Serle (1969) 5: 'Your licence, mate,' was the peremptory question from a six-foot fellow in a blue shirt, thick boots, the face of a ruffian armed with a carbine and fixed bayonet.
1944 Lawson Glassop *We Were the Rats* 75: 'I'm not looking for trouble.' 'Yer may not be bloody well lookin' fer it, mate, but yer'll bloody well get it.'
1974 *Sydney Morning Herald* 14 Feb. 7: At 8.26 that evening a train arrived at Gosford. The destination sign on the platform was not shown. I asked a station attendant (attired in a dirty open-necked shirt and trousers, recognizable only by a dirty cap) if the train was the North-West Mail. 'I wouldn't have a clue, mate,' was the reply.

mate, my little   see **my**

mates with, to be   To have as a mate [N.Z. 1880 OED]
1900 See **rush**
1945 Cecil Mann *The River* 23: Odd little bloke; funny being mates with him.
1976 Henry Gullett *Not as a Duty Only* 8: Our truck driver, Brockley, usually marched with this section when he was not driving because he was mates with Vic Maloney and Joe.

mateship   The fellowship implied in **mate** 1, and given currency by Henry Lawson: not really a colloquialism [OED 1593]
1894 Henry Lawson 'The Cant and Dirt of Labor Literature' *Prose* ii 27: When our ideal of 'mateship' is realised, the monopolists will not be able to hold the land from us.
1932 Ion L. Idriess *Flynn of the Inland* 262: The preacher appealed to his hearers to stand up to the claims of mateship, to help all hands as well as their mates, just as does the Great Mate to whom all men are mates.
1959 Dorothy Hewett *Bobbin Up* 124: There was mateship, sharing a billy of bitter-black tea, a smoke and a yarn.
1973 Max Harris *The Angry Eye* 77: Historians have come to accept fairly calmly the notion that the Australian national philosophy of 'mateship' emerged from what was perhaps the world's only homosexual social ordering of things.

Matilda   A swag [f. woman's name: origin otherwise obscure. See Richard Magoffin *Fair Dinkum Matilda* (1973)]

1893 Henry Lawson 'Some Popular Australian Mistakes' *Prose* ii 24: A swag is not generally referred to as a 'bluey' or 'Matilda' – it is *called* a 'swag'.
1910 John X. Cameron *The Spell of the Bush* 55: 'I sling Matilda on my back and steer whichever way she slews me.' 'Matilda!' repeated O'Carroll. 'Bluey.'
1939 R. H. Croll *I Recall* 81: Mostly to me that has meant tramping the bush; often it has implied carrying Matilda, the swag.
1962 J. Marshall and R. Drysdale *Journey Among Men* 116: It was good to stretch out in the arms of Matilda at the end of the day, and slowly smoke a cigarette. Ibid. 146: We unrolled our Matildas between the dunes.

Matilda, waltzing Carrying the swag, an expression given currency by A. B. Paterson's poem with this title, composed in 1895 and published in *Saltbush Bill J.P.* (1917), since achieving the status of an unofficial national anthem
1893 Henry Lawson 'Some Popular Australian Mistakes' *Prose* ii 24: No bushman thinks of 'going on the wallaby' of 'walking Matilda', or 'padding the hoof'; he goes on the track – when forced to it.
1917 A. B. Paterson *Saltbush Bill J.P.* 23: Who'll come a-waltzing Matilda with me?
1934 Brian Penton *Landtakers* 387: 'Didn't we waltz Matilda together, work a claim together, and sweat our guts out together?'
1944 M. J. O'Reilly *Bowyangs and Boomerangs* 45: There was a vast difference between those swaggies of the early goldfields and the professionals found 'Waltzing Matilda' along the banks of the Darling, Murray or Murrumbidgee.

matinee Sex in the day time
1971 Frank Hardy *The Outcasts of Foolgarah* 3: 'Lately I'd just as soon have a cold beer and a hot matinee with old Florrie while the kids are at Sunday school.'
1980 Bob Herbert *No Names . . . No Pack Drill* 63: JOYCIE: You 'aven't made your bed. KATHY: I know. JOYCIE: (*giggling*) Have a matinee, did you?

Mavourneen, Kathleen see **Kath**

Mayblooms, the Former nickname of the Hawthorn A.F.L. club
1950 *Sun* (Melbourne) 8 Apr. 3: It was Cazaly who changed Hawthorn's nickname from the 'Mayblooms' to the 'Hawks'.

mean, so ~ he wouldn't give you a light for your pipe at a bushfire, wouldn't give a dog a drink at his mirage, wouldn't shout if a shark bit him, wouldn't give you a wave if he owned the ocean, wouldn't give you a fright if he was a ghost, wouldn't give you a shock if he owned the powerhouse, wouldn't give a rat a railway pie; still has his lunch money from school; with short arms and long pockets
1919 A. B. Paterson 'The Cook's Dog' in *Song of the Pen* (1983) 404: 'They reckon he's that mean he wouldn't give you a light for your pipe at a bushfire.'
1936 A. B. Paterson 'The Shearer's Colt' in *Song of the Pen* (1983) 707: 'He's that mean he wouldn't give a dog a drink at his mirage.'
1976 Sam Weller *Bastards I have met* 2: If he owned the ocean, he wouldn't give you a wave.
1981 *Daily Mirror* (Sydney) 23 Jan. 36: Albert wouldn't shout if a shark bit him.
1981 *National Times* 25 Jan. 23: 'He'd be too mean to give you a fright if he was a ghost.'
1983 *Sun-Herald* 23 Oct. 82: Australians don't usually rate railway tucker highly. 'He's so mean he wouldn't give a rat a railway pie', is a popular way of saying someone is parsimonious.
1984 *Toorak Sunday* 1 Jul. 24: My lunch was $10, and I forgot to tip the waiter. It's not true, as the waiter probably thinks, that I have short arms and long pockets in my Mike Treloar tailor-made suits.

meanie, grey see **grey meanie**

meat-axe, mad as a see **mad**

meat pie, as Australian as a Unmistakably Australian [f. prominence of meat pie in Australian diet and 'American as apple-pie']
1972 *Sunday Australian* 16 Apr. 4: Apart from his name and his forebears, Barassi with his wide grin and fierce desire to win is as Australian as a meat pie.
1981 Vivian Smith *Oxford History of Australian Literature* 420: In some poems he uses a dramatic voice which is Australian as a meat pie.
1984 *Sun-Herald* 4 Mar. 15: The days of the Holden being as Australian as meat pies or koalas are finished.

Mediterranean back See quot. 1981

1981 *Australian* 20 Apr. 7: For afflictions such as vertebrate disease – known by many as 'Greek back' or 'Mediterranean back' – Greeks are 15 times more likely to be disabled compared with Australians.
1982 Nancy Keesing *Lily on the Dustbin* 51: There are racist overtones to the ... 'Mediterranean back' which denotes derisive suspicion about a back-ache.

Melba, to do a   To make a habit of returning from retirement, in a number of 'farewell' performances [f. Dame Nellie Melba 1861–1931]
[**1933** Samuel Griffiths *A Rolling Stone on the Turf* 97: Crozier has become as noted as a certain famous singer for the number of his 'final' appearances.]
1971 *Australian* 20 Feb. 22: The later years were marked by a seemingly endless round of farewell performances. 'Doing a Melba', they call it.
1981 *Sunday Mail* (Brisbane) 20 Sep. 60: Scamp has been known to do a 'Melba' before. In fact he has announced his retirement four times, and yesterday's exclusive to the Sunday Mail was his fifth retirement.

Melbourne, Marvellous see **Marvellous**

merchant   Used similarly to 'artist', in combinations like 'stand over merchant', 'king-hit merchant', usually with some derogatory suggestion
1944 Lawson Glassop *We Were the Rats* 133: 'Just a top-off merchant, that's all he is.'
1951 Dymphna Cusack and Florence James *Come In Spinner* 253: 'He was nothing but a bloody stoush merchant any way.'
1954 T. A. G. Hungerford *Sowers of the Wind* 9: 'I'm no lurk merchant, Mark,' Craigie said placidly.
1965 *The Tracks We Travel* ed. L. Haylen 122: 'If these panic-merchants only knew when to leave alone!'
1973 John Powers *The Last of the Knucklemen* 17: 'You're not hired to be smart-alecs and talk-back merchants.'

merino, pure   An early colonist priding himself on his freedom from the convict taint; a member of the most affluent and socially prominent class [f. breed of sheep]
1827 *Monitor* 13 Jan. 2: A round-about story has come to us ... which, as it operates greatly to the credit of the pure Merino Bank, for which we have such an ardent regard ... we shall here detail for the amusement of our readers.
1827 P. Cunningham *Two Years in New South Wales* ii 116: Next, we have ... such as have legal reasons for visiting this colony; and ... such as are free from that stigma. The *pure Merinos* are a variety of the latter species, who pride themselves on being of the *purest blood* in the colony.
1936 Miles Franklin *All That Swagger* 262: Norah was consulted, being married and of the pure merino squattocracy.
1954 Tom Ronan *Vision Splendid* 113: 'Old Mentmore ... is one of your pure merino sportsmen: member of all the big racing clubs down south.'

metho   Methylated spirits [abbr.]
1935 Kylie Tennant *Tiburon* 23: The two metho-drinkers were escorted out firmly.
1949 Judith Wright *Woman to Man* 35: 'Metho Drinker' [poem title]
1950 Brian James *The Advancement of Spencer Button* 168: A drinking party ... had taken a supply of spirits – mostly 'metho' – to a cave on the foreshores.
1983 *Australian* 19 Apr. 9: Shopkeepers near the park defend the sale of metho to Aborigines.

Mexican   A Victorian (viewed from N.S.W.); someone from N.S.W. or Victoria (viewed from Queensland) [f. south of the border]
1980 *Sydney Morning Herald* 21 Apr. 3: Victorians – whom South Coasters affectionately call Mexicans – used to use the Hume [Highway] as the quickest route to holiday spots such as Surfers Paradise and the Sunshine Coast.
1984 *Sydney Morning Herald* 6 Mar. Good Living 1: Just over two years ago the Gold Coast went into shock. Mexicans (patois for people south of the border) had stopped crossing the Tweed River armed with retirement money. There was a depression.

mia mia   An Aboriginal bough or bark hut [Morris 1845] but used of any rude shelter constructed by a white
1855 William Howitt *Land, Labour and Gold* i 252: Then there are huts of mingled boughs and sheets of bark, and here and there simple mimies, in imitation of the mimi of the natives, that is, just a few boughs leaned against a pole, supported on a couple

of forked sticks, and a quantity of gum-tree leaves for a bed.

1883 Edward M. Curr *Recollections of Squatting in Victoria* 72: My companion had made the mia-mia with forked sticks, some pieces of bark stripped from a fallen tree, and our saddle-cloths.

see **humpy**

mick A Roman Catholic: *derogatory* [f. 'Mick' for an Irishman]
1934 'Leslie Parker' *Trooper to the Southern Cross* (1966) 89: We used to have a song at school:
   Catholic dogs
   Jump like frogs
which we always yelled at the Micks.
1964 George Johnston *My Brother Jack* 159: 'I don't care whether she's a mick or a Protestant or a holy roller.'
1972 David Williamson *The Removalists* 26: 'Five kids in seven years. Bastard's a mick.'
1987 Peter Smark *Sydney Morning Herald* 10 Dec. 77: The Micks took over whole areas of the Federal and State public services and played the mates' game to the hilt.

Mick, Crooked A mythical figure of N.T. and N. Queensland credited with prodigious feats
1945 Tom Ronan *Strangers on the Ophir* 234: Chris Christian, reared on legends of his ancestors, agreed . . . that Thor, god of the thunders, rode high. The irreverent votaries of a newer and more humorous folklore commented 'Crooked Mick was kicking the billy-cans about'.
1966 Bill Wannan *Crooked Mick of the Speewah* [book title]

mick, mad A pick [rhyming slang]
1924 *Truth* 27 Apr. 6: *Mad mick* A pick.
1953 T. A. G. Hungerford *Riverslake* 224: 'I swung a mad-mick there for eighteen months during the depression.'
1973 Frank Huelin *Keep Moving* 78: 'Well, I won't buy drinks for any bloody gangers, just for a chance to swing a mad mick.'

mickey The vulva
1970 Alexander Buzo *The Front Room Boys* in Penguin *Plays* 49: 'Barry Anderson reckons he got her in the locker room the other day. Mucked around, played with mickey, she didn't mind.'
1975 Don Townshend *Gland Time* 238:

'Can't blame her for it, 'cause her mickey was probably throbbin' for it.'

micks, a pair of The call of 'tails' in two-up. At first erroneously explained as 'heads' (see quot. 1919), an explanation as yet unsupported by any evidence. Quot. 1938 is to be interpreted in the light of the tradition that the spinner backs heads. [Origin obscure: the 'tail' of the pennies used in two-up represents Britannia and her trident]
1919 W. H. Downing *Digger Dialects* 33: *Mick* (1) The Queen's head on a coin (e.g. 'Micks are right', when two heads have turned up in a game of 'two-up'); (2) a queen in a pack of cards.
1938 John Robertson *With the Cameliers in Palestine* 198: The New Zealanders are very religious men. Their priests lead them out to a quiet spot where they can pray. The priest spreads out a holy mat with marks on it which means something they have great faith in. He kneels down beside the mat, then a row of worshippers kneel all round him, with another row bending over them. The worshippers throw their offerings on to the holy mat, and the priest places two coins on a short piece of polished wood which he calls a kip, and raising his eyes to the sky, he throws up the coins as an offering to Allah. All the worshippers raise their eyes also to the sky, and then bow solemnly over the mat, and say together, 'God Almighty', and the priest answers, 'A pair of Micks', which means that the offerings are not accepted, or he may say, 'Oh Lord, he has done 'em again', and the joyful cries of some of the worshippers show that Allah is pleased, and so they, too, are glad.
1953 T. A. G. Hungerford *Riverslake* 126: 'I got ten bob to say he tails 'em – ten bob the micks!'
1966 Baker 242: If a spinner throws two 'tails' he is said to *mick them* or throw *two micks.*

micky A bull calf, usually unbranded
1876 Rolf Boldrewood *A Colonial Reformer* in *A Town and Country Journal* 9 Dec. 924: The wary and still more dangerously sudden 'Michie', a two-year-old-bull (so called after an eminent Australian barrister famous for bringing his 'charges' to a successful issue). [1890 edition, ii. 98, reads 'micky' and omits the derivation]
1933 R. B. Plowman *The Man from Oodnadatta* 63: Taking up the headrope the boss lassoed a big micky (bull calf).

1980 Rod Ansell *To Fight the Wild* 50: We were started off on small heifers, then cows and small mickeys (young bulls, not fully grown).

micky, chuck a To throw a fit, panic
1952 T. A. G. Hungerford *The Ridge and the River* 22: 'And he don't chuck a micky every time something goes off behind him!'

middy A measure of beer: in N.S.W., 10 oz.; in W.A., 7 oz.
1945 Baker 169: The *middy*, a beer glass containing nine ounces, is a measure used only in N.S.W. hotels.
1953 Baker 138: The nearest approximation to the Queensland *pot* is the N.S.W. *middy*, which holds 10 oz. of beer. At the time of writing my previous book, the size of the *middy* was fixed at nine ounces.
1972 John O'Grady *It's Your Shout, Mate!* 15: 'A glass is five ounces [in Western Australia], a middy is seven ounces, an' a pot's ten. Got it?'
1976 David Ireland *The Glass Canoe* 150: Poor Liz . . . She didn't have the same old bounce, and she went down from schooners to middies.

Mile, the Golden see **Golden**

Mile, the Hungry see **Hungry**

milfissed the balfastards see **balfastards**

milker, busy as a one-armed ∼ on a dairy farm see **one-armed**

milko A milkman [abbr. or from cry]
[**1865** J. F. Mortlock *Experiences of a Convict* (1965) 120: He proposed that I should carry his pails round the town and shout out 'Milk O!' at the customer's doors.]
1969 Mena Calthorpe *The Defectors* 180: The milko hesitated, then he ran along the street rattling the crates and bottles.
1983 *Newcastle Herald* 19 Mar. 3: No one misses the milko on the Cessnock East run. The milko sounds his truck's horn as he delivers. But the horn doesn't 'beep', it 'moos'.

milkshake, the singing see **singing**

million, gone a In a hopeless state; utterly disadvantaged or defeated [see. quot. 1969]

1916 C. J. Dennis 'The Battle of the Wazzir' in A. H. Chisholm *The Making of a Sentimental Bloke* (1946) 131: Fer young Bill was gone a million, an' 'e never guessed the game.
1922 Arthur Wright *A Colt from the Country* 142: 'What hope would you have when that came out? You'd be gone a million.'
1942 Gavin Casey *It's Harder for Girls* 212: 'If they drop their bundles they're gone a million.'
1969 Sir Paul Hasluck *Sun-Herald* 24 Aug. 48: When I was a boy in Western Australia . . . there was a Premier, John Scaddan (1911–16) who was usually referred to among our friends as 'Gone a Million, Jack' . . . Scaddan increased spending from loan funds, which in those days meant State public borrowing, to a level with which the State was quite unfamiliar and, in answering criticism, made some such remark as 'What's a million?' and gained a nickname that was intended to brand him as a careless person.
1982 Blanche d'Alpuget *Robert J. Hawke* 297: Hawke, in conveying the common belief of the officers that Whitlam would not survive as Leader, remarked, 'Gough's gone a million'.

Ming Nickname of R. G. Menzies (1894–1978), Australian Prime Minister 1939–41, 1949–66 [f. pronunciation of Menzies as 'Mingis', and Ming the Merciless in the Speed Gordon comic strip]
c. **1954** Communist Party of Australia *Our Bob: Further Misadventures of Ming (the Merciless) Menzies* [pamphlet title]
1975 *Australian* 4 Jul. 8: The swinging vote, which ended the Ming Dynasty after 23 years, has swung back to whence it came.
1986 *Sun-Herald* 2 Mar. 184: Not only did Bob Hawke choke off the flag debate last year, he'll be 'doing a Ming' with the Queen this week as he sees her passing by.

Ming Wing, the The Robert Menzies School of Humanities, Monash University, Victoria

Minties, it's moments like these you need Slogan used in advertising cartoons (from 1927) for the sweet launched by James Stedman-Henderson in 1922: applied to anyone in extremities
1963 Frank Hardy *Legends from Benson's Valley* 162: It's Moments Like These . . . [story title]

1978 *Sydney Morning Herald* 9 Jun. 1: In a Sydney court yesterday a solicitor representing Life Savers Ltd was told by a Sydney magistrate that his clients' case could not be heard because it was not listed. 'It's moments like these,' the magistrate added, 'you need Minties.'

1983 *Sun-Herald* 5 Jun. 113: At moments like these, it isn't Minties I need, it's a pantry shelf and freezer stocked with instant or almost instant foods.

miserable Close-fisted, stingy, mean [OED 1484; E. dial. 1816–59]

1903 Joseph Furphy *Such is Life* (1944) 17: 'The more swellisher a man is, the more miserabler he is about a bit o' grass for a team, or a feed for a traveller.'

1958 Frank Hardy *The Four-Legged Lottery* 183: 'Not all bookies are miserable; some of them are happy-go-lucky, generous blokes. They make money easily and spend it easily, give to charity and so forth. Pittson is miserable.'

1976 *Australian* 20 May 6: A 'lousy dollar a day!' Could any government be more miserable?

missus, the The wife of the owner or manager on a station, from the standpoint of the employees [f. *missus* as wife, and (esp. in U.S.A.) as employer of negroes]

1845 Mary Vidal *Tales for the Bush* 76: 'Now, Marion, mind all I've told you, and obey the Missis, and be quick and handy.'

1908 Mrs Aeneas Gunn *We of the Never-Never* xi: We – are just some of the bush-folk of the Never-Never ... The Maluka, The Little Missus, The Sanguine Scot ...

1958 Nancy Cato *All the Rivers Run* 216: Annie ... tacked a piece of bright oil-baize that the missus had given her over the slab-table.

1967 John Yeomans *The Scarce Australians* 39: In the Australian outback, where the manager or owner of a station has the standard title of Boss among those who do not call him by his first name, his wife has the standard title of Missus.

1981 Maxwell Grant *Inherit the Sun* 366: 'I suppose with your father away you are the Missus?'

Mo The comedian Roy Rene, b. Harry van der Sluice (1892–1954)

mob 'A large number, the Australian noun of multitude, and not implying anything low or noisy' (Morris): used almost as a technical term of cattle, etc., but more colloquially of people, as of a group with common interests

1838 Thomas Walker *A Month in the Bush of Australia* 8: I beheld a level plain, as even as a bowling green, not a rise nor a tree nor an object of any kind to interrupt the view, with the exception of 'mobs' of cattle scattered over the surface.

1852 G. C. Mundy *Our Antipodes* i 53: There are to be found round the doors of the Sydney theatre a sort of 'loafers', known as the Cabbage-tree mob ... an unruly set of young fellows, native-born generally.

1878 Rolf Boldrewood *An Australian Squire* repr. as *Babes in the Bush* (1900) 248: Ardmillan, Forbes and Neil Barrington, with all the 'Benmohr mob', as they were somewhat disrespectfully [1900 familiarly] called, were in the vanguard.

1918 Harley Matthews *Saints and Soldiers* 148: Big Snowy and his mob were back in camp behind the line.

1980 Rod Ansell *To Fight the Wild* 55: I just pulled up a big mob of dry grass to make a good thick padding.

1983 *NT News* (Darwin) 10 Mar. 6: Darwin City Council is heading for mobs of trouble over the swimming pool fencing by-law, set for introduction in 11 days.

mock (mockers), to put the ~ on To frustrate someone's plans; to place a hoodoo on someone, destroy his luck [see **moz**]

1911 Edward Dyson *Benno, and Some of the Push* 33: 'All toms is 'erlike t'me,' he said ... 'but, all the same, it's up t'me t'put a mock on that tripester.'

1923 Con Drew *Rogues and Ruses* 115: 'They'll have to race without me tomorrow. I've got a mocker hung on me.'

1938 Xavier Herbert *Capricornia* 473: 'Comin' here to put the mocks on us,' said Kit. 'Might be there's a reward.'

1941 Lawson Glassop *Lucky Palmer* 62: 'It's that sheila,' he said. 'She's put the mocker on us ... We'll never have a good trot until you get rid of her.'

1983 *Bulletin* 2 Aug. 34: The double loss put the mockers on everything.

mocker Clothes [Partridge lists *mockered up* dressed in one's best: low: late C.19–20]

1953 Baker 106: *mocker* Clothes in general.

1961 Frank Hardy *The Hard Way* 77:

'They're fulla new mocker, see. Good clothes I got from mugs in Pentridge.'
1976 David Ireland *The Glass Canoe* 55: 'Now who's got good mocha on?' he says, looking round . . . Danny's gone mad for the occasional and has his grey suit on that he wears to weddings, funerals and smokos.

mole A girl or woman: *derogatory* [? variant pronunciation of *moll*]
1965 William Dick *A Bunch of Ratbags* 270: 'Just because you've got yourself some rich bloke's mole of a bloody daughter, don't come telling me and the boys what to bloody do.'
1979 Rae Desmond Jones *Walking the Line* 19: Give us a hand you lazy mole!
1983 *Sun-Herald* 15 May 51: 'If a girl does it all the time then she's a mole. Moles are scum, worse than dirt.' . . . 'I know one girl who goes out with someone for one night and hops into bed with them – I'd call her a mole.'

moll at a christening see **christening**

molly-dooked, molly-dooker Left-handed; a left-handed person [? f. *mauly* fist OED 1780]
[**1926** J. Vance Marshall *Timely Tips for New Australians: Mauldy* Left-handed.]
1941 Baker 47: *Mollydooker* A left-handed person. Whence, 'molly dook' (adj.) left-handed.
1975 *Sydney Morning Herald* 30 Aug. 11: A word of good cheer to all molly-dookers.

monarch, monaych Aboriginal term for the police: W.A. [see **manatj**]
1961 Nene Gare *The Fringe Dwellers* 35: 'Skippy gets off. An ya know the first thing e says ta them monarch? E turns round on em an yelps, "An now ya can just gimme back that bottle." '
1975 Richard Beilby *The Brown Land Crying* 10: Myra was terrified. The coppers! Monaych! The native word contained a history of oppression: the Men with Chains!
1981 Archie Weller *The Day of the Dog* 91: 'Let's clear off out of this before the monaych come.'

Monday, yellow see **yellow Monday**

mong 1 A dog of mixed breed [abbr. of mongrel]
1923 Jack Moses *Beyond the City Gates*

152: 'What does it matter? He was only a mong!'
1944 Jean Devanny *By Tropic, Sea and Jungle* 227: It takes a good mong dog to catch a rat-kangaroo in the bush.
2 Any dog
1957 R. S. Porteous *Brigalow* 16: An irritable voice called, 'Go and lie down, you rotten mong.'
1982 *National Times* 21 Feb. 29: The only victim I can recall is a mong. A redback sank its fangs into an Australian fox terrier.
3 A human being: *derogatory*
1933 *Bulletin* 16 Aug. 39: 'Most likely he just felt faint, same as you get on *any* job, and went out to it for a minute. And the mong fired him!'
1967 *Southerly* 199: The bludging, dirty mong to whom she had . . . entrusted heart and hand.

monkey 1 A sheep
1881 A. C. Grant *Bush-Life in Queensland* i 88: Sheep lost on Saturday imperatively constrained every one on the head-station to look for them . . . and no one felt better pleased than he did to see the last lot of 'monkeys', as the shearers usually denominated sheep, leave the head-station.
1905 'The Wallaby Brigade' in *The Old Bush Songs* ed. A. B. Paterson 126: You've only to sport your dover and knock a monkey over – / There's cheap mutton for the Wallaby Brigade.
1942 Sarah Campion *Bonanza* 161: 'If only a man could breed sheep with fifty ribs apiece instead of – well, however many ribs the bleeding monkeys *do* have – he'd make his fortune!'
2 See quot. 1959 [cf. *monkey-rope* U.S. 1851 OED]
1911 E. S. Sorenson *Life in the Australian Backblocks* 207: Novices and others who lack proficiency use . . . a monkey (a strap looped between the D's for the right hand to grip).
1959 Desmond Martin *Australia Astride* 194: *Monkey.* Also known as a Wagga grip or jug handle. It is used by weak riders to mount, or to try and ride buckjumpers.
3 The vulva
1970 Patrick White *The Vivisector* 111: 'Too much dirty water. That's what's wrong with Spargo. 'E'd carry 'is bed any time a woman up an' showed 'im 'er monkey.'

monte, monty A certainty, 'a sure thing' [f. card game U.S. 1841 Mathews]

1894 Henry Lawson *Verse* i 269: 'I've got a vote for Hughie – but it ain't no monte yet.'

1908 E. S. Sorenson *The Squatter's Ward* 122: 'It's a monty the little squib would let out a yell jest as I was gettin' clear.'

1930 K. S. Prichard *Haxby's Circus* 41: 'She's the chance of a life-time,' he yelled. 'The biggest bloomin' monty ever started on a racecourse.'

1950 Brian James *The Advancement of Spencer Button* 230: 'You make a monty of that mark, and get to Sydney.'

Monts The Claremont (W.A.) Australian Rules football team (also the Tigers) [abbr.]

1978 *Australian* 4 May 17: 'Every match is now a tough one for Monts as every team in the League tries to stop us winning.'

moosh Gaol porridge [variant of *mush*]

1945 Baker 141: *moosh* Jail food.

1967 B. K. Burton *Teach Them No More* 17: Moline took his plate back to his cell, where he pushed his unwilling spoon into glutinous material. The food resisted the spoon's assault. 'What's this muck?' 'That's mush,' Ted explained. 'I knew an old lagger once. He was quite famous. He made little statues out of his mush.'

1973 Jim McNeil *The Chocolate Frog* 117: Mush pronounced to rhyme with push, prison porridge.

mopoke A dreary or stupid fellow [see quot. 1845]

1845 Richard Howitt *Impressions of Australia Felix* 233: 'A more-pork kind of fellow' is a man of cut-and-dry phrases; a person remarkable for nothing new in common conversation. This, by some, is thought very expressive; the more-pork being a kind of Australian owl, notorious for its wearying nightly iteration, 'More pork, more pork.'

1876 Rolf Boldrewood *A Colonial Reformer* (1891) 125: 'What a regular more-pork I was to be sure, to go and run my neck agin' a roping-pole, and all for a false jade, who'd have come to see me hanged.'

1910 H. H. Richardson *The Getting of Wisdom* 205: At the idea of shutting herself up wholly with such mopokes, of cutting herself off from her present vital interests, Laura hastily reconsidered her decision.

moral A 'moral certainty' (OED 1646) i.e. certain to win, esp. in horseracing

[**1847** Alexander Harris *The Emigrant Family* ed. W. S. Ramson (1966) 279: It was a moral certainty that the three white cattle were from the same stock.]

1878 Rolf Boldrewood *An Australian Squire* repr. as *Babes in the Bush* (1900) 175: It was understood that he was entered on the chance of the two cracks destroying each others chances, in one of the numerous accidents to which such races are liable, in which case Bargo would be a 'moral'.

1944 Lawson Glassop *We Were the Rats* 16: 'Think Tiger will win?' he asked. 'He's a moral,' I said. 'A lay-down misere. I might have two quid on him.'

1952 T. A. G. Hungerford *The Ridge and the River* 14: 'They're a moral to lamp your footprints where you came into the road from the track.'

1980 Jessica Anderson *The Impersonators* 139: 'I don't know about television. It depends on what else they have. But it's a moral for the evening papers.'

more front than Myers see **front**

more hide (arse, cheek) than Jessie see **Jessie**

Moreton Bay A **fiz-gig** or **gig**, i.e. police informer [rhyming slang for 'Moreton Bay fig']

1953 Baker 134: *Morton Bay (fig)*. Any witness who lays an information, anyone who unwarrantably attends to or meddles in the affairs of others; by rhyme on *gig*, which is used similarly, and which may be a contraction of *fizgig*, an informer.

1975 *Bulletin* 26 Apr. 46: If there were Mortons nearby (Morton Bay Figs; gigs, meaning busybodies).

1984 *Bulletin* 19 Jun. 69: Fifty per cent of the Drug Squad's arrests are based on information received and woe betide a user, a supplier or anyone else who becomes a dog, a gig, or as the police term it, a Moreton Bay.

morning glory See quots [f. the flower so called, and the occurrence of an erection on awaking]

1977 Jim Ramsay *Cop It Sweet* 60: *Morning glory*: Fornication before noon.

1979 *Sydney Morning Herald* 6 Oct. 2: The dam's second unusual feature is a 'morning glory', or trumpet-shaped tower spill-way built to handle flood discharge.

1984 Bill Reed *Crooks* 185: It makes

Stein's morning glory of an erection pull its woolly head in quick smart.

Moscow Corner   See quot. 1985
   1985 *Sydney Morning Herald* 16 May 4: When they [a delegation of Russian officials] were welcomed to Question Time by the Acting Speaker, Joan Child, an uproar broke out as Opposition members suggested they should be sitting in 'Moscow Corner' – a pet name for the back corner of the Government benches occupied by the left wing.

Moscow, gone to, in   In pawn
   [**c. 1882** *Sydney Slang Dictionary* 6: *Moskeener* To pawn with a view to obtaining more than the actual value of an article.]
   1941 Baker 47: *Moscow* A pawnshop.
   1953 *Caddie A Sydney Barmaid* 217: 'Me clobber's already in Moscow, an' so is me tan shoes.'

mossie   A mosquito [abbr.]
   1941 Baker 47: *Mossie, mozzie* A mosquito.
   1959 Dorothy Hewett *Bobbin Up* 76–7: They sat in the cool on the back verandah, slapping at the mozzies.
   1981 *National Times* 19 Apr. 52: The couple had become experimental in their lovemaking over the years; after watching Don's Party on television recently, they made love in the backyard for the first time. 'But we got bitten by mozzies,' she said.

mother-in-law's breath, cold as   Very cold
   1956 Encountered in conversation.
   1979 *Sunday Telegraph* (Sydney) 13 May 168: It's refreshing to hear an old Australian phrase amid all the government and advertising jargon. A taxi wound down a window on a freezing night this week. 'Out there, mate,' said the driver, 'it's as cold as a step-mother's breath.'
   1983 Buzz Kennedy *Australian* 9 Feb. 14: Then there are the family kisses – not only of the sort labelled 'as cold as a mother-in-law's kiss' but of the affectionate variety.

motherless   Used as an intensive, esp. in the phrase 'motherless broke'
   1898 *Bulletin* 17 Dec. Red Page: To these are prefixed the adjectives *motherless* and *dead*, thus *dead motherless broke.*
   1916 Arthur Wright *Under a Cloud* 35: 'I'm stone motherless meself an' I could do with that hundred Booth is offerin'.'

1945 Gavin Casey *Downhill is Easier* 20: 'I'd only known Reg when we were both stone motherless broke.'
   1972 Alexander Macdonald *The Ukelele Player under the Red Lamp* 247: Happy, full as a boot, and stone motherless broke.

motorbike, useful as an ashtray on a
see **useful**

motser, motza   A large gambling win; a 'certainty' that would ensure such a win [? f. Yiddish *matzo*, bread]
   1936 A. B. Paterson 'The Shearer's Colt' in *Song of the Pen* (1983) 739: 'It's a motzer. It's a schnitzler. We'll have to pack 'em in on the roof of the grand-stand.'
   1950 *Australian Police Journal* Apr. 116: *Motza* A lot of money.
   1977 *Bulletin* 24 Dec. 46: The lady on my left, blonde, beautiful and making a motza out of retailing.
   1983 *Australian* 19 Feb. 5: 'Win a motza on the footy' is the slogan for the new game [Footy TAB] which will be launched to-morrow.

mountain men, the   The Penrith Rugby League team
   1985 *Australian* 4 Sep. 28: The long drought broke for rugby league's mountain men from Penrith last night when the club's first grade team qualified for the Winfield Cup semi-finals for the first time.

mousetraps in one's pocket, to have
see **pocket**

Movement, the   The Catholic Social Study Movement established in 1945 as 'a loose national alliance of Catholic actionists, particularly unionists, with the object of fighting communism in the union movement' (Patrick O'Farrell *The Catholic Church in Australia* (1968) 264)
   1951 Frank Hardy *Power Without Glory* 634: 'I have here the most recent report of 'The Movement' which, as you know, is the arm of Catholic Action in the Trade Unions' ... 'In each diocese or suburb we have set about establishing cells of The Movement and in many factories and Trade Unions we have similar groups.'
   1974 Desmond O'Grady *Deschooling Kevin Carew* 13: He was exasperated that they accepted church involvement in politics through 'the Movement', which was an

off-shoot of Catholic Action designed to fight Communist influence.

see **grouper**

moves, if it ~, shoot it; if it doesn't, chop it down Reputedly an Australian national motto

1963 Alan Ross *Australia 63* 202: The country had still to be conquered. The general attitude was: 'If it moves, shoot it. If it stands still, chop it down.'

1971 Bill Hornadge *A Squint Down Under* 24: If it moves, shoot it. / If it doesn't, chop it down. Australian Motto.

1986 Matthew Strassberg *Sydney Morning Herald* 20 Sep. 26: Wendy Machin, despite her professed love of the bush, is no exception to the National Party credo – 'If it stands, cut it down. If it moves, shoot it.'

mozz As for **put the mozz on**
1941 Baker 47: *Moz* To interrupt, hinder.

1965 Frank Hardy *The Yarns of Billy Borker* 107: 'Don't mozz a man,' I tells him. 'You're well named, I'll say that for you, Calamity.'

1974 John Powers *The Last of the Knucklemen* 49: 'Don't let him mozz you, Monk.'

mozz, to put the ~ on To prejudice someone's chances, place a 'jinx' on something [f. *mozzle*]

1924 C. J. Dennis *Rose of Spadgers* 75: 'Too much soul-ferritin' might put the moz / On this 'ere expedition.'

1956 Alan Marshall *How's Andy Going/* 200: 'Looking ahead like that never does any bloody good to any man,' observed Pat. 'It puts the moz on him.'

1974 Keith Stackpole *Not Just for Openers* 32: She felt she put the moz on him . . . She couldn't bear to go in case she was a jinx.

mozzie see **mossie**

mozzle Luck, back luck [f. Heb. *mazzal* luck]

1898 *Bulletin* 17 Dec. Red Page: *Mozzle* is luck . . . *Good mozzle* = good luck; *Kronk mozzle* = bad luck.

1903 Joseph Furphy *Such is Life* (1944) 280: 'And how much do you stand to lose, if your mozzle is out?' I asked.

1919 Edward Dyson *Hello, Soldier!* 32: 'Twas rotten mozzle, Neddo. We had blown out every clip.

muck, sing 'em Supposed advice of Nellie Melba to Clara Butt on undertaking a tour of Australia

1928 W. H. Ponder *Clara Butt: Her Life Story* 138: 'So you're going to Australia!' she [Melba] said. 'Well, I made twenty thousand pounds on my tour there, but of course *that* will never be done again. Still, it's a wonderful country, and you'll have a good time. What are you going to sing? All I can say is – sing 'em muck! It's all they can understand!'

1934 Vance Palmer *The Swayne Family* 170: 'Show you're higher organism by adapting yourself. Appeal to sense of fun. Turn dark cloud inside out. Sing 'em muck.'

1977 Sumner Locke Elliott *Water Under the Bridge* 295: 'I want to hear all you girls in the balcony "There's a *track* winding *back* to an oh-*old*-fashioned *shack* . . ." Sing 'em muck,' he often told Maggie.

1988 *Sydney Morning Herald* 12 Jun. 8: Joan Vivian . . . told the true story of Dame Nellie's supposedly infamous comment . . . 'muck' was the term for popular ballads and light music – sung then by Nellie and Clara, now by Dame Joan and Dame Kiri.

muck up day The last day at school before the final examinations, marked by an absence of restraint, practical jokes etc.

1979 *Sun-Herald* 4 Nov. 123: Performers wrapped each other up in alfoil, like a large cut-lunch, and coated themselves in shaving cream (they'd obviously never got over their sixth-form muck-up day).

1980 Barbara Pepworth *Early Marks* 272: Muck-up Day is here at last . . . My form races around in a frenzy. They're celebrating our last day at school before the exams start . . . hurling eggs and rotten tomatoes at one another, sifting flour bombs, releasing pent-up nervous energy.

muddie A Queensland mudcrab
1977 *Australian* 8 Jan. 1: Each year the people of N.S.W. eat 200,000 of the prize Queensland muddies, which is all right except that they are eating mud crabs that Queenslanders are not allowed to eat.

1982 *NT News* (Darwin) 27 Jul. 10: Muddies will be ropable [heading] One of Darwin's unique tourist attractions - the mudcrab tying contest - will be staged at Lim's Hotel on August 4.

Muddy, Little The river Yarra, Victoria [f. colour of water. *Big Muddy* is the Missouri]

1965 *Nation* 3 Apr. 10: Few people could draw the breath of conscience and describe the Yarra as a proud river sweeping southward to the sea, Little Muddy nevertheless commands great local affection, whatever is said about it in another place.

mudlark   See quot. 1941 [variant of *mud-runner*]
1914 A. B. Paterson 'Racehorses and Racing' in *Song of the Pen* (1983) 312: Some horses revel in mud . . . The mudlark contingent are generally horses with good loin power, that keep their legs under them while racing.
1941 Baker 47: *Mudlark* A racehorse that runs well on a muddy course. Also footballers who play on a sodden field.
1984 *Sun* (Sydney) 27 Jan. 68: If the track is rain-affected it will suit Rustglow even better as he is a real mudlark.

mud map   A sketch drawn by a bushman on the ground, to give directions
1919 E. S. Sorenson *Chips and Splinters* 14: The mud maps that Phineas draws on the road with a stick when directing some unfortunate wanderer.
1936 Ion L. Idriess *The Cattle King* 102: He built up the fire, then sat back on his heels, and with a stick scraped the ground clear. 'I'll make you a mud map.'
1962 J. Marshall and R. Drysdale *Journey Among Men* 37: 'I'll draw yer a mud map the way they went.'

mulga   A species of acacia: colloquially **the mulga** may refer to uninhabited or inhospitable regions generally
1928 Vance Palmer *The Man Hamilton* 26: Manager of this isolated place in the mulga, a hundred miles away from anywhere.
1946 Rohan Rivett *Behind Bamboo* 397: *Mulga*, the surrounding jungle.
1973 Alexander Buzo *Rooted* 87: 'Gary's gone away for the weekend, cavorting in the mulga with the Werris Creek push.'
1983 Peter Bowers *Sydney Morning Herald* 5 Nov. 13: The mulga mafia [the National Party in Queensland] has come out of the sticks to the extent that it has broadened its electoral appeal to embrace city votes.

mulga wire   As for **bush telegraph** 2
1899 T. Quinn *The Well Sinkers* 100: 'How do you hear it, Micky?' 'Mulga wires, missus, mulga wires.'

1913 Henry Lawson 'Triangles of Life' *Prose* i 658: Tom had been out early, or had got what we call a bush telegraphy or mulga wire.
1933 R. B. Plowman *The Man from Oodnadatta* 21: The padre was not surprised to find that Stan was aware of his coming. Throughout the Inland news travels far and fast by means of the 'mulga wire'.
1950 K. S. Prichard *Winged Seeds* 297: 'The troops 've had it all by mulga.'

mullet, like a stunned   Dazed, so unaware as to be almost unconscious
1953 Baker 267: *Dullness* (looking) like a stunned mullet.
1963 John O'Grady *The things they do to you* 147: I returned and lay on the bed like a stunned mullet.
1974 Jack Hibberd *Dimboola* 46: 'Just look at him! Just look at him. Looks like a stunned mullet.'
1980 *Daily Mirror* (Sydney) 22 Apr. 34: The storyline is impossibly interwoven, the actors wander around like a group of stunned mullets and even that old pro Glenn Ford looks bewildered.

mullock, to poke   To mock, ridicule [f. *mullock* the rubbish heaped at the top of a mineshaft]
1916 C. J. Dennis *The Moods of Ginger Mick* 74: I own me eyes git brighter / When I see 'em pokin' mullock at the everlastin' sea.
1931 Vance Palmer *Separate Lives* 210: 'D'you think I'm going to sit in that galley with Curran and the other blokes all poking mullock at me?'
1957 Ray Lawler *Summer of the Seventeenth Doll* 71: 'Oh, so that's what you got me in for, is it – to poke mullock?'
1962 John Morrison *Twenty-Three* 86: 'I heard what you said when you grabbed that rope. Poking mullock at us because we won't go out over an empty hatch.'
see **borak**

munga (mungaree, mungareer)   Food (Army slang) [f. Fr. *manger*, adapted into Arabic as *manjaria*, with poss. influence of English dialect *mung*]
[**1787** Francis Grose *A Provincial Glossary: Mung* Food for chickens.
1859 Hotten 65: *Mungarly* bread, food.]
1919 W. H. Downing *Digger Dialects* 34: *Mungaree* (Arab.) – Bread. *Mungy* (Fr., Manger) – Food; a meal.

1944 G. H. Fearnside *Sojourn in Tobruk* 74: 'The mungaree has arrived,' he said. 'The Ration Party is to report to Company Headquarters and pick it up.'
1963 Lawson Glassop *The Rats in New Guinea* 149: 'Sit down and have some *munga,* John,' I said.
1965 Patrick White *Four Plays* 123: 'Okay, Nola! Shan't keep anyone waiting when the *mungareer's* on the table!'
1982 Leo Schofield *Sydney Morning Herald* 27 Nov. 28: There were odd complaints about the food . . . from mouths that nonetheless wrapped themselves gleefully around the free munga and booze.

mungo A devotee of Rugby League, as a counterpart to the Rugby Union **rah rah** [f. an uncouth character in the film *Blazing Saddles*]
1990 Andrew Slack *Australian* 10 May 22: The rugby players . . . are annoyed at being constantly referred to by our mungo mates as those rah-rah tweed coat types.

Murphy's law A U.S. expression ('If anything can go wrong, it will') given currency in Australia when Senator Lionel Murphy was Attorney General
1977 *Sydney Morning Herald* 31 Dec. 23: Murphy's Law – 'if something can go wrong, it will' – is all too familiar to oilmen.
1983 *Australian* 23 Apr. 11: The RAAF's handling of orders to photograph work on the Franklin dam site had turned into a classic application of Murphy's law, the Attorney-General, Senator Evans, told the Senate yesterday. (Murphy's law states that if anything can go wrong, it will.)

Murray cod, on the On the nod, i.e. on credit [rhyming slang]
1977 *Australian* 23 Jul. Mag. 1: A punter, well known in Sydney, who bets on 'the murray cod' (the nod) walked into City Tattersalls on Monday settling day carrying $240,000 cash.

murree, murri An Aborigine (often applied by Aborigines to themselves)
1911 E. S. Sorenson *Life in the Australian Backblocks* 160: They [the drovers] are hemmed in on all sides, and where once only King Murri was concerned about their movements they are now closely watched by boundary riders, mounted troopers, and stock inspectors.

1963 Xavier Herbert *Larger Than Life* 82: Half the crowd were 'murris', people of aboriginal stock.
1983 *Sydney Morning Herald* 14 Feb. 7: There are two Aboriginal words for the races in Moree. One is 'murri', an Aboriginal word for themselves, which is quite acceptable. The other, for whites, is 'gubber', which is derogatory.

Murrumbidgee whaler A swagman camping in the bends of the Murrumbidgee or any other river, and a byword for indolence [see **whaler**]
1873 J. C. F. Johnson *Christmas on Carringa* 16: Men when on the tramp through the Riverina country often carry a piece of twine and a hook to catch cod or blackfish. This is termed Murrumbidgee Whaling.
1878 G. H. Gibson *Southerly Busters* 177: Murrumbidgee whalers are a class of loafers who work for about six months in the year – i.e., during shearing and harvest, and camp the rest of the time in bends of rivers, and live by fishing and begging.
1911 Edward S. Sorenson *Life in the Australian Backblocks* 70: There was a well-known Murrumbidgee whaler in the Wagga district, who had been doing the one circuit – embracing Gundagai, Hay, and Wagga – for thirty odd years, and during the whole of that time had never done a scrap of work.
1953 Archer Russell *Murray Walkabout* 147: He was a 'Murrumbidgee whaler', the river prototype of the tramping sundowner.

mush see **moosh**

muster, bangtail, Tambaroora, tarpaulin see **bang-tail, Tambaroora, tarpaulin**

Muswellbrook, things are crook at see **Tallarook**

mutton, underground see **underground mutton**

Myers, more front than see **front**

my little mate Phrase given currency by the allegation in 1983–4 that Mr Justice Lionel Murphy, in a telephone conversation with the NSW Chief Stipendiary Magistrate, Mr C. R. Briese in 1982, sought to influence a court case involving the Sydney solicitor,

Mr Morgan Ryan, in the remark 'Now what about my little mate?'

1984 *National Times* 27 Jul. 3: Briese said that he had enlisted Murphy's support in his attempts to have the Government grant independence to NSW magistrates, who were then, and still are, public servants. According to Briese's statement, on one occasion Murphy rang him and told him the Government would support the independence proposition. Murphy then said, 'Now what about my little mate?' Briese says that Murphy had referred to Ryan as his 'little mate' in an earlier conversation. Briese claims he did not respond to these alleged attempts to intervene in the case against Ryan.

1984 *National Times* 5 Oct. 2: After a few words from these luminaries, the author [Ron Tandberg] ascended the podium. 'Thank you, my mate Creighton, and thank you, my mate Bob,' the cartoonist said graciously. 'I won't call either of you "my little mate", since I know you're both sensitive about your height.'

my word Used for agreement or emphasis (given extra currency in Australia from occurring in Pidgin)

1865 Henry Kingsley *The Hillyars and the Burtons* 68: Some of the young ladies said: Their word – they were surprised.

1887 *All the Year Round* 30 July. 68: 'My word' is an exclamation in constant and universal use.

1903 Joseph Furphy *Such is Life* (1944) 229: 'That's just the sort o' thing would put a hump on me. Sort o' off-sider for a gang o'Chinks! My word!'

1934 Vance Palmer *Sea and Spinifex* 213: 'Big sea running there outside t' reef. My word!'

1981 *Sun-Herald* 13 Dec. 192: There are lots of Pakistani shopkeepers in London, oh my very word.

myall 1 An Aborigine who has had little or no contact with whites [Ab. The relationship between senses 1 and 3 is uncertain]

1798 David Collins *An Account of the English Colony in New South Wales* ed. B. H. Fletcher (1975) i 507: My-yal* A stranger *This word has reference to sight; Mi, the eye.

1838 T. L. Mitchell *Three Expeditions into the Interior of Eastern Australia* i 20: Those who still remain in a savage state ... are named *'myalls'* by their half civilized brethren.

1864 Rachel Henning *Letters* ed. David Adam (1963) 185: They were myalls (i.e. wild blacks).

1902 Henry Lawson 'A Bush Publican's Lament' in *Prose* i 468: 'He's been on the roads this forty year, till he's as thin as a rat, and as poor as a myall black.'

1969 W. E. H. Stanner *After the Dreaming* 12: On the outskirts of the settlement there were a few groups of 'myalls' (bush natives) who were as wild as hawks, timid and daring by turns, with scarcely a word of English.

2 Any 'untamed' creature

1934 Vance Palmer *Sea and Spinifex* 222: 'Eight hundred bloody head. Scary brutes that hadn't seen a white man all their days – nothing by myalls and buffaloes.'

1938 Xavier Herbert *Capricornia* 72: Anna chased him through mud and mangroves and brought him home thrice before it occurred to her that he was what she called a Myall, a wild creature.

1941 Sarah Campion *Mo Burdekin* 203: In truth she was appalled, this myall who was at her happiest in bush.

3 Varieties of acacia, esp. *A. pendula*

1845 Edward John Eyre *Journals* i 47: Late in the afternoon we reached a watercourse, which I had previously named 'Myall Ponds', from the many and beautiful *Acacia pendula* trees that grew upon its banks.

1882 A. J. Boyd *Old Colonials* 2: It is a magnificent stock whip ... to its elaborately carved handle of scented myall.

1901 Rolf Boldrewood *In Bad Company* 450: The glaucous-foliaged myall, 'intense and soulful-eyed', with its swaying arms and drooping habit, looks like a tree out of its mind. It boasts with its more sturdy cousin, the yarran, a strangely-powerful violet perfume.

1938 Francis Ratcliffe *Flying Fox and Drifting Sand* 229: We ran first through red bluebush country with scattered myalls (one of the endless regiment of Acacias).

myxo Myxomatosis, disease used to exterminate rabbits [abbr.]

1953 *Daily Telegraph* (Sydney) 22 Jan. 6: Trappers said tonight that the incidence of 'myxo' was waning, and the rabbit population was increasing.

1966 *Coast to Coast 1965–1966* 135: 'The myxo'll look after the rabbits ... Them C.S.I.R.O. blokes did a good job there.'

1982 Max Harris *Australian* 6 Mar. Mag. 4: Restaurant critics are spreading like myxo.

N

naga, narga Waistcloth worn by an Aborigine, esp. in North-West Australia [f. Macassarese]

1907 Alfred Searcy *In Australian Tropics* 81: I . . . paid them with tobacco and rice, and Turkey-red for the women for nargers (waist cloths).

1930 J. S. Litchfield *Far-North Memories* 46: 'Might be you got it naga (loin-cloth) you give it longa me?'

1945 Elizabeth George *Two at Daly Waters* 100: I am reminded of the time, in our very early storekeeping days, when a myall, clad simply in a naga (length of cloth wound about him from the waist), came up to the verandah with silver in his hand, burning to buy something.

1961 Noni Braham *The Interloper* 123: A toddler, a brilliant red narga tied about her merry face, caught with one hand at her mother's flying skirts.

nailrod A coarse dark tobacco: *obs.*

1890 A. J. Vogan *The Black Police* 200: He hands our black friend a piece of 'nailrod' with which to charge his evening pipe.

1896 Henry Lawson 'Drifted Back' *Prose* i 235: 'You can give me half-a-pound of nailrod,' he said.

1967 Julian Stuart *Part of the Glory* 157: I could smoke or leave it alone, and as the jail weed was 'nail rod' or 'sheep dip' I left it severely alone.

namma hole See quots [Ab.]

1842 G. F. Moore *A Descriptive Vocabulary of . . . the Aborigines of Western Australia* 2: Amar, subst. A hole or pool of water in a rock. Ibid. 167: Water, standing in a rock – Gnamar.

1893 *Australasian* 5 Aug. 252: The route all the way from York to Coolgardie is amply watered, either 'namma holes' (native wells) or Government wells being plentiful on the road. [Morris]

1901 May Vivienne *Travels in Western Australia* 339: Native wells as 'namma-holes' have saved many a prospector from death by thirst.

1946 W. E. Harvey *North of 23°* 69: Handed on by tradition is the secret of the namma wells . . . These are the secret watering places of the desert blacks.

nan nan A straw hat; a young man affecting this as part of a mode of dress; a **lair**: *obs.* [origin obscure: cf. *nana*]

1899 Henry Lawson 'If I Could Paint' *Prose* ii 38: A boarding-house keeper, with two or three grown-up white-shirted, stand-up-and-turn-down collared (mother does all their linen herself), straw-hatted, cigarette-smoking sons . . . I'd like to paint her and the children – and the 'nan-nan' sons.

1899 W. T. Goodge *Hits! Skits! and Jingles!* 39: One little maid with a bashful smile / Given for a salutation; / Two little dudes of the nan-nan style / Bent on captivation.

1900–10 O'Brien and Stephens: *Nan-nan* A straw hat for men's wear.

nana 1 The head, in such expressions as 'off one's nana', 'do one's nana' [? f. *banana*]

1894 A. B. Paterson 'Hughey's Dog' in *The World of Banjo Paterson* ed. C. Semmler (1967) 29: 'Off his nanny again,' thought the boss, 'the sooner he goes the better.'

1968 *Coast to Coast 1967–1968* 9: 'Arright, Mister Mighty Boss. Don't do your narna.'

1975 *Australian* 8 Feb. 13: 'We've all learned to laugh at ourselves and our predicament,' Trevor England said. 'If we hadn't we'd all be off our nanas.'

2 A fool, an ass [listed by Partridge as English, a *softy* f. soft fruit]

1965 Graham McInnes *The Road to Gundagai* 148: Although he was obviously a gent, he was not a 'tonk' or a 'nana' . . . he was all right.

3 Applied to haircut [? f. resemblance to banana shape]

1941 Baker 48: *Nana (hair) cut* A utilitarian haircut in which the back of the head is closely shaved.

1966 *Coast to Coast 1965–1966* 35: If you used a brush-back, wore the hair long, or horror of horrors, had a *nana* haircut.

nanto A horse: *obsolescent* [? Ab. see quot. 1957]

1889 *The Arrow* 20 Jul. 2: And then the cove looks at our / 'Nantos' and says he, 'Well, I'm your man.'
1904 A. W. Howitt *The Native Tribes of South-East Australia* 299: He [the Aboriginal] walked with me for some miles on our next day's journey round Lake Hope, and was much amused at my remark, when the horse I was leading suddenly terrified him by neighing close to his ear, – 'Wotta yappali yenni, nanto yattana,' that is, 'Do not fear; the horse is talking.' [recalling a period before 1889]
1911 Sydney Partrige *Rocky Section* 12: 'Take old Vagabond and run him on the section, and you'll always have a second nanto if anything happens to the other.'
1924 *Observer* (Adelaide) 14 Jun. 17: He [an old Aborigine] would go on to tell how some of the tribe lower down south had seen these strange people . . . and the wonderful nantoes (horses).
1957 W. E. Harney *Life Among the Aborigines* 12: They saw many . . . with their strange 'nantus' (a word in reference to the distended nose of a horse after it has been ridden hard).

nap Blankets, bedding etc. [f. *nap* the pile on a fabric OED c. 1440]
1892 Barcroft Boake 'A Song from a Sandhill' *Bulletin* 2 Apr. 13 repr. in *Where the Dead Men Lie* (1897) 59: Drip, drip, drip! and one's 'nap' is far from dry.
1918 C. Fetherstonhaugh *After Many Days* 279: That night he could not catch the donkey, and he had to camp without any 'nap' (blankets).
1933 R. B. Plowman *The Man from Oodnadatta* 2: The blackboy's nap (blankets, waterproof sheet, etc) filled in the rear compartment.
1968 Walter Gill *Petermann Journey* 24: I knew where to put my 'nap', the Territory word for a 'swag'.

nap, go ~ on In Australia, most often used negatively, meaning 'not to be keen on', not to favour, not to care for [f. card game: *to go nap* to stake all one can, to speculate heavily OED 1884]
1918 *Kia Ora Coo-ee* 15 Dec. 3: Talking of souvenirs, I don't go nap on any of the ordinary kind which lose their interest after they have been looked at once or twice.
1923 Con Drew *Rogues & Ruses* 164: 'My trainer goes nap on Sunshine, but I'm wanting Bright Gleam to win.'
1939 Miles Franklin and Dymphna Cusack *Pioneers on Parade* 105: 'She knows I don't go nap on him, and I have to be careful not to seem prejudiced.'
1955 Patrick White *The Tree of Man* 80: 'I never went nap on the priest meself.'

narangy Joseph Furphy's term for those whose status on stations entitled them to be quartered in the **barracks** q.v.; hence a subaltern on a station, someone with authority lower than that of the manager [Ab.]
[**1793** J. Hunter *Historical Journal* ed. J. Bach (1968) 273: *Narrong* Any thing small.
1855 John Lang *The Forger's Wife* 121: He had mixed a good deal with the blacks . . . when he used the word 'narang' (small) but 'bidgee' (good), the groom did not quite comprehend the gentleman's praise of his horse.]
1903 Joseph Furphy *Such is Life* (1944) 254: Being a little too exalted for the men's hut, and a great deal too vile for the boss's house, I was quartered in the narangies' barracks.
1947 *Bulletin* 6 Aug. 4: Miles Franklin, who has made a close study of *Such is Life* and written a book about the author, believes that 'narangy' is synonymous with 'jackeroo': probably a blackfellow's word. She knows it only in *Such is Life*, where it is always used for the jackeroos, otherwise 'gentleman apprentices', on a station and others who were entitled to eat with them. They ate in the barracks at big places like Runnymede and with the family on small stations such as she grew up on.

narga see **naga**

nark *n.* A spoilsport [f. *nark* a police informer OED 1865]
[**1859** Hotten 57: *Knark* A hard hearted and savage person.]
1898 *Bulletin* 17 Dec. Red Page: An informer or mar-plot is a *nark* or a *Jonah*.
1919 W. H. Downing *Digger Dialects* 35: *Nark* A malevolent or bad-tempered person; a spoil-sport.
1928 Vance Palmer *The Man Hamilton* 94: 'Oh, don't be a nark, Miss Byrne,' he coaxed her.
1946 Kylie Tennant *Lost Haven* 369: Here

he was spoiling things for two kids, like a crabby old nark.

1959 Dorothy Hewett *Bobbin Up* 33: 'You're turnin' into a real nark,' Hazel said sulkily.

nark *v.* To annoy, thwart [f. *nark* to annoy, vex, irritate, exasperate EDD 1888]

1975 Richard Beilby *The Brown Land Crying* 200: 'Ya'd do anything to nark me, anything to put me down, wouldn't ya?'

narked Peeved, angry

1896 Henry Lawson 'The Shearing of Cook's Dog' *Prose* i 96: The cook usually forgot all about it in an hour . . . But this time he didn't; he was 'narked' for three days.

1911 Louis Stone *Jonah* 9: 'Orl right, wot are yer narked about?'

1946 Margaret Trist *What Else is There?* 135: 'Gee, Mum's going to be narked,' said Billy. 'You'll have to stick up for me, Ruby.'

1963 A. W. Upfield *The Body at Madman's Bend* 180: 'She raised it to half the wages this morning. Then looked narked 'cos we went slow.'

Nar Nar Goon Byword for any remote locality [f. place name]

1918 *Kia Ora Coo-ee* 15 Sep. 18: Jimmy was thinking of home, how his mother would be feeling, what his father would say about him, and how things in general were at Nar Nar Goon. Yes, dead, old, sleepy Nar Nar Goon.

1963 Lou Richards *Boots and All!* 176: They've had some shockers, too, players who would have struggled for a game with the South Nar Nar Goon fifths!

1981 *Age* (Melbourne) 8 Jun. 2: Television football commentaries generally tend to be about as rewarding as a night game at Nar Nar Goon football ground in a power strike.

Nasho Compulsory military training (abolished in 1972); a youth undergoing such training [abbr. of *National Service*]

1954 *Bulletin* 20 Oct. 9: 'I'm a Nasho,' he said. 'Got a bivouac this weekend.'

1966 Bruce Beaver *You Can't Come Back* 5: Sam, the new one, was just eighteen and due for his Nasho training.

1975 David Malouf *Johnno* 70: Now the Grand Central was the drinking place of 'Nashos'.

1980 *Sunday Mail* (Brisbane) 10 Feb. 5: Joh wants 'Nasho' back [heading] The Premier, Mr Bjelke-Petersen, yesterday suggested renewed national service to help boost the defence of northern Australia.

national game, Australia's 1 Two-up

1930 L. W. Lower *Here's Luck* 70: He had a small piece of wood in his hand, on which were balanced two pennies. The national game was in progress.

1944 Stan Arneil *One Man's War* (1980) 188: 'Two-up', our national game is severely frowned upon in the camp and all efforts are made to suppress it.

1976 *Bulletin* 10 Jan. 45: There's no greater humiliation than being a failure at the national game.

1983 *Sun-Herald* 23 Jan. 35: 'You can't wipe out two-up; it's our national game.'

2 Australian Rules Football

1889 Arthur Streeton *The National Game* [painting in Art Gallery of N.S.W.]

native A native plant

1977 Rodney Pybus *Times Literary Supplement* 14 Oct. 1213: A notice by the gate will stop / the stranger short: 'Australian natives', it says, / 'one dollar each'.

1979 *National Times* 4 Aug. 39: Although a wide variety of Australian natives has become available to gardeners in recent years, there is still comparatively little use made of native climbers.

naughty Sexual intercourse [f. *go naughty, do the naughty* OED 1869]

1959 Eric Lambert *Glory Thrown In* 106: 'Until I met Thelma, I always thought that sheilas had to be talked into a bit of a naughty.'

1963 Frank Hardy *Legends from Benson's Valley* 11: He put his arm around her, patting her buttock. I smiled, remembering his oft-repeated remark: 'I get a lot of knock backs but I get a lot of naughties.'

1975 Xavier Herbert *Poor Fellow My Country* 439: 'I'll give you a new dress . . . and we'll 'ave a bit of a party, and then another naughty, eh?'

1983 *Sun-Herald* 27 Mar. 29: Colin Chapman, of the ABC radio program Midday, scooped the sensation-peddling international press with his comment on Charles and Diana's giving the newshounds the slip at Alice Springs. 'My goodness, where were they off to?' asked Chapman. 'A nice cold beer and a naughty?'

neck, go under someone's To forestall an action contemplated by another, usurp someone else's prerogative [? f. horse racing]

1953 T. A. G. Hungerford *Riverslake* 61: 'I wouldn't want to go under your neck,' Randolph said sarcastically.

1961 Mena Calthorpe *The Dyehouse* 120: 'She knew she was going under Patty What's-her-name's neck. We can't shed tears of blood over these dames.'

1982 *NT News* (Darwin) 7 Dec. 7: Bob-a-job Boy Scouts in England have got under the neck of the Pommie Post Office by starting a cheap Christmas card delivery service.

neck-to-knees An old-fashioned bathing costume

1910 *Daily Telegraph* (Sydney) 20 Jun. 17: Neck to knee costumes have been for some time past insisted on at all popular resorts.

Ned Kelly 1 A name applied to anyone with 'bushranging' attributes [f. the famous bushranger (more strictly, bank-robber) hanged in 1880]

1941 Baker 41: *Kelly, Ned* Any person of bucaneering business habits.

1953 *The Sunburnt Country* ed. Ian Bevan 129: Phrases such as 'do a Ned Kelly' . . . lend so much verve and colour to the Australian serviceman's vocabulary.

1956 Tom Ronan *Moleskin Midas* 307: 'Tell that Commissioner of Taxation that Ned Kelly was a jackeroo alongside him.'

2 The belly: *rare* [rhyming slang]

1951 Dal Stivens *Jimmy Brockett* 86: I got his arm and rammed a right into his Ned Kelly.

1969 Alec H. Chisholm *The Joy of the Earth* 302: Those lads who customarily referred to . . . the belly as 'the Ned Kelly', to boots as 'daisy roots', to a snake as a 'Joe Blake', and so on.

Ned Kelly, game as Extremely plucky and insouciant

1945 Roy Rene *Mo's Memoirs* 24: He was game as Ned Kelly, and he'd ride anything.

1953 Dymphna Cusack *Southern Steel* 41: 'Is that kid game? Game as Ned Kelly.'

1966 Don Crick *Period of Adjustment* 66: 'Are you game?' 'As Ned Kelly.'

neddy A horse; in plural, usually race horse [f. *neddy* a donkey OED 1790]

1887 *Tibb's Popular Songbook* 9: So they saddled up their Neddys / And like loafers sneaked away.

1918 Bernard Cronin *The Coastlanders* 74: A hot cinder lit on my neddie's rump.

1965 William Dick *A Bunch of Ratbags* 40: My old man was backing the neddies as usual.

1975 Les Ryan *The Shearers* 69: 'Joe Clement's neddy – Wingay. Station hands reckon he's home and hosed.'

ned, red see **red**

neg driving The offence of driving negligently [abbr.]

1973 Alexander Buzo *Rooted* 44: 'Remember the time . . . when Hammo had a prang in his B and got dobbed in for neg driving?'

NESB See quot.

1988 *Sydney Morning Herald* 17 Dec. 10: There are about 4,000 inmates in the prison system of NSW. About 24 per cent of them are of non-English-speaking background (NESB).

Never-Never, the The regions remote from civilization, and as yet unsettled or unexplored, at first referring to north-western Queensland or northern Australia, generally. The term was given currency by Mrs Aeneas Gunn's classic *We of the Never-Never* (1908) [see quot. 1857]

1857 F. Cooper *Wild Adventures in Australia* 68: I had the cattle mustered, and the draft destined for the Nievah vahs* ready for the road. *Nievah vahs, sometimes incorrectly pronounced never nevers, a Cameleroi term signifying unoccupied land.

1875 Rolf Boldrewood *A Colonial Reformer* (1890) 174: 'But here it seems to be the Never-Never country, and no mistake.'

1901 Henry Lawson 'Shall We Gather at the River' *Prose* i 509: He was known from Riverina down South in New South Wales to away up through the Never-Never Country in Western Queensland.

1959 Dorothy Hewett *Bobbin Up* 21: 'I can remember when Bondi was just a heapa sand hills and scrub, goin' dirt-cheap. Nobody'd buy it then. We thought it was out in the never-never. An' look at it now.'

1979 *Australian* 29 Sep. Mag. 1: The new Never Never [heading] The most burning issue in the Northern Territory today is that of Aboriginal land rights.

new chum 1 A newly arrived prisoner in a gaol or hulk [English thieves' slang]

1812 Vaux: *Chum* A fellow prisoner in a jail, hulk, &c; so there are *new chums* and *old chums*, as they happen to have been a short or a long time in confinement.

1830–1 Henry Savery *Quintus Servinton* (1962) 287: 'There's near a thousand chaps here [in the hulk] . . . 'twont do to draw no distinctions like, with new chums.'

c. **1845** James Tucker *Ralph Rashleigh* (1952) 51: As Ralph and his associates in punishment marched past these dens [in the hulk], they were saluted by obstreperous shouts of 'New Chums! New chums!' from both sides.

2 Any new arrival, inexperienced in the conditions into which he has come

1838 T. L. Mitchell *Three Expeditions* i 99: He was also what they termed a 'new chum', or one newly arrived.

1849 Alexander Harris *The Emigrant Family* (1967) 141: Indeed, no one but a 'new chum' could have missed the course from the feeding ground to the hut.

1873 A. Trollope *Australia* ed. Edwards and Joyce (1967) 413: The idea that Englishmen, – that is, newchums, or Englishmen just come from home, – are made of paste, whereas the Australian, native or thoroughly acclimatized, is steel all through, I found to be universal.

1901 Henry Lawson 'Send Round the Hat' *Prose* i 474: A new-chum parson, who wanted a subscription to build or enlarge a chapel, or something, sought the assistance of the Giraffe's influence with his mates.

1929 Jules Raeside *Golden Days* 50: We were all new chums, and very indifferent bushmen, but our enthusiasm over-ruled our ignorance.

1957 Sydney Hart *Pommie Migrant* 159: 'You a new chum?' he asked. It was the first time I'd heard the expression.

1971 Rena Briand *White Man in a Hole* 132: Newchums at opal mining, they were soon involved talking 'shop' with Johnny while I set the billy on the fire.

New South, sunny An affectionate or jocular way of referring to New South Wales: *obsolescent*

1905 *The Old Bush Songs* ed. A. B. Paterson 61: Sunny New South Wales [ballad title]

1922 Arthur Wright *A Colt from the Country* 83: 'With that finished . . . we can kiss good-bye to sunny New South for a spell.'

nick To move smartly, to decamp [cf. E. dial. *nip* to move rapidly or nimbly OED 1825; *nit* to depart hurriedly]

1894 Ethel Turner *Seven Little Australians* 141: 'Meg could talk to father,' Bunby said, 'and Pip could keep teasing the General till Esther would be frightened to leave the room, and then me and Judy would nick down and have a run, and get back before you let them go.'

1938 Xavier Herbert *Capricornia* 257: 'You're only humming for a drink. Nick off home.'

1946 K. S. Prichard *The Roaring Nineties* 94: 'Guess you're dying for a cup of tea . . . I'll nick over to the camp and put on the billy.'

1969 Osmar White *Under the Iron Rainbow* 105: 'You haven't got to nick off on my account.'

1981 *Sydney Morning Herald* 11 Apr. 13: There is no lavatory so the Labor candidate . . . and his helpers nick across the road to use Ansett's.

Nifty Nev Mr Neville Wran, N.S.W. Premier 1976–87 [see quots]

1977 *Bulletin* 20 Aug. 35: Nifty Nev gave a farewell party for Diamond Jim at the Wrans' Woollahra pad.

1979 *Sun-Herald* 25 Mar. 176: Nifty trip [heading] And how did he get that nickname 'Nifty'? According to the Premier it happened when the young Neville Wran lived in Balmain and his mother gave him two pennies each day to catch a tram into the city and back. He regularly returned home with a penny in his pocket – that's nifty.

1983 *Sun-Herald* 18 Dec. 20: He [Wran] worked as a junior to Lionel Murphy who was then often briefed by Sydney solicitor Morgan Ryan. It was Ryan who gave Wran the nickname 'Nifty'.

night A nightgown [abbr.]

1969 Thomas Jenkins *We Came to Australia* 124: Waltz nights were not evenings with Strauss, but short nighties.

1979 *Sydney Morning Herald* 26 Dec. 14: Waltz or long nights $4 & $8 Pure cotton waltz length floral print nights, sizes 12–18, $4.

1983 *NT News* (Darwin) 4 Apr. 19: Ladies Nights 6.48 Short nights with lace trim and shirt tail hem in sizes 12–20.

night's a pup   see **pup**

niner   A nine-gallon keg of beer

1951 Dal Stivens *Jimmy Brockett* 304: I had a belly now like a niner.

1964 George Johnston *My Brother Jack* 111: 'Does he know how to breach a niner and get the bung in, that's the point?' He waved at the nine-gallon keg of beer, which had been propped up on the sofa.

1973 Alexander Buzo *Rooted* 77: 'He backed five winners at the picnic races, floored three locals in a brawl, demolished a niner, and torpedoed the minister's daughter.'

ning nong   see **nong**

nips, to put in the   As for **bite** q.v.

1919 W. H. Downing *Digger Dialects* 35: *Nip* To cadge (or 'Put in the nips').

1937 *Best Australian One-Act Plays* 398: 'He came along to put the nips in, so I gave him a couple of bob.'

1949 Lawson Glassop *Lucky Palmer* 230: 'You can't put the nips into old Alf. He's got death adders in his pockets.'

1955 D'Arcy Niland *The Shiralee* 41: 'He was here yesterday, too. Put the nips into me for tea and sugar and tobacco in his usual style. The biggest bludger in the country.'

1973 Frank Huelin *Keep Moving* 48: Parsons, priests, doctors, lawyers and professional people generally were legitimate prey, and we had no scruples about 'putting the nips' into them.

nit   A cry to warn of the approach of some authority; (as a verb) to decamp hurriedly

[**1864** Hotten: *Nix!* The signal word of schoolboys to each other that the master, or other person in authority, is approaching]

1882 *The Sydney Slang Dictionary* 10: *Nit* Get away (usually from a foe), make tracks.

1899 Henry Lawson 'If I Could Paint' *Prose* ii 38: I'd call it 'Nit! There's Mother'.

1911 Louis Stone *Jonah* 8: Suddenly there was a cry of 'Nit! 'Ere's a cop!' and the Push bolted like rabbits.

nit, to keep   To act as sentinel (or **cockatoo** q.v.) esp. for someone engaged in some illegal activity

1940 Ion L. Idriess *Lightning Ridge* 20: Bill kept nit for his elder brother who was courting a girl, and earned a shilling.

1952 T. A. G. Hungerford *The Ridge and the River* 10: 'Send two men a couple of hundred yards up and down the track to keep nit.'

1963 Gunther Bahnemann *Hoodlum* 79: Jerry, the lookout man stayed there, to keep nit.

nitkeeper   One who **keeps nit**

1935 *Bulletin* 22 May 21: That outlaw the sulphur-crested cockatoo is not the only bird to post a 'nit-keeper' when transgressing against society.

1943 *Khaki and Green* 101: Outside a window an abo was acting in a mysterious manner, reminiscent of a nit keeper in the days of S.P. bookies.

1963 Frank Hardy *Legends from Benson's Valley* 108: An elaborate network of nit-keepers on all sides frustrated the new policeman for three weeks.

1981 Maxwell Grant *Inherit the Sun* 183: Red knew there would be a nit-keeper, a man keeping watch who could slip out for the police if there was trouble.

Noah   A shark [f. rhyming slang *Noah's Ark*]

1952 A. G. Mitchell Suppl. to *Chamber's Shorter English Dictionary* 800: *Noah's Ark* n. (*slang*) a shark.

1966 Roger Carr *Surfie* 116: I've seen a four-gallon tin squashed in by the force of the water when a big Noah got caught and dragged it down. But mostly a four-gallon drum will drown any shark.

1978 John Hepworth *His Book* 82: The sun-bronzed ones refused to dunk their pinkies in the surf while the Noah's Ark was also in it.

1982 *Bulletin* 13 Jul. 65: 'I'll tell you what's worse than the Noahs,' said Edgar. 'What about those bloody dragon-flies?'

nobbler   A glass of liquor, usually spirits and water [origin obscure]

1851 *Illustrated Australian Magazine*

Nov. 248: The public houses are crowded with friends taking their last nobbler.
1873 A. Trollope *Australia* ed. Edwards and Joyce (1967) 660: A nobbler is the proper colonial phrase for a drink at a public-house.
1885 Mrs Campbell Praed *Australian Life* 103: Having accepted at my hands the customary 'nobbler', he would sit down for half-an-hour, talking.
1905 'The Shepherd' *The Old Bush Songs* ed. A. B. Paterson 116: He was going a pace, / Shouting nobbler after nobbler, with a smile upon his face.

no-hoper A horse with no prospect of winning; a man of whom nothing can be expected; a general term of contempt
1943 Baker 53: *No-hoper* An outsider (Racing slang).
1957 Ray Lawler *Summer of the Seventeenth Doll* 53: 'There's no excuse for that sort of thing, you're just a no-hoper.'
1966 Patrick White *The Solid Mandala* 18: 'A couple of no-hopers with ideas about 'emselves,' he would grumble, and then regurgitate: 'The Brothers Bloody Brown!'
1970 Jon Cleary *Helga's Web* 8: His mother had prayed that he might become a priest, but God in his wisdom had recognised a religious no-hoper when he saw one.

nong Someone stupid or ineffectual: *derogatory* [? f. E. dial. *nigmenog* a very silly fellow OED 1700: see also quot. 1865]
[**1865** Hotten: *Ning-nang* Horse-couplers' term for a worthless thorough-bred.]
1953 Baker 171: *nong* A simpleton or fool. [as World War II slang from New Guinea and the islands]
1959 Dorothy Hewett *Bobbin Up* 127: Stan had never carried a bunch of flowers in his life before, and said he felt like a nong-nong.
1969 Leslie Haylen *Twenty Years Hard Labor* 210–11: The continuance of compulsory voting means that the 'nongs', the indifferent and the plain bloody stupid, will continue to dominate the voting in the Commonwealth and the States for years to come.
1982 Mike Carlton *Sydney Morning Herald* 21 Jul. 8: If The Price is Right has one small virtue, it is that the show quite happily and honestly appeals to nongs, without in any way trying to disguise the fact.

noodle, noodling To prospect for opal in mullock heaps
1902 *Queensland Department of Mines Geological Survey* No. 177 cit. J. S. Gunn *An Opal Terminology* (1971) 30: Some splendid opal is found . . . by turning over and searching the old heaps and mullock – 'noodling'.
1921 K. S. Prichard *Black Opal* 73: They went noodling together, or gathering wild flowers. Ibid. 157: Potch gave him some scraps of sun-flash, and colour and potch to noodle, and he sat and snipped them contentedly.
1971 Rena Briand *White Man in a Hole* 27: 'Why don't you have a go at noodling*?' he suggested. *Local term for scraping the rubble heaps in search of opal.

norks A woman's breasts [origin uncertain: the wrapping on Norco butter shows a cow's udder]
1962 Criena Rohan *The Delinquents* 157: 'Hello, honey, that sweater – one deep breath and your norks will be in my soup.'
1970 Barry Oakley *Let's Hear it for Prendergast* 71: 'Wow, she's peeled right off. What norks!'
1980 Thomas Keneally in *Days of Wine and Rage* ed. Frank Moorhouse 252: 'All Maureen's got to do is trail one of her big lovely norks at him and the bugger dashes off another one of his press releases.'

Norm 1 The cartoon figure in the **Life Be In It** (q.v.) commercials conceived by Phillip Adams: see quot. 1975
1975 *Australian* 24 Nov. 2: Brian Dixon, Victoria's Minister for Youth, Sport and Recreation, has commissioned a new ocker character to help him in his latest campaign to get people off their backsides and into fitness activity. His name's NORM and he appeared for the first time last night on TV. Norm's idea of activity is sitting in front of his own set with a beer watching other people wear themselves out.
1990 *Sydney Morning Herald* 27 Jun. 3: Hold the vodka mate, it's Norm [heading] Under an agreement with the Bulgarian Union for Physical Culture and Sport, Bulgarians will have access to the 77 television commercials, starring overweight Norm.
2 Generic term for any inactive Australian male
1981 *Australian* 26 Oct. 3: For most 'Norms' it [daylight saving] means an extra hour in the pub.

North, the Deep Queensland: *derogatory*
[f. the 'Deep South' and its associations of in-
tolerance in U.S.A.]
1974 Peter Porter *Australian* 5 Oct. 13: I
learned that things have changed but not
enough to placate the southerners, for whom
Queensland in general and Brisbane in particular are sources of scorn and contempt.
'The Deep North' is the phrase used in Sydney.
1980 *Sunday Mail* (Brisbane) 12 Oct. 3:
The forthcoming elections will take the
smile off the faces of those southerners who
laugh at our so called 'deep north' politics.

northern myth, the The belief in north
Australia as having vast potentialities awaiting exploitation, attacked by B. R. Davidson in
The Northern Myth (1965)
1969 Osmar White *Under the Iron
Rainbow* 50: Kununurra . . . is the focal point
of hope for all those whose faith in the northern myth remains unshaken by the repeated
failure of large agricultural projects in the
Australian tropics.

Northern Territory champagne See
quots
1973 *Sunday Telegraph* (Sydney) 26 Aug.
112: Evidence was given that many Aboriginals drink 'Northern Territory champagne'
– methylated spirits mixed with health
salts.
1979 *Australian* 1 Dec. 13: When the
recipe for Territory champagne is 'metho
and Sal Vital', it is hardly surprising our
spirit consumption almost trebles the
national average.

nose, on the Ill-smelling; offensive, viewed
with disfavour (popularized as World War II
slang)
1941 Baker 49: *Nose, on the* (Said of
things) disliked, offensive.
1944 Lawson Glassop *We Were the Rats*
273: 'One of them base wallopers . . . He's on
the nose.'
1960 Nancy Cato *Green Grows the Vine*
46: 'You know, pongs. It means something's
on the nose.'
1974 *Australian* 12 Dec. 13: Australian
singer Helen Reddy has become a naturalised U.S. citizen. In a small ceremony in a
Los Angeles Federal court building this
week, she renounced her Australian citizenship and swore everlasting loyalty to the

Stars and Stripes. A bit on the nose, we
think.
1983 *NT News* (Darwin) 3 Feb. 7: Ever
noticed how some of Darwin's street bins are
a bit on the nose first thing in the morning
when they should be empty?

note A £1 note
1867 J. R. Houlding *Australian Capers*
131: 'Mr Buckles had not half a dozen notes
(pounds) when he landed here three years
ago.'
1923 Con Drew *Rogues & Ruses* 129:
'Where's the cow who's shook my 'alf-note?'
he demanded.
1934 F. E. Baume *Burnt Sugar* 353: He
took one look at the cheque and dashed for
the 'phone. 'A hundred notes, Maise. A
hundred notes.'
1942 Gavin Casey *It's Harder for Girls* 18:
I gave mum a score of notes, and she bought
a new outfit and went down for the wedding.

novel, the great Australian see **Australian**

nuddy, in the In the nude
1953 Baker 104: *nuddy* Nude, especially
in the phrase *in the nuddy*.
1959 Dorothy Hewett *Bobbin Up* 42:
'Take your bloody clothes and quit standin'
there half in the nuddy.'
1963 John Cantwell *No Stranger to the
Flame* 15: 'Been swimming – in the nuddy
and on me pat.'
1975 Xavier Herbert *Poor Fellow My
Country* 116: 'You're not shocked by my
bathing in the nuddy, are you?'

nugget *n.* 1 A lump of gold [f. *nug* a lump,
a block; *nugget* a lump of anything EDD
1853]
1852 G. C. Mundy *Our Antipodes* iii 322:
Gold was not so plentiful as was anticipated,
– not to be picked up on the hill-sides in an
afternoon's stroll; nor were nuggets* to be
dug up, like potatoes, by the bushel. *The
word nugget among farmers signifies a small
compact beast – a runt; among goldminers a
lump, in contradistinction to the scale or dust
gold.
2 An unbranded calf
1882 Rolf Boldrewood *Robbery Under
Arms* (World's Classics 1949) 21: So, as Jim
had lighted the fire, we branded the little red

heifer calf first – a fine fat six-month-old nugget she was – and then three bull calves.

nugget *v.* 1 To pick out nuggets of gold
1852 Lord Robert Cecil *Goldfields Diary* (1935) 31: He himself was snugly 'nuggeting' (picking out nuggets with a pen-knife or oyster knife) on his own behalf.
1857 F. Cooper *Wild Adventures in Australia* 103: The speaker . . . had been there, nuggetted from the surface-rocks three ounces of the pure metal in two days.
2 To appropriate unbranded calves
1881 Mrs Campbell Praed *Policy and Passion* 25: 'It is said that she has an eye to business, and does not disdain nuggeting*.'
*To *nugget*: in Australian slang, to appropriate your neighbours' unbranded calves.

nuggety Stocky, thickset
1874 Charles de Boos *The Congewoi Correspondence* 141: He's just oner them short, square-built, nuggetty kinder fellers.
1901 Henry Lawson 'Poisonous Jimmy Gets Left' *Prose* i 354: He was a short, nuggety man, and could use his hands, they said.
1924 Gavin Casey *It's Harder for Girls* 16: Molly was tall and dark . . . The chap she got hold of was just the opposite, a nuggety, fair little bloke.
1969 Osmar White *Under the Iron Rainbow* 107: He was a nuggety little bloke and moved as if he could handle himself in a blue.

Nullarbor nymph A semi-naked woman reported near Eucla in 1972
1972 *Sun-Herald* 2 Jan. 7: An Adelaide railway worker said today he thought the elusive 'Nullarbor Nymph' reported to have been seen handfeeding giant kangaroos near Eucla, was his missing 27-year-old daughter . . . She matched the description of the half-naked blonde reported to have been seen several times.
1973 *Australian* 31 Jan. 1: 'If,' he [Prince Charles] said at an Australia Day dinner, 'I've put my foot in it, I should probably be given a compulsory exit visa to the Antipodes and there find my name linked romantically (in the best traditions) with the naughty Nullarbor Nymph.'
1980 *Sydney Morning Herald* 31 Mar. 1: Sightings of the Nullarbor Nymph, a blonde girl who ran wild with the kangaroo, were reported widely here and overseas until the township of Eucla owned up to the publicity stunt.

numbers are up, when the When the results of a horse race are declared, hence when some issue is resolved
1890 Tasma *In Her Earliest Youth* 349: 'Yes, we've got two,' said George meditatively; 'and as for the family, it's the same as with everything else – you never can tell till the numbers are up.'
1920 Frank A. Russell *The Ashes of Achievement* 199: 'My guess is as good as his, before the numbers go up.'
1969 Mena Calthorpe *The Defectors* 181: 'You can expect a few sharp counter moves . . . You'll be hard at it until the numbers go up.'
1982 Joe Andersen *Winners Can Laugh!* 123: The numbers were up and that's what the bookies pay on.

Nyoongar A West Australian Aborigine (see quot. R. M. Berndt 1982); sometimes applied to those who are not full blood
1845 E. J. Eyre *Journal* ii 396: Men or people Yoon-gar [Western Australia]
1965 Colin Johnson *Wild Cat Falling* 10: Mum's always at me about this Noongar mob . . . A few of them are as light coloured as herself [a half caste], some even as near white as me but most of them are pretty dark skinned. None of them are real aboriginal, though sometimes a full blood relative will drift in.
1982 R. M. Berndt in Jack Davis *Kullark* xv: At first European settlement there were probably at least 6,000 Nyungar people . . . They occupied, roughly, all inland and coastal country of the south-west of Western Australia, from a line drawn diagonally from Mullewa to the north toward Kellerberrin and south-east to a little beyond Esperance. The whole area was divided among about thirteen dialectal/language territorial units, later consolidated under the general label of *nyungar*, meaning 'man' or 'person'.
1984 *ANU Reporter* (Canberra) 27 Apr. 3: Archie [Weller] describes himself as an 'octoroon', being one-eighth Aborigine. But in conversation he uses the Aboriginal word 'Nyoongah', meaning 'people' or 'man', when referring to his mates and himself. He says this is considered more appropriate than the European title of 'part-Aborigine'.

O

ocker The uncultivated Australian, a term superseding **Alf** q.v.; the nickname of anyone called Stevens [A colloquial form of names like Oscar, made a generic term by a character called Ocker played in a series of T. V. sketches by Ron Frazer (see quot. 1975)]

1927 *Sun* (Sydney) 1 May: 'Us Fellers' [comic strip in 'Sunbeams'] 1: 'And you know what I did to 'Ocker' Stevens at school on Wednesday don't you?'

1939 Kylie Tennant *Foveaux* 122: 'Will you get out of this, Okker,' Miss Montague requested irritably . . . Oscar responded in brotherly fashion.

1948 Sumner Locke Elliott *Rusty Bugles* in *Khaki, Bush and Bigotry* ed. Eunice Hanger (1968) 60: 'I've been talking to some of the RSD blokes and Occa Stevens is going to be in it.'

1971 George Johnston *A Cartload of Clay* 71: The big man would be a good player, a vigorous clubman, a hearty participant in the companionship of the club bar. He was a type Julian had sometimes talked to him about, what the boy called an 'Ocker'.

1975 Ron Frazer *Sun* (Sydney) 20 Aug. 37: 'Back in the Ocker days, guys would come up to me in their thongs and shorts and with a can in their hand and say, 'Y'know, mate, I know a guy just like that Ocker character.'

1982 *NT News* (Darwin) 25 Aug. 7: Traveller, arriving late at the airport to find the flight fully booked, was told by the cheerful airline worker: 'Sorry, ocker, the Fokker's chocker.'

off like a bride's nightie see **bride**

off one's kadoova, pannikin see **kadoova, pannikin**

off shears see **shears**

office bike, the see **bike**

offside To act as an **offsider** q.v.

1883 Let. in Mary Durack *Kings in Grass Castles* (1959) 272: I have put up a yard on Galway since Uncle Jerry left. Pumpkin and Kangaroo offsiding.

1917 R. D. Barton *Reminiscences of an Australian Pioneer* 93: I met a black-fellow who was offsiding for the horse-driver, and was called Archie.

1954 Tom Ronan *Vision Splendid* 284: He could always offside for Block and Carlson on Big House renovations if there was nothing to do in the store or the office.

offsider The assistant to a bullock-driver, walking on the offside of the team; a helper of any kind, in a subordinate position; an understudy

1880 Henry Kendall 'Jim the Splitter' *Poetical Works* ed. T. T. Reed (1966) 159: And, as to a team, over gully and hill, / He can travel with twelve on the breadth of a quill, / And boss the unlucky 'offsider'.

1905 'The Old Bullock Dray' *The Old Bush Songs* ed. A. B. Paterson 8 note: An offsider is a bullock-driver's assistant – one who walks on the off-side of the team and flogs the bullocks on that side when occasion arises. The word afterwards came to mean an assistant of any kind.

1919 E. S. Sorenson *Chips and Splinters* 14: He was able to ride after bullocks and act as offsider at pinches for his father.

1953 *Caddie A Sydney Barmaid* 211: 'I'll get me offsider. He's outside in the cart.' He trotted outside, returning with a lad of about fourteen.

1962 Gavin Casey *Amid the Plenty* 196: 'They want a storeman . . . Not a boss storeman to run it, just an offsider.'

oil Reliable information, esp. in expressions like 'the dinkum oil', and 'the good oil'

1916 C. J. Dennis *The Moods of Ginger Mick* 87: Now that's the dinkum oil from Ginger Mick.

1922 Arthur Wright *A Colt from the Country* 126: 'That's Dreamy Dan's owner,' remarked Knocker; 'we'll get the oil in a minute.'

1934 F. E. Baume *Burnt Sugar* 346: 'You're O.K. That's why I'm giving you the right oil.'

1953 *Caddie A Sydney Barmaid* 179: Ivy gave me the oil about him. 'Better look out for the old ram, he walks in his sleep.'

1970 Richard Beilby *No Medals for Aph-rodite* 279: 'I told ya, son. We're goin' to Crete. I got the good oil.'

1982 *NT News* (Darwin) 4 Jun. 7: We've got the good oil . . . that Humpty Doo school fete tomorrow is going to be even better than the first one.

oil rag, to live on the smell of an Metaphor for the ability to survive on minimum food or income [listed as a characteristic Irish expression in P. W. Joyce *English as We Speak it in Ireland* (1910) 129]

[**1893** Simpson Newland *Paving the Way* 228: 'I'd rather live on the smell of a greasy rag here than make millions in a climate like that.']

1900 Let. 28 Oct. in *Audrey Tennyson's Vice-Regal Days* ed. Alexandra Hasluck (1978) 125: The Germans are universally acknowledged to be the best colonists, they live on nothing – the saying is 'they live on an oiled rag', hardworking and so thrifty and keep a good deal to themselves.

1951 Dymphna Cusack and Florence James *Come In Spinner* 149: 'Oh, Bridie always could live on the smell of an oil rag.'

1983 Laurie Clancy *Perfect Love* 258: 'How are you going to support her? . . . She can't live off the smell of an oil rag, you know.'

Old Barn, the see **barn**

old boiler 1 A woman of mature age, 'no chicken': *derogatory* [f. the classification of poultry]

1959 *Bulletin* 25 Mar. 8: The steward put his head through the serving-hatch and inquired [of the lady bowlers] 'How are all my old boilers getting on? Ready for another round?' . . . Some of the old boilers are still simmering, but not getting any more tender in their regard for that steward.

1979 Colleen Klein *Women of a Certain Age* 109: He let her go. His eyes narrowed. 'Who wants an old boiler?' he said.

1987 David Foster *Testostero* 51: 'You're not trying to tell me my son's shacked up with some old boiler?'

2 An air hostess (now flight attendant) [f. Sir Reginald Ansett's description of air hostesses on strike in 1975]

1975 *Courier-Mail* (Brisbane) 3 Apr. 5: Sir Reginald Ansett: 'A batch of old boilers. We can do without them' [heading] It wasn't so much Sir Reginald's crack about hostesses

being 'old boilers' that needled the girls, but his suggestion that they were 'glorified waitresses'.

1981 *Sunday Mail* (Brisbane) 5 Jul. 2: Those 'old boilers' stay as trim as ever . . . Any woman who has ever been an air hostess seems to have that special something about her. As if she's been to a very good finishing school.

1989 *Sydney Morning Herald* 22 Apr. 4: According to the evidence presented to the tribunal . . . female flight attendants were allocated the worst hotel rooms among flight crew, were relegated to more menial tasks such as cleaning toilets, were encouraged to retire at 35 and were referred to as 'old boilers' after that.

old boy, the The penis

1972 Geoff Morley *Jockey Rides Honest Race* 172: 'Well what is it, your old boy fall off?'

1982 *Bulletin* 9 Mar. 96: I'll never forget the look on guests' faces in a Manchester hotel one night, when they arrived back to find a well known Australian player draped on a chaise-longue in the public lounge, having what is commonly referred to as his 'old boy' autographed by a member of the opposite sex.

see **old fellow**

Old Bus, the Sir Charles Kingsford-Smith's name for his aircraft *The Southern Cross*

1934 *The Old Bus* [title of film directed by Jack Percival, screened at the Liberty Theatre, Sydney, Aug. 1934]

1980 *Australian* 20 Feb. 9: Construction will begin in a few weeks on a full-scale replica of Sir Charles Kingsford-Smith's most famous aircraft – the original Southern Cross – the 'Old Bus' in which he made most of his historic flights.

old chum The converse of **new chum** q.v. (quot. 1812)

1846 C. P. Hodgson *Reminiscences of Australia* 22: Remember it may soon be your turn to act the same part, and give an asylum and 'Bush' education to the 'New Chum'*. *'New Chum' in opposition to 'Old Chum'. The former 'cognomen' peculiarizing the newly arrived emigrant, the latter as a mark of respect attached to the more experienced Colonist.

1855 Raffaello Carboni *The Eureka Stockade* ed. G. Serle (1969) 13: I frequently saw horrid scenes of blood; but I was now an old chum and therefore knew what was what in colonial life.

1905 'The Squatter of the Olden Time' *The Old Bush Songs* ed. A. B. Paterson 108: And quaffs his cup of hysonskin, the beverage old chums choose.

Old Dart, the   England [origin obscure]
1908 E. S. Sorenson *Quinton's Rouseabout* 206: Murty unexpectedly came in for something like £800 by the death of a distant and almost forgotten relative in the old dart.
1923 Jack Moses *Beyond the City Gates* 170: Bring it to the notice of those chaps with a bit of cash in the 'Old Dart'.
1941 Sarah Campion *Mo Burdekin* 89: 'Still as green,' interjected Dad, 'as a pommy straight from th' "Old Dart"'!
1962 Stuart Gore *Down the Golden Mile* 261: 'Gettin' too much of the good Aussie beer into you, instead of that warmed-up bilge water they sell in the Old Dart.'

old fellow, the   The penis
[**1957** D'Arcy Niland *Call Me When the Cross Turns Over* 110: 'The day you're defenceless, sister,' he said, 'that's the day me and the big feller are waiting for.]
1972 Dorothy Hewett *The Chapel Perilous* 61: 'When she takes off her clothes it'll make the ol' feller stand up.'
1983 Clem Gorman *A Night in the Arms of Raeleen* 44: 'Chock-a-block. Old feller was in there, right up to the maker's name.'
see **old boy**

old hand   1   An ex-convict
1837 James Mudie *The Felonry of New South Wales* 180: The more knowing ones, – that is, the very worst characters amongst the convicts, – seldom undergo any real punishment at all ... they bring out with them letters to some of the 'old hands' in the colony, so as to ensure their being applied for as assigned servants by persons of the *right sort.*
1845 C. Griffith *The Present State ... of Port Phillip* 76: The old hands are men, who, having been formerly convicts (or lags as they are generally termed) have become free by the expiration of their sentences.
1901 Henry Lawson 'The Golden Graveyard' *Prose* i 324: Mother Middleton was an awful woman, an 'old hand' (transported convict) some said.
2   Someone long established in a particular

place or mode of living; a person of particular experience
1843 John Hood *Australia and the East* 215: The *amor patriae* is strong among the 'old hands', as the fathers of the colony are called; but then it shows itself merely in the wish to sell their share of it for an enormous price!
1862 Arthur Polehampton *Kangaroo Land* 60: It was and is a constant source of ambition among 'new chums', especially the younger ones, to be taken for 'old hands' in the colony.
1916 Let. in Bill Gammage *The Broken Years* (1974) 116: My new men are all frightfully keen and anxious to get into a scrap – and I will admit that many of us 'old hands' are beginning to hanker after powder again.
1959 Dorothy Hewett *Bobbin Up* 149: Alice and Lil, both old hands, were all tidied up, waiting for the signal to switch off.

oldie   A member of the older generation [OED 1874]
1960 A. W. Upfield *Bony and the Kelly Gang* 168: 'The oldees can natter and gossip and tell tales.'
1972 Geoff Morley *Jockey Rides Honest Race* 210: 'Things are getting better, but it's a slow process. You've got to give us oldies a chance.'

old man   Of exceptional size (from the term applied to the fully grown kangaroo)
1834 George Bennett *Wanderings in New South Wales* i 286: Many persons when alone are afraid to face a large 'old man' kangaroo.
1845 R. Howitt *Impressions of Australia Felix* 233: I stared at a man one day for saying that a certain allotment of land was 'an old-man allotment': he meant a large allotment – the old-man kangaroo being the largest kangaroo.
1903 Joseph Furphy *Such is Life* (1944) 122: A picaninny alternative, that, you say? I tell you, it proved an old-man alternative before it ran itself out.
1934 Archer Russell *A Tramp-Royal in Wild Australia* 190: Central Australia was experiencing ... its usual climatic respite from days of blistering heat in an 'Old Man' sand storm.

old man, the   The penis
1969 D'Arcy Niland *Dead Men Running* 284: He told her that just the look of her at

times made the old man stand up like a brick chimney, and he hoped it would be the only thing ever to come between them.
see **old boy, old fellow**

Old People, the   The Aborigines, esp. in a tribal state
1859 Frank Fowler *Southern Lights and Shadows* 105: The oldest aborigines know nothing about the origin of these strange relics: they always tell you they were the work of the 'old people'.
1938 Xavier Herbert *Capricornia* 364: The elegant half caste nephew and heir had gone on walkabout with the Old People.
1974 Donald Stuart *Prince of My Country* 4: Beyond the woolshed . . . there are the humpies of the Old People, his mother's people.

Old Tin Shed, the   see **Tin Shed**

Old Viceroy, the   see **Viceroy**

on   In agreement, willing to take part, often in the expression 'Are you on?' 'You're on' denotes the acceptance of a bet [cf. *on* adv. 13c OED 1812: having a wager on something]
1883 George Darrell *The Sunny South* (1975) 29: 'What do you say if we throw them into the fish pond?' 'I'm on!' 'So am I!'
1903 Joseph Furphy *Such is Life* (1944) 128: 'If each of you gives me a kiss, of her own good will, I'll promise not to tell. Are you on?'
1939 Kylie Tennant *Foveaux* 350: 'Are you on?' Herb asked impatiently as he began to remove his coat. 'I'll give it a go.'
1949 Lawson Glassop *Lucky Palmer* 89: 'I'll have a pony on it.' 'You're on,' said Lucky, turning to him with a beaming smile.

on the improve   see **improve**

on it   sc. the liquor
1938 Eric Lowe *Salute to Freedom* 38: He knew how drink affected Brand, and he muttered to his wife, 'He's on it proper to day, mother.'
1945 H. M. Moran *Beyond the Hill Lies China* 105: For days, while he was 'on it' he did everything horrible except beat his wife.
1956 Patrick White *The Tree of Man* 141:

'It is him,' she said finally. 'It is that bastard. He is on it again.'
1968 *Coast to Coast 1967–1968* 157: 'You've got the shakes,' he said. 'Been on it, have you?'

on, it was ~ (for young and old)   An expression for an outbreak of disorder, any general absence of restraint
1951 Eric Lambert *The Twenty Thousand Thieves* 258: Peter Dimmock bounded between the tents leaping into the air at every few paces and whooping: 'It's on! It's on for young and old!'
1969 William Dick *Naked Prodigal* 49–50: Just before closing time a brawl started when some bloke walking by spilt beer on Ackie so Ackie's young brother king hit him and the bloke's mate stepped in so Archie hit *him* – and then it was on.
1979 *Bulletin* 10 Apr. 60: He picked up a bottle, and hurled it back into the crowd – and it was on again for young and old.

on the track   see **wallaby track**

on week   See quot.
1986 *Australian* 30 Aug. 17: This week [in Bourke] was 'On Week', when locals receive their fortnightly social security cheques and an estimated $45,000 passes through the pub and shop tills within three days of them being cashed.

oncer   See quot.
1976 *Sun-Herald* 12 Dec. 15: A 'oncer' is the term coined by politicians for those elected in a landslide and can only expect to serve one term in Parliament.

one-armed bill-poster (milker), busy as a   Extremely busy or harassed ['As busy as the devil in a high wind' Grose 1811]
1951 Dal Stivens *Jimmy Brockett* 214: I was as busy nowadays as a one-armed bill-sticker in a gale.
1971 Frank Hardy *The Outcasts of Foolgarah* 216: 'I'm in more trouble than a one-armed bill-poster in a high wind.'
1983 *NT News* (Darwin) 29 Jan. 21: Ask her if she's busy and likely she will reply: 'As busy as a one-armed milker on a dairy farm.'

one day of the year, the   Anzac Day (25 April) commemorated as a public holiday
1945 Cecil Mann *The River* 149: 'As you all heard the Padre and Premier both say at

the service, it is the one day in the year which we, with very great pride, can call our *own* Day.'
1962 Alan Seymour *The One Day of the Year* [play title]
1971 Frank Hardy *The Outcasts of Foolgarah* 211: A retired officer of high rank . . . out late celebrating the One Day of the Year.
1974 David Ireland *Burn* 115: I never went to a march on Anzac Day. I can always remember the kids that died up there in the slush . . . I don't have to wait for one day of the year.

one-roomed house, couldn't find a grand piano in a see **couldn't**

one them, to In two-up, to throw a head and a tail
1949 Lawson Glassop *Lucky Palmer* 168: The pennies hit the canvas. One jumped in the air, landed and lay flat. It was a tail. 'And he's –' began the fat man. The other penny ran a few feet and stopped. It was a head. '– one'd 'em!' finished the fat man.

ones, two The cry in two-up when the spinner throws a head and a tail
1911 Louis Stone *Jonah* 217: He set two pounds of his winnings, and tossed the coins. 'Two ones!' cried the gamblers, with a roar.
1951 Frank Hardy *Power Without Glory* 324: 'Two ones!' Rand said as the two pennies thudded down, one head and one tail showing.
1979 *Bulletin* 14 Aug. 36: If one head and one tail showed, then it was 'ones', meaning that the spinner must continue spinning until two sides showed together.

onion See quot. 1969
1969 *Sydney Morning Herald* 16 Jul. 13: When he had passed the circle of men, he knew an 'onion was going on' . . . The Court was told on Monday that the expression 'onion' meant a girl was available for sexual intercourse with two or more men.
1984 Brian Singleton *National Times* 30 Nov. 17: 'If the girl alleges the tradition on-i-on or onion as it is sometimes incorrectly pronounced, by a group of motor bike riders in a disused gravel pit after several hours of riotous drinking I suppose the spinsters will do [as jury members].'

onka 1 Finger: *rare* [rhyming slang Onkaparinga (place-name) = *finger*]
1975 *Bulletin* 25 Apr. 46: onka (short for Onkaparinga; finger).
1979 *Sun-Herald* 27 May 78: The tote clerk heard the bell ring for closing time, and slammed the window on his 'onkaparinga'.
2 An Onkaparinga brand blanket
1984 *Age* (Melbourne) 23 Mar. Weekender 10: You will need to have tested the thermos for leaks . . . and shaken the summer's sand from the Onka.

onkus Disordered, out of action, gone wrong
1924 *Truth* 27 Apr. 6: *Onkus* Unpleasant; absurd.
1941 Baker 51: *Onkus* All wrong, incorrect; (of machinery) out of order.
1947 Norman Lindsay *Halfway to Anywhere* 84: He took a pull at it, adding: 'A bit onkus, but drinkable. Have a swig.'

Oodnagalahbi Imaginary place which is a byword for backwardness and remoteness, given currency in the Mavis Bramston show [? f. *Oodnadatta* and *galah*]
1969 *Sydney Morning Herald* 1 Dec. 6: Last night the show [Hard Day's Week] was firmly bogged down in Oodnagalahbi (may it be eaten by grasshoppers) and Dad and Dave and Mabel wore felt hats pulled down on their foreheads and cracked jokes about carpet snakes in the dunny.
1972 Geoff Morley *Jocky Rides Honest Race* 93: 'Fifty per cent of the Australian population only buy their newspaper to see if Nancy and Sluggo finally get married. The other fifty per cent want to find out who won the third race at Oodnagallabi.'
1981 *Canberra Times* 30 Jul. 15: Canberra was chosen for the premiere season of 'Centrespread' in an effort to qualify the film for this year's Australian Film Institute awards. It would have been better to have opened it in Oodnagalahbie, where it could have sunk without trace as it deserves.

open slather see **slather**

open, they were sc. the pubs (when times of business are prescribed by law)
1942 Sarah Campion *Bonanza* 19: It was eleven – 'they' were open.
1954 *Bulletin* 2 Jun. 9: 'They were open', and . . . the homburged Australian and I spend an hour.

Orchid, Blue see **Blue**

oscar Cash: *obsolescent* [rhyming slang from Oscar Asche (1871–1936) the Australian actor]
1919 W. H. Downing *Digger Dialects* 36: *Oscar* Money.
1931 William Hatfield *Sheepmates* 161: 'Sit in, some o' yous that aint flyblown . . . an' their I.O.U.'s is good, if there's no real Oscar about the joint.'
1942 Leonard Mann *The Go-Getter* 16: 'Get the oscar off Tom soon's I see him. He's honest.'
1959 D'Arcy Niland *The Big Smoke* 21: 'If you'd been fighting all those blokes in the ring you'd have more oscar in your kick now than the Prime Minister himself.'

O.T., the The Overland Telegraph line from Adelaide to Darwin
1898 A. B. Paterson *Bulletin* 31 Dec. 31: The Overland Telegraph ends at Palmerston and employs a large staff known as the O.T. men.
1933 F. E. Baume *Tragedy Track* 36: A telephone system as far north as Ryan's Well, 78 miles along the O.T.
1942 Charles Barrett *From a Bush Hut* 38: I followed the O. T. (Overland Telegraph) down to the Alice, where I hopped the rattler.

Our Glad, Harbour see **Glad, Harbour**

out of the box see **box**

outback *adv.* Out in or to the regions remote from the settled districts of Australia
1875 Rolf Boldrewood *The Squatter's Dream* repr. as *Ups and Downs* (1878) 31: The whole party . . . rode silently along the indistinct trail which led 'out back'.
1892 Henry Lawson 'In a Dry Season' *Prose* i 80: Somebody said to me, 'Yer wanter go outback, young man, if yer wanter see the country. Yer wanter get away from the line.'
1930 Edward Shann *An Economic History of Australia* 15: They fenced paddocks which grew larger and larger as the carrying capacity grew lighter 'out-back' – where paddocks of 20 or 40 thousand acres are not rare.
1972 Ian Moffitt *The U-Jack Society* 122: 'His dream was to get some land outback.'

outback *adj.* Pertaining to the regions remote from the settled districts
1893 Henry Lawson 'Some Popular Australian Mistakes' *Prose* ii 25: We wish to Heaven that Australian writers would leave off trying to make a paradise out of the Out Back Hell.
1911 C. E. W. Bean *The 'Dreadnought' of the Darling* 99: Boundary riders on the outback runs are seldom permanent hands – not because they are not wanted to stay, but more because the life is such that they are always ready for a change.
1935 R. B. Plowman *The Boundary Rider* 71: It was a peculiarly Australian outback community at Wooltana in its dependence and interdependence.
1962 Cynthia Nolan *Outback* 92: A quite erroneous opinion, generally held in the cities, is that wives on these outback stations are eager to have a visit from another white woman.

outback *n.* The regions remote from the settled districts
1897 Henry Lawson 'The Bush and the Ideal' *Prose* ii 31: No one who has not been there can realise the awful desolation of Out Back in the ordinary seasons; few even of those who have tramped there can realise it.
1913 W. K. Harris *Outback in Australia* 1: There is no limit to the hospitality of the far Outback.
1958 Russel Ward *The Australian Legend* 68: There is substance . . . in the traditional belief that the 'true' or 'typical' Australians were the men of the outback.

outbackery The conscious cultivation of 'outback' values
1966 Tom Ronan *Once There Was a Bagman* 124: The phase of life, now sneered at by our pharisaical, suburban, scholarship-nurtured intelligentsia – 'Outbackery' they call it – has its intervals of excellence.

outer, on the Not favoured to win, not given a chance; disliked, ostracized [? f. the outside track or the outer ground in racing]
1924 *Truth* 27 Apr. 6: *Outer, on the* To be poor; to be outside.
1928 Arthur Wright *A Good Recovery* 157: 'You told me yourself that you were the cause of my being on the outer.'
1944 Jean Devanny *By Tropic, Sea and Jungle* 97: He had been thrown on the 'outer' at the completion of a job for Cinesound

Studios, Sydney, and with his few remaining pounds he had made his way north.

1953 T. A. G. Hungerford *Riverslake* 174: 'And you're on the outer for sticking up for him?'

1970 Ivan Southall *Bread and Honey* 54: Warren had always been on the outer, like a stray dog, always getting pushed.

outside Relating to the interior of Australia, beyond the settled regions near the coast (the **inside** country, q.v.)

1864 See **inside**.

1884 A. W. Stirling *The Never Never Land* 123: One talks of . . . the wretched hut in which the manager of an outside station lives, as the 'house'.

1895 George Ranken *Windabyne* 216: We had not found it easy to learn much about the outside country, but the nearer we got to the actual frontier we found that information was the more difficult to get.

1901 Rolf Boldrewood *In Bad Company* 271: 'Why don't you go outside . . . I mean *real outside country*, beyond the settled districts, in Queensland, Western Australia, Kimberley – anywhere.'

1910 C. E. W. Bean *On the Wool Track* 47: The men who owned 'outside' runs before the drought, and who own the same runs still, may almost be counted on the fingers.

over the fence see **fence**

overland *v.* **overlanding** *n.* To drove cattle long distances

1871 Marcus Clarke *Old Tales of a Young Country* 163: 'Overlanding' was a profitable and, withal, romantic occupation. Young men of spirit, wearied of the capital, and prompted by love of gain and adventure, purchased cattle and sheep in New South Wales, and drove them 'overland' to the 'New Orleans' of Colonel Torrens.

1923 Jack Moses *Beyond the City Gates* 119: When I met him first he was in charge of a mob, overlanding from the Gulf to Vic.

1971 Keith Willey *Boss Drover* 48: The big road trains have taken the work away from the drover nowadays but at one time overlanding cattle paid big money, provided you knew your job.

overlander A man droving cattle over long distances, and so one of the more dashing of the bushworkers

1841 George Grey *Journals of Two Expeditions of Discovery* ii 183: The Overlanders are nearly all men in the pride of youth, whose occupation is to convey large herds of stock from market to market and from colony to colony.

1863 Rachel Henning *Letters* ed. D. Adams (1962) 136: Two atrocious young 'overlanders', first-rate specimens of the free-and-easy Australia.

1907 Alfred Searcy *In Australian Tropics* 125: If a crowd of overlanders and backblockers happened to be present, things would be made lively.

1933 F. E. Baume *Tragedy Track* 85: The grave . . . stands mutely to remind the overlander of the tragedy.

oyster, Kimberley see **Kimberley**

Oz Australia [abbr. of *Aussie*]

1981 Buzz Kennedy *Australian* 14 Dec. 2: They can say what they like about The Overseas . . . but the Old Oz will do me.

1983 Leo Schofield *Sydney Morning Herald* 3 Sep. 31: Computer Customs check-in and plane spraying are unique to Oz.

P

Pacific peso The Australian dollar, after the deregulation of the currency by the Hawke government

1986 *Bulletin* 2 Sep. 102: How the Pacific peso was shaped [heading]

1987 *Sydney Morning Herald* 25 Sep. 27: Controversial Budget balancer, the Reserve Bank, has emerged bloodied from a confrontation with the razor-sharp foreign exchange market that started with its aggressive selling of the Pacific peso on Wednesday.

pack, go to the The lapse into a lower

state; deteriorate, fall into disrepute [listed by Partridge as a New Zealandism]

1916 Let. of 17 Apr. in Bill Gammage *The Broken Years* (1974) 116: A big mistake is being made in keeping us here too long, for we are 'over-trained', and we have the d——s own job to keep our men from 'going to the pack' through staleness.

1938 Francis Ratcliffe *Flying Fox and Drifting Sand* 245: I learned of areas which had gone completely to the pack, where man had given nature best, and the holdings had been abandoned one by one.

1958 Gavin Casey *Snowball* 118: 'You wait till he gets a bit older. Them abos always go t' the pack.'

1984 Ian Leslie *National Times* 20 Apr. 4: Susan Peacock was extremely attractive, she shone and had great appeal. But now she looks matronly, frumpish, she's gone to the pack a bit.

packapoo ticket see **pakapoo**

packing them, packing death Scared i.e. holding back nervous diarrhoea (Services Slang in World War II)

1951 Eric Lambert *The Twenty Thousand Thieves* 132: 'He's packing them badly. He's quite useless.'

1961 Russell Braddon *Naked Island* 44: 'Who's panicking?' 'You are, son. Fair packing 'em, y' are.'

1982 *Sydney Morning Herald* 10 Jul. 12: Of course, girls would be 'packin' it', going down an aisle in front of about thirteen hundred people, including photographers and TV cameras, which would be a very nerve-wracking experience for any 17-year-old girl.

1983 Sun-Herald 24 Jul. 118: Some banks, long scared of competition, have been West-packing death.

pad A track trodden by bullocks, horses etc.

1898 David W. Carnegie *Spinifex and Sand* 82: Sometimes the pads of wallabies, kangaroos, or emus, may serve as a guide.

1910 C. E. W. Bean *On the Wood Track* 101: The pads he [the rabbit] makes going down to drink in the Darling River are in places two feet deep.

1935 R. B. Plowman *The Boundary Rider* 238: A pad ran off the main track and branched to the right. The big horse followed it.

1942 Gavin Casey *It's Harder for Girls*

155: 'I was through a dozen times when the track was just a camel-pad.'

1964 Tom Ronan *Packhorse and Pearling Boat* 158: A main horse pad (bridle path, to you) led from the far end of this swamp.

Paddo Paddington, the Sydney suburb

1945 *Coast to Coast 1944* 163: 'Just down the road a piece I live, down in Paddo.'

1974 *Australian* 14 Aug. 3: Paddo gets a National Trust rating.

paddock Playing field

1978 *Australian* 3 Jul. 17: 'Hage is open season. Sure he's vigorous. The general opinion is to get him off the paddock and the game will be all right,' Glossop said.

1981 *Canberra Times* 24 Jul. 16: 'My doctor is a beaut and he is giving me great confidence in myself,' he [Len Pascoe] said. 'I'm sticking to his guidelines and he promises me I'll be back on the paddock ready to go if I work along with him.'

1984 *Daily Mirror* (Sydney) 6 Apr. 85: Young set the example for the team when it mattered most in the centre of the paddock.

paddock, heifer see **heifer**

paddock, the long see **long**

paddock, saddling see **saddling paddock**

paddock, wouldn't be seen (dead) with someone in a (forty-acre) An expression of extreme dislike [Australian version of 'not being seen dead in a ten-acre field']

1900 Henry Lawson 'Andy Page's Rival' *Prose* i 362: 'You needn't think you're goin' to cotton on with me any more after this! I wouldn't be seen in a paddock with yer.'

padre's bike, gone for a ride on the Jocular reply to any request for someone's whereabouts (World War II slang)

1953 *The Sunburnt Country* ed. Ian Bevan 129: '*He went mad and they shot him*' is the routine answer to any superior seeking the whereabouts of a subordinate. An alternative version is that he has '*gone for a ride on the padre's bike*'.

1968 Stuart Gore *Holy Smoke* 80: 'Shot through on the Padre's bike,' she says to the rozzers when they show up.

see **went for a crap and the sniper got him**

Painter, Jack the see **Jack the Painter**

pakapoo ticket, like a Untidy, disordered: *obsolescent* [f. the difficulty in deciphering a Chinese betting slip]

[**1911** Louis Stone *Jonah* 92: He had come down early to mark a pak-ah-pu ticket at the Chinaman's in Hay Street.]
1951 Eric Lambert *The Twenty Thousand Thieves* 144: Henry opened Dooley's paybook, the pages of which showed liberal sprinklings of the red ink in which fines and convictions were entered. 'What a paybook!' he sighed. Dooley grinned. 'Like a pak-a-poo ticket,' he agreed.
1968 Stuart Gore *Holy Smoke* 86: 'You wouldn't have a clue where to start once you got a pen in your hand – your paper'd be marked like a pakapoo ticket!'
1972 Alexander Macdonald *The Ukelele Player under the Red Lamp* 227: His bi-weekly betting lists made an average pakapoo ticket look like a model of stark simplicity.
1983 *Sydney Morning Herald* 3 Jan. 6: Pakapoo ticket to register a car [heading] The Department of Motor Transport's Application for Renewal of Registration of Motor Car would have to be the worst form designed by a bureaucracy. The numerous boxes, underlinings, bold printing, shaded areas and arrows do not really assist ...

pan out To 'turn out', yield results [f. the pan used in washing alluvial gold U.S. 1868 Mathews]
1898 D. W. Carnegie *Spinifex and Sand* 70: Plans so simple on paper do not always 'pan out' as confidently expected.
1908 *Australian Magazine* 1 Nov. 1250: 'Pan out' obviously comes from the old alluvial worker.
1911 Alfred Searcy *By Flood and Field* 78: The sun was low in the west as we wended our way back to camp, all hands being satisfied that the crabbing expedition had 'panned out' in rare style.
1928 Vance Palmer *The Man Hamilton* 146: 'If you don't worry about it, it's got a knack of panning out right.'
1988 *Age* (Melbourne) 10 Jun. 24: 'We'll wait and see how the race pans out.'

pannikin boss, overseer Someone with minor authority over his fellow-workers: *derogatory*

1898 Morris: *Pannikin-boss*, or *Pannikin-overseer*, n. The term is applied colloquially to a man on a station, whose position is above that of the ordinary station-hand, but who has no definite position of authority, or is only a 'boss' or overseer in a small way.
1918 George Dale *The Industrial History of Broken Hill* 74: Some miles from Grassmere they met a pannikin overseer, who by some means conveyed the news of their approach to the station.
1959 Dorothy Hewett *Bobbin Up* 72: All their unshakable distrust of the pannikin boss, the boss's man . . . the lowest of the low in a world where dog ate dog.
1969 D'Arcy Niland *Dead Men Running* 121: Father Vaughan seemed to project himself as no more than the mouthpiece of a pannikin boss of a God who sounded like a brutal and violent pirate.

pannikin, off one's Out of one's mind [variant of 'off his head', the pannikin being a familiar utensil to the bush-worker]
1895 Cornelius Crowe *Australian Slang Dictionary* 56: *Off his pannikin* Silly.
1899 Steele Rudd *On Our Selection* 107: 'I seen 'im just now up in your paddick, an' he's clean off he's pannikin.'
1916 C. J. Dennis *The Moods of Ginger Mick* 126: 'Per'aps I'm orf me pannikin wiv' sittin' in the sun.
1934 Brian Penton *Landtakers* 383: 'He's gone raving off his pannikin in Sydney with the guts half crushed out of him.'

panno Abbr. for **pannikin boss**: *derogatory*
1957 Tom Nelson *The Hungry Mile* 50: So we decided to follow the 'panno' and tracked her to the Australian Stevedoring Industry Board Office.
1960 Ron Tullipan *Follow the Sun* 31: 'I thought he might have been a panno. Perhaps it's only the panno blood makes him choose his drinking mates with such care.'
1965 Frank Hardy *The Yarns of Billy Borker* 24: Within a week [of having won the lottery], he jobbed the panno, snatched his time and bought an air ticket to gay Paree.

Panthers, the 1 The Penrith, N.S.W., Rugby League team [f. club emblem]
1976 *Sun-Herald* 9 May 68: Manly try blitz tames the Panthers.
2 The South Adelaide Australian Rules team

1979 *Advertiser* (Adelaide) 7 May 18: Panthers leap to the lead.

3   Wests, Q., Rugby League team
1979 *Courier-Mail* (Brisbane) 25 Jun. 15: Panthers on top [heading] A mighty defensive effort . . . took Wests to an upset 24–12 win over Rugby League premier Easts at Purtell Park yesterday.

4   Morningside, Q., Australian Rules team
1979 *Courier-Mail* (Brisbane) 2 Jul. 14: Panthers in upset win over premiers [heading] Morningside had a shock three-point win over Australian Rules premiers Western Districts at Hawthorn Park yesterday.

paper bag, couldn't fight one's way out of a   To lack strength, fighting skill [also U.S.]
1918 N. Campbell and L. Nelson *The Dinky-di Soldier* 5: W'y, you can't fight yer way thro' a brown paper bag!
1955 Alan Marshall *I Can Jump Puddles* 136: 'Skeeter couldn't fight his way out of a paper bag,' Joe asserted.
1974 David Ireland *Burn* 44: 'Billy, you're not worth a bumper,' Joe said. 'You couldn't fight your way out of a paper bag.'
1978 *Sunday Telegraph* (Sydney) 9 Jul. 128: Millions of women might fancy actor Robert Redford, but not Colleen Mc Cullough. She greeted reports that Redford would play Father Ralph in the movie of The Thorn Birds with: 'I don't think Robert Redford can act his way out of a paper bag.'

para   See quots [abbr.]
1967 John Yeomans *The Scarce Australians* 56: 'I used to be in pretty good condition for a para, you know, but I've gone to the pack now.'
1979 David Ireland *A Woman of the Future* 55: 'Hey, para!' Para was the word for paraplegic. Kids shouted it at football matches if someone missed the ball, or just for the sound of it.

paradise, the working man's   see **working man's**

parcel post   Epithet applied to the newly arrived and inexperienced, esp N.T. [see quot. 1946]
1931 William Hatfield *Sheepmates* 118: Hallett took charge of the three 'parcel post' men and showed them a bunk where they could deposit their belongings.
1946 W. E. Harney *North of 23°* 23: Young lads bursting with romance and itching to be out in the wide open spaces, would sign on in the cities to work on far inland stations. 'Parcel post men' they called them; that is, they were labelled and addressed to a certain place, and travelled as a parcel does in the mail.
1951 Ernestine Hill *The Territory* 431: 'He come up by parcel post,' they still say. 'He don't know nothin'.'

Parra   See quots
1979 *NT News* (Darwin) 24 Nov. 14: *Parra* A term to describe people from the western suburbs (derived from Parramatta).
1981 *Sydney Morning Herald* 19 Dec. 26: Western Suburbs foreigners are as loathed as a disease [at Palm Beach]: 'They should clean up the Parras, shoot them or something.'

Parramatta   1   A cloth originally manufactured in the gaol factory at Parramatta, N.S.W.
1826 James Atkinson *An Account of the State of Agriculture and Grazing in New South Wales* 131: The coarse woollens are known in the Colony by the appellation of Parramatta cloth, having been first made there.
1840 J. Pitts Johnson *Plain Truths* 54: There is at Botany Bay a very coarse cloth manufactory; it is termed Parramatta cloth, and is solely used for convicts' clothing, it is manufactured by Mr Simeon Lord, and is very cheap.
2   Parramatta gaol
1941 Kylie Tennant *The Battlers* 7: 'I went to Parramatta. I was in an' out up to the time I was eighteen.'
1951 Dymphna Cusack and Florence James *Come In Spinner* 269: 'Whether you done it for love or for cash, you'll end up in Parramatta just the same.' . . . 'If they stick me back in Parra, I swear I'll beat it again.'
1973 Jim McNeil *The Chocolate Frog* 10: In the midst of life we are in Parramatta. That is to say, in prison.

parson, the flogging   Rev. Samuel Marsden (1764–1838), noted for his severity as a magistrate
1983 *Sydney Morning Herald* 13 May 1: Justice Hope is a descendant of the redoubtable 'flogging parson' of Parramatta, the Rev Samuel Marsden.

pass in one's marble   see **marble**

passage, saloon   see **saloon**

pat, on one's   Alone [rhyming slang for 'Pat Malone']
1908 *The Australian Magazine* 1 Nov. 1251: 'On my own' (by myself) became 'on my Pat Malone' and subsequently 'on my Pat' a very general expression nowadays.
1920 Louis Esson 'The Woman Tamer' in *Dead Timber* 29: 'I can't live without you. It's lonely on your pat.'
1938 Xavier Herbert *Capricornia* 132: 'Who's paying?' asked Oscar. 'Abo Department?' 'Oh no,' said Lace lightly. 'I'm doing it on my pat.'
1959 D'Arcy Niland *The Big Smoke* 146: 'On the way he's got to make a bit of a call, so he leaves you on your pat in the car.'
1981 *Australian* 7 Oct. 18: Was John Snow the most ferocious bowler he faced? ... 'I had probably as much trouble as anyone against him when we lost the Ashes in 1970–71, but I was not on my Pat Malone,' he [Doug Walters] said.

Patch, Cabbage   see **cabbage**

Paterson's Curse   *Echium plantagineum* or *echium vulgare* (viper's bugloss), a spreading, blue-flowered weed [f. the Patersons said to have introduced it as a garden flower at Cumberoona, near Albury, c. 1880]
1905 J. H. Maiden *Agricultural Gazette of New South Wales* xvi 268: That 'Paterson's Curse' produces some feed is undoubted, but it is a smothering, rough, coarse plant ... the vernacular name 'Curse' shows what many people think of it.
1918 P. G. Gilder *The Farmer's Handbook* 795: Weeds proclaimed Noxious within Municipalities and Shires in the State of New South Wales up to May, 1917 ... *Echium plantagineum* (Paterson's Curse, or Purple Bugloss, or Blue Weed).
1978 *Sun-Herald* 10 Sep. 176: Grazing interests have been lobbying the Federal Government to wipe out Paterson's Curse, which they consider a threat. Now the honey industry has described it as a valuable honey and pollen source.
1982 Max Harris *Australian* 6 Mar. Mag. 4: What ... I don't understand is how, after rabbits, grasshoppers, Paterson's curse, and mice, this nation has come to be plagued by restaurant critics.
see **Lady Campbell, Salvation Jane**

Patty Duke   see **flogger**

pav   Pavlova [abbr.]
1980 *Sydney Morning Herald* 4 Oct. 4: The big breakthrough from the board [the NSW Egg Marketing Board] is a never-fail pavlova mix. You open a packet, add water and whip like blazes. The technologists at the board assure me it's so easy that even a kid of six could get a perfect 'pav' every time.
1983 *Australian* 9 Jul. Mag. 20: The food ... included the best pav I've had in years (although the topping of kiwi fruit somehow departed from the WA theme).

payback   Retaliatory action taken according to a tribal code, esp. in Papua New Guinea and among Australian Aborigines; the imitation of this in white society [Pidgin]
1929 Patrol report in Penelope Hope *Long Ago is Far Away* (1979) 103: The Ferimi natives had killed one of the Niai natives some time ago and the Niai people are waiting to pay back.
1980 *Sun-Herald* 26 Oct. 11: Someone rang the police and the mob think it was me. The bricks – and the rest – are a payback.
1982 *NT News* (Darwin) 12 Mar. 4: Wilson, in evidence, said their lives had been threatened after they had interfered with a payback at the prison.

pay dirt, to strike (bottom on)   To reach the object of one's search, achieve success [f. goldmining U.S. 1856 Mathews]
1892 Henry Lawson 'The Bush Undertaker' *Prose* i 53: He set to work to dig it [the gravel] up, and sure enough, in about half-an-hour he bottomed on payable dirt.
1946 Kylie Tennant *Lost Haven* 331: Mr Cassell's party was the only one that approached anything like payable dirt.
1965 David Martin *The Hero of Too* 73: It was a pity, but not unexpected; a man did not strike pay-dirt at the first attempt.
1982 *Sun-Herald* 1 Aug. 67: Bart's boy hits pay-dirt ... Anthony Cummings said he could not recall a better day for the stable since they switched operations from Melbourne.

pea, the   The one likely to emerge as the winner in a competition; the person in a favoured position; the person in a position of authority [Partridge lists *pea* The favourite; one's choice: low: 1888]
1911 Edward Dyson *Benno, and Some of*

the Push 206: Mr Dickson ... ran his eye down the card and chanced it. 'Dandy's the P,' he said. 'Put yer whole week's wash on Dandy, 'n' hold me responsible if the goods ain't delivered.'
1953 Baker 118: Other expressions used by racing fans include *pea*, a horse that is being ridden to win, especially when there is doubt about the genuineness of other runners.
1969 Mena Calthorpe *The Defectors* 17: 'For the time being, I'm satisfied.' 'You're the pea,' Mick said.
1982 *Sunday Mail* (Brisbane) 31 Jan. 2: We still think Eddie Kornhauser and Sir Leslie Thiess are the peas for the casino licences.

pea, on the Deranged (like cattle driven mad by eating the **Darling pea** q.v.)
[**1864** Rachel Henning *Letters* ed. David Adams (1963) 180: Biddulph showed him the poison plant that grows in the desert between here and the Flinders and which killed so many of our sheep ... The sheep went quite mad after eating it. It is a pretty shrub with whitish leaves and a crimson pea-shaped blossom.]
1903 Joseph Furphy *Such is Life* (1944) 288: 'Ill-natured, cranky beggar, Alf is – been on the pea – but there's no end of grass in his paddock.'
1908 Giles Seagram *Bushmen All* 224: 'He's got the Darling Pea right enough. Mad as a hatter.'
peastruck
1981 Eric Rolls *A Million Wild Acres* 111: It [Darling Pea] is not only poisonous but addictive and does not provide enough nourishment to support life. Pea-struck animals eat nothing else. They lose condition rapidly. Their gait changes to a high-stepping stagger and their expressions to a fixed stare.

peacock 'To peacock a piece of country means to pick out the eyes of the land by selecting or buying up the choice pieces and water frontages, so that the adjoining territory is practically useless to anyone else.' (Morris 1898)
1916 Macmillan's *Modern Dictionary of the English Language* 793: *peacocking* The selection and purchase of the best and most conveniently situated lands in a district, *esp.* those which give access to a stream, the object of this land-grabbing process being to render the other areas of little or no value.
1938 *Smith's Weekly* 3 Apr. 1: The story of Italian infiltration into Queensland and the 'peacocking' of the rich irrigation lands of the Murrumbidgee (N.S.W.) by Mussolini's colonists has been revealed by *Smith's Weekly* as it has happened.
1982 Humphrey McQueen in *A Bunyip Close Behind Me* by Eugénie McNeil v: It would be possible to produce a sparkling review by peacocking all the best anecdotes.

peacocks flying out of one's backside see **sparrows**

pea soup, if it was raining see **raining**

pebble An indomitable or incorrigible man or beast: *obsolescent*
1842 *The Hobart Town Courier and Van Diemen's Land Gazette* 4 Feb. 3: 'I say, Bill,' began a mysterious and surly-looking fellow, *'he* died game, and no mistake!' 'Yes, Jim,' returned the other, on whose brow the propensity for destructiveness was strongly indicated, though perhaps deficient on his cranium, 'now *didn't* he die a pebble!'
1870 Marcus Clarke *His Natural Life* ed. S. Murray-Smith (1970) 627: 'You're not such a pebble as folks seem to think,' grinned Frere.
1916 C. J. Dennis *The Moods of Ginger Mick* 114: They wus pebs, they wus narks, they wus real naughty boys.

pebble, game as a Courageous, with staying-power (often of horses): *obsolescent*
1893 K. MacKay *Outback* 188: Cabbage Tree Ned is as game as a pebble, and may try to dash through in spite of us.
1906 K. S. Prichard *The New Idea* 6 Jul. 45: He's firm and upright on his old grey nag, and game as a pebble.
1918 C. Fetherstonhaugh *After Many Days* 223: Traveller was game as a pebble, and he just passed Quadrant on the post and no more.
1974 Donald Stuart *Prince of My Country* 166: 'He was hard as nails and as game as a pebble.'

Peckers The Woodville (S.A.) Australian Rules team [abbr. of *Woodpecker*]
1979 *Advertiser* (Adelaide) 4 Apr. 26: Pecker coach likely to play [heading] Coach Barry Goodingham is likely to lead Woodville on Saturday.

pee in the same pot, to Feminine equivalent of **to piss in each other's pockets** q.v.: to be on terms of great familiarity

peewee, couldn't pull the tail out of a see **couldn't**

pelican shit, a long streak of Applied to anyone exceptionally tall; an expression given currency from occurring in the film *Gallipoli* (1981) scripted by David Williamson
1973 Alexander Buzo *Norm and Ahmed* in *Three Plays* 12: 'Tall bloke, he was. A long thin streak of pelican shit.'
1982 *Sydney City Monthly* Jun. 30: One of his [Alex Buzo's] favourites was overheard in a pub: *He's like a long streak of pelican shit.*
1984 *Sydney Morning Herald* 16 May 10: 'Logie lips', [Graham] Kennedy called him [Ross Symonds], 'a long, tall streak of Pelican ... er ... deliciousness.'

People, the Old see **old**

perenty A large goanna, *Varanus giganteus* [Ab.]
1889 Ernest Giles *Australia Twice Traversed* ii 8: We saw ... one of those very large iguanas which exist in this part of the country. We had heard tales of their size and ferocity from the natives near the Peake (Telegraph Station). I believe they call them Parenties. The specimen we saw today was nearly black, and from head to tail over five feet long. I should very much have liked to catch him; he would make two or three good meals for both of us.
1946 W. E. Harney *North of 23. . .* 80: I listened wide-eyed to his tales of 'parintis', giant monitor lizards, that would attack a man.
1983 G. E. P. Wellard *Bushlore* 114: This particular bungarra was what is known as a perenty. They can grow about eight feet long ... they have very sharp, long, claws and a good set of teeth and know how to use both.

Peril, the Yellow see **Yellow**

perish (perisher), to do a To come near to death, esp. from lack of water or food; to suffer any kind of deprivation or ordeal
[**1882** Rolf Boldrewood *Robbery Under Arms* (World's Classics 1949) 499: He was as sober as a judge between one burst and another . . . Then he most times went in an awful perisher – took a month to it, and was never sober day or night the whole time.]
1894 *The Argus* 28 Mar. 5: When a man or party has nearly died through want of water, he is said to have 'done a perish'. [Morris]
1910 Henry Lawson 'A Tale with Horns' *Prose* i 714: 'It was cold 'n' I did a perish because I'd come without me big coat.'
1929 K. S. Prichard *Coonardoo* 60: 'We near done a perish for water.'
1955 Mary Durack *Keep Him My Country* 281: 'A man could do a perish before anyone would know. I'd like a quid for all the blokes I buried on that track.'
1979 Dorothy Hewett *The Man from Mukinupin* 45: 'He hasn't been right since he did that perish in the desert.'

persuader The jockey's whip
1956 *Bulletin* 3 Oct. 24: 'Put away the persuader, Smithy – hands and heels will do for now!'
1989 *Sunday Telegraph* (Sydney) 12 Mar. 121: Eddery was called before stewards so they could inspect his 'persuader'.

perv n. 1 A pervert [abbr.]
1949 Ruth Park *Poor Man's Orange* 38: 'That dirty old cow, always making up to kids ... Merv, Merv, the rotten old perv.'
1959 Eric Lambert *Glory Thrown In* 18: 'He was a perv. Special attention given to small boys.'
1961 Patrick White *Riders in the Chariot* 399: 'Hannah ... took an intelligent interest in the private life of any perv. The old whore would nearly pee herself watching a drag act in some of her own clothes.'
2 Someone given to 'perving'; the act of 'perving'
1963 John Cantwell *No Stranger to the Flame* 15: 'Never even saw him. Might have been a spook.' She did up the top button on the green blouse. 'Even spooks like a bit of a perv.'
1974 Keith Stackpole *Not Just for Openers* 38: After the next ball had been bowled, the blokes' heads would turn around unobtrusively so they could have a 'perv' at a bird in a mini-skirt walking down the aisle.
1980 Patrick White *Sydney Morning Herald* 20 Sep. 11: I remember hearing Sydney ladies who had gone to ingenious trouble and considerable expense to smuggle Nabokov's classic satire into Australia – to enjoy a perv – afterwards protesting with disgust: 'It's so boring you can't read it.'

perve *v.* To act as voyeur; to observe and relish the female form or the intimacies of others
1944 Lawson Glassop *We Were the Rats* 183: 'Doing a bit of perving again?' I asked, looking at the gallery of nudes he had gathered from all sorts of magazines.
1962 David Forrest *The Hollow Woodheap* 153: He had ... sunglasses on, through which he was making a careful inventory of every bikini-clad female ... 'Well,' said Paddy reasonably, 'if you're going to perv, you might as well be honest about it.'
1970 Patrick White *The Vivisector* 233: 'You're a kind of perv – perving on people – even on bloody rocks!'

peter 1 A till, cash register (thieves' slang) [f. *peter* a portmanteau or trunk OED 1668]
[**1812** Vaux: *Peter* A parcel or bundle, whether large or small; but most properly it signifies a trunk or box.]
1895 Cornelius Crowe *The Australian Slang Dictionary* 57: *Peter* A till.
1944 Randolph Bedford *Naught to Thirty-three* 171: 'Looking Glass Fred', whose speciality was 'Peter touching'; which is the vulgate for robbing tills.
1983 James McQueen *Uphill Runner* 68: 'I've been tickling the peter, and I'm into my trust funds for about sixty thousand.'
2 The witness box
1895 Cornelius Crowe *The Australian Slang Dictionary* 56: *Peater* The witness box.
1958 Vince Kelly *The Greedy Ones* 14: 'Mounting the peter. Going into the witness box.'

petrol-head A devotee of motor racing, fast cars
1987 Max Harris *Australian* 28 Nov. Mag. 2: A drug-sponsored Formula One Grand Prix provides an orgiastic social outbreak of hoons, goons, and petrol-heads.

phantom broadcast, meeting Simulation of an 'actuality' broadcast, with studio effects, like the 'synthetic' broadcasts of Test cricket in England by the A.B.C. in 1934; other sporting fixtures conducted on similar principles
1975 *Sun-Herald* 26 Jan. 58: Many people will remember the 'phantom' fight description of 1946 when Vic Patrick and Tommy Sands were contesting the welter-weight championship at Sydney Stadium. Permission to broadcast the fight direct was refused, and ... from a small cottage near the stadium, Cliff Carey staged his amazing 'phantom' broadcast. Inside the stadium, Bill Delaney made punch-by-punch notes, which were rushed to Garth Carey, Allan Toohey and others to Cliff at the cottage ... Sound effects were fed in from the studio.
1983 *NT News* (Darwin) 4 Jan. 23: Yesterday, the first of nine phantom meetings to be held by the Darwin Turf Club during the current racing season was a qualified success ... Admission was free with all services operating including seven bookmakers who reported satisfactory holdings in the circumstances [i.e. betting on races interstate, in the absence of any actual races on the course].

piano player in a brothel Someone implicated in an activity, but accepting no moral responsibility for it [also U.S.]
1972 *Hansard* 21 Sep. 1741: Mr Bury: Have the trade union leaders paid any more than lip service to decrying violence? Have they taken any effective action, or have they adopted the general, traditional attitude of the man playing the piano on the ground floor of the brothel and affecting neither to know nor care what goes on upstairs?
1977 Fred Daly *From Curtin to Kerr* 90: 'Well,' replied Wentworth, 'if you don't know what is happening in Victoria you are like a pianist in a brothel, you do not know what is happening upstairs.'
1981 *Australian* 4 Apr. Mag. 20: Robert Hughes, art critic for *Time* magazine, who's been back on homeground for a month promoting his book on modern art, *The Shock of the New*: 'I'm just the piano player in the whorehouse of art.'

Piccadily bushman See quots
1941 Baker 53: *Piccadilly bushman* A wealthy Australian who lives (or lived) in the West End of London.
1961 Ray Lawler *The Piccadilly Bushman* [play title]

piccaninny Tiny, little [a West Indian term for a child (OED 1657) applied to Australian Aboriginals]
1833 G. F. Moore *Diary of ... an Early Settler in Western Australia* (1884) 203: He at once understood me, and said 'piccany cow? yes! yes! yes!' and seemed quite satisfied.

1844 Let. 6 Nov. cit. *No Place for a Nervous Lady* ed. Lucy Frost (1984) 167: The blacks still say as they said the last flood, 'this is only piccaniny – big one coming'.
c. 1905 Joseph Furphy *The Buln-Buln and the Brolga* ed. R. G. Howarth (1948) 107: 'Blackfellers mostly goes in for a piccaniny fire – jist three sticks, with the ends kep' together.'
1975 *Sydney Morning Herald* 15 Sep. 1: 'Nambawan pikinini b'long Misis Kwin' is the pidgin English term for his [Prince Charles'] position as first son of the Queen and heir apparent to the throne.

piccaninny dawn (light) The approach of dawn, first light
1848 W. Westgarth *Australia Felix* 104: Great numbers were mustering from the surrounding country, and . . . the hut would be attacked before 'piccininni sun'.* *About daylight in the morning.
1903 Randolph Bedford *True Eyes and the Whirlwind* 321: By pickaninny daylight, the mounted men were in motion, and Quinn and his camel went with them.
1945 Tom Ronan *Strangers on the Ophir* 12: That first pale flush of dawn which the bushman calls 'Piccaninny daylight' showed in the eastern sky.
1958 Gavin Casey *Snowball* 125: He was up before the piccaninny dawn, and in the first gentle glow of it he slid out of the house on his bare feet.
1970 Richard Beilby *No Medals for Aphrodite* 219: It was almost dawn, the 'piccaninny daylight' of the Big Country back home.
pick the eyes out see **eyes**

pick a seat at the pictures, couldn't see **couldn't**

pick handle As for **axe handle**, q.v.
1979 *Sun-Herald* 11 Mar. 93: He was just over six feet tall, about three pick handles across the shoulders and had muscles on the muscles in his arm.

picker-up A shed-hand, lower in the hierarchy than the shearer, who gathers the fleece after it has been shorn
1870 Rolf Boldrewood 'Shearing in Riverina' *Town and Country Journal* 12 Nov. 13: The wool-press-men – the fleece-rollers – the pickers-up – the yarders – the washers' cooks – the hut cooks . . . paid off.
1892 G. L. James *Shall I Try Australia?*

99: The 'picker-up' stands over the filmy looking rug which lies in a heap on the floor, gathers it up deftly, and bearing it to the table, flings it neatly out full length, with the cut side downwards.
1910 C. E. W. Bean *On the Wool Track* 166: The rouseabouts, the pickers-up, and sweepers, and tarboys, and the rest are paid by the day . . . the shearers . . . are not being paid when not shearing.

picnic A troublesome experience [f. *picnic* used ironically]
1898 Morris *Picnic*, n. Besides the ordinary meaning of this word, there is a slang Australian use denoting an awkward adventure, an unpleasant experience, a troublesome job.
1906 A. J. Tompkins *With Swag and Billy* 69: Decent grassland is scarce where this sort of country is pressed into service, and what a picnic it must be to muster.
1945 Baker 263: We call a wild confusion or a particularly difficult task a *picnic*.
1955 D'Arcy Niland *The Shiralee* 38: 'All I know is I'm going to have one helluva picnic if she doesn't find it.'

picnic races Race meetings held in country areas, and regarded as a social occasion
1896 Nat Gould *Town and Bush* 224–5: Picnic race-meetings are got up in various parts of the country. These meetings are for amateur riders only . . . The owners of the horses running at picnic races are generally men of means.
1911 C. E. W. Bean *The 'Dreadnought' of the Darling* 294: Up country they seem to judge their towns by two infallible criteria. If a town has picnic races or a polo week, it is 'alive'. If it has not, it is 'dead'.
1939 Miles Franklin *All That Swagger* 470: She was . . . familiar to the public through the pictures of her . . . leading-in her father's winners at picnic races.
1972 *Sunday Telegraph* (Sydney) 15 Oct. 132: And what is the big event? Why everyone, but everyone, is getting ready for the Bong Bong Picnic Races next Saturday. Mr Richmond assures us it's 'a very, very toney' event. 'We get our young socialites stalking around with woolly terriers,' he said.

pie-eater (biter) Someone who is 'small-time', of little account (? living on meat pies instead of proper meals): *derogatory*
1911 Edward Dyson *Benno, and Some of*

the Push 144: 'Little Benny's frenzy when the game got goin' would freeze yer blood. He was that angry with the South pie-biters, he didn't care what 'appened to 'em.'
[**1922** Arthur Wright *A Colt from the Country* 122: 'They're meat-pie bookies, all right,' he exclaimed displaying a bunch of tickets. 'Had to make four bets of it.']
1949 Lawson Glassop *Lucky Palmer* 96: 'The trouble is, Mr Hughes, you're too good for the pie-eating bookmakers round these parts. You bet too well for them, Mr Hughes.'
1953 Kylie Tennant *The Joyful Condemned* 166: 'He's one of those big he-men that go sneaking around the park waiting to switch some chromo's hand bag. Just a pie-eater.'
1975 Keith Miller *Sun* (Sydney) 10 Jan. 52: A bunch of pie-eaters. Excuse me if I find an expression from my old mate, the late Siddie Barnes, but that's what the English team has turned out to be.
1980 *Sydney Morning Herald* 5 Sep. 2: 'Some of the goods are not the best quality. If you are a connoisseur you know the difference. If you are what we call a pie eater, then you don't.'

pie-face See quot. 1985
1985 *National Times* 26 Apr. 26: It was not enough to stop him shouting 'There's pie-face in the audience!' when he spotted an Asian sitting in the front row . . . Jackson told The National Times later that pie-face was a nickname for Asians, because pies had little marks in the top of them like 'slant eyes'.

Pies, the 1 The Collingwood A.F.L. team [abbr. of Magpies]
1979 *Herald* (Melbourne) 7 Apr. 34: Lions Devour Pies [heading]
2 In Tasmania, the Glenorchy Australian Rules club
1980 *Mercury* (Hobart) 21 Jun. 56: Pies to send Roos up river [heading] Glenorchy will beat Clarence in a reply of last year's TFL grand final at Bellerive today.

pigeon, ha ha see **ha ha**

pigeons, he couldn't lead a flock of homing see **homing**

pig-iron Bob Nickname given to 1 Mr R. G. Menzies, Attorney-General in the Lyons Government, after he invoked the Transport Workers Act in 1935 when watersiders refused to load the *Dalfram* with iron for Japan
1965 Thomas Keneally *The Fear* 127: The Japanese and Pig-Iron Bob Menzies ('Thank God he's finished with politics for good,' said the priest. 'I'd prayed for that.')
1975 *Australian* 1 Nov. 21: Remember the days when 'Pig Iron Bob' decorated every railway siding?
2 Bob Hawke, Australian Prime Minister 1983–, from his negotiations with the steel industry in China
1984 *Sydney Morning Herald* 10 Feb. 7: Pig Iron Bob makes a deal with the future [heading] As a result of talks yesterday between Mr Hawke and Premier Zhao Australia and China have agreed to establish a working party to investigate the possibility of Australian exports of crude steel to the world's potentially biggest market.

pigs Expression of disagreement or derision [abbr. of 'in a pig's eye (arse)', listed by Partridge as U.S.]
1919 W. H. Downing *Digger Dialects* 38: *Pig's ear* A contemptuous ejaculation.
1933 Norman Lindsay *Saturdee* 124: 'Pigs to you, yer old man's got the stringholt.' Ibid. 165: Peter had to cover his confusion by saying 'Pigs to you' as he went out kicking the door.
1951 Eric Lambert *The Twenty Thousand Thieves* 322: 'Pig's arse to that!' another voice cried. 'A jack-up – that's the shot.' [In 1963 edn, 198, 'Pig's to that!']
1965 John Beede *They Hosed Them Out* 192: I said defensively, 'The wheel slipped off the run-way.' 'Pig's bum,' he replied.
1975 Les Ryan *The Shearers* 119: 'Ar, pigs to you!' 'In your dinger, too!'

pimp *n.* A sneak, tell-tale (mainly juvenile); an informer to the police or other authority: *derogatory* [f. *pimp* pander OED 1607]
1938 Xavier Herbert *Capricornia* 567: 'I'm not a pimp.' 'What you mean pimp?' 'I'm not a police-informer.'
1941 Gavin Casey *It's Harder for Girls* 51: 'I just say I'm not a pimp,' Brownie insisted, beginning to blubber.
1958 Frank Hardy *The Four-Legged Lottery* 182: 'Don't worry, I've drummed him. We have ways of dealing with pimps and squealers.'
1963 Alan Marshall *In Mine Own Heart* 205: 'I'm a wake-up to pimps.'

pimp *v.* To act as a pimp
  1938 Xavier Herbert *Capricornia* 524:
  'He reckons I pimped on him – and that's
  how the johns went out and grabbed 'em
  both.'
  1948 K. S. Prichard *Golden Miles* 28:
  'There was a man pimping for the boss, a
  while ago. Fell down a winze on the two
  hundred foot level. Nasty accident it was.'
  1957 Judah Waten *Shares in Murder* 155:
  'You made up to me so you could get me to
  pimp on Charlie for you.'

pineapple, the rough end of the Hostile
or unfair treatment
  1961 Ray Lawler *The Piccadilly Bushman*
  37: 'He'll know what I mean when I talk of
  getting the wrong end of the pineapple.'
  1979 David Williamson *Age* (Melbourne)
  29 Sep. 19: Despite the club's glorious past,
  your modern Collingwood supporter has, to
  be absolutely frank, had the rough end of the
  pineapple. I got home from Denmark and the
  buggers lost again.
  1983 *Sydney Morning Herald* 6 Jun. Guide
  16: Back in World War II, we sent bundles to
  Britain. Now, as repayment, their producers
  are sending back jolly World War II thrillers,
  such as Danger UXB, The Fourth Arm and
  Tenko. I think we got the rough end of the
  pineapple.

ping pong, aerial see **aerial**

pink To shear closely so that the colour of
the skin shows through
  1899 W. T. Goodge *Hits! Skits! and
  Jingles!* 113: The leathery necks he pinked
  'em too, / Did Gentleman Jack of Jambe-
  roo.
  1905 'Flash Jack from Gundagai' *The Old
  Bush Songs* ed. A. B. Paterson 27 and note:
  I've pinked em with the Wolseleys and I've
  rushed with B-bows, too. 'Pinking' means
  that he had shorn the sheep so closely that
  the pink skin showed through.
  1959 *Bulletin* 11 Feb. 33: He was the fastest and best shearer I have known. Every
  sheep was 'pinked' and seldom did he cut
  one.

pink-hi, pinkeye A 'walkabout': holiday
celebration [Pidgin]
  1929 K. S. Prichard *Coonardoo* 34: Every
  year at midsummer, for as long as Coonardoo could remember, the tribes for a
  hundred miles about had gathered for pinkeye on Wytaliba.

1936 H. Drake-Brockman *Sheba Lane*
  131: He found his natives in good tucker and
  clothes and gave the faithful Jimmy – most
  wonderful gift – a horse and cart for the
  yearly pink hi, when he visited his tribe.
  1962 J. Marshall and R. Drysdale *Journey
  Among Men* 89: We talked with a party of
  aborigines camped in the river bed. They had
  quit their station jobs, as they are prone to
  do, and had gone on a hunting walkabout and
  a 'pink-eye'.
  1976 Max Brown *Black Eureka* 87: When
  pinkeye came – six weeks holiday over the
  hot time – he was handed a half-bag of
  flour.

pinkie Cheap wine [? f. colour]
  1935 Kylie Tennant *Tiburon* 93: Staines,
  nodding his fat, puffy face into his cup of
  pinkie . . . hadn't a very good head for the
  cheap raw wine he was drinking.
  1941 *Coast to Coast* 23: 'Better put that
  bottle away . . . If the trooper comes round
  somebody'll be getting into trouble for selling Charley pinkeye again.'
  1959 Dorothy Hewett *Bobbin Up* 69: He'd
  drink anything they reckoned, plonk, pinkie,
  straight metho.

piss in someone's pocket, to To ingratiate oneself, be on very familiar terms
with [*Pissing down anyone's back* Flattering
him Grose 1811]
  1967 Kylie Tennant *Tell Morning This*
  283: 'Soon's they knew you was in with
  Numismata, they all want to piss in your
  pocket.'
  1971 Frank Hardy *The Outcasts of Foolgarah* 77–8: 'I appeared before him many a
  time when I worked for the Union. If we piss
  in his pocket, he's just as apt to come our
  way.'
  1983 Rob George *Sandy Lee Live at Nui
  Dat* 45: 'That's right, a word in the right ear,
  piss in the right pocket, that's how the world
  operates.'
  see **pee in the same pot**

pissant around To mess about
  1945 Baker 87: Someone is *pissanting
  around* when he is messing about.
  1951 Dymphna Cusack and Florence
  James *Come In Spinner* 307: 'I been pissan-
  tin' round the Northern Territory most of
  the time.'
  1959 Gerard Hamilton *Summer Glare*
  138: 'Struth, you pissant around like a rooster that's too old.'

pissant, game as a   Very brave or angry [**1934** Archer Russell *A Tramp-Royal in Wild Australia* 115: 'Must be nearly eighty ... Straight as a gun-barrel an' game as an ant.']

1945 Baker 87: *game as a piss ant.*

1962 Ron Tullipan *March into Morning* 59: 'The old white lady [q.v.] makes you as game as a pissant.'

1975 Richard Beilby *The Brown Land Crying* 82: 'Ho! Real piss-ant, ain't 'e,' Bamma jeered. 'I like ya, boy. Ya got guts.'

pissing on your swag, the dogs are   see **pull out**

Pitt Street or Christmas (Palm Sunday), not to know whether it's   To be in a state of confusion

1951 Dymphna Cusack and Florence James *Come In Spinner* 330: 'She's that pie-eyed, she don't know whether it's Pitt Street or Christmas.'

see **Tuesday or Bourke Street, Thursday or Anthony Horderns**

Pitt Street farmer   See quots [f. Pitt St as one of the main streets of Sydney's business life]

1945 Baker 198: In Sydney a business man with minor farming interests is called a *Pitt Street farmer.*

1971 *Sunday Australian* 6 Jun. 8: Australia's 9000 Pitt Street farmers – the businessmen, stockbrokers, doctors, barristers and solicitors who make a tidy profit on the side by owning or sharing a farm. Most earn at least $16,000 a year from the venture, although few visit their properties.

1983 *Sun-Herald* 27 Mar. 3: The Hawke Government is planning a tougher crack down on 'Pitt Street farmers'.

see **Collins Street farmers**

Pivotonians   Former nickname of the Geelong A.F.L. club [see quot. 1859]

[**1859** W. Kelly *Life in Victoria* 160: The Pivot City is a sobriquet invented by the citizens of Geelong to symbolise it as the point on which the fortunes of the colony would culminate and revolve.]

1981 Jack Hibberd *National Times* 26 Apr. 64: Geoffrey Blainey, a supporter of the Pivotonians (Geelong).

place for a village, the   see **village**

plant *n.*   1   'A hoard of stolen goods; also

the place where they are hidden' (OED 1796)

[**1812** Vaux: The place of concealment is sometimes called *the plant ... To spring a plant*, is to find any thing that has been concealed by another.]

1853 John Sherer *The Gold-Finder of Australia* 166: He informed me that he had a 'plant', which he would make over to me, as it might be 'sprung' whilst he was in gaol.

1882 Rolf Boldrewood *Robbery Under Arms* (World's Classics 1949) 55: 'So take care and don't act foolishly, or you'll lose a plant that may save your life, as well as keep you in cash for many a year to come.'

2   The portable equipment of a drover, bullockdriver or other bushworker [f. *plant* The fixtures, implements, machinery and apparatus used in carrying on any industrial process OED *sb.* 6, 1789]

1903 Joseph Furphy *Such is Life* (1944) 311: 'Stewart has bought his plant, and engaged him permanently.'

1951 Ernestine Hill *The Territory* 445: *Plant* A station or drover's outfit – horses, drays, cars, saddles.

plant *v.*   To conceal, secrete, usually with illegal intent [f. English thieves' slang OED 1610; recorded earlier in *Twelfth Night* II.ii.162]

1798 David Collins *An Account of the English Colony in NSW*, ed. Brian Fletcher (1975) i 331: These [stolen articles] must have been planted (to use the thief's phrase) a considerable time; for every mark or trace which could lead to the discovery of the owner was entirely effaced.

1848 Charles Cozens *Adventures of a Guardsman* 142: The practice ... of *planting* the bullocks of the various teams on the road and so keeping them until their owners are induced to offer a reward for finding them.

1882 A. J. Boyd *Old Colonials* 74: He loads up a keg of rum, and to make sure it wouldn't be touched he plants* it in a barrel of sugar. *To *plant* in bush parlance is *to hide.*

1936 Dal Stivens *The Tramp and other stories* 143: 'Of course she'll hang around you ... she knows you've got the money planted ... don't be a bloody fool.'

1958 H. D. Williamson *The Sunlit Plain* 234: 'That's why I planted these bottles in this here tent – so I'd have somewhere for a quiet gargle.'

1983 Georgia Savage *The Tournament* 9: I nicked around the house and planted myself behind the mile-high pile of fruit cases standing there.

plate A plate of sandwiches etc. brought by each person attending a social gathering as a way of catering for it

1962 Stuart Gore *Down the Golden Mile* 110: 'We might start by having some sort of social. Nothing elaborate, you know. Just perhaps all the ladies could bring a plate.'

1984 Ned Manning *Us or Them* 25: 'Bring your own if you drink anything sophisticated, otherwise we'll hit you for a couple of bucks for beer and wine, and ladies bring a plate.'

pleuro Pleuropneumonia (as a disease of cattle)

1874 Rolf Boldrewood *My Run Home* (1897) 176: 'Do you ever have any pleuro among your cattle?' said I, 'I heard something about it in England.'

1892 Henry Lawson 'The City Bushman' *Verse* i 214: Did you fight the drought and pleuro when the 'seasons' were asleep?

1964 Tom Ronan *Packhorse and Pearling Boat* 68: 'I'd say that war is like pleuro in cattle: whenever you think it's eradicated it breaks out in a fresh place.'

plod *n.* 1 The piece of ground on which a miner is working; the work card relating to this: W.A.

1941 Baker 55: *Pitching the plod* 'The exchange of words' between miners 'on the state of the ground when coming on or going off shifts.'

1948 K. S. Prichard *Golden Miles* 72: He had to go to the office for his plod – the card on which he filled in particulars of the work he was doing, its position in the mine, and the hours he was working. Ibid. 74: He held an 'unofficial' plod, because he was bogging for a machine man.

2 A yarn, a 'spiel' (see quot. 1941 above) [f. *plod* a short or dull story; a lying tale EDD]

1945 Gavin Casey *Downhill is Easier* 136: 'I suppose he told you the whole plod?' I sneered.

1954 T. A. G. Hungerford *Sowers of the Wind* 241: 'That's the plod he put up, anyway.'

1970 Richard Beilby *No Medals for Aphrodite* 158: 'What sort of a plod are you going to put up about her?'

plonk Cheap wine, or any improvised alcoholic drink; wine, from the standpoint of the beer drinker [Franklyn records *plink plonk* = *vin blanc*]

1938 Francis Ratcliffe *Flying Fox and Drifting Sand* 217: His drink at the bar had been 'plonk', and not the beer of his companions.

1946 Dal Stivens *The Courtship of Uncle Henry* 72: 'Jessie's been on the plonk again ... Goes round the wine bars at the Cross.'

1960 John O'Grady *Cop This Lot* 210: 'Wot's better than beer?' Pat asked. 'Vino rosso. Vin rouge. Rotwein. The civilised and incomparable juice of the grapes.' 'Gees,' Pat said. 'Yer don' mean bloody plonk, do yer?'

1980 Craig McGregor *The Australian People* 143: In the last few years the really astonishing growth has been in the consumption of wine, which used to be dismissed as 'plonk', but is now one of the nation's fastest-growing industries.

plurry Pidgin version of **bloody**

1907 Charles MacAlister *Old Pioneering Days in the Sunny South* 236: The blackfellow stipulated that I should 'go longa pound, and gib it money to Missus, too, or the Boss plurry well beat 'em both.'

1984 Bert Kelly *Bulletin* 3 Apr. 106: When Ginger was asked whether he preferred the infantry or the cavalry, he thought for a while and then voted for the infantry. Asked why, he replied, 'One day, the retreat will be sounded and then I don't want to be hindered by no plurry horse!'

pocket, to have death adders (mousetraps, scorpions) in one's To be a reluctant spender

1944 Lawson Glassop *We Were the Rats* 118: 'Why doancher buy a drink? Get them death adders outa ya pockets.'

1977 Colleen Klein *The Heart in the Casket* 139: 'He bought me some pink carnations ... He must be really keen, he's usually got a scorpion in his pocket.'

1978 *Sydney Morning Herald* 21 Oct. 18: 'Your old man would shout even when it wasn't his turn. No mousetraps in *his* pocket!'

pocket, to piss in someone's see **piss**

pocket, useful as a hip ~ in a singlet see **useful**

poddy (calf) A hand-fed calf; any creature at an early stage of growth

1879–80 Ned Kelly 'The Jerilderie Letter' in Max Brown *Australian Son* (1956) 275: If a poor man happened to leave his horse or a bit of a poddy calf outside his paddock they would be impounded.

1904 Henry Fletcher *Dads Wayback: His Work* 118: She had brought up all these cows with almost the watchfulness a mother gives to a child; she knew their every trick of temper since they were poddies.

1934 Brian Penton *Landtakers* 479: 'I'll soon have him nursed up as fat as a poddy calf.'

1956 Brian James *The Bunyip of Barney's Elbow* 154: Taking the milk in and bringing back the skim for pigs and poddies.

1982 *Sun-Herald* 7 Mar. 141: The use of poddy mullet is illegal in NSW because they are less than legal size.

poddy *v.* See quot.

1892 Henry Lawson 'A Day on a Selection' in *Prose* i 45: Then he 'poddies' – hand feeds – the calves which have been weaned too early. He . . . seizes a calf by the nape of the neck with his left hand, inserts the dirty forefinger of his right into its mouth, and shoves its head down into the milk. The calf sucks, thinking it has a teat.

1956 Patrick White *The Tree of Man* 59: Amy Parker . . . began to poddy her newborn calf, that was soon mumbling at her fingers in the bucket.

poddy-dodger A cattle-duffer who appropriates unbranded calves [f. *poddy* a hand-fed calf]

1937 Ernestine Hill *The Great Australian Loneliness* 83: Keep poddy-dodgers from the glen, / For Jesus Christ's sake, Amen.

1946 W. E. Harney *North of 23°* 93: Some of the small struggling 'poddy dodgers' would now and then bring in a few bullocks and sell them to the butcher, who would give them a credit at the store.

poddy-dodging

1945 Tom Ronan *Strangers on the Ophir* 9: 'He'll be a doctor or a lawyer or a banker with no need to go poddy-dodging for a living like his old jail-bird of a Dad.'

point the bone see **bone**

pointer Someone who 'works points', takes an unfair advantage

1941 Baker 55: *Point, to* To take an unfair

advantage of a person, to loaf, impose on, to malinger. Whence, 'pointer': one who does these things.

1954 Tom Ronan *Vision Splendid* 164: There was no nark or pointer in the camp.

poisoner A cook, esp. for a collection of men

1905 E. C. Buley *Australian Life in Town and Country* 23: The shearers' cook is always a competent man and supplies his clients with the best fare obtainable, utterly 'belying' the name of 'poisoner', usually bestowed upon him.

1936 Archer Russell *Gone Nomad* 14: I had to take my turn at butchering the ration sheep and as 'slushy' to 'Dough-boy' Terry, the cook – 'camp poisoner', as we affectionately called him.

1969 Lyndall Hadow *Full Cycle* 208: 'I'm not much good at cooking but I'll try.' 'Never you mind about that. Up north we've got the best poisoners in the country.'

see **doctor**

poke borak, mullock see **borak, mullock**

poke in the eye with a burnt stick, better than a An expression of qualified pleasure, usually a retort [f. Staffordshire dialect]

1974 *Bulletin* 6 Jul. 44: An Australian way of expressing ecstasy is to say: 'It's better than a poke in the eye with a burnt stick.'

1986 *Bulletin* 6 May 63: She won the $15,000 Grace Bros Prize in the Australian Singing Competition . . . That was better than a poke in the eye with a burnt stick.

poke a stick at, more than one could see **stick**

pokies, the Poker-machines [abbr.]

1967 Donald Horne *Southern Exposure* 44: In the clubs of Sydney the poker machines ('the pokies') stand up in dozens and more beer flows than in a hotel.

1975 *Bulletin* 9 Aug. 23: Bingo is rapidly assuming the place in the Queensland lifestyle that is held by the pokies in New South Wales.

polar bear's behind, as cold as a Very cold

1944 Randolph Bedford *Naught to Thirty-three* 187: I knew [in the 1890s] . . . Billy Evans, the newspaper man who wrote a ribald definition of cold, while freezing in

the press gallery of the South Australian Parliament. It began 'cold as the Esquimaux, gloomy and glum . . .'
1944 Lawson Glassop *We Were the Rats* 5: 'I . . . sneaks in just in time to see Jerry knock Binghi as cold as a Polar bear's backside.'
1971 John O'Grady *Aussie Etiket* 85: In the words of an anonymous poet of genius, 'Cold as an iceberg, gloomy and glum, / Cold as the hair on a polar bear's bum.'

pole on To impose, sponge on someone [? f. *poll* practise extortion OED 1521–1613]
[**1859** Hotten 76: *Poll, or polling* One thief robbing another of part of their booty.]
1906 Edward Dyson *Fact'ry 'Ands* 66: 'What rot, girls, why don't yer get a shift on?' cried Feathers virtuously . . . 'polin' on the firm like this.'
1938 Xavier Herbert *Capricornia* 529: 'Call me a wastrel, would ya? You – why you're poling on Jesus Christ!'
1953 *Caddie A Sydney Barmaid* 220: 'And while there's anything in the Sutton cupboard, Caddie,' he assured me when I said I couldn't stay and pole on them, 'it's yours.'

pole, up the In error, in disorder, confused [cf. *up the pole* in the wrong, tipsy OED 1896, 1904]
1906 Edward Dyson *Fact'ry 'Ands* 188: Then, as a bright afterthought, she added, 'Yer fair up the pole!'
1915 C. J. Dennis *The Songs of a Sentimental Bloke* 47: The dreams I dreamed, the dilly thorts I thunk / Is up the pole, an' joy 'as done a bunk.
1950 Jon Cleary *Just Let Me Be* 108: 'If I go and see 'em now, tell 'em what I done and why I done it, I'd be well and truly up the pole.'
1965 William Dick *A Bunch of Ratbags* 92: 'Right,' said Curly, agreeing with Ronnie's logic for once. He generally thought Ronnie was all up the pole when giving advice to someone.

pole, wouldn't touch it with a forty-foot An expression of extreme aversion or complete rejection [? variant of the English 'wouldn't touch it with a barge pole']
1903 Joseph Furphy *Such is Life* (1944) 27: 'The young feller he used to come sometimes an' just shake hands with her, but otherways he wouldn't touch her with a forty-foot pole.'
1937 *Best Australian One-Act Plays* 248:

'I wouldn't have touched those girls, myself, with a forty-foot pole!'
1958 E. O. Schlunke *The Village Hampden* 26: Business of the more or less shady sort that our reputable men wouldn't touch with a forty-foot pole.
1965 Graham McInnes *The Road to Gundagai* 180: 'I wouldn't touch it with a forty foot pole!' he gulped.

poler 1 The horse or bullock harnessed alongside the pole of the wagon
1863 Samuel Butler *A First Year in Canterbury Settlement* ed. R. A. Streatfield (1914) 95: The leaders . . . slewed sharply round, and tied themselves into an inextricable knot with the polars, while the bloody bullocks . . . slipped the yoke.
1870 Marcus Clarke *His Natural Life* ed. S. Murray-Smith (1970) 617: The huge waggons, the white body of a camping 'poler', and the three ragged figures round the glowing logs.
1919 W. K. Harris *Outback in Australia* 18: We had to blindfold that poler before we could put him in the 'body-lead'.
2 Someone given to 'poling on' others
1938 Xavier Herbert *Capricornia* 528: 'You long-jawed poler,' Norman roared. 'Living on the fat of the land, while your poor damn flock feeds on soup and coconuts and what they can root out of the bush.'
1985 Peter Bowers *Sydney Morning Herald* 21 Sep. 27: There is the odd poler, but collectively politicians work hard and earn their money.

pollies Politicians [abbr.]
1973 H. Williams *My Love Had a Black Speed Stripe* 28: I reckon they should keep argument out of politics altogether, but the pollies would never wear it.
1982 *Sunday Mail* (Brisbane) 29 Aug. 2: Our good State pollies have been given an extra phone with a silent number for their electorate offices.

Pom Abbr. of **Pommy**, q.v.
1919 W. H. Downing *Digger Dialects* 38: *Pom* – See Pommy.
1956 F. B. Vickers *First Place to the Stranger* 133: 'Move over, Pom. D'you want all the bloody fire?'
1973 Prince Charles [at an Australia Day dinner in London] *Sydney Morning Herald* 3 Feb. 2: All the faces here this evening seem to be bloody Poms.
1980 *West Australian* (Perth) 29 Jan. 6:

What has 100 years of playing cricket against the Poms brought about? We hate them and we have T-shirts with such friendly goodwill messages as 'Keep Australia beautiful – shoot a Pom'.

Pommy An English immigrant; an English national: *derogatory* [see quot. 1920]
1913 *Pommy Arrives in Australia* or *Pommy the Funny Little New Chum* [title of film directed by Raymond Longford and screened at Snowden Theatre, Melbourne, 13 Sep.]
1920 H. J. Rumsey *The Pommies, or New Chums in Australia* (Introduction): Few people seem to know the origin of the word, but I can well remember its introduction in the early seventies . . . Thousands of immigrants were arriving by the old clipper ships, and the colonial boys and girls, like all school-children, ready to find a nickname, were fond of rhyming 'Immigrant', 'Jimmygrant', 'Pommegrant' and called it after the new chum children. The name stuck and became abbreviated to 'pommy' later on.
1931 William Hatfield *Sheepmates* 271: 'Not a bad sort of a poor coot, either, for a Pommy.' (The odious word had just drifted out [c. 1912] from the wharves and the railway construction camps.)
1963 Xavier Herbert *Disturbing Element* 90–1: He still wore the heavy clumsy British type of clothing of the day. When we kids saw people on the street dressed like that [before 1914] we would yell at them: 'Jimmygrants, Pommygranates, Pommies!'
1983 L. Johnston *Sydney Morning Herald* 15 Aug. 8: In 1911, 1912, and 1913, I attended Granville Public School. In those three years, 200,000 migrants entered Australia, virtually all from Britain. Granville was expanding with industrial development and it seemed almost daily that migrant children appeared at the school, many of them with the rosy cheeks of their English complexions, which suggested the pink glow of the pomegranate, then not uncommon. Children have always chanted at one another and the native-born and earlier arrivals imitated the accents of the newcomers and chanted at them. The chant was simple and spontaneous: 'Immigranate, pomegranate, pome-granate, immigranate.' From this the natural abbreviation was 'Pommy'.

Pommy bastard
1951 Dal Stivens *Jimmy Brockett* 214: Like most of these pommy bastards, he had

funny ways but he wasn't a bad old bloke at heart.
1968 George Mikes *Boomerang* 66: It is always the Pommy Bastards who, instead of being grateful, keep on complaining.
1975 *Sunday Telegraph* (Sydney) 9 Feb. 96: A Sydney man will appear before the Royal Commission into Human Relationships later this month and allege that the fashionable T-shirts emblazoned with the words Pommie Bastards are libellous and discriminatory.

Pommyland England
1957 Randolph Stow *The Bystander* 21: 'I'm a Pommy. And going back to Pommy-land, after twenty-four years.'
1984 *Weekend Australian* 21 Apr. Mag. 20: Pommieland has just been hit by a new magazine called the *Royal Magazine* which informs a breathlessly waiting public that 'Princess Anne's favorite ploy at parties is to dress up as charlady and go about dusting chairs and tables'.

Pommy shop steward A phrase given currency by the apparent prominence of English migrants in trade unions
1982 *National Times* 4 Apr. 16: The perennial, but unproven, 'pommy shops stewards' charge whenever strikes threaten to cripple the country.

Pommy's towel (bath-mat), dry as a Very dry
1981 *National Times* 4 Jan. 5: Humphries had McKenzie downing his first beer and exclaiming he had been 'as dry as a Pommie's towel'.
1982 *Sydney Morning Herald* 13 Mar. 47: It was dry as a Pommy's bathmat in Adelaide last week.

Pommy, whingeing
1962 J. Marshall and R. Drysdale *Journey Among Men* 189: The British national pastime of 'grousing' . . . has given rise in Australia to the derisive expression *wingeing pommy*.
1972 Thomas Keneally *The Chant of Jimmie Blacksmith* 17: 'Pass a law to give every single wingeing bloody Pommie his fare home to England. Back to the smoke and the sun shining ten days a year and shit in the streets. Yer can have it.'
1984 *Sydney Morning Herald* 3 Feb. 8: What happened to the 'whingeing Pom'

school of thought, and jokes like 'Grow your own dope – plant a Pom'?

Pong A Chinese: *rare* [f. frequency of Chinese names like Wong]
1938 Xavier Herbert *Capricornia* 339: 'Your grandmother was a lubra and your grandfather was a Pong.'
1957 Dal Stivens *The Scholarly Mouse* 65: We saw he was too tall to be a Pong or an Eyetoe, though there was something about him that made us think of both.

pongo An infantryman in World War I; an Englishman [? f. *pong* smell]
1919 W. H. Downing *Digger Dialects* 38: *Pongo* A soldier; one of the rank and file.
1956 *Australian Signpost* ed. T. A. G. Hungerford 185: 'I don't think it woulda come to much if the mug Pongo hadn't bought in.' 'Private Smith,' I told the major, 'thinks the situation was aggravated by the interference of an English soldier.'
1982 *Australian* 30 Jan. Mag. 6: It came from somebody in the British Legion (the pongo equivalent of the RSL).

pony 1 The sum of £25 [OED 1797]
1895 Cornelius Crowe *The Australian Slang Dictionary* 60: *Pony* £25.
1975 Les Ryan *The Shearers* 69: 'I have a pony to say he can win.'
2 A small glass of beer: in N.S.W., 7 oz.; in Victoria and W.A., 4 oz. [U.S. 1849 Mathews]
1895 Cornelius Crowe *The Australian Slang Dictionary* 60: *Pony* A small glass of beer.
1953 *Caddie A Sydney Barmaid* 87: He . . . leaned on the counter, and ordered a pony of lager.
1965 Graham McInnes *The Road to Gundagai* 222: Mr Watson . . . poured himself a tiny glass of beer. 'Just a pony,' he said.

poofter The commonest term for a male homosexual, or man of effeminate appearance: *derogatory* [Partridge lists *puff* a sodomist c. 1870]
1900–10 O'Brien and Stephens: *Pouf or poufter* A sodomite or effeminate man.
1953 T. A. G. Hungerford *Riverslake* 49: He hawked disgustingly and spat on the floor between his feet. 'They want men in the unions, not poofters.'
1965 Hal Porter *Stars of Australian Stage and Screen* 280: During the last ten years or more, there have been imported a coterie of

untalented English homosexuals, English tonks unheard of outside their home country, to dominate sections of the Australian theatrical scene. If one cannot protest against the employment of the Pommy poofter instead of the Aussie poofter, one can record dismay at the employment of fifth raters who got nowhere near even spear-holding in Drury Lane.
1973 Keith Dunstan *Sports* 232: The Tigers were five goals down but pulling up fast. Professor Turner heard a thirtyish, beer-gutted supporter scream: 'You bloody Commo, poofter, mongrel bastard.' This, he said, brilliantly released racial, political, sexual and male chauvinist prejudices.

pooh, in the Euphemism for 'in the shit'
1961 Jack Danvers *The Living Come First* 177: 'I guess it's my fault if you're rather in the pooh with the Adelaide police.'
1970 Richard Beilby *No Medals for Aphrodite* 229: 'If they catch you with her, then you're really in the pooh.'
1975 Xavier Herbert *Poor Fellow My Country* 873: 'She'll put you in the poo if she writes anything 'bout you.'

pool To inform upon, incriminate; to involve someone against his will [cf. **put in**]
1919 W. H. Downing *Digger Dialects* 39: *Pool* To involve; cast blame or a burden on.
1928 Arthur Wright *A Good Recovery* 117: 'Leave the sheilas alone; they're sure to pool a man sooner or later.'
1942 Leonard Mann *The Go-Getter* 313: 'I got pooled into it,' he explained.
1967 Kylie Tennant *Tell Morning This* 85: 'A man thought he'd do the decent thing and tide a girl over a patch of trouble and she pools him every time. You can't prove it isn't your kid.'

pool of unemployment Phrase given currency by Labor Party advertisements in the Federal election of 1949 that the Liberals supported the concept of a 'pool of unemployment' as allegedly advocated by Professor T. Hytten ('You'll be cool in Professor Hytten's pool')
1949 *Sydney Morning Herald* 25 Nov. 4: The Vice-Chancellor of the University of Tasmania, Professor T. Hytten, may take action to stop the publication of some Labour Party election advertisements. These advertisements suggest that Professor Hytten

advocated a '6 per cent. pool of unemployment' in a paper he read to the Science Congress in Hobart in January. On Tuesday, Professor Hytten denied that he had ever advocated an unemployment pool.
1983 *Sydney Morning Herald* 21 Apr. 7: It casts considerable doubt on the old 'pool of unemployed' approach.

poon Equivalent to **nong**, but less commonly used [? f. *poind* (*poon*) a silly, useless, inactive person; one easily imposed on EDD]
1941 Baker 56: *Poon* A lonely, somewhat crazy dweller in the Outer Beyond (2) A simpleton or fool.
1974 David Williamson *Jugglers Three* 69: 'What possessed Keren to shack up with a poon like you?'
1984 Jack Hibberd *Squibs* 134: 'Consorting with a toff. The kind of poon that gets out of the war his father is trying to promote!'

pooned up Flashily dressed
1943 Baker 60: *Poon up* To dress up, especially in flashy fashion.
1951 Dal Stivens *Jimmy Brockett* 48: Some of 'em were young lairs, all pooned up to kill.
1972 Arthur Chipper *The Aussie Swearer's Guide* 48: *Pooned up* Dressed to impress, often with sexual success in view.

poor fellow my country An Aboriginal lament
1946 W. E. Harney *North of 23°* 79: Next to go on watch would be the 'blackboy', a native stockman droving in strange parts. He sings his tribal songs – those plaintive themes that tell about the greatness of his race, murmuring every now and then: 'Poor fellow my country, poor fellow my country!'
1975 Xavier Herbert *Poor Fellow My Country* [book title]
1989 Charles Perkins *Sydney Morning Herald* 18 Aug. 15: We have to overcome the often self-inflicted 'poor bugger me' syndrome. And we can. The time for crying in our beer is over.

popping up, how are you How are you getting on?: *obs.*
1894 Henry Lawson 'The Mystery of Dave Regan' *Prose* i 328: 'How are yer?' 'Oh! I'm all right!' he says. 'How are yer poppin' up?'
1907 Nathan Spielvogel *The Cocky Farmer* 16: 'Whatto, Joe. How are you popping up?'

1942 Sarah Campion *Bonanza* 207: 'Howya poppin', cobber?'

poppy, tall 1 A person with a high income: given currency by J. T. Lang in N.S.W. in the 1930s by his policy of 'taxing the tall poppies' [? f. Tarquin's decapitation of the tallest poppies at Gabii]
1931 *Sydney Morning Herald* 6 Aug. 8: 'I'll put it on the shoulders of those able to bear it,' he [Mr Lang] shouted when it was pointed out to him by the Opposition that 'lopping the tall poppies' meant in some cases 80 or 90 per cent.
1961 Mena Calthorpe *The Dyehouse* 143: 'We've got more useless ornaments on the payroll than we can carry as it is. Too many tall poppies waiting to be cut down.'
1973 *Sydney Morning Herald* 7 Aug. 1: Mr Cameron said the Public Service Board had developed a 'compulsive urge' to lavish public funds on the 'tall poppies' of the Public Service.
2 Anyone eminent in any way
1967 John Yeomans *The Scarce Australians* 85: The average city Australian is a complete conformist. If there is one place where the genuine eccentric is crushed, the tall poppy lopped and the penetrating discussion stifled, it is Australia.
1976 *Bulletin* 28 Feb. 25: In local slang he [Mr Whitlam] is a 'tall poppy', someone egregious in stature and therefore vulnerable to the scythe.
1984 Les Murray *Sun-Herald* 25 Mar. 17: 'They call me a tall poppy – with secateurs behind their backs – only to find I have a wire stem.'

pork and bean A queen i.e. homosexual [rhyming slang]
1970 Richard Beilby *No Medals for Aphrodite* 189: 'I never been happy about this bloke. Looks a bit of a pork-an'-bean to me. That why ya shepherding 'im? Mates, eh?'
1977 Jim Ramsay *Cop It Sweet* 72: *Pork and bean* Quean, female homosexual.

port Portmanteau [abbr.]
1908 E. G. Murphy *Jarrahland Jingles* 82: Silently they packed their 'ports' and flitted to the West.
1915 J. P. Bourke *Off the Bluebush* 122: They see a young chap with a 'port' on his back.
1942 Eve Langley *The Pea-pickers* 100: 'If they got their hands on my portmanteau

that'd be the last of it. I got things in that port that might interest them.'
1954 Tom Ronan *Vision Splendid* 262: He dragged his ports up to the tram stop and took them to the railway cloakroom.
1983 Patrick White *Signal Driver* 7: He carries a large port with his left hand, and with his right an unwieldy wooden chest with a handle to it. The chest appears much heavier than the port. [stage direction]

possie (pozzy) A chosen position (given currency by the Gallipoli campaign) [abbr.]
1915 Tom Skeyhill *Soldier Songs from Anzac* 16: But 'e [the sniper] never shows 'is pozzy.
1925 Arthur Wright *The Boy from Bullarah* 99: 'Quick, get a pozzy with the machine.'
1932 Myrtle Rose White *No Roads Go By* 160: Dogs lay in wet hollowed-out holes, digging themselves possies wherever they could find a damp, shady spot.
1970 Patrick White *The Vivisector* 620: 'Should have got here early – got us a good pozzy. Never be in the picture now.'
1981 *Australian* 26 Sep. Mag. 1: Thousands camped out from Thursday night to make sure of a good possie when the turnstiles opened.

possum, stir the To liven things up, create a disturbance; raise issues that others wish left dormant [? f. *playing possum* U.S. 1822 Mathews and son *Possum up a Gumtree* 1831]
1907 Charles MacAlister *Old Pioneering Days in the Sunny South* 51: Sometimes a strong sailorman, just off a six months' cruise, would favour us with 'Nancy Lee' or other jolly sea-songs, or an ambitious carrier or drover would 'rouse the 'possum' by giving some long-winded ditty of the time.
1908 E. S. Sorenson *The Squatter's Ward* 144: 'I mean to stir the 'possum in Sultan Susman from this out. I'm a different woman now.'
1949 Ruth Park *Poor Man's Orange* 9: A mission was like a tonic. It stirred the 'possum in the people, and for months afterwards they could still feel the enthusiasm.
1981 *Age* (Melbourne) 18 Jul. 15: Treasury secretary John Stone has a grand way of stirring the possum.

post-and-rail tea A bush tea in which the floating particles resemble a post-and-rail fence

1851 *The Australasian* 298: *Hysonskin* and *post-and-rail* tea have been superseded by Mocha, claret, and cognac.
1852 G. C. Mundy *Our Antipodes* i 329: A hot beverage in a tin pot which richly deserved the epithet of 'post and rails' tea; it might well have been a decoction of 'split stuff' or 'iron bark shingles'.
1904 Tom Petrie *Reminiscences of Early Queensland* 243: The tea then was all green tea, and very coarse, like bits of stick – indeed it was christened 'posts and rails'.
1936 Archer Russell *Gone Nomad* 24: Flour, 'post and rail' tea (the cheapest kind), black sugar, salt and meat, were the only rations provided.

posted, to be To be 'stood up'
1975 *Bulletin* 26 Apr. 46: Limp wouldn't brass or post you (leave you for dead).
1979 *Sydney Morning Herald* 30 Apr. 24: Not once was Beetson left 'posted' with no one to get the ball to.

postie A postman [abbr.]
1957 D'Arcy Niland *Call Me When the Cross Turns Over* 99: 'Don't forget to watch for the postie,' she called.
1970 Patrick White *The Vivisector* 202: 'He was a postie. The kind that turns scraggy later . . . always hurryin' ter reach the next box.'
1981 *Sydney Morning Herald* 29 Jan. 10: Australia Post is testing packs with aluminium frames to try to take some of the weight from posties' shoulders.

post, parcel see **parcel**

pot A measure of beer: in Victoria and Queensland 10 oz.; in W.A. various sizes
1918 N. Campbell and L. Nelson *The Dinky-Di Soldier* 12: I'd buy them a pot or a shandy, / (An' they'd always allow me to pay.)
1946 Dal Stivens *The Courtship of Uncle Henry* 76: Three pots had never made me see things before. It got me worried.
1974 S. H. Courtier *Listen to the Mocking Bird* 76: Across from the Flinders Street entrance to the station, I entered the bar of a pub and ordered a pot of beer.
1984 *Age* (Melbourne) 4 May 5: Beer prices will rise by at least two cents a 200ml glass and three cents a 285ml pot.

pot, put someone's ~ on To inform upon;

destroy someone's prospects [? f. *pot* to outdo, outwit, deceive OED 1562]

[**1868** 'The Song of the Sundowner' *Sydney Punch* 14 Nov. 195 repr. in *Old Bush Songs* ed. Stewart and Keesing (1957) 231: To refuse us tucker, our game they'll kill, / And no doubt at last will 'pot us'.]

1879–80 Ned Kelly 'The Jerilderie Letter' in Max Brown *Australian Son* (1956) 274: Hall has been tried several times for perjury but got clear as this is no crime in the Police force it is a credit to a Policeman to convict an innocent man but any mutt can pot a guilty one.

1911 Arthur Wright *Gamblers' Gold* 138: 'Why should I pot the bloke? He done me a good turn, an' th' police is no good to me.'

1935 F. D. Davison and B. Nicholls *Blue Coast Caravan* 178: He saw some blacks with whom he was familiar standing on the platform under guard of a policeman. 'Hullo, what's up?' One of them replied, 'Aw somebody's been putting our pot on.'

1957 Vance Palmer *Seedtime* 119: 'There's an election coming on, and there's a chance I'll be dumped . . . This afternoon's work has probably put my pot on.'

1978 Ray Lawler *The Doll Trilogy* 29: 'Oh . . . looks like then I've put their pot on.'

potato, not the clean Of bad repute (sometimes with reference to a convict background) [? negative of the English expression *the potato* the (very, real or proper) thing, what is correct or excellent OED 1822–80]

1877 Rolf Boldrewood *A Colonial Reformer* (1890) 384: 'Well,' said Mr Cottonbush, smiling and wincing slightly, 'it ain't quite the clean potato, of course [to travel one's sheep and steal a neighbour's grass]; but if your sheep's dying at home, what can you do?'

1908 Giles Seagram *Bushman All* 318: 'He's an awful fool, and – and not exactly the clean potato.'

1921 K. S. Prichard *The Black Opal* 148: 'I ain't always been what you might call the clean potato.'

1962 Tom Ronan *Deep of the Sky* 42: Some of the grand old pioneers and land-takers of history were not quite the clean potato.

poultice 1 A mortgage

1932 K. S. Prichard *Kiss on the Lips* 184: Mick Mallane . . . sayin' if the bank wanted his farm, poultice or no poultice, it'd have to go out and take it from him, and he'd be waitin' for 'm with his gun loaded.

1934 Thomas Wood *Cobbers* 134: Men talked about their blister, or their poultice, which means a mortgage, with complacency.

1958 *Coast to Coast 1957–1858* 137: When the farm was free of its 'poultice' her father had promised to hand over to Sam . . . But droughts and a fall in the price of wheat kept him battling to pay even interest on the mortgage.

2 A large sum of money

1951 Eric Lambert *The Twenty Thousand Thieves* 235: 'It's only two days to pay day and I've got a poultice in that pay-book of mine.'

1957 D'Arcy Niland *Call Me When the Cross Turns Over* 33: Like another time I got paid off, and it was a whacking big poultice, and I went into Pirie.

1979 *Sun-Herald* 24 Jun. 143: Singleton and Laws have another crony in their bid for a whack of television control, a bloke who made a poultice in recent weeks when he sold Rupert a quarter of a million Channel Ten shares.

Poverty Point Corner of Park and George Streets, Sydney, as the meeting-place of out-of-work theatricals

1889 *Bulletin* 15 Jun. 7: At Poverty Point [heading to theatrical column]

1974 *Sydney Morning Herald* 5 Jun. 1: The north-east corner of Park and George Streets was the gathering place of out-of-work theatricals who met to gossip and discuss local productions at the turn of the century. The memory of 'Poverty Point', as it was known, is to be perpetuated. On Monday night, Sydney City Council will set aside $120 for a bronze footpath plaque to mark the site.

1982 *Australian* 18 Aug. 10: Miller took his turn down at Poverty Point with all the other entertainers and managed to get work as a singer and violin player on the Tivoli circuit.

pox doctor's clerk, dressed up like a Dressed nattily, but in bad taste

1957 Nino Culotta *They're a Weird Mob* 106: Joe said, 'Gees, Nino, yer done up like a pox doctor's clerk. Yer don' need no coat an' a coller an' tie. Too hot, mate. Take 'em orf.'

1965 Eric Lambert *The Long White Night* 136: 'They was all dressed like they was at Buckingham Palace and Foran was done up like a pox doctor's clerk.'

1973 *Nation Review* 8–14 Jun. 1064: Good money was laid among the better class workingmen that he [Mr Don Dunstan] would, on this auspicious occasion, come up with an outfit to be the envy of every pox-doctor's clerk in the land.
1983 Mike Carlton *Sydney Morning Herald* 2 Nov. 11: Young Simon Thing was togged out as a pox-doctor's clerk for his wedding to Vicki Thing on Seven's *A Country Practice*.

pozzy see **possie**

prawn, come the raw To try to impose on someone (Services slang in World War II)
1942 *Salt* 25 May 8: *Don't come the raw prawn* Don't try to put one over me.
1959 Eric Lambert *Glory Thrown In* 41–2: 'Don't ever come the raw prawn with Doc, mate. He knows all the lurks.'
1975 Les Ryan *The Shearers* 85: 'What do you think I am, a drongo? I take hundreds of bets and we get blokes who try to come the raw prawn.'

prawn night Food and entertainment for a predominantly male clientele, esp. at a licensed club. 'Ladies' prawn nights' have also been reported, featuring male strippers.
1988 Tom Raudonikis *Sydney Morning Herald* 9 Jul. 64: 'To raise funds the girls have to bake cakes and . . . I had to arrange a horn and prawn night.'

prayers, to know more than one's Not to be as innocent as one may seem
1934 F. S. Hibble *Karangi* 167: 'Claudie knows more than her prayers.'
1957 Ray Lawler *Summer of the Seventeenth Doll* 12: 'She's a good kid, that.' 'Yeh. I'd say she knows more than her prayers, just the same.'
1976 Glen Tomasetti *Thoroughly Decent People* 116: 'She may be plain but she knows more than her prayers.'

prego Pregnant [abbr.]
1951 Dymphna Cusack and Florence James *Come In Spinner* 226: Guinea's face lighted with unholy glee. 'A Parker prego? Did I hear right?'
1965 Patrick White *Four Plays* 94: 'Can't resist the bananas.' 'Yeah. They say you go for them like one thing when you're preggo.'

premier state, the N.S.W., from the legend on vehicle registration plates

1980 *Sydney Morning Herald* 17 Apr. 1: NSW – The Premier State, will soon be adorning vehicle number plates in NSW.

Presbo A Presbyterian [abbr.]
1965 Leslie Haylen *Big Red* 78: Methos were Methodists, Presbos were Presbyterian.
1978 *Bulletin* 28 Nov. 35: My sympathies are with the 'continuing' [as distinct from 'uniting'] Presbos, who decided they weren't going to have any truck with the Methos, and the Congros and so on.

prezzie A present [abbr.]
1961 Jon Rose *At the Cross* 141: 'I bought you quite a lot of prezzies.'
1978 Patrick White *Big Toys* 18: 'Darling, I brought you a prezzie from the Other City.'
1983 Barry Humphries [as Edna Everage] *Australian Women's Weekly* Dec. 261: Even though I'm a fanatical Republican, the royal family always send me gorgeous prezzies, but as you can imagine *they're* terribly hard to buy for.

prick and ribs, all ~ like a drover's dog see **all**

pricker, to have the To be in an angry state: *rare* [variant of *get the needle*]
1945 Baker 121: A man in a temper is said . . . *to have . . . the pricker*.
1955 D'Arcy Niland *The Shiralee* 102: 'You've got the pricker properly, eh? You'll knock him into next week, will ya?'

Prince Albert, Alfred see **Albert, Alfred**

prop To pull up unexpectedly (originally of a horse)
1844 *Georgiana's Journal* ed. Hugh McCrae (1966) 127: Suddenly my pony propped, and I just had time to disengage my limb from the pommel before he started to roll himself on the beach.
1908 W. H. Ogilvie *My Life in the Open* 83: Playful or vicious . . . almost all of them 'prop' or 'go to market' in some form or other.
1929 K. S. Prichard *Coonardoo* 67: 'The horse shied, propped and shot Ted fair over his head.'
1969 Thomas Keneally *The Survivor* 70: Seconds later a university sedan, driven by George the university guard, wheeled fast

through the gate and propped at the front of the house.

1981 *Sydney Morning Herald* 31 Oct. 16: The inability to go in or out of any room without propping, like a sheep at a gate, and then perhaps lolling for a bit on the frame may be a feature of one school of method acting, but in my view is best used sparingly.

property, the smaller the ~, the wider the brim   see **brim**

public   A public (i.e. government) school, as distinct from a Catholic one; a child attending such a school

1956 Brian James *The Bunyip of Barney's Elbow* 140: People spoke of keeping their children at home, or . . . 'putting them to the convent', or 'the public', as the case might be.

1972 Philip Hickie introduction to Peter Kenna *The Slaughter of St. Teresa's Day* 7: They [the Irish and Italians of Paddington in the 1950s] were even further isolated by the Roman Catholicism into which they were born. The world was divided into Catholics and 'Publics'.

1984 Gabrielle Lord *National Times* 20 Apr. 13: These were known as the Publics. They went to public school, they ran about in the streets, they didn't believe in the Pope, and they went to something called Sunday school instead of Mass.

pufterlooner   A kind of scone made of dough and fried in fat [f. the way it rises during cooking]

1870 Marcus Clarke *His Natural Life* ed. S. Murray-Smith (1970) 577: 'Have a puff-terlooner, Master Dick,' suggests Derwent Jack, 'or a bit o' sweetcake.'

1906 A. B. Paterson *An Outback Marriage* 149: A tin plate of light, delicately browned cakes of the sort known as 'puftalooners'.

1935 F. D. Davidson and B. Nicholls *Blue Coast Caravan* 186: There was bush honey and a great platter of puff-de-loonies, all warm and crisp and golden brown.

1964 Tom Ronan *Packhorse and Pearling Boat* 140: A camp oven full of 'puff de loons' (fried scones to the uninitiated).

1975 *The Commonsense Cookery Book* 181: Puftaloons (Fried Scones) [recipe]

pull the coat   see **coat**

pull your head in   see **head**

pull out dig, the dogs are pissing on your swag   Advice to someone to abandon the tack he is on, as though by calling attention to some circumstance he has overlooked [f. message passed by Alan MacDonald to Eric Harrison in Parliament in the days of the Chifley government: see quot. 1977]

1977 Howard Beale *This Inch of Time* 39: When his speech – a little heavy-handed – had gone on for some time, I saw Alan MacDonald, the opposition whip who sat next to me, scribble something on a piece of paper and bustle down the aisle and hand it to Harrison in full cry at the table. It was usual to give a colleague a helping hand by passing him a note on some point which he might have forgotten, and so Harrison took the paper gratefully and read it. Then he threw it down on the table, completed his speech in one sentence, and sat down abruptly. What MacDonald had written was, 'Pull out digger, the dogs are pissing on your swag.'

pull the tail out of a peewee, couldn't   see **couldn't**

punched, bored or   see **bored or punched**

pup, the night's a   It's early yet

1915 Henry Lawson 'A Foggy Night in Antwerp' *Prose* i 913: The night was not even a pup yet – it was broad daylight, being Northern summer.

1934 Vance Palmer *Sea and Spinifex* 165: 'What about coming out on the water for awhile? Night's still a pup.'

1968 Geoffrey Dutton *Andy* 198: 'Are you thinking of driving out to Hanging-stone to-night?' 'It's only forty miles and the night is a pup.'

1983 *Newcastle Herald* 26 Apr. 2: So far the national shearers' strike is only a pup. Four weeks may be a long time without work in most industries, but in shearers' terms it is nothing.

pure merino   see **merino**

purler   Something exceptional in its class [f. *purl* To turn upside down OED 1856]

[**1908** *Australian Magazine* 1 Nov. 1251: purler, a heavy fall.]

1935 R. B. Plowman *The Boundary Rider* 149: 'My face was covered in blood and I had a pearla of a headache.'

1941 Baker 57: *Purl, purler* Something excellent, outstandingly good.

1980 *Australian* 16 Aug. 13: Flo's 35-minute speech was a pearler.
1980 *Mercury* (Hobart) 12 May 22: Shane Gifford . . . climbed over the pack to pull down a pearler.

push A crowd; a band of larrikins; an intellectual and cultural clique or others with some bond of association (see quot. 1896) [f. English thieves' slang]
1812 Vaux: *Push* A crowd or concourse of people, either in the streets, or at any public place of amusement &c., when any particular scene of crowding is alluded to, they say, *the push*, as *the push*, at the *spell* doors; *the push* at the *stooping-match*, &c.
1892 Henry Lawson 'The Captain of the Push' *Verse* i 186: As the night was falling slowly down on city, town and bush, / From a slum in Jones's Alley sloped the Captain of the Push.
1917 A. B. Paterson *Three Elephant Power* 31: He had originally been quartered at Sydney, and had fought many bitter battles with the notorious 'pushes' of Bondi, Surry Hills and The Rocks.
1942 Tip Kelaher *The Digger Hat* 25: I've spent it on the beaches with all the surf-club 'push'.
1963 John Cantwell *No Stranger to the Flame* 74: 'My mother and uncle and brother are well up in the holy Roman circles of this town. You one of their push?'
1963 *Sunday Telegraph* (Sydney) 20 Jan. 2: The Royal George Hotel, at the corner of King and Sussex Streets . . . has for some years been the headquarters of members and ex-members of the Sydney University Libertarian Society known simply as 'The Push.'
1973 Alexander Buzo *Rooted* 87: 'Gary's gone away for the weekend, cavorting in the mulga with the Werris Creek Push.'

pussy's bow, up to See quot. 1945
1945 Baker 207: Among nursery expressions which have acquired a fairly stabilized currency in this country are . . . *up to pussy's bow and dolly's wax*, to denote a surfeit, especially of food.
1983 T. A. G. Hungerford *Stories from Suburban Road* 58: I got swamped up to pussy's bow with their troubles.
1988 Faith Richmond *Remembrance* 30: My father asked . . . if she'd had enough to eat and she touched her white throat and laughed 'Oh yes thank you sir – up to pussy's bow'.

put in To make a proper effort, esp. in team sport
1939 See **shiner**.
1987 Wally Lewis *Rugby League Week* 29 Jul. 4: I wasn't too pleased with quotes I saw from someone high up that some of our blokes didn't try . . . If there was some bloke out there in green and gold not putting in, I didn't see him.

put someone in To inform against, implicate
1922 Arthur Wright *A Colt from the Country* 153: 'I might have a chance with the girl again.' 'After what you did to put her in?' laughed the detective. 'I like your hide.'
1951 Seaforth Mackenzie *Dead Men Rising* 52: 'Nothing would give me greater pleasure than to put you in, only that's about the one thing I've never done in my life.'
1966 Peter Cowan *Seed* 106: 'I suppose when they make you a prefect you'll put us in.'
1987 *Sun* (Sydney) 30 Jan. 11: Mark had boasted to neighbours 18 months ago about informing on someone. 'He had been skiting about how he would be putting somebody into the police.'
see **dob in, pool, pot**

putty, up to Worthless, useless (sometimes abbr. to **upter** q.v.)
1919 W. H. Downing *Digger Dialects* 52: *Up to putty* Bad; useless; ineffectual.
1924 C. J. Dennis *Rose of Spadgers* 119: Once let 'em tangle, an' you take the blame / You're up to putty, an' yeh've lost the game.
1955 *Bulletin* 2 Mar. 35: Our balance-of-payments is heading for the stage when it could be described in non-economic terms as 'up to putty'.

pyjama cricket One-day cricket [f. coloured uniforms worn by players, and because it is sometimes played at night]
1982 *Sun-Herald* 31 Jan. 35: He [Ernie Cosgrove, Australian Cricket Board official scorer for visiting teams] feels indulgent to 'pyjama' cricket, the name he gives to the one-day variety, but prefers the challenge that Test cricket poses.
1983 *Sun-Herald* 9 Jan. 5: The very mention of 'pyjama' cricket – a name born of the players' multi-coloured uniforms – makes veteran observers like former Test bowler, Bill O'Reilly, cringe.

Q

quack A doctor, without the implication that he is unqualified

1918 George Dale *The Industrial History of Broken Hill* 76: The 'quack' in charge at the time of the Wilcannia Hospital mounted the witness stand.

1946 Dal Stivens *The Courtship of Uncle Henry* 150: 'The nearest quack was in Myralie, twenty miles away.'

1960 John Iggulden *The Storms of Summer* 169: 'I'll get the quack at the Bush Hospital to have a look at it in the morning.'

quandong Someone disreputable, living by his or her wits [? because the quandong grows as a parasite]

1939 Kylie Tennant *Foveaux* 311: In this crowd of low heels, quandongs and ripperty men, she looked at her ease and yet not of them.

1977 Jim Ramsay *Cop it Sweet* 75: *Quandong* Female who makes a practice of remaining virtuous after being wined and dined.

1980 *Sun-Herald* 27 Jan. 66: The way my luck is I'd finish up with a quandong ... A beer and food bandit.

quanger A quince (juvenile)

1977 *Sydney Morning Herald* 5 Mar. 11: We had an abandoned quince orchard where we used to wage the most fantastic quanger wars.

Queensland salute A variant of the **Australian salute** q.v.

1981 *Sunday Mail* (Brisbane) 30 Aug. 2: The flies stick to you, and you suddenly realise what they mean when they talk about the Queensland salute.

question, if it's a fair An apparent apology for curiosity [also Irish, in Joyce's *A Portrait of the Artist as a Young Man* ch. 4]

1902 Henry Fletcher *The Waybacks* 90: 'So here's another taken down. How much, if it's a fair question?'

1903 Joseph Furphy *Such is Life* (1944) 30: 'Who's this Mother Bodysark – if it's a fair question?' asked Cooper.

1955 D'Arcy Niland *The Shiralee* 86: 'I don't want to be quizzy, Mac, but, if it's a fair question what's the drum?'

quid, not the full Not 'all there', deficient [f. *quid* pound]

1953 Baker 132: *full quid* In full possession of one's faculties; a person who is said to be *ten bob* or *ten deaners* or even *tuppence* in the *quid*, is held to be a few shingles short.

1975 *Sydney Morning Herald* 5 Jul. 9: It's perfectly clear that not all members of our community are the full quid.

1982 Ian Moffitt *The Retreat of Radiance* 59: 'Best to stay clear of him. I'm beginning to think he's not the full quid.'

quietly, just Confidentially, between ourselves

1938 Xavier Herbert *Capricornia* 145: 'He'd love to see you 'fore you goes. Thinks a lot of you, just quietly.'

1951 Eric Lambert *The Twenty Thousand Thieves* 161: 'Just quietly, he's up for a decoration.'

1979 *NT News* (Darwin) 17 Oct. 6: Apparently the term has nothing to do with houses and just quietly, doesn't agree with the present policy.

quilt To clout with the fist [E. dial. 'to beat, thrash, flog' OED 1832]

1945 Baker 120: *quilt* and *stoush* a person. [as fighting terms]

1973 Donald Stuart *Morning Star Evening Star* 111: More than one bloke I've seen Joe quilt good and proper for trying to make a joke of it.

quince, get on one's To irritate, exasperate [unexplained]

1941 Baker 58: *Quince, get on one's* To annoy or aggravate deeply.

1959 Gerard Hamilton *Summer Glare* 45: 'That kid gets on my quince.'

1979 Ron Barassi *Bulletin* 11 Sep. 72: 'There are times I get on the player's quince. A coach isn't there to be liked.'

Quist, to be Adrian To be pissed i.e. drunk [rhyming slang on name of tennis player]

1978 *Australian* 31 May 9: I'm on the turps again – got Adrian Quist somethin' terrible the other night.

quoit Buttocks [Partridge: 'ex roundness']
1941 Baker 58: *Quoit* The buttocks.
1951 Eric Lambert *The Twenty Thousand Thieves* 165: 'See those jokers sitting on their quoits over there?'
1972 John Bailey *The Wire Classroom* 82: 'I think he needs a good kick up the coit,' says Cromwell.

quoits, go for one's See quots [unexplained]
1941 Baker 58: *Quoits, go for one's* To travel quickly, go for one's life.
1952 Jon Cleary *The Sundowners* 34: 'Going for the lick of his coit up the street.'
1968 Stuart Gore *Holy Smoke* 80: 'Away they go for their quoits – flat out like a lizard drinking.'

R

rabbit-killer A blow to the back of the neck, like a karate chop [f. *rabbit punch* from the way a game-keeper puts a rabbit out of pain OED 1915]
1942 Gavin Casey *It's Harder for Girls* 23: I took a rush and gave him a rabbit-killer that must have nearly broken his neck.
1951 Dal Stivens *Jimmy Brockett* 99: 'He told me he was going to use a rabbit-killer punch on Hill.' 'If he does, I'll disqualify him.'
1963 Criena Rohan *Down by the Dockside* 255: He . . . had accounted for a couple more before he collected the rabbit killer that finally put him out of action.
1981 *Alan Marshall's Australia* 39: 'His cobber barges in and Ted downs him with a rabbit-killer.'

rabbit-oh A hawker of rabbits for eating [f. the cry]
1904 A. B. Paterson 'Humours of a Horse Bazaar' in *Song of the Pen* (1983) 223: Dealers who know where they can place purchases at a profit – possibly with rabbit-oh vendors.
1911 Arthur Wright *Gambler's Gold* 75: Engaged in the hopeless task of trying to win the Rabbit-O man's money.
1943 Kylie Tennant *Time Enough Later* 181: Mrs Drew knew all about her neighbours from the butcher and the grocer and the rabbito.
1983 Ruth Park *National Times* 22 Apr. 27: The 'rabbit-oh' was also a godsend [during the war], as rabbits were off the ration. You always bought a rabbit with the pelt on, as otherwise you might get a cat.

Rabbit-ohs, the The South Sydney Rugby League team ['The nickname has its origins in the 1930's Depression when club officials raised money for the players by raffling and hawking rabbits' *National Times* 4 Aug. 1975 36]
1975 *Australian* 21 Jul. 16: Rabbitohs hit rock bottom.

rabbit-proof fence A fence marking the borders between certain Australian states, therefore used as a point of reference
1957 Randolph Stow *The Bystander* 29: God! he thought. That's the coldest little bitch this side of the rabbit-proof fence.
1962 John O'Grady *Gone Fishin'* 24: 'You wouldn't find a politer bloke this side of the rabbit-proof fence.'
1976 Dorothy Hewett *Bon-bons and Roses for Dolly* 28: 'Best little ticket takers this side of the rabbit-proof. Oh! We were a great team.'

race, not in the Given no chance at all
1945 Margaret Trist *Now That We're Laughing* 73: 'With you and Daffy dressed up, none of us others will be in the race,' said Maureen.
1956 J. T. Lang *I Remember* 34: The trade unions realised that if the Chinese could get away with long hours and low pay they would not be in the race to get better conditions.
1984 *Sydney Morning Herald* 10 May 18: 'How could three men fight 50? They were not in the race.'

race off To seduce; whisk away with a view to seduction
1965 William Dick *A Bunch of Ratbags* 185: Three of Knuckles's boys had raced Sharon off to the park to see if they could do any good for themselves.

1971 Rena Briand *White Man in a Hole* 30: 'If I don't race a sheila orf at night, I start thinkin' and can't sleep.'
1984 *Sydney Morning Herald* 3 Dec. 5: Saturday night, in a huge crush outside the Southern Cross Hotel, she [Mrs Peacock] started for the party rally holding Andrew's hand, then found she was attached to the hand of a minder from Liberal Headquarters. 'I could have been raced off,' she grins.

racehorse   See quots
1977 Jim Ramsay *Cop it Sweet!* 76: Racehorse: Very thin cigarette.
1986 James McQueen *The Floor of Heaven* 182: He rolls the smoke, an incredibly thin racehorse, sucks it into the corner of his mouth, cups his hands round a match to light it.

rack, to put one's cue back in the   see cue

rack off   To go missing; as an imperative, 'Get lost' [? variant of *nick off, fuck off, piss off*]
[**1786** William Beckford *Vathek* 70: Vathek ... was still employed [i.e. urinating], not having quite racked off his wine.]
1975 *Sun-Herald* 29 Jun. 83: 'Rak Off Normie' [title in list of pop records]
1981 Angelo Loukakis *For the Patriarch* 32: 'What'll we do now?' asks Bill. 'Let's rack off for a while,' I say.

Rafferty (Rafferty's) rules   No rules at all [? *reffatory* refractory EDD]
1928 *Bulletin* 5 Jan. 37: M.Q. (and Rafferty) Rules [title of paragraph on boxing match]
1935 *Sydney Morning Herald* 28 Dec. 11: Rafferty rules may suit Mr Keenan and the Communist party, but they are repugnant to the trade union movement.
1964 H. P. Tritton *Time Means Tucker* 34: The Show adjourned at noon for the races. They seemed to be run on the 'Rafferty Rules' principle, but I heard no complaints.
1984 *Australian* 7 Feb. 16: Marylebone Cricket Club rules could become 'Rafferty's rules' if a cricket umpire's decision was not obeyed, a Queen's Counsel told the Supreme Court in Perth yesterday.

rage, maintain the   Mr E. G. Whitlam's advice to the crowd on the steps of Parliament House on 11 November 1975 after the reading of the proclamation dissolving Parliament
1976 Frank Moorhouse *Conference-Ville* 64: I thought to myself that it was those at the heart of the Labor Party who had not been able to 'maintain the rage'. They seemed to have been the most damaged in spirit by it all.
1979 Gough Whitlam *The Truth of the Matter* 119: I concluded: 'Maintain your rage and your enthusiasm through the campaign for the election now to be held and until polling day.'
1985 *Australian* 15 Aug. 3: Asked if he had 'maintained the rage' after the sacking of Mr Whitlam by Sir John Kerr, Mr McClelland replied: 'It's as hard to maintain the rage as it is to maintain an erection.'

rah rahs   Players and supporters of Rugby Union football [f. *rah rah*, 'characteristic of the spirit or feeling of college students, esp. in respect to sporting and social activities' U.S. 1914 Wentworth and Flexner]
1980 *Sunday Mail* (Brisbane) 29 Jun. 3: The 'rah rah' rugger boys of Ballymore really turned it on at yesterday's Test.
1983 Mungo MacCallum   *Sun-Herald* 5 Jun. 72: Your basic Rugby Rah Rah in his tweed jacket with the leather patches on the elbows and the red setter as his constant companion may snort into his hip flask in disgust, but in this world all things change. Even Rugger.

Raiders, the   The Canberra Raiders Rugby League club
1982 *Sun-Herald* 7 Feb. 73: Raiders make great start [heading] Canberra Raiders marked their entry into the Sydney Rugby League competition with a sound display last night.

rainbow   See quots
1919 W. H. Downing *Digger Dialects* 40: *Rainbow* A reinforcement, or member of non-combatant corps, who joined a fighting unit after the Armistice. (Rainbow after the storm.)
1938 Eric Lowe *Salute to Freedom* 433: 'Were you at Mesalaba?' he asked. 'No,' Robin said, and added rather bitterly, 'I'm a rainbow – came over after the storm.'
1944 Lawson Glassop *We Were the Rats* 153: We remembered, too, how, when we had passed them [the Sixth Division] on the way up, they had called us the 'long thinkers' and 'rainbows'. 'Rainbows?' we had asked.

'Yeah,' they replied, 'you're rainbows all right. You always see a rainbow after a storm.'

raining, if it was ~ pea soup, I'd get hit on the head by a fork An expression (with many variants) of habitual ill luck [f. proverb 'If it should rain porridge, he would want [lack] his dish' OED 1670]
1944 Randolph Bedford *Naught to Thirty-three* 110: 'I'm that unlucky that if it rained soup, everybody else would have a spoon and I'd be left with a fork.'
1950 K. S. Prichard *Winged Seeds* 29: 'Unluckiest man I ever knew. If it was raining pea soup, he'd only have a fork.'
1954 T. A. G. Hungerford *Sowers of the Wind* 69: 'If it was rainin' palaces I'd get hit on the head with the handle of the dunny door.'
1970 Richard Beilby *No Medals for Aphrodite* 169: 'Gawd, we're an unlucky battalion, we are. If it was rainin' virgins we'd be washed away with a poofta, dinkum!'

ram *n. & v.* A trickster employed to 'set up' victims for another [*ramp* to rob or swindle OED 1812]
[**1812** Vaux: *Ramp* To rob any person or place by open violence or suddenly snatching at something and running off with it.]
1941 Baker 59: *Ram* A trickster's confederate.
1952 *Coast to Coast 1951–1952* 199: Siddy might have been ramming for you, but what you didn't know, my lad, was that he was helping me to hook you. You were a goner from the start.
1964 H. P. Tritton *Time Means Tucker* 33: A gentleman with an umbrella, three thimbles and a pea was demonstrating how 'the quickness of the hand deceives the eye' and was raking in the money at a great rate. When business slackened, another gentleman would pick up the pea with surprising regularity. This would bring the crowd back to try their luck again. No one seemed to wake up to the fact that the second gentleman was 'ramming' for the first gentleman. see **amster**

rammies Trousers: *rare* [? f. Malay *rami* a fibre or garment woven from it]
1919 W. H. Downing *Digger Dialects* 41: *Rammies* Breeches.
1953 T. A. G. Hungerford *Riverslake* 42: 'Elastic for the old girl's rammies.'
1987 Beatrice Faust *Women on Men* ed.

Margot Hilton 48: He would cap all his jokes with 'Oh yes. I know how many gussets a nun's got in her rammies (panties)'.

rap A 'boost', a commendation (interchangeable with **wrap** q.v.)
1939 Kylie Tennant *Foveaux* 176: 'Everyone wants to be seen with a high-up feller. When I pass the time of day to a cove he feels that's a rap for him, see?'
1959 D'Arcy Niland *The Big Smoke* 12: 'His old man give him a rap, and that's all I know.'
1963 Football coach reported in Keith Dunstan *Sports* (1973) 229: 'And if someone does something good, takes a good mark, give him a rap. Tell him.'
1974 *Sun* (Sydney) 19 Feb. 12: A few raps in the right places and I was chosen for City first against Country and then for NSW against Queensland.
1990 *Sydney Morning Herald* 10 Feb. 35: Sciacca is getting big raps from some of the factional heavies, but his short time in Parliament (three years) may count against him.

rap up To speak highly of, 'boost' (interchangeable with **wrap up** q.v.)
1957 D'Arcy Niland *Call Me When the Cross Turns Over* 138: 'You dream and feel hopeless, I don't.' 'Rapping yourself up a bit, aren't you?' Ibid. 174: 'They couldn't rap him up enough then.'

rapt Overjoyed, carried away (interchangeable with **wrapped** q.v.)
1974 Keith Stackpole *Not Just for Openers* 114: Poor O'Keefe wasn't so rapt; he took none for 121.
1976 *Australian* 21 Jan. 1: Thommo tops the PM with $63,000 a year. 'All I can say is I'm rapt.'

rat *v.* To act as a sneak thief, esp. from a mining claim, swag
1919 W. H. Downing *Digger Dialects* 59: *Rat, to* To steal: ferret through someone's belongings (2) to take property from a dead body.
1921 K. S. Prichard *The Black Opal* 69: If claims are ratted it is said there are strangers about, and the miners deal with rats according to their own ideas of justice.
1940 Ion L. Idriess *Lightning Ridge* 109: Two claims had been ratted in the night.
1964 David Ireland *Image in the Clay* 65:

'Soon as my back's turned, you've ratted my bags!'

rat, cunning as a (sewer) shithouse Extremely cunning
1894 Henry Lawson 'Stiffner and Jim (Thirdly, Bill)' *Prose* i 124: He was meaner than a gold-field Chinaman, and sharper than a sewer rat.
1962 Criena Rohan *The Delinquents* 36: Mrs Hansen called Lola a dirty little half-bred, over-sexed slut, no better than the bloody blacks and cunning as a shithouse rat.
1971 George Johnston *A Cartload of Clay* 158: 'Real bastard. Doesn't do a tap. Cunning as a shithouse rat, too.'
1981 *Sunday Mail* (Brisbane) 25 Oct. 19: He was as cunning as the well known Australian dunny rat.

rat up a drainpipe, like a Quick to seize an opportunity, esp. sexual
1959 Eric Lambert *Glory Thrown In* 104: 'First time we spoke she turned it on – I was like a rat up a rope!'
1962 Criena Rohan *The Delinquents* 76: 'He'd be up you like a rat up a drain-pipe, given the chance.'
1972 Geoff Morley *Jockey Rides Honest Race* 98: 'How'd you go?' 'Like a rat up a drainpipe.'
1983 Clem Gorman *A Night in the Arms of Raeleen* 40: 'I used to get up them sheilas down there like a rat up a drainpipe!'

rat with a gold tooth see **flash**

ratbag An eccentric or stupid person [see **rats**]
1937 William Hatfield *I Find Australia* 138: 'You brought one rat-bag *in*,' said Ewens to me, 'so now do me a favour by taking one off my hands.'
1959 Gerard Hamilton *Summer Glare* 129: I told myself I had been a bloody ratbag for letting myself get worked up over Dookie.
1965 Patrick White *Four Plays* 185: 'It's that Miss Docker.' 'That old rat-bag!'
1981 *Age* (Melbourne) 1 Oct. 2: His first 'Piggy' act of the day was to hang up on radio person Derryn Hinch because 'I don't talk to ratbags'.

rathouse The lunatic asylum [see **rats**]
1922 Arthur Wright *A Colt from the*

Country 83: 'He'll be the long-lost boy, instead of the guy that's missed and landed in the rat-house.'
1943 Margaret Trist *In the Sun* 44: 'Livin' so much alone's no good to anyone. It'll drive you to the rat house.'
1963 Brian James *Hopeton High* 174: 'This place is growing more like a circus or a rathouse every day,' stormed Mr Rudder.
1971 Frank Hardy *The Outcasts of Foolgarah* 108: Poor devil, she ended up in the rathouse eventually.

ratpower Derisive measure of a bowler's speed [cf. *horsepower*]
1974 Keith Stackpole *Not Just for Openers* 93: 'You've got nothing to grumble about. If you were quick, you might have, but you are only half rat-power.'
1983 *Australian* 12 Feb. 15: Some may see Geoff Lawson and Rodney Hogg bowling at what fellow players quaintly call 'half-rat power' as a sign of adapting successfully to the limited-over game.

rats, to have (be); ratty To be odd, eccentric, irresponsible [? f. *ratty*, wretched, mean, miserable OED 1885]
1894 Henry Lawson *Prose* i 57: 'Rats' [story title]
1922 Arthur Wright *A Colt from the Country* 86: 'There was a rough-up in a pub; he got a knock, had a fit, and went real ratty, and that was the end of him.'
1942 Sarah Campion *Bonanza* 17: Mo had watched all this ... imagining what it must be like to be mad. Not raving, dangerous, mad but simple rats, like Bogy.

Rats, the Green see **Green**

ratshit General term of opprobrium
1974 David Williamson *Three Plays* 153: 'In all fairness she used to have some sort of spark; but the word around the industry is that she's gone ratshit.'
1980 Rod Ansell *To Fight the Wild* 105: Some days I felt ratshit, depressed about getting weaker, worried ... and lonely.
1984 *Sun-Herald* 29 Jan. 9: Just the other day London asked if he [Bryan Brown] was interested in playing the lead in Guys and Dolls and what was his voice like? He said yes to the first question and 'ratshit' to the second.
see **RS**

raw prawn, come the see **prawn**

razoo, not a (brass) No money at all. The expression is always negative (no one is ever mentioned as *having* a razoo, and no coin of the name exists) [? f. *not a sou*]

1931 William Hatfield *Sheepmates* 268: 'Richards never has a rahzoo.'

1957 Ray Lawler *Summer of the Seventeenth Doll* 35: 'I picked him up in Brisbane a week ago. By then he hardly had a razoo.'

1964 Jon Cleary *A Flight of Chariots* 361: 'Poor bastard,' he heard one of the men nearby say. 'I wouldn't give a brass razoo for his chances out there.'

1975 Jessica Anderson *The Commandant* 155: The pile had been stolen. Every penny. Every last brass razoo.

Razor Gang Committee for Review of Commonwealth Functions chaired by Sir Phillip Lynch 1981; any similar body, esp. the Expenditure Review Committee of the Hawke Cabinet

1981 *National Times* 9 Aug. 17: The Public Service Board says there have been extensive redeployments as a result of the Razor Gang report, but is unable to give the exact figures.

1984 *Age* (Melbourne) 23 Jul. 4: Labor's razor gang gets the strop out [heading]

RBT Random breath testing, introduced in N.S.W. on 17 Dec. 1982

1983 *Sydney Morning Herald* 23 Dec. 6: RBT is not all that it seems [heading]

read, you wouldn't ~ about it Expression of mingled incredulity and disgust

1949 *As You Were* 14: *Tonight we are to be evacuated from Tobruk!* You wouldn't read about it!

1950 Jon Cleary *Just Let Me Be* 135: 'Everything I backed ran like a no-hoper. Four certs I had, and the bludgers were so far back the ambulance nearly had to bring 'em home. You wouldn't read about it.'

1962 Dymphna Cusack *Picnic Races* 249: He drew a deep breath. 'You wouldn't read about it.'

1973 H. Williams *My Love Had a Black Speed Stripe* 69: You wouldn't read about it. A bloke his missus reckoned was a doctor of philosophy, whatever that was, and just about the biggest dill you could meet.

Red Centre, the Central Australia [f. the iron oxide colouring the soil]

1936 H. H. Finlayson *The Red Centre:*

Man and Beast in the Heart of Australia [book title]

1982 *Age* (Melbourne) 28 Jun. 14: Camel trek in the red Centre [heading]

Redfern, getting off at *Coitus interruptus* [f. Redfern as the station immediately before Sydney Central; see quot. 1970]

1956 Heard in conversation.

1970 *Times Literary Supplement* 4 Dec. 1422: *To get off at Redfern* . . . is dull and unoriginal. Since the nineteenth century, natives of Newcastle upon Tyne have described the procedure alliteratively as *getting out at Gateshead*. [A correspondent commenting on a review of Partridge]

1976 Jack Beasley in foreword to Dorothy Hewett *This Old Man Comes Rolling Home* vii: 'Getting off at Redfern', the penultimate rail stop, was a euphemism for *coitus interruptus.*

Red Heart, the Central Australia [f. the presence of iron oxide in the soil]

1931 Miles Franklin *Back to Bool Bool* 45: The dawn was murky. Particles of the red heart of Australia had reached the pampered city, staining the arum lilies and irritating the housewives.

1944 Frank Clune *The Red Heart: Sagas of Centralia* [took title]

1984 *Australian* 8 Oct. 3: It starts in the Waltzing Matilda country where the song was written . . . It ends in the red heart. The proposed Outback Highway is now a corrugated track.

red hot Extreme, unreasonable, 'over the odds'

1896 Henry Lawson 'Jones's Alley' *Prose* i 38: When . . . she paused for breath, he drew a long one, gave a short whistle, and said: 'Well, it's red-hot!'

1907 Arthur Wright *Keane of Kalgoorlie* 107: 'It's red hot,' put in Dave, 'th' way these owners makes 'er pore man give 'em a lump in th' sweep.'

1920 Louis Esson 'The Woman Tamer' in *Dead Timber* 24: 'That's red hot. You can't book me for the Vag.'

1980 *Sun* (Sydney) 22 Feb. 21: Tomato prices are red hot.

red hots The trots [rhyming slang]

1955 *Bulletin* 31 Aug. 25: The sport – dubbed the 'red hots' – struggled along there till quite recent times before the boom happened.

1979 *Herald* (Melbourne) 24 Feb. 35: It's not often I'd consider giving the red hots a miss on Saturday night – especially when I've got a couple of certainties.
1983 *Sydney Morning Herald* 22 Apr. 27: The reason for the press conference was to defend trotting and lay to rest the 'red hots' stigma. It is an unjustified tag which has remained with the industry since the late 1920s and early 1930s when, Judge Goran pointed out, someone with a penchant for rhyming slang coined the term.

Redlegs, the 1 The Melbourne A.F.L. team, in 1930; since the Red Demons, then the Demons [f. team colours]
2 In South Australia, the Norwood Australian Rules team
1979 *Advertiser* (Adelaide) 9 Mar. 20: Barton joins Redlegs [heading] Sturt rover Robert Barton has joined Norwood.
3 In Queensland, the Kedron Australian Rules team
1979 *Courier-Mail* (Brisbane) 17 Apr. 23: The Redlegs lifted their game in the second term.
4 In Tasmania, the City-South T.F.L. team
1980 *Mercury* (Hobart) 14 Apr. 18: Redlegs' hopes crash [heading] City-South's hopes of making the Winfield Cup finals took a nosedive . . . at Devonport Oval on Saturday.

red ned Cheap red wine
1953 T. A. G. Hungerford *Riverslake* 35: 'There's a bottle of Red Ned in my room – slip down and hit it. You need a kick!'
1966 Hal Porter *The Paper Chase* 41: Plonk, steam, bombo, Red Ned, or Red Nell are among the derogatory names for wine. [in the 1930s]
1983 *Australian* 29 Jun. 9: Research indicates red wine may help control – and even prevent – that social inhibitor, herpes simplex II. It seems the specific ingredient that tackles the virus is tannin, 'the astringent mouth-puckering compound' found in abundance in Red Ned.

Reds, the (Dirty) The Drummoyne, N.S.W., Rugby Union team [f. team colours]
1974 *Sunday Telegraph* (Sydney) 8 Sep. 87: The complete lack of flair in the whole Drummoyne outfit raises doubts that the Dirty Reds could have done anything if given more chances.

red steer (bull), the A bushfire
1930 *Bulletin* 21 May 20: There had been a number of grass fires in the district, and suspicion falling on 'Monkey' Brown . . . he was accused of loosing the 'red bull' on the community.
1941 Baker 59: *Red Steer, the* Fire, esp. a bushfire. (Bush slang.)
1963 John Cantwell *No Stranger to the Flame* 12: The cane-cutter, made negro by sun and by soot from fires (Red Steers, they called them).
1971 Frank Hardy *The Outcasts of Foolgarah* 118: Like the bushfires: hadn't he patented the special extinguisher to end the blight of the red steer for all time?

reffo A European refugee: *derogatory* [abbr.]
1941 Baker 59: *Reffo* A refugee from Europe.
1951 Dymphna Cusack and Florence James *Come In Spinner* 278: 'The woman's a Viennese.' 'Oh, a reffo?'
1961 Patrick White *Riders in the Chariot* 221: He was, in any case, a blasted foreigner, and bloody reffo, and should have been glad he was allowed to exist at all.
1981 Frank Devine *Sydney Morning Herald* 10 Jan. 6: I half suspect Channel 0 of being both a mean Australian practical joke on the reffos and yet another example of the Government's tight fistedness.

Reg Grundys, reginalds Undies [rhyming slang]
1981 *National times* 1 Feb. 14: Reg Grundies (undies).
1984 *Sydney Morning Herald* 7 Aug. Good Living 1: The masseuse, Debbie, said nonchalantly: 'Just pop all your clothes off and I'll be right back.' I should have known she meant everything, even the reginalds.

rego Motor vehicle registration [abbr.]
1975 *Sydney Morning Herald* 15 Nov. 67: Austin 1800, 8 mths rego. Gd tyres, radio. Heater. Goes well. $450 o.n.o.
1983 David Foster *Plumbum* 309: Jason gave his car to a certain notorious character, even paid to transfer the rego.

rels, rellies, rellos Relatives [abbr.]
1981 *Sydney Morning Herald* 18 Apr. 32: Physician to both mob and swells, / He loved his wife but not her rels.
1981 *Bulletin* 22 Dec. 208: Dreaded rellies are not so easily disposed of.

1982 *Sydney Morning Herald* 16 Dec. 6: It is very easy for dinkum Aussies to assert that we can't afford at present to let migrants bring out all their rellos.

remittance man Someone sent out to the colonies by his family, and sustained there by funds remitted at regular intervals; 'one who derives the means of an inglorious and frequently dissolute existence from the periodical receipt of money sent out to him from Europe' (Morris)
1897 Mark Twain *Following the Equator* 33: He was a 'remittance man', the first one I had ever seen or heard of ... dissipated ne'er-do-weels belonging to important families in England and Canada were not cast off by their people while there was any hope of reforming them, but when that last hope perished at last, the ne'er-do-weel was sent abroad to get him out of the way ... When he reached his destined port he would find a remittance awaiting him there. Not a large one, but just enough to keep him a month. A similar remittance would come monthly thereafter.
1905 Joseph Furphy *Rigby's Romance* ed. R. G. Howarth (1946) 81: 'You uncivilized animal; you're just about fit to associate with remittance men.'
1946 Judith Wright *The Moving Image* 17: 'Remittance Man' [poem title]
1972 Alexander Macdonald *The Ukelele Player under the Red Lamp* 180: For then, as now, the A.B.C. never failed to cater for its homesick English listeners, including remittance men, out-of-work actors and retired plumbers from Wapping.

reo A reinforcement: Service slang in World War II
1944 Lawson Glassop *We Were the Rats* 224: 'Where's our reos?' asked Eddie.
1952 T. A. G. Hungerford *The Ridge and the River* 22: 'He's on'y a kid, ain't he? I wonder if he's a reo for us, or something?'
1959 Eric Lambert *Glory Thrown In* 207: Doc was talking to the 'reos' in his platoon.

rep Representative, esp. a union representative [abbr.]
1899 Henry Lawson 'A Rough Shed' *Prose* i 465: The shearer's rep. requests both apostles to shut up or leave.
1956 F. B. Vickers *First Place to the Stranger* 235: Curly our Union rep, had gathered up all our returns and sent them into Cranston as evidence.

1965 Leslie Haylen *Big Red* 5: To the rural worker in the nineteen-thirties the initials A.W.U. were the alphabetical abbreviation of a way of life in the country. The 'rep' was its vicar, its apostle, its propagandist, its dues collector.

Repat Repatriation, the government department concerned with the welfare of ex-servicemen and women [abbr.]
1951 *Argus* (Melbourne) 99 Aug. 5: Repat. Wards Wanted for Mothers [heading]
1959 Vance Palmer *The Big Fellow* 15: 'Repat would see me through.'
1971 Frank Hardy *The Outcasts of Foolgarah* 42: He had come to the Repat. Hospital to take Moss away.
1984 Germaine Greer *Sydney Morning Herald* 9 Feb. 4: My father was listed as totally disabled by the Repat when he came back from the war.

Reps, the The House of Representatives [abbr.]
1954 *Bulletin* 20 Oct. 7: Tipsters now say Menzies may seek a dissolution of the Reps early in 1956, so that Senate and Reps may be elected together in April or May of that year.
1982 *Bulletin* 19 Oct. 70: A private member's Bill on industrial democracy passed through the Senate. It will be considered soon in the Reps.

retread 1 A World War I soldier re-enlisting in World War II
1941 *Salt* 22 Dec. 36: *retread* A 1914–18 soldier enlisted a second time.
2 A retired schoolteacher returning to a temporary appointment
1950 Brian James *The Advancement of Spencer Button* 267: There were three 'retreads' among the men.
1984 *Sydney Morning Herald* 9 Jul. 3: Mr Culgin did work with some retired teachers for brief periods and they were referred to as 'retreads'.

returned man A returned serviceman
1935 H. R. Williams *Comrades of the Great Adventure* 305: Civilian life has failed to furnish many returned men with all they deserve.
1943 Herbert M. Moran *Beyond the Hill Lies China* 145: The Returned Soldiers' vote had, at the beginning, been an important factor at every Election. But soon their

brief solidarity weakened and Returned Men voted on the old party lines.

1974 Barry Humphries *A Nice Night's Entertainment* (1981) 141: I'm reminded of a very dear old friend of ours, Pat Hennessy, a Returned man.

1981 A. B. Facey *A Fortunate Life* 289: He said that if I wasn't a returned soldier he would have had to fail me but they could not reject a returned man on war injuries.

rev head   See quot. 1979

1979 *Sydney Morning Herald* 3 Mar. 13: Harkins points out the 'rev heads' (fast driving teenage yobos) and the 'loweys' (equally fast young girls) he knows lolling about outside the Commercial Hotel.

1984 *The Open Road* (Sydney) Apr./May 4: I still insist that being booked for speeding didn't force me to make the momentous decision to stop driving like a teenage revvy.

revolving door, couldn't go two rounds with a   Vince Gair's opinion of Billy Snedden

1974 *Australian* 3 Apr. 5: Mr Daly said Senator Gair had described Mr Snedden as a man who 'could not go two rounds with a revolving door'.

1982 *Australian* 24 Feb. 9: He [Russ Hinze] told Senator Bonner on national television: 'You couldn't go two rounds with a revolving door.'

revvy   see **revhead**

ribs, all prick and ~, like a drover's dog   see **all**

ribuck   see **ryebuck**

Rice, a roll Jack ~ couldn't jump over   See quot. 1945

1945 Baker 107: A man well supplied with cash ... may even be fortunate enough to have *a roll Jack Rice couldn't jump over*. Jack Rice was a racehorse noted for his performances over hurdles.

1954 Tom Ronan *Vision Splendid* 119: 'I've got a roll Jack Rice couldn't jump over.' Marty produced one of those wads of currency Mr Toppingham had seen only in the cruder American films and started peeling off ten-pound notes.

1970 Jon Cleary *Helga's Web* 267: 'I never seen twenty thousand in cash before. Somehow you'd think it'd amount to a pile Jack Rice couldn't jump over.' Helidon wondered

who Jack Rice was, then remembered it was famous hurdle horse with a prodigious leap.

rice pudding, couldn't knock the skin off a   see **couldn't**

ridge (ridgie-didge)   Genuine, 'on the level' [f. *ridge* gold OED 1665 (thieves' slang)]

[**1812** Vaux: *Ridge* Gold, whether in coin or any other shape]

1945 Baker 126: We also describe something especially good as ... *ridge*.

1953 Kylie Tennant *The Joyful Condemned* 294: 'He'll tell you himself I'm ridgey-dige. I worked for him.'

1971 David Ireland *The Unknown Industrial Prisoner* 130: 'I convinced her the whole thing was ridge! She went away thinking up recipes, how to get some variety into roast sparrow.'

1986 *Australian* 6 Sep. 64: Warwick Capper ... donated his jock-strap to be auctioned at a galah ball in aid of the Swans. But, as you suspected, it wasn't the sweaty ridgedidge. No, in true Swannies, Powerplay style, he got exclusive designer Christopher Essex to sew sequins and pearls on to it.

Ridge, the   Lightning Ridge

1940 Ion L. Idriess *Lightning Ridge* 157: I arrived back at the Ridge full of beans.

1978 *Australian* 4 Oct. 7: Opal Fever Rush Hits The Ridge [heading]

right, she'll be   An expression of general reassurance

1958 H. D. Williamson *The Sunlit Plain* 77: Eddie West smiled faintly at Deborah Tindall and whispered, 'She'll be right'.

1968 *Coast to Coast 1967–1968* 125: 'She'll be right, mate,' the man consoled him.

1971 Henry Williams *Australia – What is it?* 114: If the madmen triumph and the button is pressed and this earth is reduced to a smouldering radioactive cinder, maybe, out on the old Barcoo or somewhere out west, there will be a survivor, a lone battler to emerge from his timber-and-corrugated shack, look out across the ruined planet, roll up his sleeves and roll himself a smoke, and say, 'She'll be right, mate'.

ring *n.*   The buttocks, anus [f. shape]

1952 T. A. G. Hungerford *The Ridge and*

the River 130: 'I'd get shot in the ring, that's what I'd get,' said Wallace.
1965 Randolph Stow *The Merry-go-Round in the Sea* 174: 'I bet I would have booted him in the ring if he hadn't run.'
1974 Jack Hibberd *Dimboola* 9: 'Where do I sit?' 'On your ring.'
1982 *Sydney Morning Herald* 10 Jul. 16: The answer . . . explains, in a nutshell, why the critics will never kiss their rings.

ring *v.* 1 Used of cattle forming themselves into a mass, with those on the outside circling the herd; used of horsemen riding about such a herd
1868 C. Wade Brown *Overlanding in Australia* 77: After an hour's amusement of this sort, they stop of their own accord. This evolution is termed 'ringing'. It is a good sign rather than otherwise.
1906 A. B. Paterson *An Outback Marriage* 169: By degrees, as the horses went round them, the cattle began to 'ring', forming themselves into a compact mass, those on the outside running round and round.
2 To prove oneself the fastest shearer in the shed [f. **ringer** 1]
1895 A. B. Paterson *The Man from Snowy River* 88: They had rung the sheds of the east and west, / Had beaten the cracks of the Walgett side.
1905 'Flash Jack from Gundagai' in *The Old Bush Songs* ed. A. B. Paterson 27: And once I rung Cudjungie shed, and blued it in a week. [note] i.e. he was the ringer or fastest shearer of the shed, and he dissipated the earnings in a single week's drunkenness.
1923 Jack Moses *Beyond the City Gates* 47: In his third year of shearing, Gray 'rung' Wetherina, out west.
3 To **ringbark** q.v.
1853 S. Mossman and T. Banister *Australia, Visited and Revisited* 197: He destroyed the trees by 'ringing' them; that is, cutting off a strip of bark round the butt of the tree, which prevents the sap ascending, and thereby kills them.
1885 Mrs Campbell Praed *Australian Life* 34–5: [Blacks] were only pressed into service when shepherds were scarce, or 'rung' trees (that is, gums which had been barked and allowed to wither) required felling.

ringbark To kill a tree by cutting off a strip of bark around the trunk [f. **bark** *v.*² 3 To strip off the bark from (a tree); to cut off a complete circle of bark from it, so as to kill it 1545 OED]

1877 Rolf Boldrewood *An Australian Squire* repr. as *Babes in the Bush* (1900) 50: 'Dead – every one of 'em, Miss,' explained their ruthless conductor. 'They've been ringbarked, more's the pity.'
1890 Henry Lawson 'Skeleton Flat' *Verse* i 64: When the squatter's men came with the death-dealing axe, / And ringbark'd the Skeleton Flat.
1930 *Bulletin* 8 Jan. 20: Two new hands . . . were ringbarking on Blade's selection.
1981 *Age* (Melbourne) 15 Jan. 16: Each tree [on Rottnest Island] has to be fenced for five years, otherwise the quokkas will ringbark them.

ringer 1 The fastest shearer in a shed; the outstanding man in any activity [f. *ringer* anything superlatively good EDD 1896]
1870 Rolf Boldrewood 'Shearing in Riverina' *In Bad Company* (1901) 313: The 'Ringer', or fastest shearer of the whole shed ['assembly' in 1901].
1892 Henry Lawson 'At the Tug-of-War' *Verse* i 114: 'Twas in a tug-of-war where I – the guvnor's hope and pride – Stepped proudly on the platform as the ringer of my side.
1910 C. E. W. Bean *On the Wool Track* 196: The man who shears most sheep is the 'ringer'.
2 A stockman, drover, general station hand [f. **ring** *v.* 1]
1910 John X. Cameron *The Spell of the Bush* 48: Dam-sinkers, fencers, scrub-cutters, ringers, and other men doing contract work in the vicinity.
1937 Ernestine Hill *The Great Australian Loneliness* 330: *Ringers* Drovers' men, wheeling round the cattle day and night on the road.
1964 *Sydney Morning Herald* 25 Apr. 11: If a mob of ringers (station hands) . . . start 'heading 'em' in the bar.
1983 *Sydney Morning Herald* 8 Oct. 37: 'There are young cowboys (called ringers) and a bunch of old-timers settling in.

ringie The ringkeeper in two-up [abbr.]
1941 Baker 60: *Ringie* The keeper of a two-up school.
1951 Frank Hardy *Power Without Glory* 323: Red Ted was 'Ringie'. He supervised the game in the ring itself, seeing that the pennies were spun fairly, and calling the results.
1978 Richard Beilby *Gunner* 298: With the

centre set the ringie called for the side bets.

ringtail 1 A ringtail possum
2 A 'ring in' in horseracing
1945 Tom Ronan *Strangers on the Ophir* 88: Blue Bonnet was a ring-rail. A flea-bitten gray, grandson of Snowdon, he had won hurdle races in Melbourne under another name.
1982 Joe Andersen *Winners Can Laugh* 175: Ringing in occurred regularly at local ARC meetings. In fact, it was said that the 'ringtails' there would outnumber the combined total to be found in the zoos of Australia.

ring the tin See quot.
1972 *Sydney Morning Herald* 24 Feb. 12: A foreman at the mine is the subject of a 'ring the tin' ruling by members of the Workers' Industrial Union of Australia, the city's [Broken Hill] largest union with 2,500 members ... According to union officials, 'ring the tin' ruling means that the foreman will not be spoken to by WIU men who work under him. The ban will apply 24 hours a day on and off the mine lease.

ring wobbler A horse subject to fluctuations in the betting ring
1990 *Sun-Herald* 4 Mar. 66: Unlucky Rory a ring wobbler [heading] After being responsible for a savage blow from 5–4 to 4–1, Prince of Rory ended up an unlucky fourth.

rip you, wouldn't it see **wouldn't it**

ripper As for **beaut** [OED 1851]
[**1859** Hotten 82: *Ripper* A first-rate man or article *Som.*]
1951 Eric Lambert *The Twenty Thousand Thieves* 182: 'Good letter, Chips?' A gurgle. 'It's a ripper!'
1973 *Australian* 7 Jul. 16: I love this ripper country / Of funnel webs and sharks / With blowies big as eagles / Where your car gets booked by narks.
1981 *Australian* 15 Dec. 14: 'Jeez, what a night. What a ripper bloody night,' they shouted at each other in parting.

rise, make a To achieve some kind of prosperity: *obs.*
1876 Rolf Boldrewood *A Colonial Reformer* (1890) 183: 'I haven't seen my poor

old mother for five years good, and I must go, if I was never to make a rise again.'
1916 C. J. Dennis *The Moods of Ginger Mick* 18: Ginger Mick's bin at the races, an' 'e'd made a little rise.
1940 Ion L. Idriess *Lightning Ridge* 99: Andy sank five hundred shafts, toiled for years and years, and never made a rise.

rivers, Hawkesbury see **Hawkesbury**

river, the only ~ in the world that flows upside down see **upside**

Riverina Bluebell An alternative name for **Paterson's Curse** q.v.
1979 *Sydney Morning Herald* 21 Jul. 10: Its loss [the loss of Paterson's Curse] will be a great blow to bee-keepers as it is a later winter flowering plant. It is also sold in flower markets under the name of Riverina Bluebell.
1980 *Australian* 25 Apr. 3: The war on Paterson's Curse, also known as Riverina Bluebell and Salvation Jane, was ordered by the Australian Agricultural Council and has caused a furore in the local honey industry.

roaring days, the The period of the gold discoveries, romantically viewed
1897 Henry Lawson 'The Lights of Cobb and Co.' *Verse* i 339: But these seem dull and slow to me compared with Roaring Days.
1907 Charles MacAlister *Old Pioneering Days in the Sunny South* 197: It is well over half a century since I wished my first rich dish at Spring Creek, but it seems only yesterday, so strongly have the glorious annals of those 'roaring days' burned themselves on the camera of memory.
1936 William Hatfield *Australia Through the Windscreen* 53: In its roaring days 'The Duchess' was better than many a goldmine.

roar up To rebuke, upbraid
1919 W. H. Downing *Digger Dialects* 42: *Roar up* Upbraid; abuse.
1947 Norman Lindsay *Halfway to Anywhere* 69: Bill was able to roar him up, anyway, for having the blinkin' cheek to come shoving his nose into Bill's affairs.
1958 H. D. Williamson *The Sunlit Plain* 191: 'I'll tear the tripe out of that bank manager. I'll give him such a roaring-up that he won't know whether he's coming or going.'

robber's dog, head like a see **head**

Robbo, four bob See quots
1897 *Bulletin* 23 Jan. 11: 'Four Bob Robbo' – four shillings Robinson, who lived in the classic suburb of Waterloo, Sydney . . . came into a bit of money and bought a horse and trap. The money was spent, and Robinson tired of the horse, which got poor; so he then sometimes let out the horse and trap (both somewhat worse of wear) for 4s. per half-day. There was a run on the cheap hire, and Rob. bought two other horses and traps, which he let out at the same price. A neighbouring livery-stable keeper and his employees resented Rob's cutting-down prices and, when any of the rival's equipages passed, used to cry out, in derision, 'Four Bob Robbo!' The cry was taken up by the kids, and has now become a Waterloo classic.
1906 A. J. Tompkins *With Swag and Billy* 51: Right out of the haunts of the motor, the bike and the Robbo.

robe A wardrobe [abbr.]
1969 Thomas Jenkins *They Came to Australia* 138: I had had an unsublimated ambition to possess a huge built-in wardrobe – or as the advertisement said, 'enormous floor-to-ceiling robes'.
1980 *Daily News* (Perth) 27 Sep. 29: The big master bedroom has a three-door built-in robe with a deep shelf.

Rock, the Ayers Rock
1979 *Sun-Herald* 28 Oct. 31: $32m project to save the Rock [heading] More than $32 million of public money and private money will be spent to save tourist-blighted Ayers Rock from environmental ruin.

rock-ape 1 Derogatory term for an Aboriginal
1983 *Australian* 5 Feb. Mag. 1: 'Coons, spiks , boongs, rock-apes, sunshines, I can't stand them,' he said. 'Namatjira's in the right place, six feet under.'
1985 Xavier Herbert *National Times* 25 Jan. 22: 'To be a Territorian, you've got to talk about rock apes and black bastards, things like that.'
2 Anyone else viewed with disfavour, esp. a teenager
1984 Marian Eldridge *Walking the Dog* 217: 'Who's walking you home, not those rockapes, I trust?'
1985 *Sun-Herald* 27 Jan. 18: Up North Palm Beach way they call them the 'rock apes' – the nude sunbathers who hide among the rocks and the sand hills so as not to offend the affluent family set a few hundred metres away on Palm Beach proper.

rockchopper A Roman Catholic (sometimes abbreviated, as an adjective, to *chopper* e.g. 'He went to a chopper College'): *derogatory*
1982 Alan Gill *Sydney Morning Herald* 27 Aug. 7: A rock chopper is a Roman Catholic. It is a slang word used privately in some Protestant circles in the 1940s and 1950s. Its origin remains uncertain, but it may refer to the convict beginnings of Catholicism in Australia.
1982 Edmund Campion *Rockchoppers Growing up Catholic in Australia* 2: A symbol of such unfriendliness was the nickname 'rockchoppers'. Unknown to most Catholics, the word was used privately by ascendant Protestants to express their dislike of the Irish-Australians whose proletarian roots went back to the convict rockchoppers . . . the *Macquarie Dictionary* gave it an entry, guessing (wrongly, in my view) that its origins lay in the initials RC.

Rocket The tennis player Rod Laver (b. Rockhampton, Queensland)
1976 *Australian* 21 Apr. 21: Rodney George Laver, alias the Rockhampton Rocket, has been the most prolific winner of major tournaments in the history of tennis.

rockhopper See quot. 1959
1959 Baker 140: *rock-hopper* A person who fishes from rocks on a sea coast.
1978 *Sydney Morning Herald* 29 Dec. 16: Fishermen who assume that the sea will be placid all day can get a rude shock if they have broken the first rule of rock-fishing. That rule is that somebody in the party must be looking seaward. Alert rock-hoppers seldom come to grief.

rocking-horse manure, as scarce as Very scarce
1944 G. H. Fearnside *Sojourn in Tobruk* 33: Australian cigarettes were as rare as rocking-horse manure hereabouts.
1954 Tom Ronan *Vision Splendid* 41: 'Tailormade smokes are as rare as rocking-horse manure around here.'
1981 Max Harris *Bulletin* 16 Jun. 81: The price in Australia, allowing freight and costs, is nearly par with the sterling price. And that, these days, is as rare as rocking horse manure.

rock spider A child molester (prison slang)

1986 *Sun-Herald* 19 Sep. 9: Darcy Dugan, Australia's most celebrated ex-criminal, knows exactly how other prisoners treat 'rock-spiders' – jail slang for hated child molesters.

1990 *Sydney Morning Herald* 7 Mar. 9: A prisoner found bashed and strangled in his cell had been known as a 'rock-spider', or child molester, a Supreme Court jury was told yesterday.

roley-poley See quots 1859, 1911

1859 Daniel Bunce *Travels with Dr. Leichhardt* 167–8: Very common to these plains, was a large-growing *salsolaceous* plant, belonging to the *Chenopodeaceae*, of Jussieu. These weeds grow in the form of a large ball, to the height of five or six feet, and, being annuals, die away in the autumn, and, as they do not speedily decay, lie loose on the surface . . . No sooner were a few of these balls (or, as we were in the habit of calling them, 'roly-poleys') taken up with the current of air, than the mules begin to kick and buck.

1911 Edward S. Sorenson *Life in the Australian Backblocks* 112: The simple-looking roley-poley, a huge white ball of burrs and grass. It is met with everywhere in the north-west, and rolls for miles across the plains, banking up against fences and filling up the corrals.

1935 R. B. Plowman *The Boundary Rider* 252: In the meantime we had made a roaring fire, mainly of dry roley-poley – there was not much in the way of firewood on those sandhills.

1984 *Sydney Morning Herald* 27 Jan. 2: I find the fields full of prickly saltwort, commonly known as rolly-polly because it breaks off in the wind and rolls across country.

roll up A mass meeting of workers to deal with some issue of common concern; any assembly of people

1861 *Sydney Morning Herald* 20 Jul. 8: On Sunday, the 30th June, the residents of Tipperary Gully were aroused by cries of 'Roll up', and in the course of a very short time upwards of a thousand men, armed with bludgeons and pickhandles, no forearms as yet appearing, were assembled around the 'No Chinese' standard.

1898 D. W. Carnegie *Spinifex and Sand* 120: A 'roll-up' would be called, and those who cared to put themselves forward, would form judge, jury, police and all. The general verdict was notice to quit within so many hours – an order that few would dare to neglect.

1937 Miles Franklin *Back to Bool Bool* 248: 'We are all making for the grand roll-up at Bool Bool.'

1984 Janise Beaumont *Sun-Herald* 15 Jul. 120: Per usual, the roll-up included a fair share of ladies who occasionally still wear silk scarves on their heads and shoes with little chains on the front. It has been said that the polo set need the scarves to keep their mouths from falling open.

roll Jack Rice couldn't jump over see **Rice**

Rookwood, crook as Very crook [f. Rookwood cemetery and crematorium N.S.W.]

1985 *Australian* 15 Mar. 3: Mr Wran had to admit that . . . donations [to N.S.W. political parties] could probably be channelled through Queensland to disguise their real origin. 'I'm sure they would be welcome in Queensland, because they are as crook as Rookwood up there,' he said. 'Everyone knows the price of a knighthood and you can't open up a new business unless there are donations.'

1985 Janise Beaumont *Sun-Herald* 5 May 174: By Wednesday night the Big Wet had me feeling as crook as Rookwood and it took a very small but special party to get the sparks going again.

Roos see **Kangaroos**

Rooshians see **Russians**

rooster one day and a feather duster the next see **feather duster**

Roosters, the 1 The Eastern Suburbs (N.S.W.) Rugby League team (also the Tricolours) [club emblem]

1974 *Sunday Telegraph* (Sydney) 15 Sep. 96: Roosters flying high.
2 In S.A., the North Adelaide Australian Rules team

1979 *Advertiser* (Adelaide) 23 Apr. 13: Roosters' full back cages Tigers [heading]

root *n.* 1 An act of intercourse, esp. from the male point of view [? f. *rut*. Not included in the OED, although implied in the word-play in *The Merry Wives of Windsor* IV.i.42–6 cf. *root* male member]

1938 Encountered in conversation.
1958 Sir Roderic Chamberlain *The Stuart Affair* (1973) 111: He heard Moir ask Stuart, 'Did you have a root?' and Stuart reply, 'I had a tight one.'
1974 Peter Kenna *A Hard God* 33: 'Have you ever gone all the way with a girl? . . . You know what I mean. Have you ever had a real root?'
2 A partner in intercourse
1971 Frank Hardy *The Outcasts of Foolgarah* 196: 'You're not only the best root in Foolgarah but good-natured as well.'
1974 Barry Humphries *Barry McKenzie Holds his Own* 4: 'Going back to Oz, mate? What route are you taking?' 'No one, sport. I'm travelling with me Aunty Edna.'
1976 David Ireland *The Glass Canoe* 147: Johnny Bickel . . . thought she'd be an easy root and began to take notice of her.

root *v.* 1 To copulate with, esp. from the male standpoint [see **root** *n.*]
1958 Sir Roderic Chamberlain *The Stuart Affair* (1973) 12: I took her bathers off. Then I raped her. She was hard to root.
1966 Patrick White *The Solid Mandala* 185: 'We'll root together so good you'll shoot out the other side of Christmas.'
1974 David Williamson *Three Plays* 14: 'Country tarts would root a wombat if they thought he was going to be a doctor one day.'
1981 Ken Linnett *Sequences from the Seventies* 17: We'll go into the lounge, get a couple of women, take them home, and root them silly. Just like old times.
get rooted Insulting advice, like 'get stuffed'
1961 Mena Calthorpe *The Dyehouse* 186: 'He can get rooted, for all I care,' Collins said bitterly.
1974 David Ireland *Burn* 29: 'I can tell anyone in the world to go and get rooted.'
2 To cause an upheaval, consternation esp. in the expression 'Wouldn't it root you!' (World War II slang) abbr. to **Wouldn't it!** q.v.
1945 Baker 152n: The authentic digger form is *Wouldn't it root you!* A regimental paper 'Wiry' (1941) took its name from the first letters of the words in this phrase.
1964 George Johnston *My Brother Jack* 306: 'You know, and how they always wanted me to join 'em? Well – this'll root you – I bloody *have*, sport.'
3 To worst, disable, put out of commission esp. in the p.pl. *rooted*

1951 Dal Stivens *Jimmy Brockett* 244: 'It looks as though we're rooted, smacker,' I told Herb.
1973 *Sydney Morning Herald* 16 Nov. 17: Mr Snedden said to Mr Whitlam across the house table; 'You are gutless'. Mr Whitlam replied; 'It is what he (Dr Forbes) puts in his guts that has rooted him!'
1981 *Australian* 21 Feb. Mag. 19: A roadside sign near Sunningdale, Berkshire. 'Rooted Xmas trees, £4.' Apparently better ones cost £8.

root, mallee see **mallee**

ropeable Enraged (i.e. needing to be tied up, put under restraint)
1870 J. R. Houlding *Rural and City Life* 74: 'An' iv ye know'd what I am afther thinkin' about yerself jist now, ye'd be ropeable, so ye wud.'
1898 Rolf Boldrewood *A Romance of Canvas Town* 322: 'Your aunt would be ropeable?' 'I believe you,' answered his companion. 'Blew me up sky high.'
1945 Kylie Tennant *Ride on Stranger* 122: 'When I think of that rat, it makes me just *ropeable!*'
1956 Patrick White *The Tree of Man* 278: 'I often remember how you broke that washstand at Yuruga. Mother was ropeable.'
1981 *National Times* 9 Aug. 51: Having Malcolm back in town unexpectedly means half the permanent heads have had to rearrange their golf games, and they tell me that some of the chaps from Treasury were absolutely ropeable.

rort 1 A rowdy party; a 'stunt' (World War II slang) [f. *rorty* fine, splendid, jolly OED 1864]
1952 T. A. G. Hungerford *The Ridge and the River* 81: 'Out we go on another bloody rort, so what's the use of saving a day?'
1963 John Cantwell *No Stranger to the Flame* 31: Life at the pub was one long postoperational rort, a perpetual celebration of imagined kills.
1982 Thea Astley *An Item from the Late News* 71: I can see a bunch of cattlehands who have driven in for a Friday night rort sitting up at the far end of the curved counter.
2 A deception, racket, dodge
1936 Jean Devanny *Sugar Heaven* 20: 'The cockies are supposed to pay this retention money into the bank . . . but normally they don't pay it in. They keep the use of it

through the season and we draw the bare amount at the end of the cut. It's the greatest rort ever.'

1954 T. A. G. Hungerford *Sowers of the Wind* 141: 'He could take lessons from old Craigie – he's well in on all the rorts?'

1988 *Courier-Mail* (Brisbane) 20 Feb. 2: Police probe insurance rort [heading]

rorting

1981 *Sydney Morning Herald* 10 Jun. 6: Both sides blamed the other for massive 'rorting' in party branches. Rorting, in Labor jargon, is a charmingly flexible term to cover such practices as stacking branch membership, rigging elections, cooking branch records and, as a last resort, losing all branch records to frustrate a head office inquiry.

rorter 1 See quot. 1941

1941 Baker 61: *Rorter* A professional sharper: a hawker of worthless goods: one who practises sly dodges to obtain money.

1962 Alan Marshall *This is the Grass* 64: 'He's a small-time rorter. I know him.' Ibid. 159: Rorters like Flogger prepared to fleece any man who stood staring around him.

2 A perpetrator of rorts in politics, trade unions etc.

1971 Frank Hardy *The Outcasts of Foolgarah* 56: None other than Call-me-Jack Wrorter himself.

1981 *National Times* 6 Dec. 18: On balance the Right – because they have much more experience and also happen to run the party's head office – are more accomplished rorters.

rosella 1 A sheep losing its wool, and therefore easy to shear (The pink skin showing through could recall the plumage of the parakeet so called.)

1910 C. E. W. Bean *On the Wool Track* 193: If there is an old ewe in the pen, a 'rosella' as they call her, with most of the lower wool worn off, she goes the first.

1964 H. P. Tritton *Time Means Tucker* 119: Among the sheep were three 'rosellas'. These are sheep with the wool falling off, and are very popular with shearers. In fact, a shearer's idea of Paradise is a shed full of 'rosellas'.

2 See quot.

1898 Morris: 'In Northern Australia, it is a slang name for a European who works bared to the waist . . . The scorching of the skin by the sun produces a colour which probably suggested a comparison with the bright scarlet of the parakeet so named.'

rosiner A stiff drink; any enlivening influence [f. *rosin* to supply with liquor; to make drunk OED 1729 (from the resin applied to violin strings)]

[**1865** Hotten: *Rosin* Beer or other drink given to musicians at a dancing party.]

1945 Baker 170: *rozner* is a stiff pick-me-up.

1947 H. Drake-Brockman *The Fatal Days* 114: 'I've not had a solitary spot since four. I need a rosiner.'

1973 Donald Stuart *Morning Star Evening Star* 53: There's no harm in a bit of a rosiner after a hard day's travel, just once in a while.

rotate you, wouldn't it see **wouldn't it**

rotten Drunk [f. *rotten* as 'over-ripe', 'saturated with']

[**1910** P. W. Joyce *English as We Speak it in Ireland* 126: A person considered very rich: That man is rotten with money.]

1941 Baker 61: *Rotten, to get* To become exceedingly drunk.

1953 T. A. G. Hungerford *Riverslake* 135: 'Monday to-morrow – blasted work again. God, could I get rotten!'

1971 Johnny Famechon *Fammo* 145: A reporter from one of the Sydney papers – he was the last to leave, rotten.

Rotto Rottnest Island, W.A. [abbr.]

1981 *Daily News* (Perth) 26 Jan. 2: 7 charged from Rotto [heading] Seven people were charged in Fremantle Court today over alleged incidents at Rottnest.

rough as bags, guts see **bags, guts**

rough end of the pineapple see **pineapple**

roughie 1 Something 'hard to take', unfair

[**1907** Nathan Spielvogel *The Cocky Farmer* 51–2: 'Don't we have to stiffen the sinews when we are up to it with a roughie to shear?']

1939 Kylie Tennant *Foveaux* 122: 'Kelly put a roughie over Charlie to-day.'

1970 Richard Beilby *No Medals for Aphrodite* 269: 'I bluffed him, put a roughie over him.'

2 A horse at long odds, an outsider that wins

1934 Steele Rudd *Green Grey Homestead* 155: Those who had lost a wager or two will

turn to Bell and say: 'You knew something about the roughie!'
1951 Dymphna Cusack and Florence James *Come In Spinner* 40: 'He's a roughie so 'e'll go out at long odds.'
1975 *Sun-Herald* 10 Aug. 57: Smith Roughie Upsets Crowd [heading] Punters demonstrated after trainer Tom Smith won the Second Tennyson Graduation with 20–1 outsider Alterego at Rosehill yesterday.

rouse (roust) on, to To upbraid, berate [? *roust* to shout, roar OED 1513]
1900–10 O'Brien and Stephens: *Rouse* Abuse or vilify.
1904 Henry Fletcher *Dads Wayback: His Work* 20: Dads was always 'rousing' at Mums because, just as certain as the roads were very bad from rain, or the teams were all wanted in the field, she would spring a sudden demand for flour or sugar.
1934 Vance Palmer *Sea and Spinifex* 182: 'Combo's one of those sulky devils that forget nothing . . . Can't take a bit of rousing as part of the day's work.'
1961 Ray Lawler *The Piccadilly Bushman* 31: 'Don't rouse at me, Alec.'
1984 Marian Eldridge *Walking the Dog* 145: 'The silly bitch can't even keep the fire going without I have to rouse on her.'

rouseabout (roustabout) An unskilled labourer in a shearing shed or on a station; any general employee of low status; a worker on an oilfield [*rouseabout* a restless creature never easy at home OED 1778; *roustabout* a wharf labourer or deckhand U.S. 1868 OED]
1881 *Chambers' Journal* 5 Mar 157: During shearing . . . there are thirty-six hands employed on Greenwood, together with about the same number of 'Rouseabouts'; these being men and boys who pen the sheep, pick up the fleeces as they are shorn, and sort and pack the wool, &c.
1902 Henry Lawson 'Two Sundowners' *Prose* i 100: They struck West-o'-Sunday station, and the boss happened to want a rouseabout to pick up wool and sweep the floor for the shearers.
1951 Dymphna Cusack and Florence James *Come In Spinner* 39: 'They'll probably stick you in as rouseabouts in a lunatic asylum, seeing the experience you've 'ad 'ere.'
1971 Colin Simpson *The New Australia* 518: The average young oilfield worker, called a 'roustabout', needed to have more

than muscles. Technical competence was also called for and most, I was told, had had five years of secondary education.
1984 *Sydney Morning Herald* 13 Mar. 3: Mr McInerney claimed that the Western District manager of Grazcos . . . had made statements about the town that he will not get local shearers into the sheds and will employ New Zealanders with their Maori girlfriends as rouseabouts.

Roy The 'trendy' Australian, opposite to **Alf** q.v.
1960 Murray Sayle *Encounter* May 28: The Australian business-man or big land-owner, the button-down shirt, lightweight suit type of smoothie from the North Shore Line in Sydney or Toorak Road in Melbourne, with his spurious 'taste' and 'culture' . . . In current Australian terminology, this is the 'Roy' type.
1965 *Nation* 27 Nov. 21: Middle-class 'Roys' in sports cars and yachting jackets.
1971 Frank Hardy *The Outcasts of Foolgarah* 143: The young executives, the in-people, call them what you like, the Roys, the jet set, the status seekers from Perisher Valley to Palm Beach, and none of them worth a pinch of shit if it comes to doing an honest day's work.

Royal Alfred see **Alfred**

Royals The East Perth (W.A.) Australian Rules football team [f. royal blue colours]
1980 *West Australian* 26 May 68: Royals oust tired Tigers [heading] An effervescent East Perth ran the legs off a match-weary Claremont side at Perth Oval on Saturday.

Roys, the The Fitzroy A.F.L. team [abbr.]
1916 C. J. Dennis *The Moods of Ginger Mick* 33: Wot time the footer brings the clicks great joy, / An' Saints er Carlton roughs it up wiv 'Roy.
1979 *Age* (Melbourne) 7 Jul. 40: Roys to run on [heading] Fitzroy's long winning sequence will end soon . . . But they are hoping it lasts for at least two more matches.

RS Ratshit q.v. [abbr.]
1976 David Ireland *The Glass Canoe* 46: 'Who wants to be old,' he'd say. 'You're RS these days if you're old. You've gotta be young.' RS means ratshit.
1982 *Sun-Herald* 5 Sep. 133: 'If you don't

get it [the HSC], you're RS. You need it to get a job – unless you know someone.'

RSL, the The Returned Services League: the abbreviation is used colloquially to apply to the licensed clubs

1953 *Bulletin* 7 Oct. 34: Then, suddenly, Ronnie was spending his evenings at the R.S.L., waiting until she was asleep before he came home.

1958 Barry Humphries *A Nice Night's Entertainment* (1981) 16: I went to the R.S.L. the other night and had a very nice night's entertainment.

1973 Alexander Buzo *Norm and Ahmed* in *Three Plays* 16: 'It's the good times I miss, Ahmed, those magic moments that make life seem worthwhile. Like the time we danced all night at the Bronte R.S.L.'

rubbery Imprecise, uncertain (from Mr Phillip Lynch's account of 1977 budget estimates) later used as equivalent to unreliable, 'shonky'

1977 Phillip Lynch (addressing National Press Club on 17 August on the 1977 budget, and answering a question on the projected cost of certain tax changes in 1978–9): If you look into 1978–9, well of course the figures, whatever they have put down in whatever document, must be, if I use my own term, somewhat rubbery, for the simple reason that they must depend necessarily on a series of assumptions made during the course of 1978–9 as to things like growth, inflation, et al. [transcript in Australian National Library]

1984 *Age* (Melbourne) 5 Oct. 3: Professor Blainey suggested that official figures on immigrants in the population were 'rubbery'.

rubbish To disparage, dispose of contemptuously

1953 T. A. G. Hungerford *Riverslake* 20: 'If Verity was going to tramp you for burning the tucker . . . he would have rubbished you long before this.'

1969 Alan O'Toole *The Racing Game* 120: Andrew Killburn rubbished the very notion.

1971 David Ireland *The Unknown Industrial Prisoner* 352: They rubbished him every chance they got, why should he always go back for more?

rubbity A pub [rhyming slang *rubbity-dub*]

1898 *Bulletin* 17 Dec. Red Page: *Drum* –

derived from the kettle-drums (evening parties) of the days of the Georges – was a high-class word, but it fell. The cockney turned it into *rub-a-dum-dum*; the Australian now calls the same thing a *rubadey*.

1957 D'Arcy Niland *Call Me When the Cross Turns Over* 101: 'How about a gargle? Down to the rubberdy, come on.'

1983 *Daily Telegraph* (Sydney) 2 Apr. 8: They are hopeful the prince (if not the princess) will grace them with a royal presence around the bar of one of the local 'rubbidies' over Easter.

Rules As for **Aussie Rules** q.v.

1946 Dal Stivens *The Courtship of Uncle Henry* 18: In those days . . . they played Rules in long pants that reached below the knee.

1976 *Sydney Morning Herald* 27 May 22: Rules penalty upsets Saints.

Rules, Rafferty's see **Rafferty's**

Rum Rebellion The deposition of Governor Bligh in 1809 by officers of the N.S.W. Corps, noted for their trafficking in rum

1855 William Howitt *Land, Labour and Gold* ii 118: From the date of this 'rum rebellion', and the forcible deposition of poor Bligh . . . the system of political grants went on swimmingly.

1871 Marcus Clarke *Old Tales of a Young Country* 38: The Rum-Puncheon Revolution [chapter title]

1938 H. V. Evatt *Rum Rebellion* [book title]

run 1 A tract of land for grazing; a sheep or cattle station; the station as distinct from the homestead

1804 *Sydney Gazette* 5 Feb. [4]: A Commodious DWELLING-HOUSE, with a fine Garden containing two Acres and a half of excellent Land, and a number of capital Fruit-trees of various kinds, the whole fenced in with seven-foot paling; a good run for stock, and plentifully supplied with water; eligibly and delightfully situate on the Brickfield Hill.

1826 James Atkinson *An Account of the State of Agriculture and Grazing in New South Wales* 66: A trace of land, or grazing *run*, as it is termed in the Colony.

1883 R. E. N. Twopeny *Town Life in Australia* 244: A 'run' is the least improved kind of land used for sheep, but the word is used almost alternatively with 'station', which denotes an improved run. The run may be a mere sheep-walk, but a station is bound to have a house attached to it, and fenced 'paddocks' or fields.

1901 Miles Franklin *My Brilliant Career* 10: I felt cramped on our new run. It was only three miles wide at its broadest point.
1954 Tom Ronan *Vision Splendid* 270: 'Things aren't so good on the run, so I'll have to keep moving for a while. I'm turning the homestead end over to you.'

2 In shearing, the uninterrupted stretch of work between meal breaks
1911 E. S. Sorenson *Life in the Australian Backblocks* 241: A run is anything from seventy-five to ninety minutes, when the bell rings for smoke-o, lunch, afternoon tea, or knock off.
1966 Ronald Anderson *On the Sheep's Back* 89: The day is divided into two-hour 'runs' and the rests are treasured.
1975 Les Ryan *The Shearers* 154: A day consists of 4 'runs' each of two hours' duration, with a half-hour 'smoko' morning and afternoon, and an hour for lunch. Work starts at 7.30 a.m., and finishes at 5.30 p.m.

run a drum see **drum**

run over the bastards see **bastards**

rush The sudden migration of people to a gold discovery
1855 William Howitt *Land, Labour and Gold* i 174: Very little, if any, gold will be got out of the whole of this rush.
1900 Henry Lawson 'The Story of the Oracle' *Prose* i 279: 'My Uncle Bob was mates with him on one of those 'rushes' along there – the 'Pipeclay', I think it was, or the 'Log Paddock'.
1915 K. S. Prichard *The Pioneers* 152:

'Hear Pat and Tom Kearney have cleared out to the new rush? Eaglehawk, isn't it?'

Russians (Rooshians) Wild cattle [? f. *rush*]
1845 D. Mackenzie *The Emigrant's Guide* 118: These wild Russians, as they are here called, will . . . clear at the first leap a stockyard six feet in height.
1861 H. W. Wheelwright *Bush Wanderings of a Naturalist* 58: I always looked out on the plains, and whenever I saw a bullock standing sulking by itself, I always gave it a wide berth; such a one is generally a 'Roosian.'

rustbucket A car in a dangerously rusted condition [f. application to ships]
1965 *Daily Telegraph* (Sydney) 23 Apr. 20: It was a rust-bucket. That means a very badly rusted car.
1983 *Bulletin* 2 Aug. 34: It is not the classiest of limousines – in fact, it is an old rust bucket – but it worked in its own rather eccentric way.

ryebuck (ribuck) Possessing some degree of excellence; genuine; as a retort, an expression of full agreement: *obs.*
1895 *Bulletin* 9 Feb. 15: I'm ryebuck and the girl's okay.
1911 Louis Stone *Jonah* 11: 'Oh, I don't suppose you'll be missed,' replied Chook graciously. 'Rye buck!' cried Jonah.
1915 C. J. Dennis *The Songs of a Sentimental Bloke* 72: 'E'n in the days when she's no longer fair / She's still yer wife,' 'e sez. 'Ribuck,' sez I.
1943 Charles Shaw *Outback Occupations* 17: 'Ribuck, boss,' he says; 'but y're wastin' y'r time.'

S

saddling paddock The bar in the Theatre Royal, Melbourne, known in the nineteenth century as a resort of prostitutes; any known place of rendezvous [f. *ride* for the male role in intercourse]
1868 Marcus Clarke 'Melbourne Streets at Midnight' *Argus* 28 Feb. repr. in *A Colonial City* ed. L. T. Hergenhan (1972) 102:

That door leads to the 'ladies' refreshment-room', but is known to its fast frequenters by another name.
1876 Julian Thomas 'The Theatre Vestibules' *Argus* 1 Jul. 4 repr. in *The Vagabond Papers* ed. Michael Cannon (1969) 232: The stranger, strolling out during an entr' acte [at the Royal], would be still more surprised

at Melbourne manners and customs, as witnessed in the Vestibule. This is generally crowded with men and larrikins, smoking and chaffing the loose women who pass in and out ... The stranger sees that the women, possibly picking up a male companion, all enter the compartment which was previously closed, and which is now guarded by swing doors. Curiosity will doubtless prompt him to enter, and he will find himself in the far-famed 'saddling paddock' of the Royal. It is a small bar, presided over by a man – the proceedings here are too unpleasant for a barmaid to witness. Here the most notorious women of Melbourne nightly throng, and run in the companions they have caught in the stalls or in the vestibules.

1958 Gavin Casey *Snowball* 29: The ribald, popular name of the enclosure round the Government Dam was 'the saddling paddock'.

1958 Jack Lindsay *Life Rarely Tells* 213: After a while he smoothed his hair . . . 'Back to the good old saddling-paddock' – by which he meant Maisie's bedroom.

safety, mantle of   see **mantle**

Saints, the   1   In N.S.W., the St George Rugby League team (also the Dragons)
1974 *Sydney Morning Herald* 3 Aug. 63: Exit of a great Saint.
2   In Victoria, the St Kilda A.F.L. team
1916 C. J. Dennis *The Moods of Ginger Mick* 33: Wot time the footer brings the clicks great joy, / An' Saints er Carlton roughs it up wiv 'Roy.
3   In N.T., the St Mary's Australian Rules team
1979 *NT News* (Darwin) 8 Dec. 32: Saints above [heading] Tigers tipped to lose.

saloon passage   1   An unimpeded run on the race track
1982 *Australian* 5 Nov. 24: Dittman's saloon passage along the rails prompted . . . Bart Cummings to observe: 'Only once in 50 years do you see a run like that in the Melbourne Cup.'
2   An easy win in sport
1983 *Sun-Herald* 4 Sep. 70: Manly earned themselves a saloon passage through to the grand final.

salts, go through like a dose (packet) of
To move very quickly, demolish opposition [f. Epsom salts as an aperient]

1941 Baker 25: *Dose of salts, go through (something, someone) like a* To accomplish a task very rapidly: to deal drastically with a person.
1974 David Ireland *Burn* 10: He'd go through this town like a packet of salts.
1982 Ian Moffitt *The Retreat of Radiance* 59: 'The Communists aren't mucking around. They'll go through China like a packet of salts.'

salty   A salt-water crocodile in the N.T.
1982 *Bulletin* 5 Oct. 31: I used to imagine that all the sharks up here had been eaten by the crocs ('salties', as they are known to the locals).

salute the judge   To win or finish a horse race
1953 *Bulletin* 1 Jul. 7: They had exchanged racing information; Doyle had always told him when his wife's horses 'were ready to salute the judges'.
1979 *Herald* (Melbourne) 8 Jun. Heraldform 8: Toroa has not saluted the judge in his seven runs since August, but showed something like his true form last start.

Salute, Australian, Barcoo, Queensland
see **Australian, Barcoo, Queensland**

Salvation Jane   Alternative name for Paterson's Curse (q.v.) esp. in S.A. [f. resemblance of flower to Salvation Army bonnet, or for providing fodder when vegetation is scarce]
1935 Francis Birtles *Battle Fronts of Outback* 211: Every waterhole, creek and billabong . . . was fringed with the bright heliotrope of Salvation Jane – a desert wild flower.
1979 *Sydney Morning Herald* 21 Jul. 10: The name Salvation Jane was given to this plant by sheep owners who greatly valued it in hard times as valuable fodder.

Salvo (Sally)   A member of the Salvation Army
1896 *Bulletin* 31 Oct. 27: The Salvo's Error [story title]
1908 C. H. S. Matthews *A Parson in the Australian Bush* 256: 'Well, I was rared a Carthlick, but I haven't followed it up much. To tell ye the truth, I class 'em all alike – priests, parsons, "salvos", and all the lot of 'em.'
1951 Dal Stivens *Jimmy Brockett* 249: He gasped . . . like the Salvo bloke the time I put

a fiver in his collection plate at Central Railway.
1984 *Alice Springs Star* 8 Aug. 1: When the Salvos call on Sunday morning, dig deep and remember some of the services they provide.

sandgroper   A native of Western Australia [see quot. 1963]
1896 Henry Lawson *Letters* (1970) 62: W.A. is a fraud. The curse of the country is gold . . . The old Sand-gropers are the best to work for or have dealings with. The Tother-siders are cutting each others' throats.
1902 J. H. M. Abbott *Tommy Cornstalk* 2: In delicate reference to the nature of their country the West Australians are 'Sand-gropers'.
1963 Xavier Herbert *Disturbing Element* 2: The name Sand Groper measured the contempt of the easterners for the comparative infertility of the West and the social backwardness of its first settlers.
1981 *Australian* 22 Jun. 1: It was a big match for sandgropers. In a devastating display of fast bowling . . . West Australians Dennis Lillee and Terry Alderman each claimed three English victims.

sandshoe, head like a twisted   see **head**

sandy blight   Name given to trachoma or any kind of conjunctivitis, when the eyes smart as though filled with sand
[**1834** George Bennett *Wanderings in New South Wales* i 302–3: There is an affection of the eye . . . called by the colonists the 'blight' . . . The integuments surrounding the orbit were puffed up so much, as totally to close the eye, which was found much inflamed, as in acute ophthalmia, and attended with symptoms, in some degree similar, with severe itching and pricking pain, as if sand had been lodged in it, with a profuse flow of tears.]
1846 *Georgiana's Journal* ed. Hugh McCrae (1966) 228: Cuts, splinter wounds, boils, and sand-blight, have been successfully treated.
1892 G. L. James *Shall I Try Australia?* 242: One pest of the bush and plains is 'Sandy Blight' or inflammation of the eyes – it is, I believe, called 'sandy' owing to the pain being exactly similar to that which grains of sand upon the eyeball could cause.
1964 Tom Ronan *Packhorse and Pearling*

Boat 7: In the time we lived in Derby I had sandy blight three times.

sangar   A dugout
1941 Diary 20 Apr. cit. *Sunday Mail* (Brisbane) 9 Nov. 1980 Mag. 4: We live in the ground here and the boys have become first class at repairing and rebuilding their cubby houses, called sangars, here [Tobruk]. First a hole is dug into the ground until one meets rocks, at about 6 in., then sandbags and stones are used to build up the sides.

sanger   A sandwich
1969 John Kiddell *Euloowirree Walkabout* 21: 'I fixed a few sangos for you.'
1974 Jim McNeil *How Does Your Garden Grow* 26: 'Nothing like the old cheese sanger for a man on the go.'
1980 *Sunday Mail* (Brisbane) 24 Aug. 3: A colleague went to order a chicken 'sanger' and decided to ask the serving lady why they seemed 'a little thin of late'.

sav   Saveloy [abbr.]
1949 *As You Were* 58: The cook's home port was Boston, and he'd just managed to get the savs covered with cold water before blowing through.
1968 Geoffrey Dutton *Andy* 229: 'Broughtcher buncher savs,' he shouted, and held out his arms so that each pair of dancers could stop and dip their saveloys in sauce.
1970 Patrick White *The Vivisector* 216: 'I bought a few savs I thought we'd do for supper.'

save, have a saver   See quot. 1882 [f. *To make saver* To insure against or compensate for a loss OED 1613 *obs.*]
c. **1882** *The Sydney Slang Dictionary* 7: *Save* To give part of one bet for part of another. A and B have backed different horses, and they agree that in the event of either one winning he shall give the other, say 5. This is called 'saving a fiver', and generally is done when scratchings and knockings-out have left the field so that one of the two speculators must be a winner. Form of hedging.
1891 Nat Gould *The Double Event* 123: 'Wells says Perfection will win,' said Lady Mayfield to Jack Marston, 'but I've put a saver on Caloola.'
1917 A. B. Paterson *Three Elephant Power* 17: 'I had a quid on,' he says. 'And,' (here he nerves himself to smile) 'I had a saver on the second, too.'

1983 *Sydney Morning Herald* 12 Mar. 13: The electorate clearly has had a 'saver' on the Democrats and the Senate. While giving the Labor Party a clear mandate to govern in the House of Representatives, voters have left 'the minders' in control of the Senate, just in case the Government should get out of line.

scale To practise some kind of fraud, obtain something without paying: now used most often of travelling on public transport without paying a fare [? f. *scale* to split off scales or flakes from (coin) for purposes of fraud OED 1576]

1916 Arthur Wright *Under a Cloud* 32: 'How'd that happen,' asks Bill Odzon. 'Didn't think anyone could scale you.'

1941 Baker 63: *Scale, to* To ride on a train, tram or bus without paying a fare: esp. to ride a tram footboard in this way.

1953 *Bulletin* 25 Mar. 13: The Gippsland boarding-house-keeper seemed to think we'd scale him. Every pay-day we'd no sooner get in from our road-job than he'd be on to us for our dough.

1984 *Sydney Morning Herald* 7 Jan. 31: The tram guards ... were generally much admired by little boys, even though we did our best to outwit them by 'scaling' a ride, crouching unseen on the footboard on the other side of the tram.

scarce as hen's teeth see **hen's teeth**

scarce as rocking-horse manure see **rocking-horse**

school A two-up school, or any company of gamblers; a group of drinkers

[**1812** Vaux: *School* A party of persons met together for the purpose of gambling.]

1890 A. G. Hales *Wanderings of a Simple Child* 10: As I pushed my way through the throng, I at once perceived that 'school' was in.

1910 C. E. W. Bean *On the Wool Track* 226: A few sharpers with a slight knowledge of shearing often get into a big shed, and get a 'school' going – a nightly gamble.

1935 H. R. Williams *Comrades of the Great Adventure* 184: We had just been paid, and the 'school' was a large one. Gathered around the ring were several hundred men, all deeply interested in the game.

1980 Emery Barcs *Backyard of Mars* 185: 'He is in school,' continued Freedman with a meaningful grin. Then to make it quite clear, he murmured, 'Poker school, of course.'

schoolie 1 A schoolteacher

1907 Nathan Spielvogel *The Cocky Farmer* 33: The prettiest of all the girls was the schoolie, and didn't she lead the lads a dance.

1958 Gavin Casey *Snowball* 17: 'Tough type for a schoolie, he is.'

1966 Hal Porter *The Paper Chase* 118: The Tretheways are the only ones poor enough ... to accept a boarder. The schoolie always stays with them.

2 Fish not yet full size, esp. jewfish, shark

1979 *Courier-Mail* (Brisbane) 1 Jun. 21: Several catches of 'schoolies' to 10 kg were taken during the week.

schooner A 15 oz. glass of beer in N.S.W., a 9 oz. glass in S.A. [f. *schooner* a tall glass of beer U.S. 1877 Mathews]

1939 Kylie Tennant *Foveaux* 52: The cries of 'Two of half and half', 'Schooner of new', 'Pint of old'.

1954 *Sydney Morning Herald* 8 Nov. 2: 'In Adelaide we call that a schooner' ... I expressed sympathy at such extreme myopia. 'A schooner, my friends, is a large glass,' I told him.

1983 *West Australian* (Perth) 31 Dec. 1: Other recommended new prices are: 140ml (pony) 48c (up 1c). 285ml (middy) 95c (up 3c). 1125ml (schooner) $1.30 (up 5c).

scone The head, esp. in such expressions as 'off his scone': N.Z. 1942 OED [? f. *sconce*]

1946 *Sunday Sun* (Sydney) 29 Sep. Suppl. 15: One of the schemozzles which nearly drove Mac off his scone.

1977 Ruth Park *Swords and Crowns and Rings* 402: 'This bloody well won't do. A man could go off his scone this way.'

1985 Janise Beaumont *Sun-Herald* 7 Jul. 131: Ross Willis finally used his scone and married Margaret.

scone hot See quot. 1941

1938 Xavier Herbert *Capricornia* 530: Halfcaste Shillingsworth goes Copra Co scone-hot!

1941 Baker 63: *Scone-hot* An intensive to describe great vigour of attack, scolding or speed, e.g. 'Go for someone scone-hot', to reprimand severely. (2) Exorbitant, unreasonable. (3) Expert, proficient, e.g. 'He's scone-hot at shearing'.

1974 David Ireland *Burn* 136: 'When he finds out he'll go me scone-hot.'

scoot, on the On a spree [? f. *scoot* to go away hurriedly]
1924 *Truth* 27 Apr. 6: *Scoot* To clear out; also continued bout of drunkenness.
1936 Ion L. Idriess *The Cattle King* 131: 'I'm sorry to hear Eureka is on the scoot.' 'He's not. They don't go on the scoot out there. They drink dynamite and bust.'
1962 Stuart Gore *Down the Golden Mile* 120: 'Make mine a glass this time, seein' I have to go on the scoot with you booze artists to-night.'

score between the posts Have intercourse with a woman [f. football]
1973 Alexander Buzo *Rooted* 89: 'Oh I get it, you're setting up for a naughty to-night, are you? . . . Gunna score between the posts, are you?'

scorpions in one's pocket, to have see **pocket**

scrammy Nickname for a man with a defective hand or arm [f. E. dial. *scram* (*skram*) awkward; stiff, as if benumbed OED 1825]
1822 *HRA* x 776: A Man, who goes by the name of Scrummy Jack. [described by another deponent p. 775: 'he was a little Man, and has a dun or withered Arm']
1895 James T. Ryan *Reminiscences of Australia* 353: He was familiarly called 'Scrammy Jack'. He had only one hand (the right), and where the other had been he wore a leather covering, into which a ring was attached when he was driving tandem.
1902 Barbara Baynton *Bush Studies* 44: Scrammy 'And [story title]
1906 A. B. Paterson *An Outback Marriage* 33: Scrammy Doyle (meaning Doyle with the injured arm).

scrape *n. & v.* To copulate with
1959 Donald Stuart *Yandy* 4: Like Jessie, Larrian was ready to scrape with the whitefellers.
1969 Osmar White *Under the Iron Rainbow* 64: She said she didn't mind lying down for white men at three dollars a time . . . All the girls got scraped by someone . . . She'd give the old sergeant a scrape for free and he'd make things easy for her while she was in the lockup.
1975 Robert Macklin *The Queenslander*

43: 'We rolled her over on the beach and started scraping.'

scratch, be scratching To be struggling, in difficulty
1930 Vance Palmer *The Passage* (1944) 65: He and Bob had to scratch for a living the best way they could. Ibid. 160: 'We'll have to scratch for another year or two to pay off the new boat.'
1953 T. A. G. Hungerford *Riverslake* 202: 'If his mob gets in next election they'll whip up a nice old depression, just like they did the last time, and we'll all be scratching for jobs again. The only difference is that there'll be a million or so of these bludgers scratching with us.'
1962 Alan Marshall *This is the Grass* 202: 'Not that I read much. I've been too busy scratching for a crust.'

scratchies Instant lottery tickets: scratching the surface reveals the prize
1989 *Australian* 29 Jul. Weekend 20: Occasionally I've won $2 in the scratchies.

screamer In Australian Rules football, an exceptionally high mark ['A very powerful shot in a game' 1896 OED]
[**1859** Hotten 87: *Screaming* First rate, splendid. *Theat.*, but now applied generally.]
1963 Lou Richards *Boots and All!* 175: The only thing he did all day was to take a screaming mark.
1984 Les Carlyon *Age* (Melbourne) 30 May 39: The Melbourne Cricket Ground, citadel of Aussie Rules, the very place where international figures with names like Jezza take things called screamers.

screamer, two-pot Someone very susceptible to alcohol
1959 Dorothy Hewett *Bobbin Up* 21: 'Look at Lou. She's a two-pot screamer, always 'as been.'
1972 John de Hoog *Skid Row Dossier* 95: 'It says experienced and sober, ya bloody two-pot screamer.'
1981 George Hutchinson *No Room for Dreamers* 10: And there's no need for poofters or two-pot screamers / And there's no room for bludgers – and no room for dreamers.

scrub, the Anywhere remote from civilization, or in expressions like 'head for the scrub', 'out in the scrub', any place to which one might abscond, or avoid contact with one's fellows [f. *scrub* as a wooded but inhospitable region]

1956 Kylie Tennant *The Honey Flow* 270: If Col had won the toss and proposed first, I don't think it would have made any difference, except that Elsie might have taken to the scrub.

1962 John Morrison *Twenty-Three* 194: 'You just get up in the morning, pack whatever you can lay hands on, and head for the scrub.'

1984 Garrie Hutchinson *From the Outer* 228: Who knows whether the same catastrophic drop in attendances would occur in the long term if (when?) the Grand Final heads out into the scrub [VFL Park].

see **mallee, mulga, tall timber**

scrub aristocracy   People with social pretensions in 'the scrub'

1900 Henry Lawson 'The Hero of Redclay' *Prose* i 296: 'The banker, the storekeeper, one of the publicans, the butcher . . . the postmaster, and his toady, the lightning squirter, were the scrub-aristocracy.

scrub-bashing   Driving a road through the scrub

1967 Len Beadell *Blast the Bush* 151: I was not surprised at the end of forty miles of scrub-bashing that there was still no evidence of the other road.

1982 *NT News* (Darwin) 5 Aug. 7: The drongo club . . . went scrub-bashing in their four-wheel drives.

scrub bull   A 'loner' [cf. **scrubber**]

1959 Vance Palmer *The Big Fellow* 268: What she had roused in him then had kept him from being quite the tough scrub-bull that he might have been.

1967 Barry Oakley *A Wild Ass of a Man* 68: 'I'm different from the herd, and at that school they don't like the wanderers, the scrub bulls who forage for their nourishment in their own way, alone.'

1975 Xavier Herbert *Poor Fellow My Country* 702: The Scrub Bull, of all people, getting interested in settling the country.

scrubber   1   A term for cattle that have run wild, or never been branded [f. **scrub**]

1859 Henry Kingsley *Recollections of Geoffry Hamlyn* ii 125: 'It's lucky you've got them [the cattle] cheap, for the half of them are off the ranges.' 'Scrubbers, eh?' said the Major.

1934 Vance Palmer *Sea and Spinifex* 220: 'The worst bloody scrubbers along the Gulf . . . Horns as long as your arms, and the pace of kangaroo-dogs.'

1982 Thea Astley *An Item from the Late News* 88: A chopper that went over running out scrubbers on the property west of him.

2   A horse racing on country tracks, or considered suitable only for the bush

1958 Frank Hardy *The Four-Legged Lottery* 177: 'Got a few scrubbers. Picks up a race in the bush occasionally. Likes to run his horses in the city.'

1984 *Sunday Independent* (Perth) 1 Apr. 73: Punters don't deserve to lose their money because 'scrubbers' and unfit horses ruin the chances of fancied runners when they drop back through the field after galloping for a couple of furlongs.

3   Any hardy individual, outside the conventional code

1984 Laurie Lawrence *Sunday Times* (Perth) 5 Aug. 96: 'He's [Jon Sieben] been a scrubber all his life, a hard boy to handle but one of the most mentally tough swimmers I've ever come across.

scungies   Bikini-style swimming trunks, or 'vees' [f. **scungy**]

1979 Kathy Lette and Gabrielle Carey *Puberty Blues* 3: The art of changing in and out of boardshorts at the beach was always done behind a towel or when your girlfriend was at the shop. The ultimate disgrace for a surfie was to be seen in his scungies. They were too much like underpants. The boys didn't want us checking out the size of their dicks.

1979 *Sun-Herald* 21 Oct. 119: The studs strut around the pool in brief scungies.

scungy   Unattractive, disreputable in appearance [f. *scunge* To prowl around looking for food 1843 OED]

1963 Barbara Jefferis *The Wild Grapes* 64: 'He's much more sensitive than all the other Russels. He couldn't live with anyone who was skungey looking.'

1980 Rod Ansell *To Fight the Wild* 56: The dressing on her leg was getting very scungy but I wasn't game to touch it until the bone had had time to begin setting.

Sea Eagles, the   As for **Eagles** q.v.

1975 *Bulletin* 9 Aug. 21: 'What would you do,' asked the notice [on a Manly church], 'if Jesus Christ came to Manly?' To which some

Sea Eagle-fancier had replied: 'Play him in the centre alongside Fulton and move Branighan out to the wing.'

seagull A casual wharf labourer [f. the bird's habit of waiting for and swooping on scraps]
1965 Frank Hardy *The Yarns of Billy Borker* 115: He was a casual wharfie at the time I'm telling you about . . . and they call casuals 'seagulls'.

Seagulls 1 In Queensland, the Wynnum-Manly R.L. club
1979 *Courier-Mail* (Brisbane) 5 Mar. 14: Seagulls in fighting comeback [heading] Wynnum-Manly's team of country youngsters staged a determined comeback to power their way to a 13–9 win over Valleys at Neumann Oval yesterday.
2 In Tasmania, Sandy Bay Australian Rules club
1980 *Mercury* (Hobart) 21 Apr. 22: Gulls saw it slip away [heading]

seat at the pictures, couldn't pick a see **couldn't**

secko A sex pervert [abbr.]
1949 Ruth Park *Poor Man's Orange* 38: 'Just look at that dirty ole secko, will you?' he said disgustedly.
1969 William Dick *Naked Prodigal* 13: 'You look like you'd be the sorta bloke who'd take little kids down a lane and give 'em two bob, yeh bloody secko.'
1984 *Bulletin* 20 Mar. 47: A risk of being identified with a 'sekko' (sex offender).

see you later see **later**

semi 1 A semi-detached house
1959 Dorothy Hewett *Bobbin Up* 5: Always fighting a losing battle with life in the grey, warped, weatherboard semi in Maddox Lane.
1980 Natalie Scott *Wherever We Step the Land is Mined* 22: Semi, comprising two-and-a-half bedrooms, kitchen, bath, inside W.C., rear access, very handy position.
2 A semi-trailer
1959 Dorothy Hewett *Bobbin Up* 2: A big shiny car had forced them over, to sideswipe an oncoming semi.
1979 *Advertiser* (Adelaide) 3 May 3: Tourists stranded by semi accident.
3 A semi-final
1950 Gavin Casey *City of Men* 197: 'They

reached the semis last year, with just about the same team.'
4 A semi government authority, loan etc.
1979 *Australian* 29 May 10: Acid test for semi market [heading] Two leading semi-government bodies are about to provide an important test of the market's ability to fund the 1979–80 borrowing requirements of the authorities.

send her down, Hughie see **Hughie**

septic A Yank [f. rhyming slang *septic tank* = *Yank*]
1976 *Cleo* Aug. 33: Even before R and R, Americans [at King's Cross] were septics (septic tanks – yanks). Septic is now general usage.
1983 Clem Gorman *A Night in the Arms of Raeleen* 73: 'Some compliment, eh, comin' from a Septic Tank on Fifth Avenue?'

serve An adverse criticism, reprimand [? f. tennis, or serving a summons]
[**1812** Vaux: To *serve* a man, also sometimes signifies to maim, wound, or do him some bodily hurt, and to *serve* him *out and out*, is to kill him.]
1967 *King's Cross Whisper* (Sydney) xxxix 4: *Serve*: To give a person a thrashing. 'Give the mug a serve.'
1974 Keith Stackpole *Not Just for Openers* 104: I continued to give Snow a bit of a serve. He was foolish to bowl short on such a good wicket.
1981 *Age* (Melbourne) 1 Oct. 2: He gave the Commonwealth Secretary-General, Mr Ramphal, a serve over their differences in interpreting the Gleneagles Agreement.

session A period of steady drinking, in a group
1949 Lawson Glassop *Lucky Palmer* 215: 'I'll join you in a beer later, but I don't want to get into a session.'
1969 Christopher Bray *Blossom Like a Rose* 8: 'The pub's bin open five minutes! The session's begun!'
1983 Laurie Clancy *Perfect Love* 102: He had missed out on his session but he could at least bring some bottles home.

settler's clock The kookaburra, or laughing jackass [see quot. 1827]
1827 P. Cunningham *Two Years in New South Wales* i 232: The loud and discordant noise of the *laughing jackass* (or *settler's clock*, as he is called), as he takes up his roost

289

on the withered bough of one of our tallest trees, acquaints us that the sun has just dipped behind the hills.
1856 G. Willmer *The Draper in Australia* 224: The settlers prize this bird very much and do not destroy it, as it not only kills snakes, but rouses the inmates of the huts at day-break, while at night it is heard just as it is getting dark. From these circumstances it is called the settler's clock.

seven   A 7 oz. glass of beer
1967 Noel Ottaway *The Pub and I* 28: I had just drunk a seven of new with a customer.
1976 David Ireland *The Glass Canoe* 151: She went down ... to middies, then to sevens, and finally got so low they moved her to hospital.

seven, throw a   To die; to faint; to have a vomiting attack [f. *six* as the maximum score marked on dice]
1894 Henry Lawson 'Martin Farrell' *Verse* i 269: 'I am pretty crook and shaky – too far gone for hell or heaven, / An' the chances are I'm goin' – to "do the seven".'
1926 L. C. E. Gee *Bushtracks and Goldfields* 32: They all reckoned that it was touch and go with me, that I was a 'goner', that I was bound to 'throw a seven'.
1958 Vince Kelly *The Greedy Ones* 104: 'Throwing a seven?' 'Collapsing – having a fit – fainting.'

shag on a rock, like a   Isolated, deserted, exposed [OED records *wet as a shag* 1835]
1845 R. Howitt *Impressions of Australia Felix* 233: 'Poor as a bandicoot', 'miserable as a shag on a rock' &c.; these and others I very frequently heard them make use of.
1929 Jules Raeside *Golden Days* 16: The flood waters did not subside, and we were there like three shags on a rock.
1952 T. A. G. Hungerford *The Ridge and the River* 53: 'I got no time to be standin' here like a flamin' shag on a rock!'
1987 *Times on Sunday* 14 Jun. 7: His media minders left him [Mr Hawke] isolated under the TV lights like a shag on a rock.

shake   To steal [f. *shake out* to rob OED c. 1412]
1812 Vaux: *Shake* To steal, or rob.
1854 W. Shaw *The Land of Promise* 33: There commenced a torrent of interrogation, mostly in slang, 'what's he shook?' 'has he sloped?' and other flash phrases.

1906 Joseph Furphy *Rigby's Romance* ed. R. G. Howarth (1946) 251: 'What's come o' them two black horses o' yours?' 'Gone.' 'Sold?' 'Shook.'
1965 Patrick White *Four Plays* 105: 'You don't think I'd shake anything off Ern? 'E's my mate!'
1979 Ted Schurmann *The Showie* 107: 'You're not going to take his pliers!' 'Heck, I'm only borrowing them, not shaking them.'

shake a stick at, more than one could   see **stick**

shanghai   A catapult [f. *shangan (shangie)* A stick cleft at one end for putting on a dog's tail EDD]
1863 *The Leader* 24 Oct. 17: Turn, turn thy shangay dread aside, / Nor touch that little bird. [Morris]
1910 H. H. Richardson *The Getting of Wisdom* 205: Home was, alas! no longer the snug nest, in which she was safe from the slings and shanghais of the world.
1982 *Sun-Herald* 17 Oct. 18: School holidays were spent 'down the bush', swimming all day or shooting a shanghai at whatever innocent wildlife crossed the track.

shanty   A public house, esp. unlicensed; a 'sly-grog shop' [OED] [f. the structure so called]
1864 J. Rogers *New Rush* 52: The Keepers of the stores and shanties grieve.
1880 Rolf Boldrewood *The Miner's Right* (1890) 64: Any attempt to limit the licensing produced such a crop of 'shanties' or sly-grogshops.
1894 Henry Lawson 'The Spooks of Long Gully' *Prose* i 249: The son did die that night in the 'horrors' in a shanty.

Shark, the Great White   see **Great**

sharkbait(er)   Someone who swims further out than the other surfers, as though tempting the sharks
1912 Arthur Wright *Rung In* 34–5: It might be only some foolhardy 'shark baiter' as he heard the more venturesome of the bathers termed.
1930 *Bulletin* 13 Aug. 45: By swimming past the first line of breakers Alma had declared herself to be that disquieting disturber of peace, a sharkbaiter.
1967 K. S. Prichard *Subtle Flame* 99: 'I'm no good at shark baiting!'

Sharks, the 1 The Cronulla-Sutherland Rugby League team, N.S.W. [f. club emblem, and proximity of Cronulla to the sea]
1975 *Sydney Morning Herald* 21 Jul. 13: Rogers kicks Sharks home.
2 The East Fremantle (W.A.) Australian Rules team
1983 *Sunday Independent* (Perth) 14 Aug. 37: Sharks savage the Falcons [heading] East Fremantle . . . did it again yesterday.
3 In Queensland, the Southport Australian Rules team
1986 *Courier-Mail* (Brisbane) 7 Jul. Sports Extra 9: Windsor-Zillmere's win over Southport yesterday enabled them to get over a 'mental block' against the Sharks.

sharpie Member of a teenage cult with 'short back and sides' haircut, the counterpart of the English 'skinhead'
1965 William Dick *A Bunch of Ratbags* 202: The more a sharpie protested he was not a bodgie, the more they [the police] laughed and belted him.
1975 *Sun-Herald* 13 Apr. 7: A sharpie is usually aged between 14 and 19 years. The boys wear their hair cropped short on the top and sides and longer at the back. The girls often wear 'dolly' makeup and have their ears pierced. Tattoos are often worn by both sexes. The sharpies wear blue jeans or high-waisted slacks supported by old-fashioned braces, matched with a tee shirt and sometimes a woollen cardigan . . . They usually keep well clear of the beachside suburbs, the home of their arch enemies, the surfies.

she's apples, jake, sweet see **apples, jake, sweet**

shearer's dog, all prick and ribs like a see **all**

shears, off (the) Used of sheep just shorn
1896 Thomas W. Heney *The Girl at Birrell's* 69: Now and again a buyer visited the stations to get cheap sheep 'off shears'.
1903 Joseph Furphy *Such is Life* (1944) 64: I camped with a party of six . . . bound for Deniliquin, with 3,000 Boolka wethers off the shears.
1983 Arthur Cannon *Bullocks, Bullockies and Other Blokes* 127: Stations usually sold sheep 'off shears' – that is, after shearing.

shed A shearing shed

1857 F. Cooper *Wild Adventures in Australia* 105: 'He was bound for the shearing through New England. By this time, most likely, he has set in at some of the sheds on the Namoi.'
1902 Henry Lawson 'Two Sundowners' *Prose* i 96: The number of men employed is according to the size of the shed – from three to five men in the little bough-covered shed of the small 'cockatoo', up to a hundred and fifty or two hundred hands all told in the big corrugated iron machine shed of a pastoral company.
1934 F. E. Baume *Burnt Sugar* 249: 'You might be a shed hand or just a hobo.'

sheila A girl or woman. Not derogatory, although no woman would refer to herself as a 'sheila' [f. *Sheela* as generic name for an Irish girl, counterpart of *Paddy* for a man]
[**1828** *Monitor* 22 Mar. 1053: Many a piteous Shela stood wiping the gory locks of her Paddy, until released from that duty by the officious interference of the knight of the baton.
1859 Hotten 90: *Shaler* A girl.
1910 P. W. Joyce *English as We Speak it in Ireland* 320: *Sheela* A female Christian name . . . Used in the South as a reproachful name for a boy or man inclined to do work or interest himself in affairs properly belonging to women.]
1895 Cornelius Crowe *The Australian Slang Dictionary* 72: *Shaler* A girl.
1919 W. H. Downing *Digger Dialects* 44: *Sheila* A girl.
1928 Arthur Wright *A Good Recovery* 117: 'Leave the sheilas alone, they're sure to pool a man sooner or later.'
1965 Patrick White *Four Plays* 111: 'We used to lie and talk about what we was goin' ter eat. An' the sheilas we was goin' ter do.'
1973 H. Williams *My Love Had a Black Speed Stripe* 17: Beats me how any bloke can enjoy himself talking with women. Sheila talk has always driven me up the wall.

shelf *n. & v.* An informer; to inform upon [? to put away on a shelf]
[**1859** Hotten 70: *On the shelf* To be transported.]
1926 J. Vance Marshall *Timely Tips for New Australians: Shelf* A slang word denoting an informer.
1947 C. K. Thompson *Yes, Your Honour!* 142: 'What is a top-off?' . . . 'An informer, a

pimp, a shelf, and so on,' replied the police prosecutor.

1953 T. A. G. Hungerford *Riverslake* 20: 'If you spoil this one I damn well will shelf you.'

1984 *Sun-Herald* 9 Sep. 63: For all the pre-planning and agreements not to 'shelf' one another by being seen to start a rush to back Fine Cotton, several of those in the know could not contain their greed.

shelleys, a A function at which only soft drinks are served [f. Shelleys, the soft drink firm]

1983 Encountered in conversation.

shells, bag of Something easily accomplished [cf. a piece of cake]

1978 Ray Lawler *The Doll Trilogy* 125: JOSEF: That would be kind. NANCY: A bag of shells.

she-oak Colonial beer: *obs.* [? f. the native oak, a species of casuarina, and *oak = cask*]

1873 J. C. F. Johnson *Christmas on Carringa* 1: Able to put away at a sitting a larger quantity of colonial 'sheoak' than any man of his inches.

1881 G. C. Evans *Stories told round the Campfire* 17: 'Perhaps so,' he remarked, 'but when a man expects a drink of brandy, it is a great sell to find it is only sheoak.'

1893 J. A. Barry *Steve Brown's Bunyip* 282: Hastily finishing his pint of 'sheoak'.

shepherd To hold a mining claim without working it, in order to deny others; (sporting) to ward off a player tackling a member of one's own team

1855 William Howitt *Land, Labour and Gold* i 172: It is common practice for them to mark out one or more claims in each new rush . . . But only one claim at a time is legal and tenable. This practice is called shepherding.

1895 Nat Gould *On and Off the Turf in Australia* 122–3: 'I got jammed in,' said Martin, with a smile. 'One horse kept me in all down the straight; in fact, this horse was 'shepherding' me all through the race.'

1965 Frank Hardy *The Yarns of Billy Borker* 21: 'Did the players in the other team run across and stop him?' 'No fear, his team mates shepherded them off.'

1982 *Sun-Herald* 4 Apr. 87: The bloke beside me yelled out: 'Didn't you see the

shepherd? Where'd you get a ticket, ref, out of a cornflakes packet?'

sherbet Beer: *jocular*

1917 Henry Lawson 'Romani' *Verse* iii 214: And beer that *we* called 'sherbet'.

1965 John Beede *They Hosed Them Out* 204: At mid-day I hit myself with a few sherbets.

1981 *Bulletin* 5 May 52: Hayden's only chance of hanging on to the leadership would be for Hawke to slip back on to the sherbet.

shicer A mining claim that proves unproductive; a swindler (shyster) [G. *scheisser* and English (see quot. 1859) and U.S. slang (*shyster* 1846 Mathews)]

[**1859** Hotten: *Shice* Nothing; 'to do anything for *shice*', to get no payment. The term was first used by the Jews in the last century . . . *Shicer* A mean man, a humbug, a 'duffer', – a worthless person, one who will not work.]

1855 Raffaello Carboni *The Eureka Stockade* ed. G. Serle (1969) 8: The whole flat turned out an imperial shicer. Ibid. 14: A hole was bottomed down the gully, and proved a scheisser.

1867 J. R. Houlding *Australian Capers* 127: The hole was no good, or what they called a 'shicer'.

1898 Morris: *Shicer* (2) A man who does not pay his debts of honour.

1958 Jack Lindsay *Life Rarely Tells* 213: 'There's nothing I hate more'n a shicer.'

shick, shickered, shickery Drunk [Yiddish and Ger. *beschickert*]

[**1859** Hotten: *Shickery* Shabby, badly]

1878 Rolf Boldrewood *An Australian Squire* repr. as *Babes in the Bush* (1900) 121: 'I'm always that fresh after a good night's sleep, when I've had a bit of a spree that I could begin again quite flippant. Old Tom had a goodish cheque this time, and was at it a week afore I came in. He was rayther shickerry.'

1898 *Bulletin* 17 Dec. Red Page: *shiker* Drunk.

1911 Louis Stone *Jonah* 124: 'Whose cart is it?' inquired Pinkey. 'Jack Ryan's,' answered Chook, "e's bin shickered since last We'n'sday, an' I'm takin' it round fer 'is missis an' the kids.'

1945 Gavin Casey *Downhill is Easier* 9: They sat outside the pub in the sun every day, and most of them got a bit shickered on pension day.

1961 Patrick White *Riders in the Chariot* 261: 'I'm gunna get out of this!' he announced at last. 'I'm gunna get shickered stiff!'

1973 *Sydney Morning Herald* 25 Oct. 2: A back-bench senator referred today to the Jackson Pollock painting, 'Blue Poles' bought by Australia for $1.3 million as 'shicker art' . . . Later outside the Senate he said that by 'shicker art' he meant paintings done by people who were shickered, or drunk.

1987 Charles Buttrose *Times on Sunday* 10 May 14: 'Ita still plays the opening bars of the Grieg Piano Concerto when she gets shickered.'

shicker *n.* Liquor
1916 C. J. Dennis *The Moods of Ginger Mick* 154: *Shicker* Intoxicating liquor.
1928 Arthur Wright *A Good Recovery* 85: 'Yes, I've been on the shikker,' he answered huskily.
1958 H. D. Williamson *The Sunlit Plain* 58: 'He was on the shicker when I was there last week.'

shilling in, a As for **a bob in** q.v.
1942 Gavin Casey *It's Harder for Girls* 83: We had another shilling in, and bought some bottles to take to the restaurant.

Shinboners Former nickname of the North Melbourne A.F.L. club [f. aggressive style of play: see also quot. 1981]
1981 Leonie Sandercock and Ian Turner *Up Where, Cazaly?* 51: The 'shin-boners', as they were then [1896] known (from the practice of local butchers decorating their shop-windows on football Saturdays with shin-bones of cattle tied around with blue and white ribbons), had an established reputation.
1984 *Australian* 17 Apr. 18: North Melbourne had a collective nickname – 'The Shinboners', a wonderfully inventive description of a group of players who went straight for the jugular if they couldn't break your legs.

shiner Someone who seeks the limelight but avoids the hard work, esp. in sport
1939 Herbert M. Moran *Viewless Winds* 53: How well we got to know the shiner who was brilliant when all was going well and easy, but who was missing – hanging out on the outskirts of the ruck – when our horny-handed opponents were 'putting it in'.
1983 *Sun-Herald* 10 Apr. 69: He is not a fashionable player, he is not a shiner in the open. He is simply a player who will do his job.

shingle short, a Weak in the head [variant of the English 'a tile loose']
1852 G. C. Mundy *Our Antipodes* iii 17: The climate is productive . . . of chronic diseases rather than acute ones. Let no man having, in colonial phrase, 'a shingle short' try this country. He will pass his days in Tarban Creek Asylum.
1869 *Australian Journal* Jul. 685: *A shingle short* The colonial rendering of the English phrase, 'A tile loose'.
1895 Henry Lawson 'The Fate of the Fat Man's Son' *Verse* i 280: The Fat Man's son was an Anarchist, a couple of shingles short.
1928 Miles Franklin *Up the Country* 9: 'The only time I ever saw her, she seemed a shingle short.'
1966 Patrick White *The Solid Mandala* 82: He accepted Arthur his twin brother, who was, as they put it, a shingle short.

shinplaster A promissory note issued by bush storekeepers and others, and used as a kind of currency. The name 'shinplaster' was often associated with the brittleness of the paper, which meant that the notes would disintegrate before they were cashed [U.S. 1824 Mathews]
1852 G. C. Mundy *Our Antipodes* i 163: Paper, for the most trifling sums, is current in the provinces, like 'shin plasters' in America. A great many more of these flimsy representatives of bullion than are really requisite are issued. It is averred . . . that certain large proprietors make a practice of paying wages by orders, written purposely on small and thin scraps of paper, and that they pocket many hundreds a year by the loss or destruction of these frail liabilities in the hands of rough, careless and unsober characters.
1956 Tom Ronan *Moleskin Midas* 264: He baked all his shin-plasters in the oven so that half of them would fall to pieces before they were cashed.
1974 *Australian* 27 Dec. 7: He pulls out an old shinplaster he picked up on a trip through Hall's Creek. It was a sort of personal printed postal note storekeepers and the like used to give when there was a shortage of

coins and notes of the realm. This one was dated November 1, 1936, and signed Robert R. Smith.

shiralee A swag: rare until used as a title of novel by D'Arcy Niland in 1955
1892 Gilbert Parker *Round the Compass in Australia* 49: 'Let him down easy and slow . . . Drop in his shirallee and water-bag by him.'
1957 D'Arcy Niland *Bulletin* 25 Sep. 16: A shiralee was a particular type of swag, one shaped like a leg of mutton, carried over the shoulder by a strap or rope, which usually balanced some other load, probably a tucker-bag, on the chest. I have two pictures from the 'sixties which show this plainly, one of Bendigo miners on the way to the fields, the other of Gabriel's Gully miners (Otago, N.Z.) also on the way to the diggings. In each case the captions say these men are carrying shiralees.

shirl A female counterpart of an ocker
1973 *Australian* 20 Apr. 6: If the Okkers and Shirls in the back seat [of the taxi] launch forth on a dreary and interminable discussion . . . they can quickly and effectively be silenced by a couple of extra decibels from the radio.

shirt-and-sock night A formal occasion in Alice Springs, N.T.
1983 *Sydney Morning Herald* 18 Jun. 32: At shirt-and-sock night [in Alice Springs], where local customs would be demonstrated to city slickers, a sort of strobe lighting effect was provided by red and blue light bulbs with a loose connection.

shirt front In Australian Rules football, the tackling of an opponent whose chest is unprotected, esp. by a shoulder charge
1965 Jack Dyer *Captain Blood* 87: He collected me with the perfect shirt-front, the knee coming up, the shoulder driving into my chest and the punch to the jaw on the follow-through. It was a real Victorian job.
1984 *Sunday Independent* (Perth) 9 Sep. 86: In a series of classic shirt-front situations, the Sharks players established who was boss.
see **shoulder**

shirtlifter A male homosexual
1966 Baker 216: *shirt lifter* A sodomite.
1974 Barry Humphries *Bulletin* 19 Jan. 13: When I first seen them photos of him in

his 'Riverina Rig' I took him for an out-of-work ballet dancer or some kind of shirt-lifter.
1981 *Australian* 17 Oct. Mag. 2: It is inadvisable . . . to use age-old terms like poof, queer, faggot, fairy, shirt or shirtlifter, dyke or butch sheilah in company.

shithouse General term of opprobrium
1972 Geoff Morley *Jockey Rides Honest Race* 173: 'You're probably right on all counts Ken, but I still feel shithouse about it.'
1974 David Williamson *Three Plays* 57: *West* How's your job? *Stork* Shithouse.
1983 *Sunday Independent* (Perth) 14 Aug. 23: At his first appearance before the Perth Press Club some years back, Bob Hawke was asked what he thought of Australia's foreign policy. 'Shithouse,' he said.

shit on the liver A presumed cause of bad temper [cf. *liverish*]
[**1935** H. R. Williams *Comrades of the Great Adventure* 147: 'What's up with you, you bit stiff. Got hobnails on your liver?']
1944 Lawson Glassop *We Were the Rats* 197: 'Them Jerries oughta hunk a few lumps of – off their livers,' said Eddie.
1951 Seaforth Mackenzie *Dead Men Rising* 14: 'And how is Captain Hyacinth? I trust the Captain has no more'n 'is usual amount of s – t on the liver this morning?'
1981 Archie Weller *The Day of the Dog* 81: 'Judge must of 'ad shit on 'is liver that day, unna?'
see **S.O.L.**

shivoo A party, celebration, esp. if noisy [cf. *shivoo (shebo)* a disturbance, 'row', shindy EDD]
[**1823** Jon Bee *Slang. A Dictionary of the Turf, the Ring* &c. 49: *Chevaux* Dinner, wine, song, and uproar, constitute a *chevaux*.]
1849 Alexander Harris *The Emigrant Family* (1967) 62: A 'Shiveau' at the Hut.
1908 Henry Fletcher *Dads and Dan between Smokes* 56: A real tip-top Rookwood shivoo is worth a terrace o' houses to ther undertakers.
1926 K. S. Prichard *Working Bullocks* 14: 'There's a shivoo at Marritown,' he cried teasingly, 'Me and Red's thinkin' of going on in.'
1970 Patrick White *The Vivisector* 625: On the morning after the big shivoo at the State Gallery.

shonky Deceptive, unreliable, unsound [? f. Yiddish *shoniker*, a petty trader or pedlar, or *shoddy* + *wonky*]

1970 Richard Beilby *No Medals for Aphrodite* 116: 'You shonkie sod!'

1978 *Sun-Herald* 9 Jul. 49: With the growing ground-swell of anti-communist feeling – and some fairly shonky electioneering from the Nixon camp – Richard M., then nicknamed 'Tricky Dicky', stormed in against the hapless Mrs Douglas.

shonk

1987 *Times on Sunday* 15 Mar. 15: Lionel Bowen says he's willing to create a more effective, nationally co-ordinated body to investigate the shonks.

shook on, to be To be enthusiastic about, infatuated with

1882 Rolf Boldrewood *Robbery Under Arms* (World's Classics 1949) 87: 'I am regular shook on this old moke.' Ibid. 602: When he saw how handy I was in the yard he got quite shook on me.

1901 Henry Lawson 'Joe Wilson's Courtship' *Prose* i 546–7: He was supposed to be shook after Mary too.

1926 K. S. Prichard *Working Bullocks* 301: 'What's 'took Deb?' Mrs Pennyfather exclaimed . . . 'Didn't know she was so shook on Mark Smith.'

1957 Ray Lawler *Summer of the Seventeenth Doll* 31: 'She's not too shook on the whole thing.'

1975 *Sunday Telegraph* (Sydney) 29 Jun. 49: Like Chappell, I'm not all that shook on cocktail parties myself.

shoot it, if it moves see **moves**

shoot through As for **go through** q.v.

1951 Seaforth Mackenzie *Dead Men Rising* 37: 'I'm shooting through – my woman's sick and I've waited longer than I should have.'

1962 John Morrison *Twenty-Three* 181: 'And – let us have it in plain Australian – while he was taking the call you shot through.'

see Bondi tram

shoot your own dog, you See quot.

1983 *Sydney Morning Herald* 23 Dec. 1: 'There's an old saying in the bush: "You always shoot your own dog",' Lin Gordon, Minister for Local Government and Lands, said yesterday [on a report that Mr Wran would be asking for his resignation] . . . 'It's

not a very good way to go when you get the information in the paper as to how you are going to be asked to drop out,' he said. 'I have been about for a long time and if I have any bad news to give anyone I have always done it myself.'

Shop, the The University of Melbourne

1889–90 *Centennial Magazine* ii 218: It related how 'a medical student came up to the Shop' as a freshman, and 'thought through his exams, he would speedily pop'.

1964 George Johnston *My Brother Jack* 260: 'The years at the Shop gave me nothing except a worthless B.A. and the privilege of being thrown into the University lake.'

1974 Desmond O'Grady *Deschooling Kevin Carew* 105: 'You've bought the Pommy idea of culture at the Shop,' said Moynihan.

short of a sheet of bark see **bark**

shot At the end of one's tether [? f. shooting one's bolt]

1945 Gavin Casey *Downhill is Easier* 183: It was eight miles along the track to the Bordertown road, and late at night you could easily walk the twelve miles along that to Bordertown without seeing a vehicle. I realized I was shot.

shot, have a shot at To try to 'get at' or 'take a rise' out of someone [f. *shot* a remark aimed at someone, esp. in order to wound OED 1841]

1915 K. S. Prichard *The Pioneers* 150: He was working for a shot at Donald Cameron through Young Davey.

1945 John Morrison *Sailors Belong Ships* 38: Mick, standing in the square, can't resist a shot at Beck. 'You were a long time making up your mind about this!' he yells.

1971 Keith Willey *Boss Drover* 28: We all knew him as Alec. If you called him 'Sir Alexander' he would reckon you were having a shot at him.

shot, that's the Expression of approval

1953 T. A. G. Hungerford *Riverslake* 143: 'That's the shot – buy a bit of land, and grow things.'

1963 Jon Cleary *A Flight of Chariots* 370: 'I think a good strong cuppa brew would be the shot.'

1982 *NT Times* (Darwin) 5 Aug. 7: Blaring stereo, foul language and much boozing made it just the shot for a quiet weekend for everyone.

shoulder (drop a ~ on) In Australian Rules football, the tackle delivered as a shoulder charge

1965 Jack Dyer *Captain Blood* 106: I caught him straight down the middle with a perfect shoulder.

1981 *Age* (Melbourne) 11 Aug. 34: Irrepressible Brent Crosswell yesterday came out strongly in support of the inactive VFL umpires and dropped a shoulder on the VFL for its handling of the dispute.

see **shirt front**

shouse A lavatory [abbr. of *shithouse*]

1941 Baker 66: *Shouse* A privy.

1951 Dal Stivens *Jimmy Brockett* 214: I seen that now as plain as a country shouse although I didn't like it when she told me so.

1968 Thomas Keneally *Three Cheers for the Paraclete* 84: 'I'd like some trees on it, pines, and gums, so you don't have to see your neighbour's shouse first thing each morning.'

1975 Les Ryan *The Shearers* 98: Dewlap, who had been standing at the back of the ring, all alone like a country s'house, now sidled up.

shout *v.* To buy drinks for others, or to stand any similar 'treat' [f. *to stand shot* to meet the expenses, pay the bill (for all) OED 1821; *shot* the charge, reckoning OED 1475]

1855 Raffaello Carboni *The Eureka Stockade* ed. G. Serle (1969) 92: 'You shouted nobblers round for all hands – that's all right; it's no more than fair and square now for the boys to shout for you.'

1876 A. J. Boyd *Old Colonials* (1882) 268-9: This 'shouting', as 'treating' is termed in the colonies, is the curse of the Northern goldfields. If you buy a horse you must shout, the vendor must shout, and the bystanders who have been shouted to must shout in their turn.

1939 Kylie Tennant *Foveaux* 140: Any time Tommy tried to shout the family to the picture show there was a unanimous firm refusal.

1969 William Dick *Naked Prodigal* 75: 'Like to come and have a beer with me? I'll shout.'

1981 *Daily News* (Perth) 23 Jan. 36: Bill has declared that Albert wouldn't shout if a shark bit.

shout *n.* 1 A free drink, or free round of drinks

[**1853** *Letters from Victorian Pioneers* ed. T. F. Bride (1898) 127: On regaining his senses ... he applies to the landlord, who tells him that he is in debt; that the £60 is expended. On asking how – 'How?' repeats the host, 'do you forget the shout you stood – the shout for all hands?']

1877 Rolf Boldrewood *A Colonial Reformer* (1890) 421: I threw my money about – must have a round of drinks for luck. I never saw a publican yet that could refuse to serve a 'shout'.

2 One's turn to buy drinks; in the expression 'my shout', the acceptance of this or any similar expense

1902 Henry Lawson 'Send Round the Hat' *Prose* i 472: He was almost a teetotaller, but he stood his shout in reason.

1946 Dal Stivens *The Courtship of Uncle Henry* 197: We all drank together and ordered again. It was my shout.

1974 John Powers *The Last of the Knucklemen* 22: 'I'll drink to that. Whose shout?'

show 1 (Now only U.S. and Austral.) An opportunity for displaying or exerting oneself; a chance, "opening". Phr. *to give* (a person) *a show*; *to have* or *stand a* (or no) *show* (OED): *obsolescent*

1876 Rolf Boldrewood *A Colonial Reformer* (1890) 183: As he's a gentleman, he's bound to give you a show.

1893 Henry Lawson *Letters* 54: I could not get a show in Auckland, so I spent my last pound to come down here.

1906 Joseph Furphy *Rigby's Romance* ed. R. G. Howarth (1946) 258: 'I stand a good show, if there's a vacancy.'

2 A mining claim, esp. if worked by an individual

1946 W. E. Harney *North of 23°* 205: Far and wide over the West Arm field the little men worked at their shows, exploiting the aboriginals and being exploited by them in turn.

1962 Stuart Gore *Down the Golden Mile* 263: The car that passed them that day on the way to Dutch George's show.

shower A dust-storm, in such expressions as 'Bedourie shower', 'Darling shower', 'Wilcannia shower' [f. place-names]

1898 Morris: *Darling Shower* A local name in the interior of Australia, and especially on the River Darling, for a dust storm, caused by cyclonic winds.

1933 A. B. Paterson *The Animals Noah Forgot* (1970) 38: Nature visits the settlers' sins / With the Bogan shower, that is mostly dust.
1936 Ion L. Idriess *The Cattle King* 195: 'That Bedourie shower yesterday was a beauty. There must have been thousands of tons of dust flying through the air.'

shower (rain), I didn't come down in the last A claim to a larger share of experience and shrewdness than one is being credited with
1906 Joseph Furphy *Rigby's Romance* ed. R. G. Howarth (1946) 256: 'He didn't come down with the las' rain. Pity that sort o' bloke ever dies.'
1944 Lawson Glassop *We Were the Rats* 51: 'Listen, Mr Wilkerson,' I says, 'I'm awake-up, I am. Ya doan need ter come that stuff with me. I didden come down in the last shower.'
1962 Alan Seymour *The One Day of the Year* 56: 'How did you know?' 'I didn't come down in the last shower.'

shower, to take an early To be sent off in a football match
1980 *Sydney Morning Herald* 11 Nov. 28: I have often seen Rugby League referees point to the dressing room for some errant player to take an early shower.
1982 *NT News* (Darwin) 10 Sep. 27: If he had thrown a couple of haymakers the Australians were certain the referee would have waved him to an early shower.

shrapnel Small change [f. appearance]
1919 W. H. Downing *Digger Dialects* 44: *Shrapnel* (1) Pork and beans; (2) Tattered French bank notes of small denominations.
1977 *Camera and Ciné* Nov. 24: 'I don't suppose you'd have a bit of shrapnel . . . ?' I shook fifty cents out of my purse and handed it to him.

shrewdie A shrewd person [abbr. of *shrewd head*]
[**1915** C. J. Dennis *The Songs of a Sentimental Bloke* 43: Now, this 'ere gorspil bloke's a fair shrewd 'ead.]
1916 Arthur Wright *Under a Cloud* 35: 'Look here, Wilson, you're not such a shrewdie as you imagine.'
1945 *Coast to Coast 1944* 85: He nudged Sam. 'A shrewdie, this bloke, eh? You can tell by his dial.'

1975 Xavier Herbert *Poor Fellow My Country* 365–6: Shrewdies, that they were . . . they joined forces after years of enmity.

shrimp on the barbie, I'll slip an extra ~ for yer An invitation to overseas visitors in a tourist commercial by Paul Hogan
1986 *Times on Sunday* 5 Oct. 3: 'And another thing,' he [the American sailor] added, 'that skinny, blond guy who puts a shrimp on the barbie, he said there'd be kangaroos. Well, we've been to Brisbane and we've been here and there ain't any.'

shut the gate Recognition of a scoring stroke, winning spurt that is beyond recall [f. the proverb of shutting the gate after the horse has bolted]
1930 Jack O'Hagan 'Our Don Bradman' *The Barry Humphries Book of Innocent Australian Verse* (1968) 43: Tate and Larwood would meet their fate / For it is always *shut the gate*! / When the boy from Bowral hits four after four.
1987 *Sun-Herald* 22 Nov. 68: Burke is highly competitive and combative, straight and powerful and a 'shut the gate' proposition when he takes a half break.
1989 *Sydney Morning Herald* 25 Nov. 77: One of the lasting memories of sport is of Gasnier throwing his head back and lengthening his stride. The fans always said you could 'shut the gate' when that happened. Gaz would score.

shypoo Liquor of poor quality; a public house of low reputation [? f. Chinese for 'water-shop']
1901 *The Bulletin Reciter* 30: Paddy Grady's 'Hessian Palace' was a scene of wild delight, / And we drank the shypoo deeply, till the lateness of the night.
1936 H. Drake-Brockman *Sheba Lane* 237: 'How about managing that shipoo for me?'
1962 Tom Ronan *Deep of the Sky* 218: A hostelry . . . restricted to the sale of beer and wine. Locally this was known as the 'Shypoo Shop'. I'm not sure of the derivation of 'Shypoo'. I think it is bastard Chinese for soft drink. To the sturdy second wave of pioneers of West Kimberley, beer and wine were soft drinks.

sick canary, couldn't knock the dags off a see **couldn't**

sickie A day's sick leave, taken whether one is sick or not

1953 T. A. G. Hungerford *Riverslake* 11: Now and then there would be one or more off on a sickie – they changed their jobs so frequently that they never let their sick leave accumulate.

1969 Osmar White *Under the Iron Rainbow* 109: 'Put the bludger on a sickie, boss,' he says to me.

1984 *Age* (Melbourne) 25 Apr. 3: Has the flexitime rendered the sickie obsolete?

silent cop See quot. 1934

1934 Thomas Wood *Cobbers* 122: A circle in the middle of cross-roads . . . round which all the traffic changing direction must swing; a round yellow blob, known here as the Silent Cop, or the Poached Egg.

1959 Dorothy Hewett *Bobbin Up* 2: This was the corner, by the silent cop, where she and Roy had come to grief.

1980 Barbara Pepworth *Early Marks* 10: I'm in the middle of the busy highway that runs outside the flats. I perch on a silent cop and pretend I'm one.

silly as a two-bob watch, as a wheel see **watch, wheel**

Silver Budgie, the R. J. Hawke, Prime Minister 1983– [? f. hair-styling]

1983 *Australian* 28 Dec. 9: Bob Hawke: the Messiah. Lately, the Silver Bodgie or sometimes, mistakenly, the Silver Budgie.

1984 *Sunday Times* (Perth) 5 Aug. 67: Ripping into the Federal Government over its uranium policy, he [Patrick White] spoke of 'Hawkie, screaming from under his cockatoo hairdo the platitudes he has got by heart' . . . It is not the first time that Mr Hawke's carefully tended hair-style has produced comparisons with birds. One of his nicknames around Parliament House is the 'silver budgie'. His detractors often alter this to 'the silver bodgie'.

1989 *Sydney Morning Herald* 14 Sep. 26: The Liberal senator [Amanda Vanstone] defended her nickname of Silver Budgie, which she has bestowed on Mr Hawke. She said he was just [a] little bloke and his height plus the silver hair on top reminded her of a budgie.

Silver City, the Broken Hill, N.S.W. [f. mining of silver]

1910 *The Silver City Cup* [title of newsreel

screened by Lyceum Pictures, Adelaide in Jul. 1910]

1933 Samuel Griffiths *A Rolling Stone on the Turf* 33: The latter experience I had at Broken Hill while on a visit to the 'Silver City' to act as stipendiary steward at the annual Cup meetings.

1981 *Canberra Times* 2 Jul. 2: The Silver City is a harsh place, a frontier of civilised life, a man's town in the crude, last century 'western' sense.

silvertail Someone affluent and socially prominent: *derogatory*

1890 A. J. Vogan *The Black Police* 116: A select circle of long-limbed members of those upper circles who belong to the genus termed in Australian parlance 'silver-tailed', in distinction to the 'copper-tailed' democratic classes.

1908 E. G. Murphy *Jarrahland Jingles* 116: And when they're playing billiards in their flannel tennis suits, / We feel like heaving something at these silver-tail galoots.

1947 Gavin Casey *The Wits are Out* 125: 'Mr Fleming doesn't build for basic-wage earners,' Bill said nastily. 'He hangs around waiting his chance to build for the silvertails.'

1970 Patrick White *The Vivisector* 127: 'Come on down, fuckun little silvertail! We'll put a frill around yer!'

1981 *Australian* 30 May 17: There is no room in this State [N.S.W.] for political silvertails who look as if they belong more in the chintzy tea houses of Toorak than on the hill at the SCG.

sing 'em muck see **muck**

singing milkshake, the Olivia Newton John

1983 *Sydney Morning Herald* 26 Oct. 24: *Grease* . . . The film in which Our Olivia earned her unenviable reputation as 'The Singing Milkshake'.

singlet, useful as a hip pocket in a see **useful**

sit down 'To establish oneself in some position or place; to settle, take up one's abode' OED 1535–1817 (see quot. 1798) Obsolete in this sense in England, but preserved in Australia because adopted into Pidgin

1798 David Collins *An Account of the English Colony in New South Wales* ed. Brian Fletcher (1975) i 406: There was indeed a woman, one Ann Smith, who ran away a few days after our sitting down in this place, and whose fate was not exactly ascertained.

1849 Alexander Harris *The Emigrant Family* ed W. S. Ramson (1967) 225: 'How many black fellow sit down along a camp?' said Beck.

1937 Ernestine Hill *The Great Australian Loneliness* 192: That paper-bark tree became the Mecca of a thousand thirsty men, who 'sat down' on the banks of the pretty river for a while, and then went on.

1956 Tom Ronan *Moleskin Midas* 221: Mon Tack, who had lost his wages in one night playing fantan with his uncle at George's Yard, was quite happy to sit down at the station.

sit down money Unemployment or pension benefits to Aborigines

1978 H. C. Coombs *Kulinma* 202: Community advisers became active in some communities in assisting Aborigines to apply for unemployment benefit ... generally Aborigines have been content to accept the 'sit-down' money without working.

1984 *Bulletin* 10 Jul. 77: On every second Wednesday when the social security cheques – 'sit-down money' – are collected, the queues [for liquor] are much longer.

six-bob-a-day tourist An Australian soldier on active service in World War I: *jocular* [f. the daily rate of pay, the highest to a private in any army at the time]

1916 Tom Skeyhill *Soldier Songs from Anzac* 28: But 'e called me a chocolate soldier, / A six-bob-a-day tourist too.

1918 Let. in Bill Gammage *The Broken Years* (1974) 265–6: Its na poo war now barring a few minor little affairs ... but I don't fancy us 6/- a day tourists will be required to do any of it.

six o'clock swill see **swill**

skerrick A fragment, esp. in negative expression ('not a skerrick', etc.) [*skerrick* a particle, morsel, scrap, atom EDD 1863]

1931 Ion L. Idriess *Lasseter's Last Ride* 205: Half a goanna's tail, the long thin end with not a skerrick of meat on it.

1947 H. Drake-Brockman *The Fatal Days* 116: Eddie had rushed off without leaving a skerrick of kindling; he often did.

1961 Patrick White *Riders in the Chariot* 226: 'There ain't no 22-gauge, Harry,' the

gentleman announced. 'Not a bloody skerrick of it.'

1988 *Sun-Herald* 27 Nov. 162: Lady Renouf was so relaxed she appeared not to be wearing a skerrick of make-up.

skin beginning to crack A sign of extreme thirst: *jocular*

1957 R. S. Porteous *Brigalow* 96: 'Come on ... You know bloody well yer skin's crackin'.' We drank quite a few beers that afternoon.

1964 H. P. Tritton *Time Means Tucker* 101: 'Right now my flaming skin is cracking I'm so dry.'

1983 John K. Ewers *Long Enough for a Joke* 94: 'You can always tell when George's holidays are due. His hide begins to crack!'

skinner A horse which wins at long odds; a betting coup so brought about (a *skinner for the books* is when the bookmakers do not have to pay out on a heavily backed favourite) [f. English thieves' slang: see quot. 1812]

1895 Cornelius Crowe *The Australian Slang Dictionary* 74: *Skinner* A term in racing, signifying that a horse not backed wins the race, thereby giving the book-makers a skinner.

1934 Thomas Wood *Cobbers* 97: Charles laid down his fork and said it was a skinner for the books.

1949 Lawson Glassop *Lucky Palmer* 88: 'Didn't you hear the bookies cheer? It was a skinner.'

1974 *Sydney Morning Herald* 8 Oct. 17: Skinner for bookmakers.

skin off a rice pudding, couldn't knock the see **couldn't**

skip, skippy A child of Anglo-Saxon background: *usually derogatory* [f. the television series 'Skippy, the Bush Kangaroo']

1987 Kathy Lette *Sunday Telegraph* (Sydney) 4 Jan. 142: 'The so-called wogs call the Anglo-Saxon kids joeys or skips.'

1987 *Times on Sunday* 22 Nov. 25: Children tend to use their own ethnic language in the playground. The Anglos, also known as 'Kangas' or 'skippies', are often infuriated by this.

skite *v.* To boast or brag [f. Scottish *bletherskate* a noisy, talkative fellow OED c. 1650; U.S. 1848]

1857 *Thatcher's Colonial Songster* 18: If

ever you get into a fight, / Of course you'll not forget to skite.
1899 Henry Lawson 'The Stranger's Friend' *Verse* i 369: The worst of it was that he'd skite all night on the edge of the stranger's bunk.
1932 Leonard Mann *Flesh in Armour* 34: In such an atmosphere, it was not hard even for Frank Jeffreys to skite a bit, though he was outdone easily by Charles.
1963 Jon Cantwell *No Stranger to the Flame* 75: 'And spoil my big moment? I feel like skiting – first time I had anything much to skite about.'

skite *n.* 1 Boastful talk; showing off
1860 Charles Thatcher *The Victoria Songster* Part 5 160: You don't often see a chap given to 'skite, / Can do very much when it comes to a fight.
1910 E. W. Hornung *The Boss of Taroomba* 180: 'Then none 'o your skite, mate,' said Bill, knocking out a clay pipe against his heel.
1933 Norman Lindsay *Saturdee* 115: 'Ponk's the bloke to take the skite outer him.'
2 (*skiter*) Someone given to skiting; a boaster
1898 *Bulletin* 17 Dec. Red Page: An incessant talker is a *skiter*.
1906 Joseph Furphy *Rigby's Romance* ed. R. G. Howarth (1946) 222: 'In spite of Rigby's very complimentary insinuation that I'm a skite and a liar, the wagon was gone.'
1933 Norman Lindsay *Saturdee* 181: Taunts began to hurtle . . . 'Who's a stinkin' skite?'
1969 *Australian* 23 Sep. 2: Australians should not see themselves as boastful, arrogant skites, the Governor-General, Sir Paul Hasluck, said yesterday.

skulls As for **heads** q.v.
1964 George Johnston *My Brother Jack* 325: 'You knowing all the brass-hats and the skulls down at the Barracks . . . I don't suppose you could pull some strings for me?'

slag 1 To spit
[**1882** F. W. P. Jago *The Ancient Language, and the Dialect of Cornwall* 266: *Slag* Misty rain, sleet.]
1965 William Dick *A Bunch of Ratbags* 238: He cleared his throat and spat on the car grille. 'Hell,' muttered Ritchie, 'he's slaggin' on me car!'

2 To disparage
1989 Helen Garner *Sydney Morning Herald* 29 Jan. 14: 'They [reviewers] say "this book is about X when it should be about Y", and so they slag it.'

slather, an open A situation in which there is no hindrance to what one wishes to do
1919 J. Vance Marshall *The World of the Living Dead* 71: 'Try the races up Dingo Creek way . . . They say she's an open slather up there. Not a demon in the burg.'
1949 John Morrison *The Creeping City* 227: 'You're asking to be allowed an open slather at an essential public service without being challenged.'
1955 D'Arcy Niland *The Shiralee* 209: 'You mean that would give her open slather?'
1981 *Sun-Herald* 10 May 87: Just about everything is to become 'self-regulating', which is a free-enterprise term meaning open slather.

sledging In cricket, the taunting of a batsman by members of the opposing team in order to undermine his confidence
1975 *Sun-Herald* 21 Dec. 49: But 'sledging' . . . or the gentle art of talking a player out . . . has no place in women's cricket.
1982 *Sydney Morning Herald* 4 Nov. 10: The court has been told by Ian Chappell that the expression 'sledging' first came into vogue among cricketers in 1963–64. It came from the expression 'subtle as a sledgehammer' at a time when a man called Percy Sledge had a song on the English hit parade. It meant using words to exploit an opponent's weaknesses and put him off his game.

sling To pay a bribe or gratuity, esp. as a percentage of wages or winnings
1875 Rolf Boldrewood *The Squatter's Dream* repr. as *Ups and Downs* (1878) 250: 'I dare say he'll sling me a tenner if it turns out all right.'
1923 Con Drew *Rogues & Ruses* 139: 'How do they sling?' 'Fair,' answered Paints; 'they slung me a fiver on a job I brought them in the other day.'
1949 Lawson Glassop *Lucky Palmer* 5: 'Clarrie, he ain't gone off in six months. Must sling to the cops. Wonder how much he pays 'em.'
1953 T. A. G. Hungerford *Riverslake* 130:

'Sling, Stefan!' When the Pole looked at him uncomprehendingly Murdoch whipped a ten-pound note out of the bundle and handed it to the ring-keeper. 'He don't know,' he explained. 'It's the first time he's played.'

sling (back) Any payment so made
1948 K. S. Prichard *Golden Miles* 74: 'There's some hungry bastards,' the men said, 'making big money on their ore, never give the poor bugger boggin' for 'em a sling back.'
1971 Frank Hardy *The Outcasts of Foolgarah* 34: The Garbo's margin for skill was only two bucks above the basic, but you had to take bottles into account and the sling from cafes who wanted extra tins emptied.

sling off (at) To deride, ridicule, abuse [variant of **throw off** q.v.]
1911 Steele Rudd *The Dashwoods* 24: 'I heard yer both slingin' off.'
1921 K. S. Prichard *Black Opal* 112: The rest of the men continued to 'sling off', as they said, at Bully and Roy O'Mara as they saw fit.
1942 Gavin Casey *It's Harder for Girls* 236: 'It was just some chaps'd been slinging off at him,' I said.
1975 Mary Rose Liverani *The Winter Sparrows* 232: She glowered at the driver suspiciously. Was he slinging off at her?

slip into To attack
[**1860** Hotten 218: *Slip*, or *let slip* 'to *slip into* a man', to give him a sound beating, 'to *let slip* at a cove', to rush violently upon him, and assault with vigour.]
1973 Jim McNeil *The Old Familiar Juice* 66: 'I'll slip inter you inner minute!'
1974 Keith Stackpole *Not Just for Openers* 83: He turned to the grandstand and expressed his feelings. The Press slipped into him over that.

slipper, put in the Variant of **put in the boot**, q.v.
1982 *Australian* 9 Mar. 12: It's time the do-gooders stopped putting the slipper into the league violence.

Slipper, the The Golden Slipper Stakes, a race for two-year olds inaugurated in 1957; the richest Australian race, with the Melbourne Cup
1979 *Courier-Mail* (Brisbane) 4 Apr. 26: How the Slipper was born [heading]

slops Beer

1947 Gavin Casey *The Wits Are Out* 55: 'He goes the slops too heavy, though' ... They agreed that it was a pity Ray drank so much.
1969 Osmar White *Under the Iron Rainbow* 33: 'What else is there to do in this godforsaken country except work and go on the slops?'

slug *n. & v.* (To make) a heavy charge or demand [? analogous to *sock*, *sting*]
1941 Baker 68: *Slug* A heavy bill. Also, 'get slugged': to be charged excessively.
1946 K. S. Prichard *The Roaring Nineties* 326: Alf knew the mine-owners were slugging the prospectors and alluvial diggers.
1970 Alexander Buzo *The Front Room Boys* in Penguin *Plays* 39: 'Ar jees, another slug at the wallet.'
1984 *Sun* (Sydney) 27 Jan. 3: New slug on petrol, beer and smokes [heading]

Slug, Silver see **Silver**

slushy Unskilled assistant to a bush cook; any unskilled kitchen help [f. *slush* refuse fat or grease obtained from meat boiled on board ship OED 1756]
[**1859** Hotten: *Slushy* A ship's cook.]
1899 Henry Lawson 'A Rough Shed' *Prose* i 465: 'We hate the boss-of-the-board as the shearers' "slushy" hates the shearers' cook.'
1936 Archer Russell *Gone Nomad* 14: I had to take my turn at butchering the ration sheep and as 'slushy' to 'Dough-boy' Terry, the cook.
1953 *Caddie A Sydney Barmaid* 25: Nellie, a wisp of a girl who was slushie at Mrs Murphy's boarding-house. Slushie was the name given to anyone who worked at a camp boarding-house.

sly grog (shop) Liquor sold without a licence; a place where it is sold
[**1812** Vaux: *Sly* Any business transacted, or intimation given, privately, or under the rose, is said to be *done upon the sly*.]
1829 H. Widowson *The Present State of Van Diemen's Land* 24: There are ... upwards of thirty licenced public houses in the town ... to these ... I may safely add a like number of 'sly grog shops', as they are called.
1901 Henry Lawson 'The Babies in the Bush' *Prose* i 415: I was beastly drunk in an out-of-the-way shanty in the Bush – a sly grog shop.

1957 Ray Lawler *Summer of the Seventeenth Doll* 44: 'Keepin' nit for the S.P. bookies, eh – drummin' up trade for the sly grogs.'
1969 William Dick *Naked Prodigal* 64: We were on our way to the sly grog joint to buy a dozen bottles.

smaller the property, the wider the brim see **brim**

smartarse An offensively clever person
1937 Heard in conversation.
1962 Alan Seymour *The One Day of the Year* 49: 'Going round with smart-arsed little sheilas from the North Shore. It's all wrong, son.'
1970 Barry Oakley *A Salute to the Great McCarthy* 28: 'That smart arse from the city.'

smell of an oil-rag, live on the see **oil-rag**

Smithy Sir Charles Kingsford Smith (1897–1935), the Australian aviator
1936 *Daily Telegraph* (Sydney) 14 Aug. 7: 'It would provide a real tribute to "Smithy" because he did not favor statues and would . . . have preferred something of a utilitarian character.'

smoke To decamp hurriedly, 'vamoose' [cf. *like smoke* very quickly, rapidly OED 1833]
1893 *Sydney Morning Herald* 26 Jun. 8: 'Smoke' . . . is the slang for the 'push' to get away as fast as possible. [Morris]
1896 Henry Lawson 'Stiffner and Jim' *Prose* i 124: 'Smoke be damned,' I snarled, losing my temper. 'You know dashed well that our swags are in the bar, and we can't smoke without them.'
1923 Con Drew *Rogues & Ruses* 178: 'Mind me havin' a look at your race book?' I says. 'I lent mine to a friend awhile ago, and he smoked with it.'
1961 Patrick White *Riders in the Chariot* 415: Dubbo had gone all right. Had taken his tin box, it seemed, and smoked off.
in smoke In hiding
1924 C. J. Dennis *Rose of Spadgers* 72: 'Jist now,' says Brannigan, 'Spike Wegg's in smoke. / Oh, jist concerns a cove 'e tried to croak.'
1967 K. S. Prichard *Subtle Flame* 252: 'Meanwhile Tony's got to be kept in smoke?'

smoke, the big The city [f. *smoke* as the mark of a metropolis: applied to London (see quot. 1864) although the Australian use – almost invariably the 'big smoke' – is recorded earlier]
[**1864** Hotten: *Smoke* London. Countrypeople when going to the metropolis frequently say, they are on their way to the Smoke, and Londoners when leaving for the country say, they are going out of the Smoke.]
1848 H. W. Haygarth *Recollections of Bush Life in Australia* 6: At first he has some power of choice in fixing on a resting-place for the night; but, as he gradually leaves behind him the 'big smoke' (as the aborigines picturesquely call the town), the accommodations become more and more scanty.
1893 J. A. Barry *Steve Brown's Bunyip* 21: 'You want to get away amongst the spielers and forties of the big smoke?'
1964 David Ireland *Image in the Clay* 81: 'Fresh from the big smoke, too. Learn anything in the city?'

smoko 1 A break from work for smoking and refreshment; the food and drink then taken
[**1855** R. Caldwell *The Gold Era of Victoria* 129: A curious practice exists in the Colony of taking a 'smoking time' in the forenoon for a quarter of an hour, and again in the afternoon for a quarter of an hour. All the men leave off work and deliberately sit down and smoke.]
1881 *Adelaide Observer* 31 Dec. 46: 'I must go to "smoke O".'
1899 Henry Lawson 'A Rough Shed' *Prose* i 464: 'We go through the day of eight hours in runs of about an hour and twenty minutes between smoke-ho's . . . I've worked from six to six with no smoke-ho's for half the wages.'
1930 Vance Palmer *The Passage* 247: At smoko, when they took a spell in the middle of loading the boat.
1947 John Morrison *Sailors Belong Ships* 50: Half-past three. Smoko. We get thirty minutes . . . Many stevedores don't leave the hold during smoko; they just curl up on the softest bit of cargo they can find and go to sleep.
1954 Tom Ronan *Vision Splendid* 179: 'If you blokes aren't coming down for your smoko I'll throw it away.'
2 An informal social gathering, concert etc. [f. *smoking-concert* OED 1886]
1918 G. A. Taylor *Those Were the Days* 30:

The State Governor was present, and it was a rare incident for that distinguished party to grace an Art Society 'Smoko'.

1939 E. H. Lane *Dawn to Dusk* 89: I well remember a smoko of the Meat Industry Union held in the old Centennial Hall, Adelaide Street. There was an attendance of several hundred members and, of course, the beer flowed freely.

1976 *Australian* 24 Apr. 18: The Leader of the Opposition, Mr Whitlam, worked in his Sydney office and attended a 'smoko' at Wentworthville RSL club last night.

smoodge (smooge) To ingratiate oneself, make a display of affection [f. *smudge* to kiss (cf. smouch); to covet, long for; to sidle up to; to beg in a sneaking way EDD 1839]

1908 E. G. Murphy *Jarrahland Jingles* 111: Amid the pop of the champagne cork, / The smoodgeful speech and cheers.

1910 C. E. W. Bean *On the Wool Track* 170: 'We reckon 'e smoogged [smoodged in later editions] for a bit after that. But it wasn't any good.'

1915 C. J. Dennis *The Songs of a Sentimental Bloke* 39: 'Lady, be yonder moon I swear!' sez 'e. / An' then 'e climbs up on the balkiney; / An' there they smoodge a treat.

1939 Kylie Tennant *Foveaux* 49: He patiently disentangled himself from her embrace and set about cutting the sandwiches. 'Don't smooge to me.'

1973 Patrick White *The Eye of the Storm* 480: She came smoodging up at her father and he answered, but gently . . . and kissed her.

snack Something easy to accomplish, 'a piece of cake'

1941 Baker 68: *Snack* A certainty.

1952 T. A. G. Hungerford *The Ridge and the River* 138: There was nothing to it . . . It was a snack.

1970 Richard Beilby *No Medals for Aphrodite* 274: 'How could I do that, Harry?' 'Easy. It'll be a snack.'

snagger 1 A rough shearer [see quot. 1969]

1887 *Tibb's Popular Songbook* 11: I found a lot of snaggers / Not a shearer in the mob.

1885–1914 'Click Go the Shears' *Australian Ballads* ed. Russel Ward (1964) 120: The ringer looks round and is beaten by

a blow, / And curses the snagger with the bare-bellied yeo.

1956 F. B. Vickers *First Place to the Stranger* 240: 'You've had the run of the good sheep up North. But I'm just a snagger. I don't get the long runs.'

1969 Bobbie Hardy *West of the Darling* 106: Since they were slow, inexpert, and rough in their performances, the poorest shearers in the shed were nick-named 'snaggers'.

2 A sausage, esp. in W.A. (elsewhere **snags**, q.v.)

1953 T. A. G. Hungerford *Riverslake* 199: 'Give him a hand to open up some more snaggers, Randy.'

1983 *West Australian* (Perth) 23 Dec. 20: Come the day after Boxing Day, the left-over Christmas fare will have lost its appeal, and the humble snagger will come into its own.

1985 *Kalgoorlie Miner* 2 Oct. 7: Watsonia Dinky-di's 8 Hearty Snaggers 375g 99c [advt.]

snags Sausages (rarely used in the singular)

1941 Baker 68: *Snags* Sausages.

1949 Ruth Park *Poor Man's Orange* 33: 'I know. Let's have sausages.' The tension in Mumma's housewifely heart disappeared. Good old snags. They were always there to be fallen back on.

1982 *Sydney City Monthly* Jun. 32: Someone of less-than-perfect mental facilities is *a few snags short of a barbie*.

see **snagger** 2, **snarler** 2

snake A sergeant, esp. in the term 'snake pit' for sergeant's mess

1943 Baker 73: *Snake pit* A sergeant's mess (War slang)

1948 Sumner Locke Elliott *Rusty Bugles* in *Khaki, Bush and Bigotry* ed. Eunice Hanger (1968) 91: 'Andy Edwards has been promoted and moved up to the snake pit with you and the other snakes.'

1951 Eric Lambert *The Twenty Thousand Thieves* 314: 'Baxter reckoned the officers and snakes are pinching our beer.'

snake charmer A fettler

1937 A. W. Upfield *Mr. Jelly's Business* 16: 'And what are the Snake Charmers?' 'They are the permanent-way men.'

1969 Patsy Adam-Smith *Folklore of the Australian Railwaymen* 279: Fettlers are invariably referred to as 'snake charmers'.

Snake Gully   The locale of the radio serial 'Dad and Dave' q.v.

1945 Baker 198: *Woop Woop* and *Snake Gully*, as fictitious names for a remote outback settlement, the home of the most rustic of rustics.

1965 Leslie Haylen *Big Red* 88: People rushing through the countryside by car would grin as they raced through Cooee. Here was the authentic bush town. Here was Snake Gully.

snake juice   Any improvised alcoholic drink; strong liquor generally

1903 Joseph Furphy *Such is Life* (1944) 108: Illicit snake-juice for them, and golden top for the other fellow.

1916 C. J. Dennis *The Moods of Ginger Mick* 26: 'I've arf a mind to give cold tea a go. / It's no game pourin' snake-juice in yer face.'

1973 Roland Robinson *The Drift of Things* 290: Broke into Eric's hut, threw the 'pickled' specimens out of the jars, and drank the methylated spirits. That must have been the real 'Snake-Juice'. This is a name for the various kinds of beverages some of the alcoholics in the various camps used to concoct.

snake, mad as a cut   see **mad**

snake's belly, lower than a   Despicable

1932 Leonard Mann *Flesh in Armour* 290: 'It was a dirty trick. He knew about me and her.' 'Dirty! Lower than a snake's belly.'

1957 D'Arcy Niland *Call Me When the Cross Turns Over* 181: My opinion of you is lower than a snake's belly.

1979 *Australian* 2 Mar. 1: Mrs Fraser reacted to the allegation last night by saying that anyone criticising her father, Mr Sandford Beggs, over rural loans was 'lower than a snake's duodenum'.

snakey   Bad-tempered, irritable

1919 W. H. Downing *Digger Dialects* 46: *Snaky* (adj.) (1) Angry (e.g. to turn snaky); (2) Irritable.

1941 Kylie Tennant *The Battlers* 86: 'Don't go snaky on the kid.'

1974 David Williamson *Three Plays* 34: 'What are you snaky about this time?'

snarler   1   'Services no longer required': applied to a serviceman sent back as a failure from a theatre of war

1943 Baker 73: *Snarler* A soldier or flier

sent back home from overseas service because of some misdemeanour.

1952 T. A. G. Hungerford *The Ridge and the River* 49: If he just couldn't make the grade, then Lovatt would bundle him back south for a Snarler.

1983 *Sun-Herald* 17 Jul. 57: In the Navy's Weekly Postings he receives an official 'snarler' which is nautical slang for 'services no longer required' notification.

2   A sausage

1982 *Sydney Morning Herald* 18 Sep. 28: At the end of the dispensing line little chaps from the Boys' Brigade ejaculated a blob of rich red Fountain Tomato Sauce on top of each snarler.

snatch it, snatch one's time   To demand the wages due and leave the job

[**1934** J. M. Harcourt *Upsurge* 258: 'Load that barrow or go and take your time. Any man here who doesn't care to load his barrow can take his time.']

1944 Alan Marshall *These Are My People* 158: 'I suppose you struck some bad bosses in your time?' 'If they're bad, I snatch it.'

1962 Tom Ronan *Deep of the Sky* 55: 'What's more, when we pass Silverton I'm snatching my time.'

1973 Frank Huelin *Keep Moving* 83: 'What are yous goin' to do? Snatch it or stay?'

snip   To 'bite', exact a loan

1959 *Bulletin* 21 Jan. 32: 'Can you snip Sorrowful?' 'No, he's got a death-adder in his kick.'

1984 *Sunday Telegraph* (Sydney) 1 Apr. 58: The battlers used to line up to 'snip' him [Roy Higgins] after the last. He would simply smile and hand over, and have his hand in his pocket for the next 'snip'.

snipe   An election poster [? f. the bird's long bill]

[**1860** Hotten 220: *snipe* A long bill; also a term for attorneys – a race remarkable for their propensity to long bills.]

1966 Baker 355: *snipe* A political election poster, the size of which is limited to 10 in. by 6 in.

1977 Fred Daly *From Curtin to Kerr* 75: He posted snipes on nearly every post and on the day had his booths well manned.

sniper   A non-unionist on the wharves, 'sniping' the jobs of unionists

1945 Baker 248: A waterfront term of

fairly recent origin is *sniper*, a non-union labourer.

1955 John Morrison *Black Cargo* 14: Plenty of Federation men also know him by sight, and it will need only one shout of 'Sniper!' and Lamond will be lucky to get out without being knocked down.

1957 Tom Nelson *The Hungry Mile* 72: The W.W.F. had preference of work, wharf by wharf. The outsiders (snipers) would stand back at the gate until the W.W.F. men were all used.

sniper, went for a crap and the ~ got him Jocular reply to request for anyone's whereabouts

1965 Eric Lambert *The Long White Night* 94: I looked around me at the dark figures in the dusk and called Clancy's name. From behind the top of a lighted cigarette an anonymous voice told me: 'He went for a shit and the sniper got him.'

1971 David Ireland *The Unknown Industrial Prisoner* 90: 'Where's he gone?' 'Went for a crap and a sniper got him.'

see **he went mad and they shot him, shot through on the padre's bike**

snob The 'cobbler', the sheep left to the last as the most difficult to shear [see quot. 1945]

1945 C. E. W. Bean *On the Wool Track* The sheep most difficult to shear, which naturally is left last in the pen, is also called the 'snob'. As early as in Elizabethan times 'snob' was slang for cobbler ('Shakespeare had 'snip and snob' for tailor and cobbler). The terms have persisted in old-fashioned English, and 'snob' has added to its several meanings this peculiarly Australian one.

1975 Les Ryan *The Shearers* 49: 'Get on to this wrinkled bludger!' he said. It was the last sheep in the pen . . . 'Real snob ain't it?'

snout, have a ~ on As for **have a nose on** q.v.

1916 C. J. Dennis *The Moods of Ginger Mick* 155: Snout To bear a grudge.

1949 Lawson Glassop *Lucky Palmer* 212: 'He's got a snout on the Kid for something.'

1982 *Bulletin* 20 Jul. 17: I enjoy Semmler's occasional contributions to *The Bulletin* but I have a feeling that he has a 'snout' on Aunty and takes every opportunity to criticise her.

snouted Rebuffed, in disfavour; annoyed with

1919 W. H. Downing *Digger Dialects* 46: *Snouted* Under disfavor.

1924 C. J. Dennis *Rose of Spadgers* 117: Don't mind my sulks . . . But gittin' snouted ain't wot I expeck.

1944 Alan Marshall *These Are My People* 155: 'I was sore as a snouted sheila for weeks.'

1960 John Iggulden *The Storms of Summer* 122: 'They're getting a bit snouted on fellers from the Inlet around here.'

Snowy, the 1 The Snowy River
1944 Archer Russell *Bush Ways* 67: We make our camp by the swift-rushing waters of the Snowy.

2 The region of the Snowy Mountains and Snowy River in S.E. N.S.W. used as a ski and fishing resort, officially the Kosciusko National Park

1967 Barbara Mullins *Kosciusko National Park* 17: Though camping is not encouraged in the higher altitudes . . . facilities are provided in many areas of the lower Snowy.

1975 Alex Buzo *Tom* 2: 'Where did you go fishing? The Snowy?'

3 The Snowy River hydro-electric scheme
1953 T. A. G. Hungerford *Riverslake* 2: He had been working up on the Snowy River scheme, and . . . he remembered what the chef at the Snowy had said.

soap, not to know someone from a bar of To be completely unacquainted with someone

1938 *Smith's Weekly* 26 Nov. 23: [cartoon caption] 'I don't know you from a bar of soap.'

1945 Kylie Tennant *Ride on Stranger* 309: 'Why doesn't she marry the child's father?' . . . 'It's my belief she doesn't know him from a bar of soap.'

1970 Jon Cleary *Helga's Web* 130: 'I've never met any of his – interests. Certainly not this girl. I dunno her from a bar of soap.'

Socceroos Members of a team representing Australia internationally at soccer (by analogy with the Kangaroos, the representatives in Rugby League)

1973 *Sydney Morning Herald* 15 Nov. 1: Now that the Australian Soccer team is basking in honour and glory after its World Cup victory over South Korea it can surely do without the name 'Socceroos' which is being increasingly applied to it.

sod A damper that has not risen [f. *sod* ill-raised bread OED 1836]
1900–10 O'Brien and Stephens: *Sod* Badly cooked damper.
1957 R. S. Porteous *Brigalow* 206: His dampers were leaden sods.
1975 Xavier Herbert *Poor Fellow My Country* 838: 'I want to cook our own damper, too ... I don't want one of their sods.'

soda Something easily done, a 'pushover' [? f. card game U.S. 1843 Mathews]
[**1895** Cornelius Crowe *The Australian Slang Dictionary* 98: *Zodiac*, or *Soda* The top card in the box in faro.]
1930 Vance Palmer *The Passage* 83: 'They're getting ready for the long dive now, and it ought to be a soda for you.'
1943 G. H. Johnston *New Guinea Diary* 151: 'The Middle East was a soda beside this,' one of them told me.
1966 Hal Porter *The Paper Chase* 74: The job, for which I have no really specialized training, is nevertheless a soda.
1981 *Sun-Herald* 12 Apr. 65: Once politicians trembled at the thought of facing Mike Willesee on television. These days they must think it's a soda.

S.O.L. Abbreviation for **shit on the liver** q.v.
1951 Dal Stivens *Jimmy Brockett* 137: 'I had a bit of S.O.L. the other day.'
1954 Jon Cleary *The Climate of Courage* 222: 'Sorry, chum. I've got a touch of S.O.L., I think.'
1978 Ronald McKie *Bitter Bread* 119: This was the first human sign for hours. Blue must be improving, getting rid of his s.o.l.

solid Severe, excessive, unreasonable
1916 C. J. Dennis *The Moods of Ginger Mick* 155: *Solid* Severe; severely.
1917 Let. of 6 Dec. cit. Bill Gammage *The Broken Years* (1974) 215: Just before the poor fellow got killed he said to me that it was a bit solid and the sooner it finished the better.
1948 Ruth Park *The Harp in the South* 62: 'After all, Auntie Josie's got all them kids to look after. It must be pretty solid for her with Grandma as well.'
1951 Frank Hardy *Power Without Glory*

41: 'I got fined fifty quid, Joe twenty-five.' 'Bit solid, wasn't it?'

sollicker Something very big, a 'whopper' [cf. *sollock* impetus, force (He fell down with such a sollock) EDD]
1898 Roland Graeme *From England to the Backblocks* 82: 'Who was it I heard that in cutting-out some cattle on one of the Methvin plains, did come down a soliker and broke his horse's knees?'
1908 *Australian Magazine* 1 Nov. 1251: *sollicker* Very big.
1939 Miles Franklin and Dymphna Cusack *Pioneers on Parade* 168: 'She gave me a sollicker of a dose out of a blue bottle.'
1956 Patrick White *The Tree of Man* 91: 'You can jump down, can't you? You're quite big, you know.' 'Of course he can ... he's a sollicker.'

sook 1 A timorous person, a 'softie', a crybaby (juvenile) [? f. *suck* a 'muff'; a 'duffer'; a stupid fellow EDD]
1941 Baker 69: *Sook* A coward, a timid person.
1950 Brian James *The Advancement of Spencer Button* 9: If he nervously declares he can't fight, and shows that he doesn't want to fight, then he is a 'sook' or a 'sissy.'
1970 Patrick White *The Vivisector* 11: He wasn't a sook. He could run, shout, play, fight, had scabs on his knees, and twice split Billy Abraham's lip, who was two years older.
1984 Allan Caton *Age* (Melbourne 22 Sep. 12: Who wants a sook for PM? I do not. If the heat gets too much for blubbing Bob, he should get out of the kitchen.
2 A timid horse
1980 *Sydney Morning Herald* 2 Aug. 59: White, answering charges that Panamint is unsound, described the horse as a 'big sook' ... 'Invariably when he is taken in and out of the box he is timid.'
1983 *West Australian* (Perth) 17 Dec. 184: 'He is a real sook unless there is another horse with him ... If there is not another horse alongside him, he starts to weave and get a bit uptight.'
sooky
1953 Dymphna Cusack *Southern Steel* 328: 'Get along with you: you're getting real sookey.'

sool To incite someone to a course of action, from the command 'Sool him' to a dog to attack or harass some quarry [f. *sowl* to pull roughly . . . In later use esp. of dogs OED 1607]

1849 Alexander Harris *The Emigrant Family* (1967) 135: 'Hey! hey! sowl her boys!' roared Morgan: and on went the whole pack, seizing the poor beast by the ears, nose, and even eyelids.

1903 Joseph Furphy *Such is Life* (1944) 130: 'Soolim, Pup!' I hissed.

1911 Louis Stone *Jonah* 31: The Push gathered round, grinning from ear to ear, sooling the women on as if they were dogs.

1920 Frank A. Russell *The Ashes of Achievement* 116: 'The author'll sool a lawyer on you first thing you know.'

1961 Mena Calthorpe *The Dyehouse* 83: Oliver Henery had sooled the Unions on to Renshaw over the loads that the girls were humping about.

sooler

1963 Xavier Herbert *Disturbing Element* 141: She had been sending white feathers round . . . She had become what her former comrades of the I.W.W. called a Sooler.

1982 Anthony Splivalo *The Home Fires* 49: A few residents on the goldfields . . . resented the coercion of young men into military ranks. They referred to the coercers as 'soolers', which is the Australian slang for persons who incite others to actions against their will.

sorry, you'll be Jocular greeting to new army recruits in World War II

1944 Lawson Glassop *We Were the Rats* 66: Every soldier we passed on the road yelled, 'You'll be sorry'. Every soldier we encountered in camp until we got our issue clothes said, 'You'll be sorry'.

1951 Dymphna Cusack and Florence James *Come In Spinner* 185: A voice called derisively 'You'll be sorry!' Crooked smiles split the soldiers' faces.

sort A girl or woman (at the same level of usage as **sheila**); applied rarely to men also.

1933 Frank Clune *Try Anything Once* 93: 'Look here, George,' I said. 'Lend me a suit of civvies. I've got to meet a great little sort, and her father has a dead nark on soldiers.'

1941 Kylie Tennant *The Battlers* 276: 'Hey, Bob!' Dick Tyrell gave a low whistle. 'Take a look at that good sort.'

1968 Kit Denton *A Walk Around My Cluttered Mind* 137: They'd told me, 'Don't

worry about bringing anything except a bottle. The sorts are laid on.' Even after only ten months I understood this to mean that there would be feminine company.

1983 Janise Beaumont *Sun-Herald* 23 Oct. 128: Others included that divine Nick Shehadie (I've always thought he was the best sort in town).

soul-case, belt (worry, work) the ~ out of To subject to extreme hardship or punishment

1901 F. J. Gillen *Diary* (1968) 34: Fliers were celebrating some festival all night and worried the very soul cases out of us.

1937 K. S. Prichard *Intimate Strangers* 288: 'Eviction was what I got after clearing two thousand acres of virgin land: sweating my soul case out to grow wheat.'

1951 Dymphna Cusack and Florence James *Come In Spinner* 152: 'If you've been going in for any of them beach girl competitions, Peggy my girl, I'll belt the soul case out of you.'

1962 Ron Tullipan *March into Morning* 13: 'Then he got the bright idea of bringin' in orphan kids and working the soulcase off them until they turn eighteen and have to be paid more money.'

southerly (buster) The cool, gusty wind that springs up at the end of a hot day, sometimes bringing a shower of rain (originally in Sydney)

1850 B. C. Peck *Recollections of Sydney* 132: It is almost a corollary, that the evening of a hot-wind day brings up a 'southerly buster', as we have heard the vulgar call it, very chill indeed . . . as the wind comes from the southerly region of the Australian Alps.

1896 Nat Gould *Town and Bush* 96: The southerly buster is well named. The wind comes in bursts and whirls the dust about . . . The buster, however, makes up for the inconvenience it causes by clearing the heated atmosphere, and is generally followed by a refreshing shower of rain.

1949 Ruth Park *Poor Man's Orange* 146: After the unbearably hot day, the old men on the balconies were sniffing the air and saying, 'Here she comes!' The southerly buster, the genie of Sydney, flapped its coarse blusterous wing over the city . . . The women undid the fronts of their frocks, and the little children lifted up their skirts and let it blow on their sweaty bottoms.

souvenir To purloin [listed by Partridge as military slang (1915)]

1918 *Aussie* 18: Jan. 11: *Souvenir* – Is generally used in the same sense as salvage, but of small, easily portable articles. *Salvage* – To rescue unused property and make use of it.

1932 Leonard Mann *Flesh in Armour* 85: Artie Fethers bent down and souvenired the officer's pistol.

1951 Dymphna Cusack and Florence James *Come In Spinner* 395: Val stared at the cases. 'How on earth did you get those?' 'Souvenired 'em,' said Lofty with a broad wink.

1970 Cynthia Nolan *A Bride for St Thomas* 95: I was just in time to prevent Sister Seymour's brass inkstand being souvenired.

spag An Italian: *derogatory* [abbr. of *spaghetti*]

1966 Baker 344: *Spaggie* An Italian. [as Victorian slang]

1974 *Bulletin* 1 Jun. 399–40: 'And [Al Grassby] brought in all those migrants . . . y'know, those coons and spags.'

1982 *Sydney Morning Herald* 6 Aug. 10: 'Basically, we've got the wog problem under control . . . we are aware of what these wogs, spags and dagoes want.'

sparrows (geese, peacocks, swallows) flying out of one's backside An expression for the male orgasm

1959 Gerard Hamilton *Summer Glare* 94: 'What's it like? . . . You just wait, son. You'll think a flock of geese are flyin' out yer backside.'

1972 Geoff Morley *Jockey Rides Honest Race* 204: I exploded with feeling and a million sparrows flew out of my backside.

1977 Robert Close *Of Salt and Earth* 38: I clutched the girl passionately and jammed her against the truck. Then it seemed my navel sprang unscrewed, and a thousand peacocks flew backwards out of my arsehole.

1979 David Ireland *A Woman of the Future* 258: 'They said that when it happened I'd feel as if swallows were flying out of my arsehole.'

spaso See quot. 1979

1979 David Ireland *A Woman of the Future* 55: The other word like para [q.v.] was spaso, short for spastic.

1984 Helen Garner *The Children's Bach* 74: 'He's got something wrong with him. Spazzo.'

spear, get the To be sacked from a job [variant of the English 'get the bullet']

1912 'Goorianawa' *The Lone Hand* 1 Oct. 27 repr. in *Old Bush Songs* ed. Stewart and Keesing (1957) 273: I've been many years a shearer and I fancied I could shear, / I've shore for Rouse of Guntawang and always missed the spear.

spear To dismiss

1911 Steele Rudd *The Dashwoods* 13: 'If I was the boss here I would. I'd spear him without warnin'.'

spear tackle See quot. 1978

1978 *Sydney Morning Herald* 16 Mar. 7: There is nothing edifying about the spear tackle in Rugby League football – the player with the ball is inverted and goes down head first.

special A convict who is educated or well connected, and who is therefore given special treatment

1843 James Backhouse *A Narrative of a Visit to the Australian Colonies* 406: Port Macquarie . . . still is a depot for that description of educated prisoners, denominated 'specials'.

1867 John Morrison *Australia As It Is* 213–14: A laudable consideration was shown by the Government to a class of convicts belonging to what are usually styled 'the upper classes of society', and who were known by the name 'specials'. A settlement was set apart for them, and they were exempted from severe manual labour. One of them made himself very useful . . . by teaching in families.

speck To search for gold in small quantities near the surface

1888 Henry Lawson 'His Father's Mate' *Prose* i 4: A pick and shovel, and a gold dish . . . with which he used to go 'a-speckin'' and 'fossickin'' amongst the old mullock heaps.

1901 May Vivienne *Travels in Western Australia* 171: Almost everyone in the camp went out for an afternoon's specking (looking on the ground for nuggets).

1932 K. S. Prichard *Kiss on the Lips* 219: Charley Beck and his old woman had specked a thirty-ounce slug.

1978 *Australian* 4 Oct. 7: Now and then he reaches down for a piece of shale, spits on it, rubs it then casts it aside. He's specking [for opal].

Speck, the Tasmania [f. size in relation to mainland Australia]
1930 *Bulletin* 11 Jun. 21: N.S.W., V., Q., S.A., W.A. and the Speck.

speedball In shearing parlance, a meat rissole with laxative qualities
1966 Baker 84: *speedball* A rolled ball of mincemeat.
1975 Les Ryan *The Shearers* 155: Speed ball: Rissole moistened with bore water (containing a high mineral content).
1981 Keith Garvey *Slowly Sweats the Gun* 18: Ned Lynch forked an extra speed-ball onto his plate.

speedo The odometer (mileage indicator) in a car
1969 Mena Calthorpe *The Defectors* 140: He glanced at the speedo ... He'd driven almost five miles.
1978 *Bulletin* 3 Oct. 108: Winding back the speedo remains an Australian car sharp's practice, according to the latest Trade Practices Commission Report.

Speewaa A legendary station used as the locale for tall tales of the outback
1944 Alan Marshall *These Are My People* 144: He suddenly grinned. 'I cooked on Speewa.' I had heard of Speewa, that mythical station used as a setting for all the lies put over on new-chums. I knew many of the tales, so I answered him: 'It's a big place. When I was there they had to get two Chinese to mix the mustard with long-handled shovels. The shearing shed was so long the boss rode up and down the board on horseback.'
1951 Ernestine Hill *The Territory* 445: *On the Speewaa* A legendary station of doughty deeds – 'I bet that happened on the Speewaa'. The original Speewaa Station is near Swan Hill on the Murray River, home of great men and tall tales in the very earlies.
1979 *Courier-Mail* (Brisbane) 12 May 1: Each [contestant] must tell a speerwah, or bush yarn, for more than four minutes.

spell *n.* A period of rest, interrupting work [f. *spell* a turn of work taken by a person ... in relief of another OED 1625]
c. **1845** James Tucker *Ralph Rashleigh* (1952) 140: Ralph taking one of their tools, Bob took another and worked awhile, to give the children a *spell*.
1861 Horace Earle *Ups and Downs* 214: After the dray had departed Tom declared his intention 'to take a bit of a spell, and have a pipe'.
1918 Harley Matthews *Saints and Soldiers* 84: They sat on a hill during a spell in their practice manoeuvres.
1942 Gavin Casey *It's Harder for Girls* 171: You've worked hard for a long time and ought to be able to afford a spell.
1980 *Sun-Herald* 1 Jun. 63: Happy Landing would have one more run and then go for a spell.

spell *v.* To rest from work
1846 J. L. Stokes *Discoveries in Australia* ii 42: In order to spell the oars, we landed at a point on the east side. [Morris]
1865 Rachel Henning *Letters* ed. David Adams (1963) 199: He went down to Mr Paterson's ... to 'spell' his horses before starting on a long journey southward.
1926 K. S. Prichard *Working Bullocks* 101: When the team had spelled a day Red brought the big whim into action.
1975 Xavier Herbert *Poor Fellow My Country* 1314: By rights the horses should have been spelled for a couple of days before being pushed further.

spider Brandy with lemonade or ginger beer; a fizzy soft drink with icecream added
1854 C. H. Spence *Clara Morison* ii 67: 'I must have a nobbler or a spider to put me to rights.'
1859 Frank Fowler *Southern Lights and Shadows* 52: *A Spider* Lemonade and brandy.
1942 Gavin Casey *It's Harder for Girls* 233, 4: 'You've had your drink, so now you've got to buy us all a spider at Smith's.' ... I didn't want to go back and sit in Smith's and drink silly coloured muck with ice-cream floating in it.
1962 Criena Rohan *The Delinquents* 122: Mavis had Sharon Faylene, clad only in a damp napkin, on her hip, and both were enjoying a raspberry spider.

spiel *n.* 1 The dishonest scheme of a **spieler** 1
1932 William Hatfield *Ginger Murdoch* 175: 'I reckon you were thinking you had shaken me off, and could go about your spiel, whatever it is.'
1954 T. A. G. Hungerford *Sowers of the Wind* 174: 'This isn't a spiel, Colonel,' McNaughton said desperately ... 'I know this bloke, and he's on the level.'

1987 Bill O'Reilly *Sydney Morning Herald* 5 Dec. 66: Why people should pay to come through the gates for such so-called entertainment must surely be one of the greatest spiels of modern times.

2 The utterance of a **spieler** 2, a prepared line of talk

1957 Judah Waten *Shares in Murder* 62: 'I get you Brummel. Go on with your spiel.'

1962 Alan Marshall *This is the Grass* 125: Spruikers in braided uniforms strutted up and down before foyers extolling the virtues of the pictures within ... I often stood watching them, listening to every word of their spiel.

1981 *Australian* 22 Jul. 22: In his official welcome to delegates, Alderman Sutherland gave a spirited spiel about the beauties of Sydney.

spieler 1 Someone who lives by his wits; a gambler, 'con-man' [f. G. *spielen* to play U.S. 1891 Mathews]

1885 *The Australasian Printers' Keepsake* 72: Who eyed Bob very suspiciously, muttering 'spieler' and 'Murrumbidgee whaler'.

1896 Henry Lawson 'Stiffner and Jim' *Prose* i 124: He was cracked on the subject of spielers. He held that the population of the world was divided into two classes – one was the spielers and the other was the mugs.

1935 H. R. Williams *Comrades of the Great Adventure* 234: The spielers worked the three-card trick on the 'mugs'.

1957 Judah Waten *Shares in Murder* 156: You could match your wits against smart con-men and spielers.

2 A 'barker' for a sideshow; anyone with a plausible tongue [U.S. 1891 Mathews]

1975 Max Williams *The Poor Man's Bean* 33: A spieler calls, 'Come in; come on; come over'.

spill In politics, the declaring of a number of offices in the party vacant as a result of one vacancy occurring.

1956 J. T. Lang *I Remember* 311: There had to be an annual election of leader. That made it inevitable that some members would intrigue against the leader hoping for a Cabinet spill.

1975 *Australian* 18 Mar. 1: It will be left to Mr Fraser's supporters to force the issue and move against Mr Snedden through either a spill of leadership positions or a motion of no confidence.

spin 1 A piece of experience (always with an adjective: 'rough spin', 'fair spin', etc.) [? f. *spin* for the toss of a coin OED 1882, or *spin* in various uses implying duration OED 1856, 1875]

1917 Diary entry 10 Jan. cit. in Bill Gammage *The Broken Years* (1974) 259: Out of the line at last ... by jove she's been a crook spin this trip.

1942 Leonard Mann *The Go-Getter* 243: 'I had a rough spin during the depression and bad luck since.'

1974 Desmond O'Grady *Deschooling Kevin Carew* 107: He knew Kevin had had a rough spin since the withdrawal of the Education Department scholarship.

2 £5, esp. in gambling

1949 Lawson Glassop *Lucky Palmer* 15: 'Not a five bob. A spin,' said the carpenter, fishing a five pound note out.

1962 Stuart Gore *Down the Golden Mile* 261: 'Backed Sweet Friday for a spin,' replied Tug. 'But it never run a drum.'

spin out, to In two-up, to throw tails [f. the rule that the spinner backs heads]

1959 *Bulletin* 7 Oct. 8: On spinning-out after a long run of ins, Smithy counted among his winnings two football grandstand-tickets.

1983 *Sun-Herald* 23 Jan. 35: Bluey ... once spun 13 heads before spinning out (threw tails).

spine basher, spine bashing A loafer (World War II slang): *obsolescent*

1944 Lawson Glassop *We Were the Rats* 208: 'She's sweet,' I said. 'Go and do some spine bashing.'

1946 Rohan Rivett *Behind Bamboo* 399: *Spinebasher*, one always on his back, always resting.

1976 *Sydney Morning Herald* 20 Mar. 14: The elbow-benders, spine-bashers, eternal babblers keep one ear to the loudspeakers, an ear to the ground.

spinner, come in The cry in two-up that clears the way for the tossing of the coins, all bets having been placed

1945 Tom Ronan *Strangers on the Ophir* 119: Cries of 'Another quid to see him go. Get set on the side. All set, come in Spinner.'

1965 Leslie Haylen *Big Red* 101: Outside he could hear the gamblers: 'Come on, I want a dollar in the guts.' 'Who'll put a dollar in the guts.' Laughter, shouts, and then silence. 'Come in spinner.'

1975 Les Ryan *The Shearers* 97: 'All set?' Lofty asked. 'Set!' Sandy said. 'Come in, spinner!'

spit, go for the big To vomit (given currency by the Barry McKenzie comic strip)
1967 Frank Hardy *Billy Borker Yarns Again* 40: Don't tell me the Gargler went for the big spit.
1973 Alexander Buzo *Rooted* 43: 'Remember the time he got sick at Davo's twenty-first and went for the big spit? He said me "Jees I feel crook", and then he raced across the room, shoved his head out of the window and burped a rainbow.'

spit chips, to 1 To be extremely thirsty
1901 *The Bulletin Reciter* 108: While you're spitting chips like thunder . . . / And the streams of sweat near blind you.
1946 Alan Marshall *Tell us about the Turkey, Jo* 142: I was spitting chips. God, I was dry!
2 To be in a state of anger and frustration
1947 John Morrison *Sailors Belong Ships* 189: 'Old Mick Doyle's with them. He's spitting chips because they're not using sea water.'
1986 *Sun-Herald* 16 Nov. 82: Greg Norman was spitting chips over a reference to him in *The Age* by Peter Thomson as the 'Great White Fish Finger', as Jack Newton once dubbed him.

split, the (great) The split in the Labor Party in 1955 which was marked by the formation of the DLP
1955 *Bulletin* 8 Jun. 6: He [Henry Bolte] is not carried away by the conviction that 'Labor' has been wrecked. Indeed, he holds that the effects of the 'split' have been exaggerated.
1970 Kylie Tennant *Evatt* 338: After the election Evatt was again elected leader of the Parliamentary Labour Party by 58 votes to 20 . . . The Party was settling into shape after the split.

sport A form of colloquial address
1923 George S. Beeby *Concerning Ordinary People* 305: 'All right, sport. No offence meant.'
1941 Kylie Tennant *The Battlers* 105: 'Now lay off, sport.'
1975 Richard Beilby *The Brown Land Crying* 80: 'Come on, sport,' the doorman was

saying patiently. 'You can't stop here. You've had a skinful.'

sport back on the front page, to get Paraphrase of a remark by Malcolm Fraser during the 1975 election campaign, to indicate a desirable state of political stability
1975 *National Times* 1 Dec. 12: On the Sydney radio station, 2SM, Mr Fraser responded to one question about the turbulence of the last three years by remarking on the placidity of the long Liberal regime. 'It may have been dull,' he said, 'but I'm not sure they didn't prefer to have a dull government so they could go straight to the sports pages and not have to worry about what the politicians were doing.'
1980 *Australian* 26 Jan. 5: If Mr Fraser's determination to 'put sport on the front page' was regarded as something of a cynical exercise at the time it is certainly no less cynical than the demand by sporting leaders to keep 'politics out of sport'.

spruik To hold forth like a showman [unexplained]
1915 C. J. Dennis *The Songs of a Sentimental Bloke* 42: 'E'll sigh and spruik, an' 'owl a love-sick vow – / (The silly cow!)
1934 Vance Palmer *The Swayne Family* 250: 'Wonder you didn't get a job spruiking for the pictures down there in town.'
1975 Hal Porter *The Extra* 244: Hollow-chested men . . . who sell agitated toys on street corners or spruik outside strip-tease joints.

spruiker A speaker attracting custom outside a theatre or sideshow; any loquacious person
1924 *Truth* 27 Apr. 6: *Spruiker* A speaker.
1951 Dal Stivens *Jimmy Brockett* 82: A spruiker outside was dressed up like a train conductor and he told you about the tour.
1971 Craig McGregor *Don't Talk to Me About Love* 159: He declaimed in the voice of a Royal Easter Show spruiker.

spunk, spunky *n.* Someone attractive to the opposite sex [f. *spunk* semen]
1967 *King's Cross Whisper* (Sydney) xxxix 4: *Spunky* Young female.
1979 Kathy Lette and Gabrielle Carey *Puberty Blues* 5: It was Darren Peters – the top surfing spunk of sixth form.
1981 *Age* (Melbourne) 21 Aug. Weekender 11: The show attracts a lot of 'spunk

mail' from younger viewers (i.e. Dear John, you are a real spunk, please send me a photo).

1984 *Sydney Morning Herald* 6 Oct. Mag. 28: Gynaecologists in Sydney have been known to leave their wives for younger, spunkier patients.

squatter 1 Someone taking up his abode in the bush and living by preying on the flocks of others, dealing in sly grog, etc. [f. *squatter* One who settles upon land, esp. public land, to which he has no legal title U.S. 1788 Mathews]

1830 J. Betts *An Account of the Colony of Van Diemen's Land* 39: The means of rooting out a class of people called 'Squatters'. These were generally emancipated convicts, or ticket-of-leave men, who, having obtained a small grant, under the old system, or without any grant at all, sat themselves down in remote situations, and maintained large flocks, obtained, generally, in very nefarious ways, by having the run of all the surrounding country.

2 A respectable pastoralist; a pastoralist occupying a tract of land with a licence from the Crown (from 1836)

1840 Gov. Gipps to Lord Russell *HRA* xxi 130: A very large proportion of the land, which is to form the new district of Port Phillip, is already in the licensed occupation of the Squatters of New South Wales, a class of persons whom it would be wrong to confound with those who bear the same name in America, and who are generally persons of mean repute and small means, who have taken unauthorized possession of patches of land. Among the Squatters of New South Wales are the wealthiest of the Land, occupying with the permission of Government thousands and tens of thousands of acres; Young men of good Family and connexions in England, Officers of the Army and Navy, Graduates of Oxford and Cambridge are also in no small number amongst them.

1848 J. C. Byrne *Twelve Years' Wanderings in the British Colonies* i 186: A squatter obtains his temporary right to what land he requires by producing a licence from the Crown land Commissioners in the colony, for which he pays annually, the sum of £10; besides being subject to a small annual assessment on his sheep, cattle and horses, for the support of a border police. The squatters are the great producing class of the colony: their vast herds and flocks out-number by many degrees the scanty numbers depastured on the purchased, or granted, land of the country.

3 A pastoral magnate, whether occupying land as tenant of the Crown or as owner, regarded as one of the privileged or affluent

1900 Let. of 21 Sep. in *Audrey Tennyson's Vice-Regal Days* ed. Alexandra Hasluck (1978) 118: Squatters in the colonies are our aristocracy – as being the people who came out from home in early days. 'Oh he is an old squatter, or, she is a daughter of a squatter' means that nothing more need be asked.

1902 Henry Lawson 'Lord Douglas' *Prose* i 494: 'You're allers findin' excuses for black-legs an' scabs, Mitchell,' said Barcoo-Rot . . . 'Why, you'd find a white spot on a squatter.'

1934 Tom Clarke *Marriage at 6 a.m.* 46: *Squatter* a station owner (corresponds almost to 'squire' in English).

1958 H. D. Williamson *The Sunlit Plain* 42: She might have been a squatter's wife, the way she was dressed, Leo reflected.

squatter's chair A canvas-backed chair with the arm-rests extended to support the full length of the legs

1901 Miles Franklin *My Brilliant Career* 130: Harold was stretched in a squatter's chair some distance away.

1961 Noni Braham *The Interloper* 5: She flung herself into one of the squatter's chairs, stretched out her legs on its extended arms.

1982 *Sydney Morning Herald* 3 Jul. 29: Membership of the Queensland Club puts you at the top of Queensland's highly structured social heap. From the squatters' chairs on its balconies, one can look across Alice Street onto the Botanical Gardens, a riot of tropicality snuggling into a bend in the lolling Brisbane River.

squattocracy The squatters (senses 2 and 3) collectively regarded as a colonial aristocracy, often with a derogatory implication

1846 C. P. Hodgson *Reminiscences of Australia* 118: Throughout the Colony generally English are the most numerous, then the Scotch, then the Irish, amongst the squattocracy.

1865 Henry Kingsley *The Hillyars and the Burtons* iii 265: A miserable and effete Squattocracy (with their wretched aping of the still more miserable and effete aristocracy of the old world).

1891 Francis Adams *Fortnightly Review* Sep. 398: One has not endured all these years the rule of the squattocracy, as voiced in a hopelessly subservient and corrupt legislature, for nothing.

1939 Miles Franklin and Dymphna Cusack *Pioneers on Parade* 2–3: She had canonized anyone who held more than ten thousand acres, and lumped pure merinos and the poorer goats in the one romantic squirearchy known as the squattocracy.

1975 Hal Porter *The Extra* 91: Here, you find Petty's Hotel, once the haunt of squattocracy, now a Red Cross Blood Transfusion Centre.

squib 1 A coward, or someone lacking in nerve [f. *squib* a mean, insignificant or paltry fellow OED 1586–1653 *obs.*]
1924 *Truth* 27 Apr. 6: *Squib* A coward.
1936 Archer Russell *Gone Nomad* 55: 'There's no place in this town for squibs,' he was told.
1942 Gavin Casey *It's Harder for Girls* 200: 'He shut up, just like th' bloody squib he is.'
1969 D'Arcy Niland *Dead Men Running* 26: 'You're a squib, son. You're yellow.'
2 A horse without staying power, esp. in the expression 'speedy squib'
1923 Con Drew *Rogues & Ruses* 107: 'He's only a long-legged squib.'
1984 *Sun-Herald* 26 Feb. 78: It has been said, among other things, that the Golden Slipper is a race for speedy squibs.

squib it
1918 George Dale *The Industrial History of Broken Hill* 170: All the employers had agreed to fight the Union, but had squibbed it at the last moment.
1949 Lawson Glassop *Lucky Palmer* 222: 'What, are yous squibbin' it?' asked the man incredulously.
1978 Keith Garvey *Tales of My Uncle Harry* 22: Tiger's supporters couldn't believe that their champion had squibbed it.

squiz An inquisitive look [? f. *squint* + *quiz*]
1913 C. J. Dennis *Backblock Ballads* 199: *Squiz* A glance.
1946 Dal Stivens *The Courtship of Uncle Henry* 69: He put the chops down and took a squiz at me.
1968 Geoffrey Dutton *Andy* 282: 'You're mad, you blokes, not to go and have a decent squiz at it.'
1975 Don Townshend *Gland Time* 142:

He put his hand in his pocket and produced a small box. 'Have a squiz at that.'

SS Social Security i.e. the payments to the unemployed and others
1982 Jack Davis *The Dreamers* 132: 'Lend me five bucks.' 'Here you are. I don't mind collecting it out of your next SS.'

stack on To put on, 'stage', perpetrate (usu.) an *act, blue, turn*
1949 Lawson Glassop *Lucky Palmer* 175: 'Don't stack on no blue,' he said. 'I'm runnin' this game and I'm runnin' it proper.'
1969 Mena Calthorpe *The Defectors* 11: She was prettier than he had thought, swinging about on her heels and stacking on an act.
1970 Jack Hibberd *White with Wire Wheels* in Penguin *Plays* 159: 'How was she? Stacking on a turn?' 'Not Sue. She's as placid as they come.'
1981 *Australian* 21 Nov. Mag. 19: For reasons best known to himself, Mr Bjelke-Petersen stacked on a turn and the negotiations broke down.

staggering bob see **bob**

stand The place allocated to one man on the board of a shearing shed, with the accompanying equipment
1901 Rolf Boldrewood *In Bad Company* 21: 'It's hard on a chap, when he comes to a shed after travellin' three or four 'undred mile, to be told that all the stands is took up.'
1911 E. S. Sorenson *Life in the Australian Backblocks* 227: Stands are sometimes booked weeks and months prior to date of shearing, applications being accompanied in many cases with a sovereign as a guarantee of good faith.
1964 Tom Ronan *Packhorse and Pearling Boat* 147: There was a shearing shed with eight stands rapidly disintegrating from the combined effects of white ants, rust and general neglect.

stand over To extort money etc. by intimidation; to domineer over someone
1939 Kylie Tennant *Foveaux* 173: 'I just had Thompson in here and he stood over me for three quid.'
1950 *The Australian Police Journal* Apr. 119: *Stand over* To threaten, menace, or use duress on someone for the purpose of gain.

1958 Frank Hardy *The Four-Legged Lottery* 192: We'll have to stand over him to get our money.

standover man A criminal using force, or the threat of force, to intimidate or extort
1939 Kylie Tennant *Foveaux* 174: He didn't deserve to be a 'standover man' if he couldn't move quicker.
1962 Alan Marshall *This is the Grass* 60: I guessed he was a stand-over merchant and that he had brought these two men with him like a hunter who goes out with his dogs.

stanza A half or quarter in a football match [U.S. Wentworth & Flexner]
1978 *Australian* 19 Jun. 25: St George ... were aided in their fightback by a huge 12–2 penalty count in the second stanza.
1981 *Canberra Times* 21 Sep. 16: Both sides looked nervous in the opening stanza.

starve the bardies see **bardies**

starver A saveloy
1941 Baker 71: *Starver* A saveloy.
1959 D'Arcy Niland *The Big Smoke* 211: 'I know what the things I eat cost me. Starvers, crumpets, stale cakes, specked fruit, pies.'

station, there's movement at the Expression for hurried activity, esp. portending some imminent event [f. the opening line of A. B. Paterson's 'The Man from Snowy River' (There was movement at the station, for the word had passed around) 1895]
1918 George Dale *The Industrial History of Broken Hill* 79: He is still the rebel of yore, and is seen in the forefront of any movement on the station for the betterment of conditions.
1966 Tom Ronan *Once There Was A Bagman* 225: There was movement on the station, of course, as soon as old Harry showed over the skyline.
1984 Paul Kelly *The Hawke Ascendancy* 339: By Monday 13 December Hayden had received sufficient reports to know trouble was brewing. Bowen had told him earlier: 'Watch it, there's movement at the station.'

statistics, the In football, the count of points scored, errors made, tackles completed, penalties awarded, scrum wins etc., according to the code
1978 David Williamson *The Club* 23: 'He

only got twelve kicks last week. I saw the statistics.'
1979 *Advertiser* (Adelaide) 11 Jun. 14: Statistics illustrate his dominance – 35 hit outs, 11 marks, four hand-passes and 23 kicks.

steam Cheap wine; methylated spirits
1941 Baker 71: *Steam* Cheap wine, esp. laced with methylated spirits.
1953 T. A. G. Hungerford *Riverslake* 185: 'I've got a bottle of steam if you'd like a snort, Kerry.'
1968 Stuart Gore *Holy Smoke* 60: 'Top quality plonk ... Not this round-the-world-for-a-dollar steam that *you* go for.'
1978 Max Richards *Sadie and Neco* in *Can't You Hear Me Talking to You?* ed. Alrene Sykes 147: *Neco* Is that bottle of steam still there? ... *Sadie* What bottle? *Neco* The Meths.

steamed up In a temper, in a state of excitement
1941 Baker 71: *Steamed up, get* To become angry or frenzied.
1953 T. A. G. Hungerford *Riverslake* 109: 'Holy cow, was he steamed up!'
1966 Roger Carr *Surfie* 80: I just sat around the kitchen thinking and getting all steamed up, mostly at her folks pushing me around and making me stay the night.
1984 *Age* (Melbourne) 16 Apr. 24: 'We were prepared to see St Kilda come out steamed up after what happened last week,' said Quade.

steam, like Rapidly, vigorously, energetically
1901 Let. 20 Mar. *Letters from Irish Australia 1825–1929* ed. Patrick O'Farrell (1984) 107: They [the kangaroos] fight like steam and even with the leg broken can make nasty little rushes.
1923 Con Drew *Rogues & Ruses* 180: 'Sparkle's got a break on the field and is leatherin' it out like steam.'
1944 Lawson Glassop *We Were the Rats* 129: 'We reefed watches and rings off 'em like steam.' Ibid. 179: 'She comes across. Turns it on like steam. She pulls her dress off.'
1979 Bobbie Hardy *The World Owes Me Nothing* 102: I hammered at the door like steam and over he came and opened it.

Steelers, the The Illawarra Rugby League

Club, whose home ground is in Wollongong, 'the Steel City'

1982 *Sun-Herald* 7 Feb. 73: Lack of playing depth, and an inadequate home ground, will be two of the biggest problems for the Illawarra Rugby League Club in their first year in the Sydney premiership. The Steelers' home ground, Wollongong Showground, with a capacity of about 13,000 could be taxed to the limit at some home matches this season.

steer, the red   see **red**

sterks, the   The shits [see **sterky**]

1959 David Forrest *The Last Blue Sea* 24: 'He just gives me the sturks.'

1968 Stuart Gore *Holy Smoke* 26: 'You'd give a man the sterks, bludgin' there in bed as if it was the Palace Hotel.'

sterky   As for **packing them** q.v.: *rare* [abbr. of *stercoraceous*]

1944 Jean Devanny *By Tropic, Sea and Jungle* 162: The croc disappears, and there's Ernest, standing up to his waist in the water, looking for him – scared as hell, but too game to come out. He yells for us to come in ourselves, so my dad goes in. He's a bit sterky too.

1953 Baker 104: *sterky* Frightened.

sterling   English immigrants, as distinct from the native born [see quot. 1827]

1827 P. Cunningham *Two Years in New South Wales* ii 53: Our colonial-born brethren are best known here by the name of *Currency*, in contradistinction to *Sterling*, or those born in the mother-country.

1844 Louisa Meredith *Notes and Sketches of New South Wales* 50: The natives (not the aborigines, but the 'currency', as they are termed, in distinction from the 'sterling', or British-born residents) are often very good-looking when young.

see **currency**

stick, more than one could poke (shake) a ~ at   An inordinate amount

1905 Joseph Furphy *Rigby's Romance* ed. R. G. Howarth (1946) 42: '"What the (adj. sheol) did you want fetchin' us out of Egypt, where we had as much meat and vegetables as you could shake a stick at?" says they.'

1944 Lawson Glassop *We Were the Rats* 104: 'I been in more drums than ya could poke a stick at,' he said.

1967 Frank Hardy *Billy Borker Yarns*

Again 15: Your tips have cost me more money than I could poke a stick at.

stick one's bib in   see **bib**

sticker licker   A parking policeman in S.A.

1982 *Bulletin* 2 Mar. 32: Sticker lickers in South Australia are called brown bombers in New South Wales.

stickybeak *n.*   1   An inquisitive person (sticking his beak in)

1924 Steele Rudd *Me an' th' Son* 7: 'Did y' hurt yourself – stick-beak?' he sez.

1938 *Bulletin* 6 Jul. 48: 'Then you'll spoil your life and hers for what some old stickybeak and scandalcat has said.'

1953 *Caddie A Sydney Barmaid* 25: The stickybeaks were dying to know who was the father of the baby, but Nellie wouldn't tell.

2   The act of stickybeaking

1983 Peter Kocan *The Cure* 13: She's just having a sticky-beak into the yard.

1988 Barney Roberts *Tales I carry with me* 107: Bugger him, she thought, he's only come over for a sticky-beak.

stickybeak *v.*   To act as a stickybeak, to pry into the affairs of others

1935 Kylie Tennant *Tiburon* 111: 'Ain't I got enough trouble,' he roared, 'with them stickybeakin' round 'ere gettin' me up before the court.'

1945 Margaret Trist *Now That We're Laughing* 142: 'It's so good of them to come.' 'Why is it?' demanded Mrs Henderson. 'They only come to stickybeak.'

stiff   Out of luck

1919 W. H. Downing *Digger Dialects* 27: *Stiff* Unlucky.

1922 Arthur Wright *A Colt from the Country* 124: 'On'y just got cut out of second place,' declared Knocker. 'Ain't a man stiff?'

1945 Cecil Mann *The River* 137: 'It's damn' stiff you can't march this year, but you will next year.'

1970 Richard Beilby *No Medals for Aphrodite* 77: How stiff could you be? The truck gone, the bridge blown, and now her, packing up like this!

1980 *Sun-Herald* 23 Nov. 103: A man would be as stiff as a board not to get a lift home with one of the boys.

stiffen the lizards   see **lizards**

sting *n.* 1 A strong drink [f. *stingo* strong ale or beer OED 1635]

1929 K. S. Prichard *Coonardoo* 60: 'I'm through with prospectin'!' 'Misses his three square meals a day and sting,' Bob explained.

1954 T. A. G. Hungerford *Sowers of the Wind* 263: He drained his glass [of whisky], and filled it again immediately . . . 'Feel the need of a bit of sting, eh?'

1972 John de Hoog *Skid Row Dossier* 4: You can share a bottle of sting (methylated spirits) down a lane.

2 Dope, esp. in racing

1950 *Australian Police Journal* Apr. 118: *Sting* Dope.

1958 Frank Hardy *The Four-Legged Lottery* 173: The 'smarties' soon found stings that didn't show on a swab.

sting *v.* 1 To exploit someone by extracting a loan; to overcharge

[**1812** Vaux: *Sting* To rob or defraud a person or place is called *stinging* them, as, that *cove* is too fly; he has been *stung* before; meaning that man is upon his guard, he has already been trick'd.]

1919 W. H. Downing *Digger Dialects* 47: *Sting* (vb.) Make a request for a loan or gift. So, also, 'Put in the stings'.

1928 Arthur Wright *A Good Recovery* 161: 'Suppose he wants to put the stings in for a few quid.'

1945 Kylie Tennant *Ride on Stranger* 63: 'In this world you've got to sting or get stung,' he pointed out.

1970 Patrick White *The Vivisector* 331: 'Who sold you the paintings?' he asked . . . 'Diacono? Then he must have stung you!'

2 (*give the sting*) to dope a racehorse

1949 Lawson Glassop *Lucky Palmer* 36: 'It's a moral. They're going to give it the sting. They'll hit it with enough dope to win a Melbourne Cup.'

stipe Stipendiary steward (controlling horse-racing) [abbr.]

[**1860** Hotten 228: *Stipe* A stipendiary magistrate. *Provincial.*]

1949 Lawson Glassop *Lucky Palmer* 163: 'You was going to do all sorts of things to us. Going to call in the stipes and everything.'

1977 *Australian* 15 Jan. 20: The racing page screamed STIPES PROBE JOCKEY.

1983 *Newcastle Herald* 14 Jan. 14: The stipes have wide-ranging powers to banish undesirables from tracks, quiz jockeys about

riding performances, hold inquiries into so-called 'form reversals'.

stir To act in a way provocative to authority or upholders of the status quo; to create a minor disturbance (juvenile) [? f. *stir the possum* q.v. or the proverb 'The more you stir a turd, the worse it stinks' 1546]

1972 John de Hoog *Skid Row Dossier* 110: Excitement was whipped up over the tiniest incident and when several youths went 'stirring' one day – riding up and down the lifts of large office blocks – conversations dwelt on and enlarged every action.

1978 Kevin Gilbert *Living Black* 38: When I started to stir, people began to wake up to what conditions we lived in.

stir the possum see **possum**

stirrer Someone given to 'stirring'

1971 Frank Hardy *The Outcasts of Foolgarah* 88: That'd be him, thought the Dean, a shit-stirrer from way back. Ibid. 109: The lurk men and stirrers weren't the only ones burning the midnight oil.

1979 Bill Scott *Tough in the Old Days* 16: The new bloke was a stirrer, with all his talk at lunch time about how the lunchroom was too small.

1983 *Australian* 14 May 11: Mr Paul Everingham, in boots-and-all fashion, immediately claimed protests were motivated by stirrers, white radicals and those opposed to Northern Territory development.

stone the crows see **crows**

stonker To defeat, thwart, put out of commission [cf. *stonk* the stake in a game EDD; *stunk* (stonk) to pant, gasp, groan with exertion SND]

1917 Diary cit. in Patsy Adam-Smith *The Anzacs* (1978) 215: We just go into the line again and again until we get knocked . . . Just in and out, in and out, and somebody stonkered every time.

1942 Sarah Campion *Bonanza* 42: 'Now you're stonkered all right, if Clancy ever gets on yer track.'

1981 Dorothy Hewett *The Golden Oldies* 46: 'That was the day when I felt so stonkered and stayed in our suite.'

stores, on, off the Applied to convicts either drawing rations from the government stores in Sydney, or subsisting independently of them

1798 David Collins *An Account of the English Colony in New South Wales* ed. B. Fletcher (1975) i 193: Having taken himself off the stores to avoid working for the public, he was frequently distressed for food. Ibid. 392: All these depredations were chiefly committed by those public nuisances the people off the stores.
1809 *HRNSW* vii 141: A general muster of male prisoners, on or off the stores . . . will be taken on the following days.

stoush *v.* To clout, punch [see **stoush** *n.*]
1893 J. A. Barry *Steve Brown's Bunyip* 66: 'I'll get stoushed over this job yet. Brombee's got it in for me.'
1896 Henry Lawson 'Shooting the Moon' *Prose* i 150: 'Now look here,' I said, shaking my fist at him, like that, 'if you say a word, I'll stoush yer!'
1934 'Leslie Parker' *Trooper to the Southern Cross* (1966) 69: 'He had a bit of turn-up with the military policeman and stoushed him.'
1965 Eric Lambert *The Long White Night* 79: 'Get out of that bloody car while I stoush yer!'

stoush *n.* Fighting, violence [? f. *stashie (stash)* an uproar; a commotion, disturbance, quarrel EDD 1851]
1908 Henry Fletcher *Dads and Dan between Smokes* 32: 'He looked as though he liked bein' hit an' took stoush fer breakfast every mornin'.'
1935 H. R. Williams *Comrades of the Great Adventure* 247: He returned to France and participated in some more 'real stoush' – as he called a battle – before the war came to an end.
1971 Frank Hardy *The Outcasts of Foolgarah* 82: Here they are now with their mob looking for a bit of stoush.
1981 *Sun-Herald* 19 Apr. 135: Personally, I like a good stoush at Brookvale Oval, or wherever.

streaker's defence See quot. 1983
1983 *Australian* 22 Apr. 1: The Attorney-General, Senator Evans, yesterday explained that his decision to allow RAAF spy flights over the Franklin dam had been taken because 'it seemed like a good idea at the time'. He told the National Press Club he had adopted what was known in legal circles as 'the streaker's defence: it seemed, your worship, like a good idea at the time'.

street, to To outdistance, esp. in horseracing
1983 *Newcastle Herald* 20 Apr. 36: Rosebrook streeted the opposition in yesterday's $10,000 Rocket Stakes (900m) at Broadmeadow.
1990 *Sun-Herald* 4 Mar. 65: Avenue streets the field [heading] Brilliant three-year-old Shaftesbury Avenue produced a record win . . . at Warwick Farm yesterday.

strength, the ~ of The essential facts about, reliable information upon [? f. *strength* the force, tenor, import (of a document) OED 1425–1602 *obs.*]
1904 Henry Fletcher *Dads Wayback: His Work* 34: 'About this forchin-tellin' game, it takes er bit o' knowin' ter get ther full strength of it.'
1939 Kylie Tennant *Foveaux* 154: 'What's the strength of it? Any idea?'
1959 K. S. Prichard *N'Goola* 153–4: 'A trapper camped further along the road gave me the strength of them.'
see **strong**

strife A 'literary' term often given a colloquial use
1931 Miles Franklin *Back to Bool Bool* 320: 'Laleen does not want to come back here and make strife amongst her relatives,' he said.
1944 Lawson Glassop *We Were the Rats* 113: 'Some blokes aren't nominated,' he said dismally. 'They cop all the strife that's goin'.'
1958 Barry Humphries *A Nice Night's Entertainment* (1981) 16: Had a bit of strife parking the vehicle.
1972 David Williamson *The Removalists* 105: 'You're in the shit I'm afraid, Ross . . . You're in real strife, boy.'

strike a blow see **blow**

strike, strike a light See quot. 1913
1913 C. J. Dennis *Backblock Ballads* 200: *Strike* An exclamation expressing astonishment etc.
1959 D'Arcy Niland *The Big Smoke* 14: 'Strike me pink, Chiddy, what are you doing with all that money behind you, mate?'
1984 Helen Garner *The Children's Bach* 58: 'Strike a light. Look, Poppy. What does it say here?'

strike paydirt see **paydirt**

string   To form a string, move in a string, esp. of cattle [f. *string* to move or progress in a string or disconnected line OED 1824]
1887 W. S. S. Tyrwhitt *The New Chum in the Queensland Bush* 192: He sees through the darkness a line of cattle slowly stringing away across the flat.
1895 A. B. Paterson 'Clancy of the Overflow' *The Man from Snowy River* 21: As the stock are slowly stringing, Clancy rides behind them singing, / For the drover's life has pleasures that the townsfolk never know.
1905 E. C. Buley *Australian Life in Town and Country* 26: After the cutting out is done, the beasts have been sorted in mobs according to their classes, each mob is made to 'string' or move in single file, in order that a count may be made.

strong, the ~ of   As for **the strength of**
1910 Arthur Wright *Under a Cloud* 31: 'Don't yer want to own up? Some reason for wantin' to preserve yer incog. I suppose. What's the strong of it?'
1938 Xavier Herbert *Capricornia* 566: 'What's the strong of you? What's the questioning for? I've done nuthin'.'
1959 Eric Lambert *Glory Thrown In* 161: 'What's the strong of this joint?' demanded Doc brusquely. 'Not an undertaker's is it?'

stroke, Government   see **Government**

stubby   1   A beer bottle smaller than the usual size, esp. 375 ml [f. shape]
1968 Frank Hardy *The Unlucky Australians* 49: He threw an empty stubby into the box and went to the refrigerator for a full one.
1979 *Courier-Mail* (Brisbane) 12 May 1: If you can roll a cigarette in one hand, play a gumleaf, saw or comb, crack a whip and drink a stubbie in 10 seconds, then make tracks for Winton and the Mr Outback quest.
2   *Stubbies* A brand of men's shorts
1977 *Australian* 7 Apr. 3: Stubbies – the football shorts with pockets – have become an international fashion ... Although the Stubby is a very Australian name – thought of in the context of short shorts to go with short bottles of beer – Mr Phillips is confident they will become as American as apple pie.
1983 David Foster *Plumbum* 176: Australian tourists ... are recognisable throughout Asia by their characteristic

attire of thongs and stubbies, and their self-satisfied expressions.

stuck into, to get   1   To attack someone, physically or verbally
1942 Gavin Casey *It's Harder for Girls* 228: 'A bit o' peace after ... you an' Winch nearly getting stuck into each other at the pub.'
1953 T. A. G. Hungerford *Riverslake* 120–1: 'What was the trouble, Con? I saw you stuck into a Balt across the press as I come down.'
1977 Jeff Thomson *Sunday Telegraph* (Sydney) 27 Feb. 60: 'They're getting a bit cocky, the Poms. So I'd like to get stuck into 'em again.'
2   To apply oneself energetically to a task
1955 John Morrison *Black Cargo* 65: 'All right, grab those knives and get stuck into it.'
1975 Les Ryan *The Shearers* 124: 'Righto, you blue-tongues!' he bellowed out. 'Get stuck into it!'
3   To consume (food or drink) with gusto
1947 Gavin Casey *The Wits are Out* 89: 'Come on,' Syd said. 'What about getting stuck into it?' They gathered round the barrel for some serious drinking.
1973 Alexander Buzo *Rooted* 30: 'Davo got stuck into the grog, didn't he?'

students, the   The members of one of the University sporting teams in N.S.W.
1957 *Bulletin* 14 Aug. 39: In a cut throat game ... which ended University's chances, Randwick, scoring five tries to one, 'failed' the Students 18–14.
1976 *Sunday Telegraph* (Sydney) 24 Oct. 76: Boycott thrashes Students [heading] Geoff Boycott, the veteran English test batsman, scored a casual century for Waverley against University of NSW yesterday.

stump, the black   see **black**

stung   Drunk, tipsy [f. **sting** 1]
1919 W. H. Downing *Digger Dialects* 48: *Stung* (adj. or p. part.) (1) Drunk; (2) having been induced to lend.
1952 T. A. G. Hungerford *The Ridge and the River* 62: 'The old bloke's stung already, and the pubs aren't even opened yet!'
1965 William Dick *A Bunch of Ratbags* 219: We had arrived at Doreen's sister's wedding-reception about an hour ago and by now we were all half stung.

1982 *National Times* 22 Aug. 11: To be drunk, I learn, is to be 'stung' or 'rotten'.

stunned mullet, like a see **mullet**

Stupenda, La The soprano Joan Sutherland [f. the applause (*È stupenda*, She's stupendous) when she sang Handel's *Alcina* at the Fenice Theatre, Venice, in February 1960]
1960 *Daily Express* (London) 22 Feb. 4: Noel Goodwin flies to Italy and hears them call Joan Sutherland LA STUPENDA [heading] Pink carnations which decorated the boxes and galleries of the graceful Fenice Theatre . . . were showered last night on the woman the audience cheered as 'La Stupenda'. She was Joan Sutherland, Covent Garden's star soprano.
1984 *Sydney Morning Herald* 16 Feb. 16: La Stupenda, in a rare burst of public talking, reveals that, like Kate Fitzpatrick, she too enjoys a decent game of cricket.

subbie A sub-contractor
1978 *Sun-Herald* 4 Jun. 21: Most owner-drivers or sub-contractors, as they are known in the business, have to overload if they want to make ends meet. For the independent 'subbie' a couple of extra tonnes over the legal limit is often the only thing separating a profitable run from a straight-out loss.

Such is life An expression given a special Australian currency from being the supposed last words of Ned Kelly, and from being adopted by Joseph Furphy as the title of his famous novel
1880 J. Jenkins *Diary of a Welsh Swagman* (1975) 100: Ned Kelly, the Bushranger was hanged today [9 Nov.] at 8 a.m. His last words at the scaffold were, 'Such is life'.
c. **1897** Joseph Furphy *Such is Life Being certain extracts from the diary of Tom Collins* (1903)
1969 *Such Was Life Select Documents in Australian Social History 1788–1850* ed. Russel Ward and John Robertson.

suds Beer
1945 Cecil Mann *The River* 139: By the look of you, Jim, you've put away a quart or two since last Day. Always were pretty good on the suds.
1984 *Sunday Independent* (Perth) 29 Apr. 3: WA beer drinkers, faced tomorrow with the fifth price increase in a year, can take

solace in the fact that suds-lovers in the eastern states pay quite a bit more.

sugar bag A nest of wild honey in a tree; honey [Pidgin]
1830 Robert Dawson *The Present State of Australia* 136: The strange native . . . pointed with his tomahawk to the tree and nodding his head and smiling at me, repeated the words, 'Choogar-bag, choogar-bag, choogar-bag!' (sugar-bag) their English expression for honey, or anything sweet.
1901 F. J. Gillen *Diary* (1968) 288: Honey or as the blacks call it 'Sugar bag' appears to be fairly plentiful for the boys cut out two lots yesterday.
1941 Charles Barrett *Coast of Adventure* 109: Grigalalok already had found 'sugar bag' in a rock cavity, bringing a mass of dripping honeycomb to our conchologist.

sunbeam An item of cutlery or crockery laid on the table but not used, and so not needing to be washed up
1982 *Sydney Morning Herald* 24 Dec. 19: In Australian households sunbeams still lighten the washing up.

sunburnt country, the Australia [f. Dorothea Mackellar's poem: see quot. 1914]
1914 Dorothea Mackellar 'My Country' in *The Witch Maid* 29: I love a sunburnt country / A land of sweeping plains.
1953 Ian Bevan ed. *The Sunburnt Country Profile of Australia* [book title]
1979 Thea Astley *Hunting the Wild Pineapple* 106: 'To stop the brain-drain, that's for what. Keep the old genius located right here in the sunburnt country.'
1981 *Australian* 3 Dec. 16: The sunburnt country's droughts and flooding rains have had a marked effect on the end-of-year result for our second largest pastoral company, Dalgety Australia.

Sunday too far away An expression given currency by a film of this title (see quot. 1975), but part of the lore of the shearer much earlier
1963 *Sydney Morning Herald* 17 Aug. 11: A lot of greasies (shearers) get hen trouble. Some shearers' wives reckon we shearer blokes are either too tired, too drunk, or too far away.
1975 *Times* (London) 20 May 9: The title [of the film] is from a song, the complaint of the shearer's loveless wife: 'Friday he's too

tired, Saturday too drunk, and Sunday too far away.'

1984 *Sydney Morning Herald* 8 May 4: The jibes of Mick Young, who described the Thredbo weekend as 'Friday too tired, Saturday too drunk, Sunday too far away' . . . did not hit home.

sundowner A swagman who arrives at a station at sundown, too late in the day to do any work, but in time to draw rations

1887 W. S. S. Tyrwhitt *The New Chum in the Queensland Bush* 82: There is a class of men in Australia called 'sundowners' from the fact that they always turn up at stations, nominally in search of work, at sundown, never coming in before for fear of having to work for their rations.

1901 Henry Lawson 'A Double Buggy at Lahey's Creek' *Prose* i 596: 'What do you want me to come at sunset for?' asked James. 'Do you want me to camp out in the scrub and turn up like a blooming sundowner?'

1913 John Sadleir *Recollections of a Victorian Police Officer* 109: 'Sundowners', swagmen who travelled without any settled purpose from station to station, obtaining fresh supplies of food at any station where they might chance to find themselves at sunset.

sunnies Sunglasses

1981 *Sun-Herald* 11 Jan. 9: On his head was a top hat adorned with dark glasses ('sunnies').

1984 *Sydney Morning Herald* 4 Feb. 35: A mob in mirrored sunnies (essential accessories at Narara).

sunny New South see **New South**

sunshine state, the Queensland, in the language of tourist advertising

1962 Criena Rohan *The Delinquents* 128: 'If you ask me, all Brisbane's full of coppers and all of them bastards,' she said, expressing in one concise sentence the full theory of central government of the sunshine state.

1970 *Coast to Coast 1969–1970* 115: 'We had such fun, remember? And somehow it never seemed to rain. Good old Sunshine State.'

1982 *Sunday Mail* (Brisbane) 19 Sep. 3: Once most definitely taboo in the Sunshine State, male strippers are now performing under the nose of the police and, according to promoters, they can't keep the girls away.

sunstruck bone, like a Extremely dry, thirsty

1894 Henry Lawson 'Stiffner and Jim (Thirdly Bill)' *Prose* i 123: We comes to Stiffner's Hotel . . . with throats on us like sun-struck bones, and not the price of a stick of tobacco.

1962 Dymphna Cusack *Picnic Races* 168: 'Spend yer day riding round 9,000 bloody acres with a thirst on yer like a sunstruck bone, and the heat frying the brains under yer hat.'

1977 F. A. Reeder *Diary of a Rat* 39: Hot as a couple of hells, dry as a sunstruck bone, with huge sand hills everywhere.

super 1 The superintendent of a station [abbr.]

1857 F. Cooper *Wild Adventures in Australia* 59: 'Scotchy' . . . introduced me as a particular friend to Wilder the owner of that run, under the impression that a 'super' was required, as Wilder had from some time spoken of his intention to reside in Brisbane.

1888 'The Jackeroo' *Bulletin* 10 Mar. 14 repr. in *Old Bush Songs* ed. Stewart and Keesing (1957) 79: When I got to the station I saw the super there.

2 Superphosphate

1931 *Southern Cross Times* 25 Jul. cit. G. C. Bolton *A Fine Country to Starve In* (1972) 142: Oh, kind hearted creditors, / don't start repossessing the super bags yet!

1959 K. S. Prichard *N'Goola* 142: The bottom fell out of the market for wheat. Prices were so low they would not pay for seed and super.

1975 *Australian* 12 Aug. 1: Restore super bounty, says IAC.

3 Petrol with an octane rating above 'standard'

4 Superannuation

1978 *Sydney Morning Herald* 20 Jun. 13: Super board funds $30m project [heading] The State Superannuation Board is to provide finance for Lend Lease Development Pty Ltd's new regional shopping centre at Campbelltown.

surf, surfie A young habitué of the beaches, long-haired and given to surf-board-riding, seen as a cult figure

1963 *Sun-Herald* 10 Mar. 1: Police will maintain a constant alert today on Sydney's 15 beaches to prevent gang warfare between Rockers and Surfies.

1975 *National Times* 13 Jan. 40: If you are a 14-year-old schoolgirl and you have just discovered boys are not the same thing as your brothers, what really sends your heart into a turmoil is the sight of a blond, long-haired, blue-eyed, sun-bronzed surf wearing board shorts and bare feet.

1982 *Sun-Herald* 11 Apr. 15: 'People automatically think of a surfie as a brainless twirp with bleached blonde hair who takes drugs and sleeps around. It's such a terrible generalisation.'

Susso Government sustenance for the unemployed during the depression; a man drawing his dole [abbr.]

1942 Leonard Mann *The Go-Getter* 10: Five shillings were five shillings and a handsome help to the sustenance. 'We're on the Susso now.' That was the song they knew and did not sing.

1947 Vance Palmer *Cyclone* 8: 'He thinks it puts hair on his chest knocking about with the sussos.'

1969 Patsy Adam-Smith *Folklore of the Australian Railwaymen* 190: When war was declared all our big 'susso' camps folded up overnight and the boys went to where they were sure to find work.

swag *n.* 1 Booty, plunder (as in English thieves' slang)

1812 Vaux: *The swag,* is a term used in speaking of any booty you have lately obtained, be it of what kind it may, except money.

2 A collection of legitimate belongings

c. **1845** James Tucker *Ralph Rashleigh* (1952) 125: The cart contained various articles of property of those kinds that generally constitute the bulk of a settler's swag. There were pipes, tobacco, the keg above named, a quantity of tea and sugar, two or three coarse cotton striped shirts, and a pair or two of duck trousers.

1852 G. C. Mundy *Our Antipodes* iii 285: A tall picturesque-looking sprig of the squattocracy has just pitched his 'swag' – a leathern valise – through the open skylight on to the cuddy table.

3 The pack carried by the traveller, usually some essential belongings rolled in a blanket

1853 John Rochfort *Adventures of a Surveyor* 49: Disregarding the state of the roads, on the 24th of August, 1852, we strapped on our 'swags',* consisting of a pair of blankets and a spare pair of trousers, and started for the diggings. *Swags, colonial word for pack.

1873 A. Trollope *Australia* ed. Edwards and Joyce (1967) 293: The man who travels on foot in Australia, whether he be miner, shepherd, shearer, or simply beggar, always carries his 'swag' with him, – which consists of his personal properties rolled up in a blanket.

1896 Henry Lawson 'Enter Mitchell' *Prose* i 132: It was a stout, dumpy swag, with a red blanket outside, and the edge of a blue blanket showing in the inner rings at the end . . . It might have been hooped with decent straps, instead of bits of clothes-line and greenhide – but otherwise there was nothing the matter with it, as swags go.

swag, the dogs are pissing on see **pull out**

swag, cigarette see **cigarette**

swag it To follow the swagman's life

1870 W. M. Finn *Glimpses of North-Eastern Victoria* (1971) 26: I was much surprised to see two able-bodied men, who informed me that for seventeen years they were swagging it from one place to another; indeed, they had travelled the colony, and had no notion of now abandoning their nomadic way of life . . . They said they were not going to work for any master, and would eke out an existence for their remaining time in the world.

1936 Archer Russell *Gone Nomad* 58: 'Swagging it' to a sheep station on the Queensland border he secured a job as a boundary rider.

swaggie A swagman q.v.

1896 Henry Lawson 'She Wouldn't Speak' *Prose* i 115: I thought a damp expression seemed to pass across her face when me and my mate sat down, but she served us and said nothing – we was only two dusty swaggies, you see.

1926 K. S. Prichard *Working Bullocks* 158: He would . . . fraternize with everyone he met, shouting all comers in the hotel bars, pick up any old swaggie and take him to dinner.

swaggie's dog, all prick and ribs like a see **all**

swagman A tramp carrying his belongings

in a 'swag'. The swagman is sometimes distinguished from the 'traveller', who is regarded as seeking work

1868 Marcus Clarke 'Swagmen' in *A Colonial City* ed. L. T. Hergenhan (1972) 32–3: The Wimmera district is noted for the hordes of vagabond 'loafers' that it supports, and has earned for itself the name of 'The Feeding Track'.

1875 A. J. Boyd *Old Colonials* (1882) 110–11: 'The Swagman' [chapter title] He tramps across the country ostensibly for work, and at the same time praying Heaven that he may not find it ... Idleness being the mainspring of the journeys of the Swagman (*anglice*, tramp).

1887 *All the Year Round* 30 Jul. 66: A 'swagman' is a different character. The name is given to any one tramping the country for work, or any other purpose, and carrying his worldly goods slung round him in a bundle, which is always known as his 'swag'.

1893 Henry Lawson 'Some Popular Australian Mistakes' *Prose* ii 24: Men tramping in search of a 'shed' are not called 'sundowners' or 'swaggies'; they are 'travlers'.

swallows flying out of one's backside see **sparrows**

swamp *v.* To act as an assistant to a bullock-driver; to travel on foot with a bullock-team, giving minor assistance or having one's swag carried; to obtain a lift for oneself and one's swag from any traveller [see **swamper**]

1926 K. S. Prichard *Working Bullocks* 101: Billy Williams the bullocky, and Ern Collins who was swamping for him, turned their team into the yards on the following Monday.

1944 M. J. O'Reilly *Bowyangs and Boomerangs* 6: My duties were to help to load and unload, bring the horses in the morning, to harness up, help to corduroy bad patches on the track, draw water for the horses at the soaks and wells, hobble out the horses at night, put the bells on, etc. These duties were then known as 'swamping' ... All this work for the privilege of having one's tucker, tools and swag carried on the waggon. Fortunately the chap I 'swamped' for was an exceptionally good sort.

swamper One engaged in the activities of swamping [f. *swamper* a road-breaker or clearer U.S. 1850; assistant to the driver of a mule team U.S. 1870 Mathews]

1901 May Vivienne *Travels in Western Australia* 284: A 'swamper' is a man tramping without his swag, which he entrusts to a teamster to bring on his waggon. Arrived at the camping-place, ... the swamper awaits the teamster's coming, recovers his swag and spends the night at the camp. While on foot the swamper will generally leave the track, and prospect.

1944 Randolph Bedford *Naught to Thirty-three* 200: A 'swamper' being a man [on the way to a gold rush] who pays for the carriage of his swag, and walks after the dray.

1966 Tom Ronan *Once There Was a Bagman* 15: My fellow swamper tossed his swag off [the mailman's truck] here; he was home.

Swans, the 1 The South Melbourne V.F.L. team, now defunct

1975 *Sunday Telegraph* (Sydney) 7 Sep. 64: Bulldogs race to big Rules win over Swans.

2 In N.S.W., the same team re-named the Sydney Swans

1982 *Australian* 25 Feb. 1: The Sydney Swans are 32 tall and muscular young men who up until yesterday went under the name of the South Melbourne Football Club.

3 In W.A., Swan Districts Australian Rules team

1980 *West Australian* (Perth) 19 May 60: Round One to Swans ... Twelve wins straight, and undefeated at the end of the first round this season – that is how Swan Districts stand.

swarm *n. & v.* A meeting of shearers, esp. a stop-work meeting

1958 *Bulletin* 2 Apr. 50: The shearers would be 'swarming' (having a meeting) or demanding waiting-time.

1962 *Sydney Morning Herald* 24 Nov. 12: After seeing them in the yards, the shearers 'swarmed' (held a meeting) and decided to ask the squatter for five bob a ram – away above the award.

1975 Les Ryan *The Shearers* 58–9: 'There's been a swarm. The shearers want to negotiate a complaint.'

sweet All right, in order, 'jake'

1898 *Bulletin* 17 Dec. Red Page: *sweet, roujig* and *not too stinkin'* are good.

1939 Kylie Tennant *Foveaux* 312: 'I

brassed a mug yesterday,' he told her, 'and everything's sweet again.' He flashed a roll of notes as big as his fist.

1949 Lawson Glassop *Lucky Palmer* 242: 'Everything jake?' he asked. 'She's sweet,' said Max.

1975 Xavier Herbert *Poor Fellow My Country* 353: Mossie came in ... to say cheerfully, 'She's sweet'.

sweetheart of song Miss Gladys Moncrieff, also known as **Our Glad** q.v.

1972 Peter Mathers *The Wort Papers* 280: Nor I, sang Gladys Moncrieff, the sweetheart of song.

sweetheart agreement An industrial agreement negotiated directly by employers and employed, without reference to the arbitration court

1974 *Australian* 12 Nov. 3: Miss Martin said Mr Jones' description of the hostesses' and stewards' award as a sweetheart agreement was farcical. The award had been decided by arbitration, not by negotiation between Qantas and the unions.

1985 *Advertiser* (Adelaide) 28 Sep. 3: Mr Colin Polites said the ACTU–Government wage-discounting agreement was a 'sweetheart' deal which the ACTU and Government were seeking to have rubber-stamped by the commission.

swifty An act of deception

1953 *Caddie A Sydney Barmaid* 224: 'You didn't work a swiftie on them, did you?' I asked suspiciously. For I was already aware that Bill was collecting three doles for himself.

1982 Malcolm Mackerras *Sydney Morning Herald* 3 Jul. 13: The point needs explaining and repeating so that the electorate will fully understand the 'swifty' being pulled by a double dissolution.

swill, the six o'clock The last minute rush for drinks in the pubs, occasioned by six o'clock closing (in N.S.W. 1916–55)

1951 A. W. Upfield *The New Shoe* 93: It wanted ten minutes to the fatal hour of six, and the enforced National Swill was in full flood.

1955 Alan Ross *Australia 55* 81: This evening ritual, known amongst Australians as the 'six o'clock swill'.

1970 Donald Horne *The Next Australia* 160: The 'six o'clock swill' before the lava-tory-tiled bars closed was one of the continuing tests of masculinity.

1980 *Sunday Mail* (Brisbane) 10 Feb. 12: Are southerners appalled at the one o'clock and six o'clock 'swills' which Queensland's two-session policy causes at some hotels?

swing the billy The action required to settle the tea-leaves

1966 D. E. Charlwood *An Afternoon of Time* 46: He put in the tea and a gumleaf and swung the billy over his head.

1981 *Sydney Morning Herald* 2 May 42: Ken Esgate has been a bushie round these parts all his life, as was his father. Esgate gave James Mason a lesson in how to swing the billy.

sword swallower Someone eating from his knife, esp. among shearers

1941 Baker 74. *Sword-swallowing* The practice of seting with one's knife.

swy The game of two-up [G. *zwei* two]

1921 *Aussie* 15 Mar. 54: 'Just done me last dollar up at the swi school.'

1961 Jack Danvers *The Living Come First* 106: 'Collecting their cut of the local swy-game.'

1981 *Australian* 26 Dec. 4: Swy school a declared gaming house, rules NSW judge [heading] Thommo's two-up school in Sydney is a declared gaming house – that's official.

Sydney or the bush All or nothing (i.e. to make one's fortune, and live in the capital, or lose it all, and seek a livelihood in the bush)

1924 *Truth* 27 Apr. 6: *Sydney or the Bush* All or nothing.

1930 E. Shann *An Economic History of Australia* 365: 'Sydney or the bush!' cries the Australian when he gambles against odds, and the slogan betrays a heart turning ever towards the pleasant coastal capitals.

1953 T. A. G. Hungerford *Riverslake* 127: 'Spin for five,' Murdoch suggested to Novikowsky. 'Sydney or the bush!'

1970 Richard Beilby *No Medals for Aphrodite* 34: 'Here we go,' Turk murmured grimly, climbing in behind the wheel. 'It's Sydney or the bush! Keep your fingers crossed.'

1983 *Sun* (Sydney) 30 Dec. 39: It's hard to pick a middle ground. The [investment] choices for next year appear to be boom or bust, Sydney or the bush.

T

tabby A woman

1916 C. J. Dennis *The Moods of Ginger Mick* 21: An' the tabbies pitch the weary Johns a tale, / 'Ow they orl is puffick ladies 'oo 'ave not been pinched for munce.

1951 Dal Stivens *Jimmy Brockett* 14: I picked a good-looker for a secretary. It added to your prestige. Most of the blokes had plain-looking tabbies, a bit long in the tooth.

1967 Alan O'Toole *The Coach from the City* 134: 'Should be a good turnout,' Badger prophesied. 'I suppose you'll be carting that little tabby of yours along.'

tack, flat as a see **flat**

tail To tend and herd stock, esp. on foot; to pursue stock that have strayed

1844 *Port Phillip Patriot* 5 Aug. 3: I know many boys, from the age of nine to sixteen years, tailing cattle. [Morris]

1852 G. C. Mundy *Our Antipodes* i 314: The stockman, as he who tends cattle and horses is called, despises the shepherd as a grovelling, inferior creature, and considers 'tailing sheep' as an employment too tardigrade for a man of action and spirit.

1919 W. K. Harris *Outback in Australia* 17: Camels will wander miles away during the night, even though they are hobbled. 'Tailing' horses, bullocks or mules is mere play compared with the task of 'tailing' camels.

tailer

1934 Mary Gilmore *Old Days: Old Ways* 242: You must not confuse the stockman with the 'tailer'. The tailer, and, for years the later rouseabout on the sheep-run, were no-account men. They were weaklings; they were menial; and could be asked to cut wood and would do it as part of their lowly, wretched, and good-for-nothing lot.

tailie In two-up, a gambler who habitually backs tails

1919 W. H. Downing *Digger Dialects* 49: *Tailie* A man who backs 'tails' in the game of two-up.

1949 Lawson Glassop *Lucky Palmer* 176: 'Gents,' he cried, 'now isn't there a tailie in the school?'

tail out of a peewee, couldn't pull the see **couldn't**

take an early shower see **shower**

take a look at see **look**

take out To win, esp. in sport

1976 *Australian* 15 Jul. 2: Helen Morse ... takes out the Australian Film Institute's top actress award tomorrow night.

1980 *Daily Mirror* (Sydney) 31 Mar. 54: Atkins, who prepares his team at Toowoomba, is hoping the colt will take out the AJC Derby.

take to the bush see **bush**

talent, the Collective term for those who stand out in any group, esp. in their own estimation, hence a **push** q.v.; likely-looking girls (to male observation) [cf. *the talent* the clever ones (racing slang) OED 1883; also *the fancy*]

1870 Rolf Boldrewood 'Shearing in Riverina' *Town and Country Journal* 29 Oct. 10: Upon the 'talent' also, consisting of men who can shear, and shear well, from fifty to seventy sheep more in a day than their fellows, the eye of watchfulness must be kept.

c. **1882** *The Sydney Slang Dictionary* 8: *The Talent* Low gamblers, sharpers, larrikins and their girls, confirmed prostitutes, and 'the fancy' generally who frequent their resorts.

1950 Jon Cleary *Just Let Me Be* 115: The thick-set detective looked after her, and Harry grinned at him. 'Not bad, eh?' he said, raising his eyebrow. 'That's a bit of the local talent.'

1979 *Sun-Herald* 7 Oct. 97: There wasn't even any 'talent' to rescue us. All the men were married, or about to be.

talk under water, wet cement, able to Extremely vociferous

1976 Sam Weller *Bastards I have met* 2: He can talk under water and eat ice cream at the same time.

1980 *Bulletin* 5 Feb. 43: McMahon was then a relatively junior minister, not that that would have bothered McMahon, of whom a contemporary once said admiringly, 'Billy can talk under wet concrete.'

tall poppy see **poppy**

tall timber, to take to the To decamp, as in 'take to the scrub'
1919 W. H. Downing *Digger Dialects* 49: *Take to the tall timber* Abscond.
1954 T. A. G. Hungerford *Sowers of the Wind* 61: 'Head for the tall timber until the grog runs out.'
1975 John O'Grady *Gone gougin'* 109: Peter removed the steel bar and said, 'Head for the tall timber, Roman.'

Tallarook, things are crook in Catchphrase for any adverse situation [f. rhyme on place-name]. Other catchphrases include: There's no work at Bourke. Got the arse at Bulli Pass. No lucre at Echuca. In jail at Innisfail. Things are weak at Julia Creek. Things are crook at Muswellbrook. The girls are bandy at Urandangie.
1963 Lawson Glassop *The Rats in New Guinea* 217: 'He says things are crook in Tallarook. He's the only soldier on his feet in his weapon pit.'
1978 *Australian* 23 Sep. 3: Things are crook in Tallarook ... and even worse at Kingaroy. One of the country's best known families, the Bjelke-Petersens, is feeling the rural pinch.
1982 *Sun-Herald* 21 Nov. 86: The number of people who ring talk-back shows asking for financial advice must surely be a good indication that not all is well in Tallarook or the North Shore's normally comfortable Ben Ean belt either.

tally 1 'The last of a specified number forming a unit of computation, on the completion of which the tally-man calls "tally" and notes it down' (OED *tally sb.* 5d)
1875 Rolf Boldrewood *The Squatter's Dream* (1878) 222: Keeping tally ... is the notation of the hundreds, by pencil or notched stick, the counter being supposed only to concern himself with the units and tens.
1886 P. Clarke *New Chum in Australia* 175: As a 'hundred' is called, one of us calls out 'tally', and cuts one notch in a stick.
2 The total number of sheep shorn by one man in a specified period
1870 Rolf Boldrewood 'Shearing in Riverina' *Town and Country Journal* 29 Oct. 10: At five o'clock the bell rings; the day's labour

is over; the men wait to see the sheep counted, and to hear their 'tallies' – the sums total of the day's shearing – read aloud.
1911 E. S. Sorenson *Life in the Australian Backblocks* 241: The quality and weight of the fleeces, and the size and condition of the sheep, have also a lot to do with the fluctuations of tallies.
1919 A. B. Paterson 'The Cook's Dog' in *Song of the Pen* (1983) 409: Each shearer has his average tally – one is a hundred-a-day man, another can only do eighty, while some run up to a hundred and fifty and even more.
3 Any other total achieved by an individual or team
1957 Ray Lawler *Summer of the Seventeenth Doll* 21: 'Roo's one of the best men they've got – runs his own gang [of canecutters] – but even down here you never get him yappin' about his season's tally.'
1960 Nancy Cato *Green Grows the Vine* 24: 'You'd better help her fill her tins for the rest of the morning, to bring up her tally.'
1982 *Sun-Herald* 25 Jul. 63: Williams, 18, booted home four winners – a tally that could have been even higher.

Tambaroora (muster) See quots. *obs.* [f. place-name]
1882 A. J. Boyd *Old Colonials* 63: It may be that the exciting name of Tambaroora is not familiar to all my readers ... Each man of a party throws a shilling, or whatever sum may be mutually agreed upon, into a hat. Dice are then produced, and each man takes three throws. The Nut who throws highest keeps the whole of the subscribed capital, and out of it pays for the drinks of the rest. The advantage of the proceeding lies in this: Where drinks are charged at sixpence, the subscription is double that amount for each ... Thus if ten Nuts go in for a Tambaroora, with nobblers at sixpence, the winner pockets five shillings by the transaction.
1895 Cornelius Crowe *The Australian Slang Dictionary* 84: *Tambaroora* A game of a shilling each in the hat and the winner shouts.

Tantanoola tiger An animal reported preying on sheep at Tantanoola, S.A. in 1889, sometimes identified with a large wild dog shot there in 1895, whose stuffed hide was preserved in a local hotel; any beast similarly reported
1907 Charles MacAlister *Old Pioneering Days in the Sunny South* 356: The old-time

system of shepherding flocks, hurdling or yarding them together at night in the days when the prowling dingo was the 'Tantanoola Tiger' of the bush.

1958 Max Harris in *The Penguin Book of Australian Verse*, ed. Thompson, Slessor and Howarth 258: 'The Tantanoola Tiger' [poem title]

tar, thumbnail dipped in see **thumbnail**

tarp A tarpaulin [abbr.]
1917 Diary cit. Patsy Adam-Smith *The Anzacs* (1978) 205: Made a shelter out of boxes of ammunition with a tarp for roof. Bad luck if a shell lands near.
1963 Alan Marshall *In Mine Own Heart* 174: 'They were open trucks with no tarps.'
1971 Frank Hardy *The Outcasts of Foolgarah* 183: 'There's plenty of tarps: we'll rig up a tent.'

tarpaulin muster See quots
1904 E. S. Emerson *A Shanty Entertainment* 26: Each one in the room to sing, recite, or shout all round, and if nobody reneged, a tarpaulin muster every half-hour for drinks, or smokes, just as the company cared.
1945 Elisabeth George *Two at Daly Waters* 102: As she had not brought a town outfit, Daly Waters had what we call in the bush a tarpaulin muster (the loan of everybody's best clothes).
1978 Wendy Lowenstein *Weevils in the Flour* 187: I rushed in there and took up a tarpaulin muster, and got enough to pay the bailiff and fix us up for another week.

tart A girl or woman. Not used in any derogatory sense, although women would not refer to themselves as 'tarts'. The juvenile 'jam tart' is obsolete [abbr. of *sweetheart*]
[**1865** Hotten 254: *Tart* A term of approval applied by the London lower orders to a young woman for whom some affection is felt. The expression is not generally employed by the young men, unless the female is in 'her best', with a coloured gown, red or blue shawl, and plenty of ribbons in her bonnet – in fact, made pretty all over, like the jam tarts in the swell bakers' shops.]
1899 W. T. Goodge *Hits! Skits! and Jingles!* 150: And his lady-love's his 'donah' / Or his 'clinah' or his 'tart'.

1915 C. J. Dennis *The Songs of a Sentimental Bloke* 34: A cove 'as got to think some time in life / An' get some decent tart, 'ere it's too late, / To be 'is wife.
1968 Thomas Keneally *Three Cheers for the Paraclete* 114: 'The mortgage office, you've got no idea . . . Little tarts with short haircuts running all over the place with folders.'
1983 Clem Gorman *A Night in the Arms of Raeleen* 25: 'You gotta bar that . . . Swearin' in front of a tart.'
see **tom, tom tart**

tartplate Pillion seat on motorbike or motorscooter, for female passenger
1982 *Southerly* 439: There may have been no disrespect in calling the pillion seat on a motorcycle or motorscooter a *tartplate*.

tartshop, dragged screaming from the Applied to politicians who have come reluctantly to face an election [attributed to W. M. Hughes, but used earlier by Alfred Deakin]
1904 Alfred Deakin *Ballarat Courier* 23 Aug. cit. J. A. La Nauze *Alfred Deakin* (1965) 378: I do not propose to reply to him [W. M. Hughes] except by saying he presents to you as undignified a spectacle as does the ill-bred urchin whom one sees dragged from a tart-shop kicking and screaming as he goes.
1974 *Sydney Morning Herald* 11 Jan. 6: It's time for the Whitlam Government, in Billy Hughes's immortal words, to be dragged screaming from the tart shop.

Tasmanian bluey A hard-wearing jacket for outdoor work
[**1891** Wilberton Tilley *The Wild West of Tasmania* 29: For about half a mile from the Silver Queen workings Zeehan is very thickly populated . . . Heavily laden drays, pack-horses and mules, form constant processions journeying to or from Dundas and Trial; miners with their swags, surveyors in their 'blueys'.]
1934 Thomas Wood *Cobbers* 86: Axemen . . . dressed in the manner of the craft – a slouch hat, trousers tucked into heavy boots, and a seamless coat of 'Tasmanian bluey', cut low round the neck and under the arms.

Tassie (Tassy) Tasmania; a Tasmanian [abbr.]
1894 *The Argus* 26 Jan. 3: Today Tassy – as most Victorian cricketers and footballers

familiarly term our neighbour over the straits – will send a team into the field. [Morris]

1915 Henry Lawson 'Fighting Hard' *Verse* iii 154: Fighting hard for little Tassy, where the apple orchards grow.

1963 Bruce Beaver *The Hot Summer* 61: 'Maybe Perth, eh? Or Tassie?'

1976 Helen Hodgman *Blue Skies* 11: 'I've come over from the mainland to give it a go in Tassie.'

Tatt's Tattersall's sweep, first promoted on the Sydney Cup in 1881 by George Adams, proprietor since 1878 of Tattersall's Hotel in Pitt St Sydney (on the model of subscription being conducted by Tattersall's in London)

1908 Henry Fletcher *Dads and Dan between Smokes* 51: 'Ther white savage plays two-up; a little better, he puts half-a-crown on ther tote; a little better, he sends a crown to Tatt's.'

1926 K. S. Prichard *Working Bullocks* 69: 'I says, "my intentions is honourable, and my prospeks – a ticket in Tat's".'

1934 *A Ticket in Tatt's* [title of film directed by F. W. Thring, screened Melbourne, Brisbane and Sydney from 6 Jan.]

1945 Tom Ronan *Strangers on the Ophir* 156: 'If we were living in a story-book, it would be simple. I'd find another Broken Hill, or win Tatts, or be discovered by a rich uncle.'

1983 *Bulletin* 26 Jul. 101: Said Paul Harris: 'It's a bit like winning Tatt's.'

taws The initial or basic position, esp. in such figurative expressions as 'right from taws', 'back to taws' [f. *taw* a marble, and the line from which play starts OED 1740]

1951 Dymphna Cusack and Florence James *Come In Spinner* 155: 'Sometimes I think we ought to shoot all the politicians and start right back from taws.'

1964 H. P. Tritton *Time Means Tucker* 18: I was under the impression that it was to be the usual sparring match, but he came at me from taws.

1977 Colleen Klein *The Heart in the Basket* 99: 'I'd gather a bunch of young architects ... and I'd start from taws.'

1985 *Sydney Morning Herald* 27 May Guide 15: If it comes down to taws, they still do make films like that from time to time.

taxi, black see **black taxi**

taxidermist, see a Get stuffed

1969 A. W. Fadden *They Called Me Artie* 39: On the Saturday before election day I met my old friend Ted Walsh who was also my opponent ... On the wall of the bar an expertly preserved crocodile was displayed ... Nellie ... asked how I expected to fare against Ted on polling day. I replied, 'I expect that Ted will do to me what the taxidermist has done to your poor crocodile.'

1981 *Australian* 10 Oct. 15: Earlier this year he [Mr Muldoon] suggested that the President of Nigeria, Mr Shagari, should see a taxidermist.

tea-and-sugar burglar A swagman who begs or 'borrows' tea and sugar; a minor predator

1899 Henry Lawson 'A Rough Shed' *Prose* i 463: 'Could I explain that I "jabbed trotters" and was a "tea-and-sugar burglar" between sheds.'

1956 Tom Ronan *Moleskin Midas* 165: 'We're pulling off a big job soon ... We'll make these tea-and-sugar bushrangers around this shanty look like a mob of schoolgirls.'

1967 *King's Cross Whisper* (Sydney) xli 4: *Tea and Sugar Bandit*: A petty thief. Usually the type of person who is too lazy to work and too frightened to steal large quantities of other people's goods.

see **frying-pan**

tea and sugar train Weekly train across the Nullarbor from Cook, S.A. to Parkeston, W.A. to service the fettlers and railway communities on the Trans-Australia line

1937 Ernestine Hill *The Great Australian Loneliness* 225: The 'Trans' and its people are a little world sufficient to themselves ... with a weekly shopping orgy on the 'Tea and Sugar' train that brings their water and supplies.

1980 *Daily News* (Perth) 11 Nov. 3: Paddy has been a fettler on the trans-line for more than 20 years. His only regular contact now with people is when the 'tea and sugar' train makes a brief stop near his house once a week, to supply him with food.

Teddy Bear A show-off, esp. a cricketer given to antics on the field [? rhyming slang for *lair* q.v.]

1953 Baker 135: *teddy bear* A flashily dressed exhibitionistic person; by rhyme on *lair*.

1965 Wally Grout *My Country's 'Keeper* 55: Umpire Col Egar was so furious at this

327

amateurish attempt at time-wasting that he snapped to the Pakistani bowler: 'Get up you Teddy Bear' (an Australian expression not meant to be complimentary).

1974 Keith Stackpole *Not Just for Openers* 128: When Parfitt made the catch Greig jumped in the air, and, as he landed, thumped his fist into the pitch . . . I said to Greig as I walked past, 'You're nothing but a bloody Teddy Bear.' He returned the pleasantries.

telegraph, bush see **bush**

tell the time if the town hall clock fell on top of him, couldn't see **couldn't**

ten, ten, two, and a quarter A week's rations in the outback: ten pounds of flour, ten of meat, two of sugar, and a quarter-pound of tea (the quantities might vary within this framework)

1867 John Morrison *Australia As It Is* 175: The rations for one man are the well-known weekly allowance of 10 lbs. of flour, 10 lbs. of meat, 2 lbs. of sugar, and a quarter of a pound of tea.

1903 Joseph Furphy *Such is Life* (1944) 104: He [the boundary rider] has some hundreds of pounds lent out (without interest or security) though his pay is only fifteen shillings a week – with ten, ten, two, and a quarter.

1956 Tom Ronan *Moleskin Midas* 332: 'Give me a humpy down there on the creek and feed me on the old ten, ten, two and a quarter.'

Tench The convict barracks in Hobart: *obs.* [abbr. of *Penitentiary*]

1859 Oliné Keese *The Broad Arrow* ii 432: 'Prisoners' barracks, sir – us calls it Tench.'

1864 J. F. Mortlock *Experiences of a Convict* (1965) 89: The Prisoners' Barracks (commonly called the 'Tench') became the abode of myself and hundreds more, who earned our food and lodging by stone-breaking, or other public labour.

tent embassy see **embassy**

tent, were you born in a Reproach to someone who has come in leaving the door open [Partridge lists *born in a barn* Canadian]

1959 H. D. Williamson *Sammy Anderson Commercial Traveller* 224: They, too, turned sorrowfully away, the last leaving the doors open . . . 'There's some people that was born in tents,' Tossington murmured testily.

1979 *Sun-Herald* 11 Nov. 119: Now that the Olds are liberated, they'll probably stop locking doors. 'What were you, born in a tent?'

Territorian 1 An inhabitant of the Northern Territory

1882 William J. Sowden *The Northern Territory As It Is* 41: Past the racecourse – for the Territorians attempt races between the animated clothes-horses dubbed equines here – you come to Sailor's Gully.

1930 J. S. Litchfield *Far-North Memories* 57: Unfortunately, a number of Territorians considered they had a right to take forcible possession of any lubra that suited their fancy.

1968 Frank Hardy *The Unlucky Australians* 11: 'The old Territorian is a good bloke, rough as guts but his heart's in the right place.'

1982 *Australian* 15 May 3: Each Territorian annually guzzles an average of 931 glasses of beer, 25 bottles of wine and 125 nips of hard spirits – a consumption twice the national average.

2 A resident of the A.C.T.

1981 *Canberra Times* 24 Jun. 21: The discovery that there is nascent shelter [from nuclear fallout] for 35,874 Territorians, or at best 150,911 of us is not especially cheering since there were 197,622 Territorians alive and kicking when the 1976 census was taken and may very well be 240,000 of us now.

Territory, the The Northern Territory

1882 William J. Sowden *The Northern Territory As It Is* 48: Capital and skilled labour must be the watch-word for the Territory.

1898 A. B. Paterson *Bulletin* 31 Dec. 31: The man who once goes to the Territory always has a hankering to get back there.

1930 J. S. Litchfield *Far-North Memories* 207: It is the exception to find the man who does not drink to excess in the Territory.

1981 *Australian* 22 Jul. 3: I was mystified by the bowl in the men's pissoir being way off-centre on its cubicle wall. Why? Denis Hornsby . . . explained: 'So the users who are, ah, tired can lean against the wall.' They look after drinkers in the Territory.

Territory confetti

1982 *NT News* (Darwin) 14 Jan. 7: It's called 'Territory confetti' and it's scattered around the countryside . . . the ring-pull tops from stubbies and cans.

Territory factor
1983 *NT News* (Darwin) 11 Jan. 7: Most of us have heard of the Territory factor – the indefinable excuse for charging more.

Territory rig
1983 *Australian* 4 Nov. 7: Mr Yunupingu, in what the tourist brochures call 'Territory rig' – open-neck shirt, shorts and long white socks.

that Used to express qualification, tentative addition to a statement (cf. **like**)
1965 D'Arcy Niland *The Apprentices* 95: 'I'll tidy up the room for you, wash the curtains and that.'
1974 Keith Stackpole *Not Just for Openers* 22: Not patting ourselves on the back or that, I think the only sound sides over the last couple of years have been the sides chosen on tour. They've been chosen on form.
1980 Rod Ansell *To Fight the Wild* 54: There wasn't much bush tucker in the area around my camp, in the way of fruit or that.

that'll be the day see **day**

they were open see **open**

thirds, on See quots
1824 E. Curr *An Account of the Colony of Van Diemen's Land* 77–8: It is common practice for persons who have not sufficient land, or who cannot attend personally to their flocks, to give them in charge to another party, who receives one third of the increase for his trouble.
1843 Charles Rowcroft *Tales of the Colonies* ii 109: I had prevailed on him to purchase . . . a hundred ewes heavy with lamb, and to put them out 'on thirds'.

Thommo's A notorious two-up school operating near Sydney [f. Joe Thomas, the organizer]
1957 *Bulletin* 28 Aug. 57: Thomo's is almost as old and exclusive as any up-town, Bligh Street club. New members have to be recommended, screened and flash a fair-sized roll. No sheilas, either.
1976 *Sunday Telegraph* (Sydney) 13 Jun. 12: Police raid Thommo's: 15 charged on two-up. Thommo's two-up school, the most famous and longest lasting game in Sydney, was raided by police early yesterday . . . Thommo's two-up school was established

during World War II and has flourished ever since. Successive police commissioners have denied the two-up school's existence, claiming it was a 'press myth'.
1981 *Sydney Morning Herald* 26 Dec. 3: Police have obtained a court order making Thommo's two-up school a 'declared gaming house' . . . Police had recently made five raids on the first floor premises at 179 Oxford Street, Darlinghurst.

throat, to have the game by the To be in full control, in a position of advantage
1947 John Morrison *Sailors Belong Ships* 15: 'We're sailors, see? Two sailors. We got the game by the throat.'
1960 Ron Tullipan *Follow the Sun* 105: 'Think we'll get it done to-day?' 'Can't miss . . . We have it by the throat now all right.'
1974 David Ireland *Burn* 58: 'So you got the game by the throat, eh?'

throw a map see **map**

throw a seven see **seven**

throw one's hat in first see **hat**

throw off To deride, ridicule; superseded by **sling off** q.v.
1812 Vaux: *Throw off* To talk in a sarcastic strain, so as to convey offensive allusions under a mask of pleasantry, or innocent freedom; but, perhaps, secretly venting that abuse which you would not dare to give in direct terms.
1911 E. S. Sorenson *Life in the Australian Backblocks* 247: Some hard case is bound to 'throw-off' at him at such times.
1935 Kylie Tennant *Tiburon* 190: 'You're not being funny are you? Sort of throwing off?'
1962 Dymphna Cusack *Picnic Races* 183: 'You're like all the townies. Throwing off at people on the land.'

thumbnail dipped in tar, written with a Catchphrase for rough penmanship, from Paterson's 'Clancy of the Overflow'
1895 A. B. Paterson *The Man from Snowy River* 20: And an answer came directed in a writing unexpected / (And I think the same was written with a thumb-nail dipped in tar); / 'Twas his shearing mate who wrote it, and *verbatim* I will quote it: / 'Clancy's gone to Queensland droving, and we don't know where he are.'

1984 Phillip Adams *Australian* 28 Apr. Mag. 2: My attention turned to home and, dipping my thumb nail in tar, I managed, I think, to evoke the cultural, social and spiritual reality for a typical suburbanite [in writing 'I Love this Bonzer Country' as a new national anthem].

Thursday or Anthony Horderns An equivalent to **Pitt Street or Christmas** or **Tuesday or Bourke Street** q.v. [f. the former Sydney retail store]
1982 Nancy Keesing *Lily on the Dustbin* 127: More to the point is her brother's remark that she'd 'forget her head if it wasn't screwed on'. Her aunt sums up: 'You wouldn't know if it was Thursday or Anthony Horderns.'

tickets, to have ~ on oneself To be conceited [? f. sales tickets advertising a high price, or prize certificates at a show]
[**1915** C. J. Dennis *The Songs of a Sentimental Bloke* 28: 'E's taken tickets on 'is own 'igh worth; / Puffed up wiv pride.]
1941 Kylie Tennant *The Battlers* 20: 'Arr,' the busker said disgustedly, 'you've got tickets all over yourself.'
1953 Gwen Meredith *Beyond Blue Hills* 84: 'I know I'm not in the same class as Danny Marks,' he announced, 'I haven't got any tickets on myself.'
1970 Jack Hibberd *White with Wire Wheels* in *Plays* 227: 'You're the bastard that's always been smug and had tickets on himself.'

tiger A toiler in a shearing-shed; any one doing rough work
1897 Henry Lawson 'The Green-hand Rouseabout' *Verse* i 322: Engine whistles. 'Go it, tigers!' and the agony begins.
1956 F. B. Vickers *First Place to the Stranger* 135: 'You're going to see something now ... Those tigers (he meant the shearers) will make you dance.'
1959 C. V. Lawlor *All This Humbug* 23: 'If you don't mind, Missus, I'd like to be sure I'm not drinking out of the same cup as the new "Tiger".'

tigering Working hard under adverse conditions; roughing it
1880–1904 'The Banks of the Condamine' *Old Bush Songs* ed. Stewart and Keesing (1957) 257: Your delicate constitution / Is not equal unto mine, / To stand the

constant tigering / On the banks of the Condamine.
1973 Roland Robinson *The Drift of Things* 385: He was a well-built young man, and a good worker as I was to find out; but then I had done my share of tigering and I reckoned I could hold my own.

tiger country Rough, thickly wooded terrain feared by airmen; any primitive area
1945 Elisabeth George *Two at Daly Waters* 89: The territory a hundred and sixty miles west of Daly Waters and thence to the Western Australian coast is also dreaded by aviators and generally called by them 'tiger country'. Dwellings are from eighty to a hundred miles apart and there are no recognizable landmarks for the flyer who is bushed.
1961 George Farwell *Vanishing Australians* 20: A Kimberley settler in the undeveloped 'tiger country', away on the wrong side of the rough-shod King Leopold Range.

tiger, for work (punishment) A 'demon' for work, someone with an insatiable appetite for it
1896 *Bulletin* 24 Oct. Red Page: His father thought a lot of Henry; he used to call him a tiger for work.
1935 William Hatfield *Black Waterlily* 15: 'Tiger for work, aren't you?' he smiled. 'A good fault, of course, if you don't carry it to extremes.'
1959 Dorothy Hewett *Bobbin Up* 79: 'He's a real tiger for his tucker,' Linnie said, smiling wanly through her tears.
1965 Eric Lambert *The Long White Night* 74: I patted her shoulder. 'Mum, you're a tiger for punishment!'

tiger, Tantanoola see **Tantanoola**

Tigers, the 1 In N.S.W., the Balmain Rugby League team [f. black and gold colours, and club emblem]
1976 *Sun-Herald* 13 Jun. 52: Tigers' semi-final spot is on the line.
2 In Victoria, the Richmond A.F.L. team
1974 *Sunday Telegraph* (Sydney) 29 Sep. 108: Tigers knock the knockers.
3 In W.A., the Claremont Australian Rules team
1980 *West Australian* (Perth) 19 May 60: Runaway Tigers swamp Demons [heading] Claremont kicked their highest score for the season against Perth at Lathlain Park on Saturday.

4   In S.A., the Glenelg Australian Rules team
   1979 *Advertiser* (Adelaide) 23 Apr. 13: Roosters' full back cages Tigers [heading]
5   In Queensland, the Easts Rugby League team
   1979 *Courier-Mail* (Brisbane) 19 Apr. 21: Tigers captain-coach Des Morris confirmed that some of his players had complained of being bitten.
   The Mayne Australian Rules team
   1979 *Courier-Mail* (Brisbane) 28 May 18: It was a disappointing performance from the Tigers, who . . . succumbed to the Kedron onslaught in the third quarter.
6   In N.T., the Nightcliff Australian Rules team
   1979 *NT News* (Darwin) 17 Nov. 40: Tigers skin safe Too strong for Buffs [heading]
7   In Tasmania, the Hobart Australian Rules team
   1980 *Mercury* (Hobart) 31 Mar. 28: The Tigers show that old snarl [heading]

Tilly Devine   Wine [rhyming slang]
   1953 T. A. G. Hungerford *Riverslake* 35: 'Right now, he'd give you half next week's pay for a snort of Tilly Devine, I bet!'

time, couldn't tell the   see **couldn't**

timothy   A brothel
   1953 Baker 124: *timothy* A brothel.
   1967 *King's Cross Whisper* (Sydney) xli 4: *Timothies*: Houses in areas where if the rent is paid two weeks in a row the law calls round to see where the money came from.
   1982 *NT News* (Darwin) 8 May 9: There were 17 men in the 'Timothy' when it 'went off'.

tin-arsed, tin-back, tin-bum   Lucky, a lucky person [? f. being impervious to kicks in the backside. Apparently unrelated to *tin* = money]
   1899 W. T. Goodge *Hits! Skits! and Jingles!* 150: And a 'tin-back' is a party / Who's remarkable for luck.
   1955 D'Arcy Niland *The Shiralee* 142: 'I come up with a stone worth five hundred quid . . . Tin-bum, they call me.'
   1971 R. F. Brissenden *Winter Matins* 25: This tin-arsed character / Hasn't there been six months before he starts / To fidget, gets to grizzling in his beer.
   1975 Les Ryan *The Shearers* 79: 'Good on yer Joe. You always were a tin-arse.'

tin-kettle, tin-kettling   The beating of dishes, etc. to celebrate a wedding or similar event
   1892 Barcroft Boake 'Babs Malone' *Bulletin* 20 Feb. 21 repr. in *Where the Dead Men Lie* (1897) 103: What cheering and tin-kettling / Had they after at the 'settling'.
   1900 Henry Lawson 'The Songs They Used to Sing' *Prose* i 380: They married on the sly and crept into camp after dark; but the diggers got wind of it and rolled up with gold-dishes, shovels &c. &c., and gave them a real good tin-kettling in the old-fashioned style.
   1931 A. W. Upfield *The Sands of Windee* 39: 'I hope you haven't forgotten that we are to tin-kettle the Fosters tomorrow night.'
   1964 *Sydney Morning Herald* 25 Apr. 11: At Dalton . . . a few weeks back there was a 'tin kettling' (first night after the honeymoon neighbours surround the house and bang tin utensils.)

tin, kick the   see **kick**

tinlid   A kid [rhyming slang]
   1954 T. A. G. Hungerford *Sowers of the Wind* 254: 'You got any tin-lids that you know of?'
   1968 Stuart Gore *Holy Smoke* 110: *tin-lid* A 'kid'; a child.
   1983 Barry Dickins *Australian Book Review* Jul. [inside front cover]: It says in the foreword that Bruce used to help out at his Dad's orchard as a tinlid.

tinned dog   Canned meat
   1895 *Bulletin* 17 Aug. 27: We gave him some 'tinned dorg' and a drink.
   1922 Edward Meryon *At Holland's Tank* 28: The jam stood on the table in its original tin, and the 'tinned dog' or tinned meat, was served likewise.
   1950 Gavin Casey *City of Men* 326: 'We'll be living in a tent and eating tinned dog. It's no place for a woman.'
   1964 Nancy Cato *The Sea Ants* 13: The welcome change in diet, with fried fish instead of tinned-dog on the menu, only whetted their appetites for more.

tinnie   1   A can of beer, usu. 375 ml
   1964 Barry Humphries *A Nice Night's Entertainment* (1981) 79: We all shacked up there with stacks of the old *glühwein*, a few crates of tinnies, a couple of little snow bunnies and no complications.
   1978 *Sunday Telegraph* (Sydney) 19 Mar.

331

35: Low-price 'tinnies' woo drinkers away from bottles.
1984 *Alice Springs Star* 7 Aug. 15: With ice cold tinnies at only $1 a good raging crowd is certain.
2 A boat with an aluminium hull (instead of fibreglass)
1979 *Herald* (Melbourne) 7 Jun. 35: The aluminium 'tinnie' has long been a major force in the Australian boat market for its low initial cost, durability and ease of use.

tinny *adj.* As for **tin-arsed**
1919 W. H. Downing *Digger Dialects* 50: *Tinny* Lucky.
1950 Jon Cleary *Just Let Me Be* 54: 'Your mother won again, Joe. Six pounds.' 'She's tinny,' Joe said.
1981 Rev. Fred Nile *Sun-Herald* 27 Sep. 9: 'I developed a technique and skills in gambling and I reckon I could still win a lot of money. As it is, I'm what you might call tinny. The only time I ever pulled the handle of a poker machine after I was converted, I won a jackpot.'

tin, ring the see **ring**

Tinsel Town Sydney, esp. from a Melbourne standpoint [f. parallel with Hollywood]
1981 *National Times* 29 Mar. 38: Seems Tinsel Town won't support elegant theatre restaurants. The Tivoli cabaret in George St, Sydney closed after two months. Pinks in Goulburn Street . . . is languishing.

to and from A Pom i.e. Englishman [rhyming slang]
1946 Rohan Rivett *Behind Bamboo* 399: *To-and-from* A Pommy, i.e. Englishman.
1978 *Daily Telegraph* (Sydney) 11 Mar. 17: The to-and-froms speak in a most peculiar way.
1982 *Australian* 6 Mar. Mag. 8: As a 'To-and-From', one of the things that baffled me . . . when I first arrived here many years ago was the esky routine.

toastrack A tram with external footboards instead of an internal corridor (discontinued in Sydney by 1960) [f. resemblance]
1941 Baker 77: *Toastrack* One of the old-style footboard trams still used in Sydney.
1961 Hugh Atkinson *Low Company* 113: The tram stop opposite where the faithful got down after riding the toast-rack trams from the smart areas uptown.

1973 *Bulletin* 17 Nov. 44: Visitors there [the Sydney Tram Museum at Loftus] can ride on an authentic toastrack for 15 cents (children 10 cents).

toby 1 A raddle stick for marking sheep not shorn to the employer's satisfaction
1912 'Goorianawa' *The Lone Hand* 1 Oct. 30 repr. in *Old Bush Songs* ed. Stewart and Keesing (1957) 273: I've been shearing on the Goulburn side and down at Douglas Park, / Where every day 'twas 'Wool away!' and toby did his work.
1964 H. P. Tritton *Time Means Tucker* 41: Till the 1902 strike, the owner had the right to raddle any sheep not shorn to his satisfaction and the shearer would not be paid for it. (Raddle was a stick of blue or yellow ochre, also called 'Toby'.)
2 A 'dab' at something: *rare*
1941 Baker 77: *Toby* A man silly of mind and clumsy of hand, but willing to do whatever asked.
1944 Alan Marshall *These Are My People* 155: 'I'm not much chop on pies, but I'm a toby on puddin's.'

toe Speed, esp. in horse racing
1889 A. B. Paterson 'The Scapegoat' in *Singer of the Bush* (1983) 103: He had what the racing men call 'too much toe' for him.
1923 Con Drew *Rogues & Ruses* 163: 'He has got two horses in the Handicap, and is bemoanin' his fate that both can't win. They're both got plenty of toe, and they're got about equal weights.'
1951 Dal Stivens *Jimmy Brockett* 166: It made me feel real good to hear that engine. It sounded as though it had plenty of toe.
1983 *Sun-Herald* 23 Oct. 73: In Lawson and Hogg we have two penetrating fast bowlers who have enough 'toe' to keep any batsman honest.

toey 1 Restive, fractious, touchy [? pawing ground]
1945 Baker 135: *toey* Worried or anxious.
1969 Patsy Adam-Smith *Folklore of the Australian Railwaymen* 82–3: We were shunting at Marree and I had a toey crew on. I knew they had booze planted somewhere and they knew I knew.
1983 *Sydney Morning Herald* 14 Jan. 1: Mr Wran returned from Lord Howe Island one day earlier than scheduled because, as he put it, 'I get toey: I was anxious to get back to work'.

1973 Jack Hibberd *A Stretch of the Imagination* (1981) 43: 'A toey winger was rendered flat of foot by a long handball over his skull on to the half-forward line.'

tom, tom-tart A girl or woman. Not derogatory, but not used by women of themselves: *obsolescent* [? f. *tomrig* a strumpet OED 1668]

c. **1882** *The Sydney Slang Dictionary* 8: *Tom-tart* Sydney phrase for a girl or sweetheart.

1906 Edward Dyson *Fact'ry 'Ands* 55: 'There's a little tom in this flat who'd give er bit t' have you hers for keeps.'

1915 C.J. Dennis *The Songs of a Sentimental Bloke* 20: A squarer tom, I swear, I never seen, / In all me natchril, than this 'ere Doreen.

1933 Norman Lindsay *Saturdee* 181: 'Who's yer tom? She must be yer sweetheart. Why don't yer up an' kiss her?'

1951 Dal Stivens *Jimmy Brockett* 102: 'You did, darling,' one of the little social toms said. She was a nuggety little sheila.

tomahawk To cut sheep while shearing; to shear roughly

1859 Henry Kingsley *Recollections of Geoffry Hamlyn* ii 25: Shearers were very scarce, and the poor sheep got fearfully 'tomahawked' by the new hands.

1878 G. H. Gibson *Southerly Busters* 179: I'm able for to shear 'em clean, / And level as a die; / But I prefers to 'tommy-hawk', / And make the 'daggers' fly.

1898 Roland Graeme *From English to the Backblocks* 189: 'I don't want small numbers,' he replied once to a squatter, who had been boasting of the high tallies his shearers made, 'but I won't have my sheep tomahawked.'

1925 E. S. Sorenson *Marty Brown* 105: 'They do a bit o' tommyhawkin' at shearin' time, an lay up with gammy wrists about three days a week.'

Tomaris Sweep conducted in Darwin on the Melbourne Cup [f. Tom Harris, who founded it in 1934]

1979 *NT News* (Darwin) 6 Nov. 1: Darwin bookmaker Gerry Monck has won the Tomaris. His last minute decision to gamble on 2000 tickets instead of his usual 1000 has won him $10,000.

Tom Collins see **Collins**

toms tits, toms, the The shits [rhyming slang: different from the English use (Franklyn, Partridge) in being always in the plural, and in not occurring as a verb]

1944 Lawson Glassop *We Were the Rats* 67: 'Break it down,' said the corporal. 'You'll give these blokes the tomtits before they get their first lot of C.B.'

1964 Thomas Keneally *The Place at Whitton* 51: 'This place,' Raddles, some way down the hall, grunted, 'and this silence business. It gives me the toms.'

1989 *Sun-Herald* 11 Jun. TV Mag. 10: 'That bloody Laws! Cripes, he gives me the tomtits. Crawls to pollies and then hangs up on some poor sod from Blacktown who can't defend himself.'

tongs Hand shears [f. shape]

1908 W. H. Ogilvie *My Life in the Open* 36: Most of the ... sheds in Australia are now fitted with machinery, but in many are still to be found the old-fashioned shears, or 'tongs' as they are familiarly called.

1961 George Farwell *Vanishing Australians* 93: Back in Jackie Howe's day there were many good men who could cut their 300 a day 'with the tongs'.

tonk A man with un-masculine characteristics; a male homosexual, esp. in the passive role: *derogatory* [unexplained]

1941 Baker 77: *Tonk* A simpleton or fool (2) A dude or fop (3) A general term of contempt.

1964 George Johnston *My Brother Jack* 65: 'You've got to get rid of those sonky bloody cobbers of yours,' he said to me one night. 'The way you lot are heading you'll end up a bunch of tonks.'

1965 Hal Porter *Stars of Australian Stage and Screen* 280: During the last ten years or more, there have been imported a coterie of *untalented* English homosexuals, English tonks unheard of outside their home country, to dominate sections of the Australian theatrical scene.

1970 Richard Beilby *No Medals for Aphrodite* 32: 'You're a good bloke, Turk, but sometimes you talk like a tonk,' one of them had told him in a moment of bibulous candour. And so he took care not to talk like a tonk ... Instead, he had adopted their sloppy, profanity-riddled speech.

Top End The northern part of the Northern Territory

1933 F. E. Baume *Tragedy Track* 93: She

looked around, stayed one day, and left again for the more human ... regions of the Top End, where at least one could drink fresh water occasionally.
1945 Tom Ronan *Strangers on the Ophir* 37: 'Those Kimberley horse-buyers wouldn't give a fiver for Carbine unless you could show a receipt. And the top-end drovers do their own stealing.'
1975 *Bulletin* 30 Aug. 10: May I protest the use of the term 'Top End' ... as applied to parts of North Queensland? This term has long been used to refer to – and only to – that portion of the Northern Territory north of Katherine, including Arnhem Land. Long-time residents of this part of the continent commonly use it with a hint of pride and manage to instil into it some feeling of the remoteness and special character of the region.

Top-ender
1941 C. Barrett *Coast of Adventure* 14: The old Top-ender drank beer, which, to the men up there, is more desirable than iced nectar is to gods.

top-off *v. & n.* To inform to the police; an informer; *derogatory* [? f. *top* to put to death by hanging OED 1812]
1941 Kylie Tennant *The Battlers* 129: 'Who topped off Chigger Adams to the cops?' he shouted angrily.
1944 Lawson Glassop *We Were the Rats* 133: 'I haven't forgot ... how he pooled me with the Q.M. Just a top-off merchant, that's all he is.'
1966 Betty Collins *The Copper Crucible* 14: 'About four o'clock in the morning some top-off rings the cops.'
1970 Richard Beilby *No Medals for Aphrodite* 177: 'Go on, shout so they can all hear, you top-off bastard.'

top paddock, kangaroos in one's see **kangaroos**

Tothersider 1 A person from Van Diemen's Land (Tasmania), from the standpoint of the mainland
[**1855** William Howitt *Land, Labour and Gold* ii 362: Scenery precisely like hundreds of miles which I have seen 'on the other side', as they call Victoria, and as the Victorians call Van Diemen's Land.]
1903 Joseph Furphy *Such is Life* (1944) 276: The ancient t'other-sider [Vandemonian Jack] oscillated his frame-saw.

2 In W.A., a person from the eastern states
1896 Henry Lawson *Letters* 62: W.A. is a fraud ... The old Sand-gropers are the best to work for or have dealings with. The Tothersiders are cutting each other's throats.
1950 K. S. Prichard *Winged Seeds* 30: 'Unemployed from all over the country swarmin' here, t'other siders as well as W.A. blokes.'
1963 Xavier Herbert *Disturbing Element* 2: My parents ... were what were called T'othersiders, meaning people who had come to West Australia from the other side of the continent.

touch of them, a 1 sc. the 'rats', the d.t.'s
1900 Henry Lawson 'The Hero of Redclay' *Prose* i 302: 'He's boozin' again,' someone whispered. 'He's got a touch of 'em.' 'My oath, he's ratty!' said someone else.
2 sc. the shits
1944 Lawson Glassop *We Were the Rats* 30: 'You tell me you're licked just because you've taken one on the chin in the first round. You give me a touch of 'em.'
1962 Gavin Casey *Amid the Plenty* 53: 'This place gives me a touch of 'em,' said Lenny.

tough as fencing wire see **fencing wire**

towel up To give someone a thrashing, verbal or physical
[**1859** Hotten 111: *Towel* To beat or whip. In *Warwickshire* an oaken stick is termed a *towel ... Towelling* A severe beating.]
1923 Con Drewe *Rogues & Ruses* 128: 'And you think Matt Barker will towel up Jumbo Lewis ... He might if he had an axe.'
1957 Ray Lawler *Summer of the Seventeenth Doll* 34: 'The kid towelled him up proper.'
1973 Alexander Buzo *Rooted* 42: 'Gary got his big serve working, I chipped in at the net, and we were laughing. Towelled them up in no time.'

towie A tow-truck operator
1984 Robert Caswell *Scales of Justice* 38: 'Any of you towies got your Authorities signed?'
1988 *Sydney Morning Herald* 13 Apr. 7:

Len . . . has been a towie for 30 years and 'on call' continuously for the last nine.

town bike, the   see **bike**

town hall clock, couldn't tell the time if the ~ fell on top of him   see **couldn't**

town, to go to   As for **go to market** q.v.
1952 T. A. G. Hungerford *The Ridge and the River* 80: 'Malise was going to town on them about their fire.'
1961 Nene Gare *The Fringe Dwellers* 142: 'Went ta town on em, e did . . . E thinks that water got put on because he ticked off them pleecemen.'
1973 Henry Williams *My Love Had a Black Speed Stripe* 120: Rose came out of the house, all ready to go, and she had really been to town on herself. Lipstick, eyeshadow, high heels, the lot.

trac   An intractable prisoner [abbr.]
1967 *King's Cross Whisper* (Sydney) xli: 4: *Trac*: Intractible [sic] prisoner.
1978 Kevin Gilbert *Living Black* 237: 'They're used to treating the tracs with the rough stuff and it rubs off on to the other prisoners so they get it rough, too, although not as rough as the tracs.'
1984 *National Times* 1 Jun. 15: Like when they sent me to the tracs and the Blockhouse.

Track, the   The Stuart Highway, joining Darwin to the south
1965 *Australian* 28 Jan. 10: Maps may tell you the thousand miles long black ribbon linking Darwin with Alice Springs and the south is the Stuart Highway. But up here it is 'the Track' or 'the Bitumen'.
1984 *Age* (Melbourne) 16 Jun. Extra 11: They call the 1500 kilometres of bitumen south [of Darwin], the track.
see **Bitumen**

track, on the   As for **on the wallaby track** q.v.
1896 Henry Lawson 'Some Day' *Prose* i 138: 'I've been knocking round for five years, and the last two years constant on the track, and no show of getting off it unless I go for good.'
1935 Kylie Tennant *Tiburon* 74: 'See 'ere, Mr Sullivan, I'm on the track, an' I'm down an' out.'
1953 *Caddie A Sydney Barmaid* 255: It

would have been impossible for him to maintain the home on a dole ration . . . He was going on the track.* *On the track – Tramping the back country in search of work.
1965 Eric Lambert *The Long White Night* 12: His clothes clearly proclaimed him as a man who had been on the track, one of that tattered, aimless, wandering band which the Depression threw up, who moved from town to town in the bush, drew their dole and then were moved on by the police.

track with   To associate with, to cohabit with
1915 C. J. Dennis *The Songs of a Sentimental Bloke* 51: I swear I'll never track wiv 'er no more; / I'll never look on 'er side o' the street. Ibid. 126: *Track with* To woo; to go 'walking with'.
1933 Norman Lindsay *Saturdee* 239: 'Who are you trackin' with now?'
1954 T. A. G. Hungerford *Sowers of the Wind* 270: 'I bet it's that cross-eyed harlot he's been tracking with.'
track square with
1919 W. H. Downing *Digger Dialects* 50: *Track square* To pursue an amorous enterprise with honourable intentions.
1964 George Johnston *My Brother Jack* 161: 'He's been at me for years about how irresponsible I am, and the first time I come back with a girl I'm tracking square with, I get hoisted!'

Tracy   The cyclone which devastated Darwin on 25 December 1974
1977 *Australian* 3 Sep. Mag. 5: John Waters explains how his house is three storeys high: 'It's the only one in Darwin. After Tracy everyone was building down, but I thought we'd go up as a mark of defiance.'

train a choko vine over a country dunny, couldn't   see **couldn't**

train, tea and sugar   see **tea**

tram, on the wrong   Following the wrong tactics, mistaken, astray
1955 John Morrison *Black Cargo* 223: 'No, son, you're on the wrong tram with me.'
1982 *Bulletin* 19 Jan. 27: What McMahon will be telling his former parliamentary colleagues is that the Fraser Government is, in his judgment, on the wrong tram economically.

trammie A tram conductor or driver [abbr.]

1946 Margaret Trist *What Else is There?* 229: 'A blue uniform, that's air force, isn't it?' 'It depends,' replied Alf cautiously. 'Maybe it was a trammie.'

1959 Dorothy Hewett *Bobbin Up* 1: Shirl had a glimpse of the trammie, swinging on the footboard.

1963 Gunther Bahnemann *Hoodlum* 146: 'There won't be much dough in a trammie's bag, Rob. Shillings, pennies, and so on.'

tramp To give someone the sack: *rare*

1941 Baker 78: *Tramped* Dismissed from employment.

1953 T. A. G. Hungerford *Riverslake* 109: 'If you come in tanked at tea-time, he'll tramp you, sure as your ring points to the ground!'

1975 Les Ryan *The Shearers* 128: 'The next day I managed to get the pen I was offered, but only after another shearer had been tramped.'

trap A policeman; in the nineteenth century, esp. a mounted policeman: a survival in Australia of English thieves' slang ('One whose business is to 'trap' or catch offenders; a thief-taker; a detective or policeman; a sheriff's officer' 1705 OED)

1812 Vaux 274: *Traps* Police officers or runners, are properly so called; but it is common to include constables of any description under this title.

1853 John Rochfort *Adventures of a Surveyor* 72: If he is taken by the 'traps', he will be sent to prison handcuffed to a common felon.

1882 Rolf Boldrewood *Robbery Under Arms* (World's Classics 1949) 2: Our 'bush telegraphs' were safe to let us know when the 'traps' were closing in on us.

1945 Tom Ronan *Strangers on the Ophir* 229: 'I never thought I'd offer to shake hands with a trap, but give me a hold of your fist, Mike Devlin.'

1974 Ronald McKie *The Mango Tree* 146: They were sorry that Scanlon was dead and knew that he had been a good trap.

trap for young (amateur) players A hazard for the unwary

1944 G. H. Fearnside *Sojourn in Tobruk* 60: 'This nuptial bliss stuff will get you in every time. It's a trap for young players.'

1957 R. S. Porteous *Brigalow* 18: I said something about the broken step being dangerous. 'That's right,' he agreed. 'She's a trap for young players.'

1962 Gavin Casey *Amid the Plenty* 80: 'You look out for the hire-purchase, that's a trap for young players, these days.'

traveller A tramp seeking work in the outback, sometimes distinguished from the **swagman** and the **sundowner**, and sometimes classified with them; one of the itinerant unemployed in the depression

[**1859** Hotten 111: *Traveller* Name given by one tramp to another.]

1868 Marcus Clarke 'Swagmen' in *A Colonial City* ed. L. T. Hergenhan (1972) 33: I remembered at one station, situated on the main road for 'travellers', that the unhappy cook was 'put on the fire' by a crowd of these gentry.

1893 Henry Lawson 'Some Popular Australian Mistakes' *Prose* ii 24: Men tramping in search of a 'shed' are not called 'sundowners' or 'swaggies'; they are 'trav'lers'.

1910 C. E. W. Bean *On the Wool Track* 65: Once a year, for a month or two, on horses, bicycles, occasionally on foot, come by the 'travellers', shearers on their way from shed to shed.

1941 Kylie Tennant *The Battlers* 23: Any sergeant will tell you that the 'locals' – that is, the unemployed residing in the town – are bad enough. But the 'travellers' – meaning the men with track-cards who wander the country in search of work, getting their food-orders from declared 'dole stations' in towns fifty or sixty miles apart – the travellers are worse.

travelling, a fine day for See quot. 1951

1951 Ernestine Hill *The Territory* 306: 'It's a fine day for travellin',' they told him – the time-honoured phrase that all over the outback is notice to quit.

1962 David Forrest *The Hollow Woodheap* 214: He was going on a long, long journey, alone and torn in half, and . . . looking out at the morning, decided it was as good a day as any for travelling.

trawler See quot.

1947 C. K. Thompson *Yes, Your Honour!* xiv: The driver of the Black Maria, the 'trawler', or in polite language, the police patrol . . . offered me a lift from the police-station to the court.

tray (trey) -bit A threepenny piece (before decimal coinage, 1966)
1898 *Bulletin* 1 Oct. 14: 3d. a 'traybit'.
1911 Louis Stone *Jonah* 98: 'Well, a tray bit won't break me,' said Chook, producing threepence from his pocket.
1918 Harley Matthews *Saints and Soldiers* 103: Come, join the army, / Make no delay, / Front seats a deener, / Back seats a tray.
1949 Ruth Park *Poor Man's Orange* 68: She wanted to say something, to tell this silly old coot that what she knew about life could be written on a tray bit.

trays, tray-bits, the The shits [rhyming slang]
1952 T. A. G. Hungerford *The Ridge and the River* 24: 'Oscar's got a touch of the trays.'

treat with ignore see **ignore**

trick, can't take a To be constantly unsuccessful [f. card games]
1944 Lawson Glassop *We Were the Rats* 211: 'He tells us we might be Aussies but we can't take a trick. He says we got a canin' in Greece an' had to get out.'
1963 D. H. Crick *Martin Place* 192–3: 'Looks like curtains for you, pal. Can't take a trick.'
1977 *Bulletin* 5 Feb. 11: The ACTU leader can't take a trick.

Tricolours, the The Eastern Suburbs (N.S.W.) Rugby League team (also the Roosters)

trifecta A set of three successes, or exceptional events [f. *trifecta* betting, the selection of the first three place-getters in correct order]
1982 Nancy Keesing *Lily on the Dustbin* 62: A Sydney woman said of a friend's daughter that she had won the daily double but missed out on the trifecta: the young woman in question was having her wedding at the fashionable St Marks, Darling Point, the reception at the Royal Sydney Yacht Squadron, but had missed out on the honeymoon in Fiji.
1983 *Sun-Herald* 6 Mar. 130: If they're super Sloanes they'll have the trifecta – a wedding at St Mark's, the reception at THE Gold Club and a honeymoon in Fiji.
1984 *Bulletin* 20 Mar. 54: The south-west of New South Wales struck the trifecta last

week – the Riverina Merino Field Day, the opening of the duck season and a visit by Prime Minister Bob Hawke.

triss A homosexual
1967 Kylie Tennant *Tell Morning This* 157: 'Think I'm going round flapping my mouth to every silly triss that gets shoved in [the cell] with me?'
1982 Mike Carlton *Sydney Morning Herald* 4 Aug. 8: This is where Brideshead fails utterly; with the one exception of the scandalously trissy but minor character, Anthony Blanche, they are all such dreary people.

trissing
1989 Debbie Spillane *Sun-Herald* 11 Jun. 96: I've turned to ABC Radio and am enjoying listening to the likes of 'Johnners', Truman and Martin-Jenkins, trissing on about tea-cakes and passing trains as well as the cricket.

troppo Mentally or nervously affected by the privations of war service in the tropics; showing any signs of being similarly affected
1943 George Johnston *New Guinea Diary* 222: 'A man must be going troppo,' he remarks quietly.
1948 Sumner Locke Elliott *Rusty Bugles* in *Khaki, Bush and Bigotry* ed. Eunice Hanger (1968) 88: 'They're taking him to the psychiatric ward.' . . . 'What's that?' 'Where they take you when you go troppo.'
1973 Roland Robinson *The Drift of Things* 266: Cecil tried to give me advice against the boredom which gripped everyone in the Territory . . . 'Don't give way to going "Troppo", as most of our fellows do.'
1984 *Sydney Morning Herald* 16 Feb. 9: According to one person, 'Neville [Wran] is troppo about Barrie [Unsworth]. He is dedicated to stopping him.'

trot A sequence of chance events, esp. betokening good or ill fortune ('a good trot', 'a rough trot') esp. sporting
1911 Louis Stone *Jonah* 216: A trot or succession of seven tails followed, and the kip changed hands rapidly.
1922 Arthur Wright *A Colt from the Country* 147: 'Luck? Hang it, no. I'm having a bad trot. Lost to-day and again to-night.'
1949 Lawson Glassop *Lucky Palmer* 177: He was 'Lucky' Palmer, having a bad trot at the moment, admittedly, but still 'Lucky' Palmer.
1965 Wally Grout *My Country's 'Keeper*

166: Most Pressmen I have found to be good coves who will lay off a player having a bad trot.
see **spin**

truckie A truck (i.e. lorry) driver [abbr.]
1954 *Bulletin* 5 May 20: Carson . . . was heading back for Murrayford when the truckie found him with his head under the wheel-hub.
1983 *Sun-Herald* 25 Sep. 152: Because we think there is more to life than sitting around waiting for our men to come home we are forming the Truckies Wives' Association.

tube 1 The downtube in a shearing shed to which the hand piece is connected
1954 *Bulletin* 27 Jan. 25: 'Yeah, boy, it really is my last season on the tube (in the shearing game).'
1963 *Sydney Morning Herald* 17 Aug. 11: Get off the tube (out of the game) while you are young enough.
2 A can of beer; given currency by the Barry MacKenzie strip in the 1960s
1964 Barry Humphries *A Nice Night's Entertainment* (1981) 77: Oh, I was down by Manly pier / Drinking tubes of ice-cold beer / With a bucket full of prawns upon me knee.
1976 *Sydney Morning Herald* 25 Jun. 12: They said 'Good on yer mate. Good on yer. Have a tube.'

tucker, to make To gain an income sufficient only to cover such necessities as food
1861 Horace Earle *Ups and Downs* 336: 'Well, we shall perhaps make tucker* out of it,' was the reply . . . for diggers never like to let their neighbours know the extent of their luck. *Food.
1901 Henry Lawson 'The Golden Graveyard' *Prose* i 344: They 'drove' (tunnelled) inwards at right angles to the fence, and at a point immediately beneath it they were 'making tucker'; a few feet farther and they were making wages.
1944 Brian James *First Furrow* 8: They spoke to Tully and begged him to throw it in. They'd never make tucker, they said, on the job. They'd starve on it.

tucker bag, box The bag in which the itinerant carries his rations
1893 Henry Lawson 'Some Popular Australian Mistakes' *Prose* ii 24: The nose (tucker) bag hangs over the other shoulder

and balances the load nicely – when there's anything in the bag.
1908 W. H. Ogilvie *My Life in the Open* 52: The 'tucker box' is taken from one of the waggons, and there in the weird silence of the brooding Bush they take their evening meal.
1941 Charles Barrett *Coast of Adventure* 36: Old man Rogers enjoyed his supper, and stowed cold roast goose in the tucker-bag, for breakfast.

Tuesday or Bourke Street see **Bourke Street**

tug the coat see **coat**

turkey 1 A swag: *rare*
1912 G. H. Gibson *Ironbark Splinters* 6: So you 'pack' your bloomin' turkey.[1] and you take the northern train. [1]'Turkey' –a bushman's slang for 'swag', a bundle of blankets and clothes. The term is sometimes also applied to a pack-horse.
2 In 'plain turkey', 'scrub turkey' etc., a swagman who tramps the plain country, the scrub [f. the birds inhabiting these regions]
1955 Alan Marshall *I Can Jump Puddles* 152: Father had humped his bluey in Queensland and was familiar with the ways of swagmen. He always called them 'travellers'. The bearded men who kept to the bush he called 'Scrub Turkeys' and those came down from the plains he called 'Plain Turkeys'.
1973 Frank Huelin *Keep Moving* 178: *Scrub Turkey* Bagman who has gone Bush. Usually slightly mental or eccentric.

turkey, head over Head over heels [? f. *tuck* the stern of a boat OED 1625]
1906 Edward Dyson *Fact'ry 'Ands* 234: 'One was dumped down two flights, 'ead over tuck, with a fat punch.'
1915 C. J. Dennis *The Songs of a Sentimental Bloke* 43: 'E swallers lysol, throws a fancy fit, / 'Ead over turkey, an' 'is soul 'as flit.
1955 Alan Marshall *I Can Jump Puddles* 46: 'I knock Sir Frederick Salisbury, or whatever his name is, head over turkey into a clump of peacocks.'

turn out To become a bushranger
1875 Rolf Boldrewood *The Squatter's Dream* repr. as *Ups and Downs* (1878) 165: 'I'm not sure that you won't get off light. You have had the good luck not to have killed

anybody that I know of since you turned out.'
1899 G. E. Boxall *The Story of the Australian Bushrangers* 274: The reward offered for the capture of Thomas Clarke was raised to £1000, while £500 was offered for his brother John, who had just 'turned out'.

turps Liquor
1865 Henry Kingsley *The Hillyars and the Burtons* 294: 'They tossed for a go of turps and a hayband – I ask your ladyship's pardon, that means a glass of gin and a cigar.'
1962 J. Marshall and R. Drysdale *Journey Among Men* 84: The Sergeant alleged that Ah Fong was a notorious drunkard, forever on the 'turps'.
1973 John O'Grady *Survival in the Doghouse* 57: He's humping a dozen cans with him. Ice cold. And he gets a great welcome. Not only because of the turps, but because with him there we can have a four-handed game.
1982 *NT News* (Darwin) 13 Mar. 6: What about the rest who are going straight back on the turps the minute the stores do open?

twang Opium [unexplained]
1898 *Bulletin* 1 Oct. 14: Tobacco is 'snout', opium 'twang'.
1945 Tom Ronan *Strangers on the Ophir* 68: The honest Chinese limits himself to his one pipe of 'Twang' per night.
1961 Ion L. Idriess *Tracks of Destiny* 94: This Chinaman was a 'runner' carrying smuggled 'twang' (opium) from Port Darwin to his compatriots in at the Creek.

tweeds Pants
1954 T. A. G. Hungerford *Sowers of the Wind* 116–17 'I take my coat off every day, and it don't stop the flaming traffic!' 'Try taking your tweeds off, boof-head!'
1973 Alexander Buzo *Rooted* 85: 'Susan was a lovely girl. She never dropped her tweeds for anyone.'
1980 Murray Bail *Homesickness* 161: 'Should always lock the door, Shiel,' he said, giving his tweeds a hitch.

twenty-four door sedan A nightcart
1978 Encountered in conversation.

twisted sandshoe, head like a see **head**

twist top A beer bottle containing 250 ml

[f. type of seal, which may be used on other sizes also]

two bob The sum of money most often used in derogatory expressions like 'not worth two bob', 'two bob lair' [cf. U.S. 'two-bit']
1930 K. S. Prichard *Haxby's Circus* 226: 'Shares in Haxby's are not worth two bob, these days.'
1944 Lawson Glassop *We Were the Rats* 144: Bert was more the 'two-bob lair' type.
1958 H. D. Williamson *The Sunlit Plain* 257: 'Cunning, too – put it over his own cobbers – sell his wife fer two bob.'
1974 John Powers *The Last of the Knucklemen* 30: 'I don't get hustled into punch-ups with two-bob lairs.'
1984 *National Times* 23 Mar. 31: Curtis used to be a two-bob revolutionary, wearing a North Vietnam badge on his school uniform and clutching Martin Sharp's Oz.

two bob each way, to have Not to commit oneself to either of two courses of action; to seek to profit from all contingencies [f. horseracing]
1973 Max Harris *The Angry Eye* 186: I suspect our elegant French trading friends are having two bob each-way in the Australian sex-aid market.
1984 *Age* (Melbourne) 16 Jul. 12: Mr Hawke has gone down in my estimation also, he seems to want two bob each way on this one [abortion].

two bob watch see **watch**

two, four, six, eight; bog in, don't wait A mock grace, esp. used by children
1936 Encountered in conversation.
1975 Les Ryan *The Shearers* 45: Clarrie stood nearby ... disapproving of the two, four, six, eight, bog in don't wait, business going on.
1984 Helen Garner *The Children's Bach* 11: 'Two four six eight, bog in don't wait,' said Dexter.

two kilometre law Law in N.T. banning the drinking of liquor within 2 km of licensed premises, contentious because taken as curbing Aboriginal drinking in public places
1982 *Australian* 28 Aug. 13: It is known throughout the Territory as the two kilometre law, and it is due to come into force at the end of the month.
1984 *Bulletin* 10 Jul. 77: 'We had this

magic thing happen,' she [the Mayor of Alice Springs] explains. 'Eighteen months ago the government brought in the two-kilometre law which makes it illegal for anyone to drink in a public place within two kilometres of a licensed outlet. Overnight it changed Alice Springs from the real rubbish dump it was becoming.'

two-pot screamer see **screamer**

two-up A gambling game based on spinning two pennies, and wagering whether they fall as two heads or two tails
1898 W. T. Goodge 'Australia's Pride' *Bulletin* 3 Sep. 32: At 'loo he'd lately scooped the pool; / He'd simply smashed the two-up school.
1916 Official memo 10 Jan. cit. Patsy Adam-Smith *The Anzacs* (1978) 151: Gambling. The game known as Two-up is not to be played.
1932 Leonard Mann *Flesh in Armour* 57: Once a bookmaker's clerk, and now a two-up king.
1959 Vance Palmer *The Big Fellow* 65: 'He showed me how I could do something better for the other fellows than keeping the two-up ring for them on Sunday mornings.'
see **grouter, heading them, kip, spinner, swy**

tyke, tike A Roman Catholic: *derogatory*
1941 Baker 76: *Tike, tyke* A Roman Catholic.
1948 Ruth Park *The Harp in the South* 268: 'I'll do what I like when I like without the interference of any bone-headed tike.'
1969 Jon Cleary *Remember Jack Hoxie* 86: 'I'm like you, a Tyke. A Catholic.'

1983 Patrick White *Netherwood* 21: 'Don't want ter listen to any of yer tyke arguments.'

tyranny of distance, the Phrase applied by Geoffrey Blainey to the dispersion of settlement in Australia, and the difficulties resulting
1966 Geoffrey Blainey *The Tyranny of Distance* [book title]
1973 Henry Williams *My Love Had a Black Speed Stripe* 19: 'It is the tyranny of distance Ronald that makes the motor car such an important adjunct to living in this empty continent.'
1983 *National Times* 8 Apr. 15: A sense of isolation affects even long-time country residents. Few are immune to the tyranny of distance.

tyrants, the last of the Lachlan Macquarie, Governor of New South Wales 1809–22 (in old-fashioned school textbooks)

Tyson, hungry (mean, rich, independent) as Expressions referring to the millionaire pastoralist, James Tyson (1823–98)
1890 *Bulletin* 4 Oct. 11: 'Hungry' Tyson gave £2000 to the Sydney Royal Naval Home.
1928 Arthur Wright *A Good Recovery* 8: 'Th' old bloke's as rich as Tyson.'
1950 *Coast to Coast 1949–1950* 190: 'No more bunging a job in at a minute's notice and walking off with a billycan and a roll of blankets, as independent as Tyson.'
1962 Tom Ronan *Deep of the Sky* 30: He never subscribed to the 'hungry Jimmy Tyson' legend.

U

uey, do a To make a U-turn
1976 *Bulletin* 28 Feb. 27: Ted Heath, like Fraser, began as a professed opponent of big government but was soon 'doing a youee' (U-turn) all over the place.
1988 Ruby Langford *Don't Take Your Love to Town* 210: When we reached Botany Road we chucked a U-ey in front of the Clifton Hotel.

ugly as a hatful of arseholes see **hatful**

ump, umpy Umpire, esp. in Victoria [abbr.]
1958 *Bulletin* 3 Sep. 39: A lone 'outer' supporter ... bawled across the ground, 'Look after 'im, Umpy, 'e's the only mate y're got'.

1979 *Herald* (Melbourne) 2 Jun. 32: Umpy kicked: boy is outed [heading] A teenage footballer has been suspended until the 1981 season for kicking an umpire.
1981 *Sun-Herald* 18 Jan. 63: The ball was going so far down the legside Howarth must have thought someone had moved the stumps when he saw the umpy's finger go up.

uncle from Fiji see **Fiji**

underground mutton Rabbit, as an edible meat
1946 A. J. Holt *Wheat Farms of Victoria* 129: 'Underground mutton' (rabbit) is almost always available for those who like it.
1965 Eric Lambert *The Long White Night* 138: 'I thought a feed of underground mutton would go all right for my tea.'
1981 *Bulletin* 22 Dec. 206: The rifle was for rabbits: we ate a lot of underground mutton in the 30s.

under someone's neck, go see **neck**

uni The university
1962 Alan Seymour *The One Day of the Year* 103: 'I think I might ditch my course. Leave Uni.'
1977 *Sydney Morning Herald* 26 Feb. 21: Sydney Uni spends up to welcome its students.
1982 Tim Winton *An Open Swimmer* 16: 'The Uni, eh?' The old man grinned. 'They tell yer anything at the Uni?'

unlock the lands The cry of those seeking to break the monopoly given to the squatters by the Order-in-Council of March 1847, esp. after the goldrush
1855 Raffaello Carboni *The Eureka Stockade* ed. Geoffrey Serle (1969) 75: The licence fee, and especially the disreputable mode of collecting it at the point of the bayonet, were *not* the only grievances the diggers complained of. They wanted to be represented in the Legislative Council; they wanted to 'unlock the lands'.
1865 Henry Kingsley *The Hillyars and the Burtons* 325: There being undoubtedly a strong necessity to attend to the cry of 'unlock the lands', the Radicals brought in their bill.

up who, who's (and who's paying the rent) See quot. 1966: World War II slang

1966 Baker 172: *who's up who (and who's paying the rent)?* Just what is happening? Who's in control? e.g. 'Nobody knows who's up who' etc., said of a complete mess-up.
1970 Barry Oakley *Let's Hear it for Prendergast* 66: 'These days you don't know who's up who and who's paying the rent.'
1981 Maxwell Grant *Inherit the Sun* 356: It all had to do with who was up who, as far as Red could see, in this business world.

uphill In difficulty
1945 Tom Ronan *Strangers on the Ophir* 184: 'Peter'll be a bit uphill getting Luke out of the cooler, won't he?'
1954 T. A. G. Hungerford *Sowers of the Wind* 141: 'He'll certainly be uphill now, trying to stack Lefevre for leave.'
1978 *Sun-Herald* 15 Jan. 44: The Opposition . . . will be uphill in persuading the voters to reject this opportunity to have the Council democratically elected.

upside down, the hut that's The symbol of the strange aspect which Australia presented to the immigrant from the antipodes (Christmas in mid-summer, trees losing bark instead of leaves, etc.) with the underlying belief that the inhabitants on the bottom of the world must walk upside down [f. ballad with this refrain]
1957 *Old Bush Songs* ed. Stewart and Keesing 269: 'The Hut That's Upside-down' [ballad title]
1961 Judith Wright *Australian Letters* Jun. 30: The Upside-down Hut [essay title]

upside down, the only river in the world that flows The Yarra River, Melbourne, from its brownish water: *jocular*
1953 Baker 275: *The only river in the world that flows upside down* A reference to the River Yarra which flows through Melbourne.
1966 Jan Smith *An Ornament of Grace* 51: Bet you're from Melbourne, the only city in the world where the river flows upside down with the mud on top.
1982 *Age* (Melbourne) 11 Jun. 3: Getting wet in the Yarra means taking your chances with a river that many believe flows upside down. It means sinking into black mud up to a metre deep and finding the odd oil slick past your face.
see **Little Muddy**

upter No good at all [abbr. of 'up to putty' or 'up to shit']

1919 W. H. Downing *Digger Dialects* 52: *Upter* A corruption of 'Up to Putty'.

1951 Eric Lambert *The Twenty Thousand Thieves* 169: Go Through slapped Happy's shoulder. 'How are yer, Hap, old feller?' 'Up to shit' ['Upter' in 1963 edn], replied Happy.

1970 Richard Beilby *No Medals for Aphrodite* 174: 'How's the feet, Private Wilkinson?' 'Upta, sir. Can't get me boots on this mornin'.'

Urandangie, the girls are bandy at see **Tallarook**

urger 1 A race tipster who seeks a bonus from the winnings of others

1924 *Truth* 27 Apr. 6: *Urger* A fraudulent race follower.

1930 L. W. Lower *Here's Luck* 85: Tipslingers, urgers and whisperers slunk like jackals through the crowd.

1946 *Sun* (Sydney) 18 Aug. Suppl. 15: Bill's got more nerve than a Randwick urger.

1950 *Australian Police Journal* Apr. 120: *Urger* A nuisance on a racecourse who will prevail on a mug to back something, usually on the pretence that the urger's brother-in-law trains it, etc., or something similar, the object being that the mug might 'sling' if the horse wins.

1967 Frank Hardy *Billy Borker Yarns Again* 14: 'An urger is a bloke who slings out tips and asks for a cut if one of them wins.'

1981 *Sunday Mail* (Brisbane) 25 Oct. 11: Last week urgers were a problem at Eagle Farm.

2 Any parasite or loafer, who incurs no risk himself

1952 T. A. G. Hungerford *The Ridge and the River* 155: 'Come on, you urgers!' he muttered. 'Sooner we get goin', the sooner we get across.'

1964 George Johnston *My Brother Jack* 325: 'I'm not saying you're an *urger* or anything like that, but this recruiting stuff, well, it *is* sort of urging in a way, don't you think?'

1972 G. C. Bolton *A Fine Country to Starve In* 231: The farmers ... resented the intrusion of pickets and urgers who came in from outside the district and attempted to run their campaign for them.

useful A general factotum in a business, pub etc.

1866 Rachel Henning *Letters* ed. David Adams (1963) 219: There are three men employed about the place [a timber-logging business]. The bullock-driver, the puntman and a 'generally useful' man.

1898 Alfred Joyce *A Homestead History* ed. G. F. James (1969) 41: Our friends had met with a trained carpenter in town, whom with his wife they had hired for £20 a year, the man as general useful, which would include his trade employment, and his wife as cook for the proprietors.

1900 Henry Lawson 'Middleton's Peter' *Prose* i 261: There were two rooms, of a sort, attached to the stables – one at each end. One was occupied by a man who was 'generally useful'.

1935 Kylie Tennant *Tiburon* 37: Roman stepped out of the room next to the laundry of O'Brien's Hotel, where he was barman, yardman and general useful.

1953 *Caddie A Sydney Barmaid* 6: The Missus called the useful to take over. A fight had started in the front parlour and women were biting and scratching in one mad mix up.

1962 Criena Rohan *The Delinquents* 31: 'I met Paddy Murphy, you know the 'useful' at your pub, and he had a look at it.'

useful/useless, as ~ as an ashtray on a motorbike, a glass door on a dunny, a handbrake on a Holden, a hip pocket in a singlet, the Yarra

1984 *Sydney Morning Herald* 9 Feb. 14: Like a bridge under troubled waters or an ashtray on a motorbike, some things come easily to lateral thinkers.

1981 *National Times* 25 Jan. 23: As useless as a glass door on a dunny.

1976 Sam Weller *Bastards I have met* 2: He's about as useful as a pocket in a singlet.

1981 *National Times* 25 Jan. 23: 'As useless as the Yarra – too thick to swim in and too thin to plough!'

ute A utility (vehicle combining the features of a sedan and a truck) [abbr.]

1944 Stephen Kellen *Camp Happy* 11: The wheel twisted in my hand and the 'ut' veered sharply, heading straight for a tree.

1951 Eric Lambert *The Twenty Thousand Thieves* 178: 'He gets pissed one night, pinches a ute from the transport lines.'

1961 Jack Danvers *The Living Come First* 17: 'Take the ute and drive in to Alice. The wire we ordered has arrived.'

1981 Dorothy Hewett *Susannah's Dreaming* 13: 'I'll give y' a lift 'ome in me ute.'

V

vag, on the According to the provisions of the Vagrancy Act
1877 T. E. Argles *The Pilgrim* ii 21: She had got three months 'on the vag.' for making a sleeping place of a prominent doorstep.
1916 C. J. Dennis *The Moods of Ginger Mick* 28: If I don't work they'd pinch me on the vag.
1959 K. S. Prichard *N'Goola* 148: 'Was you in the game, love? Or did they get you on the vag?'
vag A vagrant
1895 Cornelius Crowe *The Australian Slang Dictionary* 91: *Vag* A vagrant.
1965 Xavier Herbert *Larger than Life* 40: 'We got a prisoner, eh?' The sergeant grunted. 'Just a vag.'

vagged, to be To be arrested under the provisions of the Vagrancy Act
1930 *Bulletin* 9 Jul. 28: 'We can't have the public's mind polluted by abusive language. You're vagged.'
1941 Kylie Tennant *The Battlers* 11: 'I been vagged,' the Stray mentioned. 'Oh! you have? Well, there you are. If you ain't got any money, they run you in.'
1972 David Ireland *The Flesheaters* 156: 'You can't go out alone and penniless *these* days . . . You can be vagged if you've got no money.'

Vandemonian *n. & a.* 1 Tasmanian [f. Van Diemen's Land, the original name of Tasmania]
1832 *The Currency Lad* 25 Aug. [2]: We are no advocates for the unlimited admission of Vandemonian wheat to our market.
1840 G. Arden *Australia Felix* 9: A shrewd old Vandemonian colonist.
1903 Joseph Furphy *Such is Life* (1944) 273: Vandemonian Jack, aged about a century, was mechanically sawing firewood in the hot, sickly sunshine.
2 An ex-convict from Van Diemen's Land
1855 Raffaello Carboni *The Eureka Stockade* ed. G. Serle (1969) 90: A sulky ruffian . . . [of] the known cast, as called here in this colony, of a 'Vandemonian', made up of low, vulgar manners and hard talk.
1899 G. E. Boxall *The Story of the Australian Bushrangers* 139: It was popularly supposed that these bushrangers were all convicts from 'Van Diemen's Land', hence they were known as 'Van Demonians', 'Derwenters' from the River Derwent, and 'Tother siders'.

Vaseline Valley See quot. 1982
1982 *Sydney Morning Herald* 10 Apr. 31: When Capriccios, or International Vanities as it was sometimes known, opened its doors in the early 1970s, it started the gay development along the stretch of Oxford Street that is now known as 'The Golden Mile', or, in a cruder vernacular form, as 'Vaseline Valley'.
1987 Kathy Lette *Girls' Night Out* 69: We were deep in the heart of Vaseline Valley, so I automatically pressed the 'Walk' button with my elbow.

Vee-dub A Volkswagen car [f. abbr. VW]
1970 Alexander Buzo *The Front Room Boys* in Penguin *Plays* 48–9: 'They've got all the defects of the Vee Dub fifteen hundred and none of its virtues'.
1981 *Sydney Morning Herald* 14 Feb. 40: 'It's got a little bit of rust but nothing major and like all Veedubs the engine just keeps on going.'

Vegemite Trade name of a yeast extract, with a status like that of the meat pie or the smell of gumleaves as something typically Australian
1980 Thomas Keneally in *Days of Wine and Rage* ed. Frank Moorhouse 249: It was . . . like seeing something tribal, Vegemite say, in the window of NSW House in the Strand.
1985 *Sydney Morning Herald* 9 Feb. 59: A few hours of conversation with Holmes a Court are more than enough to instil the conviction that he sees himself as being as Australian as Vegemite.

velvet, black see **black**

verandah (under the) An exchange market conducted on a city pavement, under an awning, in Victoria; title of a serial column in the Melbourne *Leader* from the 1860s: *obs.*

1868 Marcus Clarke *A Colonial City* ed. L. T. Hergenhan (1972) 18: The Victorian broker ... begins to be known, he is seen under the 'Verandah' [illustration on facing page], and lunches at the Criterion.
1873 A. Trollope *Australia* ed. Edwards and Joyce (1967) 403: The verandah is a kind of open exchange – some place on the street pavement apparently selected by chance, on which dealers in mining shares congregate. What they do, or how they carry on their business when there, I am unable to explain.
1898 Morris 489: Verandahs ... are an architectural feature of ... most city shops, where they render the sidewalks an almost continuous arcade. 'Under the Verandah' has acquired the meaning 'where city men most do congregate.'

Viceroy, the old Lachlan Macquarie, Governor of New South Wales 1809–22, so termed by his supporters after his resignation
1824 Michael Massey Robinson *The Colonist* 5 Feb. 1835 46: 'The Old Viceroy' [song title]

Vietnamatta The Cabramatta-Fairfield area, as populated by Indo-Chinese refugees
1981 *Sydney Morning Herald* 11 Feb. 10: 'Vietnamatta', or 'Saigon City', are the terms used by local people to describe the changing face of Cabramatta.
1982 *Sydney Morning Herald* 23 Sep. 7: A sign at Cabramatta station identifying the place has been crossed out and replaced by the word Vietnamatta. Vietnamese refugees have made a new home in Cabramatta. It's called Little Saigon by the locals.

village, the place for a The site of Melbourne, as indicated by John Batman in his diary after concluding an agreement with the Aborigines giving him possession of 500,000 acres in the vicinity of the Yarra Yarra, Port Phillip
1835 John Batman Diary MS [La Trobe Library] 8 Jun: This will be the place for a village.
1959 Barry Humphries *A Nice Night's Entertainment* (1981) 20: Who has not heard of his [Batman's] famous statement: 'This is the spot for a village', or 'This is the village for a spot', as they say in the classics.
1984 *Australian* 17 Nov. Mag. 8: 150

years later, is Melbourne a good place for a suburb? [heading]

Vinnie's The Society of St Vincent de Paul, as an outlet for used clothing, etc.
1984 *Sydney Morning Herald* 7 Sep. Metro 15: Cardier ... in a suit fresh from St Vinnie's and a hat pulled low like the gangster he sometimes portrays.
1984 *Southerly* 390: 'I'll go down to Vinny's and see what they've got.'

vision splendid, the Any splendid prospect, esp. of the future (from A. B. Paterson's 'Clancy of the Overflow' and Wordsworth's 'Immortality' ode)
1895 A. B. Paterson *The Man from Snowy River* 21: And he sees the vision splendid of the sunlit plains extended, / And at night the wondrous glory of the everlasting stars.
1954 Tom Ronan *Vision Splendid* [book title]
1959 Xavier Herbert *Seven Emus* 110: Such was his acting that he took in his audience along with himself, made them share his optimism, his vision splendid, even ... against their better judgement.
1972 Ian Moffitt *The U-Jack Society* 199: I sat obediently and listened, and Sir Phillip spread his vision splendid of electricity extended with nuclear power.
1984 Mike Carlton *Sydney Morning Herald* 21 Nov. 12: We were treated to the choking sob and the glint of a tear as the Prime Minister was overcome by his vision splendid of electoral gains extended.

Volvo set, the Well-to-do environmentalists, as described by Mr Barrie Unsworth, secretary of the N.S.W. Labor Council, in the debate over the logging of rainforests in N.S.W. in 1982
1982 Barrie Unsworth *Sydney Morning Herald* 22 Oct. 1: 'The phrase Volvo set was coined by Rod Muir of 2-Day FM to describe the chic, trendy set of the middle class. What I said to the Premier on Monday was that while he is looking after the Volvo set he didn't want to lose the support of the Holden Kingswood set.'
1982 *Sydney Morning Herald* 23 Oct. 12: The image often conjured up of people lounging on their Paddington patios, drinking white wine and feeling emotional about trees – the middle-class, Volvo set, in Unsworth's terms.

W

waddy A wooden club, often improvised [Ab. 1788 Ramson 126]

  1899 Steele Rudd *On Our Selection* 19: We each carried a kerosene tin, slung like a kettle-drum, and belted it with a waddy – Dad's idea.

  1930 K. S. Prichard *Haxby's Circus* 236: The men grabbed seats, started to smash them up, and use them as waddies.

  1947 Vance Palmer *Cyclone* 79: 'They're planning to march out to the camp some night and deal it out to the lot of us with waddies.'

  1973 Frank Huelin *Keep Moving* 114: 'The only ones who wait for us are railway demons with boots and waddies.'

wadgella A white man, in W.A. [pidgin version of *whitefellow*]

  1927 A. G. Bolam *The Trans-Australia Wonderland* 79: 'Waijela bool-ga munda?' (White fellow dig big earth?)

  1969 Lyndall Hadow *Full Cycle* 157: 'Sister Merry Christmas only Waigella[2]!' [2]Corruption of 'white fella'.

  1978 Nene Gare *Bend to the Wind* 126–7: 'Oh, my people. Loveliest people in the world. Easy ta get along with. Easy going. They must be or they wouldn't a put up with the wadgellas fa so many years.'

wage-plug A worker for wages [cf. *plug* a slow horse U.S. 1860 Mathews; *wage-slave* OED 1886]

  1918 George Dale *The Industrial History of Broken Hill* 206: The wage-plug on the surface is keeping in motion the machines of production.

  1921 *NSW Police News* 7 Dec. 41: He was a mercilessly down-trodden wage-plug.

  1931 Miles Franklin *Back to Bool Bool* 154: 'The Australian working-man is the richest wage-plug on God's earth, and the most leisured.'

  1983 *Newcastle Herald* 19 Apr. 2: This package of extras . . . makes sure that the actual level of salary is less important to the MP than it is to the ordinary wage plug.

Wagga blanket, rug A covering made from corn sacks, chaff bags or similar material [f. place-name Wagga Wagga, N.S.W.: otherwise unexplained]

  1893 Henry Lawson 'The Darling River' *Prose* i 86–7: The live cinders from the firebox . . . fell in showers on deck. Every now and then a spark would burn through the 'Wagga rug' of a sleeping shearer, and he'd wake up suddenly and get up and curse.

  1938 Xavier Herbert *Capricornia* 454: The nap . . . consisted of two greasy bransacks, or, as bushmen call them, Wagga Rugs.

  1951 Simon Hickey *Travelled Roads* 52: Any bush worker in the West knows that a Wagga rug is made by top-sewing two cornsacks together, which, with any sort of blanket underneath, would keep out the cold, or even rain, at a pinch.

  1983 John K. Ewers *Long Enough for a Joke* 92: It contained his bunk covered with a couple of new cornsacks which he called his 'wagga'.

Wagga grip see **monkey** 2

waigella see **wadgella**

waist, lady's see **lady's**

wake up to, to be a To be fully apprised of a situation; to be alert to possible deception [f. thieves' slang: see quot. 1812]

  1812 Vaux: *Awake* An expression used . . . as a thief will say to his accomplice, on perceiving the person they are about to rob is aware of their intention, and up on his guard, *stow it*, the *cove's awake*. To be awake to any scheme, deception, or design, means, generally, to see through it or comprehend it.

  1924 *Truth* 27 Apr. 6: *Awake* To know all.

  1932 Leonard Mann *Flesh in Armour* 237: She would see, then, that he was no fool, and take a full wake-up to it.

  1963 Alan Marshall *In Mine Own Heart* 64: 'The trouble is that Florrie's a wake-up to me. She doesn't believe half the lies I tell her.'

  1975 Xavier Herbert *Poor Fellow My Country* 592: 'I got a feelin' he's a wake-up. Still, don't worry. We'll beat him.'

Waler 'An Anglo-Indian name for an Australian horse imported from New South Wales into India, especially for the cavalry. Afterwards used for any horse brought from Australia.' (Morris)

1863 B. A. Heywood *Vacation Tour at the Antipodes* 134: I have heard men from Bengal talk of the 'Walers', meaning horses from New South Wales.

1983 *Australian* 9 May 9: In Sydney opposite the State Library stands a modest memorial to our 'gallant horses', the Walers of World War I, which carried our boys from the Pyramids to Jerusalem.

walkabout 1 Temporary migration from one's normal habitat (originally applied to the movements of Aboriginals); any journey away from a home base [Pidgin]

1828 *Sydney Gazette* 2 Jan. 3: When the executioner had adjusted the rope, and was about to pull the cap over his eyes ... he said, in a tone of deep feeling, which it was impossible to hear without strong emotion, 'Bail more walk about', meaning that his wanderings were all over.

1908 Mrs Aeneas Gunn *We of the Never-Never* 218: The day after that was filled in with preparations for a walk-about, and the next again found us camped at Bitter Springs.

1969 William Dick *Naked Prodigal* 10: 'Hold the fort men. I'm going walkabout,' yelled Arthur, throwing down his trolley with a clang.

1976 *Sydney Morning Herald* 17 May 6: His answers to questions were garbled and grammatically walkabout.

2 A 'meet-the-people' stroll by royalty or other notable (first used of Queen Elizabeth on 12 Mar. 1970 Auckland N.Z.)

1977 *Australian* 24 Mar. 5: A fair-haired 16-year-old girl ... was the other star of the walkabout. She presented the flowers then popped her head up and kissed the Queen on the cheek.

1986 *Australian* 13 Sep. Mag. 2: The Pope will do a 40-minute 'walkabout' among security-cleared people, many of them Aborigines, on his way to the podium.

3 A lapse in concentration (first applied to the tennis player Evonne Goolagong)

1985 *Sun-Herald* 17 Nov. 77: 'You could say I went walkabout in the second set,' Shriver said. 'I did an "Evonne".'

1990 *Sydney Morning Herald* 12 Jan. 37: Becker also went walkabout in his second set

against Masur. 'My concentration went somewhere else and I had trouble for two or three games,' he said.

walk off, do a walk To abandon a rural property through inability to make it pay

1939 Leonard Mann *Mountain Flat* 76 7: 'The one who doesn't get Suttons' will have to walk off.'

1958 E. O. Schlunke *The Village Hampden* 114: 'They're so much in debt that, if the Government Relief Board wasn't carrying them on, they'd all have to walk off their farms tomorrow.'

1970 *Sydney Morning Herald* 21 Jul. 6: The manager of the Bourke Rural Bank can recall four graziers who have 'done a walk', leaving the bank to use the properties as best it could to recover the graziers' debts.

Walla Walla, further behind than At a disadvantage [see quot. 1978]

1953 T. A. G. Hungerford *Riverslake* 161: 'Chuck over that pair of strides, will you – I'm further behind than Walla Walla.'

1967 Frank Hardy *Billy Borker Yarns Again* 19–20: 'Not much use backing a two-to-one winner at this stage. You're further behind than Walla Walla.'

1978 *Sydney Morning Herald* 21 Nov. 27: Walla Walla the great pacer after whom the phrase ... was coined because he won from seemingly impossible handicaps.

Wallabies, the The Rugby Union team representing Australia internationally [f. analogy with the Kangaroos, the Rugby League team]

1976 *Australian* 22 Oct. 20: Wallabies flop in the wet.

wallaby, on the ~ track Tramping the outback in search of work (as though following the track made by the wallabies)

1861 Horace Earle *Ups and Downs* 208: He had started on the Wallaby track* more than once. *Wallaby track – tramping in search of employment.

1887 *All the Year Round* 20 Jul. 66: He perambulates the country, going 'on the Wallaby', as it is strangely termed, nightly receiving the hospitality of the farmers and station-managers whom he honours with his presence.

1891 Henry Lawson *Verse* i 134: 'On the Wallaby' [poem title]

1934 Brian Penton *Landtakers* 382: 'The

last time I saw a sky like this was in 'Thirty-nine. A lot of good men were on the wallaby after that.'

walloper A policeman [f. *wallop*]
1945 Baker 137: We also call a policeman . . . a *walloper*.
1951 Frank Hardy *Power Without Glory* 33: 'Police! Everyone out! The bloody wallopers are on their way!'
1975 *Nation Review* 5 Dec. 212: His [Ned Kelly's] skull was round for a long while being used as an ashtray by a sensitive and softly spoken walloper.
1980 *NT News* (Darwin) 23 Feb. 7: After being allowed through the door [of the casino], our man was pounced upon by the eagle-eyed security walloper.

waltzing Matilda see **Matilda**

warb 1 Someone of little acumen, or of disreputable appearance [see **warby**]
1941 Baker 80: *Warb* A low-paid manual worker.
1953 Baker 135: *warb* A dirty or untidy person; also (by rhyme) *wattle and daub*; whence, *warby*, dirty or untidy.
1956 Ruth Park and D'Arcy Niland *The Drums Go Bang!* 126: Alongside this masterpiece he felt the warbiest of the warbs.
1967 Kylie Tennant *Tell Morning This* 201: 'But it's a no-hoper's jail – a lot of old warbs and kids mixed up with coves like Amos the Cannibal and chaps that razors bounce off.'
1984 *Sydney Morning Herald* 4 Feb. 37: In Moore Park Road, she picks up an intoxicated person (police call them warbs, slang passed down from they don't know where).
2 An unskilled circus hand
1956 Ruth Park and D'Arcy Niland *The Drums Go Bang!* 174: I'm classed as a warb, but I do everything. I help pull down and put up the Big Top, play recorded music, bang the cymbals.
1967 John Yeomans *The Scarce Australians* 30: There are four general hands (known in Australian circus slang as worbs).

warby Unprepossessing in appearance or disposition; decrepit, unkempt, 'drack'
1941 Kylie Tennant *The Battlers* 264: 'Of all the warby ideas,' he said . . . 'the warbiest is you going on your own.'

1959 D'Arcy Niland *The Big Smoke* 183: A warby unshaven young man in working clothes walked through and right up to him at the back.
1973 Jim McNeil *The Old Familiar Juice* 74: 'He's down there whackin' up bumpers with a couple of 'is warby mates.'
1990 *Sydney Morning Herald* 9 Apr. 82: Mr Keating says a warb is 'someone who gets around in tatty old clothes'. We guess that Barrie Unsworth's cardigans must have been perilously close to the warby line.

warm inner glow, the politics of The ideology of the Left in the Australian Labor Party, from the standpoint of the Right: any reformist programme which seems unrealistic to its opponents [see quot. 1984]
1982 *Australian* 15 Jun. 1: The politics of the 'warm inner glow' – the right-wingers' derisive phrase for the social concerns of the Left – received a hefty beating over the holiday weekend . . . 'What we have here are the politics of the warm inner glow – making people feel good,' Mr Keating said.
1984 James McClelland *Australian* 15 Dec. Mag. 14: A few years ago when I was a practising politician I coined a phrase to describe the philosophy of those for whom the ultimate test of a policy is the feeling of personal virtuousness to be derived from its espousal: the politics of the warm inner glow.

warrigal 1 Aboriginal term for dog
1793 J. Hunter *Historical Journal* ed. J. Bach (1968) 274: *Waregal* A large dog.
2 An untamed creature (e.g. horse, native); an outlaw
1875 Rolf Boldrewood *The Squatter's Dream* repr. as *Ups and Downs* (1878) 249: 'He's a good shot, and these warrigal devils [natives] knows it, or they'd have rushed the place long enough before now.'
1892 Gilbert Parker *Round the Compass in Australia* 44: Six wild horses – warrigals or brombies, as they are called – have been driven down, corralled, and caught.'
1939 Kylie Tennant *Foveaux* 410: The people of Foveaux were Kingston's 'Warrigals', as he said with a contemptuous affection.
1948 K. S. Prichard *Golden Miles* 244: He was toddling now, a sturdy, obstreperous youngster with a shock of dark hair, and 'the wicked look in his eye of a regular young warrigul', Dinny said.

washer A face-washer, a 'flannel'
1951 Dymphna Cusack *Say No to Death*
194: Doreen had given her a washer and a
drop of warm water to wash the sleep out of
her eyes.
1962 *Southerly* 97: We add to *washer* the
meaning of *face-cloth.*
1974 Alexander Buzo *Coralie Lansdowne
Says No* 71: 'I'll get you a cold washer.'

wash-up, the The process giving a final
outcome [f. *wash-up* in gold-mining]
1957 *Bulletin* 4 Sep. 12: Frank Forde had
been thought unlucky to lose his Flinders
seat by seven votes, but in the final wash-up
the margin was narrower still.
1985 *National Times* 9 Aug. 5: In the
wash up, the settlement between ACB and
the South Africans was a reasonable legal
compromise for both sides.

watch, silly (crazy) as a two-bob Extremely silly
1954 Peter Gladwin *The Long Beat Home*
72: 'There now, I clean forgot. I'm getting
silly as a two-bob watch.'
1964 George Johnston *My Brother Jack*
58: He would describe somebody as being 'as
silly as a two-bob watch'.
1972 John de Hoog *Skid Row Dossier* 75:
'Don't buy him a beer, Johnny, he's silly as a
two bob watch,' someone advised as he tapped me on the shoulder.

water, able to talk under see **talk**

Watsons, (to bet) like the 1 To wager
large amounts [derived by Baker (1966:
73–4) from the Watson brothers, noted
bettors]
1945 *Argus* 12 Jun. 15: I have been asked
for the origin of the expression 'Betting like
the Watsons'. Thinking back, I seem to remember a previous controversy as to who
were the Watsons so famous for their betting
activities.
1949 Lawson Glassop *Lucky Palmer* 163:
'Bet well? You bet like the Watsons.'
1967 Frank Hardy *Billy Borker Yarns
Again* 140: 'That Frank Duval must be a
game punter, Billy.' 'I'd bet like the Watsons
meself if I had a million quid in the bank.'
2 At a great rate
1983 Bruce Dawe *Over Here, Harv!* 134: 'I
can just see him at the head of the turn-out,
swinging along on them crutches of his like
the Watsons!'

1985 T. A. G. Hungerford *A Knockabout
with a Slouch Hat* 8: 'I got shot through
Claremont like the Watsons. Only joined up
yesterday. What's it like here?'

wayback 1 The regions remote from
settlement
1901 F. J. Gillen *Diary* (1968) 277: Like
most stock stations in the 'wayback' there
has been no attempt made to improve the
appearance of the surroundings.
1929 Jules Raeside *Golden Days* 344: The
episode reminded me of a boarding-house
were I once stayed at in the way-back.
1973 Margaret Carnegie *Friday Mount*
218: No wonder some of the way-back towns
had that look.
2 An inhabitant of the 'wayback' regions,
unused to city life
1904 Henry Fletcher *Dads Wayback: His
Work* [book title]
1931 Miles Franklin *Back to Bool Bool* 54:
'The real old way-backs. You can't change
'em.'
1956 Tom Ronan *Moleskin Midas* 165:
'I'm only a wayback meself with no schoolin'
so I wouldn't know.'

weak as gin's piss see **gin's piss**

weekender See quot. 1941
1941 Baker 81: *Weekender* A week-end
cottage or shack.
1944 Lawson Glassop *We Were the Rats*
266: It was just a 'week-ender', just like any
of the other thousands scattered sparsely
around the edge of Lake Carraday.
1976 *Australian* 23 Feb. 9: Remember
the weekender? They haven't been building
too many of them in recent years. It used to
be a glorified garage . . . a kilometre from
the nearest sealed road, ten kilometres from
running water and 100 kilometres from the
nearest sewer pipe.

Weetbix packet see **where did you get
your licence?**

weight is right As for **correct weight**
q.v.
1989 *Sun-Herald* 21 May 74: I believe
legislation has gone through both houses of
Parliament passing Phantoms but high-ups
in the Liberal [sic] have yet to declare
'weight's right' on the issue.

well in Well established financially, prosperous, affluent

1845 Thomas McCombie *Arabin* 241: They had a pretty little farm, and were well in.

1883 Rolf Boldrewood *Robbery Under Arms* (World's Classics 1949) 568: 'My word, he's well in, is the cove' says the horse-driver; 'he's got half-a dozen stations besides this one. He'll be one of the richest men in Australia yet.'

1922 Arthur Wright *A Colt from the Country* 83: 'Said to be well in, is he not?' queried Mrs Whinston.

1948 K. S. Prichard *Golden Miles* 15: 'I'm not much to look at, ma'am,' Paddy protested. 'But I'm well in.'

1976 David Ireland *The Glass Canoe* 180: Someone saw her at the trots with some of the trotting men who were really well in, and she was regarded with awe ever after.

welter of it, make a To do something to excess [*welter* Something exceptionally big or heavy of its kind 1865 OED]

1918 *Kia Ora Coo-ee* 15 May 5: My oath! he was making a welter of it.

1947 Gavin Casey *The Wits Are Out* 55: 'He goes the slops too heavy, though . . . he makes a welter of it.'

1952 Jon Cleary *The Sundowners* 196: 'Now I don't want you to make a welter of it,' she said as she walked in behind the bar . . . 'Any-one who gets noisy drunk or tries to start a fight gets locked up until he sobers up.'

1979 *National Times* 17 Feb. 10: Whitlam lists the works of art purchased by the National Gallery that were ordered to be hung at Yarralumla . . . The Kerrs made a bit of a welter of it.

Werris, Werris Creek A Greek; a leak (urination) [rhyming slang]

1967 *King's Cross Whisper* xliii 11: *Werris Creeks*: Greeks.

1985 Robert G. Barrett *You Wouldn't Be Dead for Quids* 101: 'He's a Werris, but he's not a bad bloke.'

westie See quot. 1981

1979 *NT News* (Darwin) 24 Nov. 14: Westie: A person from the western suburbs.

1981 *Sydney Morning Herald* 20 Oct. 13: Bondi attracts all sorts. The eastern suburbs trendies, the 'westies' (anyone who lives west of the Harbour Bridge), the families, the migrants, the vagrants . . .

wet 1 Annoyed, irritated

1898 *Bulletin* 17 Dec. Red Page: To *get narked* is to lose your temper; also expressed by *getting dead wet*.

1915 C. J. Dennis *The Songs of a Sentimental Bloke* 42: Quite natchril, Romeo gits wet as 'ell. / 'It's me or you' 'e 'owls, an wiv a yell, / Plunks Tyball through the gizzard wiv 'is sword.

1941 Baker 81: *Wet, get* To become angry or irritable.

2 Used in a special sense of sheep being shorn, when any dampness in the fleece is thought by shearers to cause cramps, rheumatism or poisoning: if the sheep are voted 'wet', shearing will cease*

1910 C. E. W. Bean *On the Wool Track* 181: A shearer halfway down the board stopped and hung up his machine. The slip of a boy shearing next to him looked up. 'Reckon they're wet?' he asked. The first shearer was putting on his coat. He nodded. 'I've been thinking so too, this half-hour,' said the youngster. It spread down the shed just like fire in stubble.

1966 D. E. Charlwood *An Afternoon of Time* 55: The shearers . . . felt the ewes and lambs, declared them 'wet' and knocked off.

wet, the The rainy season in N.W. Australia (cf. **the Dry**)

1908 Mrs Aeneas Gunn *We of the Never-Never* 292: 'Not too bad, though,' he said, reviewing the year's work, after fixing up a sleeping-camp for the wet.

1938 Xavier Herbert *Capricornia* 115: People scoffed at O'Cannon's cotton, saying at first that it would never see the Wet through, then that it would never live through the Dry.

1969 Christopher Bray *Blossom Like a Rose* 14: 'Oh, it's the Wet coming on. That's what does it. Makes people edgy as can be.'

1983 *Australian* 5 Feb. Mag. 1: 'Thou shalt not kill – except coons in the wet,' said the barmaid, laughing.

wet cement, able to talk under see **talk**

wet enough to bog a duck see **duck**

whaler A bush nomad, managing to subsist without work

1883 R. E. N. Twopeny *Town Life in Australia* 244–5: A 'waler' is a bushman who is 'on the loaf'. He 'humps his drum', or 'swag', and 'starts on the wallaby track'.

1900 Henry Lawson 'The Darling River' *Prose* i 84: They grow weary of seeing the same old 'whaler' drop his swag on the bank opposite whenever the boat ties up for wood; they get tired of lending him tobacco, and listening to his ideas, which are limited in number and narrow in conception.

1911 E. J. Brady *River Rovers* 90: It was a wrinkled whaler that we camped beside on a sandspit next night . . . A wise old vagabond was this who had bearded many station cooks in his day.

1919 W. K. Harris *Outback in Australia* 144: On the Murrumbidgee we asked several questions of an old 'whaler'* as to roads and grass and water ahead. *On the Outback rivers sundowners are known as 'whalers'.

1947 Vance Palmer *Hail Tomorrow* 2: 'There's too many of these billabong whalers, like Tom says, just wandering in for the company and the rations.'

whaler, Murrumbidgee see **Murrumbidgee**

wharfie A waterside worker, docker, longshoreman [abbr. of *wharf-labourer*]

1912 *The Lone Hand* 1 May 40: The best testimonial to Hughes' ability is the fact that he has so often swayed the unruly 'wharfies', and controlled their organisation for so long.

1923 George S. Beeby *Concerning Ordinary People* 152: 'Some o' the neighbours is already beginning to look down on us because you're only a wharfie.'

1971 Frank Hardy *The Outcasts of Foolgarah* 7–8: Every job has its perquisites . . . the business executive has the expense account, the wharfie has the busted crate of cigarettes.

1981 *Sunday Telegraph* (Sydney) 8 Feb. 30: The Premier, Mr Wran, can swear like a Balmain wharfie, according to Graham Richardson, secretary of the NSW branch of the ALP.

wheel, to be on someone's As for **on someone's hammer** q.v. [? f. cycle racing]

1954 Vince Kelly *The Shadow* 89: 'I'm going back to Melbourne. Down there the cops'll give you a go. Here they're on your wheel all the time.'

1969 Osmar White *Under the Iron Rainbow* 118: 'The inspector's been on my wheel to trace him.'

wheel, silly as a Extremely silly

1952 T. A. G. Hungerford *The Ridge and the River* 57: Oscar was sound, but silly as a wheel.

1966 *Coast to Coast 1965–1966* 157: 'She was as silly as a wheel, too, but a man's got to do what he can to protect his daughters.'

1986 Bruce Pascoe *Night Animals* 26: 'Poor old Cobber, silly as a bloody wheel.'

Whelan the Wrecker Trading-name of a firm of demolition specialists, generalized to any demolition team

1953 *Bulletin* 3 Jun. 8: While bricks, mortar and timber crumbled, splintered and fell, and dust rose: Whelan the Wrecker Is Here.

1964 George Johnston *My Brother Jack* 347: One frontage was boarded up and it was in process of demolition, and there was a big sign on one wall that said WHELAN THE WRECKER IS HERE.

1976 W. K. Hancock *Professing History* 124: The government might cut its losses and call in Whelan the Wrecker to clear away the mess on Black Mountain.

1982 *NT News* (Darwin) 10 Aug. 3: John Holland (Constructions) won the $172050 contract and sub-contracted it to Whelan the Wrecker.

Where did you get your licence? An allegation of incompetence, with varying explanations

1971 Colin Simpson *The New Australia* 110: Our taximan leans out of his window: 'And where did you ever get a bloody driver's licence – out of a Weetbix packet?'

1971 John O'Grady *Aussie Etiket* 56: Because you are driving safely, you will be abused with sentences like . . . 'Where did you get your bloody licence, Woolworth's?'

1982 *Sun-Herald* 4 Apr. 87: The bloke beside me yelled out . . . 'Where'd you get a ticket, ref, out of a cornflakes packet?'

whinge To complain, gripe, protest [f. *whinge* to whine 1150 OED: Sc. and northern dial.]

1951 Dal Stivens *Jimmy Brockett* 279: Old

Misery Guts and Fuller whinged when I told them what we had to do.

1965 John Beede *They Hosed Them Out* 178: Even though I wasn't going home, I was alive and well. What did I have to winge about?

1973 Henry Williams *My Love Had a Black Speed Stripe* 23: That's a thing that gets me with sheilas: whenever they start whinging they always try and make out how reasonable they are.

1984 *West Australian* (Perth) 7 Feb. 20: Australia's farmers are weary of being seen by their city cousins as whingeing conservatives dependent on government help to keep them in clover.

whinger One who whinges
1965 John Beede *They Hosed Them Out* 210: I said, 'Doc, I'm no winger but I can't sleep with this damn thing.'

1979 Dorothy Hewett *The Man from Mukinupin* 106: 'Don't whinge. I can't stand a whinger.'

1984 *National Times* 27 Jan. 34: 'As you know, cockies are the greatest whingers in the world.'
see **Pommy, whingeing**

whippy The wallet, the pocket
1967 *King's Cross Whisper* (Sydney) xliii 11: *Whippy*: Pocket. Sometimes whip your kick, or willy, same as wallet.

1980 *Sun-Herald* 27 Jan. 66: Fair dinkum, if a man had enough in the willy, I mean whippy . . .

1984 *Sunday Telegraph* (Sydney) 8 Apr. 63: The going has been tough on the punt lately and the whippy was looking pretty bare.

whips of An abundance [f. *whips* plenty, lots EDD 1894; cf. *lashings of*]
1905 *The Old Bush Songs* ed. A. B. Paterson 24: We'd whips and whips of Rhino as we meant to push about.

1918 Bernard Cronin *The Coastlanders* 123: 'They's whips of feed and the water's not bad.'

1934 Steele Rudd *Green Grey Homestead* 97: 'And tell him I've got whips of room for him.'

1961 George Farwell *Vanishing Australians* 182: 'Then you want capital – whips of it.'

white ants, to have To be eccentric, crazy
1900–10 O'Brien and Stephens: *White ants* Silliness, madness. Any person of weak intellect or peculiar in their manner as if insane is said to have white ants.

1908 Henry Fletcher *Dads and Dan between Smokes* 64: It wants a fool or a very sane cove indeed ter live in ther lonely bush an' keep ther white ants out o' his napper.

1926 L. C. E. Gee *Bushtracks and Goldfields* 65: And so he rambles on . . . and in the unsteady glance of his honest, old eyes and his disconnected speech, I read the mark of the Australian solitudes – 'white ants' they call it up north.

1938 H. Drake-Brockman *Men Without Wives* 27: '"Get the white ants?" What do you mean?' 'Go ratty. Mad.'

white lady Methylated spirits, sometimes mixed with something else
1935 Kylie Tennant *Tiburon* 24: Two old men in the corner lying stupefied over a mixture of 'white lady' – boiled methylated spirit with a dash of boot polish and iodine.

1949 Judith Wright *Woman to Man* 35: His white and burning girl, his woman of fire, / creeps to his heart and sets a candle there.

1962 Ron Tullipan *March into Morning* 57: 'What is it?' Chappie asked, eyeing the bottle with suspicion, 'metho?' 'The white lady.'

1975 Richard Beilby *The Brown Land Crying* 225: 'Ya was on the White Lady at the finish, mixin' it with Coke' . . . 'But jees, meths'n Coca Cola.'

white leghorn See quots.
1975 Les Ryan *The Shearers* 135: *White leghorn* Colloquial term for a woman bowler.

1984 David McNicoll *Bulletin* 3 Apr. 50: I wrote recently about lawn bowlers, known affectionately as the 'White Leghorns'. Gwen Dunn, of Blakehurst, NSW, writes to tell me that they are now wearing 'mini-beige' instead of white.

white shoe brigade See quot. 1987
1987 *Sydney Morning Herald* 12 Feb. 1: The name 'white shoe brigade' has its origins in the offices of John Moore, Liberal Party President in Queensland. Mr Moore coined the term for the Queensland property developers who are close to Premier Sir Joh

Bjelke-Petersen and his senior minister, Mr Russ Hinze, and who have made fortunes in train of the Queensland Government's commitment to aiding development.

1990 *Sun-Herald* 14 Jan. 36: Both are fully paid up life members of the White Shoe Brigade – making Sanctuary Cove's Mike Gore look like only an annual subscriber.

white, the man in The referee or umpire in football [f. dress]

1973 Alexander Buzo *The Roy Murphy Show* 107: 'It's all very well to knock the men in white, Mike, but you must bear in mind that referees have many difficulties confronting them.'

1982 *NT News* (Darwin) 31 Dec. 13: 12 women umpires have been sharing the solitary shower at the Gardens Oval with the men in white (not all at the same time) while waiting for extra showers to be installed.

whizz off As for **race off** q.v.

1963 Lawson Glassop *The Rats in New Guinea* 87: 'You might have been the Wizard of Nerridale but I was the Whizzer of Nerridale.'

1978 Richard Beilby *Gunner* 308: 'Good on ya, Digger! Whizz 'er off while she's hot.'

who's robbing this coach see **coach**

who's up who and who's paying the rent see **up**

Wicks, the The Randwick, N.S.W., Rugby Union team [abbr.]

1984 *Sunday Telegraph* (Sydney) 8 Apr. 127: Wicks go down in shocker [heading]

wide brown land, the Australia, from Dorothea Mackellar's 'My Country'

1914 Dorothea Mackellar *The Witch Maid* 29: Her beauty and terror – / The wide brown land for me.

1966 Jan Smith *An Ornament of Grace* 33: A nice myth to be dusted off every Anzac Day, about bronzed heroes of the wide brown land.

1973 *Australian* 4 May 11: Migrants are staying away in droves from the widest and brownest part of this wide, brown land.

wider the brim, the smaller the property see **brim**

widgie Female counterpart of the **bodgie** q.v.

1950 *Sun* (Sydney) 5 Jul. 19: A benefit dance will be held on Friday at the Gaiety Ballroom, Oxford Street ... There'll be competitions for jitter-bugging, Charleston, and prizes for the most colorfully dressed 'bodgy' and 'weegie'. Mo and Hal Lashwood will be the judges.

1951 *Sydney Morning Herald* 1 Feb. 1: What with 'bodgies' growing their hair long and getting round in satin shirts, and 'weegies' cutting their hair short and wearing jeans, confusion seems to be arising about the sex of some Australian adolescents.

1965 William Dick *A Bunch of Ratbags* 248: I had never seen so many bodgies and widgies all together at one time before.

wild colonial boy see **colonial**

wild white man, the William Buckley (1780–1856), the convict who escaped and lived for thirty-two years with the natives, being eventually returned to the white community

1856 James Bonwick *William Buckley, the Wild White Man* [book title]

1871 Marcus Clarke *Old Tales of a Young Country* 18: William Buckley, The 'Wild White Man' [essay title]

willy A supply of money for betting; money (in criminal slang)

1949 Lawson Glassop *Lucky Palmer* 36: 'Two quid? Break it down. That's me willie. That's all I got.'

1975 *Bulletin* 26 Apr. 46: It was this woman who was guarding the willy (money) and the success of the operation rested on the Limp distracting her attention.

willy willy On land, a spiralling dusty wind; at sea, a minor cyclone: esp. N.W. Australia

1894 *The Age* 20 Jan. 13: The willy willy is the name given to these periodical storms by the natives of the north-west. [Morris]

1898 D. W. Carnegie *Spinifex and Sand* 254: Large tracts of burnt country had to be crossed from which clouds of dust and ashes were continually rising, blown up by 'Willy-Willies' (spiral winds).

1929 Sir Hal Colebatch *A Story of a Hundred Years* 168: The [pearling] industry requires that capital be risked; it takes its toll of life even in ordinary working, and in cyclones or 'willy willys' many lives and much property have been lost.

1942 Gavin Casey *It's Harder for Girls* 113: A corkscrew of sand, the beginning of a willy-willy, danced through the yard, tugging at her skirts as it went and making her drop the wood as she grabbed at the garment with both hands.

1980 *National Times* 27 Apr. 28: Again and again we see 'willy-willys' which dance friskily in the parched landscape, often more than 100 metres high. They are almost solid with sand.

Windies, the The West Indies cricket team

1965 Wally Grout *My Country's 'Keeper* 69: The Australian public was enchanted and took the 'Windies' to their hearts from that moment.

1976 *Sunday Telegraph* (Sydney) 4 Jan. 52: Windies roll with brutal pace beating.

wine dot See quot. 1966

1953 T. A. G. Hungerford *Riverslake* 35: 'Is he a wine-dot?' 'Is he hell! . . . He's never off it.'

1966 Baker 226: Addicts of cheap wine are known variously as *winedots* (a play on Wyandottes, domestic fowls of a U.S. breed).

1976 Dorothy Hewett *This Old Man Comes Rolling Home* 11: 'Gawd, you smell like an old wine dot, Laurie.'

wingy Nickname for someone who has lost an arm [f. *wing* to wound . . . in the arm or shoulder OED 1802]

[**1895** Cornelius Crowe *The Australian Slang Dictionary* 96: *Winged* One-armed, or wounded.]

1910 Henry Lawson 'The Rising of the Court' *Prose* i 660: Wingy, by the way, is a ratty little one-armed man, whose case is usually described in the headline, 'A 'Armless Case', by one of our great dailies.

1932 Leonard Mann *Flesh in Armour* 8: The figure of Nelson . . . on the top of the column, was hardly discernible in the dirty mist . . . Bill Potter waved a nonchalant greeting with 'Good-day Nelson', 'Eh?' asked his companion. 'Just passing the day to old Wingie.'

1945 *Coast to Coast 1944* 32: The only thing I haven't is a left arm . . . they can call me Wingy now.

1982 *Sydney Morning Herald* 24 Jul. 13:

John Hyde, the West Australian wheat farmer who lost an arm in a tractor accident and is called 'Wingie'.

wipe To dismiss from consideration, wash one's hands of [f. *to wipe one's hands of* OED 1785]

1941 Kylie Tennant *The Battlers* 196: Giving her money . . . in the casual manner that wiped her from all consideration as a human being.

1948 Ruth Park *The Harp in the South* 269: 'From now on he's wiped. I never want to see him again.'

1962 David Forrest *The Hollow Woodheap* 149: 'She wiped you like last week's bath mat.'

1983 Patrick White *Netherwood* 36: 'Suspended once – but they didn't wipe me.'

wire, mulga, spinifex see **mulga, spinifex**

Wolseley The name of the shearing machine which came into use in the late 1880s and the 1890s, patented 1877 [f. F. Y. Wolseley the inventor]

1897 Henry Lawson 'The Boss's Boots' *Verse* i 321: Bogan laid his 'Wolseley' down and knocked the rouser out.

1905 'Flash Jack from Gundagai' *The Old Bush Songs* ed. A. B. Paterson 27 and note: I've pinked 'em with the Wolseleys and I've rushed with B-bows, too. Wolseleys and B-bows are respectively machines and hand shears.

1964 H. P. Tritton *Time Means Tucker* 60: The old type Wolseleys, if the tension screw was a bit tight, would run hot: when jammed onto thin pants it was somewhat startling.

wombat 1 Used in expressions suggesting torpor or stupidity

1896 Edward Dyson *Rhymes from the Mines* 124: I was sullen as a wombat on such still, wan days as these.

1917 A. B. Paterson *Three Elephant Power* 31: Dooley, better known as The Wombat because of his sleepy disposition, was a man of great strength.

2 Nickname for an unappreciative male [cf. **root** *v.* 1]

1982 *Australian* 4 Dec. Mag. 11: 'Could be he's what us girls call a wombat!' An animal that eats roots and leaves.

see **koala** 2

3 See quot. 1984 [? f. animal's burrowing habit]

1984 *Bulletin* 13 Nov. 32: Men known colloquially as 'wombats', says Costigan, illegally transmit prices to an operator outside racetracks by talking into radio devices in their pockets. This information is passed in turn to an operational base and then phoned to SP operators.

wombat trail See quot.

1986 *Sunday Telegraph* (Sydney) 14 Dec. 192: Among the Christmas revelry at Parliament House . . . the annual Wombat lunch held by Ian Sinclair stands out. The lunch is traditionally held for journalists who followed the Wombat Trail – with the National Party Leader during an election.

wongi 1 A friendly yarn, esp. in N.W. Australia [Ab.]

[**1835** G. F. Moore *Diary of . . . an Early Settler in Western Australia* (1884) 271: Weeip . . . asked me to 'paper wonga' the Governor about it. *Descriptive Vocabulary* 73: Wangow – To speak; to talk.]

1916 Arthur Wilson *Mining, Lays, Tales and Folk Lore* (1944) 78: I gave them a 'good luck greeting', and then, somehow, we all fell to a wongi.

1957 Randolph Stow *The Bystander* 186: 'I just wanted a bit of a wongi with you. You know how it is, a joker gets the urge to talk sometimes.'

1984 *Sunday Independent* (Perth) 28 Oct. 8: Senator Withers plays down his role and dislikes the term 'Peacock's right-hand man'. 'Call me his "Wongi man" – I'm just someone he can have a chat with at the end of the day,' he said with a smile.

2 A native of the Kalgoorlie region

1950 K. S. Prichard *Winged Seeds* 161: 'Bob Brown'd never forgive us if he heard we'd been calling on the wongi and hadn't paid him and his missus a visit.'

1981 Archie Weller *The Day of the Dog* 61: Charley's woman, a shy dark wongi from Kalgoorlie, comes out and takes the baby. Ibid. 167: *wongi* really the people from Kalgoorlie way, but any full-blood Aboriginal.

wonk 1 Aboriginal term for a white: *derogatory*

1938 Xavier Herbert *Capricornia* 252: He went to the Dagoes and Roughs of second-class and won their friendship by buying

them liquor and telling them how he had been cast out by the Wonks of the saloon.

1958 Elizabeth Webb *Into the Morning* 116: I began remembering dirty words the boys at the River Cap used to call whites. I said aloud: 'A lot of bloody wonks – I don't care. I don't bloody well care . . . a lot of dirty wonks.'

2 A male homosexual

1945 Baker 123: An effeminate male is a . . . *wonk*.

1970 Patrick White *The Vivisector* 213: 'I'd have to have a chauffeur to drive me about – with a good body – just for show, though. I wouldn't mind if the chauffeur was a wonk.'

wood-and-water joey Someone given the menial tasks on a station, etc., having no special skills of his own [f. 'hewers of wood and drawers of water' *Joshua* 9:21]

1882 Rolf Boldrewood *Robbery Under Arms* (World's Classics 1949) 313: 'It's all devilish fine for you . . . to go flashin' about the country and sporting your figure on horse-back, while I'm left alone to do the housekeepin' in the Hollow. I'm not going to be wood-and-water Joey, I can tell ye, not for you nor no other men.'

1887 *All the Year Round* 30 Jul. 67: A 'wood-and-water Joey' is a hanger about the hotels, and a doer of odd jobs.

1906 T. E. S. Spencer *How McDougall Topped the Score* 128: He was wood-and-water Joey at the 'Star' / Where she waited, and assisted at the bar.

1955 E. O. Schlunke *The Man in the Silo* 205: A Furphy water-cart, with the wood-and-water Joey sitting unhappily on the shaft.

Woodbine See quot. 1919

1919 W. H. Downing *Digger Dialects* 54: *Woodbine* An English soldier, so called from the name of a cheap brand of cigarettes favored by Englishmen.

1937 Ernestine Hill *Water into Gold* 192: Bagtown became 'Woodbine Ave' . . . so-called for the number of English settlers in residence.

1978 Richard Beilby *Gunner* 43: 'Ingelesi,' he grinned. 'Pommies. Chooms. 'Bines. That's what we call them.'

wood duck See quot. 1984 [f. the proverbial stupidity of the woodcock]

1984 *Bulletin* 19 Jun. 69: The bigger suppliers sit back in luxurious harbourside apartments and rely instead on a network of couriers (known as wood ducks or woodies) to run all the risks in contacting and selling to users in the street.
1988 *Sun-Herald* 17 Jan. 131: The salesman . . . will recognise that you know what you want and aren't a run-of-the-mill 'wood duck'. Wood ducks are easy targets.

wooden To fell, knock out [cf. *stiffen*]
[**1908** Henry Fletcher *Dads and Dan between Smokes* 39: When misfochin' as yous can't prevent lands yer a woodener, take it smilin'.]
1911 Steele Rudd *The Dashwoods* 25: 'I never saw him any more till I see you going to wooden him with the furniture.'
1936 A. B. Paterson 'The Shearer's Colt' in *Song of the Pen* (1983) 721: Some poor inoffensive Chinaman had come into the yard . . . and his wife had 'woodened' him without giving him a chance to explain.
1974 *Southerly* 145: 'If you can't wooden 'em [kangaroos] at a 'undred yards with one I.C.I. bullet, you're not tryin'!'
1981 A. B. Facey *A Fortunate Life* 70: He had picked up a stick about four feet long and one and a half inches thick, and intended to wooden me out.

wood, have the ~ on To hold an advantage
1941 S. J. Baker *New Zealand Slang* 53: *to have the wood on a person* To have an advantage over someone.
1949 Lawson Glassop *Lucky Palmer* 156: 'She's got you taped, too, kid. She's got the wood on all of us.'
1973 *Sunday Telegraph* (Sydney) 16 Sep. 47: The Swans hold the wood on the Magpies in finals matches.
1984 Ned Manning *Us or Them* 46: 'We've got the wood on Wilkie and McKenzie . . . I caught them smoking pot in the out-of-bounds area.'

Woods, the 1 In N.S.W., the Eastwood Rugby Union team [abbr.]
1975 *Sunday Telegraph* (Sydney) 17 Aug. 57: Woods as premiers? Forget it.
2 In Victoria, the Collingwood A.F.L. team (more often 'the Magpies')
1977 *Sunday Telegraph* (Sydney) 25 Sep. 75: Once a Woodsman always a Woodsman is the rule at Collingwood – and that's the way

it will always be so long as blokes play football in black and white striped jumpers.

Woodser, Jimmy A person drinking alone at a bar; a drink taken alone [see quots 1933, 1982]
1892 Barcroft Boake 'Jimmy Wood' *Bulletin* 7 May 17: Who drinks alone, drinks toast to Jimmy Wood, sir.* *A man drinks by himself is said to take a 'Jimmy Woodser'.
1900 Henry Lawson 'They Wait on the Wharf in Black' *Prose* i 286: 'I wanted to score a drink!' he said. 'I thought he wanted one and wouldn't like to be a Jimmy Woodser.'
1933 Acland: *Jimmy* or *Johnny Woodser* Slang. A drink by yourself . . . A correspondent tells me that James Wood was a shearer on the Darling River, New South Wales, in the 'eighties. He spent the off season in Bourke. He was fond of a glass of beer but was never known to shout. He always drank on his own, so that when the shearers saw any one go to the bar by himself they always said he was having a *J. W.* Hence the saying.
1982 Heather M. Hassall *Bulletin* 27 Jul. 8: 'Jimmy' Wood was the son of James Wood who, in 1716, founded the Gloucester City Old Bank, the most ancient banking house in England with the exception of Messrs Child of Fleet Street. 'Jimmy' was a miser who, although generous to the poor – such as a gift of £200,000 to the impoverished of the City of Gloucester – was exceedingly frugal in his own living habits. His always drinking alone, led to the term 'Jimmy Woodser' for mean people who adopted the same practice. I can vouch for the accuracy of the above statements as I am connected with the Wood family.

Woolloomooloo uppercut See quots
1967 *King's Cross Whisper* (Sydney) xliii 11: *Woolloomooloo uppercut*: A strategic boot in the groin.
1985 Robert G. Barrett *You Wouldn't Be Dead for Quids* 46: Les swung his foot back and gave him a Woolloomooloo uppercut straight in the balls.

Woolworth's see **where did you get your licence?**

Woop Woop Imaginary place which is a byword for backwardness and remoteness. Sometimes defined as 'where the crows fly backward, to keep the dust out of their eyes'

1923 A. B. Paterson 'Shakespeare on the Turf' in *Song of the Pen* (1983) 436: On the Woop Woop course he ran a mile / In less than forty with his irons on!

1949 Lawson Glassop *Lucky Palmer* 94: 'I don't come from Woop Woop. Harry Hughes is known on every racecourse in New South Wales.'

1970 Sumner Locke Elliott *Edens Lost* 90: 'I was all over the country. You could drive hundreds of miles back of the beyond out into Woop-Woop or Buggeryville and there I was.'

1980 *Daily News* (Perth) 5 Nov. 68: Doesn't matter which race ... could be the Hanging Rock Cup or the Woop Woop welter ... the ritual is the same. Only the baloney is different.

see **Snake Gully**

word   To inform someone privately, tip off
1915 C.J. Dennis *The Songs of a Sentimental Bloke* 50: I met 'im on the quiet, / 'An worded 'im about a small affair.

1928 Arthur Wright *A Good Recovery* 26: 'Here's a few bob to go on with. I'll word the landlord to look after y'.'

1939 Kylie Tennant *Foveaux* 349–50: 'You word the paper-boy to send your paper up to Central.'

1949 Lawson Glassop *Lucky Palmer* 212: 'Joyce Butler's on the switch and you can word her up to make a date for you.'

1967 K. S. Prichard *Subtle Flame* 234: 'Ted worded a mate of his on the *Western Star.*'

working off a dead horse   see **dead horse**

workingman's paradise, the   Australia
1859 Henry Kingsley *Recollections of Geoffry Hamlyn* i 103–4: That was what they saw, and what any man may see to-day for himself in his own village, whether in England or Australia, that working man's paradise.

1873 Anthony Trollope *Australia* ed. P. D. Edwards and R. B. Joyce (1967) 524: I must say of this colony [Tasmania], as I have and shall say of all the others, that it is a Paradise for a working man as compared with England.

1892 William Lane *The Workingman's Paradise: An Australian Labour Novel* 38:

In Sydney, in 1889, in the working-man's paradise, she stood on the kerb, this blind girl, and begged.

1978 *Overland 71* 42: It conjures up the old image of Queensland as a workers' paradise – a kind of Australian deep south and California wrapped into one.

worries, no   i.e. there is no problem, no difficulty [f. *not to worry*]
1966 Roger Carr *Surfie* 100: I went over to the boarding house to her room. Only she wasn't there either. No worries, she'd be back.

1979 *Age* (Melbourne) 30 Aug. 20: We had a mound of luggage but the taxi driver who swept it into his cab said 'No worries, she's apples'. We were back once more in the no-worries country.

1981 Gary Disher *Approaches* 117: There was this bloke who walks into a pub and asks the barman if he wants to hear an Irish joke. 'I'm Irish,' says the barman. 'No worries,' says the bloke, 'I'll tell it slow.'

wouldn't it?   Expression of exasperation [see quot. 1945 and **root** *v.* 2]
1944 Lawson Glassop *We Were the Rats* 162: 'Do you know our divisions have even got a mobile laundry, decontamination unit? Wouldn't it you?' Ibid. 135: 'Well, wouldn't it rotate you?' said Eddie.

1945 Baker 152n: The authentic digger form is *Wouldn't it root you!*

1985 Robert G. Barrett *You Wouldn't Be Dead for Quids* 172: 'I think I've popped a bloody knuckle too, wouldn't it root you?'

wouldn't read about it   see **read**

wowser   A censorious person; a killjoy [? f. *wow* To whine; to grumble, make complaint EDD 1876]
1899 *Truth* 8 Oct. 5: The Parraween Push / A Partisan Protest / Willoughby 'Wowsers' Worried / The 'Talent' get a 'Turn' On Thursday week at the North Sydney Police Court ... ten young men were fined sums varying from £2 with costs to 7/6 with costs ... for having behaved in a riotous manner on the Military Rd.

1911 Henry Lawson 'The Song of the Heathen' *Verse* iii 65: O this is the Wowsers' land, / And the laughing days are o'er, / For most of the things that we used to do / We must not do any more!

1930 J. S. Litchfield *Far-North Memories* 182: The wife was undeniably a 'wowser'.

One could read her character in the square-toed, thick-soled boots she wore, in her thick black woollen stockings, and in her stiff black hat.

1942 Leonard Mann *The Go-Getter* 201: 'A few years ago the age [of consent] was seventeen, but some old women got a wowser government to increase the age.'

1976 *Sydney Morning Herald* 14 Aug. 10: Mr Nile does not see the Festival of Light as a puritanical neo-wowser movement.

1981 Roger Pulvers *Age* (Melbourne) 10 Aug. 11: 'I love Melbourne because it's the only city with a radical tradition in Australia, as well as being the home base for the wowsers.'

wowserdom, wowserish, wowserism

1984 *Bulletin* 17 Apr. 47: As a veteran student of wowserdom, I will watch his progress with devoted interest.

1933 Frank Clune *Try Anything Once* 122: They looked much the same although it seemed to me they had lost their dash and grown wowserish.

1918 George Dale *The Industrial History of Broken Hill* 229: Brookfield ... had arrayed against him every device known to both Capitalism and wowserism.

wrap (up) *n.* A flattering account (interchangeable with **rap (up)** q.v.)

1949 Lawson Glassop *Lucky Palmer* 54: 'Do you want a cigarette paper?' 'Cigarette paper? No, I've got the makings.' 'I thought you wanted to give yourself another wrap up.'

1958 Frank Hardy *The Four-Legged Lottery* 177: Ronnie Hutchison, a specialist in long distance races, getting the wrap up from his mates, Des Hoysted and Frank O'Brien – 'ridden in copy-book style by Hutchie'.

1973 *Australian* 7 Aug. 22: When I was at Ipswich I thought it was a great 'wrap' to be picked to play for Queensland.

1980 *Sunday Mail* (Brisbane) 22 Jun. 40: The Brisbane players destroyed the reputations of several Manly players who came to Brisbane with huge 'wraps' on them.

wrap (up) *v.* To praise (interchangeable with **rap (up)** q.v.)

1967 *King's Cross Whisper* (Sydney) xliii 11: *Wrap*: To say nice things about someone.

1973 *Sun* (Sydney) 1 May 78: Last week I wrapped him over his display of whistle blowing in the Easts-Manly game. This was virtually the 'kiss of death'. Anytime referees get a wrap they seem to get banished to the suburbs.

1975 Xavier Herbert *Poor Fellow My Country* 875: 'Does she wrap you up! Look ... "This sweet and lovely creature".'

wrapped Overjoyed with something (interchangeable with **rapt** q.v.)

1963 Criena Rohan *Down by the Dockside* 212: 'She gave me a quid now and then. I never stood over her for it. She's wrapped in me, see?'

1976 *Sydney Morning Herald* 21 Jan. 1: $1,210 a week to play cricket 'I'm just wrapped,' Thomson said. 'The offer is a fantastic one which never in my wildest dreams did I expect.'

Wrecker, Whelan the   see **Whelan**

wrestling, mobile, open-air Rugby football, from the standpoint of an Australian Rules player

1971 Colin Simpson *The New Australia* 215: Rules fans call Rugby 'open-air wrestling'.

1980 *Australian* 20 Dec. 14: You know the old chestnut. To Melburnians, rugby is no more than mobile wrestling.

wrong tram, on the   see **tram**

wrong, you're not An expression of agreement

1981 Buzz Kennedy *Australian* 18 Jul. Mag. 4: Just as one would not wear spats, so one does not wish to say, 'You're right' when the argot of the day dictates, 'You're not wrong'.

1984 *Sunday Independent* (Perth) 9 Sep. 38: Robin Leach, who fronts the programme, says: 'My show is *Dallas* come to life.' You're not wrong old son.

wurley, wurlie An Aboriginal hut (1847 OED), extended to any similar rude shelter constructed by a white

1917 F. J. Mills *Dinkum Oil* 66: And 'wurlie' cigarettes (you have all sniffed those fearful cigarettes, which effluviate like a wurlie).

1937 Ernestine Hill *The Great Australian Loneliness* 11: I have interviewed men living in wurlies of paper-bark who read Gibbon and wrote Greek.

Y

yabber *n.*   Talk [Ab.]
1855 Raffaello Carboni *The Eureka Stockade* ed. G. Serle (1969) 7: There was further a great waste of yabber-yabber about the diggers not being represented in the Legislative Council.
1908 *The Australian Magazine* 1 Nov. 1252: Others [aboriginal words] have remained, and are likely to remain in the category of slang, such as ... yabber (yabba) talk.

yabber *v.*   To talk
1848 H. W. Haygarth *Recollections of Bush Life in Australia* 102: The most loquacious of them all would bear little comparison with an Australian 'gin' when fairly moved to 'yabber'.
1890 Jane I. Watts *Family Life in South Australia* 190: He told me that he heard my father 'Plenty yabber, yabber'. I could not understand what he meant till he held up his hands, and in a serious tone uttered words as though he were reading. It then dawned across me that he was mimicking my father reading the Bible.

yabber, paper   A letter
1888 Overlander *Australian Sketches* 24: I determined to send him [a native] off first with a paper yabber to the other stockman, telling him where we had gone.
1901 F. J. Gillen *Diary* (1968) 303: The letter is carried securely tied in a cleft stick ... The blacks regard messengers of this sort as sacred; they probably have an idea that if they interfered with a 'paper yabber' some evil magic would result.
1935 H. H. Finlayson *The Red Centre* 74: In the bad old days of early settlement undesirable bucks were got rid of by giving them 'paper yabbers' to deliver to distant neighbours.

yabbie, yabby   A small freshwater crayfish (*Parachaeraps bicarinatus*) used as bait [Ab.]
1894 *Argus* 6 Oct. 11: Small crayfish, called 'yabbies' ... may be found all over Australia, both in large and small lagoons. These creatures, whilst nearing a drought, and as the supply of water is about to fail,

burrow deeply in the beds of the lagoons, water-holes, or swamps. [Morris]
1965 Graham McInnes *The Road to Gundagai* 142: Down the hill came running McLachlan kids ready to go fishing for yabbies. These small fresh water crayfish, which inhabited every muddy pool in the bush, were the easiest things to catch in the world.
1979 *Advertiser* (Adelaide) 8 Mar. 30: Fresh yabbies are at the Grote Street fishmongers for the first time in many months. Freshly cooked yabbies are $3.70 a kilogram, $1.90 less than prawns.

yachtie   A yachtsman, esp. if engaged in yacht racing
1979 *Australian* 14 Jul. Mag. 15: He admits to being a fanatic 'yachtie' and said: 'I love sailing. I live it. In fact I'd be happy to die on the boat.'

yack, yacker (Yakkitty-yak) *n. & v.*   Talk
[*yack* a syllable imitative of a snapping sound; hence as vb. OED 1861]
c. **1882** *Sydney Slang Dictionary* 9: *Yacker* Talk.
1959 *Daily Telegraph* (Sydney) 7 Mar. 2: He was a travelling yakitty-yak man in the ubiquitous presence of Mr Graham Webb.
1969 William Dick *Naked Prodigal* 16: All the girls ... yacking about clothes or some woman who'd just had her twentieth kid.
1980 Murray Bail *Homesickness* 162: 'They were all yacking in some other lingo.'

yakker (yakka, yacker)   Work [Ab.]
1866 W. Ridley *Kamilaroi* 171: work *yakka*.
1888 *Boomerang* 14 Jan. 13: The Brisbane wharf labourers ... are so accustomed to hard yacker that they can't be happy for a single day without it.
1908 *The Australian Magazine* 1 Nov. 1251: Others [aboriginal words] ... are likely to remain in the category of slang, such as ... yacker (yakka), work.
1936 Archer Russell *Gone Nomad* 74: Two days later Adams packed his blanket and his Shakespeare and left for the South ... No more 'bush yacker' for him.
1962 Stuart Gore *Down the Golden Mile*

127: 'I'm not scared of a bit of hard yakka.'
1983 Janise Beaumont *Sun-Herald* 25 Sep. 136: The overall feeling as one watched the bejewelled matrons was that a great deal of yakka had gone into redistributing flesh and tarting up faces and hair.

yamidgee An Aboriginal: W.A.
1955 *Bulletin* 15 Jun. 22: 'He no *yamatjee*, boss,' Johnnie replied. 'He white feller.'
1965 Randolph Stow *The Merry-go-Round in the Sea* 186: 'What's yamidgees?' said the boy. 'Boongs. Noogs. Coloured folk.'
1983 G. E. P. Wellard *Bushlore* 55: I was standing outside the humpy discussing the day's work with three of the Yamagee musterers. I use the word 'Yamagee' because that is the name they call themselves in that district. They never say 'Blackman' or 'Aborigine', it is always 'Yamagee'.

Yan Yean The water supply to Melbourne from the Yan Yean reservoir (originally as distinct from tank water)
1868 J. R. Houlding *Australian Tales* 260: 'We have plenty of Yan Yean water to flush our gutters in dry weather.'
1873 Anthony Trollope *Australia* ed. P. D. Edwards and R. B. Joyce (1967) 386: During the very heart of the summer of 1871 ... I moved from a house in the town to a friend's residence in the country; and neither at the one nor the other could a bath be filled. The Yan Yean was not 'running'.
1945 Baker 196: *Yan Yean* Melbourne water supply.

yandy To winnow, now in a tin-mining process [Ab.]
1929 *The Inlander* Nov. 25: A few miles from the 'Bar', we saw for the first time the native women 'yandying' tin ore. 'Yandying' is a delicate science, which only the women of the tribes seem able to master.
1944 M. J. O'Reilly *Bowyangs and Boomerangs* 48: Yandying, in the black-fellow language, means shake-about. It is the natives' method of separating the grass seeds from the husks.
1976 Roland Robinson *The Shift of Sands* 360: Maudie's yandy is an oval, concave piece of galvanised iron, coolamon shaped. With a constant yandying motion, throwing the sand into the air towards her, a backwards and forwards and sideways motion, Maudie separates the mineral sand in the yandy and pours it out.

yarpie A South African: *derogatory* [? f. Jaap as a common first name]
1986 *National Times* 30 May 36: Hacca: Ex-Pom with Yarpie Connections [heading] Robert Holmes a Court has substantial business ties with South Africa.
1987 Jeff Wells *Times on Sunday* 22 Nov. 24: Some countries ... have backed their rhetoric by officially banning their sportsmen from South Africa. Others such as Australia and Israel, which don't mind doing a little business with the yarpies on the side, indulge in so-called active but extremely selective and headline-grabbing discouragement

Yarpieland
1990 *Sun-Herald* 7 Jan. 128: Tim Fischer, shadow minister of veterans' affairs, has visited the grave of Breaker Morant in a Pretoria cemetery during a stop-over in Yarpieland.

yarra Insane [f. mental asylum at Yarra Bend, Victoria]
[**1921** Mary E. Fullerton *Bark House Days* 119: His monomania sent him at last to 'Yarra Bend', where as was gruesomely said, he walked round and round in a circle each day, whim-horse to his own imaginary invention.]
1943 Baker 89: *Yarra* (adj.) Stupid, crazy.
1973 Jim McNeil *The Chocolate Frog* 50: 'Whats'er matter? You gone yarra, or somethin'?'
1980 *Sydney Morning Herald* 20 Oct. 26: 'Kingston Town is a good horse, ... but in my opinion he would not have lived with Phar Lap. I know a lot of people will say I'm "Yarra"; but that's my belief.'

Yarra, useful as the   see **useful**

Yarra-banker A soapbox orator [f. Yarra River, Victoria]
[**1895** Cornelius Crowe *The Australian Slang Dictionary* 98: *Yarra Bankers* Vagrants living on the banks of the Yarra.]
1912 Louis Esson *The Time is not Yet Ripe* ed. P. Parsons (1973) 32: 'The man's an agitator, a red-flagger, a Yarra-banker.'
1973 Dr J. Cairns *Bulletin* 8 Dec. 13: I think that Parliament is a sort of elevated Yarra bank.

yarraman Aboriginal term for horse, used also by whites: *obs.*
1860 Mrs A. Macpherson *My Experiences*

of Australia 50: [He] was told by his black guide 'Bail yarraman (no horse) only white fellow.'

1866 W. Ridley *Kamilaroi* 20: *Horse* yaraman* *All the Australians use this name – probably from the neighing of the horse.

1875 A. J. Boyd *Old Colonials* (1882) 69: 'Then there's seventeen yarramen – call 'em thirty pounds a head.'

1891 H. Patchett Martin *Coo-ee: Tales of Australian Life* 280: He just clapped spurs to his old yarraman (horse), and never pulled up out of a gallop till he had got over the range.

1908 Giles Seagram *Bushmen All* 20: 'You accuse me of taking the yarramen. Of course I did. It was our only hope.'

yartz, the The arts, in Australia [invention of the Barry Humphries persona Les Patterson, Australian Cultural Attaché]

1978 Barry Humphries *A Nice Night's Entertainment* (1981) 183: This poem is dedicated to something Australians hold very precious beginning with Y – 'the Yartz'.

1986 Patrick White *Memoirs of Many in One* 166: Blobs of black here and there [in the theatre audience] from Cabinet Ministers doing their duty by the Yartz.

yeller fella Male half-caste in N.W. Australia [f. colour]

1937 Ernestine Hill *The Great Australian Loneliness* 206: The attitude of the lubras to these children is problematic. In some instances they treasure the 'little yellafella' as they call him.

1959 Donald Stuart *Yandy* 12: No future in being a yeller feller, down this end, or further north.

1971 Keith Willey *Boss Drover* 29: Part-Aborigines, or yeller-fellers as we called them in the old days, had a hard life.

1977 Kenneth Cook *The Man Underground* 137: 'The boongs and the yella fellas are lousing up this town so fast that it's no longer safe for a decent white woman to walk down the street.'

Yellow Monday A variety of cicada [f. colouring]

1951 Dymphna Cusack and Florence James *Come In Spinner* 163: She uncurled her fingers and showed the jewelled head of a cicada. 'He's a Yellow Mundy.'

1981 *Bulletin* 24 Nov. 110: In the unlikely event that I get to heaven, there will be no angels strumming harps. Just a band of Yellow Mondays playing summer's old sweet song and McGilvray giving cricket commentaries between the breaks.

yike A heated argument, a disturbance [unexplained]

1941 Baker 84: *Yike* A row or argument (2) A fight.

1945 Roy Rene *Mo's Memoirs* 186: 'There's that tram connie having a yike with a drunk.'

1964 George Johnston *My Brother Jack* 244: 'Sorry your party ended up in a yike.'

1980 *National Times* 12 Oct. 61: I think of my grandmother, who came from Hopetoun in the Mallee and whose utterances were few . . . An argument she referred to as a 'yike', a serious disagreement 'a decent yike'.

yonnie A stone, esp. of a size for throwing

1941 Baker 84: *Yonnie* A small stone, a pebble.

1979 *Sun-Herald* 18 Mar. 79: There were two lamp posts . . . each equipped with an electric bulb. I'd say about 45 watts. Young couples courting would smash each of them with a well-aimed 'yonnie' on pay night.

1980 *Sun-Herald* 27 Jan. 66: Yonnies are stones to Victorians. A Sydneysider will look at you blankly.

you'll be sorry   see **sorry**

young and old, it was on for   see **on**

young Harry, cop this   see **cop**

young (amateur) players, a trap for   see **trap**

you're not wrong   see **wrong**

yous, youse Perhaps derived from *yez* [You (said to more than one) *Anglo-Irish* OED 1804], but in Australia not necessarily a plural

1908 Henry Fletcher *Dads and Dan between Smokes* 39: When misfochin' as yous can't prevent lands yer a woodener, take it smilin'.

1911 Louis Stone *Jonah* 190: 'Yous are a white man, an' I always knew it.'

1944 Lawson Glassop *We Were the Rats* 81: 'Glad ter know yous both,' said Jim awkwardly.

1969 Christopher Bray *Blossom Like a*

Rose 165: 'I don't mean to piss in yer pockets, but youse blokes are all right.'
1984 Jack Hibberd *Squibs* 226: 'Mr Prime Minister . . . How would youse like your grapefruit this corker of a morn?'

yow, to keep To **keep nit** q.v.
1942 Eve Langley *The Pea-Pickers* 283: 'You keep yow,' she said in a muffled voice, 'and whistle "The Prisoner's Song" if anyone comes along.'
1965 Graham McInnes *The Road to Gundagai* 206: Molly kept a look out ('kept yow', as we used to say).

yowie Supposed Australian counterpart to the Yeti or Abominable Snowman, sometimes connected with Aboriginal legend: described as a hairy creature about two metres high
1975 Rex Gilroy *Sun-Herald* 14 Dec. 126: Australia has its own version of 'Bigfoot', known to the Aborigines for thousands of years as the Yowie ('Great Hairy Man'). The beast has the appearance of an ape. It is described as a hairy, man-like ape-like creature standing from 6ft to 8ft tall. It is stooped and moves with a loping gait, emitting a screech-ing sound if disturbed. It inhabits trees and caves, but always in the denser and generally inaccessible mountainous forest regions.
1979 *Advertiser* (Adelaide) 23 May 24: Rex's [Rex Gilroy's] main grudge against Australian academics is not that they don't believe in Yowies but that they condemn his theories without considering his research or evidence.
1984 *Sydney Morning Herald* 7 Jan. 4: Rather frightening being out in a pitch black night on a river bank in a thunderstorm. It's the sort of time when the Yowie monster of Aboriginal legend is likely to come and get you.

Yugo A Yugoslavian migrant [abbr.]
1954 *Bulletin* 19 May 21: 'Where did he hit me?' 'What!' 'The Yugo – with his gun.'
1973 Henry Williams *My Love Had a Black Speed Stripe* 46: We filled him in about Johnny, the young Yugo.
1981 *National Times* 13 Sep. 22: 'What we call Yugos,' he said, 'they seem to mix in a bit better, they come in here and have a drink.'

Z

zack Sixpence: *obsolescent* [? Yiddish (G. *sechs* six)]
1898 *Bulletin* 1 Oct. 14: 6d. a 'zack'.
1928 A. W. Upfield *The House of Cain* 89: 'When I throw a seven (die), I won't have a zac on me.'
1958 Frank Hardy *The Four-Legged Lottery* 215: 'It's mortgaged, Jim. Not worth a zac.'
1983 *Australian* 14 Jul. 5: I would be a rich man if I had a zack for every time I heard someone in ethnic broadcasting making a disparaging remark about the Public Service.

zambuck Ambulance or first aid man, esp. at a sporting fixture: *obsolescent* [f. brand name of an ointment]
1943 Baker 90: *Zambuck* A first-aid man in attendance at a sporting contest.
1956 Ruth Park and D'Arcy Niland *The Drums Go Bang* 146–7: 'I might have come home just in time to see the zambucks carting you two off in the ambulance.'
1984 *Bulletin* 6 Mar. 43: If you don't know what a Zambuck is, it's someone in the black and white uniform of the St John Ambulance Brigade doing honorary duty at a sports arena, ready to dash on the field with everything from liniment to stretcher.

Z cars 1 The Z class trams in Melbourne, painted orange instead of the former green
1982 *Age* (Melbourne) 25 May 11: The Tramways Board is now, after seven years, still forced to conduct a defence of the Z cars.
2 As for **black taxis**, q.v.
1983 *Australian* 13 Jan. 7: The car was among official Ford limos known to Canberrans as 'Z-cars', for the red Z prefix on the number plates.

ziff A beard [unexplained]

1919 W. H. Downing *Digger Dialects* 54: *Ziff* A beard.

1939 Miles Franklin and Dymphna Cusack *Pioneers on Parade* 88: Lord Cravenburn regretted his ziff.

1955 F. B. Vickers *The Mirage* 114: 'Wears a ziff, black 'un, black as the hair on his chest.'

1981 Gwen Kelly *Always Afternoon* 211: 'Better get rid of that ziff,' she said pointing to his embryonic beard.

zoo, feeding-time at the An undisciplined assault on food and drink; any disorderly but excited scene

1951 Dymphna Cusack and Florence James *Come In Spinner* 33: 'The Public Bar gets more like Taronga Zoo at feeding time every day.'

1970 Richard Beilby *No Medals for Aphrodite* 68–9: 'Gawd, you should get on that crowd ... It's like feeding time at the zoo.'

1975 *Sydney Morning Herald* 23 Oct. 6: At question time, the Prime Minister gives a daily performance. It's the highlight of the day – feeding time at the zoo. Just about every question thrown at him he appears to greet with relish.

Zorba Nickname for anyone of Greek background, esp. the N.S.W. sports commentator Peter Peters [f. the novel by Nikos Kazantzakis *Zorba the Greek*, also a film]

1985 *Sun-Herald* 7 Apr. 66: An afternoon in the commentary box with Greg 'Hollywood' Hartley and Peter 'Zorba' Peters is all about entertainment.

1987 *Sydney Morning Herald* 1 Sep. 17: Senator Bolkus, who strongly supported the move [for affirmative action], remembers being taken aback at the words of his good friend Mick Young ... 'Good stuff, Zorba, I suppose you'll be just as delighted when a boiler knocks you off for the ministry.'